Richard Rogers

Team 4
Richard + Su Rogers
Piano + Rogers
Richard Rogers Partnership

Richard Rogers

Team 4
Richard + Su Rogers
Piano + Rogers
Richard Rogers Partnership

Complete Works
Volume One
Kenneth Powell

	6	**Team 4**
		The AA, Yale and early influences
New Haven, Connecticut, 1961	20	Science Campus Project, Yale University
Feock, Cornwall, 1963	22	Pill Creek Retreat
Coulsdon, Surrey, 1965	24	Wates Housing Project
Feock, Cornwall, 1964–7	28	Creek Vean
Feock, Cornwall, 1964	38	Pill Creek Housing
Radlett, Hertfordshire, 1964–6	40	Jaffe House
London, 1965–7	44	Murray Mews Housing
Swindon, Wiltshire, 1967	50	Reliance Controls Electronics Factory
	58	**Richard + Su Rogers**
		Visions and experiments, and a commitment to research
Ulting, Essex, 1967–8	68	Spender House
London, 1968–9	72	Rogers House
1968 & 1971	82	Zip-Up Enclosures
Ashford, Kent, 1969–71	86	Universal Oil Products (UOP) Factory
London, 1969–71	88	Design Research Unit Roof Extension
	90	**Piano + Rogers**
		The Practice and the Pompidou Centre
Paris, 1971–7	102	Pompidou Centre
Paris, 1971–7	134	IRCAM
1971	140	ARAM Module
Como, Italy, 1972–3	142	B&B Italia Offices
Tadworth, Surrey, 1973–4	146	UOP Factory
London, 1973	152	Park Road Development
Melbourn, Cambridgeshire, 1975	154	PA Technology Laboratory
London, 1977	160	Millbank Riverside Housing
	162	**Richard Rogers Partnership**
		Origins, philosophy and ethos: a design community
London, 1978–86	174	Lloyd's of London
1978	210	Third Generation Office
Cambridge, 1979	212	NAPP Laboratories
Quimper, France, 1979–81	214	Fleetguard Factory
London, 1979–83	220	Coin Street Development
London, 1981	226	Free Trade Wharf Development
Newport, Wales, 1982	228	Inmos Microprocessor Factory
London, 1982	236	National Gallery Extension
Princeton, New Jersey, 1982–5	242	PA Technology Laboratories
Florence, Italy, 1983–4	248	Arno Masterplan
Maidenhead, Berkshire, 1984–5	252	Industrial Units
London, 1984–9	254	Thames Wharf
Glasgow, 1985–7	272	Linn Products
London, 1985–8	274	Billingsgate Securities Market
Nantes, France, 1986–7	282	Centre Commercial St Herblain
London, 1986	288	London as it could be
London, 1987	300	Royal Avenue
	306	Complete list of works 1961–87
	316	Index

Team 4

The AA, Yale and early influences

Richard Rogers' work is rooted in history, yet directed towards the future. His art is, by definition, social and communal and created by a community of designers. Indeed, Rogers cannot conceive of architecture without people. Human society and the city, that resilient organism which has outlived the prophets who predicted its demise, is at the very centre of everything he does and is. Bold, colourful, beautifully made, with a strong aesthetic agenda and an appeal to even the untutored eye, Rogers' architecture is popular – in the best sense – attractive, accessible, but with a complex rationale which is as radical as it is romantic. For over thirty years, Rogers' buildings have expressed a passionate, almost Ruskinian, conviction about the role of architecture in life; that passion has been with him since his youth.

Nino and Dada Rogers, 1932

Rogers was born in the great historic city of Florence on 23 July, 1933. His father, William Nino, the grandson of an English dentist who had settled in Italy, was a medical student. His mother, Ermengarde Gairinger – who was always known as Dada – was from Trieste. Her father, Ricardo, had trained as an architect and engineer, though he had subsequently given up practice to become a director of development in a large insurance company. In 1938, with war seemingly inevitable, the Rogers family moved to and settled in England and Dr Rogers, as he had become, found a job in a Surrey hospital. The young Richard Rogers subsequently attended two rather traditional English schools, where he never felt entirely comfortable – due, in large part, to undiagnosed dyslexia.

Rogers' interest in architecture might have been predicted, given his family connections, but from the start his architectural instincts were distinctive and, by contemporary British standards, unconventional. The roots of Rogers' concern for the city and quest for an appropriate urban architecture for the twentieth century are to be found in his origins and upbringing and in the mix of science, design and the arts which characterized his family. Rogers' father's cousin, Ernesto Rogers, an exceptional humanist thinker, was one of the leading architects in Italy: a partner in the respected practice of BBPR – perhaps best known for the expressive Torre Velasca in Milan. Ernesto Rogers was also an occasional editor of the major Italian journals *Domus* and *Casabella*, and a pioneering urbanist. Through Ernesto, the young Rogers came to admire the work of other Italian architects, notably Ignazio Gardella and Franco Albini.

Richard Rogers, aged two, on Dada's knee

The schoolboy Rogers

Rogers' mother was an enthusiast for modern design right up to the time of her death in 1998 and a major influence on her son throughout her life. Nino and Dada took Richard back to Italy when he was a schoolboy where he was entranced by Florence and loved the art and sculpture of the Renaissance, particularly the early Renaissance and the work of Masaccio. Rogers' lively interest in the visual arts, (which later, for example, took him to the chairmanship of the Tate Gallery trustees) was formed in his childhood. The elegant, sociable cities of Italy, with their vibrant street life, impressed themselves indelibly on him. His earliest memory of a building was that of the cathedral in Florence, and in particular Brunelleschi's dome. In due course, he discovered the famous Nolli plan of Rome,

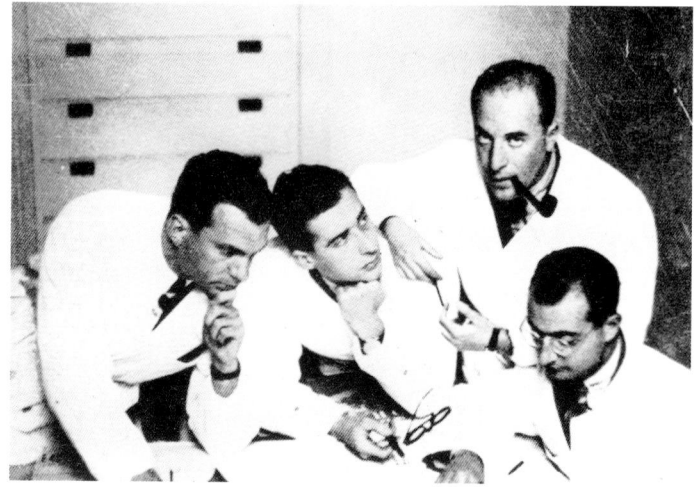
The office of BBPR in the 1950s; Ernesto Rogers is third from the left with the pipe

which shows open space not just as gaps around buildings, but as a continuum flowing through them. For Rogers, buildings were always permeable, not closed fortresses against the streets. Urban concerns fuelled Rogers' dissatisfaction with some of the classic formulae of the Modern Movement – Le Corbusier's city plans, for example, applied disastrously to many old cities – and his hopes for a different sort of modern architecture. For Rogers, a continuity was a critical concern.

Rogers went to the Festival of Britain in 1951 and was inspired by the Royal Festival Hall, designed by a team led by Leslie Martin (later, as Sir Leslie, to be a crucial supporter of Rogers' work) and equally by the Dome of Discovery, designed by Ralph Tubbs – a distinctly futuristic work. The Festival proved that modern architecture was alive in Britain. After National Service, part of which was spent in Trieste – providing an opportunity to get to know cousin Ernesto – Rogers resolved to enter the rigorous Architectural Association (AA) school in London, in the autumn of 1954. The school was, as it had been in the 1930s, a bastion of the Modern Movement and the emphasis, in the years after the Second World War, was ever more on buildings for people – the 'social' architecture of housing, new towns, schools, hospitals and health centres, which were the preoccupations of most 'serious' architects after the war. The socially-minded, indeed, socialist ambience of the AA suited Rogers whose politics, like those of his parents, were firmly to the left. 'I never had the "shock of the new" experience that most people of my age in Britain had in the 1950s', says Rogers. His cosmopolitan and progressive family background set him apart from most of his fellow students. He found inspiration from some of the tutors, notably Robert Furneaux Jordan, who combined a passion for history with a broad international outlook, and Peter Smithson, whose school at Hunstanton, Norfolk, designed with his wife and partner Alison Smithson, was one of the most talked-about new buildings in Britain. Peter Smithson was one of the progenitors of the New Brutalism, proclaimed as a route whereby modern architecture could be regenerated. Rogers describes Smithson as 'a great mentor', but also says, 'In many ways, cousin Ernesto was a greater influence. Peter was worried that I was too interested in history and too inspired by historic cities.' But the Smithsons' 'pop' vision and involvement with the coterie of artists and architects who formed the Independent Group, certainly influenced Rogers and, later, formed part of the ideology of the competition entry for the Pompidou Centre. It was Rogers' essentially modern view of history and continuity which was also to underpin his role as an urban campaigner in the 1980s and 1990s. Rogers – who found written communication and drawing difficult (his friend and later fellow student Georgie Cheeseman helped him with these) – only blossomed at the AA during his final years there, under the influences of Smithson, Alan Colquhoun, John Killick and others. He wrote two significant essays in his third year, one on the form of the city, showing the influences of CIAM; and one on the Maison de Verre by Pierre Chareau (later published in *Domus*). He won the 5th year prize for a school project, yet he left the AA in 1959, 'with no great sense of direction, save for a vague Italian influence'.

The decisive influences in Rogers' career came only after marriage and with a sojourn in the United States. In 1960, he had married Susan (Su) Brumwell, the daughter of Marcus and Rene Brumwell – all of whom were to be influences on his life and work. Marcus Brumwell was a man of great business, scientific and artistic talent whose interests came together in his running of the Design Research Unit, which had been set up in 1943 with idealistic and visionary aims as an integrated design service, equipped to tackle the demands of post-war reconstruction. Its first head had been the great critic and

Florence Cathedral – Brunelleschi's dome

Ernesto Rogers, Sanatorium, Legnano, Italy, 1938

BBPR (Ernesto Rogers and Enrico Peressuti), Torre Velasca, Milan, 1956–8

Su and Richard Rogers on 42nd Street, New York, 1961

Norman and Wendy Foster, early Team 4 days

Rogers' year at Yale – Norman Foster seated centre, Rogers lying down

Leslie Martin teaching, with Le Corbusier as guest

Serge Chermayeff – a dominating figure at Yale

Norman Foster, Richard Rogers and Carl Abbott at Yale, 1962

Laurie Abbott (right) with his wife Carol and Su Rogers' brother Joe, sailing near Creek Vean

Vincent Scully, who 'opened up' Frank Lloyd Wright's work to Rogers at Yale

James Stirling – tutor at Yale, and friend to Rogers

historian Herbert Read, who recruited a number of associates: the graphic designer and typographer Milner Gray, Misha Black (a prime player in DRU over many years), the engineer Felix Samuely and the architects Sadie Speight (later married to Leslie Martin) and Frederick Gibberd. When the war ended, Marcus Brumwell became proprietor and DRU took off: it was heavily involved in the Festival of Britain. Although run on commercial lines, DRU preserved its early ideals and its democratic, non-hierarchical organization could be compared with that of Richard Rogers' practice half a century on.

In the autumn of 1961, Richard and Su Rogers went to the USA where Richard pursued a masters degree in architecture – on a Fulbright scholarship – and Su enrolled in studies in urban planning. Although her first degree, at the London School of Economics, had been in sociology, Su Rogers' interests were increasingly architectural. Their interests neatly interacted and Richard Rogers stresses the degree to which Su informed his thinking on urban issues. The couple lived initially with the sculptor Naum Gabo and his wife, who were great friends of the Brumwells. The Gabos acted much as 'second parents' to the couple for their first semester; Richard remembers their long and lively discussions on twentieth-century art, architecture and form, and Naum Gabo's influential constructivist ideas.

It was very much an 'English year' at Yale, Su recalls. Among the young British architects then at Yale were Eldred Evans, who had also been at the AA (where Rogers thought her the brightest of his contemporaries), and Norman Foster, who had trained in the school of architecture at Manchester University – where teaching was conducted in a far more traditional manner than was the custom at the AA – and who had come to Yale on a Henry scholarship. (Foster and Rogers had actually first met back in London, at a Fulbright reception.) The head of the Yale school was the legendary irascible Paul Rudolph – 'he really cared about the look of a building – not like the AA, where the social programme was everything', Su recounts. Rudolph, then in his early forties, believed in working his students hard, even calling seminars at 2.00 am! Rogers says this of him: 'He was utterly committed to the art of architecture – a fanatic, who never seemed to sleep. It was like an army officers' training course – gruelling, testing, with no holidays. There was none of the English laid-back approach: we learned to work – all the time. The American students, who thought we were a bit too intellectual, urged us to "do more and think less!"'

Richard Rogers confirms that 'Rudolph was highly visual in his interests – his approach would have been considered very improper in Britain at the time'. Both Rogers and Foster speak with great enthusiasm of Rudolph's early Florida houses (designed with Ralph S. Twitchell), like the Siegrist House in Venice (1949) and the Healy House in Sarasota (1950), with its timber frame and roof covering of plastic. According to Norman Foster, 'Rudolph was exploring high-performance materials, innovating, looking at issues of climate. He was a highly committed practising architect as well as a fantastic teacher.' While Rudolph was a major formative influence on both Foster and Rogers there were also other 'marvellous' teachers at Yale. James Stirling, whom Rogers had met but hardly known well in London, was teaching temporarily in the school and became close to Richard and Su. Although only four years older than Richard Rogers, he was already a senior architectural figure. And there was also Serge Chermayeff who, says Rogers, 'could have persuaded us to do anything. He was a dominating figure, hugely intellectual in the best European mould and just as much an influence on me as Rudolph.' His analysis of public and private space imprinted itself on Rogers and

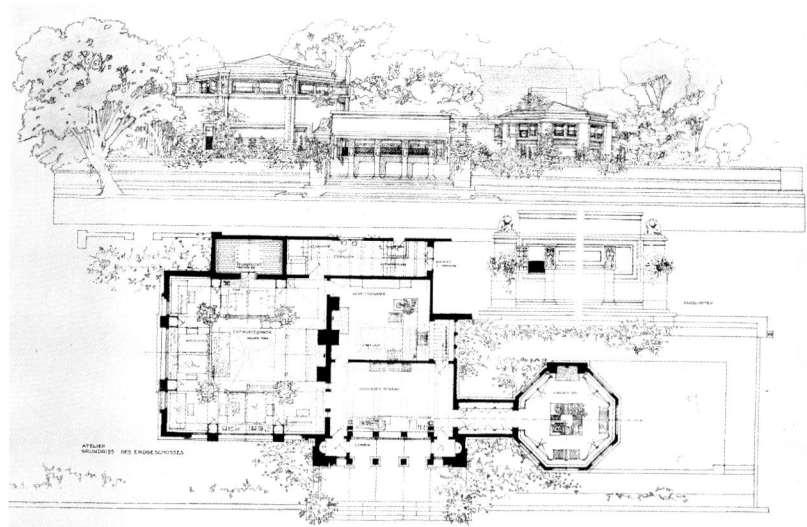
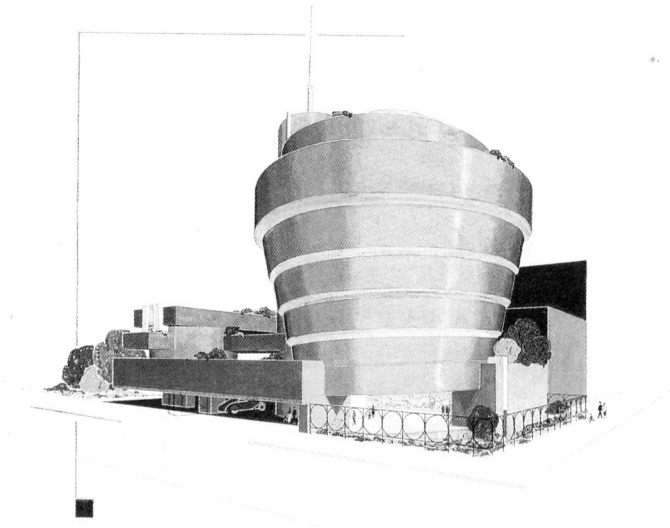

Frank Lloyd Wright Studio, Oak Park, Illinois, 1895 – plan and elevation

Frank Lloyd Wright, Solomon R. Guggenheim Museum, New York, 1943–59 – drawing of exterior

later strongly influenced the housing work done by Team 4. Meanwhile, Vincent Scully 'opened up' Frank Lloyd Wright's work, much as John Summerson had 'opened up' Georgian London at the AA, and expounded an organic view of design; of the relationship between architecture and nature. Rogers describes Scully as 'the greatest lecturer I ever heard'.

'Wright was my first god', says Rogers. He could not comprehend the isolation imposed on Wright – for example, by his sidelining at MoMA's 1932 International Style show, or the persistent undervaluing of 'the greatest architect of the nineteenth century' (as Philip Johnson scathingly described Wright) on the East Coast. 'Wright's work has to be seen, experienced as space, to be understood. It was pretty revelatory', Rogers says. 'Corb had dominated the AA while I was there ... But for me he was always a rather elusive presence, though I loved many of his buildings. Wright, on the other hand, was very real and immediate.' More than any other building, Unity Temple in Oak Park, Illinois, impressed him – 'a really stunning building ... unforgettable' – but he found his sheer range, from the early Prairie houses to Taliesin, Wisconsin, to the Guggenheim Museum, staggering. 'Wright', says Rogers, 'was an unashamed maker of form: he carried no illusions about functionalism'. The Wrightian influence was subsequently subtly apparent in Rogers' buildings and certainly his legacy of an 'organic' element is evident in every one.

The formal education which Rogers received at Yale was, however, less significant, he feels, than the whole experience of America. 'Politically, I'd tended towards anti-Americanism', says Rogers, 'but aesthetically, I was overwhelmed by the place – by its tall buildings, technology and amazing energy – the attitude of "can do".' Part of the appeal of the United States for a young man brought up in wartime austerity in Britain was its sheer modernity – the style and drive of the country mesmerized Rogers. He and Su had sailed to America on the liner, the Queen Elizabeth. 'It had towered over Southampton. In New York, it was dwarfed by the buildings', Richard recalls. In contrast to Britain, in America it was possible to live in a modern way, in a modern house uncluttered by the baggage of centuries.

With Foster (who had become a friend and collaborator already) and an American student Carl Abbott, Richard and Su went on a series of epic trips around the country, some amidst the snow and ice of the North American winter, seeing, at least externally, most of Wright's buildings. They also sought out work by Mies van der Rohe, who was to become a real influence on Foster, though Rogers found his approach somewhat constrictive. 'To me, Mies was always rather a closed book', says Rogers. 'While I loved his cool, beautiful architecture, I found it difficult in didactic terms – too closed and finite as a system.' Louis Kahn was another enthusiasm and Rogers and Foster trekked to Philadelphia to see him and to visit his Richards Medical Research Laboratories, then new. (Memories of the building were to re-emerge strongly in the designs for Lloyd's of London.) Kahn pointed the way to a new modern architecture.

Beyond Wright, it was the architecture of the American West Coast that Rogers found inspirational – after Yale, he discovered another America and a different set of architectural values. After their one-year courses had finished, Richard and Su set out for California. Both found jobs in San Francisco, Su with the government housing agency, Richard with the West Coast office of the renowned Skidmore, Owings & Merrill (SOM) practice. Rogers got to know the works of Rudolf Schindler, who was a major influence on him and the subject of an essay at Yale, and of the architects of the Case Study houses such as Pierre Koenig, Craig Ellwood, Raphael Soriano and Charles and Ray Eames. The rational machine-made aesthetic of the Case Study houses of Soriano, Ellwood and Eames offered an approach to practical fast-track construction and exemplified the advantages of prefabrication and the use of mass-made components, while the structural drama of Schindler's work was unforgettable. Their use of lightweight steel construction and interest in 'technology transfer' and prefabrication affected Rogers and, indeed, Foster. The programme

Team 4

Louis I. Kahn, Richards Medical Research Laboratories, University of Pennsylvania, Philadelphia, 1957–65

Pierre Chareau and Bernard Bijvoet, Maison de Verre, Paris, 1928–31: interior

Pierre Koenig, Case Study House # 22 (Stahl House), Hollywood, Los Angeles, California, 1960

Ezra Ehrenkrantz, SCSD project under construction, California, 1962

behind the Case Study houses (launched in 1945) strongly appealed to Rogers. 'The house', it was laid down, 'must be capable of duplication and in no sense be an individual performance.' Rogers was particularly excited by Soriano and 'the way he handled steel in a much less precious way than ... the Miesian approach'. Rogers recalls that he 'fell in love with the idea of a mass produced house, made with standard industrial components'. Rogers and Foster, who also gravitated to the West Coast for a time, were equally entranced by some of the post-war system-built schools in California, built under Ezra Ehrenkrantz's SCSD (School Construction Systems Development) programme – the prototype SCSD school, at Palo Alto, was newly opened when Rogers and his companions visited it in 1962. These deep-plan, steel-framed buildings undoubtedly made their mark on Reliance Controls some years later and embodied the inspiration of the British post-war school building programme (Ehrenkrantz had worked in Britain for a time).

The potent alliance of Rogers and Foster, forged at Yale (where, for example, they worked together on a project for university science laboratories) produced Team 4, founded on Richard, Su and Norman's return to London in 1963. According to Rogers, the partnership with Foster was 'intellectual magic, the fire of creative discussion, better than the greatest tennis match – though we were both on the same side, of course'. Georgie Cheeseman (who had married and become Georgie Wolton) and her sister Wendy (who later married Foster), a graduate of the University of London's Bartlett school of architecture, were the other partners. Georgie Wolton soon left, but the name Team 4 persisted – it was a deliberate riposte to the cult of the individual which Rogers detested – and Su Rogers, though not formally qualified as an architect, played a growing role in it.

The team established itself in Wendy Cheeseman's flat in Belsize Park, London. As jobs came along, it recruited staff. Frank Peacock was the first – 'I think Richard regarded me as a practical person', he recalls. Then came Laurie Abbott, a potent presence in the Rogers office to this day. Abbott was an accomplished draughtsman – 'he came to see us with the most exquisite portfolio I'd ever seen', Rogers recalls. Having left school at 16, Abbott studied architecture part-time and worked for the Greater London Council (GLC) and for Owen Luder before coming to Team 4. He also proved to be a highly imaginative designer. Next came John Young, a bright young AA student on his year out, who arrived, aged 22, in Autumn 1966. He had seen a picture of Team 4 – showing the team hanging out of the window of their office – in *Architectural Design* magazine and was certain that this was 'the democratic, progressive, friendly, design-orientated office' that he was looking for. 'From day one I was given responsibility for construction detail drawings, under Frank Peacock's watchful eye, assisting either Richard or Norman on a number of jobs at various stages of construction. This climate of responsibility was stimulating and I flourished', Young later recalled, 'constantly surprising myself with what I was able to do.' Mark Sutcliffe, who

The artist Ben Nicholson in 1961, one of the Brumwells' Cornwall-based friends

Barbara Hepworth, at work on sculptures for the Festival of Britain in 1951 – another friend of the Brumwells from the Cornwall arts scene

later joined Norman Foster's practice, also worked for a time at Team 4. The team's regular engineer was Anthony Hunt and they enjoyed direct contact with the excellent firms of Ove Arup and Samuely, even though such a new practice.

The practice's first significant commission, Creek Vean, for Su's parents Marcus and Rene Brumwell, predated, in its conception, the formation of Team 4. The Brumwells wished to make their principal home for retirement in Cornwall and had acquired a routine Victorian villa, Cot House, standing in ample grounds, at Pill Creek, near the village of Feock on the Fal estuary. They considered both an adaptation and extension of the existing house and a completely new house on the site. Their first choice as architect was Ernst Freud, a veteran German emigré and son of the famous psychologist, whose initial proposals for extending Cot House were duly forwarded to the couple's son-in-law, far away in Yale, for his comments. Rogers was unimpressed and wrote back to the Brumwells soon after Christmas, 1961, describing the plans as 'appalling'. He felt that his parents-in-law who, through friendships with Cornwall-based artists such as Ben Nicholson, Henry Moore and Barbara Hepworth had assembled an important personal art collection, were setting their sights too low. They should select an architect, he wrote, 'of the calibre, or at least of the potential calibre, of the artists whose art work you buy ... I feel that your beautiful works of art should have a setting which shows them off to their best advantage, at the same time harmonizing with them.' Rogers' suggestions of suitable architects included Leslie Martin, who had done a wonderful conversion of an old mill for his own occupation, James Stirling and James Gowan ('generally considered the best small house builders in England by the Americans, and by myself'), Alan Colquhoun ('very intelligent, very sensitive') and his old AA and Yale colleague, Eldred Evans who, with her then partner Dennis Gailey, had won the competition for a new civic centre in Lincoln.

For all his youth and inexperience with actual buildings, Rogers, always confident in his judgements, had no qualms about lecturing the Brumwells. A month later, he wrote again reassuring them – they had clearly expressed doubts about his suggestions – that 'the whole purpose of modern architecture is not simply to create beautiful exteriors but to combine function with aesthetics, and relate them to the spiritual and physical needs of the client, and to the site. I have never heard before this idea that good modern architects are less functional than mediocre ones, in fact the reverse is usually true.' Surely they, of all people, realized that architecture was about creating works of art as well as practical structures? 'To a retired architect like Freud, building one small house means nothing. For him, the sooner the job is completed, the better and he can get on with his retirement. But to any young architect, like any of my friends or your friends from the AA, one small house means everything. He will become completely involved in it and give you the maximum amount of thought, knowledge and attention within his ability.'

The implications were clear: a young architect like Rogers was the man for the job. In fact, Rogers added, he had only recently entered into a partnership with Frank Peacock, 'the outstanding technical student of the last decade of the AA' and a man with a lot of practical building experience. If Peacock had one failing – one guaranteed to reassure nervous clients – 'it is that he is too safe'. One major problem remained: Rogers was still a student and was, in fact, to spend another year in America. So the 'partnership' with Peacock was still-born, though the latter was soon to become a key figure in Team 4.

While at Yale, Rogers had worked frantically on a number of private projects, struggling to fit them around his course work and sometimes finding that he had to work flat out to keep up with the unending demands of his tutors. One such venture came from his old friend Michael Branch who expressed interest in building a house; plans by

Rogers and Foster, a fusion of Wrightian and Kahnian themes, rigorous yet romantic, were sent to him from Yale. While the plan never came to fruition, the Branch house was, in fact, arguably a seminal Team 4 project. Through it, Foster and Rogers found that they could work together easily – 'there was a chemistry', says Norman Foster. ('The Branch house was conceived in Naum Gabo's house … to the music of Ella Fitzgerald and Elvis Presley', Rogers later recalled.)

Back in England, Team 4 took up the Brumwells' Cornish project where Rogers had previously left off. Creek Vean took three years to design and build and Rogers recalls around fifty variant schemes being prepared before the final version was constructed. The house, says Laurie Abbott, was 'a pretty difficult job – there was nothing straightforward about it at all'. Everyone who worked on the project remembers it as problematic and, at times, nightmarish – five architects spent three years on the job. Richard Rogers describes the house as 'Wrightian – a solid, romantic house very much dug into the earth'. He might have used that old Arts and Crafts epithet, 'of the soil'. Wright was clearly the predominant influence in the design of the house. Abbott remembers clearly that the initial ideas came from both Rogers and Foster, with the latter having a significant hand in the final plan. It was Foster, too, who convinced the Brumwells to drop the idea of modernizing and extending the existing house and to go for a new building, having concluded that the former course was an expensive compromise. (Tony Hunt was also sceptical of the practicality of a conversion and extension job.) Then, as later, the two men worked in close empathy.

One of the first versions of Creek Vean provided for a house that tumbled down the steep slope of the site to the old boathouse below (retained for the Brumwells' boat). Subsequently the plan was amended to locate the house along the contours of the slope, with the main entrance across a bridge from the lane at the top. Most of the accommodation inside is arranged at a lower level along a top-lit gallery. Sliding doors allow the rooms to be fully opened up to the gallery space. The tension between the open and the closed, the public and the private, reception rooms and bedrooms, reflects the influence of Serge Chermayeff; the plan fanned out to embrace the landscape and views, while turning its blank, almost fortified, rear elevation to the road.

There is also much about the house that prefigures Rogers' later work – its flexible use of space, extendibility, awareness of public interior space and, above all, its expressive drama. Indeed, the house was for long seen as an interesting oddity, out of tune with later 'High-Tech' work – Rogers despises that label – and far less prescient of the future than, say, Reliance Controls. Laurie Abbott, who did all the working details for the house, recalls the vast amount of work that went into the big windows of frameless glass in aluminium tracks. 'We began to see the problems of being innovative', he says, 'given the conservative outlook of the building industry. We had to reinvent glazing and discovered the attractions of neoprene joints. Creek Vean was something of a test bed for new ideas.'

The problems of building Creek Vean drove Team 4 towards prefabrication and the elimination of 'wet trades' from the construction process. Although the house leaked, and some of the windows quickly ceased to open, the architects agonized endlessly about the technical problems, determined to get things right – not for them Wright's arrogant indifference to practical issues.

Before acquiring Cot House, the Brumwells had owned a house on the other side of the creek, where the village of Feock was gradually expanding in piecemeal fashion. There seemed to be scope for a compact housing development there and Team 4 duly developed the plans for such a scheme: nineteen houses on a stepped section with views to the creek. The much-reviewed Siedlung Halen housing scheme in Berne by architects Atelier 5 was certainly a key influence and, though the high density of the development supposed a strong sense of community, privacy was an equally important priority – the Italian hilltown meets Chermayeff. The scheme, however, came to nothing. Local planners, who had been uneasy with the plans for Creek Vean – passing them on condition that the concrete was painted (it never was) – were adamantly opposed to the housing scheme. The planner Max Lock advised the Brumwells on a possible appeal, but the project was dropped. 'It was a good design, but in the wrong place', Su concludes. Yet the scheme offered a viable alternative to the suburban sprawl which was spoiling Cornwall.

The Jaffe House at Radlett, Hertfordshire, built in 1966, resembled a single element of the Pill Creek scheme developed as an individual house; an attempt, perhaps, to rationalize Creek Vean and to build on the experience of it. The site was on a slope, facing north. Through a

Ray and Charles Eames on the steel frame of the Eames House, Pacific Palisades, California, 1949

series of skylights, capturing the sun from the south, Team 4 enabled as much daylight as possible to pour into the stepped levels, where room divisions were kept movable and flexible. The house had none of the romance of Creek Vean but was, if superficially straightforward, both rigorous and forward-looking – amazingly so for its routine suburban site, sandwiched between conventional villas. James Stirling admired the house greatly, not surprisingly since his own influence is to some degree evident in the designs. (The hard rigour of the brick enclosing walls takes its cue, perhaps, from the Leicester University Engineering Building, a source of inspiration for Team 4, who loved Stirling and Gowan's 'bloody-mindedness'.) Again, the inspiration of Serge Chermayeff and also Christopher Alexander can be detected in its use of public and private space – in theory, the house was the model for many, many more like it, and its progeny are distributed clearly among the later work of Foster (who once considered buying it) and Rogers.

Richard Rogers has always wanted to build housing, seeing every house he has designed, with the possible exception of Creek Vean, as a prototype for larger developments; in effect, for new urban forms. Even today, his frustration with the house-building industry is clear. During the 1960s, Eric Lyons, working with that inspired developer Span Homes, built private-sector housing that was both modern and popular. Span proved that it could be done – only when the company over-extended itself with the new commuter village at New Ash Green did it lose its sure touch. Inspired by an approach from photographer John Donat to Neil Wates, Team 4 was commissioned to prepare proposals for a housing development on a sixty-nine-acre site in Coulsdon, Surrey. The project provided for long blocks of two and three-storey houses built around a central, enclosed parking and service area, with generous areas of open space on the outside of the housing clusters, which were connected by pedestrian routes. The architecture was rationalist in inspiration, yet the qualities of the site were a key consideration. The scheme was a one-off, but universal in its implications. The architects thought hard about the treatment of external spaces and internal plans, tailored to the needs of typical families – fostering a sense of community, within the context of a proper hierarchy of public and private spaces, was the ultimate goal. Rogers sees the project – subsequently abandoned – as having 'a lot of Chermayeff's thinking in it' and considers it a key progenitor of his other work right through to the present. (The principles behind Wates later emerged in the public/private world of Coin Street, the piazza at Beaubourg and the vision of 'London as it could be'.) Rogers was disappointed by the collapse of the Coulsdon scheme, though Foster, it appears, was sceptical from the start about the intentions of the clients. The cancellation of the project, which clearly reflected a commitment to planning and urban form forged in the USA, was a body blow to Team 4 and helped to precipitate its dissolution.

The housing scheme at Murray Mews, though far smaller, was actually built. The site was in Camden Town, London and there were just three houses. The progenitor of the scheme was Dr Owen Franklin, stepson of Naum Gabo, and the houses were to be tailored to the needs of the individual clients. The aesthetic, brick and sloping patent glazing, owed a good deal to Stirling, but the interiors of the houses were spatially innovative, with striking, full-height galleried living spaces which flowed into external courtyards. The construction was essentially traditional, using concrete, brick and patent glazing. There were many problems with the job, so many, in fact, that even the normally buoyant Rogers became very depressed. 'The low point came' (according to Bryan Appleyard's biography) 'after a particularly awful day at Murray Mews when he trudged in the darkness up to Hampstead Heath, flung his head into his hands, sobbed and vowed to give up architecture'.

The experience of Murray Mews and Creek Vean undoubtedly encouraged Team 4 to look beyond brick and concrete towards a different sort of architecture – lightweight, made of mass-produced components, demountable (in theory anyway) and 'sitting lightly on the ground'. If Wright's aesthetic, infused with recent European influences (including that of Stirling) and Chermayeff's philosophy had dominated the practice's early work, the time had clearly come to explore other exemplars. Rogers and Foster looked to Craig Ellwood, Raphael Soriano, Charles and Ray Eames and others whose work they had studied on the West Coast for a new way forward. Rogers, rejecting Miesian closed systems, desired a more fluid and expressive alternative, with less striving for a 'classic' aesthetic. Moreover, the practice seemed to have chosen a hard route to success: every scheme was radically different, demanding a new start every time. 'We were desperate', Rogers recalls. 'We'd put so much into all those jobs and had no more to give. Architecture was an all-consuming passion during that intense period. We were working eighteen hours a day, seven days a week.' Then, amidst the continuing traumas of Creek Vean (not completed until 1967), Murray Mews and the rest, came the chance to do something different.

The 'something different' was the Reliance Controls Electronics Factory at Swindon which, with the Wates housing scheme, was the other key project of Rogers' early practice. After the trials of a group of houses designed for demanding individuals, the prospect of an industrial building which could set a new standard for the factories of the future was tempting. Like Creek Vean, Reliance Controls was thoroughly American in inspiration but, specifically, West Coast-American; more Eames and Soriano than Mies. Rogers has described the importance of the project in terms of 'shaking off Yale'. The Reliance Controls company was a leader in the infant – but rapidly expanding – British electronics industry and planned to open a new research and production base at Swindon. It was headed up by Peter Parker (later to become Chairman of British Rail), who saw the opportunity to build something high-profile and high-quality, a standing testimony to the company's aspirations to lead the field. But the building had to be inexpensive and, moreover, it had to be completed in ten months. James Stirling, who had been approached to be the architect himself but had turned it down as too small, drew up the short-list for the scheme, in which he included Team 4.

'Factory' is an inadequate description for Reliance Controls. Indeed, the building was something novel in Britain – a nation still dependent on heavy manufacturing – combining actual production with administration and research and development under one roof, and making a nonsense of the traditional divide between white- and blue-collar workers. As Norman Foster has suggested, 'it was an attempt to acknowledge, respect and give identity to those changes and, at the same time, to recognize social shifts in the sense that, in electronics, the person working on the assembly line is likely to be in cleaner conditions than the office worker. It is no longer a situation of "we and they", "back and front", "clean and dirty", "posh and scruffy".'

The basic brief was for 30,000 sq.ft. of space, with a flexible interior which could be reconfigured as the varying demands of the company required. There had to be provision for future expansion up to 110,000 sq.ft. should the need arise. Open, uncluttered space was vital for Reliance's operations. The company regarded itself as a progressive employer and plentiful natural light was vital. Thirty years on, it all sounds straightforward. But in the mid-1960s, Reliance Controls was something radical, pointing the way ahead to 1980s developments like Stockley Park, where manufacturing, research and office uses are inextricably mixed, and to the final breakdown of old-style planning controls on uses. Roche & Dinkeloo's building for Cummins Engines at Darlington (1962–6) was a factory pure and simple, while the later block designed for Boots' at Nottingham by SOM – it was American architects who were leading the way – contained only offices, with the production blocks elsewhere on the company's 'campus'.

Again, in retrospect Team 4's solution to the Reliance brief, developed in conjunction with Anthony Hunt, seems simple: a big shed, steel-framed and clad with profiled steel panels on the roof and extendible walls – one of which was entirely glazed and removable – with services separated out and run off a central underfloor duct. Hunt made Reliance possible where, at the insistence of the architects, everything was 'stretched to the limits'. He advocated a kit-of-parts approach, with a limited range of standard components. There was a deliberate attempt to eschew the monumentalism of Mies in favour of an almost matter-of-fact straightforwardness, a denial of rhetoric which echoed the Smithsons. (The slim, unbraced water tower at Reliance Controls – Hunt agonized over the practicality of it – was, of course, a direct quote from the Smithsons' Hunstanton school.) As Reyner Banham commented, 'Team 4 managed to eliminate the lurking monumentality of the Miesian tradition in metal framing. Whereas Mies ... stood in the Neo-Classical tradition, Team 4 had escaped from it.' The fully exposed structural frame defined the aesthetic, with the elegant cross-braces on the front elevation the only concession to 'decoration' – they are structurally redundant. Although intended to be matter-of-fact, Reliance Controls was admired as a beautiful object. Ian Nairn

Alison and Peter Smithson, Hunstanton School, Norfolk, 1949–54

Ludwig Mies van der Rohe, Crown Hall, Illinois Institute of Technology, Chicago, 1950–6

James Stirling and James Gowan, Leicester University Engineering Building, Leicester, 1963

thought its elegance 'wasted on the Greenbridge estate in Swindon ... it wouldn't shame places as traditionally beautiful as Burford or Bourton-on-the-Water', while the assessors of the *Financial Times* industrial architecture award – given to the building in 1967 – felt that it evoked 'a lost vernacular'.

Reliance Controls has been frequently – and misleadingly – depicted as a key Foster building, and only more marginally as part of the corpus of Rogers' work. Yet Reliance Controls fed directly into the separate practices established by both Rogers and Foster after the break-up of Team 4 in 1967, and symbolizes the continuity of thinking which flowed into both. 'We still share the same common language that brought us together in the 1960s', Foster declared in 1998, insisting on the integrity of Team 4's work. 'We share the same passions.' The Rogers and Spender houses, designed by Richard + Su Rogers, and the Zip-Up House programme both draw on the lessons of Reliance, as, indeed, do Norman Foster's unbuilt Newport school project and the various early industrial schemes by Foster Associates. Moreover, the determination to delineate clearly the elements of the structure and the services was to become part of Rogers' mature manner, expressed, for example, in Lloyd's.

With the completion of Reliance Controls, Team 4 appeared to have run its course – especially with the loss of the big Wates scheme – though another significant commercial project, the offices for Fletcher & Stewart at Derby, followed on. Fletcher & Stewart, like Reliance, was part of the Booker empire. ('It wasn't a great success', according to John Young, and neither Rogers nor Foster remembers the job with affection – though the Derby building, unlike Reliance Controls, survives.) As Su Rogers insists, 'we had had a good run' – a number of buildings had been completed and unbuilt projects had given the office valuable experience in working on larger commissions. Both Richard Rogers and Norman Foster, however, were dissatisfied and wanted to go their own ways. According to Rogers, 'the divorce was difficult'. Foster and his wife, Wendy Cheeseman, were a powerful team in their own right and duly formed a practice, Foster Associates. Neither Richard nor Su Rogers had any expectation that their practice would be financially underwritten by their parents, and there were no jobs, though Rogers had a modest income from teaching. Nonetheless, the new husband-and-wife Rogers practice was born, with a small group of Team 4 staff also forming part of it. 'But, frankly, we were pretty dispirited at the time', Richard Rogers recalls. 'It wasn't clear where we were going.'

According to Frank Peacock, a Team 4 stalwart who worked for both Rogers and Foster later, 'the partnership with Norman, while it lasted, really worked. Richard looked up to Norman, on account of his amazing skills as a draughtsman for example. At the same time, Richard was a remarkable leader of the practice – his ability to attract people's loyalties and retain them shone through.' John Young was another Rogers loyalist, though he had initially felt closer to Foster from an architectural standpoint. In fact, the bones of the Richard Rogers Partnership as it emerged in the 1980s were formed in 1967–8 – Marco Goldschmied, another founding director, arrived soon after the break-up with Foster.

Team 4, in its brief existence – founded in the year that 'Beatlemania' hit Britain and wound up during the 'summer of love' – had made its mark. The British architectural culture which emerged during the 1950s was inspired by pre-war Europe. Many of the leading figures, Basil Spence, Leslie Martin, Denys Lasdun and Erno Goldfinger, had practiced during the 1930s and belonged to the 'age of the masters'. Le Corbusier was their chief inspiration. Team 4's ideas, however, were forged in the USA – their experiences there allowed them to look at the tradition of European modernism in a new light. Their heroes in Britain, such as they were, were critics of the old CIAM school – like the Smithsons and Stirling, whose campaign to reinterpret Corbusier influenced Foster and Rogers, for whom Ronchamp was an icon. Coming to terms with America – with Wright, Mies, Saarinen, Kahn and the West Coast school of Eames, Schindler, Ellwood and others, was a way to renewal. There was more than one way to read America – Edward Cullinan and Richard MacCormac, for example, feasted on the riches of the West Coast and produced an idiosyncratic humanist architecture of their own; marred, Rogers feels, by a strain of sentimentality and subjectivity. (It was significant that Rogers and Foster came to the West Coast after a spell on the East Coast.) YRM, more than any practice, took up the Mies/SOM torch to excellent effect. But the real flame burned in the offices of Team 4 and was passed on to the practices that Rogers and Foster established after its demise. It took the contributions of Foster and Rogers' mentor, Stirling, to turn British eyes back to Europe and to a great historic tradition of civic and public design which informed his late master-piece, the Stuttgart Staatsgalerie, and made it a worthy companion to Lloyd's and the Hongkong and Shanghai Bank as symbols of the 'new' British architecture of the 1980s. Rogers could not sympathize with Stirling's change in direction ('Leicester was always an inspiration', he says) but was unswerving in his support for his old mentor's work – as he made clear in the 1980s by backing the hugely controversial No. 1 Poultry scheme for the City of London. By that time, Foster, Rogers and Stirling were recognized as the 'big three' of British architecture – the grouping could be traced back to Yale in the early 1960s.

A 'who did what at Team 4' exercise is pointless. A decade or more ago, it may have seemed easy to read back into the work of the practice characteristics of the subsequent work of Rogers and Foster and to allot work accordingly. At the time, it didn't quite work like that. Team 4 *was* a team, for all the tensions and disagreements that the term glossed over. Within it were the makings of two new practices who were to remake British architecture. Rogers sums up the influences which underlay his (and Foster's) architectural education: 'we were the first generation to be inspired by the Modern Masters, but not to be subservient to them. We were a lucky generation.'

Team 4 with Tony Hunt: (back row, left to right) Tony Hunt, Frank Peacock ; (front row, left to right) Sophie Read, Wendy Foster, Richard Rogers, Su Rogers, Norman Foster, Maurice Philips

Naum and Miriam Gabo (photographed in 1937)

Georgie Wolton (née Cheeseman)

Norman Foster and Richard Rogers discussing the Greenwich Millennium site in 1997

Science Campus Project

Yale University, New Haven, Connecticut, 1961

Yale University's architecture school brought Norman Foster and Richard Rogers together and forged their subsequent partnership in Team 4. During their year there (1961–2), Foster and Rogers collaborated on several design projects. Paul Rudolph, the head of school (subsequently replaced by Serge Chermayeff), emphasized practical issues and the need for good presentation of schemes through drawing and modelling. One of these collaborations involved a scheme for new science laboratories on the Yale campus at New Haven, Connecticut.

Rudolph's brief for this project insisted that it concerned not just an urban problem, but equally an architectural one. Most current development projects, the brief maintained, were the result of an obsession with scale and profitability, ignoring 'life itself and the spirit of man'.

While it may have reflected some British projects known to Foster and Rogers – for example, the Smithsons' much-published scheme for Sheffield University – the inspiration for the project was largely American, and the influence of Louis Kahn was pervasive. The scheme provided for departmental blocks stepping down in tiers from a central spine of communal facilities, with parking spaces underneath. The strongly expressed service towers, firmly disliked by visiting critic Philip Johnson, were clearly Kahnian – part of Kahn's strategy of 'served and servant spaces' which was to have a potent influence on Rogers and later be vividly expressed at Lloyd's.

Although Rogers has never counted Rudolph as a major influence, the rigour of his approach to teaching made a mark and his strong emphasis on the way buildings looked, in contrast to the more theoretical and social approach of the AA, imprinted itself. In this project, Rogers' belief that practical functions, however mundane, can and should find a strongly architectonic expression, is clearly stated. Although designed for a highly specialized use, the buildings make a dramatic gesture to the university campus and to the public domain beyond.

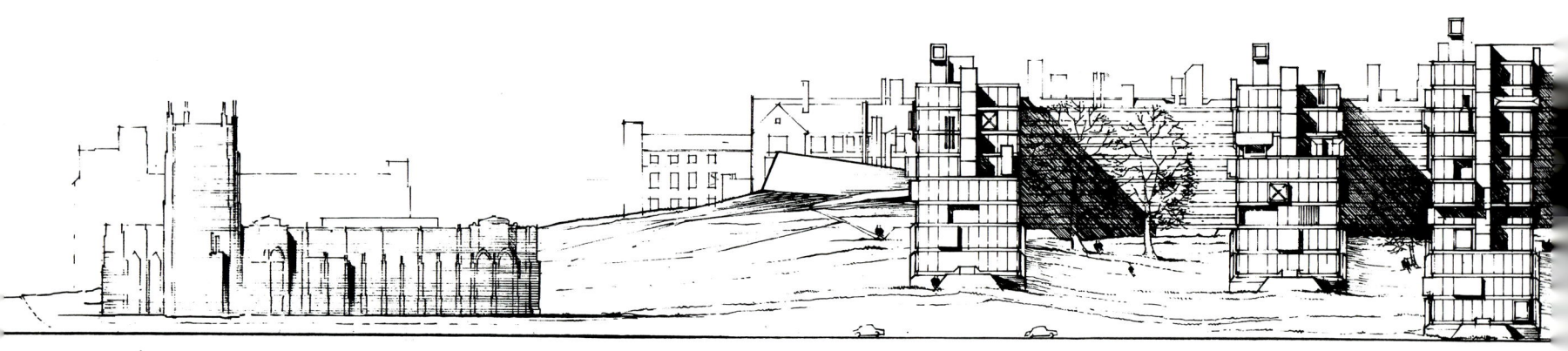

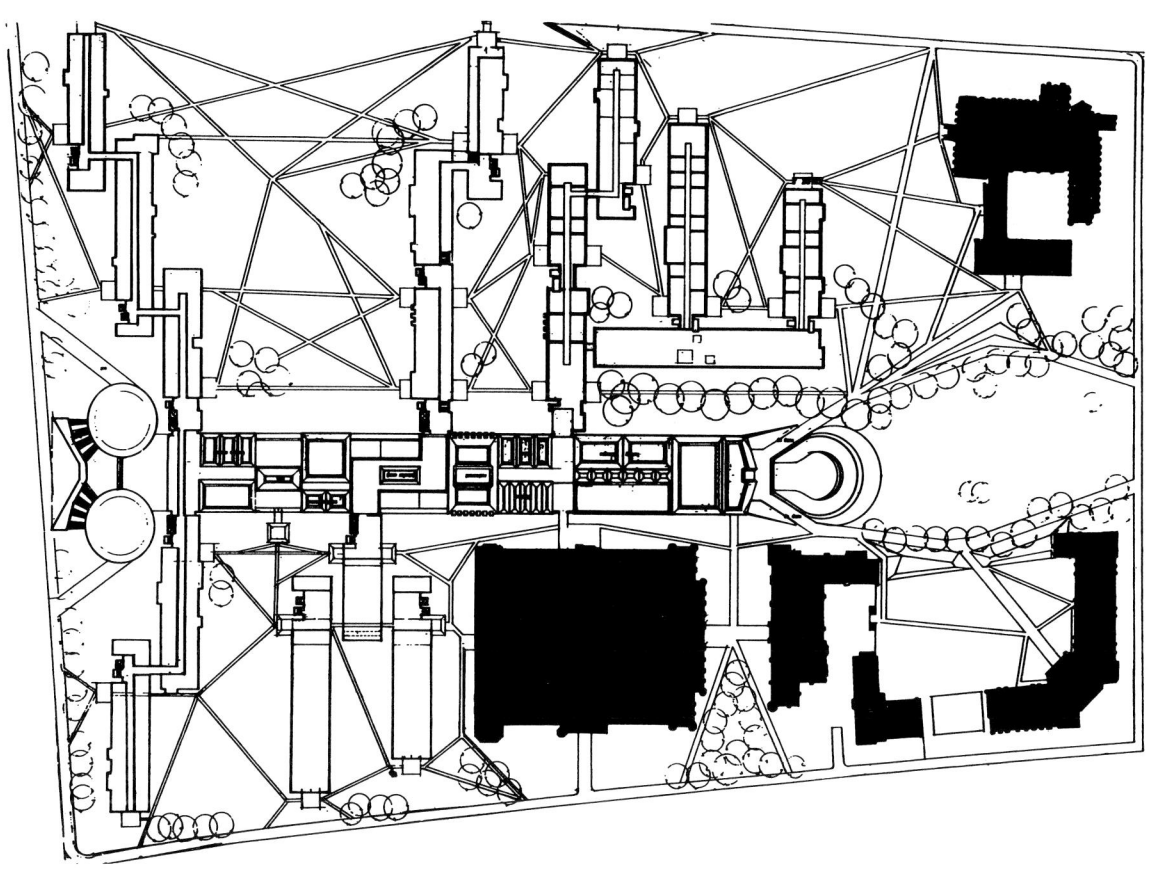

Richard Rogers' project – designed at Yale with Norman Foster – for a new laboratory complex on the New Haven campus (1 & 3) was influenced by the work of Louis Kahn. A radical intervention into the traditional layout of the campus (2), the scheme looked forward to Rogers' later urban masterplans.

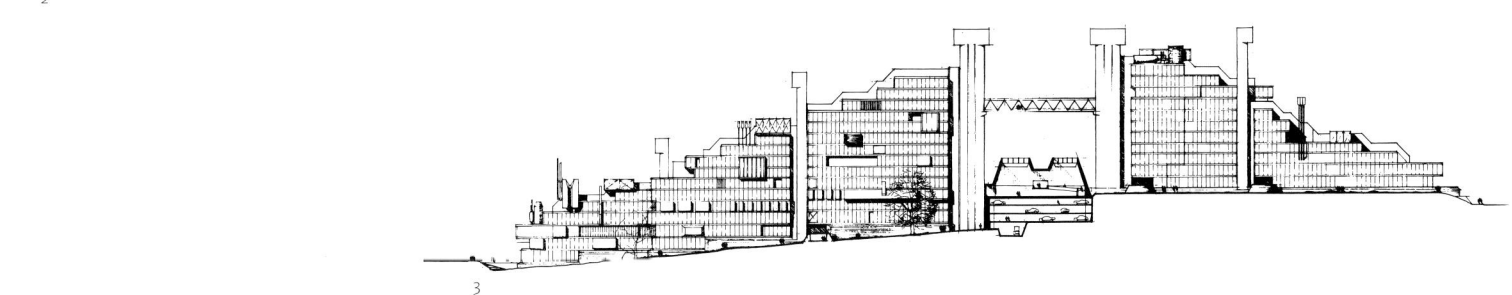

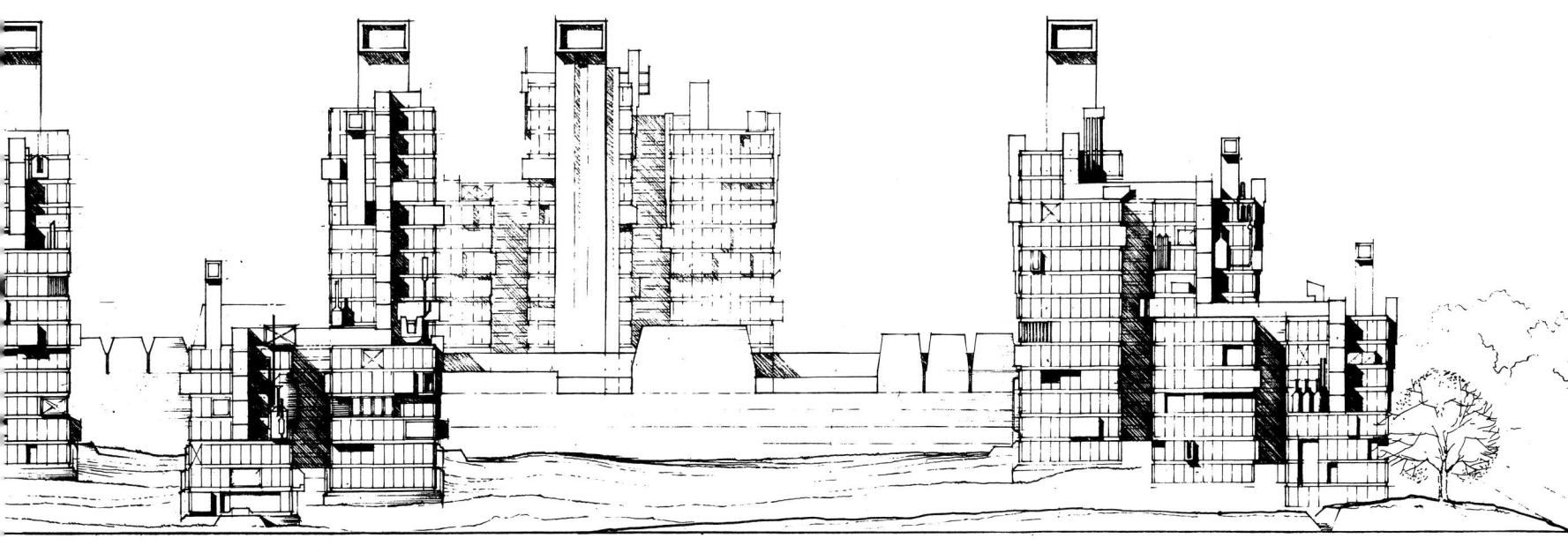

1

2

3

Pill Creek Retreat

Feock, Cornwall, 1963

4

Pill Creek Retreat was completed while the house at Creek Vean for Su Rogers' parents was under construction. Situated on the Fal estuary beyond Feock it was, simply, a retreat to which Marcus and Rene Brumwell could escape in order to read, have a picnic (whatever the weather) or just look at the view.

The Brumwells had owned a similar retreat, known as 'The Hut', in the garden of their home in Dorking, Surrey. Richard Rogers 'improved' The Hut with a big window overlooking the Surrey Downs, and stayed there from time to time making plans to build a more permanent house on the site, although these were never executed and the site was eventually sold.

For Pill Creek Retreat Rogers had ideas of building a free-standing box, of Miesian character, placed in the landscape rather than being part of it – echoing the iconic Farnsworth House in Illinois. However, as built, the Retreat resembled a cockpit dug into the earth. Entirely glazed, with built-in concrete seating and incorporating a small cooker and sink unit, it was entered through a sliding panel in the glass. The building was a house in miniature, with a flavour of the house to come across the creek.

5

Early development sketches for the Retreat (1, 2 & 4) showing a free-standing Miesian box later gave way to a cockpit dug into the cliff edge (3).
The Retreat overlooks the Fal estuary, a short distance from the site of Creek Vean. The interior of the Retreat (5 & 6) was fitted out with basic cooking facilities – it was a place to spend a day reading or looking at the beautiful view.

6

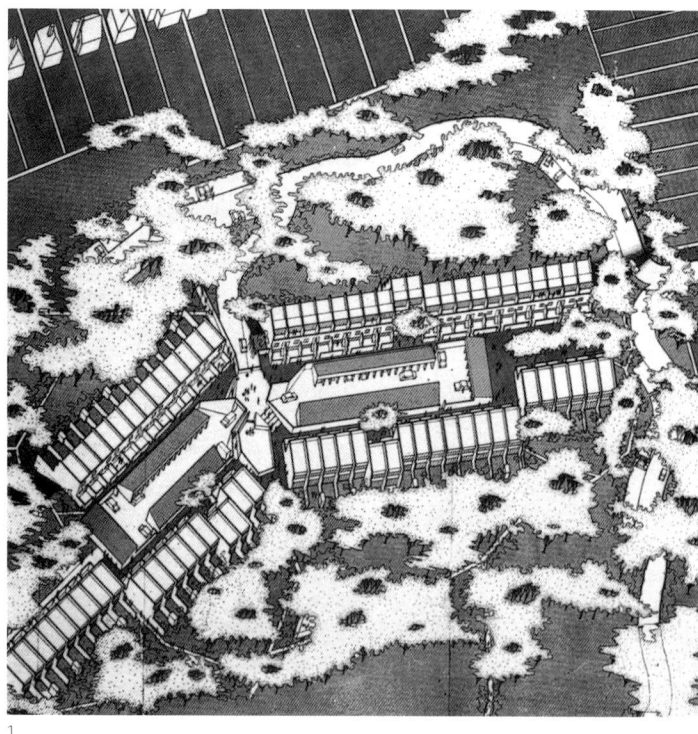

Wates Housing Project
Coulsdon, Surrey, 1965

Richard Rogers has a passionate interest in housing. Not in designing houses for relatively affluent individuals, but a concern for tackling both the shortage of houses for comparatively non-affluent people and a wish to confront the problem of the poor quality – technical and aesthetic – of what has been built by the public and private sectors in recent decades. Ironically, Rogers has yet to build this sort of housing, but the interest is well represented by Team 4's innovative, but unexecuted, project for Wates at Coulsdon, Surrey.

The background to the project was undoubtedly a reaction by Wates to the success of Span Homes, the company formed by Leslie Bilsby to build genuinely modern houses for everyman. Bilsby's alliance with the architect Eric Lyons produced some 5,000 homes in and around London. Lyons – whose architecture was soft-edged, deploying a comfortable mix of brick and timber – was an excellent planner, and the landscaping at Span developments was always outstanding. Wates felt that what Span could do, it could do too, and Neil Wates sought architects who could produce, in effect, a masterplan for a 70-acre site at Coulsdon.

The site's steep contours demanded an unconventional approach and Team 4's thinking was strongly influenced by the Siedlung Halen project of Atelier 5, as well as by the theoretical approach which underlay Chermayeff's balance of 'community' and 'privacy'. The practice's work on Creek Vean and the associated Pill Creek housing project had provided experience of working with steep, difficult sites.

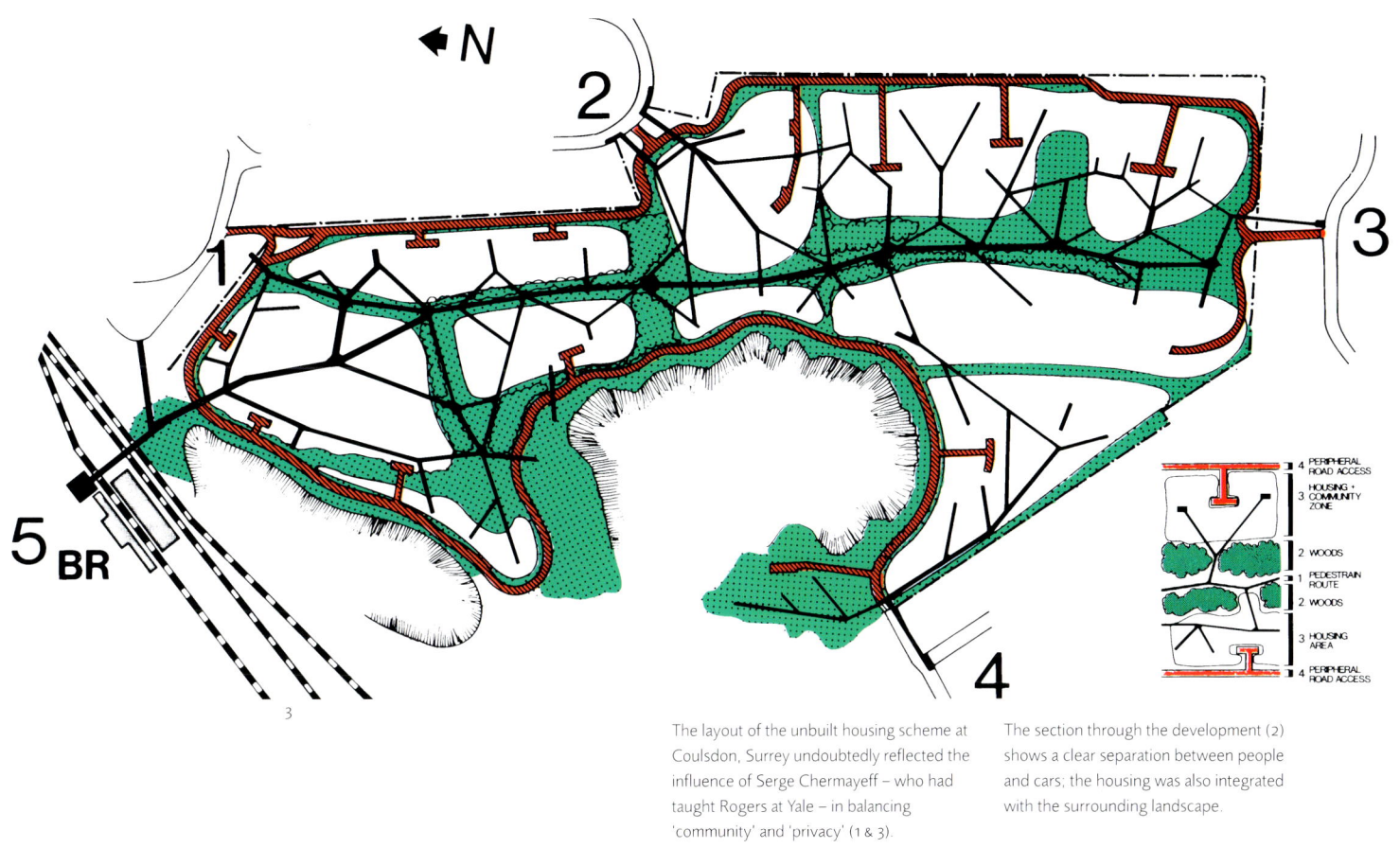

The layout of the unbuilt housing scheme at Coulsdon, Surrey undoubtedly reflected the influence of Serge Chermayeff – who had taught Rogers at Yale – in balancing 'community' and 'privacy' (1 & 3). The section through the development (2) shows a clear separation between people and cars; the housing was also integrated with the surrounding landscape.

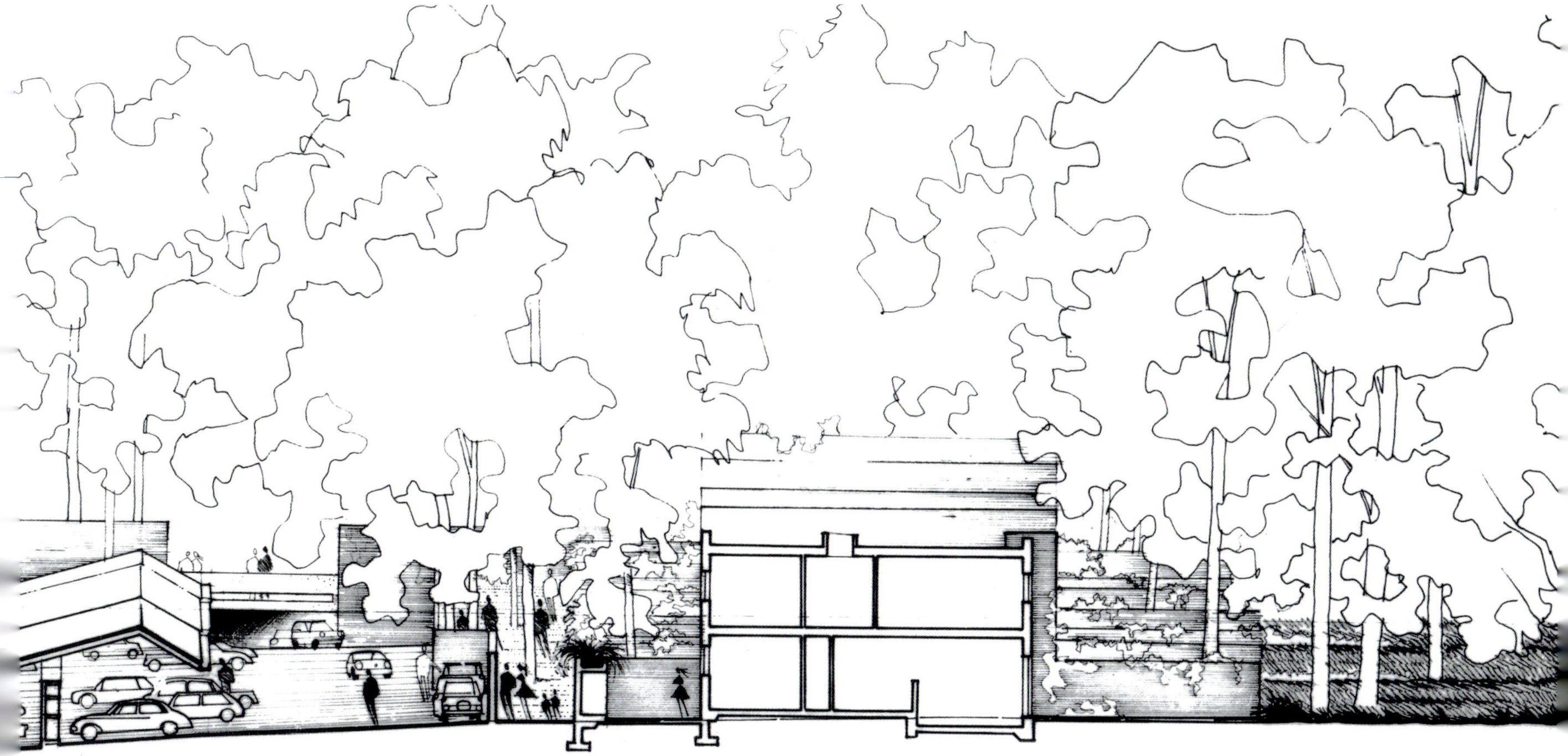

4

In line with the progressive practice of the period, traffic and pedestrians were to be rigorously segregated. The wooded strip along the centre of the site was to be preserved and developed as a pedestrian spine, with a network of footpaths leading off it to every house. There was a series of interconnected open spaces, for play areas, walks through the trees, and paths direct to the station, the schools and the shops. Vehicles would be confined to a road running around the periphery with feeder roads leading off into walled vehicle courts at the centre of the housing clusters. There was no conflict between pedestrians and vehicles at any time and cars could be driven up to the door of each house. In this way an 'urban' core was made for each group of houses, where cars could be parked and serviced, and a tight sense of community developed with the houses arranged in strings on either side of the court.

In addition to masterplanning the site, Team 4 was commissioned to design a detailed pilot scheme of 130 houses for nine acres of the site. The houses were to be of two basic types: three-storey and two-storey, the larger houses 'dug into' the slope in long terraces. Parking and servicing spaces were provided in a rear yard, and parkland extended right up to the front of the houses without the interruption of roads. Construction was to be along traditional lines - cavity walls, brick facing, timber floors and roof structures.

Wates decided not to go ahead with the scheme, a reverse which depressed Rogers who saw such backtracking as indicative of the essential conservatism of the house-building industry, whereas Norman Foster had always been sceptical about the prospects of the scheme. The failure of the Wates project drove Rogers towards a more radical approach to housing which focused on need rather than on the vagaries of the market.

5

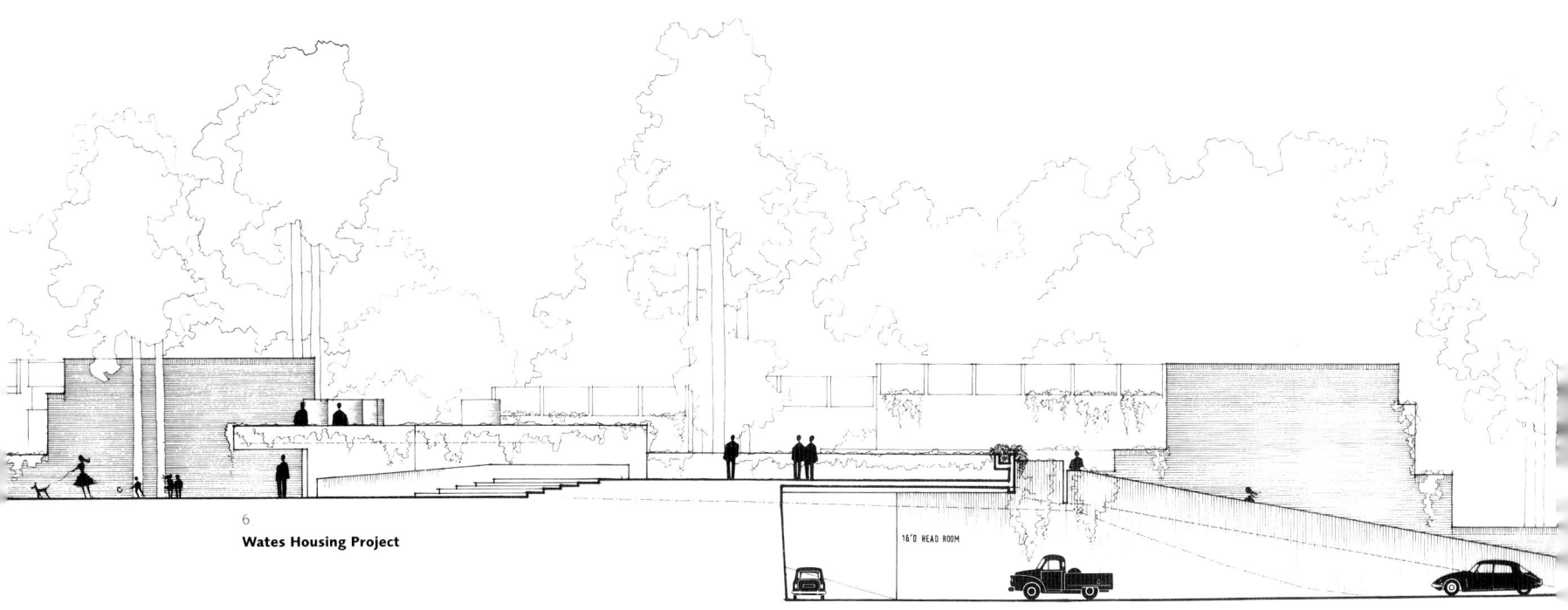

6

Wates Housing Project

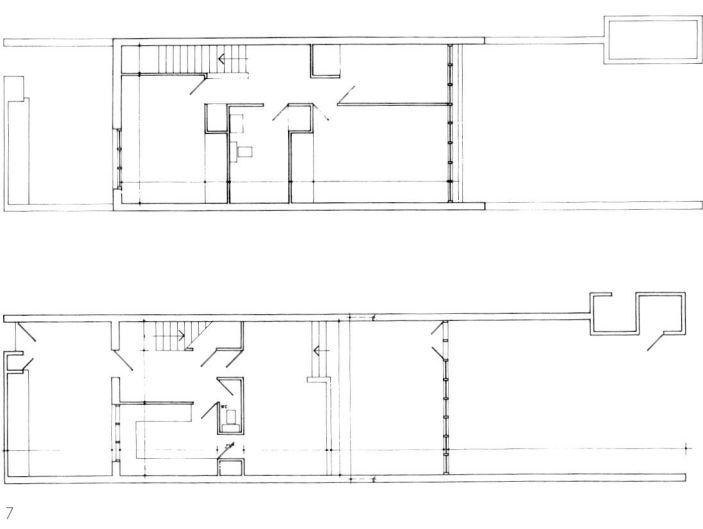

7

8

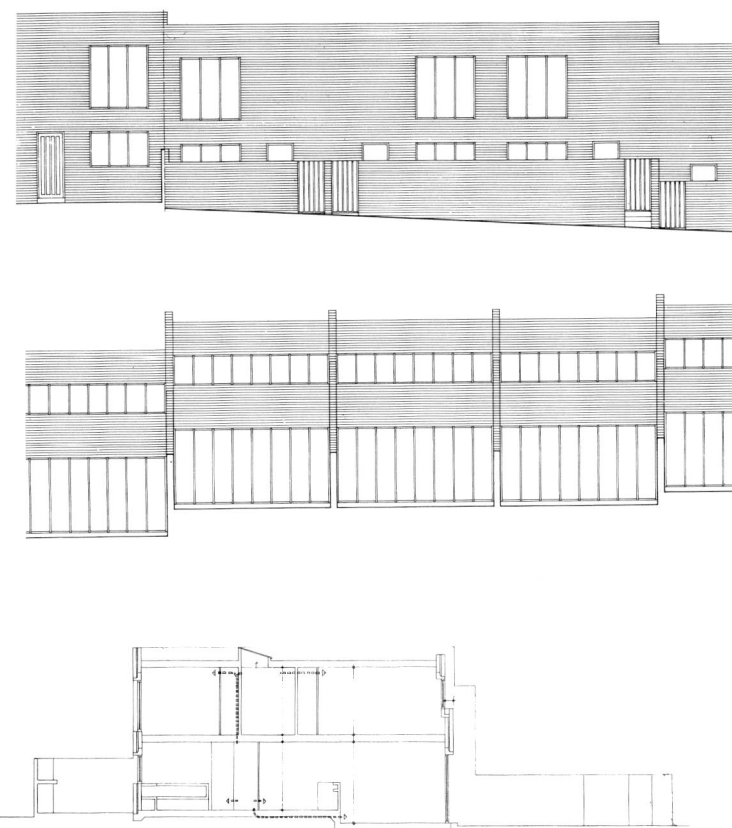

Car and pedestrian zones were rigorously separated, as shown in the model (4), sketch (5) and section (6). The houses were designed in two generic types – two-storey (7) and three-storey (9). The three-storey version incorporated a split-level living area at the top (8).

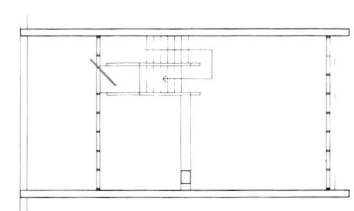

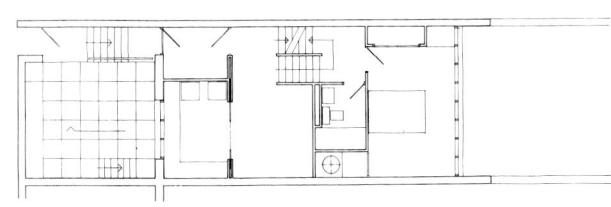

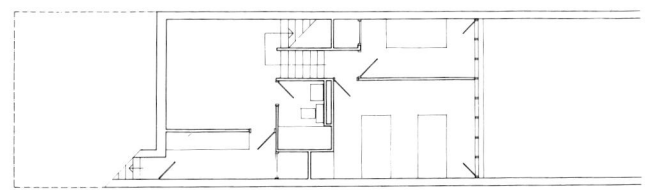

9

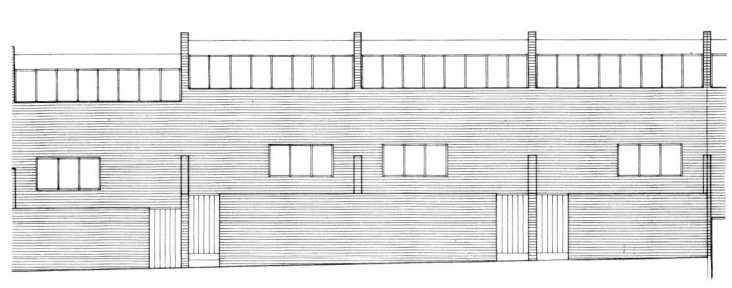

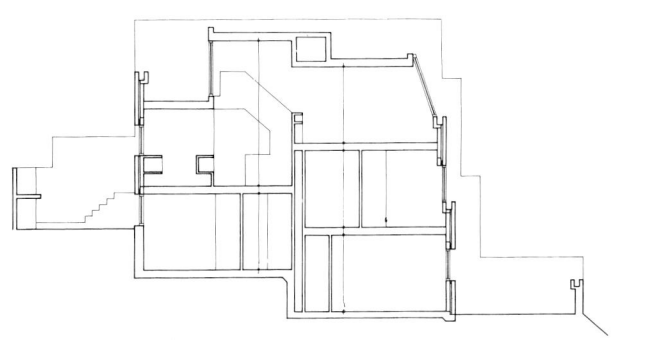

Creek Vean

Feock, Cornwall, 1964–7

Creek Vean was Team 4's first major job, begun in 1963 after Richard Rogers and Norman Foster returned to London from the USA. The clients were Rogers' parents-in-law, Marcus and Rene Brumwell, who had acquired a site with an existing Victorian villa on it close to their holiday cottage on Pill Creek near Falmouth, Cornwall. The Brumwells' aim was to create a comfortable retirement home there, with space to display their significant art collection. Converting and extending the existing house had been considered and Ernst Freud drew up proposals for an extension. However, after Rogers' return to England, Freud was dropped and Team 4 won the commission to design a new house.

The project was slow to be finalized and, when it was, slow to be constructed. The key influences were those of Frank Lloyd Wright, whose work Rogers and Foster had come to revere during their stay in America, and Serge Chermayeff, a much-respected Yale tutor. Preliminary schemes proposed a house that would step down the slope to the creek in dramatically Wrightian fashion, recalling Fallingwater. The Siedlung Halen housing project in Berne, designed by Atelier 5, was also well-known to Team 4 – and influenced its own scheme for a housing development close to Creek Vean. In its final form, however, Creek Vean makes more subtle use of the contours of the site, occupying a relatively level zone just below the road and extending along the slope rather than down it.

The house seems to be 'dug into' the land, partly as a result of the extensive planting which embraces it, but is actually free-standing and approached by a bridge from the road. From the entrance, one can go up a few steps to a living room (the only room on this level), an eyrie with splendid views across the river and out to the Fal estuary, or down to the main level with its focal point being the kitchen, open to the first floor, and the run of study and bedrooms opening off the gallery. The top-glazing provides excellent light; however, there is too much of it – particularly sensitive works have had to be moved to the study to stop them from fading.

The rooms off the gallery ('private' space) are defined by sliding partitions from the 'communal' space beyond, so that the spatial effects and the pattern of use can be varied as required. Some of the furniture was framed in concrete which was used, in the form of moulded blocks on a reinforced concrete frame, as the basic material of the house. The Brumwells wanted a maintenance-free building, and resisted local authority demands that the concrete be painted for cosmetic effect. The floors were to be of local Cornish slate, but no supplier could be found to guarantee the quantities required, so Welsh slate was used instead. Its texture adds considerably to the 'organic' feel of the interior – the house appears at one with the West Country landscape in a way that Lescaze's 1930s headmaster's house at Dartington, not far away, does not. The heating system is contained below the floors, giving a completely uncluttered look.

The traditional references of Creek Vean should not be exaggerated. As it developed, the project cast off some of its more obviously Wrightian references to become sharper in its geometry and harder in its details. The development of the plan set the kitchen/dining room at an angle to the main axis, fanning off from the route that leads straight through to the garden – making the house appear as two separate blocks from the road – infusing a dynamic into the composition of which Paul Rudolph would have been proud. Great attention was given to the design of the full-height windows, providing the extensive views required by the clients.

Marcus Brumwell, Rogers' client at Creek Vean, seen below the completed house (2, previous page). The relationship of the house to the creek is a vital element of the project (1, p28).
The entrance sequence to the house (3 & 4) takes the visitor from the lane across the bridge, from which the house can be entered; ahead is the route through the garden down to the water.

The plan (5) shows the two axes which, from east to west, lead down to the boathouse and the creek, and which, from north to south, run through the house.
Planted 'cathedral' steps (6) lead down to the boathouse and the creek.

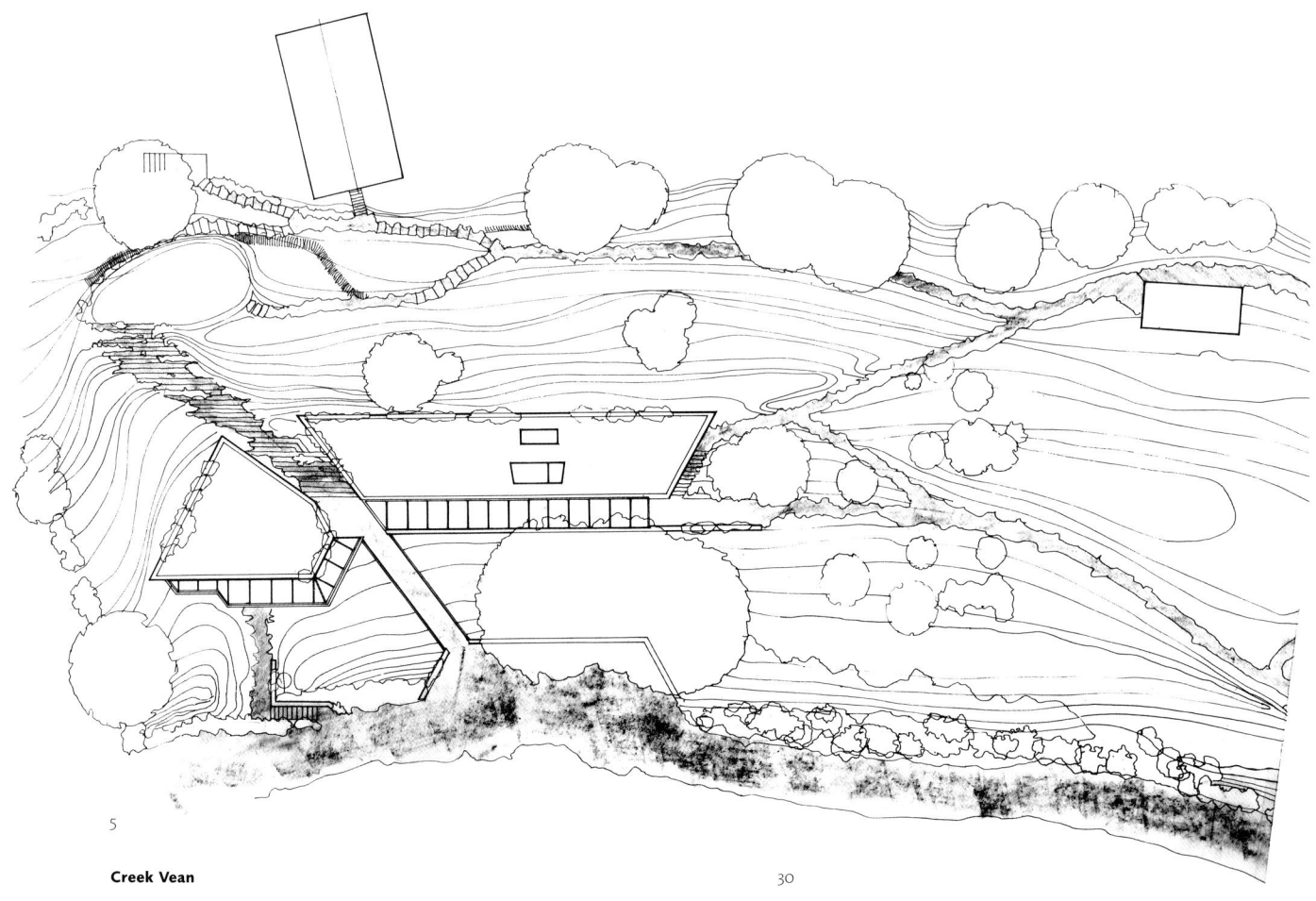

Creek Vean

The house was designed to reach out to the surrounding landscape. A roof-top vantage point, reached by very steep 'cathedral steps' from the top floor living room, provided the best views of the estuary. It was a romantic, almost Gothic, gesture, but elsewhere there were other points where the inhabitants could break down the walls of their enclosure and become part of the landscape. The river itself mattered a great deal to the Brumwells, who loved sailing and kept a boat in the boathouse below the house. The gardens down to the water are luxuriantly planted, to a scheme by Michael Branch, and the planting extends over the roof of the bedroom wing, rooting the house even more firmly to the site. The planted staircase down to the garden is a clear quotation from Alvar Aalto's Säynätsalo Town Hall.

Creek Vean has been meaningfully compared to Kettle's Yard in Cambridge, created by Jim Ede as both a house and an art gallery. Marcus and Rene Brumwell knew Ben Nicholson, Barbara Hepworth, Patrick Heron and many other artists who were inspired by and lived in Cornwall. In their youth, they had known Christopher Wood ('though he was always a difficult man', according to Rene Brumwell). Although Creek Vean has never been open to the public, its plan revolves around the display space of the gallery and staircase. The house

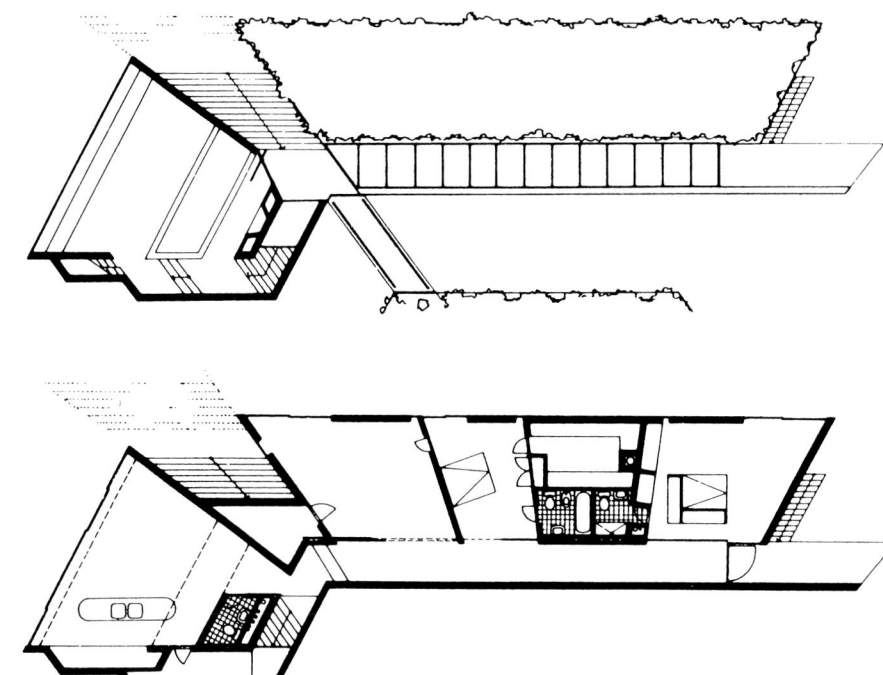

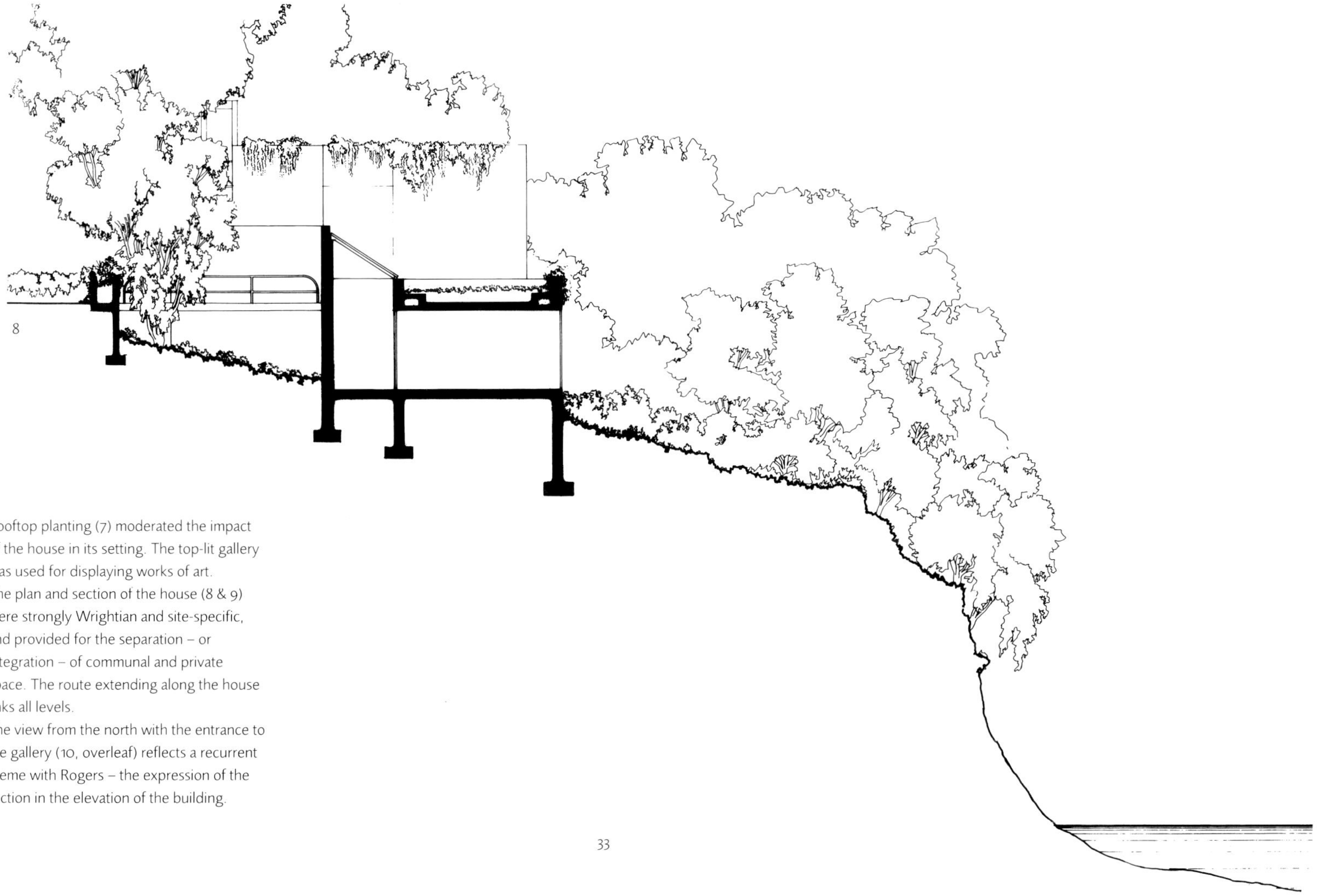

Rooftop planting (7) moderated the impact of the house in its setting. The top-lit gallery was used for displaying works of art. The plan and section of the house (8 & 9) were strongly Wrightian and site-specific, and provided for the separation – or integration – of communal and private space. The route extending along the house links all levels.
The view from the north with the entrance to the gallery (10, overleaf) reflects a recurrent theme with Rogers – the expression of the section in the elevation of the building.

represents the response of a new generation, for whom Nicholson, Hepworth and the rest were already historic figures, to the artistic climate of Cornwall as well as to the magical landscape of the county. Some of its flavour pervades the 'Tate of the West' at St Ives, a successful public encapsulation of the St Ives school designed by Rogers' old college friend Eldred Evans and her partner David Shalev in 1993.

Although Creek Vean, along with other house projects of the Team 4 period, might seem entirely detached from Richard Rogers' later work, its highly expressive, sculptural quality, use of space and light and relationship to the landscape prefigure later themes in his architecture.

Creek Vean was certainly a deeply-felt work, though it caused headaches for both architects and clients. In a newspaper interview in 1969, when Creek Vean won an RIBA award (the first given to a private house since the awards scheme began) Richard Rogers declared: 'Methods of building like this have got to end. Builders go bankrupt, architects lose money, and the client is driven to distraction', while Su Rogers added that 'the pain and anguish of it all has forced us to realize that future homes must be built much more quickly and much more simply'.

For all that, Creek Vean has been a spectacular success as a family home; moreover it has now been listed. Its spaces lend themselves to socializing as much as to domestic calm. Mrs Brumwell, who insisted from the start that kitchen and dining room be integrated, feels herself vindicated by the experience of living in the house. With its island sink/preparation unit, the first of many in houses and flats designed by Rogers including his own house at Royal Avenue, London, it is a shrine to hospitality. Rogers' children and many other members of the Rogers/Brumwell/Miller clan – Su Rogers and her present partner John Miller have a holiday house nearby – have come to regard Creek Vean as a second home. Rene Brumwell's 95th birthday in 1997 saw a spectacular three-day event, with dinners, drinks parties and teas for relatives, friends and neighbours from Feock, London and every corner of the world. It was the celebration of a life, but it also seemed like the best way to celebrate a great house.

Creek Vean is romantic, expressive and very personal, designed with two aims in mind: the display of a treasured art collection (11 & 14) and the creation of a place for socializing and extended family living. The combined kitchen/dining room (13 & 15) is the heart of the house; it is integrated with the rest of the house by means of a void (12). The private spaces (16) can either be opened up to the gallery or completely sealed off for seclusion.

Creek Vean

13

14

15

16

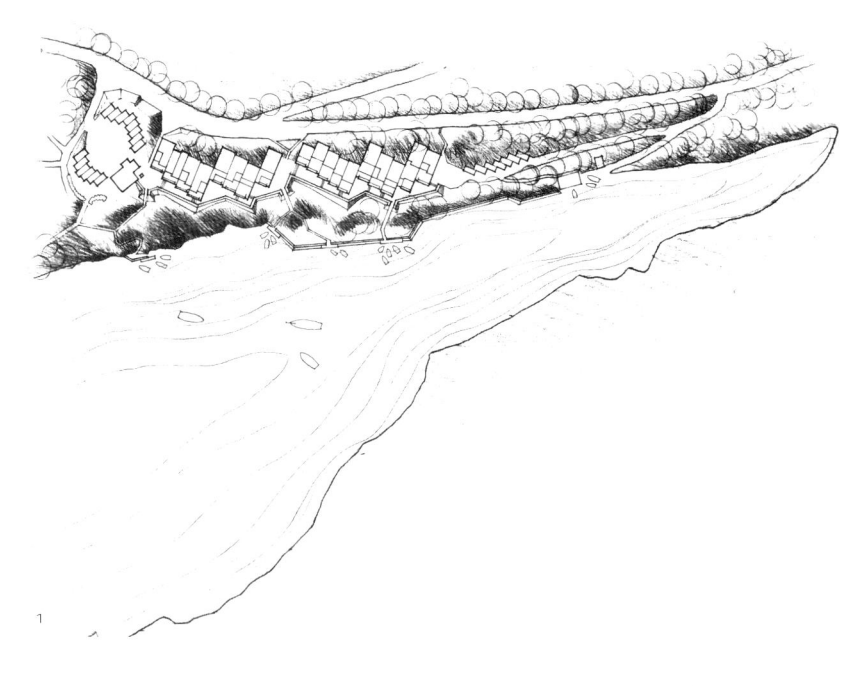

Pill Creek Housing
Feock, Cornwall, 1964

Concurrent with the design and construction of Creek Vean was a project to build a housing development on land owned by the Brumwells across the creek from their new house. The scheme was always contentious, even within the Brumwell family, and was eventually dropped after local planners opposed it strongly. However, its intentions were, if not entirely altruistic, honourable: Marcus Brumwell deplored the sprawl of new houses which was gradually spreading out from the old centre of Feock and felt it would be preferable to group new housing in a well-designed complex.

With the exception of the Span developments by Eric Lyons, new private-sector housing in Britain after the Second World War had been traditional in form – that is, based on the garden city ideal of detached or semi-detached houses in their own gardens. Innovations had been largely confined to the public sector. Architects were attracted by denser models, including the proverbial Italian hill-town (promoted as the ideal by the *Architectural Review*), with its strong connotations of the picturesque. Team 4's ideas were more radically rooted. The notion of a dense village, where individual houses could offer complete privacy yet be part of a distinct community, was in line with the ideas of Chermayeff, as taught at Yale.

The scheme carefully addressed the landscape, proposing the retention of all significant trees and the use of earth mounds to screen roads and parking areas. Planting would be encouraged to spread around and even over the houses (as at Creek Vean). A staggered section for the houses allowed maximum privacy and good views, with the nineteen houses being dug into the land. An early version of the project showed the houses with large areas of raked glazing – as later at Murray Mews. The developed scheme abandoned the glazing in favour of private open courts and terraces.

A later variant of the Pill Creek idea emerged in 1968, in the form of a proposal by Richard + Su Rogers for another seaside site. Like the Pill Creek scheme, however, it was never built.

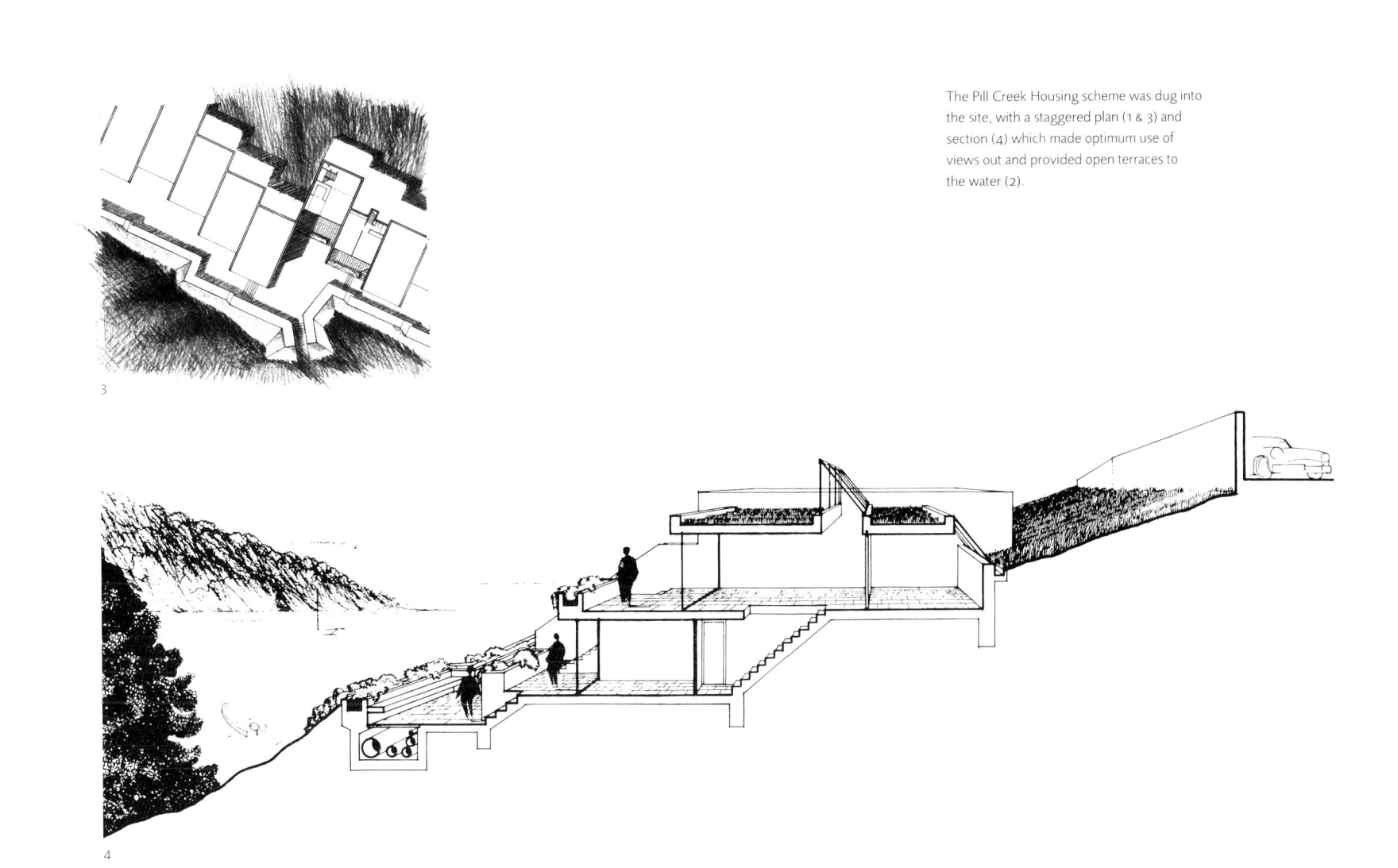

The Pill Creek Housing scheme was dug into the site, with a staggered plan (1 & 3) and section (4) which made optimum use of views out and provided open terraces to the water (2).

Jaffe House

Radlett, Hertfordshire, 1966

The romantic qualities of Creek Vean were, for better or worse, absent from the Jaffe House, designed not for a dramatic Cornish creek but for a suburban plot in mundane Hertfordshire. Perhaps it is the cool rationalism of the Jaffe House, low on emotion and expression, which makes it seem out of place in the Rogers *œuvre*. Yet the house has its place in Rogers', as much as Norman Foster's, subsequent development.

The stepped section drew on that developed for the Pill Creek housing project, though at Radlett the slope was undramatic. Inclined lights, unambitiously framed in timber, ingeniously provide a generous continuous light inside, despite the north-facing aspect of the house. Everything is contained within brick retaining walls, as if this were the first of a long terrace of such houses – a pipe dream, however, since neighbouring plots had already been filled with run-of-the-mill villas. It is the flexibility built into the house which makes it really interesting. The Jaffes wanted spaces that could be adapted for social occasions and for the changing needs of a family. The living space is divided by sliding doors into a 'public' (entertaining) zone and a family zone centred on the kitchen. Along the eastern edge of the house are the 'private' quarters and the bedrooms, though their walls are non-structural and can be relocated. The interior flows downhill, providing views along the way of sky and, as you approach the lowest level, countryside.

The Jaffe House was seen as a prototype, but, as was often the case, turned out to be a one-off. (Despite its provision for adaptation, the Jaffes later sold up and moved out.) For Team 4, the house was a testing ground for ideas in space, flexibility and materials. The mix of the latter was undoubtedly over-complex and the house helped refine Rogers' ideas about materials and to drive him towards lightweight construction. Notably, the interior of the house was chosen as the setting for Stanley Kubrick's controversial film *A Clockwork Orange* in 1971.

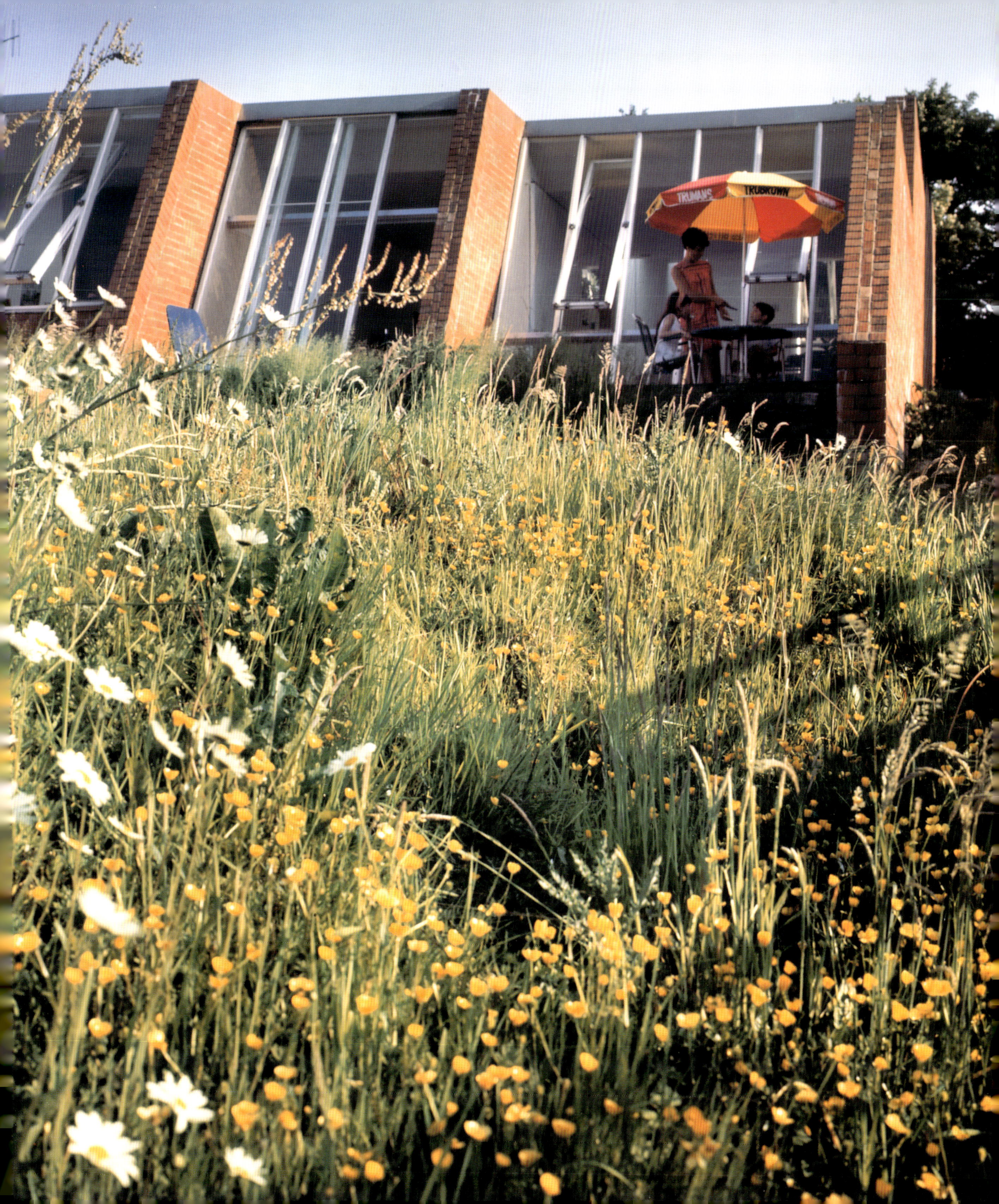
TRUMANS
TRUBROWN

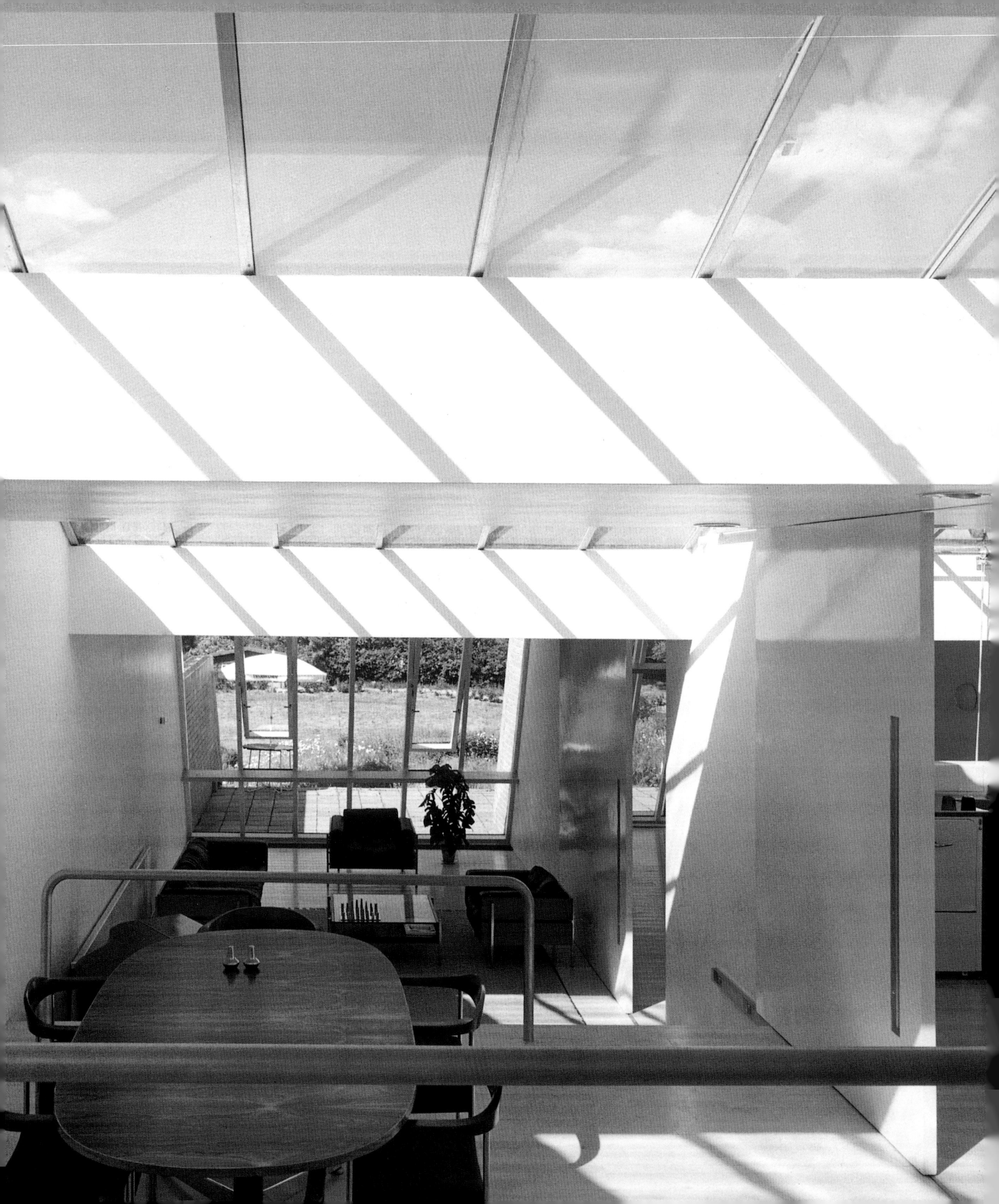

The internal layout of the Jaffe House (3, 6 & 7) made good use of the contours of the site (1, p40) to create a series of separately defined but interlocking spaces for family living, top-lit at each change in level. The three living zones within the plan (5) are also expressed through the staggered elevation (2, previous page & 4).

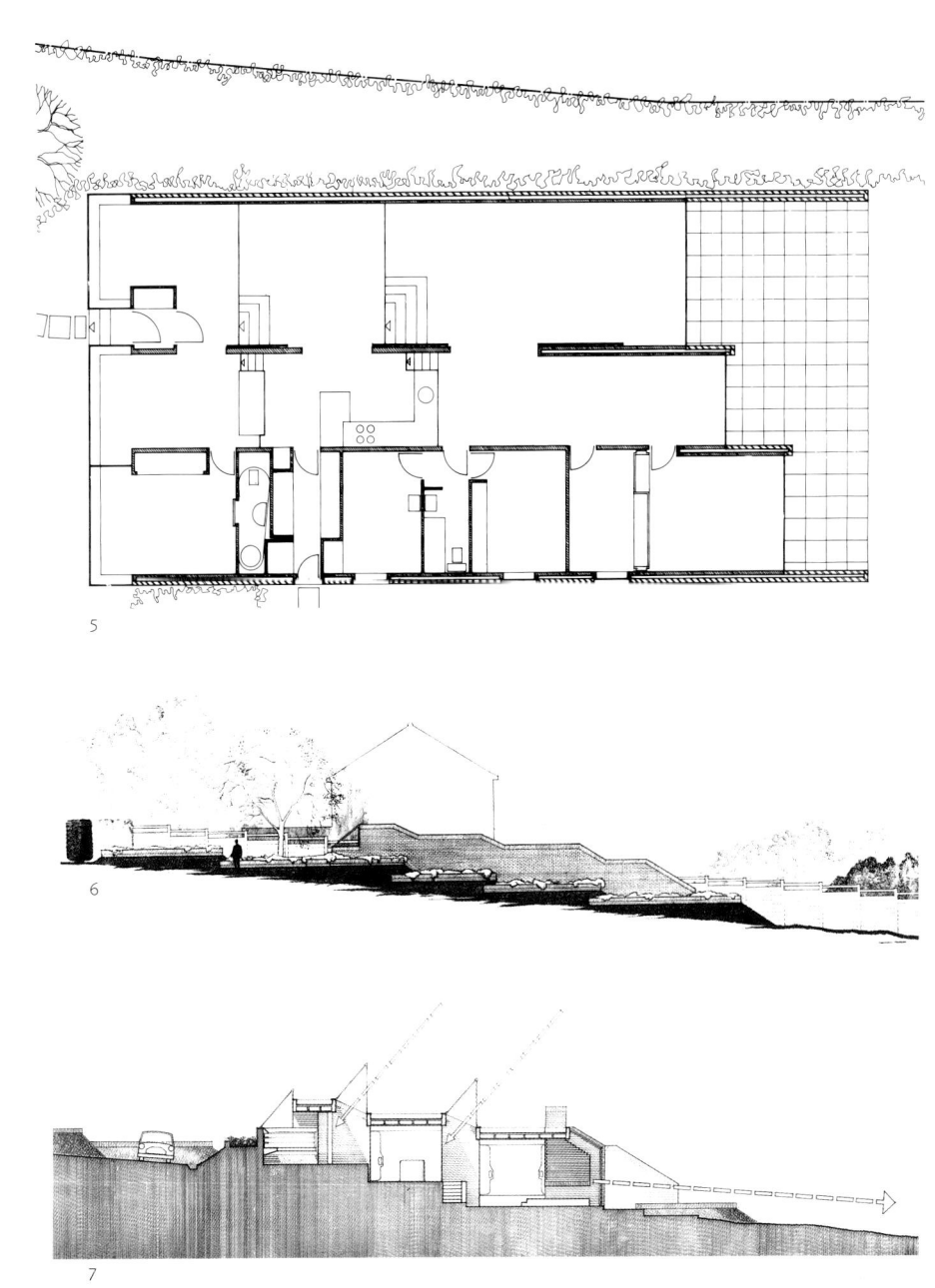

Murray Mews Housing

London, 1967

The three houses built at Murray Mews, Camden Town, London, were related to the unbuilt project for nearby Camden Mews (1964), where new studio houses were to be slotted in behind large Victorian houses. At Murray Mews, however, the houses stand directly on the street, rather than being insulated behind open courts. The only openings in the street elevations are the front door (off which the kitchen opens directly) and garage door – there are no windows. Above the street facades a great sloping wall of glazing lights the main living spaces of the houses. The living room sits underneath the three bedrooms lit by projecting bay windows, and is itself lit by generous windows to the rear private gardens, which can be glimpsed from the kitchen. On top of the bedrooms is a little gallery looking down into the living space and out to the gardens.

Built with traditional brick-faced cavity wall construction, the Murray Mews houses provided Team 4 with a number of problems, including site flooding and poor contractors. A client pointed out to the architects that a 'damp proof course' was no more than newspaper painted black. However, each of the houses was customized for the three clients, who were led by Dr Owen Franklin, a friend of the Rogers family. The aim – privacy and calm in the heart of London, at moderate cost – was kept clearly in sight throughout the project, which provides a significant example of how high densities can be combined with comfort, meriting comparison with the London housing of Darbourne & Darke and Jeremy Dixon.

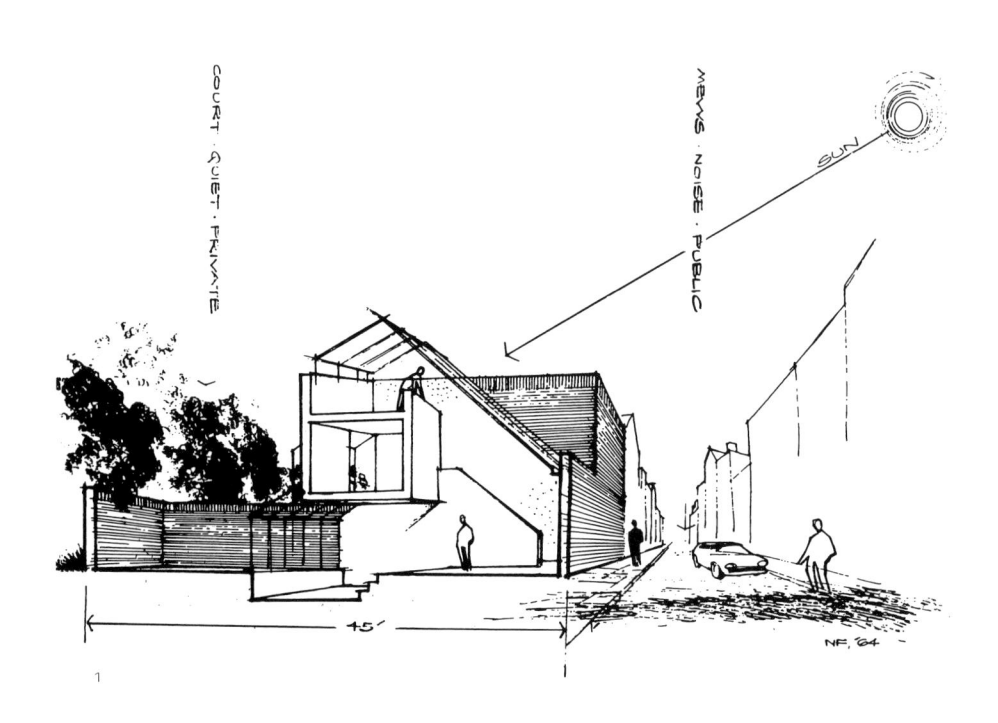

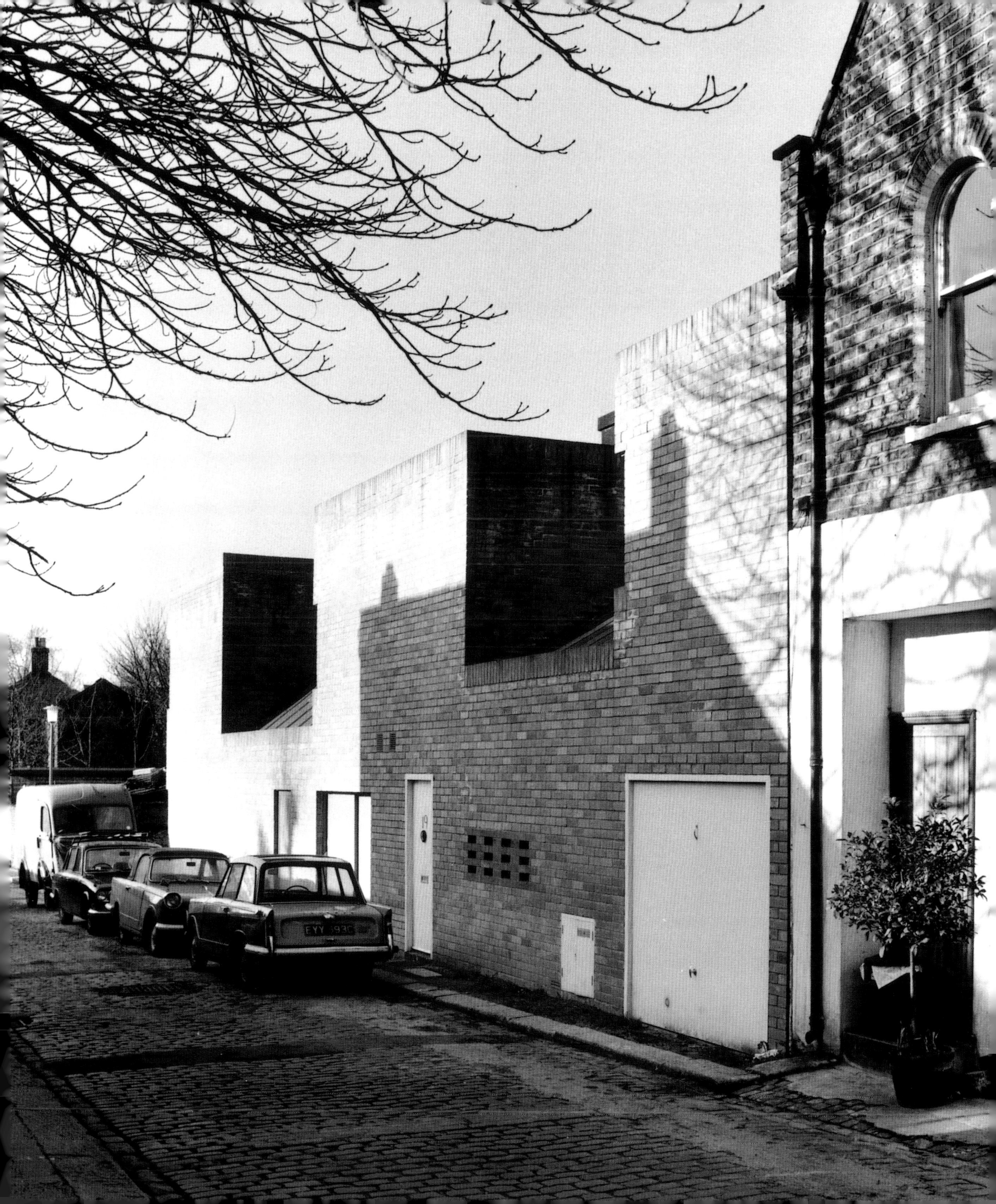
19

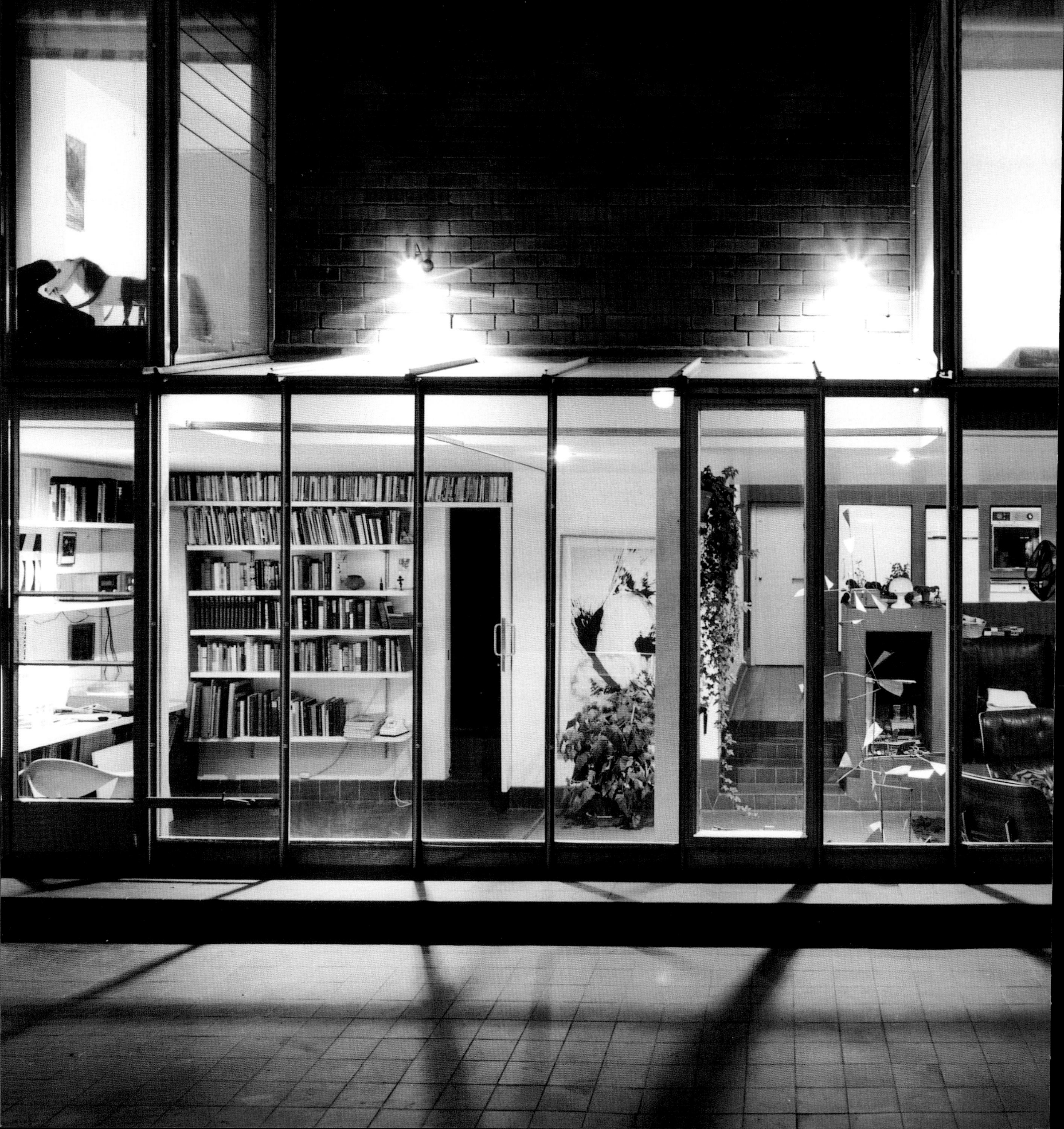

The street frontages of the Murray Mews houses (2, previous page) are discreet, even anonymous: a response to a tough urban environment. At the rear of the buildings, living rooms (3) opened up to private courtyards (4). The scheme infused drama into a flat, uneventful inner-city site (1, p44, 5 & 6).

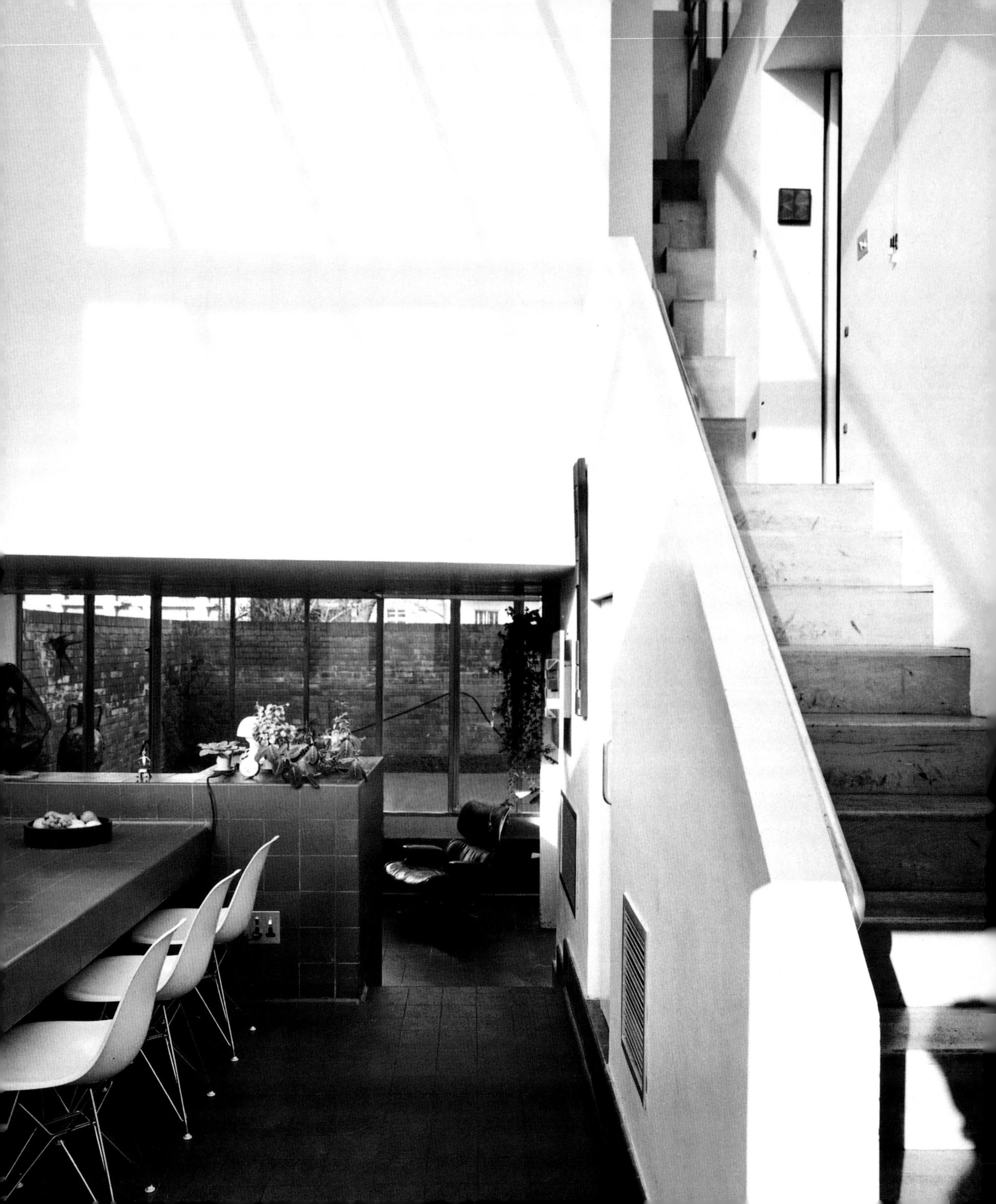

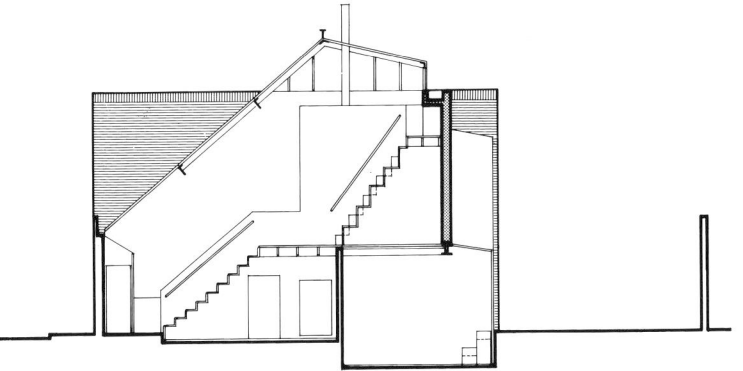

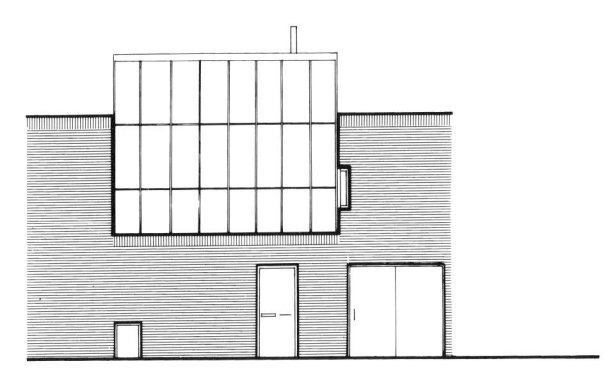

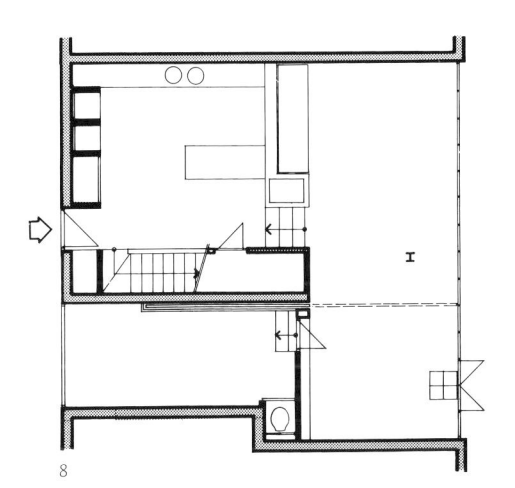

The use of top lighting in the principal living spaces (7 & 8) was a key move, allowing the exteriors to remain free of windows to the street. Interiors, though modest in scale and vertical in emphasis, are given interest by the skilful use of natural light (9 & 10).

7
8
9
10

Reliance Controls

Electronics Factory, Swindon, Wiltshire, 1967

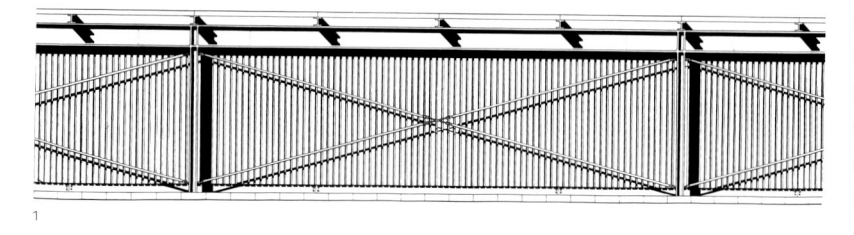

Now demolished, Reliance Controls Electronics Factory was one of the most sensational British buildings of the second half of the twentieth century. Yet the intentions underlying its design were to create not a sensation, but a common-sense model for the workplace of the future. In this context, Reliance Controls has considerable historical significance. It was neither a factory nor an office building nor a research station, but a combination of all three. By the 1980s, buildings like this were to become commonplace, but in the 1960s the ground-rules for this new building type, the stuff of business parks, had not been laid. Reliance Controls was the progenitor of the new workplace and developments like Stockley Park, where good and innovative architecture was part of the formula for success.

The client at Reliance Controls, Peter (later Sir Peter) Parker, believed in this formula from the first and had asked James Stirling for advice on the selection of an architect. He laid down strict cost guidelines and was adamant that the building must be ready within ten months – it was eventually finished early and on budget. The commission to Team 4 was daring – the practice had built only individual houses – but it was highly significant in allowing the practice to change direction and move away from traditional methods of construction towards lightweight buildings made of standardized components. In the event, Reliance Controls was the last building completed by Team 4, but the new practices which grew out of it, Foster Associates and Richard + Su Rogers, both learned much from the project. For Rogers, it provided an opportunity to build on the experience of the West Coast of America, the Case Study houses and the SCSD schools programme and to cast off the practical difficulties which had dogged Creek Vean, Murray Mews and other schemes.

The radicalism of Reliance Controls was both social – this was to be a democratic, anti-hierarchical shed, with managers and workers co-existing in one space – and architectural. The idea of the building was clearly expressed in its structure, with everything contained within the grid of the steel frame and sheltered by one large roof. Inside, partitions were made to be moveable, so that production, research or managerial space could easily grow or contract as required. Extendibility was a basic stipulation, with a series of open courts planned to light the enlarged building – the original phase was subsequently extended, but in 1991, with land prices in the UK's 'Silicon Valley' soaring, the whole complex was pulled down. (Rogers refused to lobby for its preservation, arguing that, after a quarter of a century, the building had served its purpose. Preserving it as a monument would be to deny the philosophy on which it had been founded.)

The structure of Reliance Controls consisted of steel columns, sunk into relatively shallow foundations, with 8 ft. cross heads shop-welded into position. Centre steel beam sections were site welded to produce continuous beams. Both roof and wall cladding were of corrugated steel, plastic coated and insulated, and the roof was braced against wind by means of steel braces set in the perimeter bays. Internal partitions were generally of aluminium and glass, though some private areas were demarcated by blockwork. All services were housed within

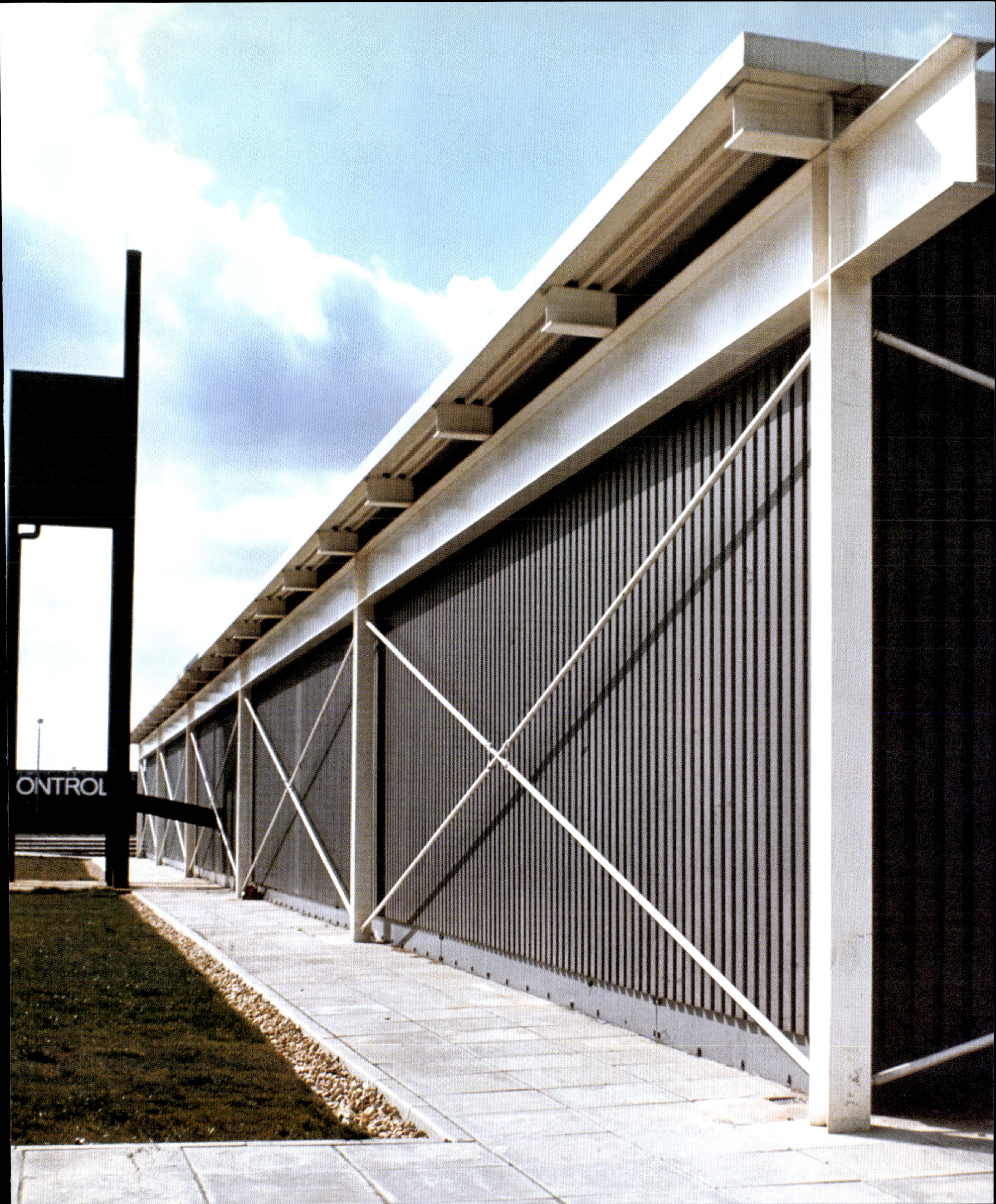
ONTROL

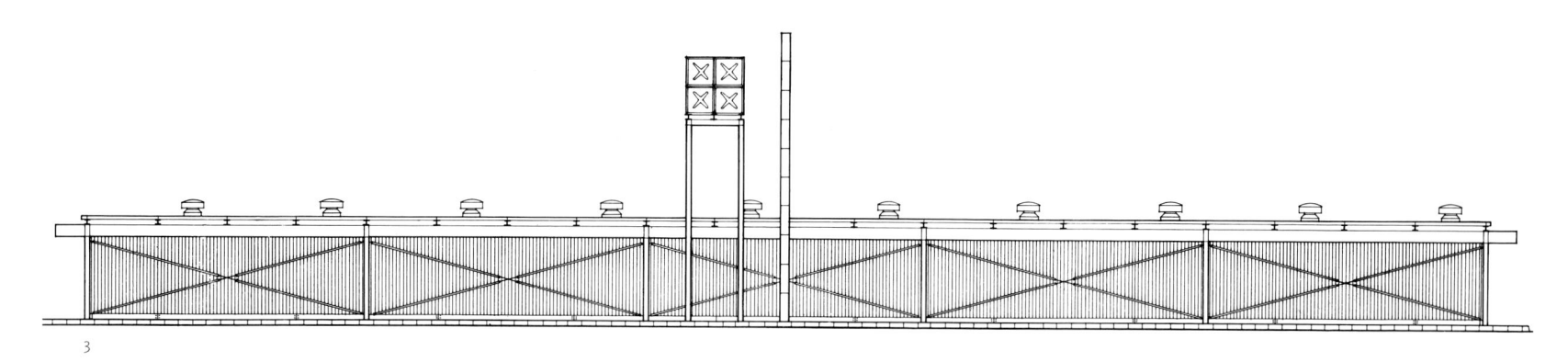

The structural logic of Reliance Controls was clearly expressed externally, though the cross-braced shed achieved a remarkable elegance through clarity of expression and finesse of detail (1 & 2, previous pages, 3 & 4). The integration of structure and services was a key element in the scheme (5). The end of the primary beams, welded to T-shaped columns on the perimeter, expressed the method of fabrication (6). The cross bracing (7 & 8, overleaf) shows clearly by day or night.

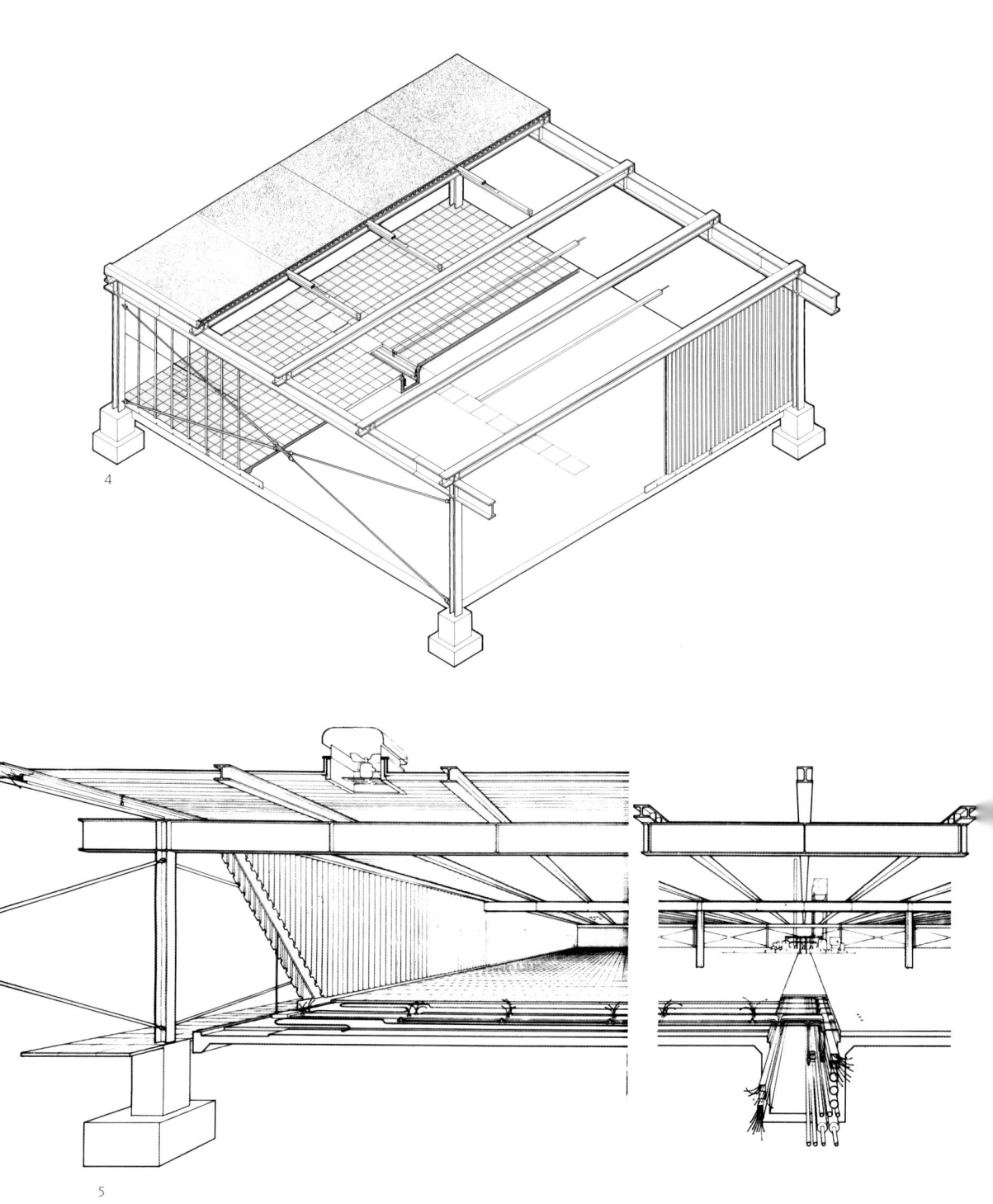

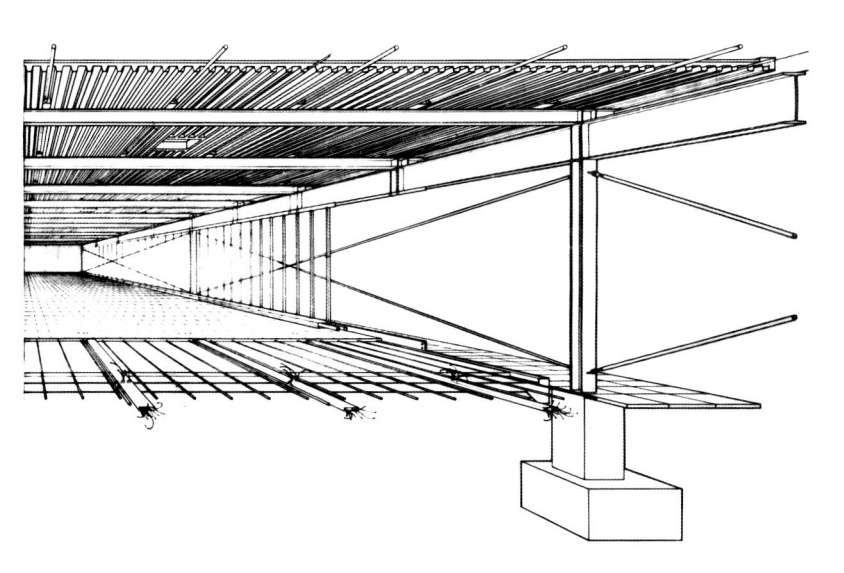

a centralized duct, with secondary distribution in the floor plate for heating, electricity, gas and telephones. Ducting was also provided in the double-skin perimeter walls. Lighting and ventilation were contained within the troughs of the roof deck.

The deceptive simplicity of Reliance Controls was the result of a close collaboration with engineer Anthony Hunt. Tony Hunt had first worked with Team 4 on Creek Vean and had become a regular collaborator. At Reliance Controls, he was able to reassure the architects that their ideas, using untried materials, were practical. Confidence restored, they proceeded to push the structural possibilities to the limit in the interests of architectural effect. The steel sheeting used as cladding, for example, had not been used in this way before in Britain – 12 ft. high panels, without intermediate support, were regarded as daring. Only one aspect of the design worried Hunt: the decision to extend the cross bracing all around the building rather than to confine it to the two elevations where it was functionally necessary. 'I am still a little embarrassed: it is not a "pure" structure, so the engineer in me can never be entirely satisfied', he has said.

The end result of the architect/engineer teamwork was, however, a

7, 8

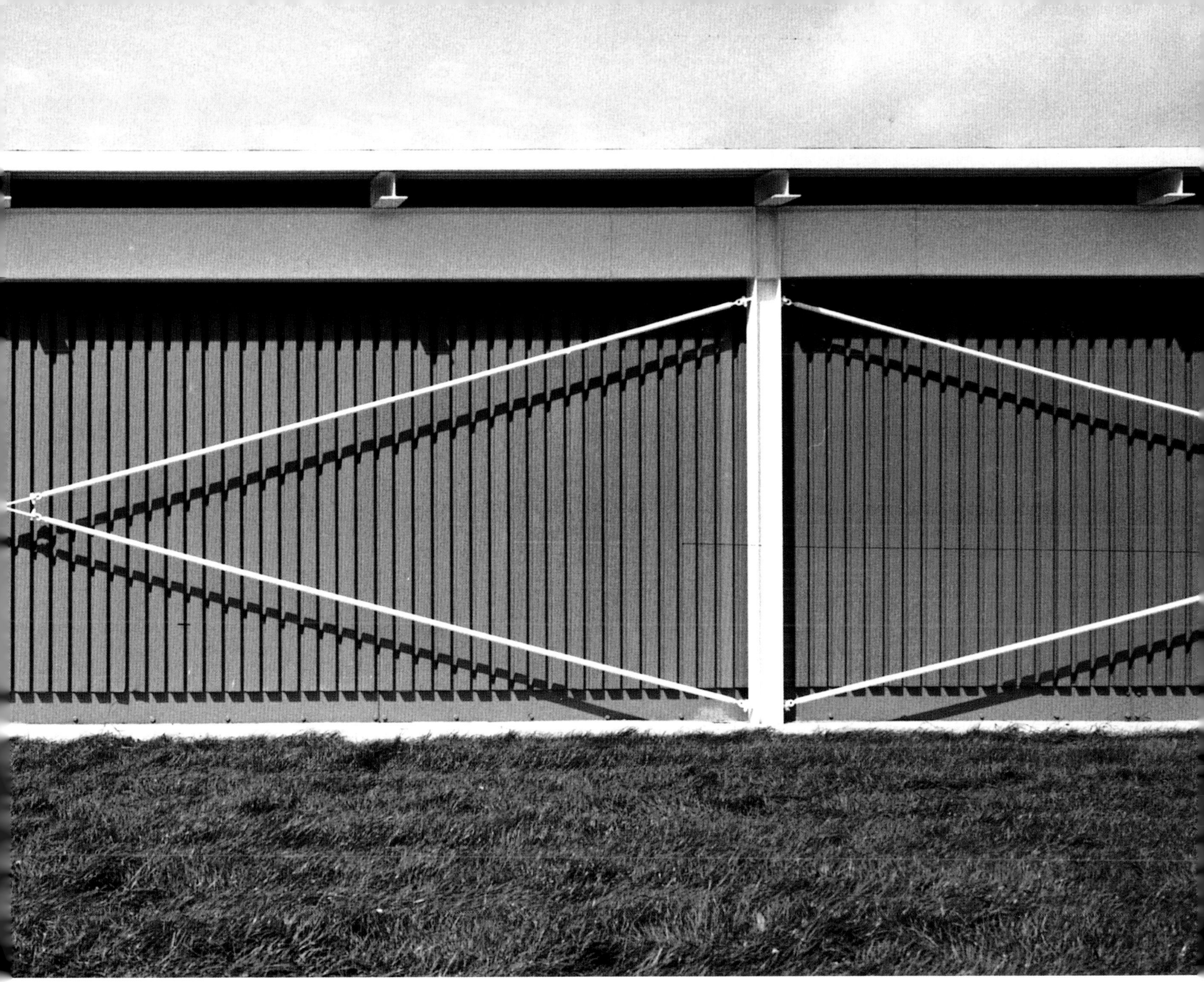

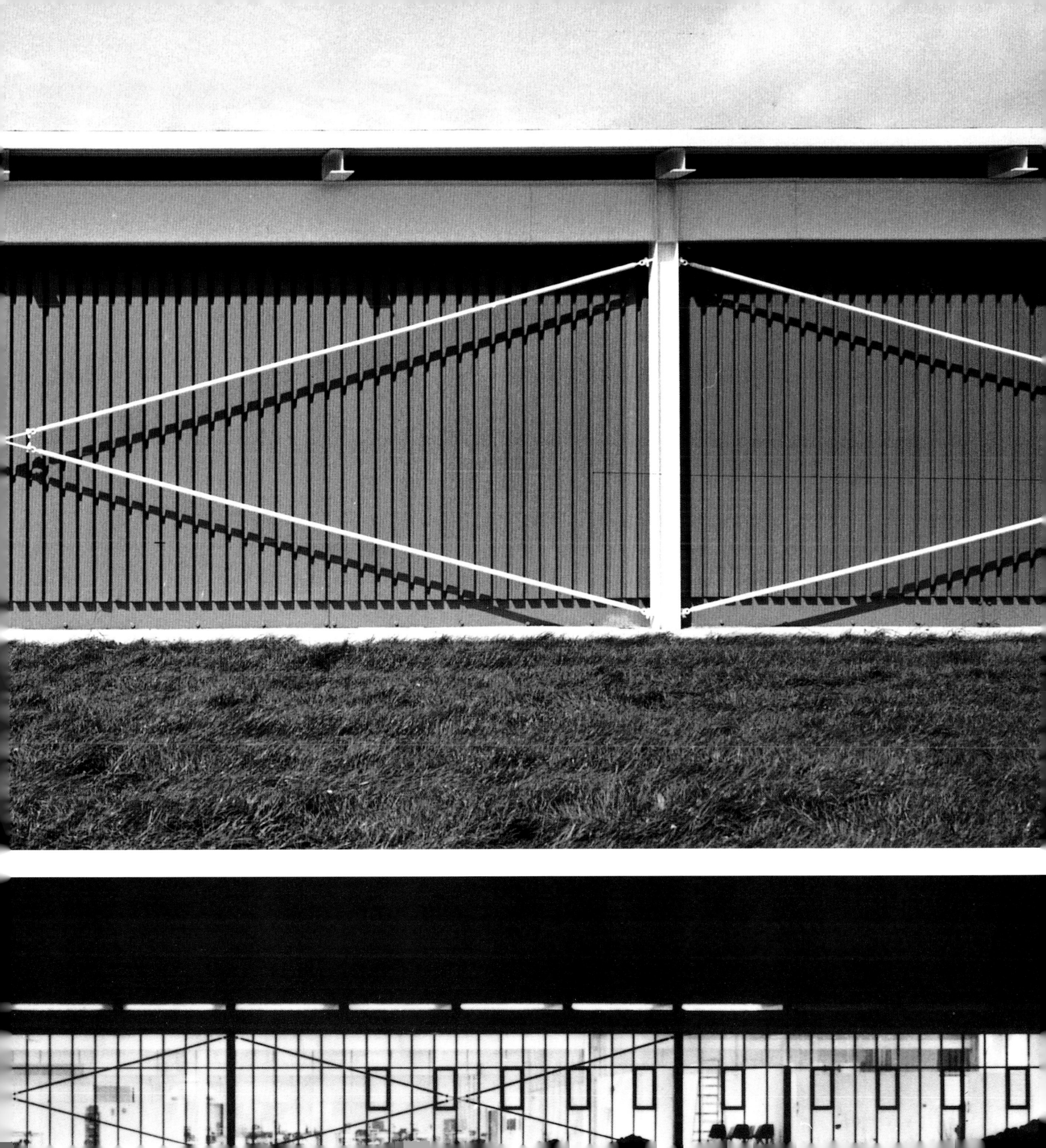

building of great elegance and fragile beauty. Actually resilient and economical (costing around £3.50 per sq.ft.) and highly effective in use, Reliance Controls was also an aesthetic *tour de force*. Although the architects were anxious to avoid what they saw as the finite monumentality of Mies – a reflection of the latter's roots in the Classical tradition of Schinkel and Behrens – in favour of the fluid improvisation of Charles and Ray Eames and the West Coast, they could not entirely cast off Miesian influences. The way in which the steel frame is detailed, notably at the corners of the building where cross heads project boldly above the stanchions, contains echoes of the primitive hut and of formal compositional roots. The containment of servicing within the floorplate helped keep the look of the building pristine and perfect. Norman Foster's later work has been characterized by an imperative for clarity and calm and the subordination of services in the interests of architectural effect. Rogers, in contrast, has revelled in the effects obtained by a frank expression of services – contrast IBM Cosham and Stansted Airport with the Pompidou Centre or Lloyd's. Only the clear link between Reliance Controls and Rogers' work in the immediate aftermath of Team 4 – the Wimbledon house, for instance – gives the lie to the idea that Reliance Controls was largely Foster's building. Both Foster and Rogers confirm that it was the result of a close collaboration. For Laurie Abbott, 'it showed just how good Norman and Richard could be when they worked closely together'. Only one aspect of the building seems at odds with Rogers' usual predilections: its colourlessness. When the *Architectural Review* featured Reliance Controls, it reported that 'the employees have recently demanded more colour' and that internal partitions were being painted to keep the workforce happy. Never again was there to be a completely colourless Rogers building. Reliance Controls saw Team 4 going out on a high note. It did not produce the commissions which could have kept the practice – one imagines temporarily – together, but, as Richard Rogers has commented, 'Reliance was a breakthrough. We had found our style.'

The Reliance Controls building was designed for possible future growth and expansion and was never conceived as a finite Miesian pavilion (9).

Flexible floor space with relocatable service cores (10) form the basis for the plan. The site plan allows for separation of goods and staff traffic (11).
Partitions were made movable so as to make the interior of the building flexible and adaptable to change (12 & 13).

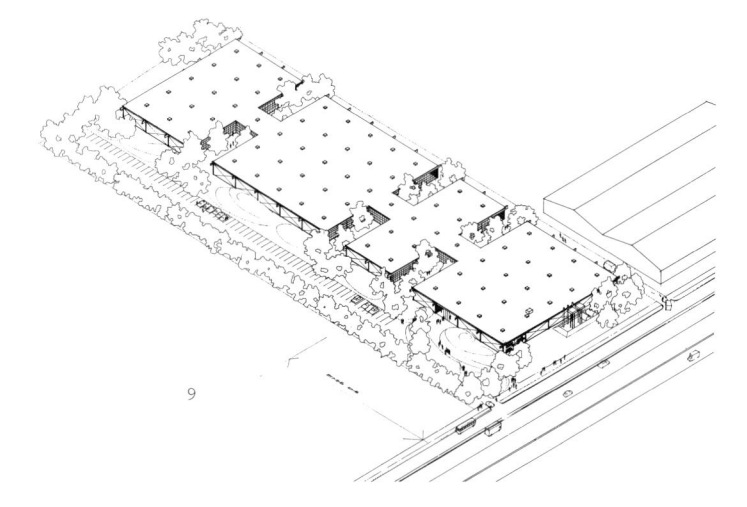

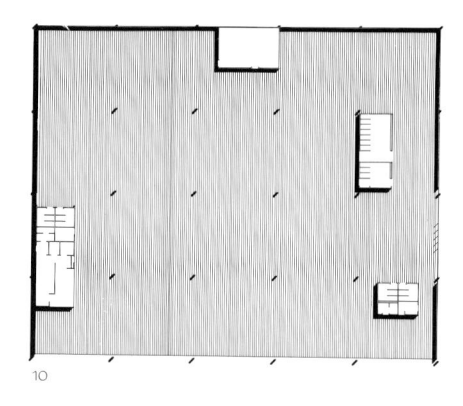

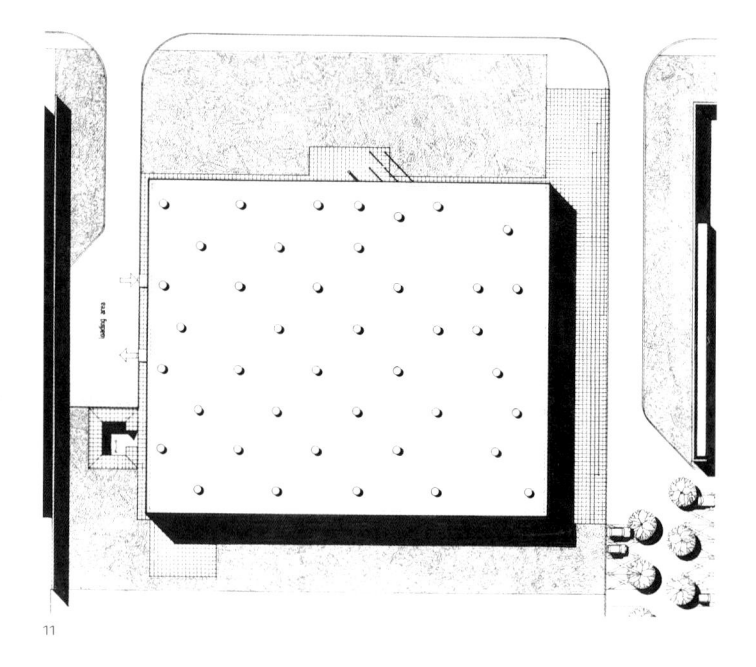

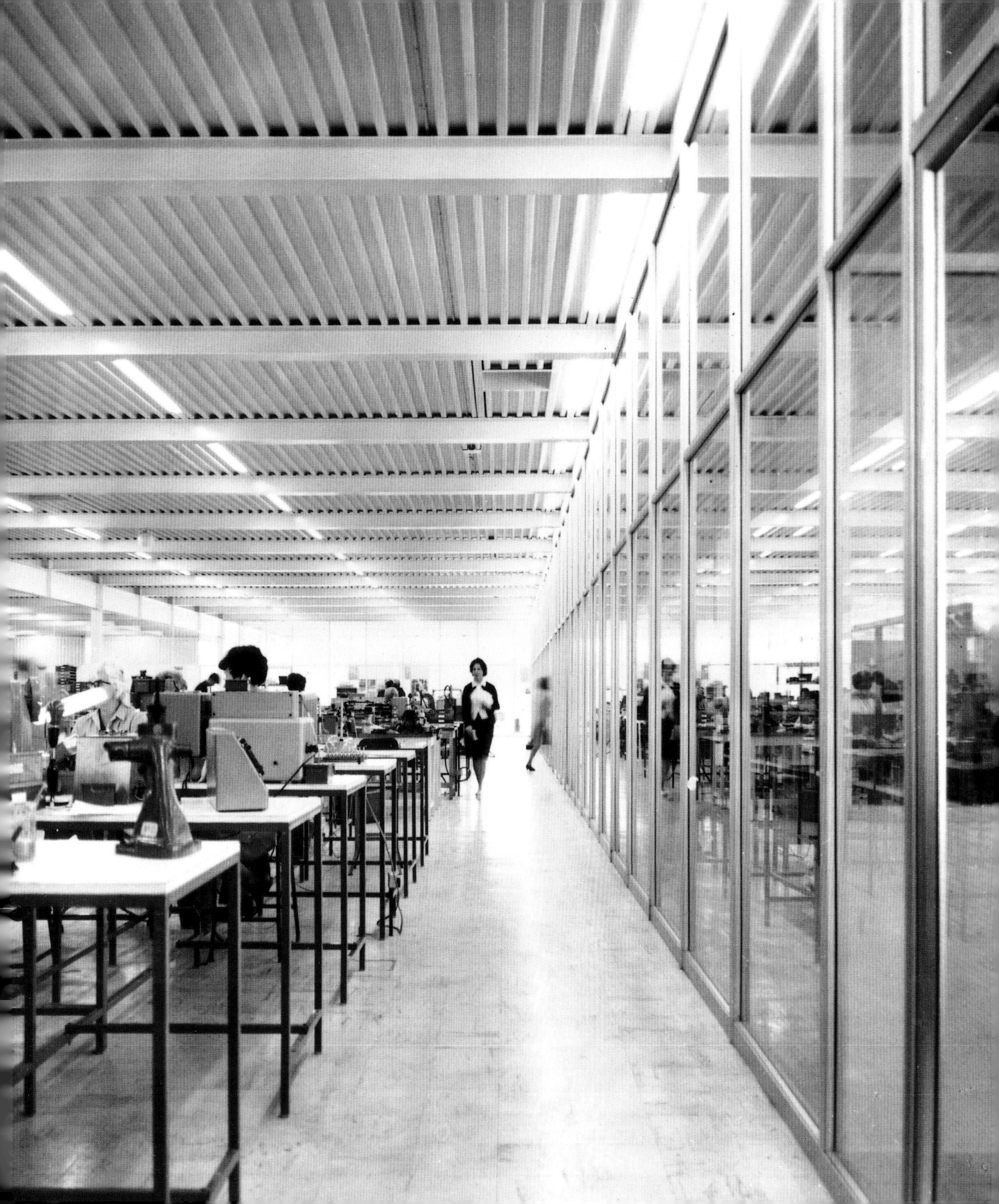

Richard + Su Rogers

Visions and experiments, and a commitment to research

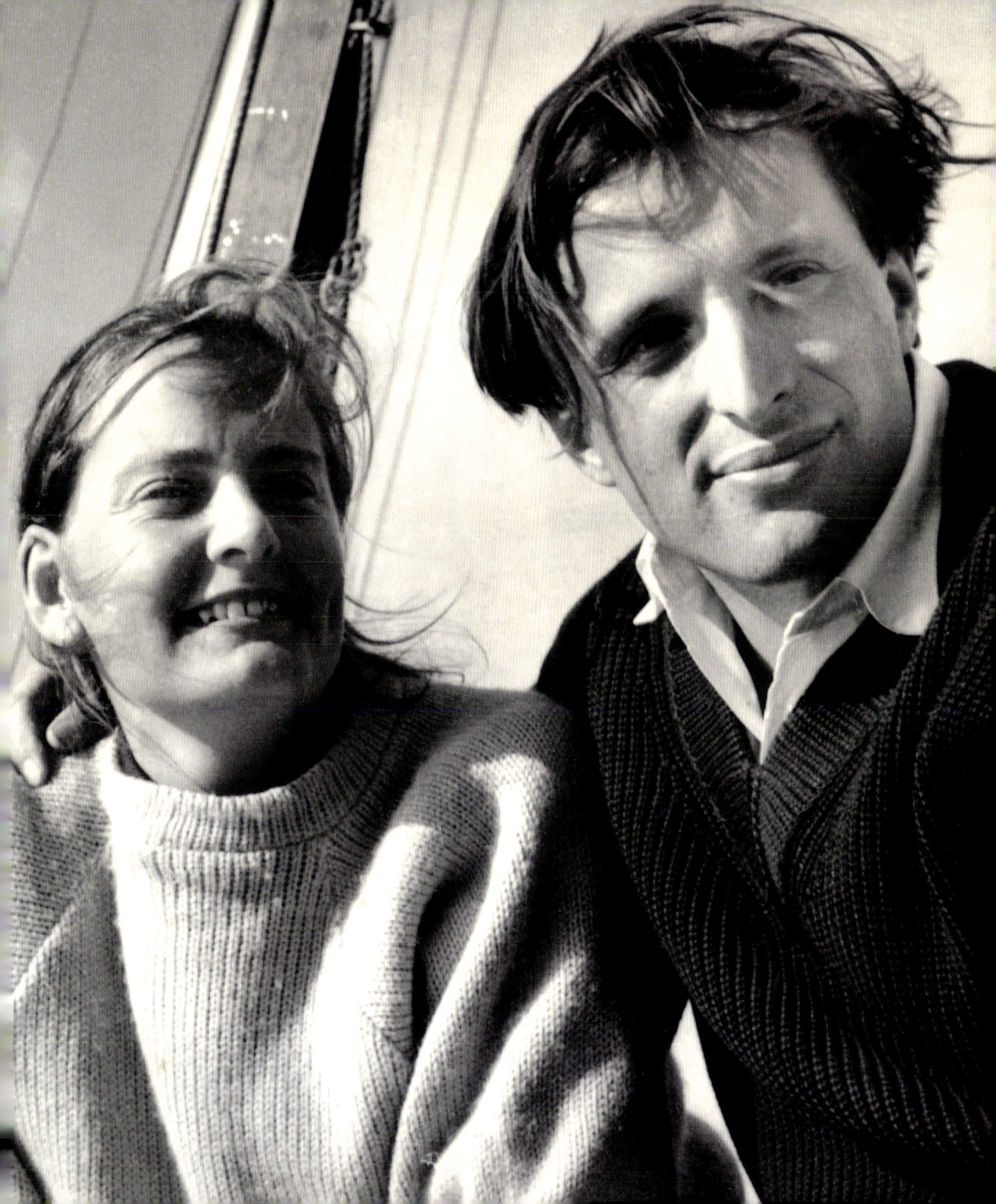

Teamwork – the holistic experience of a group of people not just working together but discussing issues, eating and relaxing together – has been one of the most significant foundations of Rogers' approach to architecture; the teams which he has formed have been based more on personal friendship and a close artistic dialogue than on conventional business relationships. With the dissolution of Team 4, and the departure of Norman and Wendy Foster to form Foster Associates, Richard and Su Rogers found themselves as the core of another new practice. Su Rogers had always wanted to be an architect. Su's mother, Rene Brumwell recalls that 'she rather resented our pushing her in another direction, I'm sure'. At Yale, Su Rogers had made the leap from sociology (in which she had graduated at the London School of Economics) to architecture via a master's degree in planning. Writing to Marcus and Rene Brumwell from Yale in January, 1962, Richard Rogers reported: 'Su has built a wonderful model of a new residential neighbourhood she has designed and has got a 'high pass' – the only non-architect to get such a high mark!'

The new practice, formally initiated on 1st May, 1967, was known quite simply as Richard + Su Rogers. At the time of the Team 4 break-up, it had no work. Leslie Martin, an acknowledged leader of the British architectural profession and old friend, to whom Rogers turned for advice, was, however, encouraging. 'I told him the score', Rogers recalls. 'No work, no money: what do we do? He said we should stick it out – it would all come out right. He believed in us and would see what he could do to help. I was much cheered.'

Marcus Brumwell, ever a friend and supporter, did give immediate and practical help at the Design Research Unit which he headed up. The DRU had always had an architectural dimension, though its commissions had been principally fit-outs and interiors rather than new buildings. It worked with architects like Richard Seifert, Hugh Casson, T.P. Bennett and Michael Rosenauer, but its aim was to secure larger jobs. Richard + Su Rogers was therefore invited to work in association with DRU. The first job was to reorganize DRU's own accommodation in London – 'we gave them lots of bright pink, yellow and green', Rogers remembers. 'And they gave us a roof over our heads. The end of Team 4 had been a pretty depressing experience and we needed a home.' In fact, Richard + Su Rogers' rigour was a tonic to a diffuse an already rather complacent organization.

The year that the new practice was launched was the year that saw the high point of Sixties pop culture in Britain, with its emphasis on colour and expression. 1967, after all, saw the 'summer of love', when the Flower Power craze spread from America's West Coast to Europe. Perhaps more significantly, Britain had a Labour government, re-elected the previous year with a substantial majority – to the delight of the Brumwells and the Rogers. Marcus Brumwell's old friend Harold Wilson was in Downing Street and housing and education were government priorities. The 'new' universities were up and running. Building them had provided more work for an architectural profession still heavily dependent and inclined to work on public commissions. Big-name architects like Basil Spence, Denys Lasdun and Peter Shepheard, and well-respected practices like RMJM, YRM and The Architects' Co-Partnership, headed by middle-aged men, were the beneficiaries of the university building boom. Leslie Martin himself had plenty of work at Oxford and Cambridge, where the colleges were expanding. Meanwhile, some of the best new college buildings were designed by Powell & Moya, whose Skylon at the Festival of Britain had inspired Richard Rogers and other young visitors. And, while the London County Council (LCC) had now become the Greater London Council (GLC), it was still commissioning plenty of architecture, including the new South Bank arts centre, next to the Royal Festival Hall, as well as schools and housing – Rogers particularly admired the estate at Roehampton. The post-war generation of good architects were still keen to meet the all-prevailing social and environmental architectural needs around the country. Yet, alongside the massive public sector, the property boom of the 1960s had rocketed a new generation of frankly 'commercial' architects to fame and wealth. The best-known of them was Richard Seifert, whose Centrepoint tower in the West End of London became a *cause célèbre* when it was deliberately kept empty for tax purposes by its developer. Seifert eschewed academic purity and politeness in favour of powerful, sometimes vulgar effects, merging Corbusian ideas with the razzmatazz of America – the America of Morris Lapidus, perhaps, rather than Mies or SOM. SOM was itself given work in Britain by image-conscious companies like Boots and Heinz, while the young Peter Palumbo had already embarked on his campaign to build a tower by Mies (who was to die in 1969) at the heart of London. But the gulf between British and American architecture remained enormous.

American architecture had been Richard Rogers' inspiration, igniting a talent reared on Italian modernism and memories of the 1951 Festival of Britain. It was not the corporate American architecture of the Mies school which attracted him, but a more informal tradition, which linked technology to an optimistic view of mankind. Rogers' socialism and political awareness were ingrained. He and Su had joined the first CND (Campaign for Nuclear Disarmament) march on the Atomic Weapons Research Establishment at Aldermaston in 1958. Ten years later, the rising of students and workers in France and demonstrations in British universities filled him with hope. 'We were very political', he says. 'It seemed possible that the West might fall – to the people.'

The respectable British architects who designed new universities tended to be at least liberal, if not left wing, in outlook. Schooled in the modernism of the 1930s, the inheritance of Tecton and the MARS Group, they had lived through the Second World War and had had their hopes rekindled in 1945. For a new generation, however, the old certainties seemed thin. Life was not entirely about housing estates, schools and health clinics. Earnestness had to be leavened with enjoyment. The founders of Archigram were radicals of a new order. They were members of Rogers' own generation, trained during the

1950s and all closely associated with Rogers' own school, the AA. Reyner Banham, the leading architectural critic of the day, backed Archigram strongly – 'Archigram is short on theory, long on draughtsmanship and craftsmanship. They're in the image business, and they have been blessed with the power to create some of the most compelling images of our time', he wrote. 'You accept Archigram at its own valuation or not at all, and there's been nothing much like that since Frank Lloyd Wright, Mies and Corb ... ' For Richard Rogers, 'they were certainly visionaries – but they weren't political in any sense. That was their failing for me.' But the outlook of Archigram, often seen as a key influence on the Pompidou Centre later, was 'in the air' and fused happily with Rogers' own essentially optimistic outlook. Rogers, after all, had been inculcated by Peter Smithson and James Stirling with the kind of Pop culture that was previewed in the 1956 Institute of Contemporary Arts exhibition 'This is Tomorrow', where Eduardo Paolozzi was another prominent contributor. It fitted in with his own inclusive, anti-puritan approach to architecture and to life.

Although the DRU tie-up with Richard + Su Rogers was never really a success – Rogers felt frustrated with the set-up from the beginning – it generated the core of what eventually became Richard Rogers Partnership. One conspicuous Rogers loyalist was John Young, who had become 'a sort of part-time associate' on his return to the AA but had subsequently quit the school without doing his diploma year in order to 'concentrate on building buildings'. Young was the key player in the first significant post-Team 4 job, the Spender House. Humphrey Spender, a veteran photographer and brother of the poet Stephen Spender, decided to sell his substantial old house in rural Essex, while keeping part of the garden on which to build a new house. Via one of Spender's students at the Royal College of Art, Richard + Su Rogers were recommended for the job. Initially, Richard Russell acted as project architect but soon quit the practice to return to college, leaving the job to Young.

Richard Rogers was clear from the start that this should be a steel house, building on the experience of Reliance Controls. It should use standardized components, in the manner of the Eames House. It should be, in essence, an industrial product. Spender endorsed these ideas enthusiastically and the house was built – or, perhaps more correctly, assembled – in nine months, beginning in the summer of 1968, at a cost of £12,500. But the project was labour-intensive – many models were made – and far from trouble-free. The structural system was that of Reliance Controls – external frame, made of six portal frames, three for the house and three for the studio (separated by an open courtyard). The frame was infilled with profiled, plastic-coated steel panels, as used at Reliance. The standard metal framed windows were supplied by Crittall. (The house was in 'Crittall country', according to John Young, and Spender was friendly with the Crittall family.) Construction was relatively straightforward, though John Young took enormous pains over detailed drawings for every element in the building.

However, 'Spender was not an easy client', says Young, 'and things weren't helped by my lack of experience.' After the house was completed, Spender found much that (he felt) needed improvement, though he admitted that 'the house is basically a pleasure to live in'. Young was subsequently called on to remedy problems, real or alleged, with blinds, the shower, flooring, kitchen fittings and many other items, even producing an immaculate drawing for a neoprene-sealed cat flap to be fitted into the all glass front door of the house! Several years after the completion of the house, Young sent Spender a thirteen-page, handwritten letter with advice on a number of

London County Council Architects' Department, Alton West Estate, Roehampton, London, 1952–5

Richard + Su Rogers (left to right): Richard Rogers, Su Rogers, John Doggart and John Young

Site visit by Richard and Dada Rogers to the Rogers House, Wimbledon, 1968

The Rogers House, as built, incorporating a carport

defects, including problems with the roof. In fact, the way that the house was built, using a number of autonomous contractors for various elements, was one of the principal causes of the subsequent problems. But it could not be otherwise – the building industry was not equipped at that time to address such a radical programme. When a new car, for example, is designed, dozens of mock-ups are made: the Rogers team was trying to apply techniques similar to those of car manufacture to housing and the problems which arose were instructive. (By the time Lloyd's was being designed, full-scale mock ups were used as a matter of course.)

The Spender House was a bold statement of the new practice's agenda, which clearly eschewed the traditional approach taken at Creek Vean or Murray Mews. Its imperfections (and they were not entirely imaginary) reflected its somewhat experimental status. Rogers saw the house not as a one-off, but as a prototype which could be multiplied as a solution to the problems of mass housing. The same was true of the house built for Rogers' parents in Wimbledon, London. Nino and Dada Rogers had been staunch supporters of their son's career – in 1965, for example, Richard designed a new kitchen for their house at Northey Avenue in Cheam, Surrey. Now they were thinking seriously of moving house as Dr Rogers was planning to retire. He had seen many elderly patients struggling on in houses far too large and inconvenient for them, so he wanted to live in a 'bungalow' which formed a positive approach to retirement, with all the accommodation on one floor.

A site was found close to Wimbledon Common, in a densely planted garden. There were the predictable problems with neighbours and planners, but the project eventually got the go-ahead. The site was an ideal location for a house which would be very private and, equally, make very little impact on its neighbours –

it cannot be seen from the road. The intention, Rogers wrote, was 'to develop a prototype for single and multiple application within the widest social and technical context'. But the needs of his parents were to be specifically addressed, firstly by creating a flexible house (Rogers' father wished to continue a degree of medical practice from it). The house should be designed for quick construction and low maintenance – and it should be relatively cheap. Like the Spender House, the Rogers House was designed on a grid, which, at Wimbledon, embraces the hard-paved landscape which surrounds and links the house proper and the 'gatehouse' or studio which adjoins it across a courtyard. (Behind the house is a lush area of grass and trees.)

Engineer Tony Hunt designed the structure using the same portal frames (14 metres in span) used at the Spender House, five for the house itself and three for the studio. At Wimbledon, the columns were, however, partly hidden externally and, instead of Reliance Controls-style steel wall panels, there were insulated sandwich panels – a plastic core sealed in an aluminium skin – jointed with neoprene. (The technology had been developed in the USA for refrigerated trucks – this was a key instance of technology transfer as pioneered by Charles and Ray Eames and Jean Prouvé.) Floor-to-ceiling glazing provided views and also access to the garden, sliding panels enabling the house and garden to be pleasingly integrated. This integration is, in fact, the key to the project. The contrast between the verdant landscape and the rigorous grid on which the buildings are laid out is striking. Privacy, balanced by transparency; a respect for site and local amenity and the pursuit of economy and flexibility are the ingredients which make the Wimbledon house a harbinger of Rogers' later work.

For Richard Rogers, the Spender House was, though highly

The American Airstream trailer: an early influence on Rogers

The insulated panel system used on the Rogers House and later the basis for Zip-Up

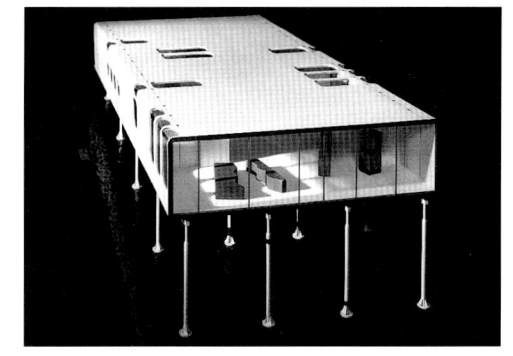

The Zip Up House

significant for the future, somewhat 'eccentric' and marred by the very small budget. Wimbledon provided an opportunity to address the same issues with more consideration and a better budget. Rogers stresses the role of his parents as demanding and critical clients. Dada Rogers was particularly influential: 'she made it what it is', he says. As a prototype for other modestly-scaled houses, the Rogers House makes sense. Typically for Rogers, the kitchen became the focus. An early version of the plan showed it buried away at the centre of the house, but it was eventually made an integral part of the main living space, in the manner of Creek Vean (and, later, Royal Avenue). Equally typical of Rogers was the bold use of colour for the steel frame and for internal elements like the kitchen island unit, blinds and sliding walls.

Both the house and the gatehouse embody the sense of continuity of use which is central to Rogers' thinking. After Nino Rogers' death in 1993, Dada Rogers lived there happily until her death in 1998, and the house is still in family use. An accomplished and gifted potter, whose work showed Italian influences and recalled the still-lifes of Morandi, Dada used the gatehouse as a working pottery and studio; it was later converted into a small house. Rogers' brother, Peter, one of his sons and John Young have all lived in it at various times. The building exemplifies Rogers' characteristic versatility: the format equally adaptable to working or domestic use.

The potential universalism of the Wimbledon house, therefore, made it a clear adjunct to Richard + Su Rogers' work on the so-called Zip-Up House – or 'enclosure' (the relevance of the idea extended beyond the residential sphere). The Zip-Up concept, based on the idea of insulated modular panels 'zipped' together with neoprene, pervaded the Rogers office for some years and has never entirely faded; a house, it suggested, was a product. The Zip-Up House was intended not for a specific client but for everyone: mobile young couples, the retired and also homeless people, lost in the conventional housing system, short of permanent structures and funds. The Zip-Up was seen as instant, affordable and adaptable, giving ordinary people a new right of choice and control over their housing conditions. Typically for Rogers, the agenda was as much social as architectural in the narrow sense, and was adamantly democratic, wedded firmly to the notion of technological progress as a key to social progress. The origins of the Zip-Up lay in the practice's work on 'The House for Today' competition promoted by plastics manufacturer Dupont and the *Daily Mail* in 1969. The Rogers entry came second, but attracted a lot of press interest. There were echoes in the concept not only of Buckminster Fuller – 'the daddy of the environmental movement', as Rogers calls him – but of Jean Prouvé, the great French *constructeur* who had designed mass-produced houses for those left homeless after the Second World War. Above all, the Zip-Up was a radical rethinking of the Case Study concept in the way that it used technology transfer and demonstrated structural innovation. Instead of using panels to infill a structural frame, as at the Spender and Rogers houses, the Zip-Up concept made the panels into the structure. They were zipped together to form a rigid box. Interior panels were entirely movable. The house did not even need foundations – it sat on adjustable feet which could take account of any ground conditions and could be moved at will.

The Zip-Up House idea was entirely practical, but it was not taken up by the housing industry. (When Rogers applied for planning permission to site one on land in Cornwall, he received a rapid refusal from the planners.) For John Young, the development of this idea confirmed his loyalty to Rogers. 'At Team 4', he recalls, 'I'd seen myself as closer to Norman Foster than to Richard, whose approach

Jean Prouvé in his house at Nancy, 1970

Jean Prouvé, Maison Tropicale, Maxeville, 1949

seemed to be typified by Creek Vean. Now Richard was taking the lead in pushing the issue of prefabrication and the ready-made.' Despite the lack of commercial interest, the Zip-Up programme rolled forward. A two-storey version, which Richard and Su Rogers considered building for themselves on an ill-fated site at Camden Mews, demanded a light steel frame contained within the depth of the panels. The Zip-Up approach informed the unbuilt industrial projects for Sweetheart Plastics near Portsmouth and for Universal Oil Products (UOP) at Ashford: the applications of the system were by no means exclusively domestic and it offered a significant advance on the technology of Reliance Controls.

UOP, whose initial contact with Rogers came through sheer chance – Su Rogers had met the managing director's wife in a hairdressing salon – became a significant Rogers client. The Ashford project (1969) was for a 30,000 sq.ft. factory/warehouse – it was planned to be doubled in size subsequently – using the Zip-Up panel system on a grand scale. With its great glazed ends, demountable to provide for future expansion, this tube-like extrusion of a building prefigured Norman Foster's Sainsbury Centre at the University of East Anglia. There were to be no walls or roof in the normal sense, just a continuous skin of highly-insulated aluminium panels, giving great energy savings, on an entirely internal structure. The *Architectural Review* commented: 'Universal Oil Products is by Rogers out of Ehrenkrantz – a wholly flexible multi-purpose extendible tube which by its sheer glamour makes package deal parcels look what they are – off the cuff, off the peg, easy-way-out, inflexible, ugly and inefficient structures for lazy minded industrialists who can't be bothered to plan nor to improve.' The scheme was not built. The client merged with another company and moved the site for the project, changing the brief in the process. The building, later completed by Piano + Rogers for UOP in 1973–4 was, according to John Young who worked on the original with the Rogers and John Doggart (who had also worked on the Wimbledon house), 'rather less radical'. The Sweetheart project, another Zip-Up variant, was for an office block attached to an existing factory (owned by the family of Peter Southgate, a member of the Rogers practice). By raising the building on columns, vehicular access to the adjacent factory was maintained, while the offices benefited from better views out. The scheme, however, also remained unbuilt.

Richard + Su Rogers had begun the association with DRU in optimistic mood and, for the few years that it lasted, the arrangement provided them with the scope to initiate the research work that has been central to the Rogers practice ever since. The Zip-Up House, for example, led to the Autonomous House project. Traditional construction tied a house forever to one site and tended to prescribe a lifestyle. The Zip-Up House opened up new possibilities of mobility and freedom. Being heavily insulated, it was also energy efficient. But houses still depended on piped-in services – power, water, waste disposal. The Autonomous House studies looked at ways in which houses could be freed from their surroundings: windmills and solar collectors to generate power, 'waste digesters' and recycling systems for used water. These elements could be incorporated into the kit-of-parts of which the house of the future would be assembled. The 'energy crisis' of the 1970s had yet to hit, but Rogers, while an enthusiast for benign technology, was already aware of the natural limits to growth and the need to protect a fragile environment.

The Rogers had formed a working relationship with Misha Black at DRU, though Richard Rogers found the 'umbrella' of the large company rather irksome. (In a group portrait of the Unit taken in 1968, he is a conspicuous figure, standing apart at the back, the only male in the picture not wearing a tie.) Black wanted to reinforce the design resources of the firm and saw the newcomers as an asset, though not everyone at DRU was happy with their 'intrusion' into the office. The office was busy with, among other jobs, packaging design for Watney's brewery, a new corporate identity for British Rail and a standard street sign (still in use today) for Westminster City Council. In 1969, when DRU, which was growing fast, decided to move to new offices in Aybrook Street, Richard + Su Rogers were given the job of designing a rooftop extension to the building, a 1900s factory. The Aybrook Street project was yet another Zip-Up spin-off.

Some new names were appearing in the Rogers office at this time. The project architect for the DRU roof extension was Jan Kaplicky, a Czech who had quit his own country in 1968 and was later one of the founders of Future Systems, a practice which carried forward many of the innovative ideas of the 1960s, and got them built. Another was Marco Goldschmied, born in Harrogate of Anglo-Italian parentage, schooled in Italy and England and trained at the AA in the same year as John Young. Goldschmied had applied to Foster Associates for a job, but was told only that 'we'll let you know'. Rogers, in contrast, offered him a job immediately. A talented designer, his organizational and managerial talents were equal assets and he was later to become a founding director of Richard Rogers Partnership. Pierre Botschi was Swiss – the Rogers office was always cosmopolitan – and remained with Rogers for some years, running, among other jobs, the DRU conversion project at Aybrook Street.

Renzo Piano also joined the team. Richard Rogers informed a client in January, 1971: 'we have taken on a brilliant, young, Italian architect, Renzo Piano, as our partner ... He works mainly in plastics and tensioned steel and is, in my opinion, the best European, younger generation, architect.' Piano had arrived in London in the summer of 1970. Four years younger than Richard Rogers, he was from Genoa, the son of a building contractor with a great interest in practical construction and new materials. His interest in prefabrication and the use of ready-made components – the timber factory he had designed in Genoa was built like a large road vehicle – encouraged him to seek out Richard + Su Rogers. The actual meeting was arranged by Dr Owen Franklin, the client for Murray Mews. Piano's arrival was timely and, for Rogers, something of the magic which had fuelled his partnership with Foster was rekindled – 'we knew where we were going, what we liked and disliked, and were driven by youthful energy and shared beliefs'. The association, which began informally, was soon regularized as a new practice, Piano + Rogers.

Marco Goldschmied, who joined the Rogers Team in 1969

Group photograph of the Design Research Unit (DRU), 1968 – Richard Rogers stands at the back, not wearing a tie

The early executed schemes by Piano + Rogers were all modest in scale. The so-called 'Fitzroy-Burleigh' project was ambitious but nothing was built, though the scheme passed through many variations before being finally abandoned in the late 1970s. The client was developer Ralph Diamond of Samuel properties who, working with the major landowner, Jesus College, Cambridge, envisaged a large enclosed shopping precinct in the run-down Kite area of Cambridge, close to its historic town centre. Marco Goldschmied, who took charge of the project soon after his arrival in the office, reflects that 'it was fortunate for us that it wasn't built – in most other towns, it would have gone ahead. It was alien to Cambridge and would have done us no good.' In 1970, however, developments of this kind were almost universally welcomed by local authorities and the enlargement of Cambridge's shopping provision by twenty per cent seemed a positive move. Moreover, the development was within the town, not a US-style suburban mall. Long and relatively low, it would not intrude on the skyline. As well as shops, there would be restaurants, several cinemas, offices, a bus station and multi-storey parking – in Reyner Banham's categorization, this would have been a megastructure. Cambridge probably did not need the scheme, but there were aspects of it which were positive and which anticipated the Pompidou Centre: the extensive use of escalators, 'clipped on' external walkways and ramps leading to upper level parking (in Paris it was people, not cars, who got to go to the top of the building), and the placing of all services along one perimeter of the building. 'Cambridge also provided our first serious brush with the planning system', says Goldschmied. 'It was a big urban intervention and was inevitably political. We learned a lot.' The experience of Cambridge helped later when the practice became embroiled in the furore over the Coin Street development. Cambridge is not remembered affectionately. 'It was too big and we weren't ready for it', John Young believes. Rogers recalls: 'it was a truly horrible experience. We fought "tooth and nail" with the clients; it was a real "shot-gun wedding". Everyone involved, apart from Jesus College, behaved abominably and we suffered.'

Another still-born project from the Richard + Su Rogers' days, was Witham Workshops, a development of light industrial units in Essex. The scheme was very simple: a long run of standardized units constructed of profiled steel panels on a lightweight steel frame, but it remained unrealized. The DRU rooftop extension was, however, built in 1971, after the conversion of the old building had been finished. Jan Kaplicky produced an extraordinary photo-montage, showing the existing building with a giant Volkswagen Beetle sitting on the roof. The reality was not so different. The extension was virtually independent of the building below. Instead of conventional walls and columns, there were steel trusses from wall to wall with

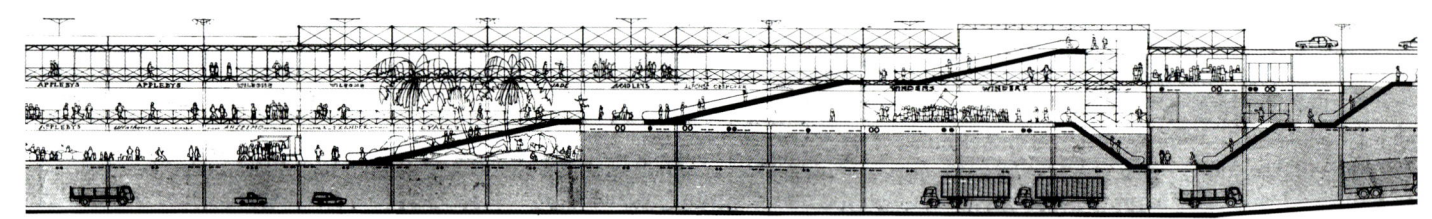

Part section through the Fitzroy Burleigh Central Area project, Cambridge, 1970

Renzo Piano's Italian Industry Pavilion, Osaka World Fair, 1970

Roof panels for Renzo Piano's Tensile Steel and Reinforced-Polyester Structure, Genoa, 1966

Exterior of Renzo Piano's office-workshop, Genoa, 1968–9

Interior of Renzo Piano's office-workshop, Genoa

panels, two to a bay, forming walls and roof. The initial idea was to make the panels from glass reinforced plastic (GRP) but fire officers rejected this proposal and subsequently they were changed to aluminium (coloured bright yellow, like the steelwork at the Wimbledon house) on a steel frame. The interior was an advanced example of the 1960s fashion for *Burolandschaft*, with the open-plan idea enhanced by the absence of structural divisions. Piano + Rogers was also commissioned to design all the furniture. Its own office was duly installed in the new building. But the tie-up with DRU was soon to end as the company decided that Piano + Rogers was not an asset, though the practice was allowed to stay on in the building (paying rent) until it moved to the Avon Trading Estate in West London.

John Young remembers that the outlook, once more, looked bleak. 'We were renting space at Aybrook Street, but we had no work to pay the rent. And the break-up of Richard and Su's marriage was having a serious impact on the practice.' Richard and Su's separation happened in 1970 and eventually led to divorce. Su Rogers, however, continued as part of the partnership.

While this period immediately preceding the Pompidou Centre competition was worrying, there were auguries of the future. The Chelsea football stadium project at Stamford Bridge ('incredibly exciting' according to Su Rogers) brought Rogers into direct contact with the great engineering practice of Ove Arup & Partners – Edmund (Ted) Happold of OAP was instrumental in the Pompidou triumph and introduced Peter Rice to Rogers. Rice became a close friend and an invaluable collaborator. The stadium project was marketing-led and eventually came to nothing, but it produced highly innovative proposals (in the spirit of Frei Otto, who was involved as a consultant) for a lightweight fabric structure to cover the entire stadium; a forerunner of the fabric structures widely used in the 1980s. However, all this was in the future; for the moment, the issue of getting work was paramount. The best opportunity seemed to be in Glasgow, where there was a competition for a building to house the Burrell Collection of art. The entry was, however, eventually unsuccessful.

In the four years between the break-up of Team 4 and the triumph at Beaubourg, Rogers and his partners had succeeded in building very little: just a couple of private houses and an office extension. But a practice and a philosophy had been forged. At Reliance Controls, the users had complained about only one aspect of the Team 4 building – the absence of colour. Colour, texture and expressive form, all perennial features of Rogers' mature architecture, were unleashed in the work that followed on from the dissolution of Team 4.

The partnership with Renzo Piano was fortuitous for Richard Rogers. It was a happy accident that Piano was an Italian – he stirred Rogers' own feelings for his roots in Italy. More important, however, were Piano's untrammelled optimism and fearless radicalism, which reinforced Richard Rogers' own instinct to experiment and innovate. Rogers remembers the time at DRU as rather dispiriting. It all ended rather badly, and the prospects seemed so poor in 1970–1 that Rogers spent much of his time teaching in the United States – at Cornell University – and occasionally at home at the AA and Cambridge. However, Rogers now knew *what* and *how* he wanted to build, and he had the makings of the team, including Piano, Young, Goldschmied, Kaplicky, Botschi and others, that he needed to achieve his aims. All that was required was the ideal commission.

Renzo Piano's Genoa team in the late 1960s

Renzo Piano with Ted Happold of Ove Arup Partnership's Structures Group 3

Spender House

Ulting, Essex, 1967–8

The Spender House was Rogers' first post-Team 4 project and, though it was problematic and not entirely successful, it set the agenda for much of the office's work during the 1970s.

The brief was for a compact house and studio for an architect turned photographer and his wife, both approaching the age of 60. They were selling their large house in Essex but retaining part of the garden, secluded but with pleasing views, as a site for their new home. Rogers' designs (in the development of which John Young was instrumental) clearly reflected the legacy of Reliance Controls. The use of a steel frame infilled with plastic-coated steel panels was seen as entirely appropriate for a domestic building and reflected the strong influence of the Case Study houses on Rogers. In particular, the Spender House was inspired by the experimental steel houses built in the 1950s by Craig Ellwood (1922–92) and Raphael Soriano (1907–88). Soriano had insisted on the necessity of modular planning: 'planning with steel must be done logically and economically, for tricks are costly and hazardous'. Soriano had equally insisted that his houses were not one-offs, but prototypes. 'If you are looking for a solution for housing in the twentieth century, which I am, the general and the individual must be identical', he declared. The Spender House therefore, while designed for the needs of specific clients, embodies an objective, universal approach to housing people. Significantly, it was intended to be low-cost, extendible and adaptable. Low maintenance was equally a priority.

The design places house, studio (with attached carport) and intermediate courtyard within a regular grid. The raw materials are six 14-metre portals, three for each building, made from standard steel sections and expressed externally, with both roof and walls of plastic-coated, profiled steel panels. Wall panels and windows (set in aluminium frames by Crittall), designed to be interchangeable, allow for maximum flexibility. Pitched glazing in the roof provides north light for the studio. All components were intended to be demountable and reusable.

Reliance Controls was the landmark of Rogers' early work and the Spender House applied some of the lessons learned there to the issues of house design, marking the abandonment of the more traditional construction techniques used in earlier projects – notably Creek Vean – in favour of lightweight construction using, as far as possible, off-the-peg components. The difficulties which arose during the project were the result of the contractual arrangements with a variety of specialist contractors responsible for various elements; the architects had to coordinate and resolve many problems. Young effectively became the project manager, dealing with every detail of the construction and fit out. Richard Rogers wrote to Spender in January 1971, two years after the completion of the house: 'we consider the advantages of the scheme far outweigh the disadvantages. In each project, we do our best to eliminate some of the problems of the last project. Sometimes doing this creates new problems, but at least we try.'

The Spender House was seen by the architects as a model for mass housing and they were disappointed that the steel industry did not promote its virtues. However, it did provide a test-bed for the Rogers House, begun before the Spender House was completed, which combined a similar diagram with a more sophisticated use of materials.

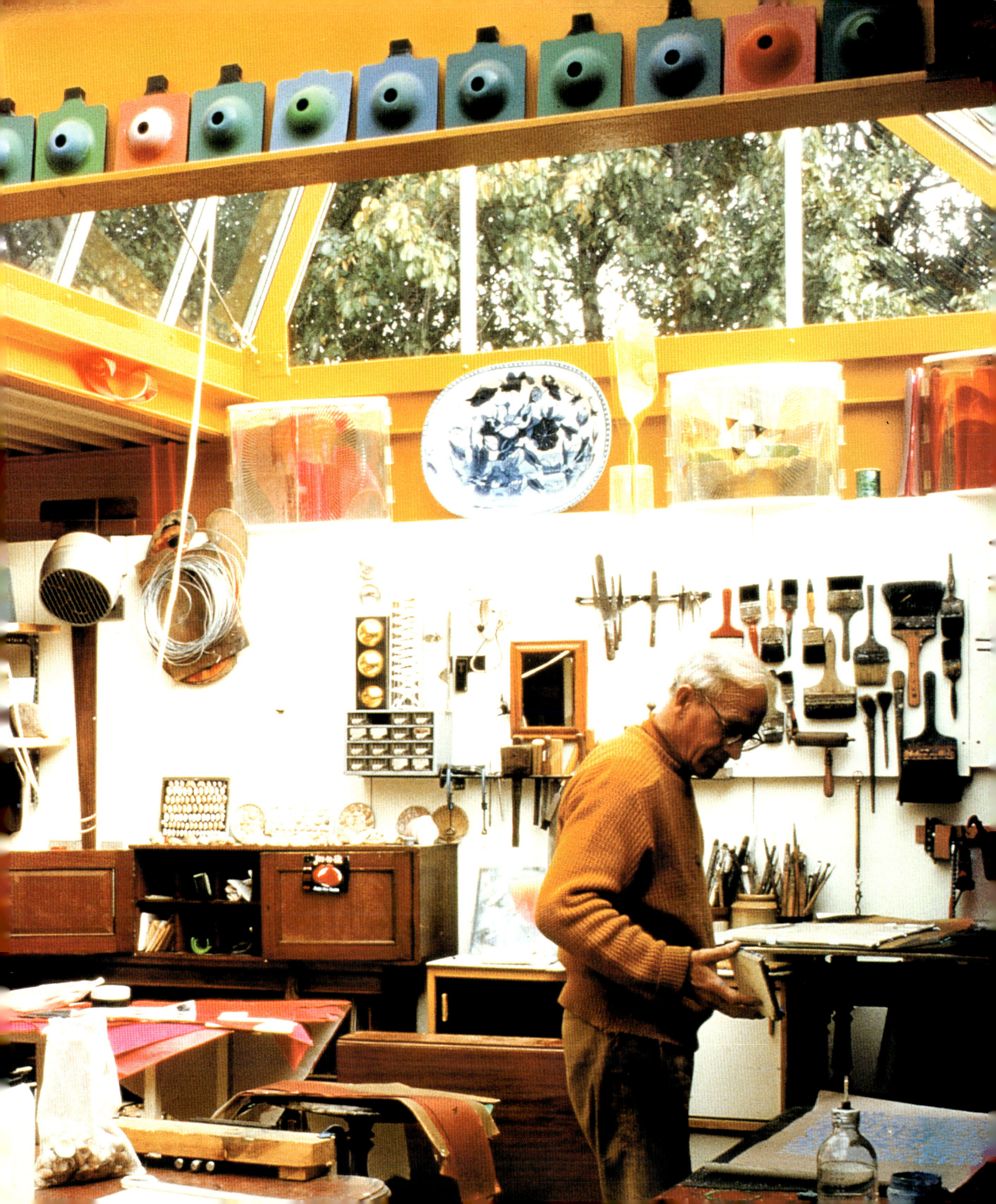

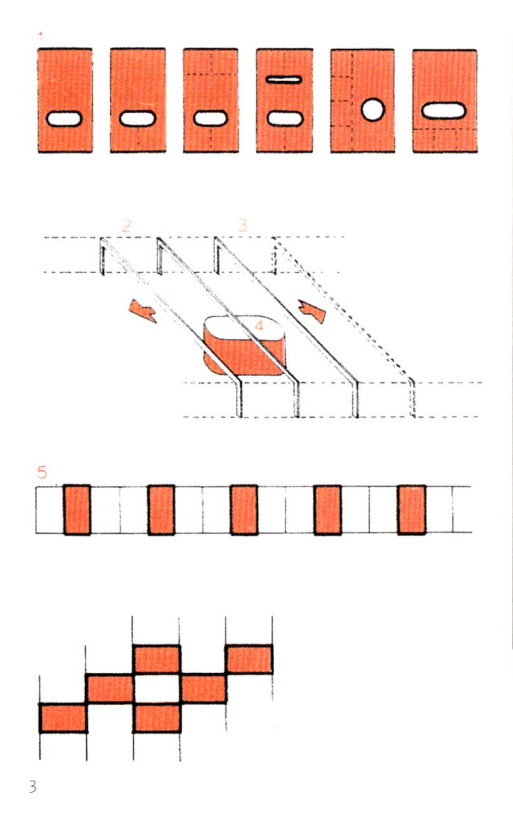

Spender House

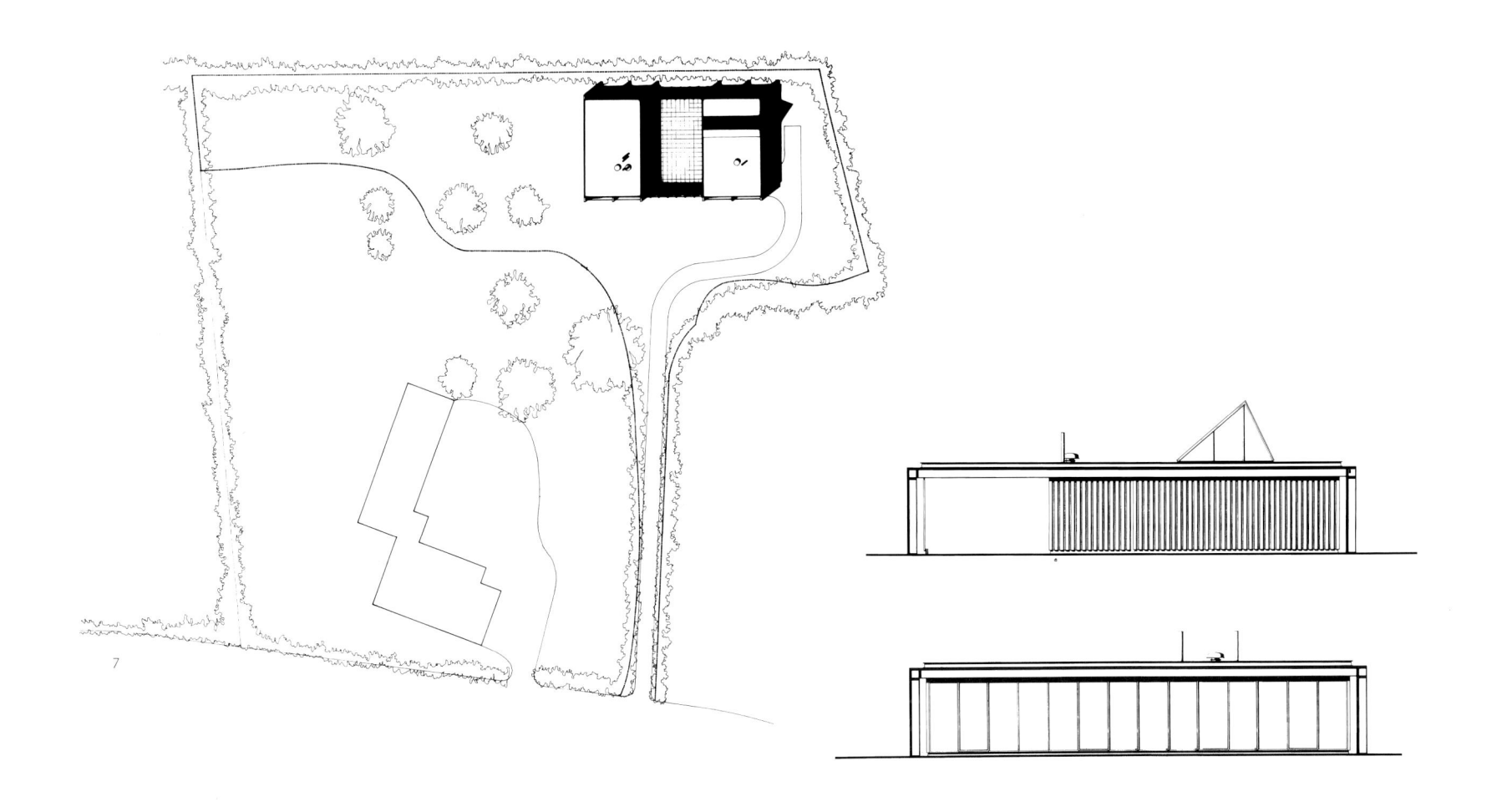

Humphrey Spender works in the studio of his house (2, previous page). Rogers applied the construction methodology of Reliance Controls to a housing programme (3 & 4).
The house and studio are built of identical components (8 & 9): the studio is differentiated by a large north-facing skylight for even illumination (1, previous pages & 5).
The site was in the garden of a former vicarage (6 & 7).

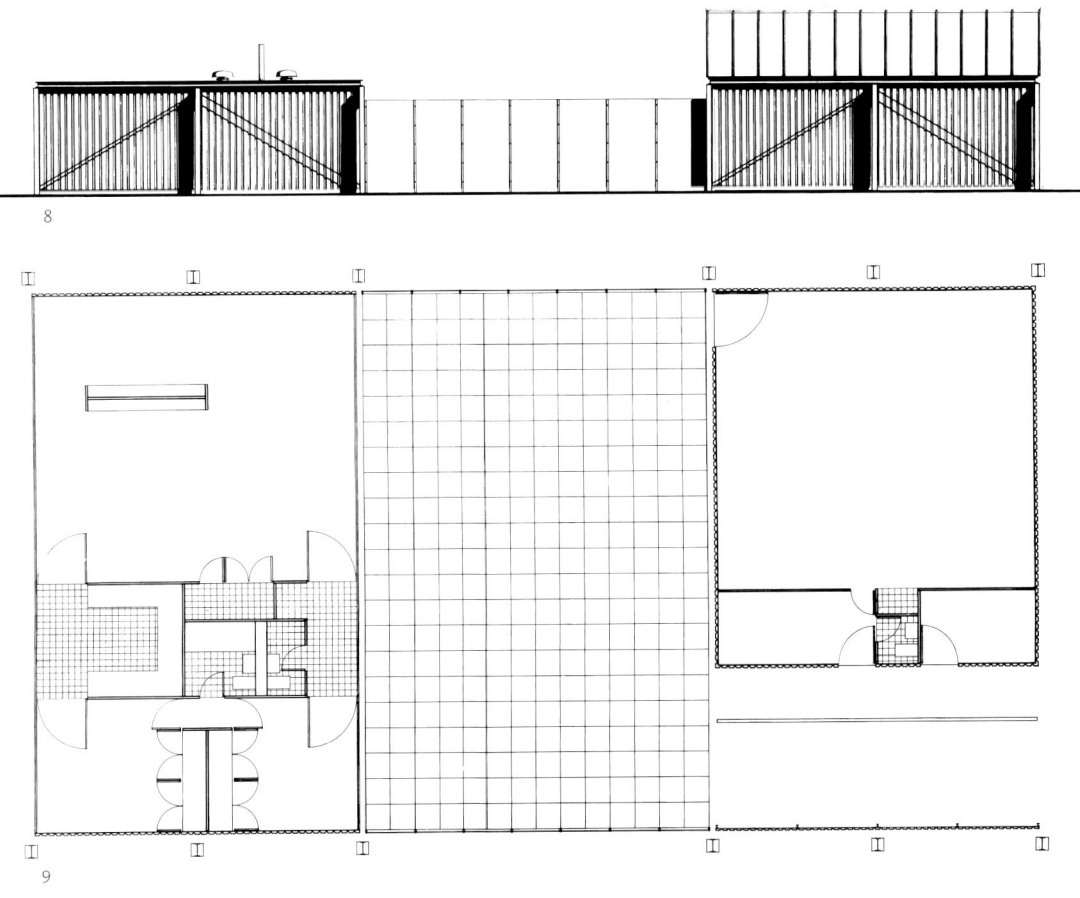

Rogers House

Wimbledon, London, 1968–9

The house built for Richard Rogers' parents on a garden site close to Wimbledon Common was a significant development of the architectural language of Reliance Controls and the Spender House. It was an affectionate evocation of the qualities which Richard Rogers had admired in some of the Californian Case Study houses.

The brief was for a retirement home to replace a conventional suburban villa in which the Rogers had lived since the early 1950s. Rogers developed it in collaboration with his parents, who had a very clear view of the house they needed. Flexibility was a high priority, since Dr Rogers wished to continue limited medical practice and needed a consulting room. The future needs of a growing family, who might wish to visit, also had to be considered. The house should enhance the sense of seclusion inherent in the site while respecting the amenities of neighbours. It should be economical to build, to maintain and to run, suitable for a couple in their 60s. His mother wanted a house with flair, a contrast to the 'sensible' suburban villa which she had never been able to love.

The strategy which developed from this brief provided for a house built using not the traditional techniques of Creek Vean and Murray Mews, but those of industrialized production: the house would be assembled rather than built. In practice, this meant a steel frame of welded rigid portals, five for the house itself and three for the studio or 'lodge' facing it across a paved court. The walls are formed of 2" thick 'Alcoa' plastic-coated aluminium panels, insulated and fixed together with a neoprene zip jointing system. The east and west elevations are entirely glazed with sliding units (specially made, in fact, rather than off-the-peg). The roof consists of reinforced wood wool slabs with a suspended plaster ceiling containing a radiant heating system (a great improvement on the blown warm air system used at the Spender House). All internal partitions are movable, except for bathroom walls and the low wall defining the kitchen. Glazed roofs, neoprene zipped and solar reflecting, enclose the bathrooms.

The Rogers House is, in many ways, an act of homage to Eames, Soriano and Ellwood, just as Creek Vean paid homage to Wright. It was always seen by Rogers as a prototype, not a one-off job. The circumstances of the Wimbledon commission naturally inspired close attention to detail, producing a far finer end product than the Spender House, but the principles behind the scheme had universal implications and the Rogers team believed that the house could have been replicated by the thousands. It remains a carefully crafted object with some elements – the custom-made windows and plaster ceiling, for example – that may seem to compromise the purity of the idea.

The use of strong colour in the house, for the steel frame and for internal elements, reflects Rogers' own tastes and those of his mother. By happy chance, his parents brought with them from Cheam a number of items of furniture designed by Ernesto Rogers, including a set of imposing dining chairs. The house neither demanded nor received a minimalist response in terms of furnishing

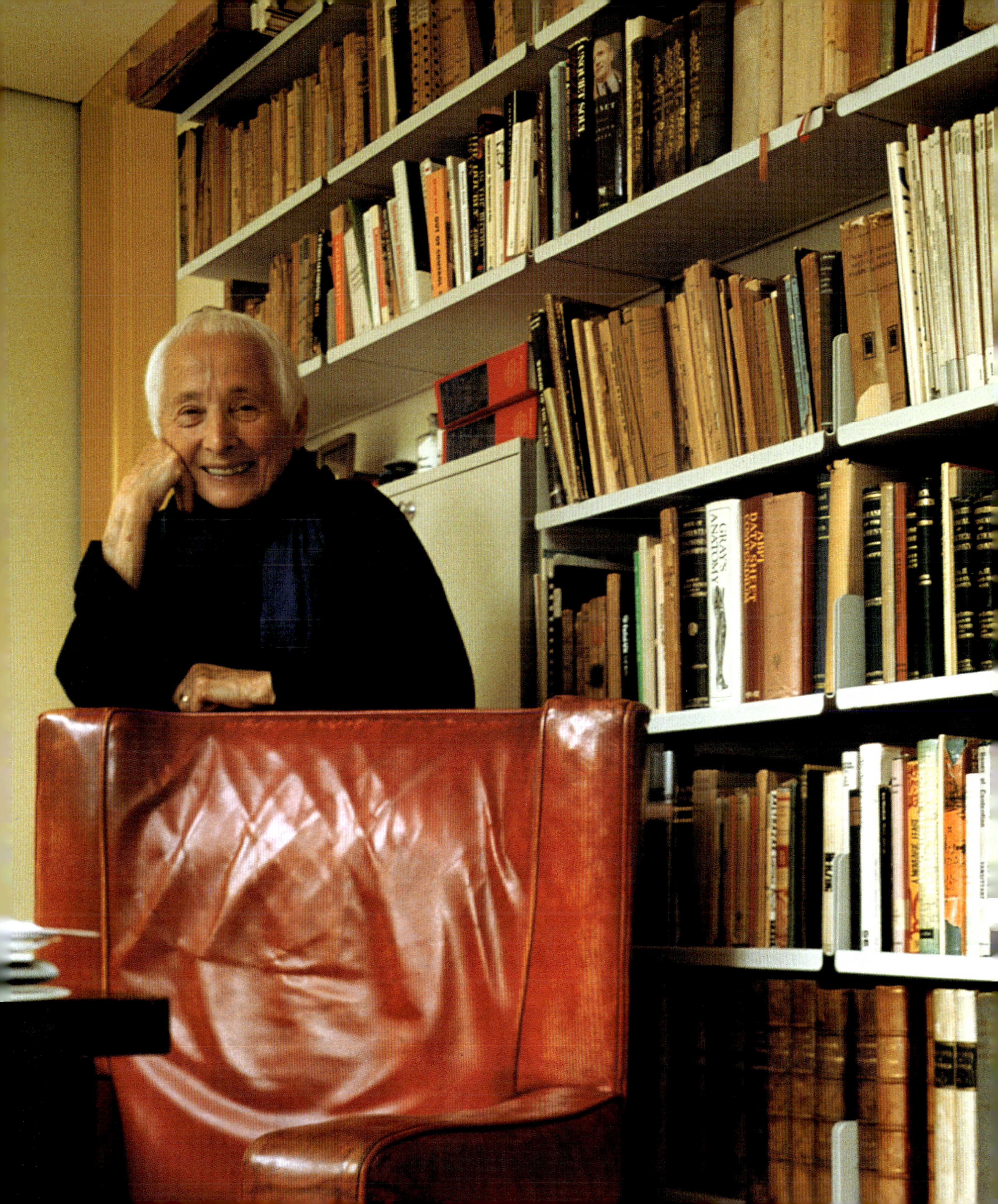
GRAY'S ANATOMY

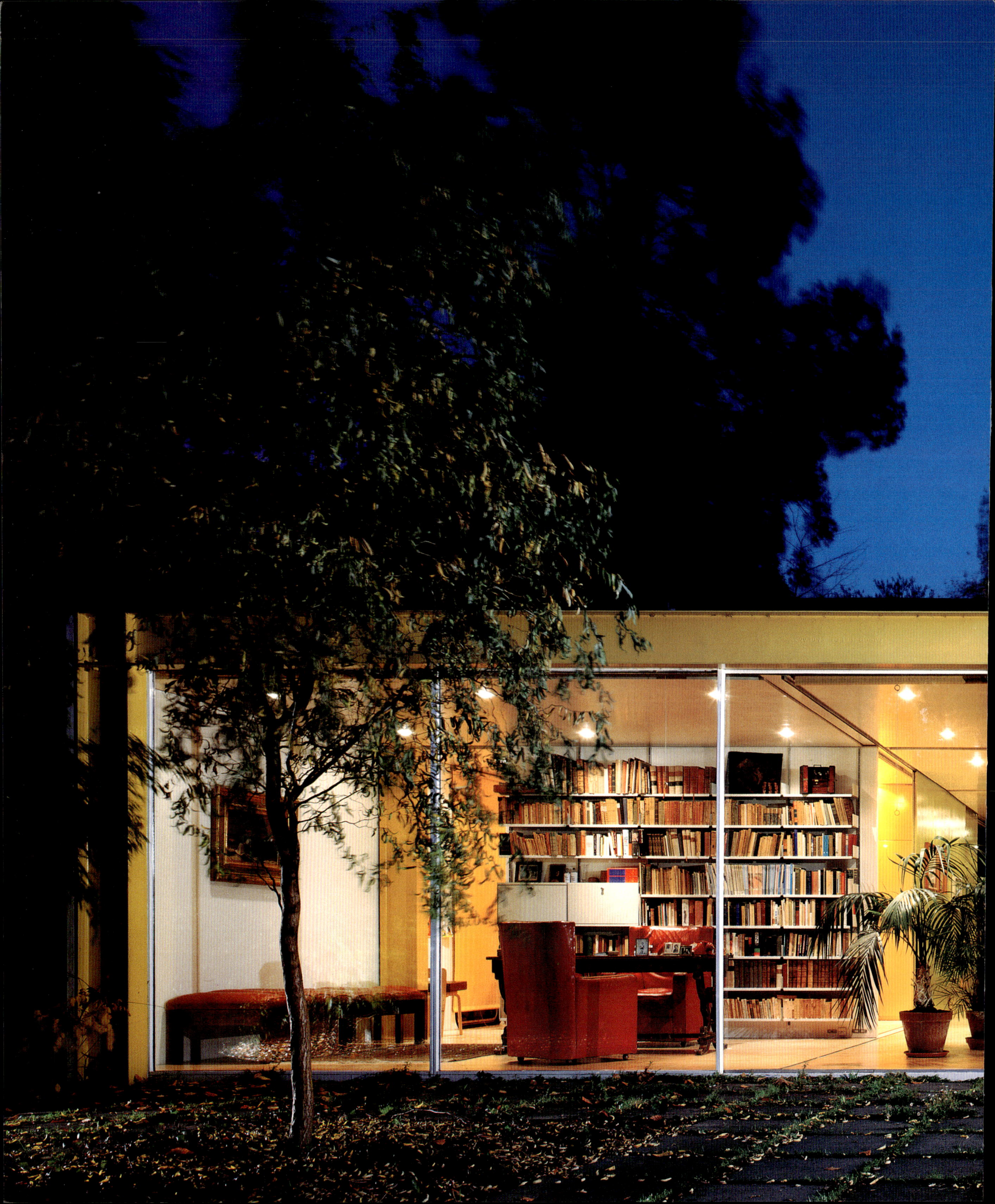

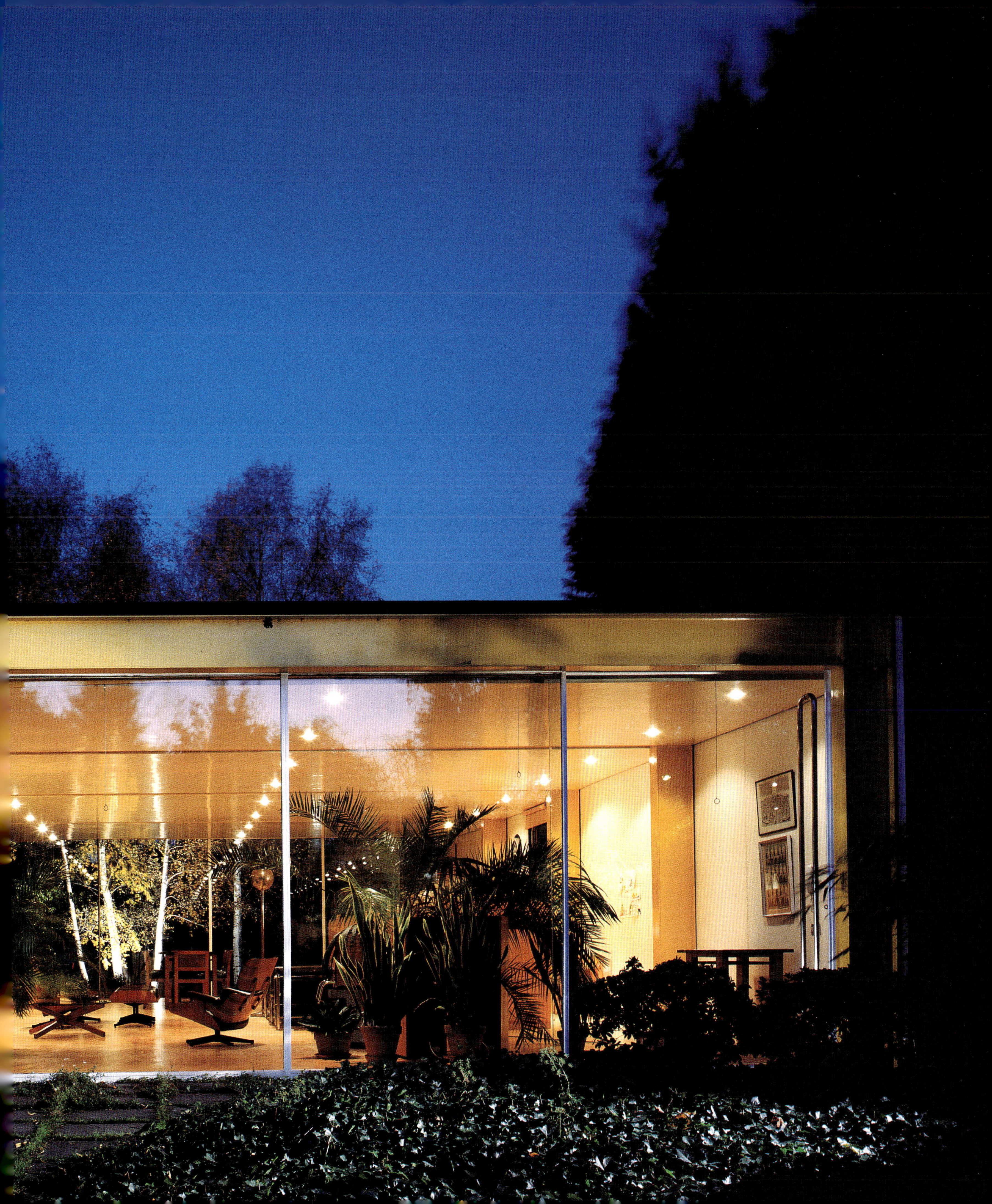

Richard Rogers' sketch shows the layering and connection of the house to Wimbledon Common beyond (1, p72).
Dada Rogers in the study of her house (2, p73), which is a glowing presence by night in the mature suburban garden in which it was built (3, previous pages).
House and lodge are laid out on a grid which makes optimum use of the relatively narrow site (4).

The garden and house are treated as a unit, both visually and in terms of the way they are used by the Rogers family (5 & 6).
In its openness and transparency, the house is an evocation of the West Coast of the USA, built on the outskirts of London (7 & 8).
In contrast to the all-glass principal facades, the boundary walls use prefabricated, storey-height, insulated panels (9).

and decoration. It is seen as a family house and encapsulates Richard Rogers' deepest feelings about family, continuity, identity and the landscape, as well as his search for a new housing aesthetic.

Richard Rogers' own account of the house stresses its relationship with the landscape. He describes it as 'a transparent tube with solid walls only on the boundary. The tube links together Wimbledon Common, the earth mound that acts as an acoustic and visual barrier, the lodge (originally carport and pottery), the beautiful courtyard (which could be filled in if the house were ever extended), the house and the wonderful garden beyond. This tube/tunnel is cut into sections by light and plants so that one is looking through a series of layers – of translucent planes. The garden has little colour, just a few wild flowers, but the house and lodge are full of colour. This is for me magical because of the near perfect relationship between client and architect. It has matured over time with Mother's constant adjustments to everything moveable, from her stunning pottery, to the furniture and plants.' For Rogers, this will always be Dada's house.

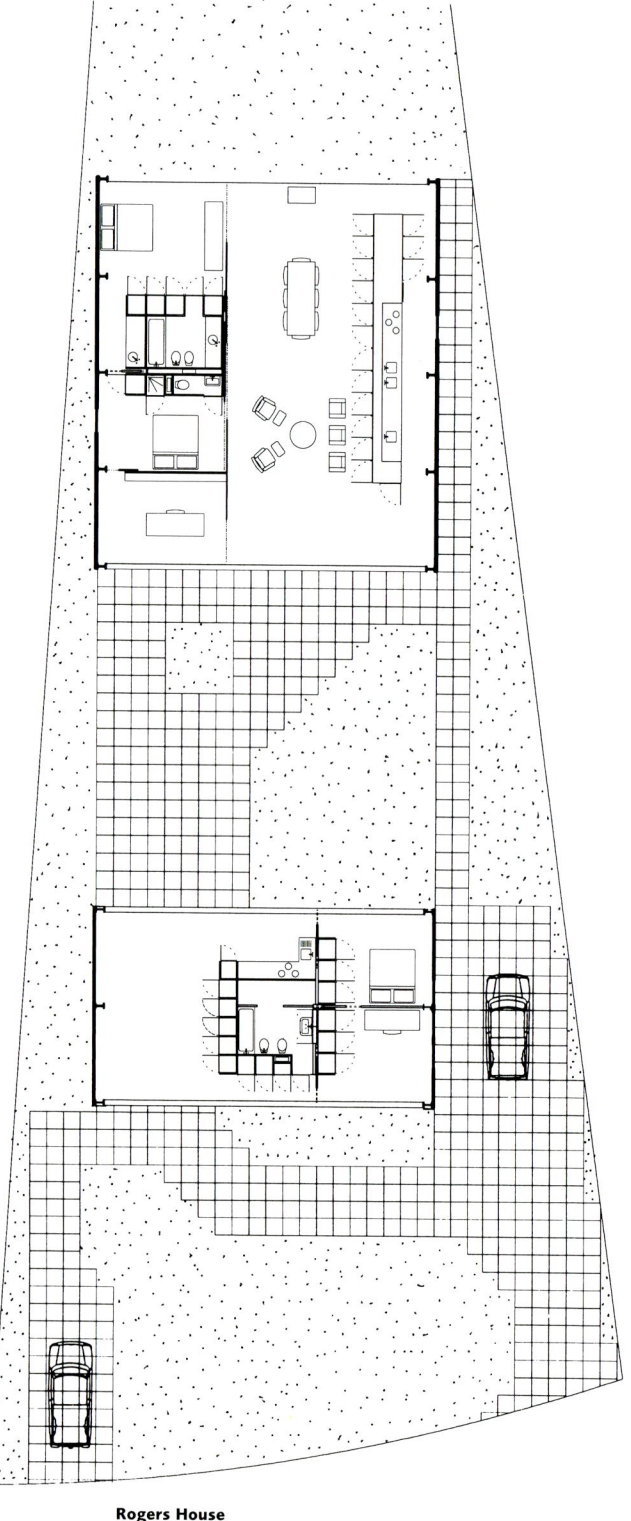

Rogers House

7

8
9

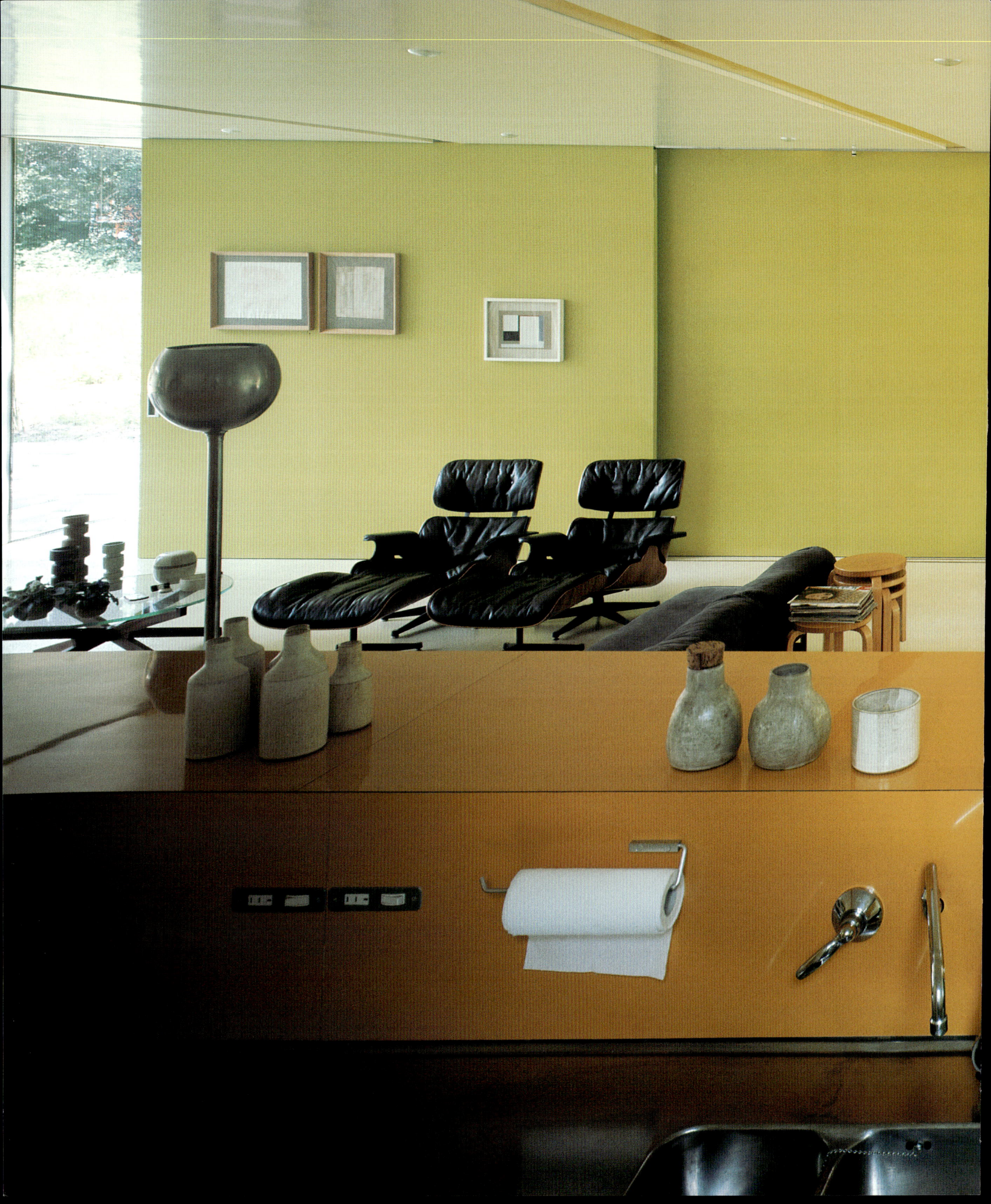

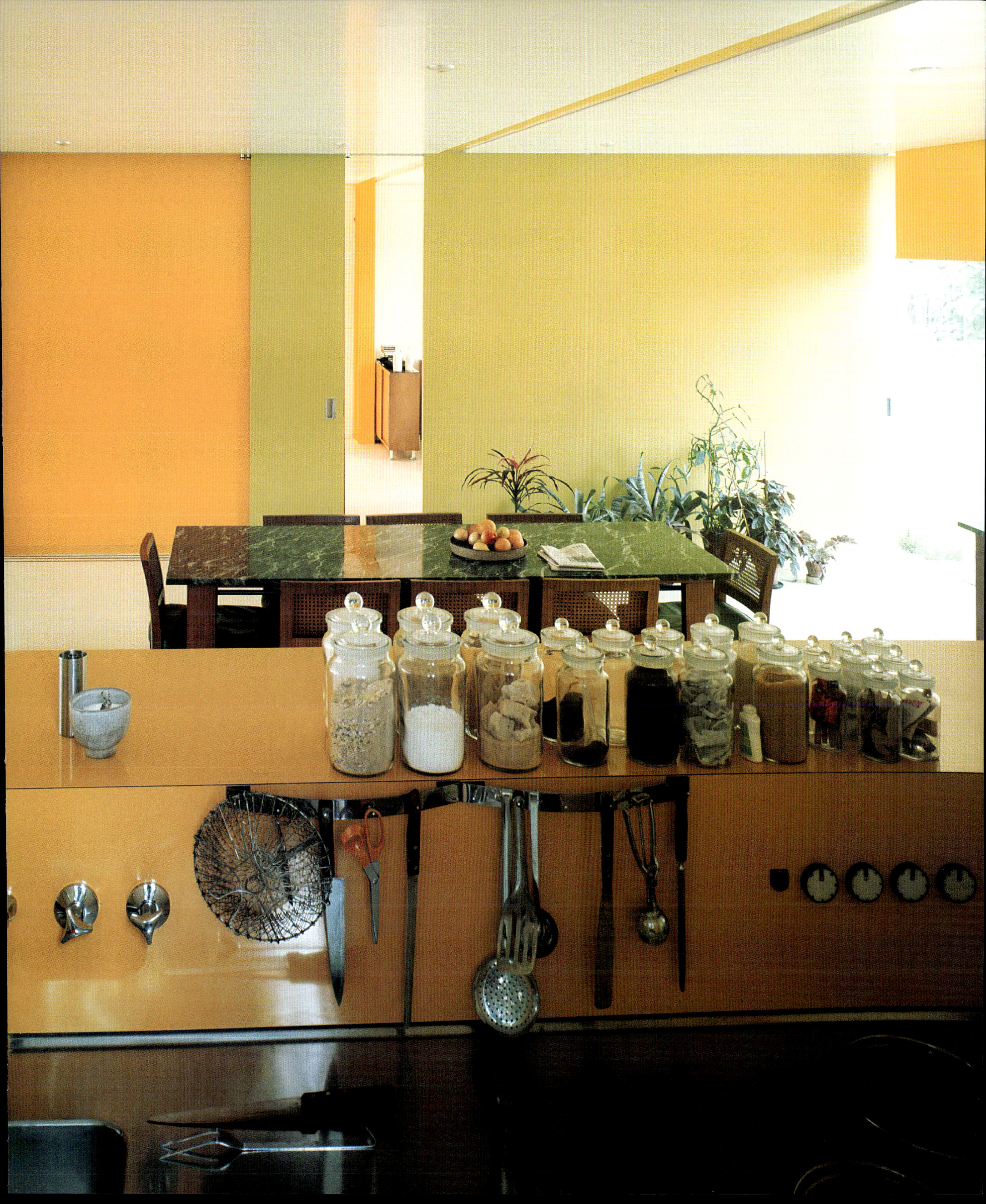

11

The interior of the house (10, previous pages, 11 & 13) is furnished with an eclectic mix of items, including designs by Ernesto Rogers and other leading designers. Examples of Dada Rogers' pottery are also on display (12).
The house is designed to offer both privacy and a sense of openness (14). Views into the green space of the garden are an essential element in the experience of the interior (15).

12   13   14

Rogers House

15

Zip Up Enclosures No 1 & No 2

Prototype Housing Unit, 1968 & 1971

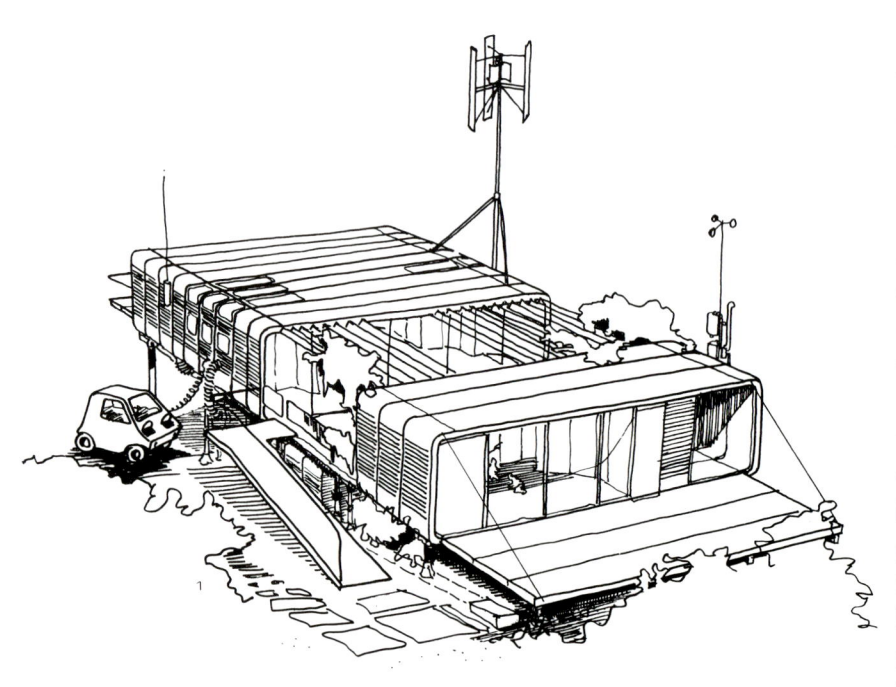

The first Zip-Up House was designed, in collaboration with engineer Tony Hunt, in response to a competition sponsored by the DuPont company for 'The House for Today', to be exhibited at the 1969 Ideal Home Exhibition in London. Richard + Su Rogers was convinced that the future of housing lay in mass production. The Spender and Rogers Houses had been seen as prototypes, but it was the Zip-Up concept which opened the way to factory production of houses, which were envisaged as portable, expandable resources, not fixed permanently to one plot of ground.

The project made use of monocoque construction, similar to cars and aeroplanes where the 'skin' of the vehicle provides its own structural support. It was based on the insulated, aluminium skinned sandwich panels used at Wimbledon, but with their structural behaviour transformed by the use of a high performance cellular PVC core (used primarily in the aircraft industry) to produce a load-bearing panel capable of spanning 10 metres. The wall, floor and roof components combined to form a structural ring which could be jointed to identical rings to form an enclosure of infinite length. The overall aim was to offer the user a wide range of choice at low building cost with minimum maintenance and running costs and a high degree of environmental control. Rogers saw the concept as rooted in DIY principles. He envisaged potential purchasers going to their local homestore to buy as many rings as they wanted or extra rings to enlarge an existing starter home to cope with an expanding family. There was no internal structure, thus permitting maximum flexibility for subdivision. The structural panels had an insulation value seven times that of a traditional house so that one 3kw heater was sufficient to heat the whole house according to Max Fordham who worked on the servicing aspects of the Zip-Up programme. The house was freed from the site by elevating it above ground level on a series of steel jacks – adjustable to the contours of the land. There were no foundations and, though the house would normally be plugged into existing services, it could, in theory, be moved at will. (Rogers' later work on the Autonomous House opened up the prospect of freeing the house entirely from dependence on piped-in services.) Within the house, all partitions were moveable – the layout could be totally changed in a day and bathrooms repositioned over a weekend – and it was envisaged that extra doors and windows could be provided by a reasonably competent householder, using a special cutting tool and standard components. End elevations could be totally glazed.

Zip-Up received much media attention, but was generally seen as 'futuristic', whereas its designers argued that it could be produced using existing materials and technology. They were dismayed by the resounding lack of interest on the part of component producers and by the hostility of planners approached about plans to place Zip-Ups on sites in Cornwall and Surrey. In retrospect, the radicalism of the concept remains striking and the bright yellow panels are still a defiant statement. Rogers remained passionate about the project – Zip-Up No 2 applied the same technology to a two-storey house, appropriate for a tight urban site (although a light steel frame, inserted into the thickness of the panels, was deemed necessary for structural stability). Nor was the Zip-Up concept applicable only to houses – factories, offices and even hotels could be assembled of standard parts in a fraction of the time required for a conventional building.

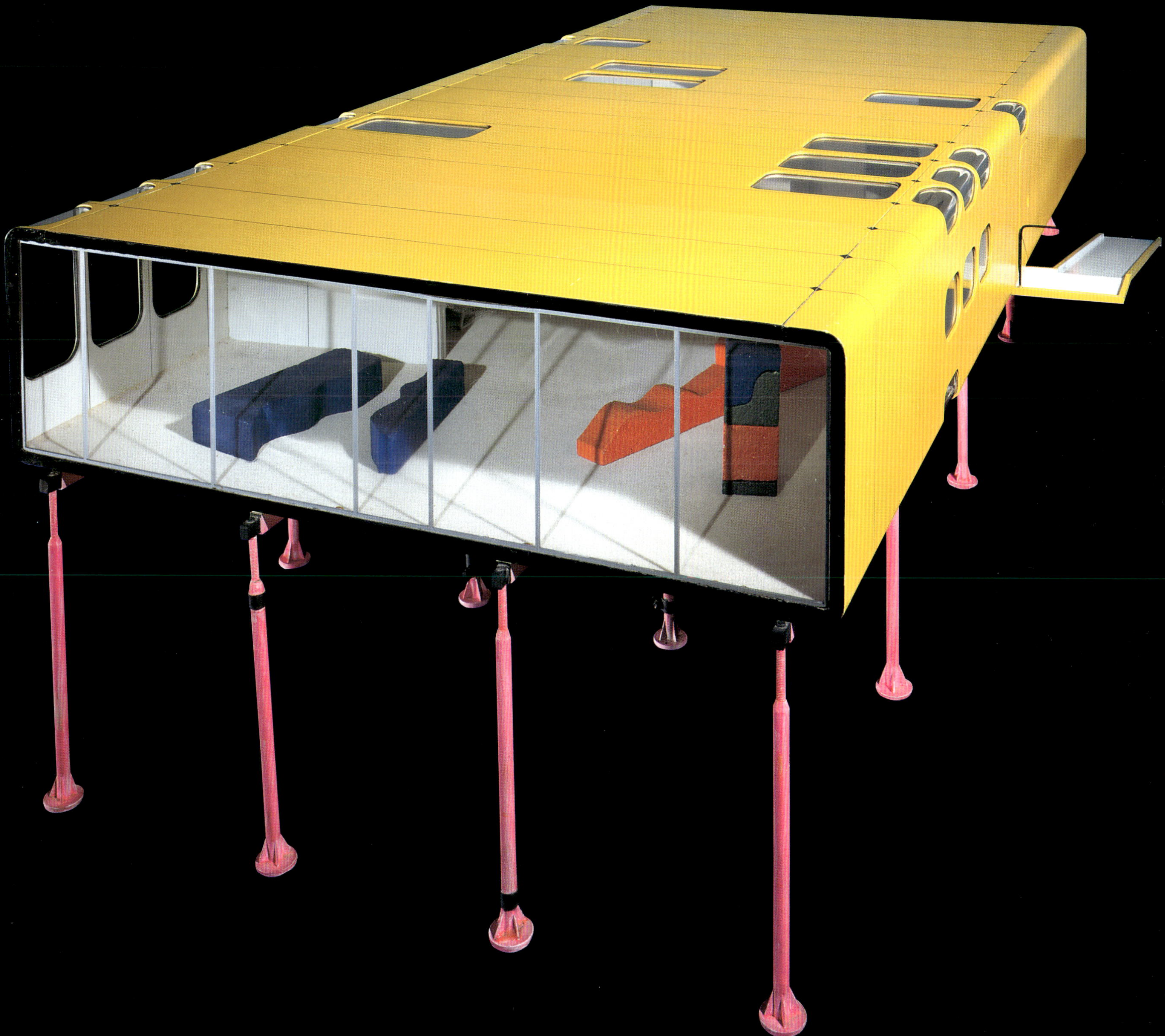

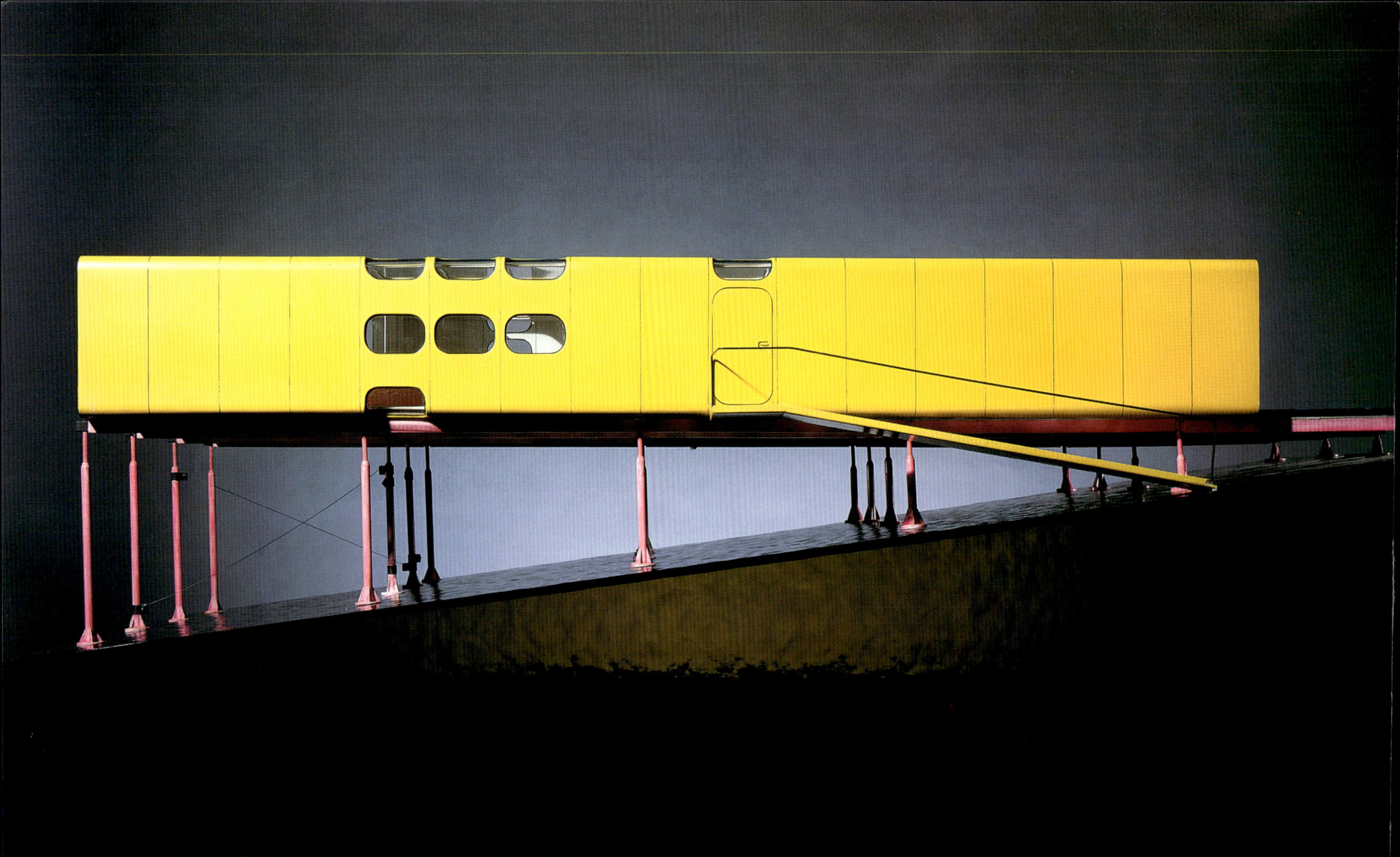

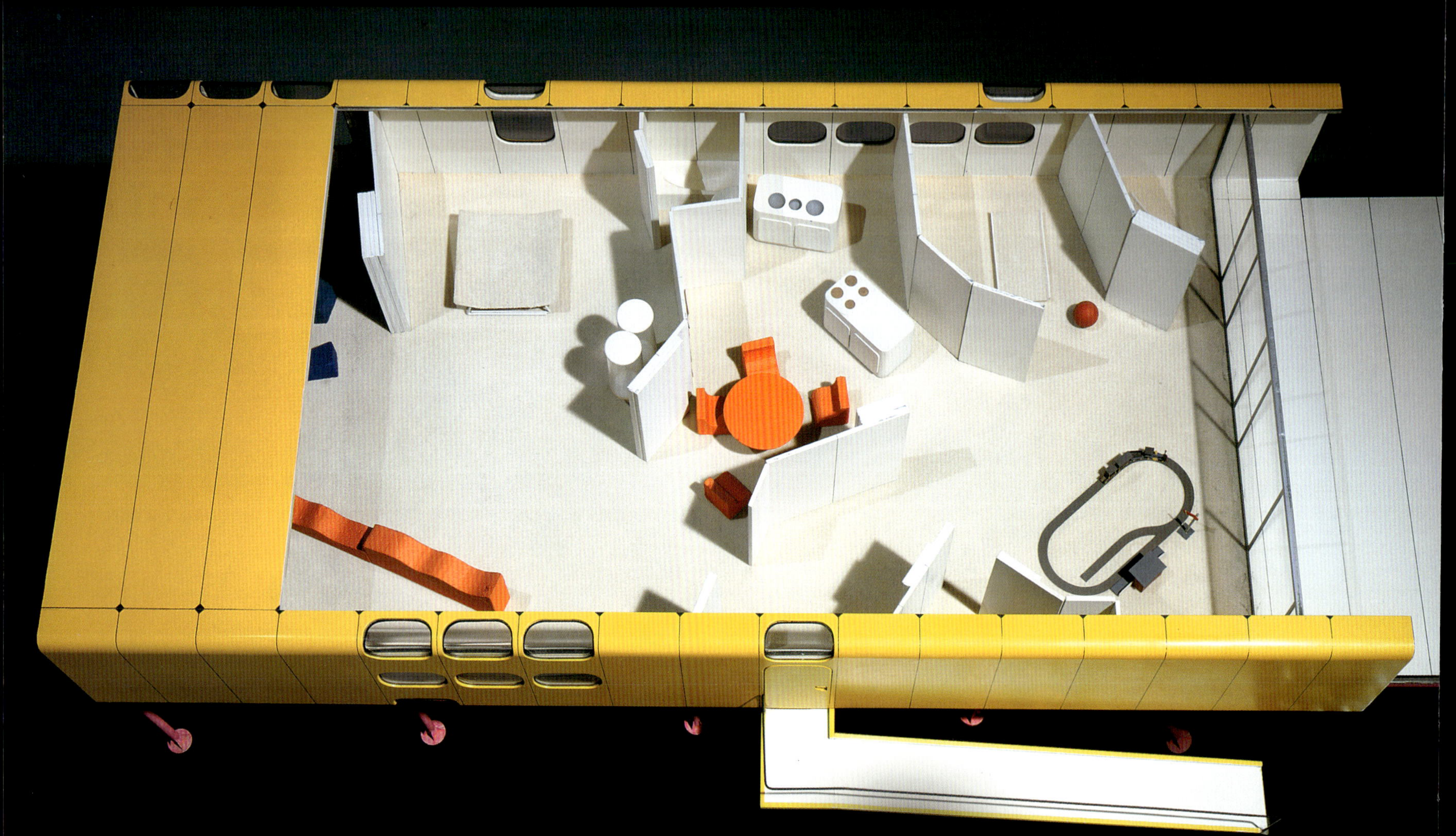

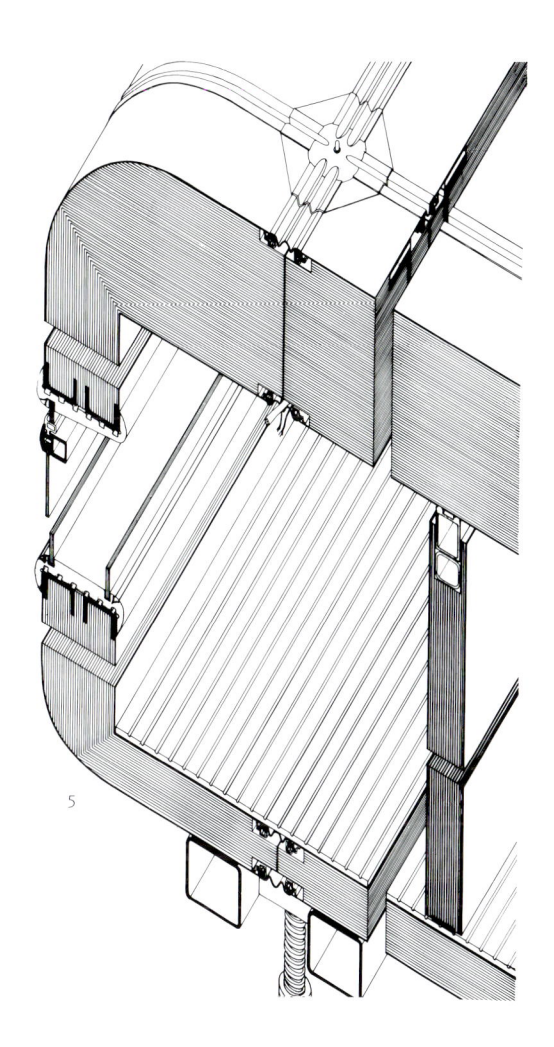

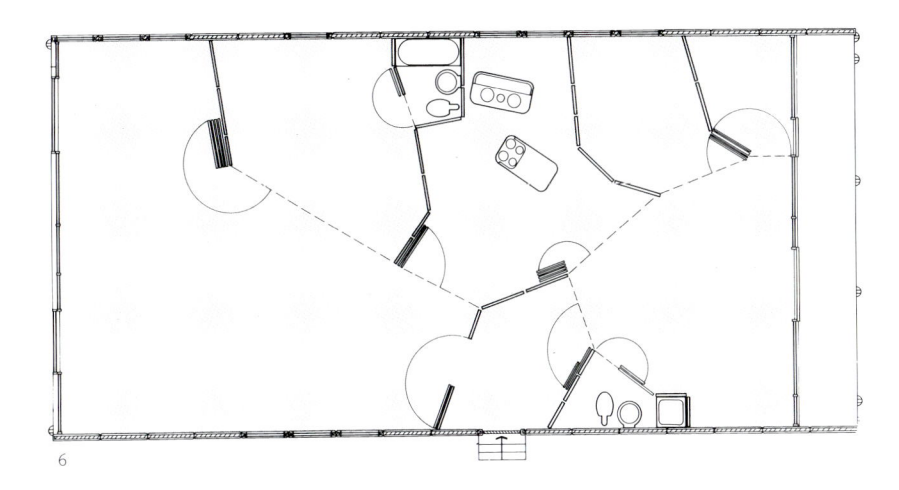

The Zip-Up House could be assembled anywhere: adjustable jacks freed it from the tyranny of the site contours (1 & 2, previous pages & 3).
The plan was intended to be completely flexible – the room spaces could be reconfigured by the inhabitants at will (4 & 6).

Even bathroom locations could be changed in a weekend. The house was fabricated of ring-shaped, insulated sandwich panels which formed its roof and walls, terms which were scarcely applicable to the radical design (5).
A two-storey version of the Zip-Up House was also envisaged (7).

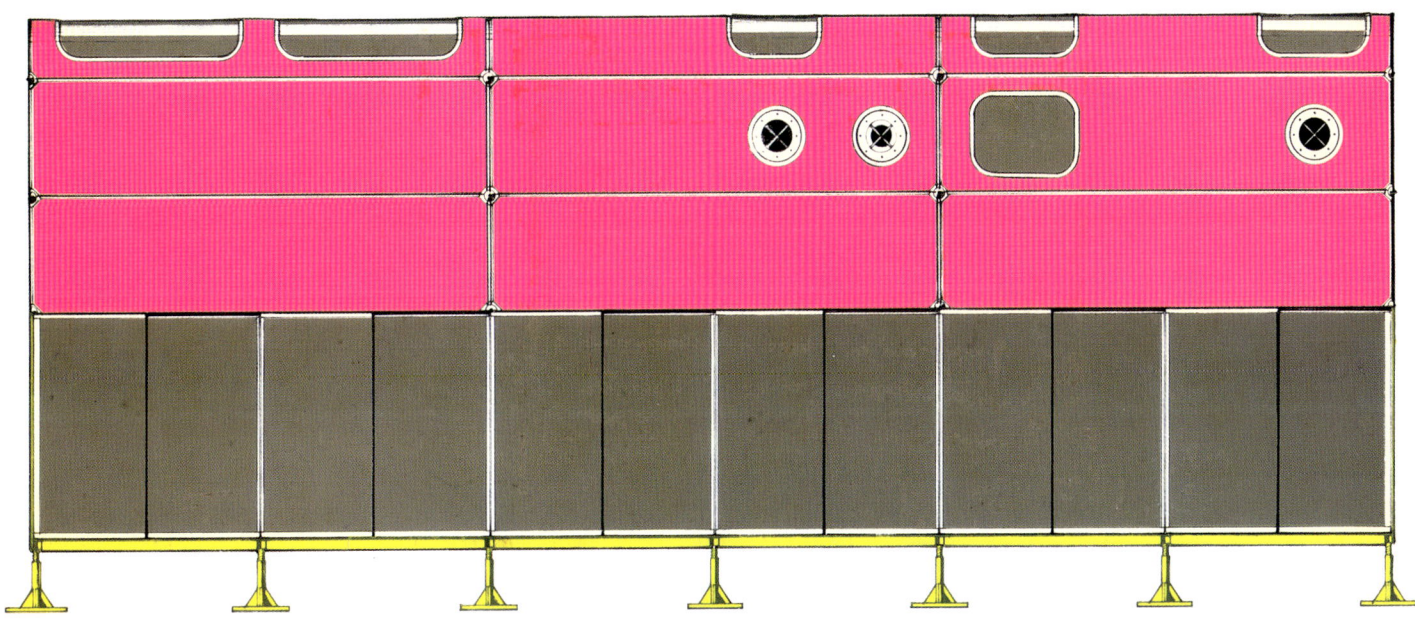

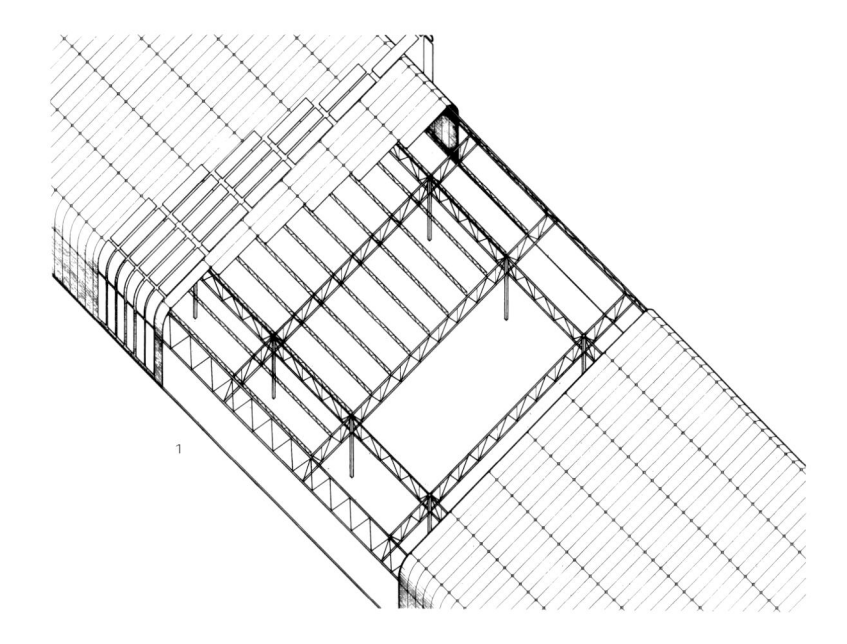

Universal Oil Products Factory
Ashford, Kent, 1969–70

The first project for UOP applied the technology of the Zip-Up House to an industrial building. The principles were unchanged, but they were now applied on a far larger scale with the aim of producing a 'low energy, loose fit' building 120 metres long and 42 metres wide; a tube of insulated aluminium panels where roof and walls were one. The factory – which remains unbuilt – represented a considerable advance on Reliance Controls. The absolute clarity of the Zip-Up House had, however, to be compromised by an internal steel structure. The great span of the building necessitated rows of supporting columns along each side, though the floor space was largely uninterrupted. The fact that the panelling system was not only strong but also relatively light meant that a long span could be achieved without deep foundations.

The advantages of the large cladding panel system were many. It could be quickly applied, providing a totally enclosed envelope for the installation of finishes and services. It also offered an exceptional degree of insulation and low running costs. The building could be readily extended and alterations, such as the insertion of new window and door openings, posed no problems. Although it was unlikely that a factory would be picked up and moved to another part of the country – the dream of mobility was central to the Zip-Up House – the UOP project addressed the needs of a new industrial order far removed from the mills and mines which still formed the backbone of the British economy in the 1960s. Richard Rogers believed that the reform of the workplace was as urgent as the reform of the home. He sought a new industrial vernacular which could be adapted to a wide variety of user needs; the best British industrial buildings of the post-war era – the Brynmawr rubber factory, Cummins Engines and Reliance Controls, for example – had been prestige, one-off projects. But his vision in this case remained unrealized, even though the collapse of traditional industry and the emergence of a new research-based, lightweight, mobile economy seemed to augur well for its realization.

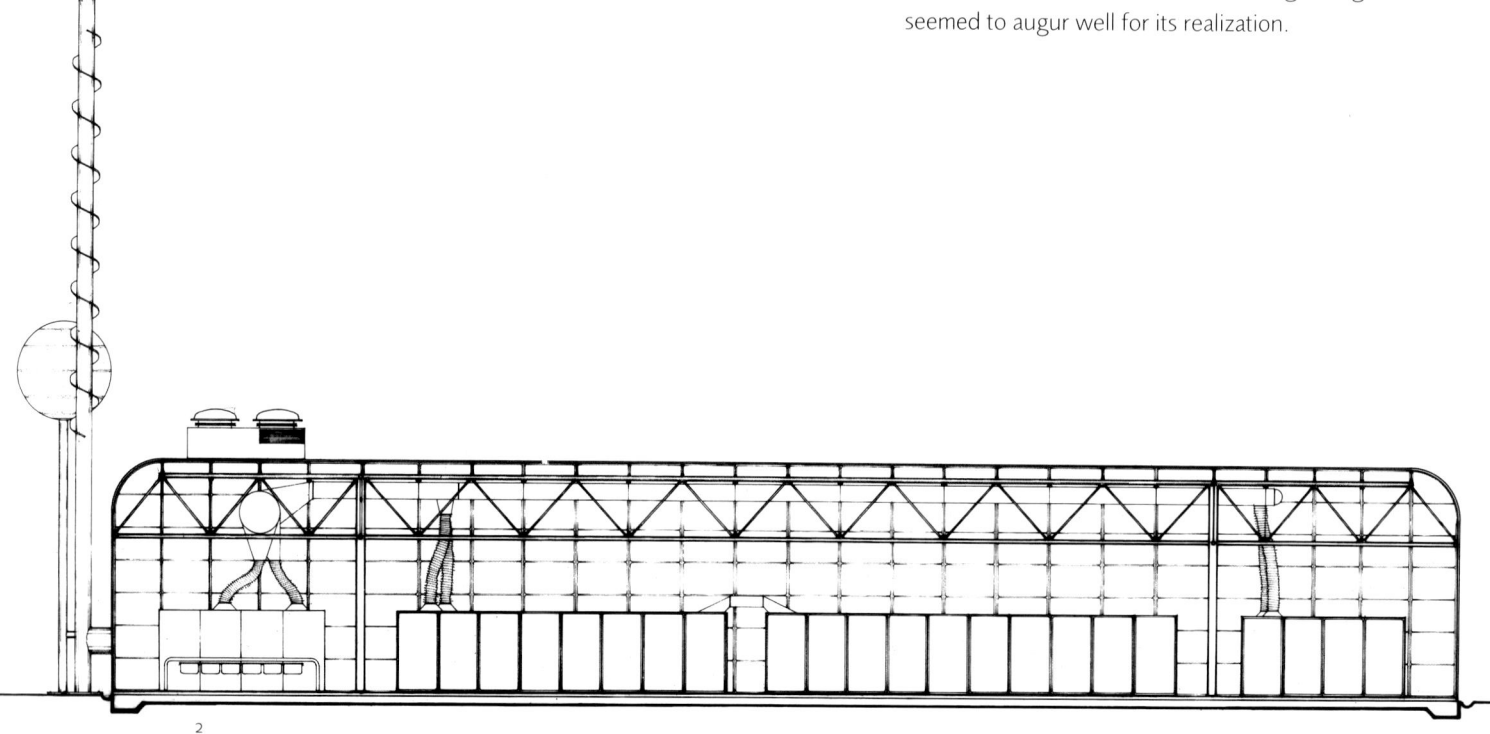

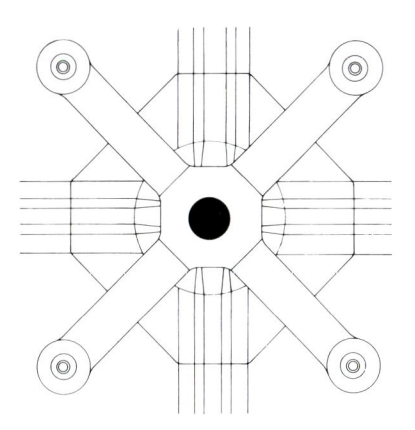

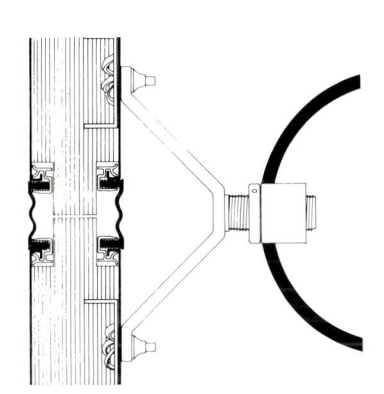

The UOP building had a wide-span steel structure and highly-insulated envelope with movable glazed ends to allow for future expansion (1, 2, 4 & 5).
Connections between the structure and the insulated wall panels were achieved with cast steel 'spiders' (3).

Extension to Design Research Unit

London, 1969–71

Design Research Unit (DRU), in which Marcus Brumwell had played a founding role, provided a welcome umbrella for Rogers' practice after the break-up of Team 4 in 1967. The company moved to new premises in Aybrook Street in 1969, acquiring a former industrial building. Richard + Su Rogers was commissioned firstly to produce a brief for converting the building and subsequently to carry out the actual conversion. The existing building, however, was scarcely large enough and in 1971 DRU asked Rogers to design a rooftop extension, for which planning consent had already been given.

The Zip-Up system was ideal for this purpose, since it was lightweight (so that the new floor could be carried on the existing structure of the building) and allowed for fast-track construction. Moreover, the uninterrupted span it provided was ideal for the nature of the work at DRU – carried out by teams who formed and re-formed in line with the projects in the office, requiring adaptable open space rather than enclosed rooms.

The scheme had to be amended in detail to satisfy the planners. The profile of the extension had to be redesigned, with sloping sides, making it a roof space rather than an additional floor, and aluminium panels had to be substituted for the proposed GRP. As executed, the panels, with a bright yellow coating, were 3 metres wide and carried on lightweight arched steel portals, without column support. Aluminium framed windows were riveted into the panels.

The Rogers office was also responsible for the furnishing of the entire building and produced a standard table (180 cm x 90 cm), together with drawing board and filing cupboard, for each work unit with steel and laminate as the basic materials.

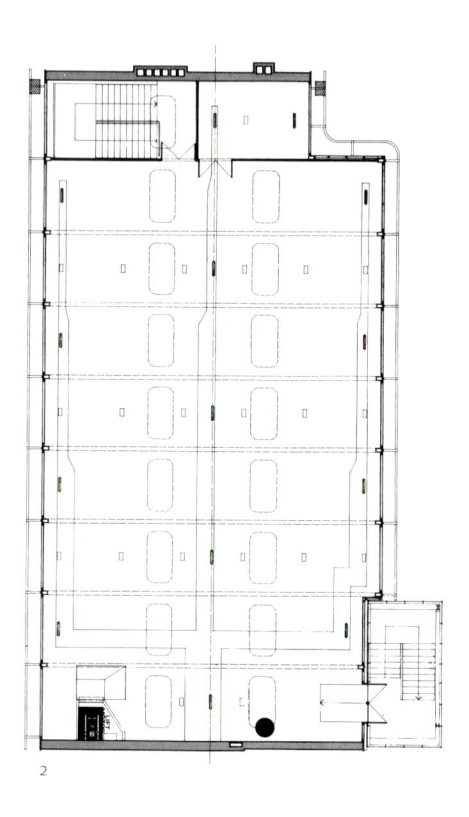

3

A photomontage by Jan Kaplicky
humorously explains the design concept (1).
The extension to the DRU building was
basically a Zip-Up structure (3); as built, it
featured aluminium panels carried on a steel
frame (4).
The extension (2) provided an open-plan,
well-lit office space (5). Rogers also designed
the new furniture system for the building.

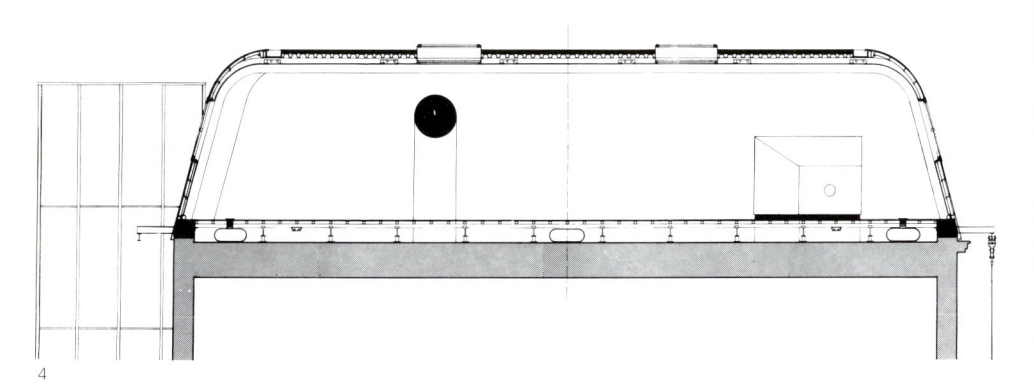

4

5

Piano + Rogers

The Practice and the Pompidou Centre

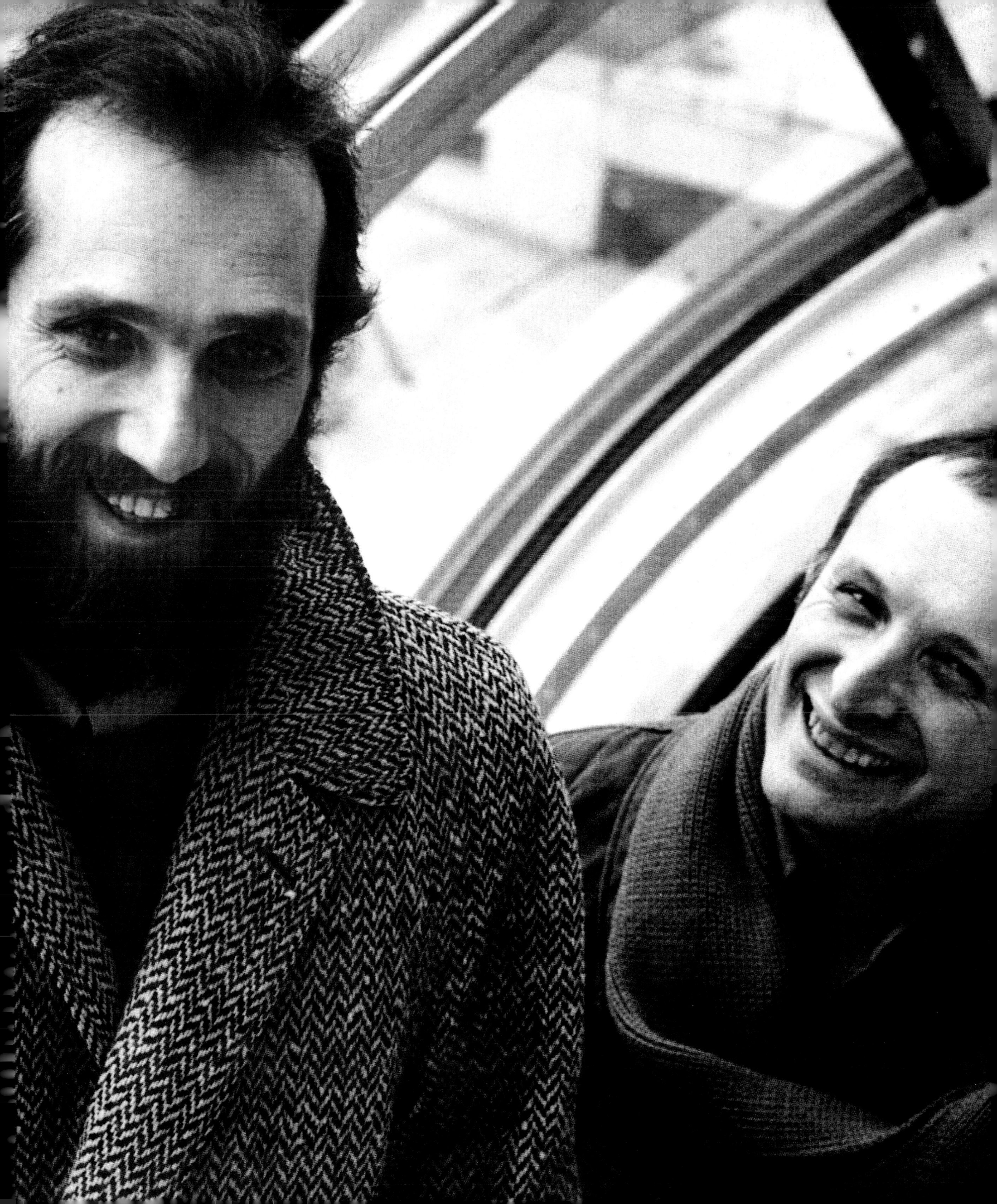

Richard Rogers' emphatic development of team-based partnerships took a new turn with Renzo Piano. Like Rogers, born in one of the major cities of Italy (although in his case Genoa), Piano was four years younger than Rogers. An important port, Genoa developed as a major industrial city during the nineteenth century and was one of the powerhouses of the Italian economy – a place for doers. Piano was, indeed, a doer. He had trained in Milan but returned to his native city to practice architecture. His family background was in the building industry and he had gained a reputation for his innovative use of materials; lightweight steel frames, plastic and GRP-panelled cladding used with the shared intentions – speed, economy, flexibility and low running costs – of Rogers in his post-Team 4 projects. For the Osaka Expo 70 Piano had designed a 38 x 38 metre demountable pavilion, assembled using a plastic skin on a tensile structure, to display the products of Italian industry. He was heavily involved in research into plastic-moulded shells and inflatable roofs, prefabrication and lightweight structures. For all this, Piano's practice at this period remained, according to the architectural writer, Peter Buchanan, 'a relatively modest and local affair', rich in ideas but with a limited number of built works.

Piano's association with Rogers, beginning in 1970, moved rapidly from an informal arrangement to a full partnership, but was cemented by the Pompidou Centre. 'Beaubourg', as Richard Rogers always calls it, was the project which made both Piano and Rogers into major players on the world architectural scene and formed the basis of two great architectural offices.

Georges Pompidou's project for a great cultural centre in the heart of Paris was born out of the radical events of 1968 when, to the delight of Richard Rogers, students and workers combined to shake the foundations of the French establishment. The French President, Charles De Gaulle, survived the challenge of the Left, but was soon forced into retirement and replaced by the shrewd and cultivated Georges Pompidou. As Mayor of Paris, Pompidou had promoted the idea of a major public library on a site (largely cleared in the 1930s) in the fourth *arrondissement*, just east of the Boulevard de Sebastopol and close to the Les Halles market area. (While the destruction of the great nineteenth-century Les Halles market was widely regretted, it was cleared independently of the construction of the Pompidou Centre.) Pompidou, now President, transformed the library project into something much bigger: an integrated arts centre designed to establish the reputation of Paris on the world's cultural scene. There was never any doubt that the Centre should be simply the best of its sort in the world. Pompidou took personal charge of the project, appointing a small team to run it. The brief – brilliantly put together by the highly professional French Ministry of Culture – was developed by the young architect/engineer François Lombard to include a library, museum of modern art, centre for industrial design and a music research centre, together with shops and cafés to cater for visitors. Pompidou had no doubt that the building should be the subject of an international competition and he appointed Robert Bordaz, a judge and senior civil servant with a great interest in the arts, to develop and control the competition. Rogers believes that 'without Bordaz, Beaubourg would never have been built'.

Richard Rogers was initially hesitant about entering the Pompidou competition in 1971. He was reluctant to design what appeared to be a politician's monument and doubtful that a non-French entry could stand much chance of winning. Piano was, however, anxious to compete for the Paris job and the balance was tipped by the intervention of the engineer Ted (later Sir Edmund) Happold, then a partner at Ove Arup & Partners, who was anxious that OAP should

Rioting in the streets, Paris 1968

Michael Webb, Entertainments Centre for Leicester Square, London (project), 1962

Piano + Rogers

enter. An alliance with an architectural practice was necessary and Happold turned to Rogers, whom he had met in connection with the abortive plan for a new stand at Chelsea Football Club. Happold and his young associate, Peter Rice, helped to overcome Rogers' doubts and the practice resolved to produce a scheme.

President Pompidou maintained a typically French respect for intellectual and artistic endeavours and was prepared for some radical proposals. Indeed, absorbing – and, in some senses, neutralizing – radical ideas were part of the agenda of the arts centre project. For Rogers, memories of 1968 were very much alive. 'The building expressed the hopes of 1968', he says. 'What happened then still mattered a lot to some of us.'

There was no shortage of unbuilt precedents for the anti-elitist public forum which Piano + Rogers eventually built on the Plateau Beaubourg. Mike Webb, one of the founders of the Archigram group, had designed a 'Sin Centre' for the West End of London as his thesis project at the Regent Street Polytechnic in 1959–62, although Webb envisaged his Centre being orientated towards entertainment rather than culture. The project, widely discussed, provided fuel for Cedric Price's Fun Palace scheme of 1962 (designed, in collaboration with engineer Frank Newby, for the radical theatre director Joan Littlewood). The Fun Palace – never realized – provided, Price declared, for 'self-participatory education and entertainment ... The activities designed for the site should be experimental, the place itself expendable and changeable.' Its physical form was of rows of steel towers containing main services and bearing great gantry cranes. By means of a system of tracks, the cranes could assemble spaces required for any event – an exhibition, a pop concert, a play or a 'happening' of the sort then in vogue – in a very short time. There were no fixed walls or floors. The entire development was

Jean Prouvé, Maison du Peuple, Clichy, 1936–9

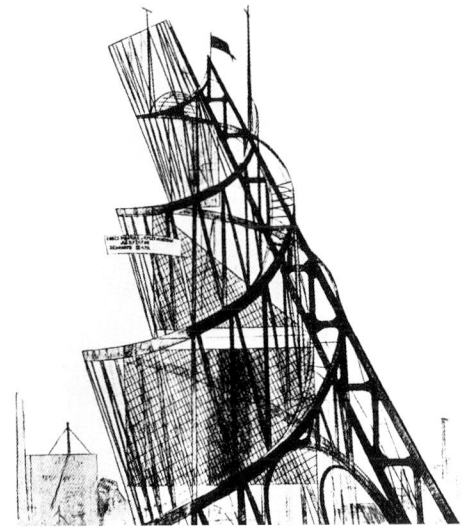

Vladimir Tatlin, drawing of the *Monument to the Third International*, 1919–20

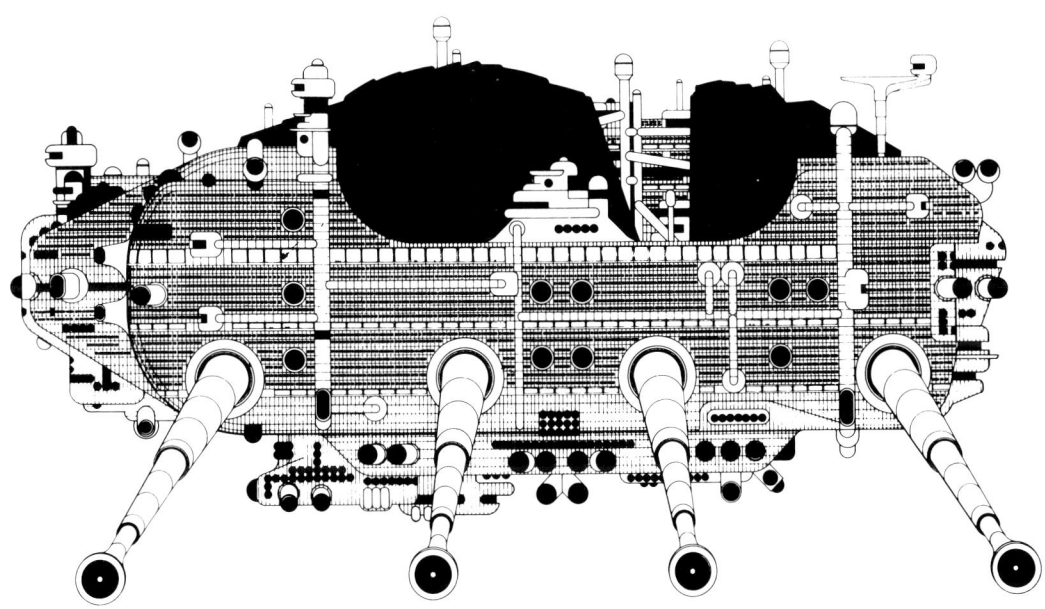

Ron Herron, Cities Moving Project, 1964

intended to have a short life – maybe ten years. Permanence was seen as reactionary. Archigram went on to promote wildly impractical, but nonetheless inspirational, visions of 'plug-in' and 'walking' cities, using collages peopled by cut-out figures from the colour magazines.

For Richard Rogers, then as now, Archigram seemed 'disturbingly apolitical', tending, if anything, towards an uncritical celebration of consumerist society, though both he and Piano acknowledge its role in creating an atmosphere of experiment in which 'fun' was reckoned among the proper attributes of a public building. Rogers says: 'As for Cedric Price – it was the spirit of his work – he was, after all, very political – rather than the form, that was an influence. And, of course, we all admired the avant-garde director Joan Littlewood. They were all there in the background to Pompidou.'

The ethos in which the Pompidou Centre was conceived reflected the world of pop culture, Archigram and street politics, all present in the world of the AA in the 1950s. But it had roots in earlier Modern Movement experiments – in the work of Antonio Sant'Elia, of the Russian Constructivists and the great engineers of the nineteenth century, who were widely acclaimed as 'pioneers of modern design'. There was also a striking antecedent in Paris itself in the form of the Maison du Peuple in Clichy, designed by Jean Prouvé with Beaudouin & Lods and featuring movable floors. Another (unbuilt) Parisian project of the 1930s, that by Oscar Nitschke for the Maison de la Publicité, provided a precedent for the use of a facade as a gigantic electronic billboard – though Rogers says that he was not aware of it at the time. The lights of New York's Times Square, which had so impressed Rogers as a student, were another real and potent memory. Rogers speaks of 'a web of ideas, an almost indivisible chain of influences' underlying Pompidou. The rhetoric of Buckminster Fuller was certainly one of those influences. 'Equally, the Case Study houses, the Maison de Verre with its fluid space and movable partitions, and Corbusier', says Rogers. Banham considered the Pompidou Centre to be 'in some ways [the] most extreme of all built megastructures'; the apotheosis of a tradition celebrated in his *Megastructure: Urban Futures of the Recent Past* (1976). He pointed to an intriguing precedent for the principal facade of Pompidou in Chamberlin, Powell & Bon's megastructural 1960s Leeds University scheme, where staircases snake up the walls of the faculty buildings as the escalators were to snake up the Pompidou Centre. But the most vital element of all in the scheme was its commitment to public space. Piano and Rogers, with their shared Italian background, were fervent advocates of city life. At the Pompidou Centre, they proposed a visionary leap forward – the creation of a really generous new public space at the heart of Paris; in the aftermath of a near-revolution. It was to become, perhaps, the most significant new public space of the twentieth century: a derelict backwater was turned into a spot which every visitor to Paris came to know.

Richard Rogers and Renzo Piano are reluctant to divide the credits for the Centre. 'It was a synthesis – we worked together, discussing

The team that won Beaubourg: (standing, l to r) Marco Goldschmied, Su Rogers, John Young, Renzo Piano (seated, l to r) Sally Appleby, Peter Flack, Richard Rogers, Jan Kaplicky (Gianni Franchini is missing from this photograph)

Gianni Franchini

Richard Rogers, Renzo Piano, Su Rogers and John Young working on the Burrell competition entry at the Aybrook Street Offices

The Paris office, housed in an inflatable on the banks of the Seine, opposite Notre Dame

Piano + Rogers

every detail', says Piano. 'Rather like allocating individual points to the winners in a doubles match in tennis', adds Rogers. The design process for the competition entry certainly involved Richard and Su Rogers, Piano, Happold, Rice, Gianni Franchini, a key player based at Piano's Genoa office, John Young and Marco Goldschmied – the last two were given the status of partners in Piano + Rogers – and was conducted in both London and Genoa. Entries for the competition were due not later than 15 June, 1971. There were 681 of them, including Piano + Rogers', which arrived only after a series of near-disastrous mishaps. The competition jury was chaired by Jean Prouvé – which seemed a good omen – and included leading figures from the museum world as well as architects like Oscar Niemeyer and Philip Johnson, the latter a former tutor of Rogers at Yale. (At a crit in the school, he had torn the service towers off a model made by Rogers and Norman Foster, but he subsequently became an admirer of Rogers' work.)

Piano + Rogers' scheme – it launched their partnership after the break from Su Rogers, who quit the office soon after the competition victory – was presented as a 'centre of constantly changing information … a cross between an information-orientated, computerized Times Square and the British Museum, with the stress on two-way participation between people and activities/exhibits.' After much debate and many re-thinks, the scheme proposed a rectangular structure, set tight against the rue de Renard on the east, with a large piazza to the west. Public space would extend right under the Centre, which would be raised on piloti. The building would be steel-framed, with the exposed frame water-filled for fire safety. It would be a vast shed, in effect, with the immense floors – which it was envisaged could be made movable – slung between the two main elevations, one providing access at all levels and acting as a giant public noticeboard for the piazza and the other equally a noticeboard, but aimed at the traffic on the rue de Renard.

The competition jury's decision, allegedly prompted by Philip Johnson, to award just one prize (to Piano + Rogers) – making it difficult to displace the winners in favour of a more conventional runner-up – was not quite unanimous, but none of the unsuccessful entries attracted much interest when all were subsequently exhibited in Paris. Upturned concrete bowls, inverted pyramids, jagged ziggurats, giant eggs and forty-storey towers could easily be dismissed, though the informal shortlist of thirty schemes included those by Moshe Safdie, Kisho Kurokawa and (a genuine Archigram product) Dennis Crompton. The winning scheme, however, had undeniable merits, including its provision of a generous open space, its lightness and transparency, flexibility and potential liveliness as a public place. It was also, the jury concluded, a practical building, which could actually be realized.

The competition won and the results duly celebrated, Rogers and Piano faced the task of developing the scheme and getting it built. A team had to be assembled – and quickly. It would work from Paris, which would become the practice's main base. Among the recruits were Tony Dugdale (a talented AA graduate) and Laurie Abbott, a former member of Team 4 in whom Rogers had enormous faith. Benedetto Merello was recruited from Italy. At 4 o'clock one morning, Mike Davies, then working in California as part of the multi-disciplinary Chrysalis practice, received a telephone call from Rogers which led to the departure, a week or two later, of Davies and his

Jørn Utzon, Sydney Opera House, 1957–73 – which Peter Rice worked on as assistant engineer

Left to right: Lennart Grut, Ted Happold and Peter Rice of Ove Arup Partnership's Structures Group 3

Piano + Rogers, Paris. Left to right: Mike Davies, Alan Stanton, Mike Dowd, Cuno Brullman, Jari Sircus, Reiner Verbitz, Alphons Oberhofer

Piano + Rogers, London, al fresco lunch in the park behind the Aybrook Street offices, 1973. Left to right: Niki van Oosten, Renzo Piano, George Xydis, Nigel Greenhill, Rita Bormioli, Alphons Oberhofer (back view), Peter Ullathorne, young Ben Goldschmied

Richard Rogers, Ruth Rogers, Marco Goldschmied

Renzo Piano (centre) with structural engineer Peter Rice (left) and services engineer Tom Barker of Ove Arup & Partners (right)

colleagues Chris Dawson (a friend of Young and Goldschmied from AA days) and Alan Stanton (who had worked with Norman Foster after the break with Richard Rogers) for Paris, where they were signed up by Piano + Rogers. Mike Davies had trained at the Northern Polytechnic, gaining a solid grounding in practical matters before going on to the AA and meeting Alan Stanton. His interests lay in lightweight structures and inflatables – it was the 'Pneu-World' issue of *Architectural Design* edited by Davies and some AA colleagues which had led to his first meeting with Rogers in 1969. After the AA, Davies went to UCLA on a scholarship and stayed on in California for several years after his formal studies were completed. With Chrysalis, he was involved in sixteen built projects, ranging from a pavilion at Expo 70 to a video van for the Watts urban workshop in Los Angeles. Davies loved the experimental and innovative ambience of the West Coast – 'in LA, traditional architecture seemed all but irrelevant', he recalls – and warmed instantly to the agenda of the Pompidou Centre.

Piano + Roger's Pompidou Centre would probably never have existed without the intervention of Ted Happold and the support of Ove Arup & Partners. Happold was to remain – increasingly peripherally – involved in the project for several years, but the key players in the engineering team were Peter Rice (d.1992), Lennart Grut and (for services) Tom Barker, all three of whom were to become long-term collaborators of Rogers. Rice's talents had first emerged when he was assistant engineer on the Sydney Opera House. The construction of the Opera House was fraught with difficulties, but Rice was overwhelmed with the poetry of Utzon's conception. He became equally fervent about the Pompidou Centre, but the circumstances were different – Rogers, Piano and colleagues had developed the competition in close collaboration with their engineers. Rice was the engineer who was instrumental in turning it into a completed building. He became the Pompidou's structural guru: intensely involved in the project, acting practically as a partner on it – much more than a facilitator. Rogers has said that his work was 'poetic', and written: 'He does not wait for the architect to develop his ideas and then offer options of how to prop them up. He is a strategist who is at his best working on understanding the nature of the client's wishes.' Robert Bordaz recalls Rice's 'championing' the project: it 'was part of himself, he loved it, and as he explained the calculations which had allowed it to be built as it should be, I realized that he fully felt its quality.'

The competition scheme posed a number of practical problems, which were addressed during 1971–2 as preparatory work on the site got underway. Firstly, the height of the proposed building was vetoed on fire safety grounds. It had to be reduced, with 42 metres stipulated as an absolute maximum. The architects' response – the only practical option if a serious loss of accommodation was to be avoided – was to delete the open space under the building, thus bringing it down a floor. In retrospect, this change was beneficial, placing the main entrance at piazza level and linking the building more clearly to the streets. Other changes which occurred as the scheme was developed were less happy. The competition scheme was notable for its magnificent clarity: two great walls consisting of double rows of steel columns, cross-braced, supporting a series of floors which looked (and were intended to be) as mobile as those in Cedric Price's Fun Palace. It was, in Rogers' words, 'an ever

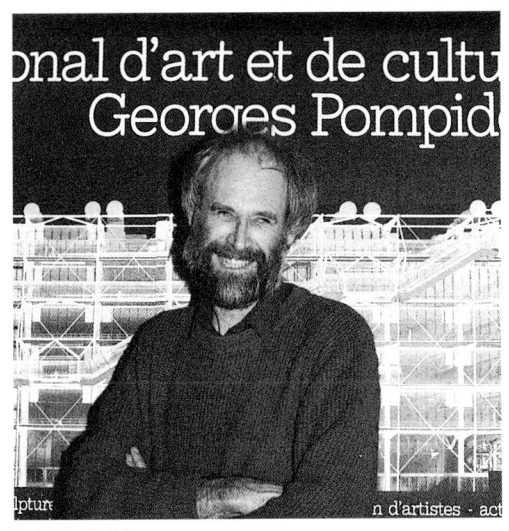

Laurie Abbott in Paris

Press conference for IRCAM. Left to right: Pierre Boulez, Robert Bordaz, Richard Rogers, Renzo Piano

changing framework, a meccano kit, a climbing frame for the old and young, for the amateur and the specialist, so that the free and changing performance becomes as much an expression of the architecture as the building itself.' The Centre was to be 'a flexible, functional, transparent, inside-out building'. As the building was condensed, and became deeper and squatter, it became less transparent and less generous in its internal spaces, with reduced floor to floor heights.

The scheme, as developed for the *avant projet sommaire* required by the French authorities, had, however, lost a good deal of its clarity. Initial attempts to simplify and economize resulted in an unsatisfactory compromise which Laurie Abbott describes as 'the jelly mould' or 'blancmange'. Abbott, who had recently joined the design team, describes the redesign as 'disastrous – we seemed to have simply lost it'. Renzo Piano, however, recalls the 'tremendous pressure' to make the scheme buildable and appealing to the client, with the underlying fear that the job could still be taken away from the competition winners. 'It was easy to lose your way. Maybe we were not being aggressive enough. Fortunately, we were told forcefully by one of the judges (Willem Sandberg of the Stedelijk Museum, Amsterdam) that things were going very wrong.' For both Rogers and Piano, teamwork and collaboration is at the heart of architecture and they were responsive to Abbott's views. Abbott was the key player who knew about the *nature* of the building, and was involved with its creative development.

The 'jelly mould' (which had duly impressed Pompidou himself) was quietly abandoned, with the backing of Robert Bordaz, in favour of a faithful reworking of the competition scheme. One gap in the

Piano + Rogers Paris Team in the excavated site for the Pompidou Centre, 1972

Ruth Rogers (centre) on an anti-Vietnam protest march in the late 1960s

Richard and Ruth Rogers with Roo, Paris, 1977

Collage of everyone in the Paris, London and Genoa offices of Piano + Rogers

Piano + Rogers proposal for the facades as giant walls of information – a key element of the competition entry

latter was the provision of a practical services strategy. Both of the main facades were intended as giant noticeboards – another idea that eventually had to be dropped. There was always an implicit acceptance that the building had a 'front' and a 'back'. Tom Barker advised that all services should be concentrated on the rear (street) elevation. According to Laurie Abbott the rear elevation, 'in effect, just happened – you couldn't produce detailed architectural drawings showing just pipes'. Placing all the services on one side freed up the 'front' elevation and avoided the need for intrusions on the roofline, which the French authorities regarded as a very sensitive matter. Bit by bit, the designs for the Centre came together. For Abbott, there was a point when 'suddenly, it all felt right'. In the 'jelly mould' scheme, the clarity of the original idea – two great walls of steel with floors slung between them – had almost vanished. With the help of Peter Rice, it was recovered. Getting the facades right was a high priority. The competition scheme provided for double rows of steel columns, giving a densely layered appearance and enclosing the services and circulation zone, but this seemed structurally illogical to Rice and his team, including Lennart Grut (later a director of Richard Rogers Partnership) and Jim Hill. The introduction of the 'gerberette' (which took its name from the engineer Heinrich Gerber) transformed the situation. The massive cast-steel gerberettes, six to each of the main columns, are an economical way of minimizing the deflection of the main floor trusses, allowing for a degree of movement in the structure while providing absolute stability. The outer layer of the facades was reduced to a framework of slender tension rods and cross braces, adding greatly to the elegance and transparency of the building. Amazingly, and against all the odds, the essence of the architects' vision was carried across into the completed building. There were

Piano + Rogers

none of the usual compromises – Rogers and Piano fought tirelessly to avoid them, so that the fire in the project remained.

Excavation work on site started in March 1972, and by the end of that year work was underway on the massive concrete substructure. The steel facade components were being fabricated at the time of Pompidou's sudden death in April 1974, but, with the help of Robert Bordaz, the scheme survived the change of presidency. President Giscard d'Estaing, Pompidou's successor, demanded dramatic budget cuts; in fact, his presidency was to prove immensely trying, with Rogers and Piano having to fight his many objections. The idea that both front and back facades act as giant noticeboards was eventually dropped on his orders: 'he saw it as a potential political weapon rather than a cultural concept', says Rogers. The steel superstructure was, however, erected between the autumn of 1974 and summer 1975. Another year and a half of fitting out preceded the opening of the Centre in January 1977. In the first year of its existence, it attracted six million visitors. The public loved it, though to the French establishment, closing ranks against pressure for reform, it was a left-over from a past regime. For the architects, it was an outstanding achievement since, despite all the political and practical pressure to compromise, the essential qualities of the competition scheme survived into the finished building. The Centre was a dramatic statement for a new sort of architecture, at odds with conventional ideas of the city, culture and the state. The Centre undoubtedly paved the way for President Mitterands' *grands projets* of the 1980s. It seemed outlandish to some, yet the sheer determination of Rogers, Piano and the rest of the team got it built. This was a pattern to be repeated in many subsequent Rogers projects.

Like any Rogers building, Pompidou was built on teamwork. Team spirit had to survive – though it was severely tested by – the numerous, well-chronicled crises, great and small, which affected the project over nearly six years. Both Rogers and Piano brought in individuals who were effective team players – Laurie Abbott ('the key Brit', according to John Young, and in charge of the superstructure and mechanical services team, working with Rice and Barker from OAP), Alan Stanton (leading an internal and external systems team), Mike Davies (who subsequently took charge of Pierre Boulez' IRCAM), Gianni Franchini (in charge of interiors), Eric Holt (d.1992), responsible for the facades, Cuno Brullmann (working on the piazza and some interiors), 'Benny' Merello, Walter Zbinden (substructure) and Bernard Plattner (general coordination and site supervision). Plattner later became the mainstay of Piano's French operation, while Shunji Ishida and Noriaki Okabe, who were recruited to work on Pompidou, also became key members of the Renzo Piano Building Workshop. The involvement and collaboration of so many people enabled the building to happen; in a structure which required so much more than producing drawings and then asking people to 'do' it, such wide collaboration was essential.

When the project began, few of the members of the team even spoke French. Paris 'seemed very foreign in those days', recalls Mike Davies (who took rooms in an eighteenth-century town house, complete with Louis XV four-poster bed). Richard Rogers, meanwhile, rented a flat in the rue de Sevigne, not far from the site, moving after a few years to a beautiful apartment in the Place des Vosges. Importantly, also, during the genesis of the Pompidou Centre, Rogers had met and (in 1973) married Ruth Elias: her political views and strong visual sense inspired him. Ruth Rogers never joined the Rogers practice, but there was never a project, from the early 1970s onwards, in which Richard Rogers did not feel the benefit of her support and critical advice.

As another part of the Beaubourg scheme, IRCAM (Institut de Recherche & Coordination Acoustique Musique) was a key element; a centre for musical experiment, linking music with scientific and sociological research, which was to be run by the French star of the musical avant-garde, Pierre Boulez. Mike Davies recalls Boulez as 'a very good client – very decisive – with a good team' (which included Nicholas Snowman, later to be Rogers' client at London's South Bank Centre). IRCAM was to be placed underground (to eliminate the noise of the city) and simultaneously create a small square just south of the Pompidou Centre. It was a completely novel project, containing spaces for the most innovative techniques and including a big studio/concert hall as well as smaller studios and public spaces. A large hole was excavated for IRCAM. However, the arrival of President Giscard d'Estaing in 1974 saw the project budget cut by an alarming thirty-three per cent. Davies recalls the chagrin of seeing part of the excavation, achieved at huge cost, filled in to allow for the reduced building. Yet IRCAM, despite this setback, became a spectacular success, technically and artistically, and was later to be extended, above ground, by Piano's practice.

Left to right: Peter Rice, Renzo Piano and Richard Rogers astride one of the first of the Centre's gerberettes

The Pompidou Centre took Richard Rogers and most of his practice to Paris: for six years, Piano + Rogers became a reality, not an ideal. The Centre engaged everyone's attentions for virtually every waking moment, yet there was the issue – which became all the more pressing as the project neared completion – of the future. Would there be enough work in Britain to keep the team employed?

John Young and Marco Goldschmied, released from working at the Pompidou Centre, had been given the task of keeping the London 'branch office' – for this was what it seemed – in operation. In 1973–4 they had overseen the construction of the UOP factory at Tadworth, Surrey, a simplified version of the scheme proposed for the same client for a site at Ashford. The striking lime green shed was a development of the Zip-Up House, using panels made of glass reinforced cement on a polystyrene core attached to a tubular steel frame. 'It was rather less radical than the Ashford scheme', says Young, modestly omitting the fact that the building was still the most radical new industrial structure in Britain, a breakthrough and not a compromise. Other projects, however, came to nothing. The Cambridge shopping centre could have been a major commission. It had come into Richard + Su Rogers' office in 1969 and was not finally abandoned until 1978. Over those nine years, there were countless meetings and revisions, but absolutely nothing was achieved. When the project was eventually pronounced dead, John Young described it as: 'my most unrewarding working experience'.

The housing projects for Park Road (1973) near the Lord's cricket ground in London, and Millbank (1977), the first scheme under-taken after the split with Renzo Piano, remained unbuilt. In the circumstances, the prospects of an important commission for a research building near Cambridge for the PA organization were cheering. The approach came from Gordon Edge of PA Technology, brother-in-law of Andrew Holmes, an ex-employee of Richard + Su Rogers. Marco Goldschmied recalls the first, crucial meeting with PA. He and Young had travelled there in the latter's 'clapped out' 2CV van (ex-Belgian post office), happy not to be seen getting out of the vehicle. They were shown into an office where, it was clear, the PA team had enjoyed a perfect view of their arrival. 'We looked like a real Mickey Mouse team', says Goldschmied. 'Which was what we felt!'

PA's ideas for the new building diverged radically from those presented by Young and Goldschmied, which was a vision of a great glasshouse, sunk into the landscape, formed of a partly glazed, partly planted roof membrane suspended from a series of steel arches, with parking underneath the great column-free space. In contrast, 'PA's ideas revolved around brickwork', says Goldschmied. He and Young were discouraged: 'we were at our wits' end, but we needed the work desperately, and Richard sent word not to give up'. Goldschmied believes that the ensuing discussions with PA provided good experience for the future – 'the issues were entirely practical, balancing cost, schedule and efficiency in operation', he says. Although there was a brick-clad version of the scheme, produced with a transparent lack of enthusiasm, what was actually built was a true Rogers building. PA Technology – one of four such centres then existing around the world – was about innovation and the development of new industrial products. The brief called for flexible space to contain laboratories, workshops and offices. There was to be scope for extension (there were later two phases of expansion). Finally, the need for the new building was urgent. As built, PA Technology retained one important element of the initial scheme – parking and loading were provided under the building, which was set in carefully landscaped grounds. The structural approach, however, was turned in a more conventional direction – a steel frame, with internal columns, on a concrete slab. Services were suspended beneath the slab, providing easy access for maintenance and upgrading. The cladding system, a mixture of glass and enamelled steel sandwich panels, was designed for change in line with those envisaged to internal layouts. This produced a 'speckled' effect – as in the later Inmos building – which, though observing a strict grid, reflects the activities going on inside the building. The readiness to subordinate overall architectural effect to the expression of function is characteristic of Rogers, who has never sought the poised perfection favoured by Norman Foster. Indeed, the work of the Rogers practice seems to reflect a positive delight in the impact of practical requirements on the building shell.

PA Technology was a striking success, winning the *Financial Times* Award for Industrial Architecture in 1975, and, more than Reliance Controls, provided a model for the high-tech industrial buildings of the 1980s, not least in its colourful and carefully-detailed interiors. It was much (and favourably) reviewed and this augured well for the future of the Rogers office. Out of it, moreover, came a semi-formal association with PA Technology, producing the Rogers Patscentre interdisciplinary research operation. Mike Davies, Alan Stanton and others were members of what became 'the R&D end of Piano + Rogers' (as Davies describes it). Energy issues, high on the architectural agenda because of the oil crisis of the 1970s, were one aspect of the work undertaken. Research into the Autonomous House was also progressed. Performance, efficiency and economy were ever more central issues.

When Richard Rogers lectured at the RIBA in June 1976, he spoke of the connection between architecture and ideology. 'It is my belief', he declared, 'that we cannot fundamentally alter the quality of architecture without changing our negative ideology, for ideology encompasses everything. We need to research and partake in a system which offers the have-nots shelter, food, education and the quality of life, whilst reducing the stress, strain, and other anxieties of the haves.' With Pompidou in mind, Rogers argued the case for buildings which could 'take on functions well beyond that of a simple container or sculpture and become true dynamic urban structure, capable of responding to man's changing needs, encouraging a rich variety of activities and extending the strict limits of the client's brief.' The lecture effectively stated the agenda for his work over the next quarter of a century, when he was to become the spokesman for a social vision of architecture in a world of change and confusion.

With the Pompidou Centre completed and opened, the project team dispersed. Officially, Piano + Rogers remained in existence. In practice, Piano retrenched in Genoa, while keeping an office in Paris, and Rogers returned to London. There was not enough work in London for everyone in the Rogers circle. Mike Davies launched 'Chrysalis II' with Alan Stanton and Ian Ritchie while doing part-time work for Rogers Patscentre. Laurie Abbott pursued his own projects, including car designs for Fiat. Jan Kaplicky had long ago departed. Beaubourg, simultaneously the climax of the inventive optimism of the 1960s and the harbinger of the new civic concerns of late twentieth-century architecture, had received enormous media coverage and become an icon for young architects. Yet for Rogers the prospects were, at best, uncertain. The energy crisis had turned into a recession, which made Beaubourg look over-optimistic. Young and Goldschmied kept the office going, but Rogers took on a teaching post in California and spent much of his time there with Ruth. John Young described the prospects in 1977 as 'grey and uncertain compared with the optimism with which architects faced up to the 1960s, at the time I nervously entered Team 4's office for the first time'. The response of British architects to demands for a more user- and environment-friendly architecture had been negative and timorous – neo-vernacular was the archetypal style of the 1970s, while Post Modernism was on the horizon. Modern architecture was widely blamed in Britain for destroying town centres and creating inhuman housing schemes. SAVE Britain's Heritage, the pressure group formed in 1975, seemed to have an anti-modernist agenda: 1975 was Architectural Heritage Year. 'Heritage' seemed suddenly more important than the present or the future. Where did this leave Richard Rogers' conviction that technology was 'the alphabet without which there is no poetry'? The future seemed to lie with what he described as 'overscaled dolls' houses'. Yet he was to become the central figure in the renaissance of modern architecture in Britain, not only as a practitioner but as a spokesman for modern values and in particular for the cause of the modern city.

Renzo Piano and Richard Rogers, of course, remained partners and in 1978 Piano came to London to support the practice's bid for a commission which rivalled the Pompidou Centre in scale. Winning Lloyd's of London confirmed Rogers' status as one of the world's leading architects. While Lloyd's, in fact, finalized the professional separation between Piano and Rogers, it produced a new multi-disciplinary partnership which built on the professional relationships that Rogers had developed over nearly twenty years.

Reunion party in Paris to celebrate the twentieth anniversary of winning the Pompidou Centre competition, July 1991

Pompidou Centre

Centre Culturel d'Art Georges Pompidou, Paris, France, 1971–77

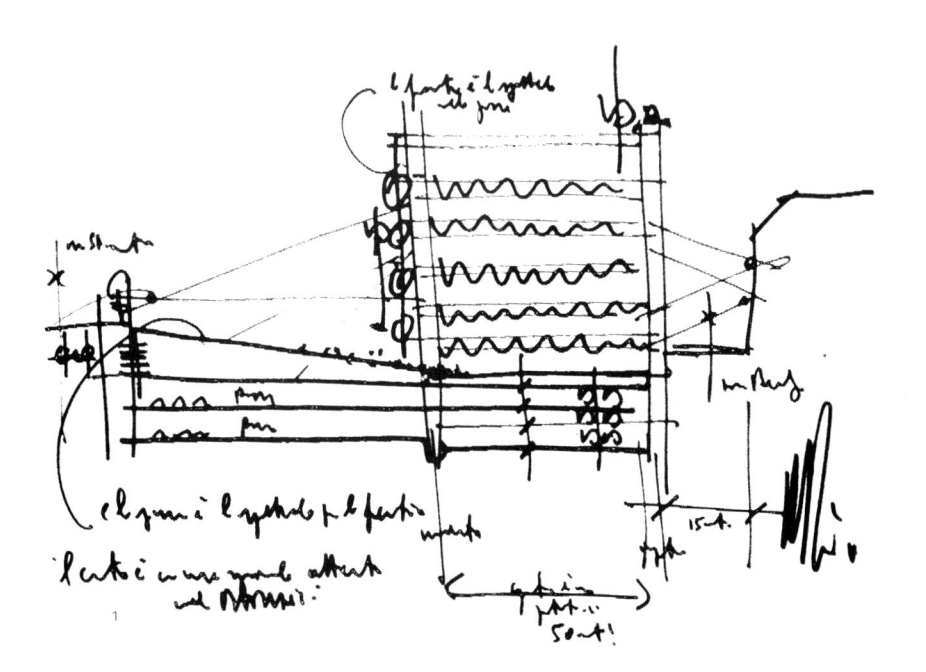

The Pompidou Centre remains, even after the *grands projets* of the 1980s, the most spectacular post-war monument in Paris. It launched the careers of both Richard Rogers and Renzo Piano as world architects. It marked a watershed in the complex relationship between politics and culture in France and was equally a passionate statement about the life of the city. It launched a whole new approach to public building and broke down the monumental elitism of usual public institutions.

The site of the Centre at the Plateau Beaubourg is close to that of the former magnificent nineteenth-century Les Halles markets which were destroyed to Rogers' dismay. (The markets were moved out of central Paris, leaving a void – eventually filled by a vast shopping centre and rail interchange.) To the east, the rundown Marais district had been reprieved from total clearance, but was far from fashionable. Beaubourg was a key connection in the renewal of the historic heart of the capital. The site for the Centre had been cleared in the 1930s and was used as an untidy car-park before it was identified as the ideal location for President Georges Pompidou's arts centre.

The idea of a major cultural amenity had emerged in the aftermath of the 1968 Paris riots, which had toppled President Charles De Gaulle and threatened the survival of the French state. Initially, the project had centred on the provision of a big library, open to all (unlike the Bibliotheque Nationale), which some argued could be housed in part of Les Halles. Pompidou inflated the project to become a comprehensive centre for the arts, including the library, a modern art museum, a centre for industrial design and a centre for research into music and acoustics (to be tailor-made for Pierre Boulez, a leader of the musical avant-garde whom the French wished to attract back from the USA). There would also be cinemas, bookshops and other visitor amenities. The project brief was developed by Francois Lombard as 'a centre for the contemporary arts', with the implicit acceptance that this would be a radical and innovative place, perhaps feeding on the energies of 1968 and the widely-acclaimed youth culture of Paris. The international competition for a building to house the centre was launched in 1970 and a senior civil servant, Robert Bordaz, was appointed to run the project from competition stage to completed building.

The competition, which attracted 681 entries, was won by the Piano and Rogers team, including Su Rogers, John Young, Marco Goldschmied, Gianni Franchini as well as Richard Rogers and Renzo Piano, and their collaborators from Ove Arup & Partners, led by Ted Happold. The Piano + Rogers competition scheme was proclaimed as 'a live centre of information, entertainment and culture', with the stress, perhaps, on information. Inspired by a number of precedents, notably Nitschke's unbuilt project for a Maison de la Publicité (1932–5), the architects proposed a building with two main facades – one to a great new piazza, which took up over half of the total site, and the other to the busy rue de Renard which would be used as gigantic public noticeboards addressing, respectively,

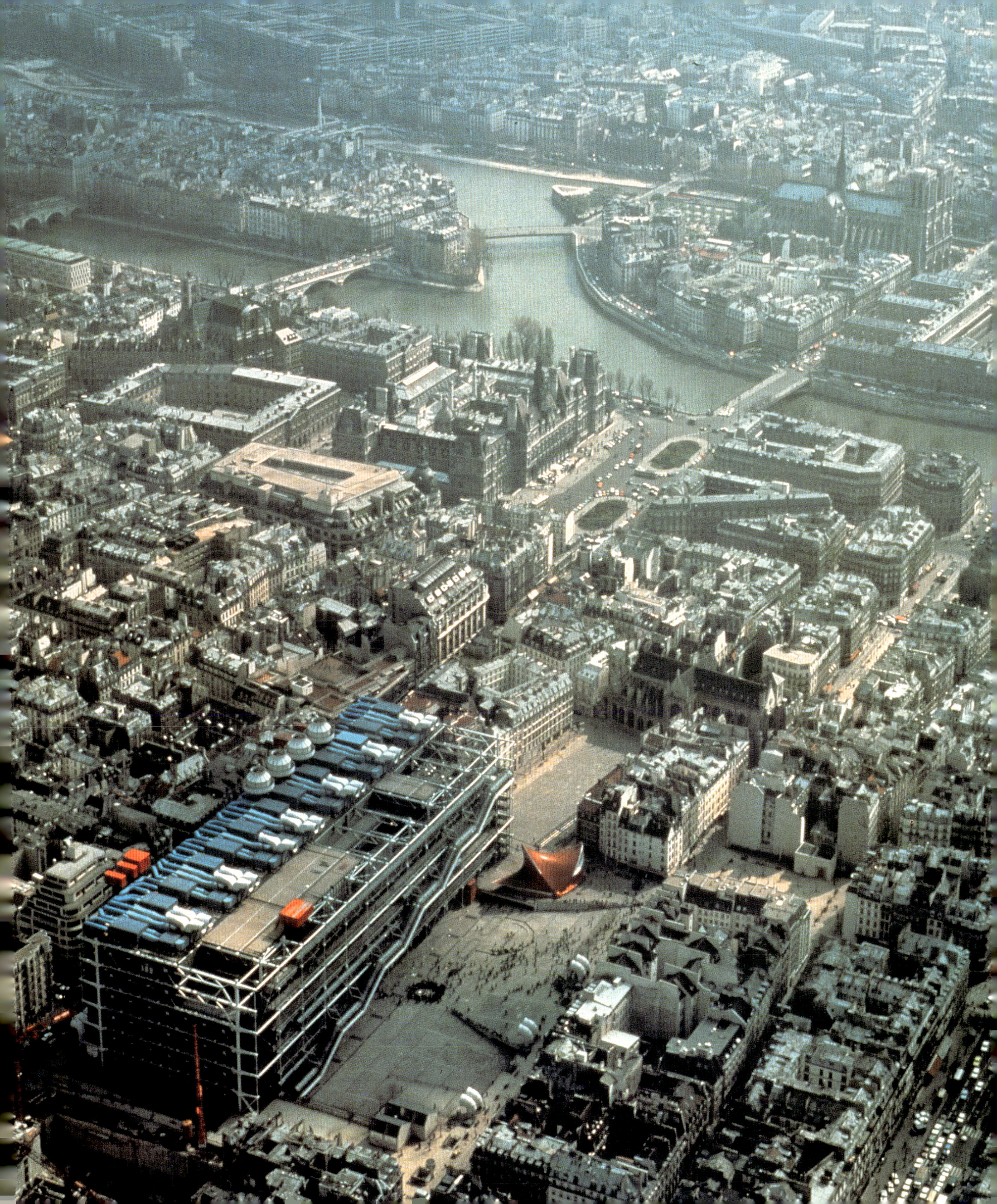

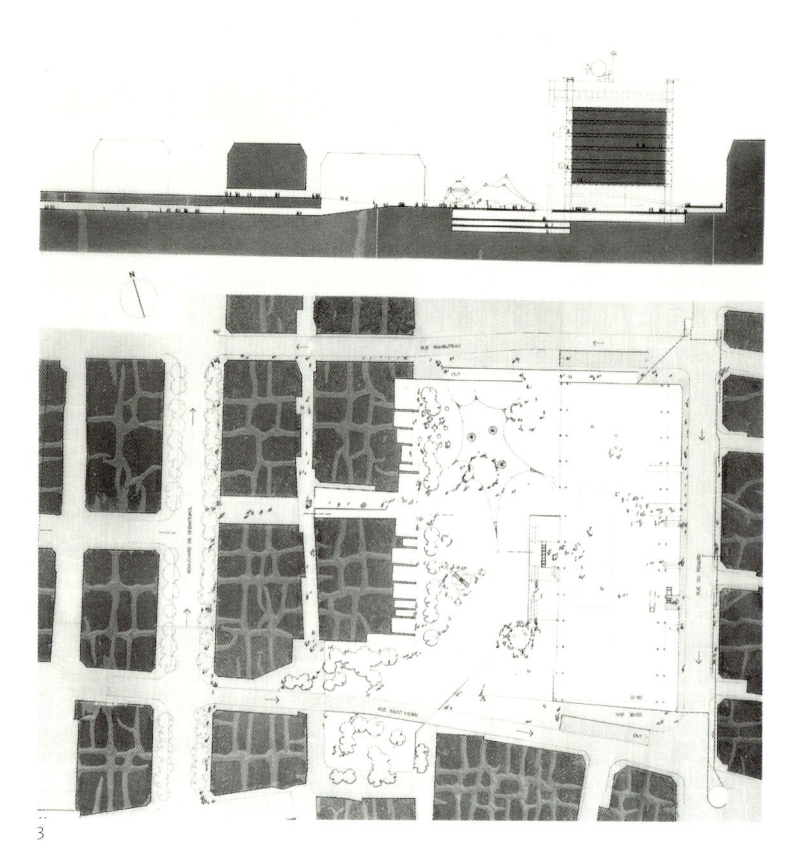

The site of the Pompidou Centre (2, previous page & 3) was a long-derelict gap in the Gothic pattern of Paris, close to the Marais quarter – the site had remained vacant since the 1930s (8). The new piazza was an integral part of the project from the start.
Extracts from the competition report (4), illustrate the concept of Beaubourg as an information centre linked to others elsewhere in France and beyond.

The Centre was conceived as a radical 'university of the streets', opening up to a public alienated by traditional museums (1, p102). Giant noticeboards, for instance, were proposed (6).
The model (5) and section (7) of the competition-winning scheme clearly show the concept of the building's two layered facades, between which were hung a series of open floors – initially envisaged as moveable.

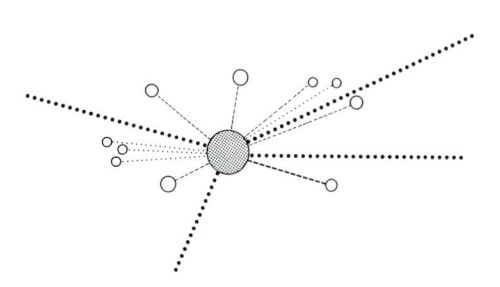

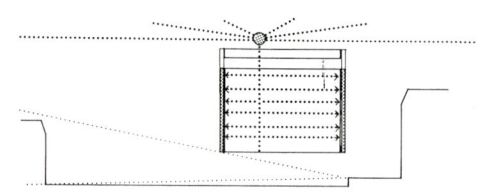

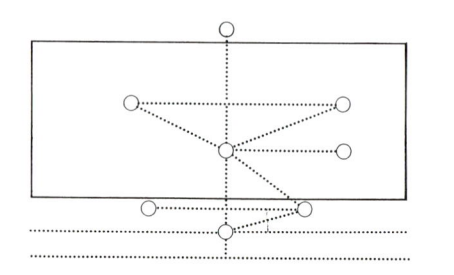

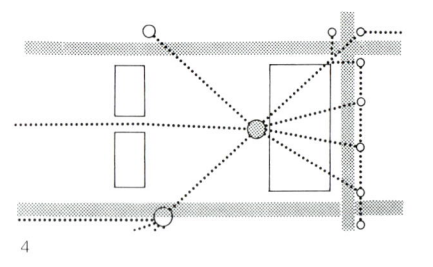

Pompidou Centre

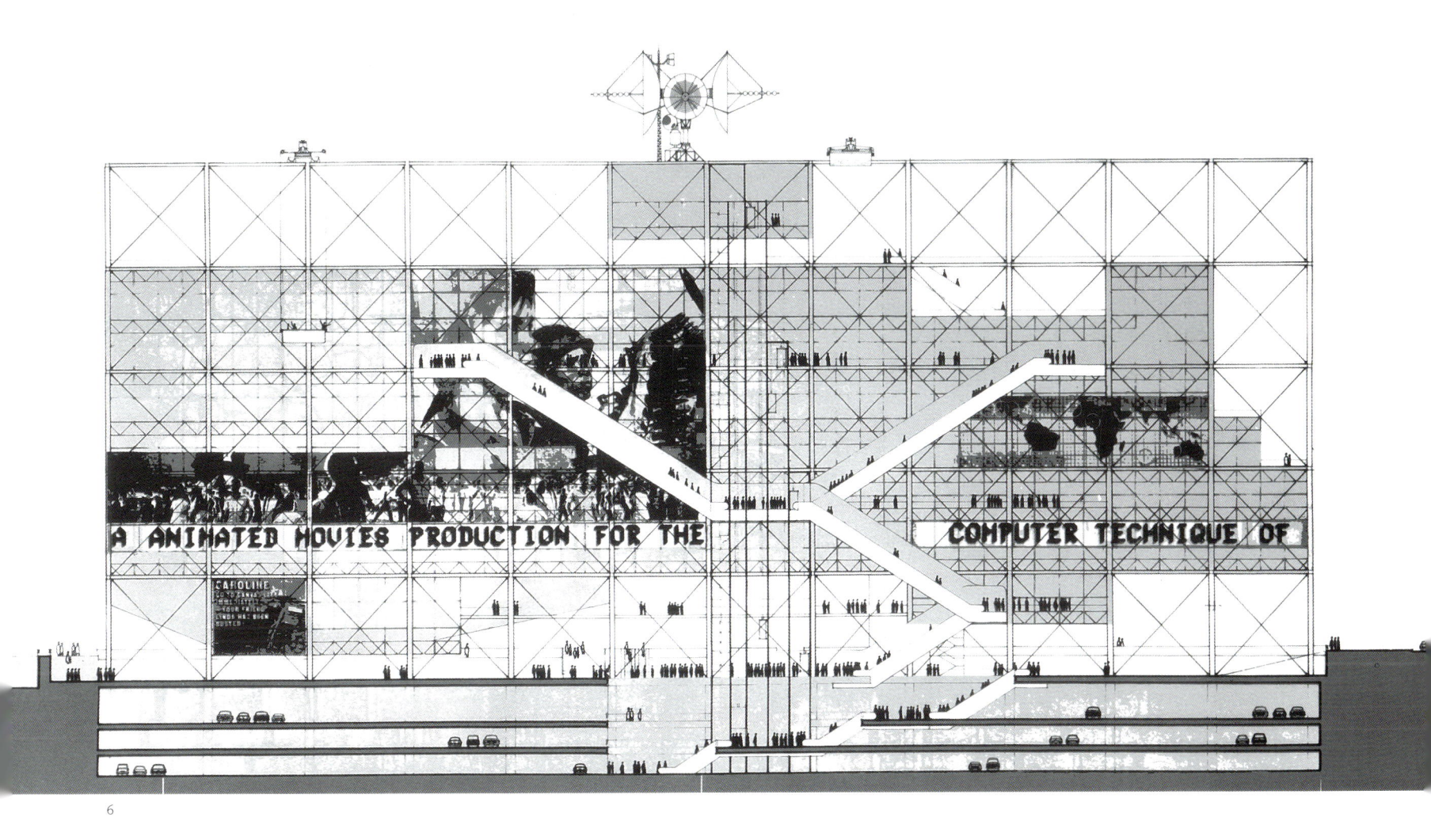

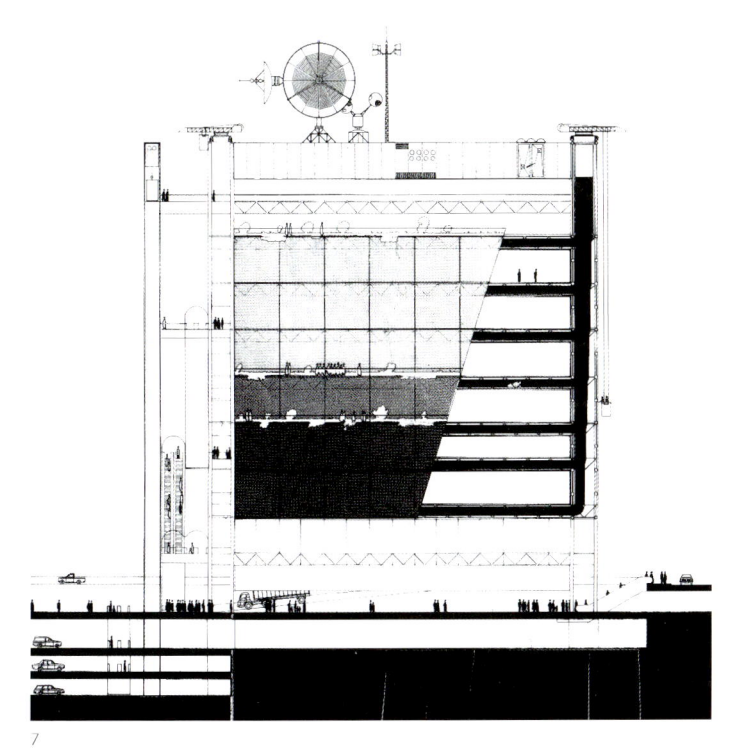

6

7   8

Philip Johnson was one of the jurors who chose the Piano + Rogers scheme for the Centre (9). The jury was chaired by Jean Prouvé.
The so-called 'Jelly-mould' scheme (ultimately abandoned) was a development of the original in which the clarity of the concept receded (10).
The scheme as built reinstated the architectonic clarity and transparency of the building (11).

pedestrians in the new piazza and passing motorists. The essence of the proposed Centre was flexibility. It would be a 'university of the streets', responding to the ever changing needs of its users. Partly inspired, perhaps, by the experimental arts and entertainment projects of Cedric Price and Archigram, and by memories of the revolutionary Russian Constructivists, the architects proposed a flexible container, where all interior spaces would be moveable within the framework provided by the freestanding structural frame. They envisaged 'an ever-changing framework, a meccano kit, a climbing frame for the old and the young...' There would be close interaction between the building and the piazza and the piazza facade of the Centre would be 'an activity container, a strongly layered, 3-dimensional structural framework with people walking on it and looking down from it, a wide variety of items clipped to it, tents, seating and audio-visual screens, etc...'

The rhetoric of the proposals impressed the competition judges, but both practical and political considerations led to major revisions as the scheme was developed. Two fundamental elements in the competition scheme – moveable floors and the interactive information facades – were dropped from the built scheme. The height of the building was also reduced (at the insistence of fire officers), resulting in the infilling of the proposed open ground floor, while there were significant changes to the structural design

10

11

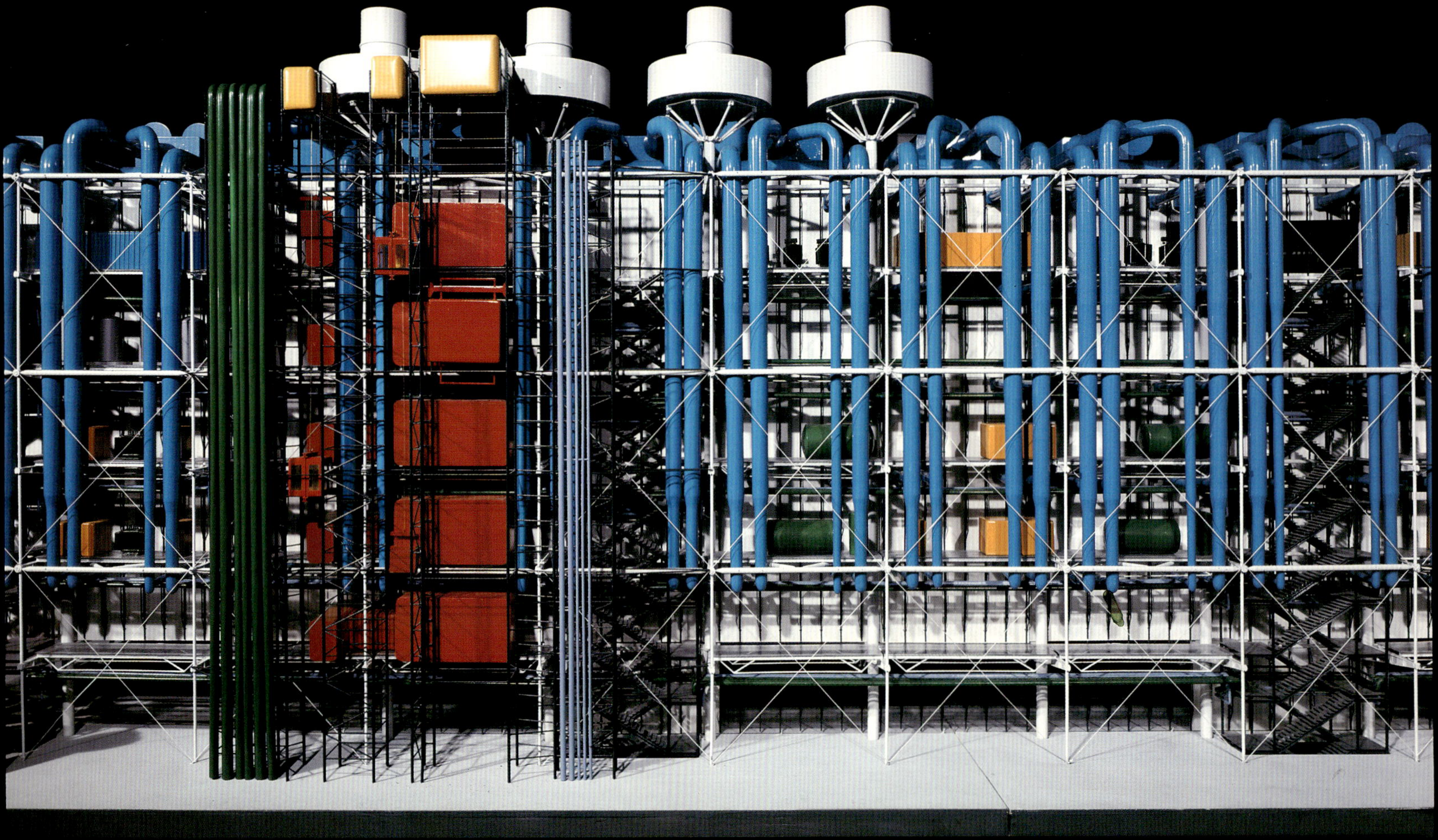

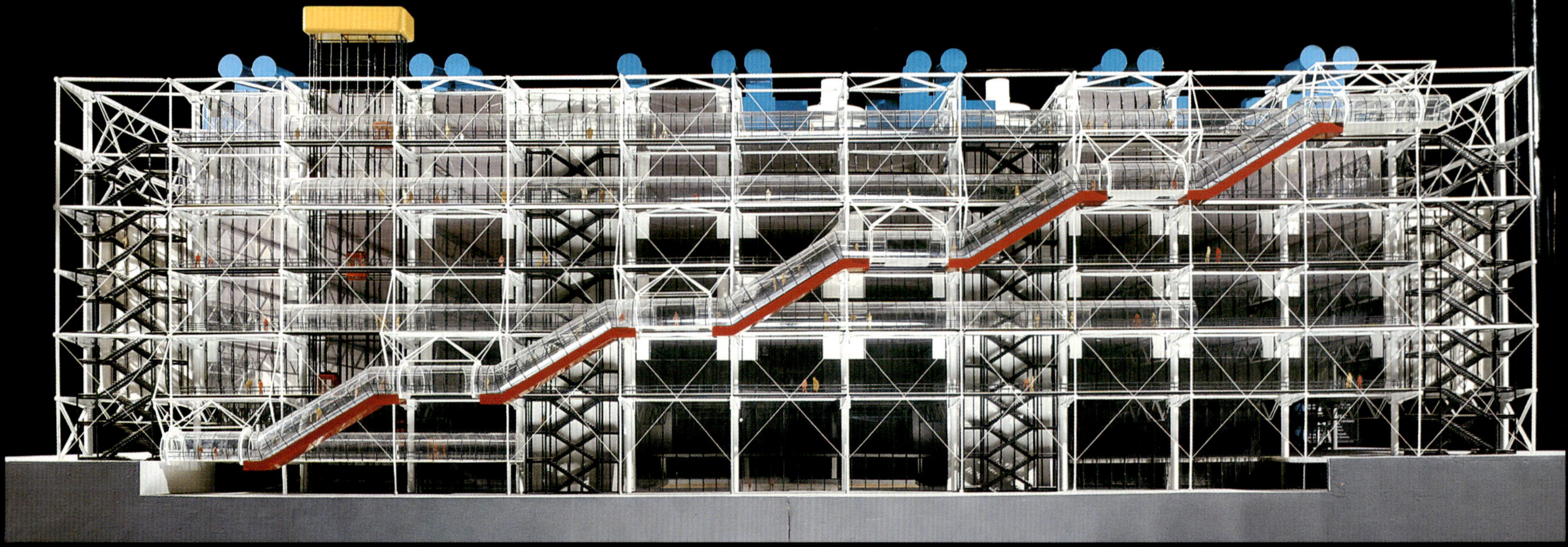

of the facades, partly in response to the needs of servicing (developed by Tom Barker of Arup) but equally in the interests of structural and architectonic clarity. But the key elements in the competition scheme remained intact and none of them was more significant than the relationship of the building to the city. The piazza was designed as a bowl (inspired, perhaps, by the Campo in Siena), gently sloping down to the ground floor of the building, with interior and exterior spaces envisaged as a continuous entity. An equally fundamental issue was that of movement – the building would not be a static monument, but would be made accessible by escalators snaking up the facade to the piazza.

Construction began with the excavation of the site in March 1972. After the death of President Pompidou caused a reconsideration of the entire project – which was cut, but not cancelled, by the new regime – work on the superstructure began in summer 1974.

The Centre opened in January 1977. IRCAM, effectively a separate project but closely linked to the Centre, was completed, albeit on a reduced scale, in summer, 1977. (Refurbishment of the entire building and reorganization of departments within it, under the direction of Renzo Piano and in consultation with Richard Rogers, culminated in its closure for two years from September, 1997.)

As built, the Centre consists of five large open-plan floors, each 170 m x 48 m and of reinforced concrete, supported on the main structural steel planes to east and west (always read as the 'back' and 'front' elevations of the Centre respectively, though not

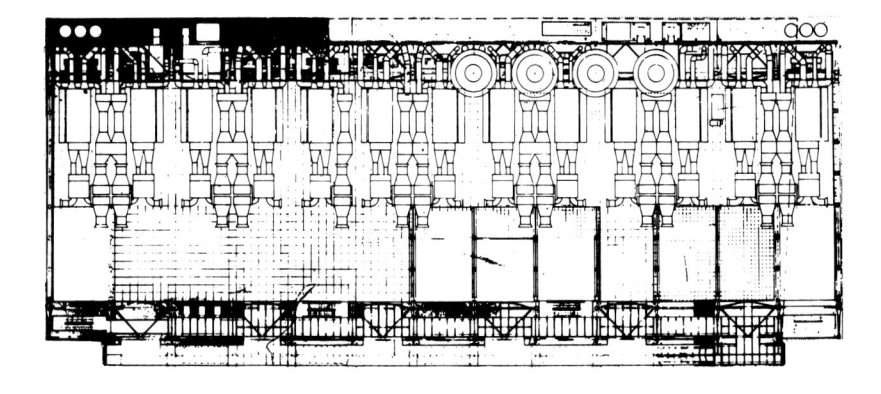

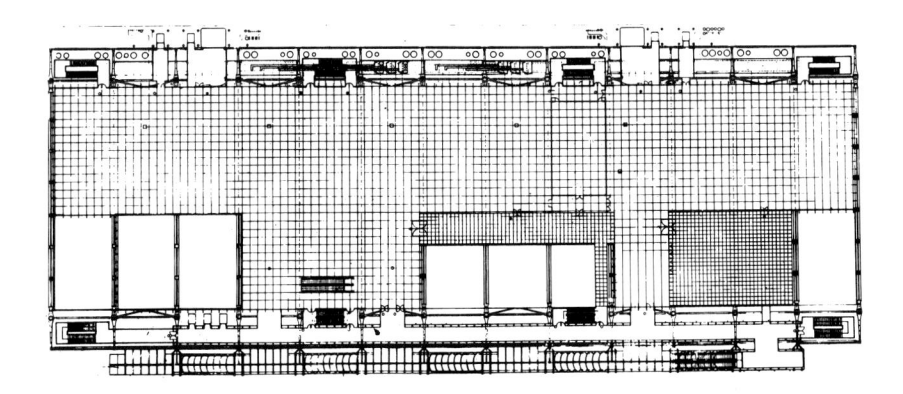

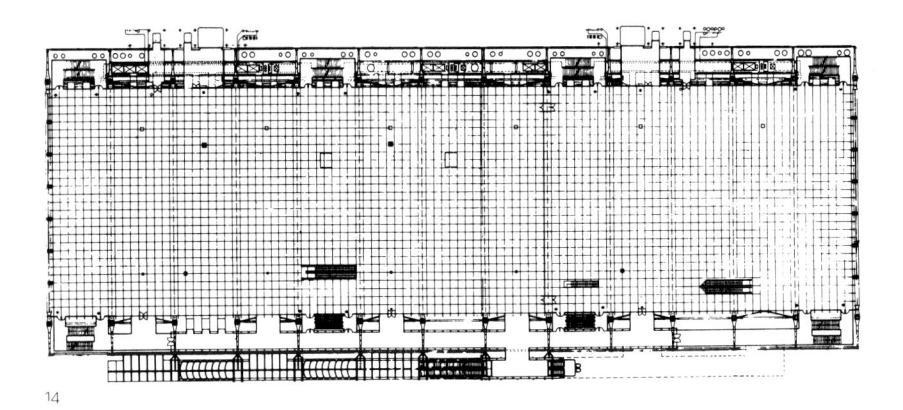

In its final form, the Centre realizes the vision of Piano + Rogers (12 & 13). The services are concentrated on the east facade to the rue de Renard. The piazza facade consists of a zone of staircases, lifts and escalators, the latter snaking up the building in a dynamic celebration of movement.
Clear floor space, uninterrupted by services and structures, offered the flexibility in usage that was key to the winning solution (14).

15

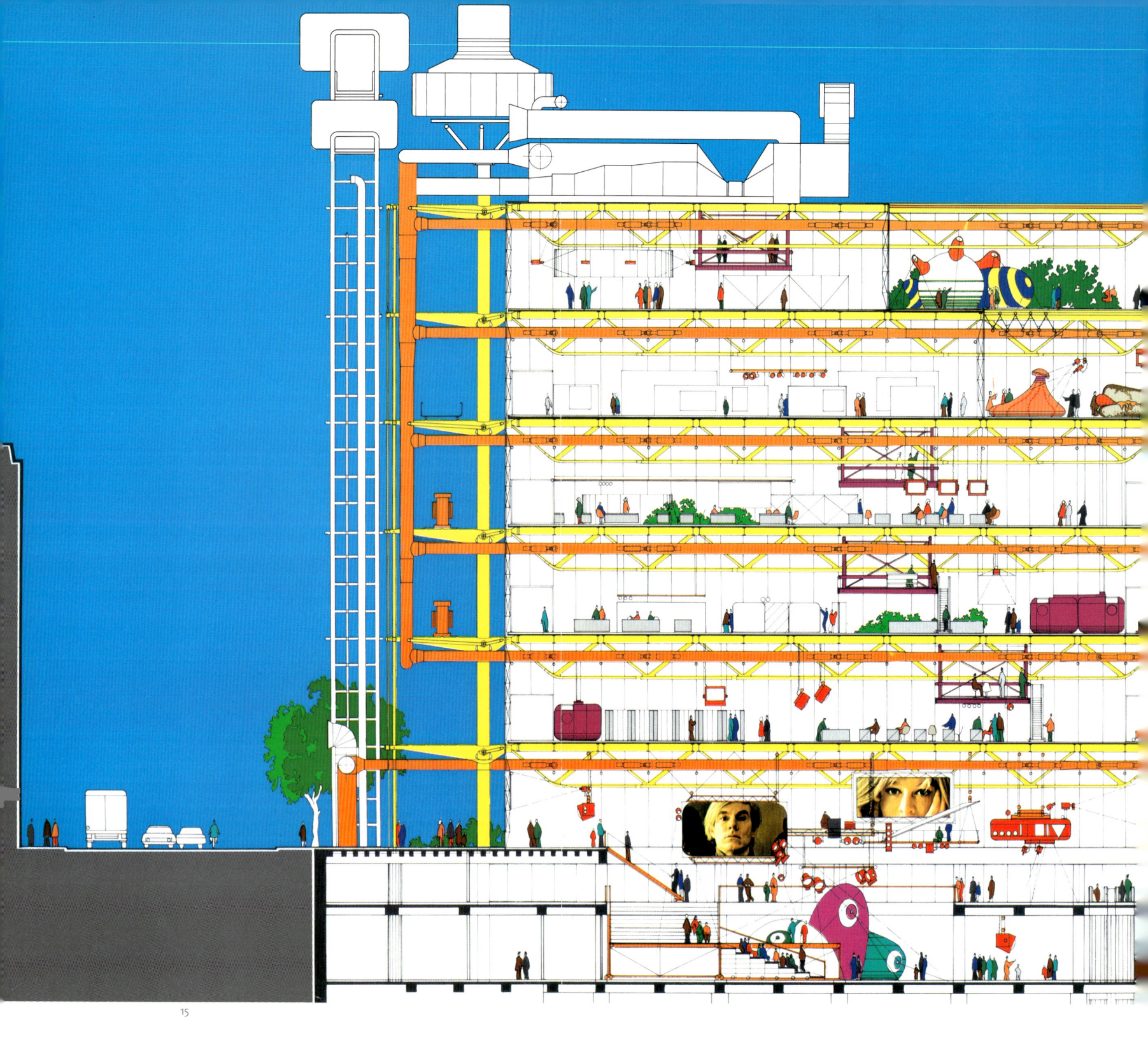

The section through the Pompidou Centre illustrates how the 'facades' are, in reality, deep zones of servicing and movement respectively. They support five floors above the ground floor 'forum', which is partly double-height. The piazza is considered a part of the ensemble, a place for spontaneous assembly and activity, with parking underneath.

Pompidou Centre

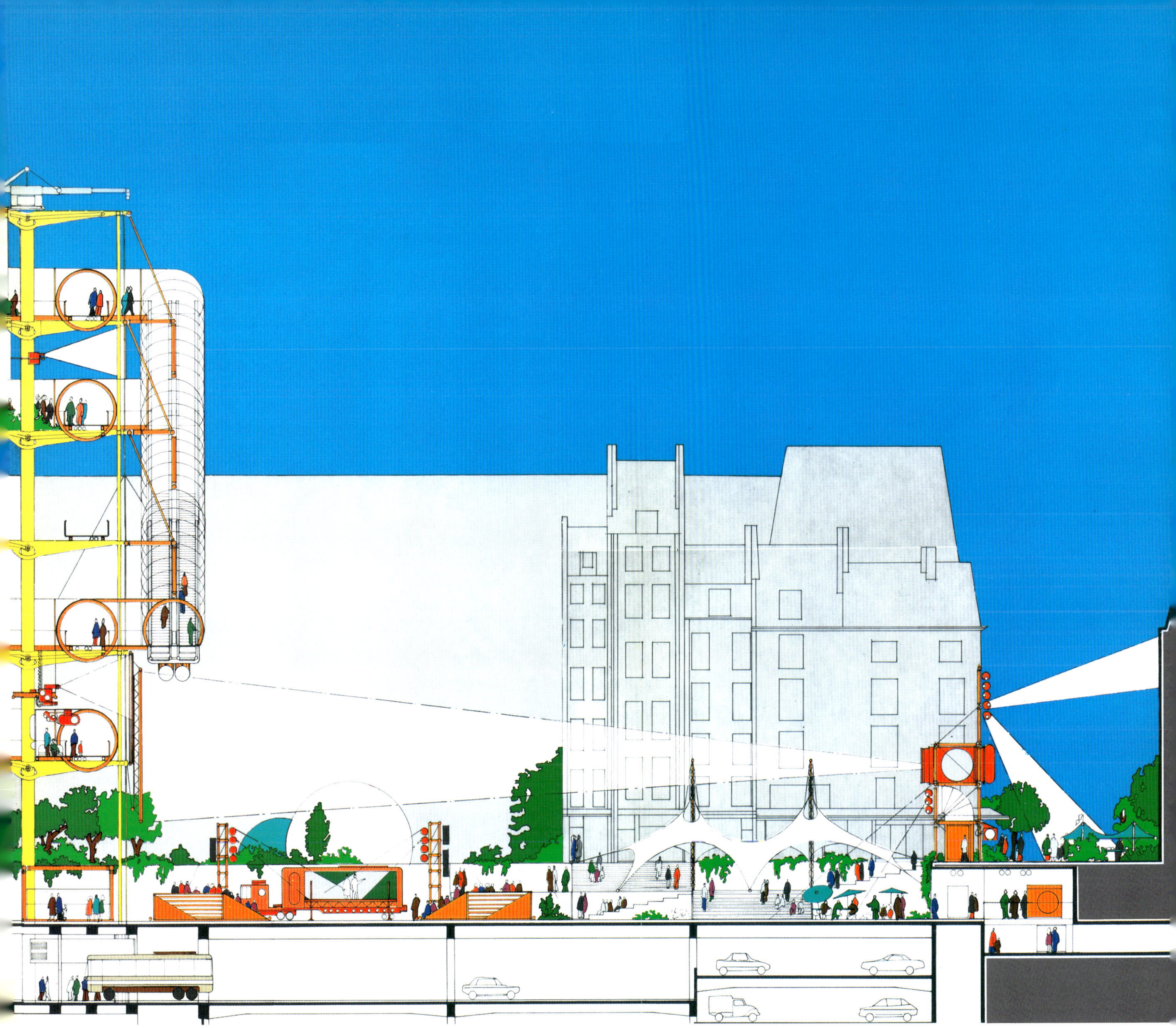

16

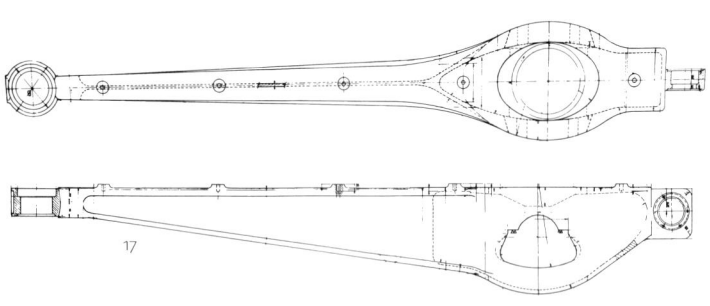

17

18

19

originally envisaged as such) and configured in thirteen structural bays, each 12.9 m wide. The ground level of the building is at the level of the street and piazza and relates to the life of both: the entrance from the piazza is into an impressive double-height space. The building sits on a four-storey reinforced concrete substructure, which contains technical and storage areas and vehicular servicing and parking space.

Access to the building is provided by lifts, escalators and staircases attached to the west facade of the Centre and capable of handling up to 3,000 people per hour. Movement is a key theme of the building – the escalators are functionally effective but also highly symbolic. The east facade is the servicing zone, containing mechanical services and access for goods. The structural frame is constructed of 800mm hollow steel columns supporting cast steel 'gerberettes' on which the main steel beams of the floor plates sit. The gerberettes are connected to outer tension members and to a series of diagonal steel wind-braces.

The cladding of the floors is a curtain wall of steel and glass, mixing glazed and solid metal panel sections, hung from the floor above, thus structurally separate from the facades and designed for change. The cladding is kept back from the edge of the building, allowing ample space for services and for human interaction and giving the building an open and transparent appearance. The idea of 'hierarchy', fundamental to the architecture of Richard Rogers, extends to the elements of the building, so that internal partitions can be moved at will, while refitting the cladding or installing new services takes longer. The architects imagined the uses of the

20

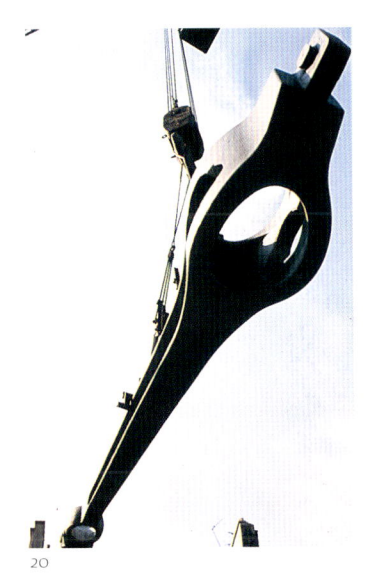

21

Like a grand Meccano set, the Centre was assembled on site out of a range of prefabricated steel parts, including the huge cast-steel 'gerberettes', each weighing ten tonnes, connecting the great trusses supporting the floors to the columns (16–22).

22

The erection of the steelwork was a massive, but highly organized, task, with 48 metre long trusses being delivered to the site at night and lowered into place on the gerberettes (23–32).

Pompidou Centre

27

28

29

30

31

32

115

33

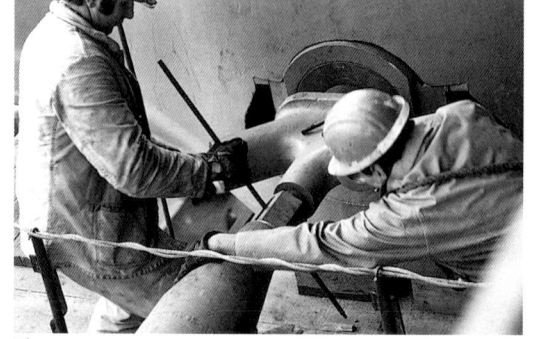

34

35

36

37

Pompidou Centre

116

38

39

40

The components and connections were of a scale rarely seen in the construction industry – more likely, in fact, to be seen in civil engineering projects or oil rigs (33–37). The construction sequence was bay by bay for the full height of the structure, rather than floor by floor (38, 39). Large prefabricated floor elements were dropped in between the primary trusses (40). The structural frame provides a number of passive means of fire protection, including water cooling in the columns, and overcladding to the beams (41–43).

41

42

43

The varied and dramatic exterior of the Centre derives from the expressed services, but the cooling towers and vertical risers were aligned with the adjacent streets to provide a striking townscape and to root the building into the existing context (44–47).

various floors changing frequently, while the technological advances, necessitating changes to services, would happen more gradually.

The detailed design and construction of the Centre represented a triumph of teamwork. Led by Peter Rice and Lennart Grut, Ove Arup & Partners, whose role in the project was crucial from the start, developed the structural concept of the facades, building in both stability and flexibility in a system which hinged on the 10 tonne, 8 metres-long cast steel gerberettes. The realization of the project was undertaken via a series of interdependent teams (each under a team leader) – for substructure (Walter Zbinden), superstructure and services (Laurie Abbott), facades (Eric Holt, who died in 1992), interiors (Gianni Franchini), systems (Alan Stanton), and the piazza (Cuno Brullmann) – with overall coordination managed by Bernard Plattner. IRCAM was undertaken as a separate project under the direction of Mike Davies. The Pompidou Centre confirmed Rogers' predilection for interdisciplinary teamwork and laid the foundations for the evolution of his office as a major centre of research and development.

Begun in the euphoric postlude of 1968 and reflecting the optimistic vision of the 1960s, Pompidou was completed in a new, and rather more pessimistic, era. Although an immediate popular success, the Centre was both politically isolated – the indifference of successive administrations in France led to underfunding and neglect – and, apparently, out of touch with an energy conscious age.

The Centre reflects, as it must, the architectural, social and political concerns of the period during which it was conceived. Many of those concerns are, however, still relevant – indeed, they possess a new relevance at a time when issues of public space, the renaissance of the city, the role of culture and the arts in urban life and the continuing need for a public and 'social' architecture are being actively debated. One of the oddest criticisms levelled at the building is that many of the millions of people visiting it come there with less than 'serious' intentions – many just ride the escalators to the top and gaze at the view (having passed the library floor, constantly packed with readers!). For Rogers, this is an irrelevant criticism, since the idea of people enjoying the building was always central to the concept – he believes that cities should provide plenty of rewarding (and free) experiences of this kind. Rogers' views were shared by the Centre's first director, Pontus Hulten, who declared: 'museums are no longer places to preserve works that have lost their social, religious and public functions, but places where artists meet the public and the public becomes creative'. Rogers recalls an illustration from a Rupert Bear annual, which he read as a child, showing a fantasy building full of pipes and escalators – Rogers is *homo ludens* personified. Despite the odium in which the Centre was held by elements of the French establishment, it has been run with verve and imagination. Long opening hours, including evenings, open it up to a very wide public, both of Parisians and of visitors from all around the world.

The Centre is a fantastic object in its own right: expressive,

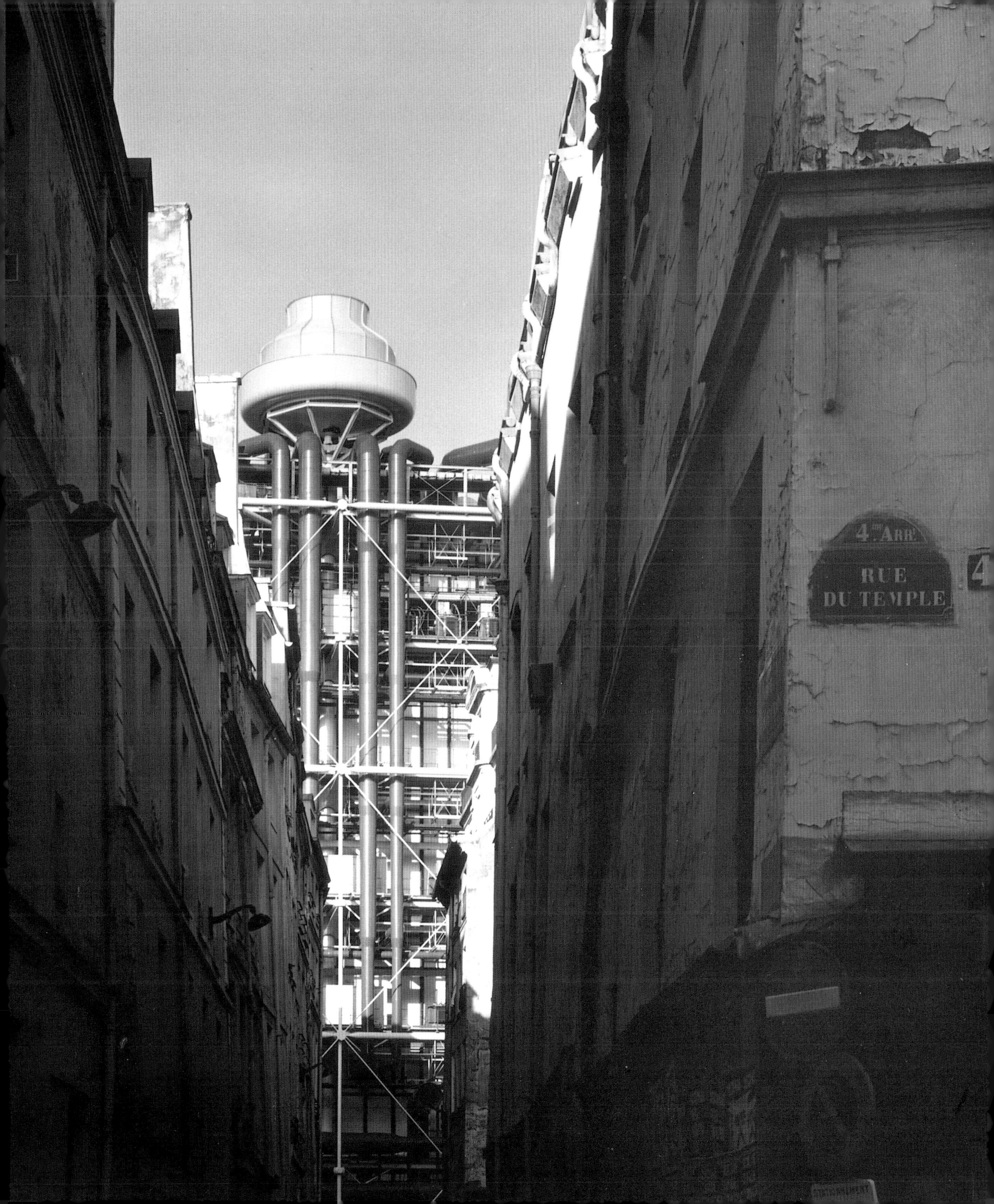
4me ARRt
RUE
DU TEMPLE

48

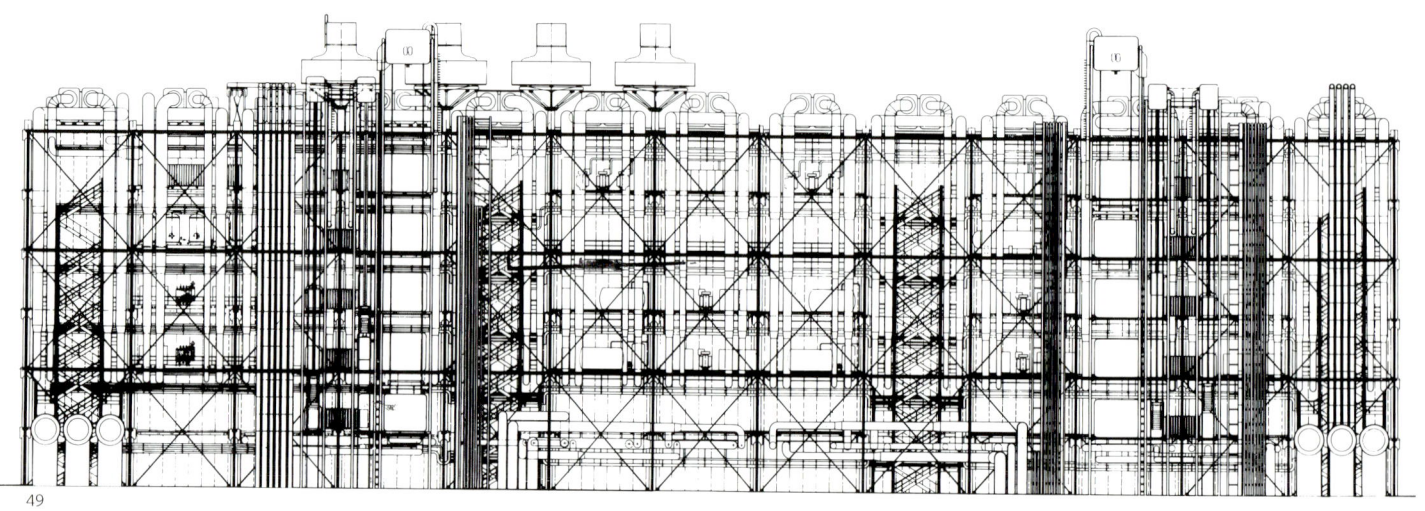

49

Pompidou Centre

The services are boldly expressed with massive components, including the nautical-looking extractors, but scale is balanced by a meticulous attention to fine detail (48). The 7 metre wide services zone on the rue de Renard is a brightly coloured and huge piece of urban sculpture, but the colours code the various services it supplies (49).

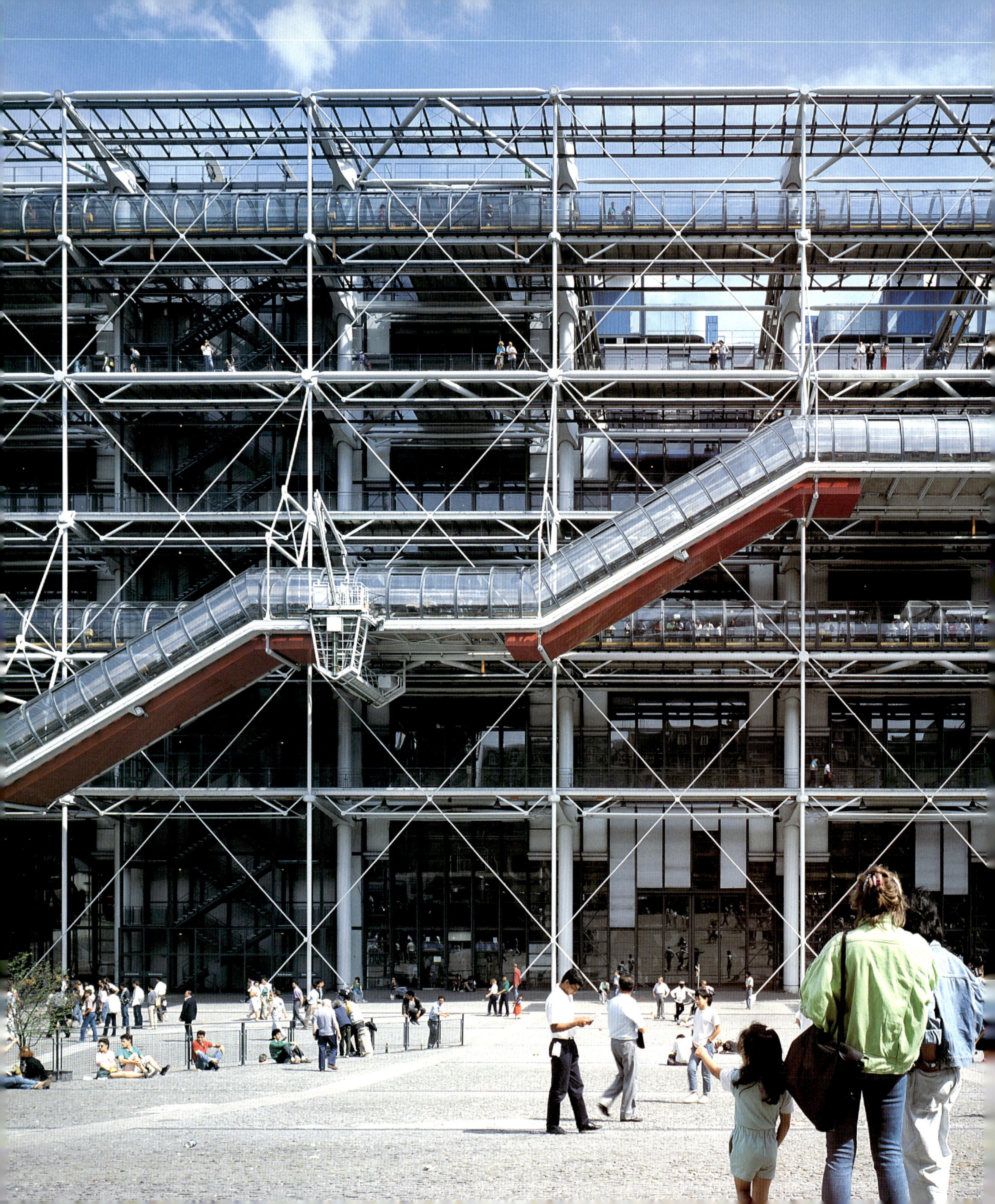

The piazza (50) has become one of the most frequented places in Paris – as its designers intended – and crowds flow in and out of the Centre, using the escalators to gain unrivalled views of the city.
The piazza has a spontaneous, ever-changing life of its own, a showcase for urban theatre (52 & 53).
Over 7 million people visit the Centre every year; some come to the piazza simply to watch other people (51).

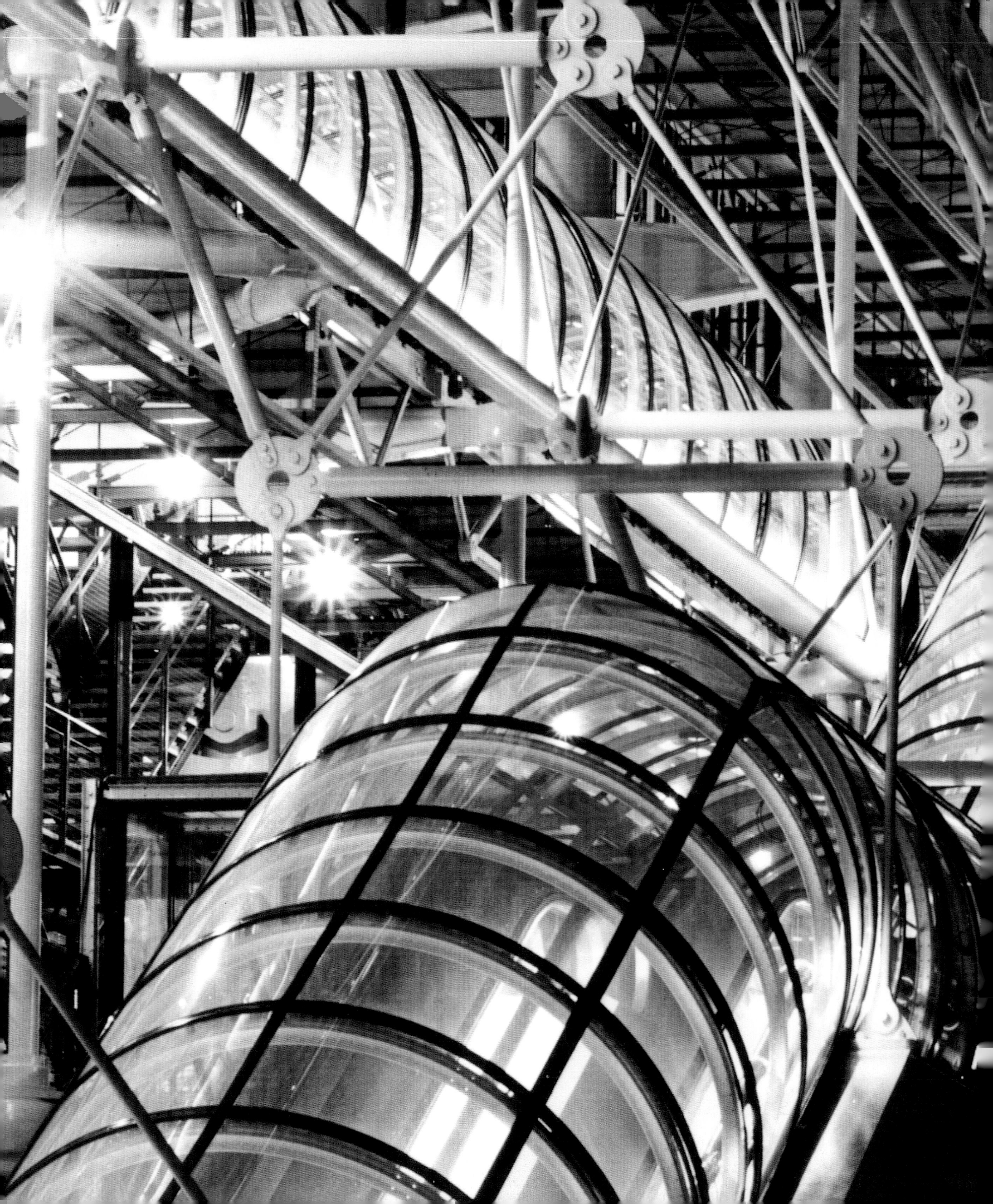

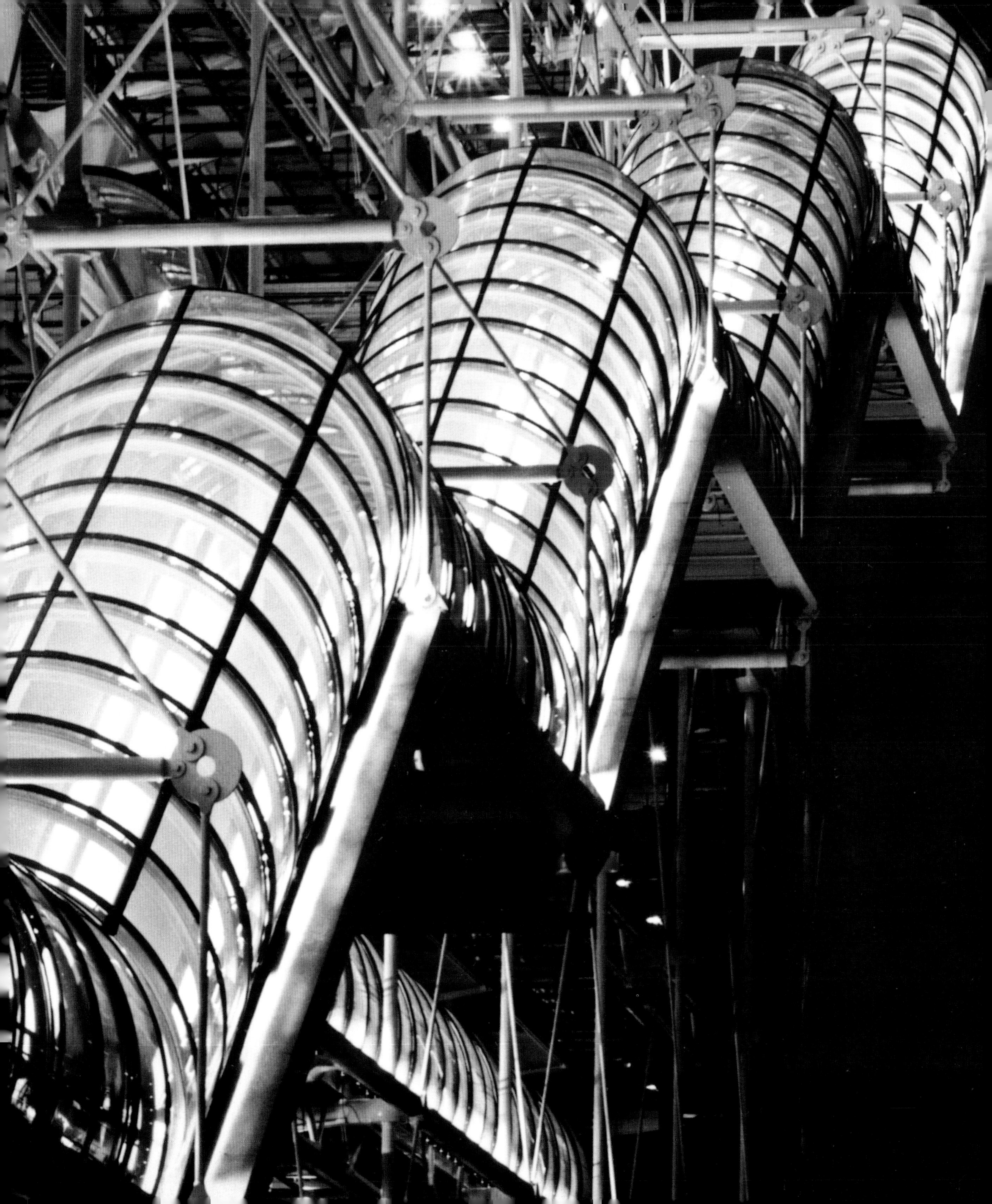

55

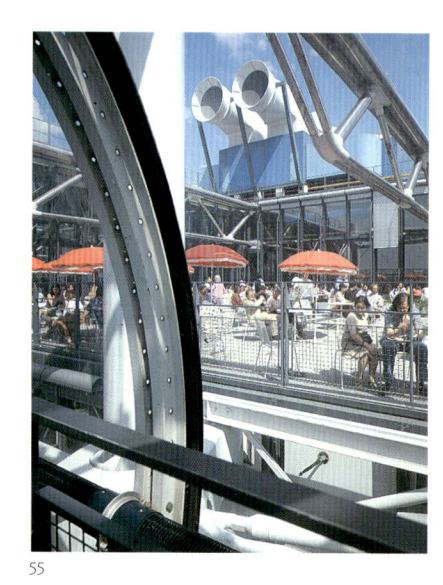

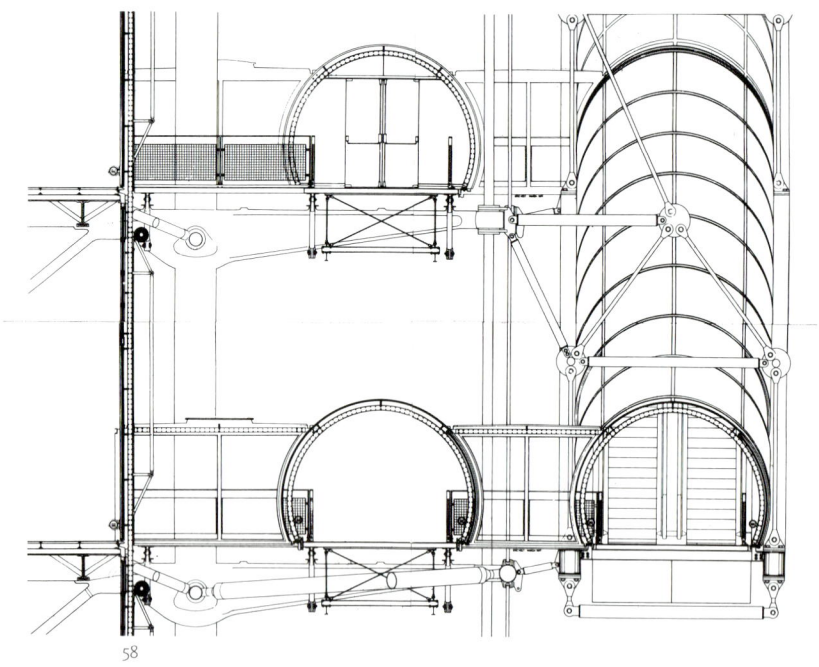

56

57

58

The escalators (54, previous page & 55–60) are set in glazed tubes which snake up the front of the building – its structure is seen at close proximity and there are magnificent views of the heart of Paris. Constructivist and Futurist visions of an architecture of movement are triumphantly realized. The movement zone acts as a 'street in the air' leading to public spaces.

59

Pompidou Centre

60

61

The ground floor double-height forum (61 & 64) is a public place – an extension of the piazza beyond. Above are a series of highly flexible, multi-use, warehouse-type spaces, containing the galleries (65), public library (62 & 63), children's museum, industrial design centre, and temporary and permanent exhibition spaces; these form a striking contrast to the formal enclosures of traditional cultural institutions and reflect the radical agenda of the architects.

Pompidou Centre

62

63

64

colourful, complex, the realization of Modern Movement visions of the building as machine. Yet there is a calm rationality at the heart of the building, partly instilled, perhaps, by Peter Rice, 'a true virtuoso', as Rogers remembers him, 'optimistic and open to new challenge, always pushing the boundaries a little further...' At the core of Rice's art was a rationalism which fuelled his rigorous reworking of the Pompidou facades. This rationalism was understood and appreciated by the French, so that Rice became involved, post-Pompidou, in major projects like the Grande Arche at La Defense and the Science Museum at La Villette. Far from being merely fantastic, the Centre stands in that tradition of rational building which encompasses the Maison de Verre, and the work of Jean Prouvé, *le constructeur*, whose genius moved easily from urban megastructures to the design of temporary homes for those left homeless after the Second World War. It is a rationalism which stretches back beyond the iron and glass architecture of the nineteenth century and the philosophy of Viollet-le-Duc to the Enlightenment. The Pompidou Centre is, perhaps, the last great product of the Enlightenment, the summation of an optimistic tradition rooted in reason.

65

66

67

68

Pompidou Centre

69

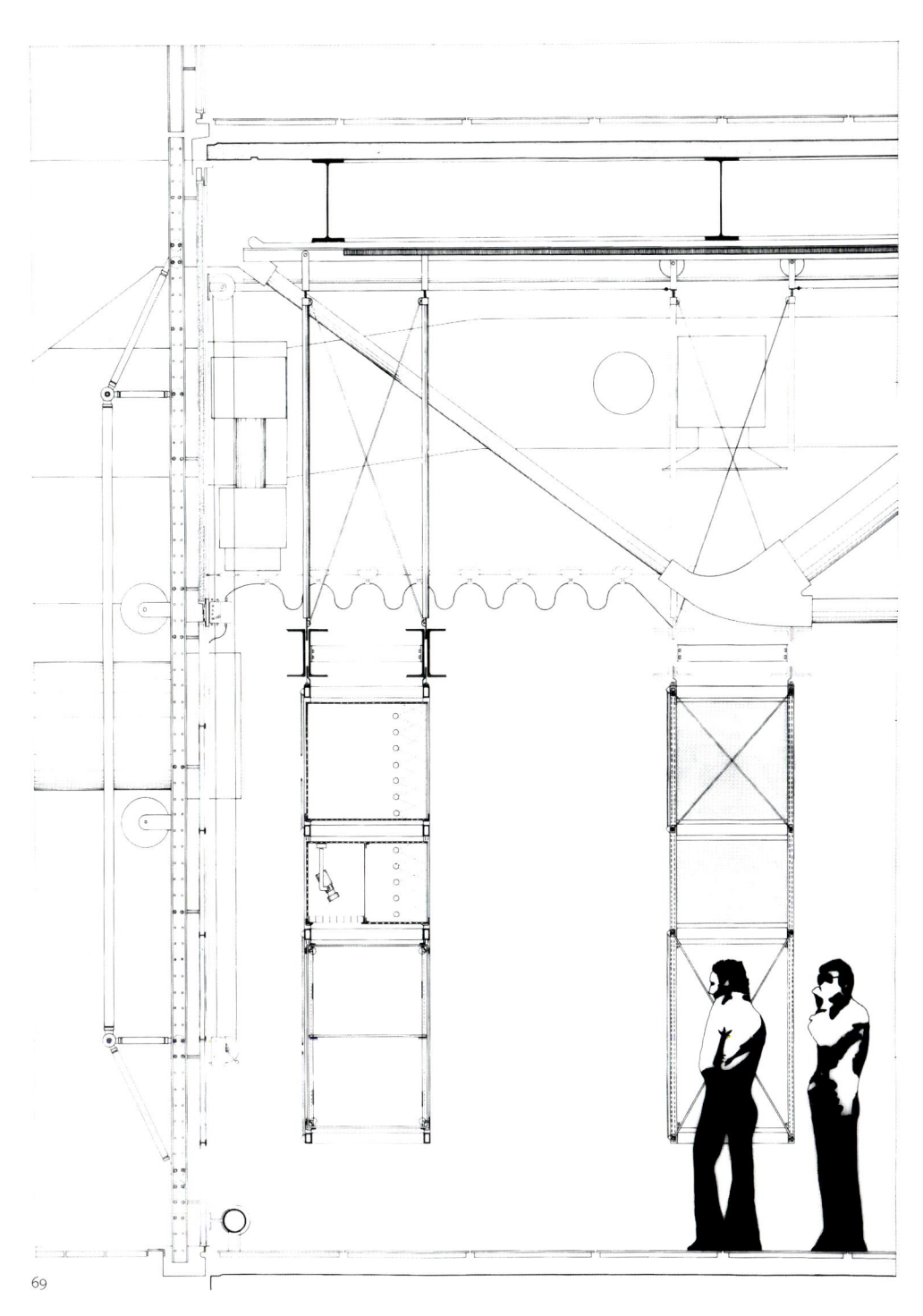

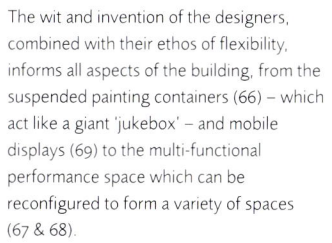

The wit and invention of the designers, combined with their ethos of flexibility, informs all aspects of the building, from the suspended painting containers (66) – which act like a giant 'jukebox' – and mobile displays (69) to the multi-functional performance space which can be reconfigured to form a variety of spaces (67 & 68).
The architects were also responsible for the design of the furniture system (70–73): a simple kit-of-parts based on wire mesh, steel-tube, perforated metal and natural hide.

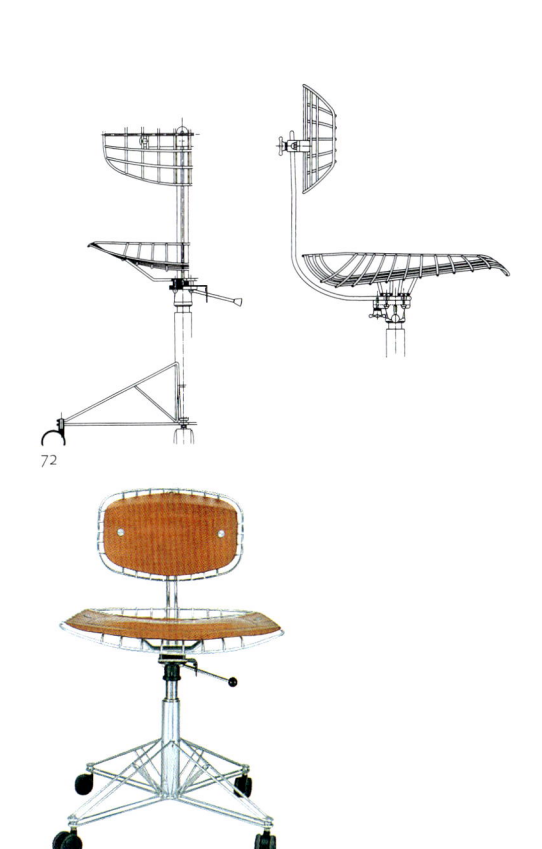

70

71

72

73

74

Pompidou Centre   132

A new square was created south of the Centre, with views to the medieval church of St Merri across a striking water sculpture by Jean Tingueley and Niki De Saint Phalle. The square sits on top of IRCAM.

IRCAM

Institut de Recherche et Coordination Acoustique et Musique
Paris, France, 1971–7

The Pompidou Centre was intended from the first to include a centre for research into music and acoustics, with Pierre Boulez selected as its director. IRCAM – the Institut de Recherche et Coordination Acoustique et Musique – was intended to be experimental and innovative, linking scientific and musical studies in a unique way. Although specialist and scholarly in character, IRCAM was to be, at times, accessible to the public, with regular concerts and demonstrations.

The project was developed in association with Boulez and his team, which included Nicholas Snowman (later a Rogers client as director of London's South Bank Centre). IRCAM was initially to be housed within the Pompidou Centre, but Boulez's pressure for more space – the allocation rose tenfold and could not be accommodated in the main building – led to its being relocated. At first, there were ideas of a separate building on the site of the Place St Merri, but the latter formed part of the setting of the Centre.

The decision was therefore taken to place IRCAM below ground, thus ensuring the complete exclusion of extraneous noise. The project, run largely by Mike Davies, provided for laboratories, studios, offices and a large public performance space. The high degree of flexibility found in the Centre itself was not appropriate in this specialist facility, where the interior assumed a more cellular character. After the death of Georges Pompidou and the accession of President Giscard d'Estaing, the project was radically cut – part of the site already excavated was filled in. A high performance building had to be achieved on a much reduced budget.

As completed in 1977, IRCAM extends to around 10,000 sq.m., contained within a concrete shell sunk up to 20 metres into the ground. Access is via a naturally lit staircase which serves all levels. Beyond this public area, the accommodation is zoned, so that offices and computer rooms are adjacent to the stairs and lobbies, with laboratories beyond and the highly sensitive studios doubly insulated away from all noise at the very heart of the building. The main public studio space, seating 400, is equipped for a wide range of events. Its volume can be changed by means of a movable ceiling. Adjustable surfaces mean that the acoustic qualities of the space can be varied. The space is completely flexible, the embodiment of 1960s ideas of an adaptable environment, and has an industrial rather than an obviously cultural character. It is a true workshop, where conventional ideas of the relationship between performers and audience are overturned.

In 1988–90, Renzo Piano added a six-storey, above-ground office extension to IRCAM, giving it a more obvious public presence and deferring to the context of an adjacent nineteenth-century school, itself used by IRCAM.

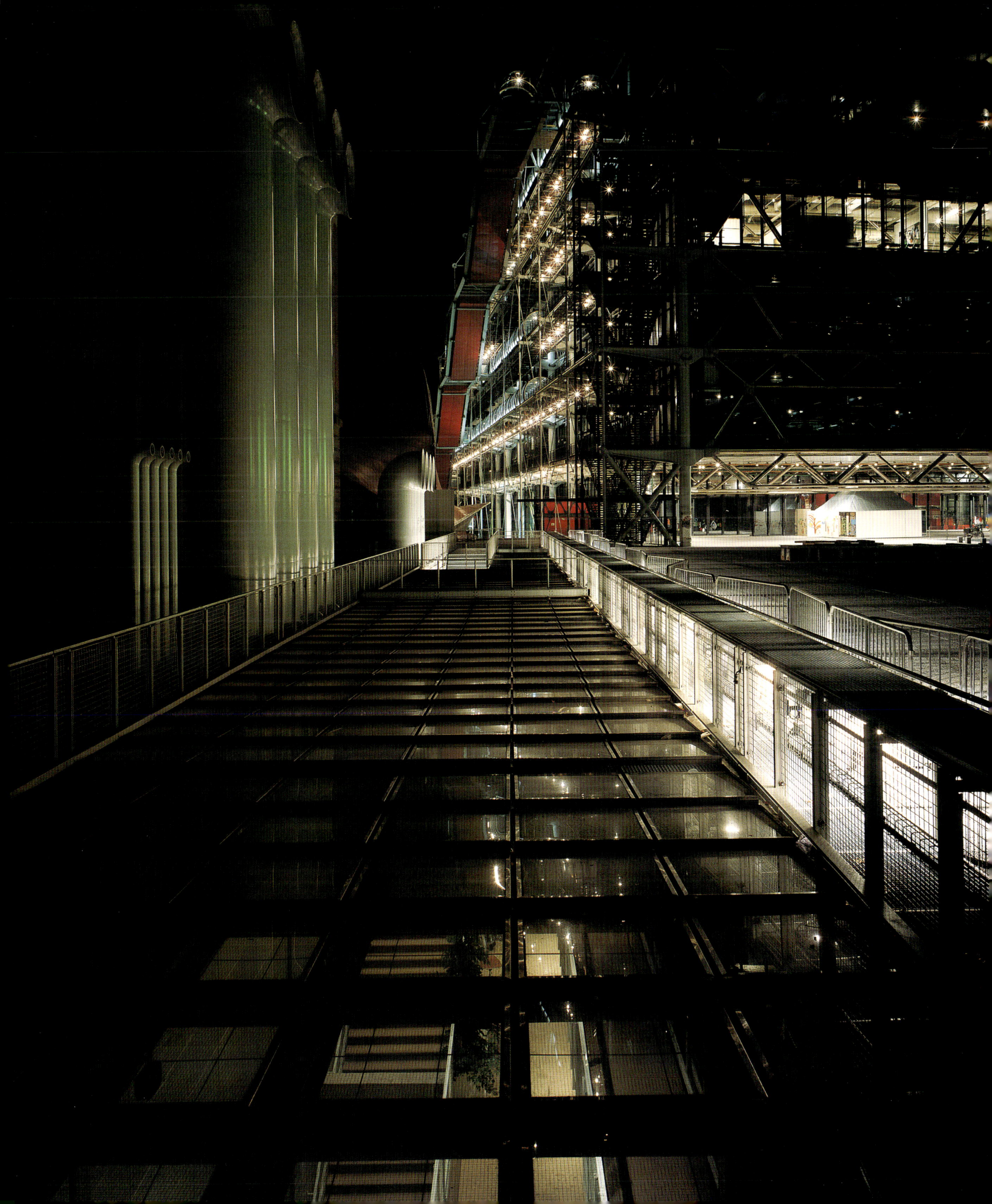

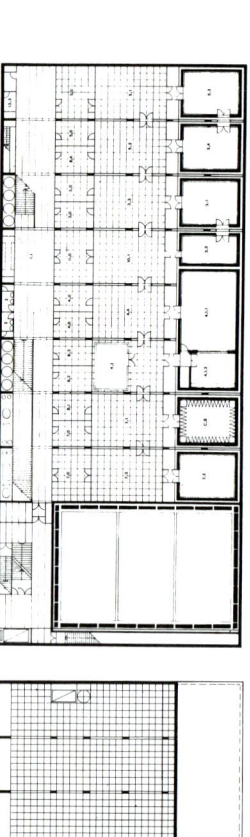

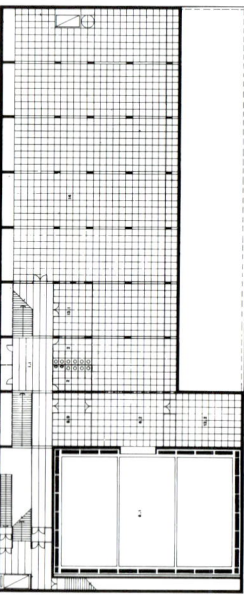

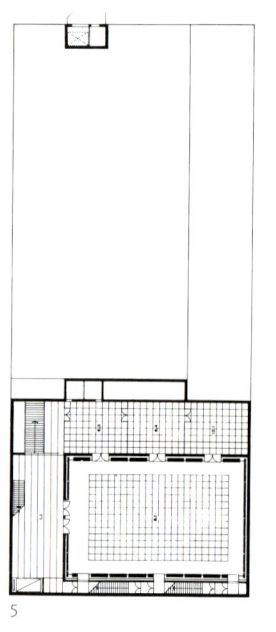

IRCAM

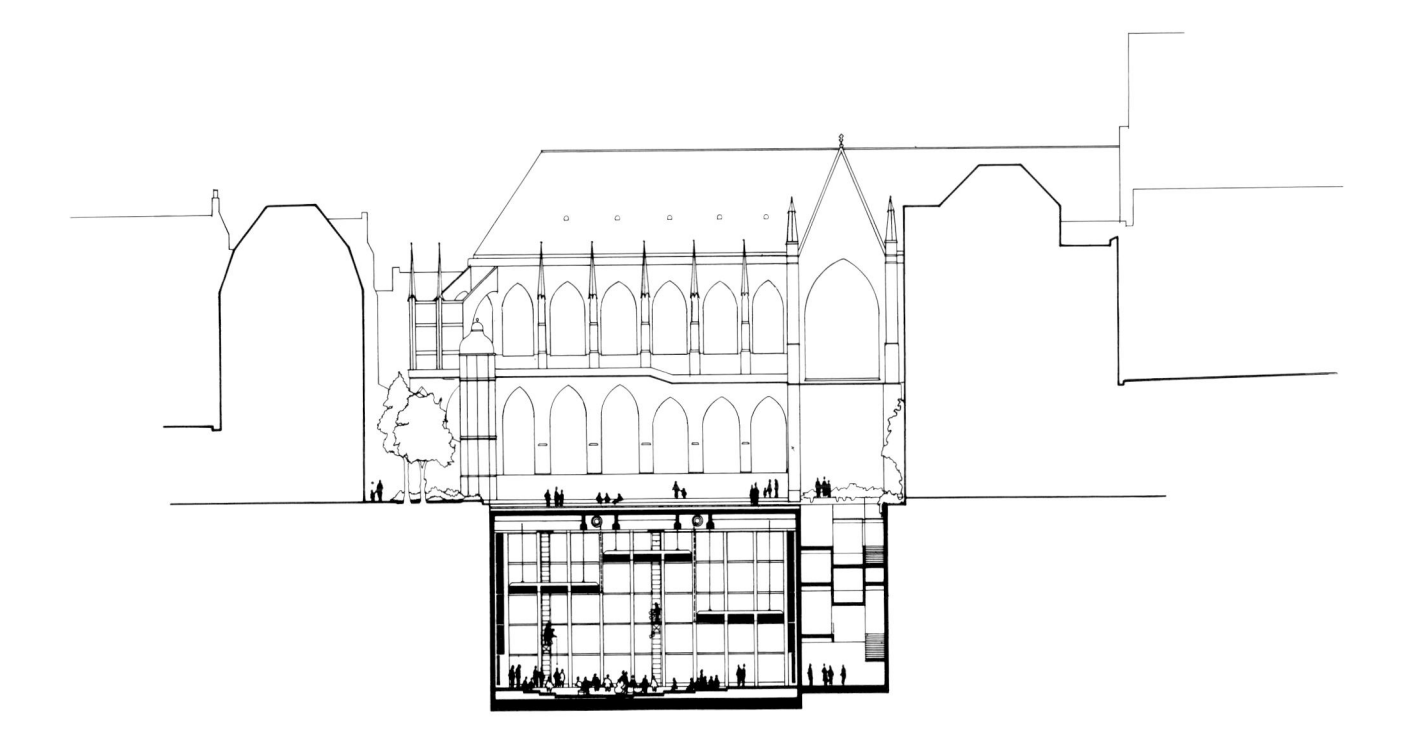

IRCAM, the innovative music and acoustic research centre run by Pierre Boulez, occupies a great concrete box sunk up to 20 metres deep into the ground – ensuring effective sound insulation even in the heart of the city.
The public zone of the great staircase (3 & 4), which serves all levels of IRCAM, is day-lit and gives access to the private world of the studios and research facilities beyond (1, p134 & 5), and views to the city above. Locating the facility underground opens up views of the church and creates a public piazza above (2, previous page & 6).

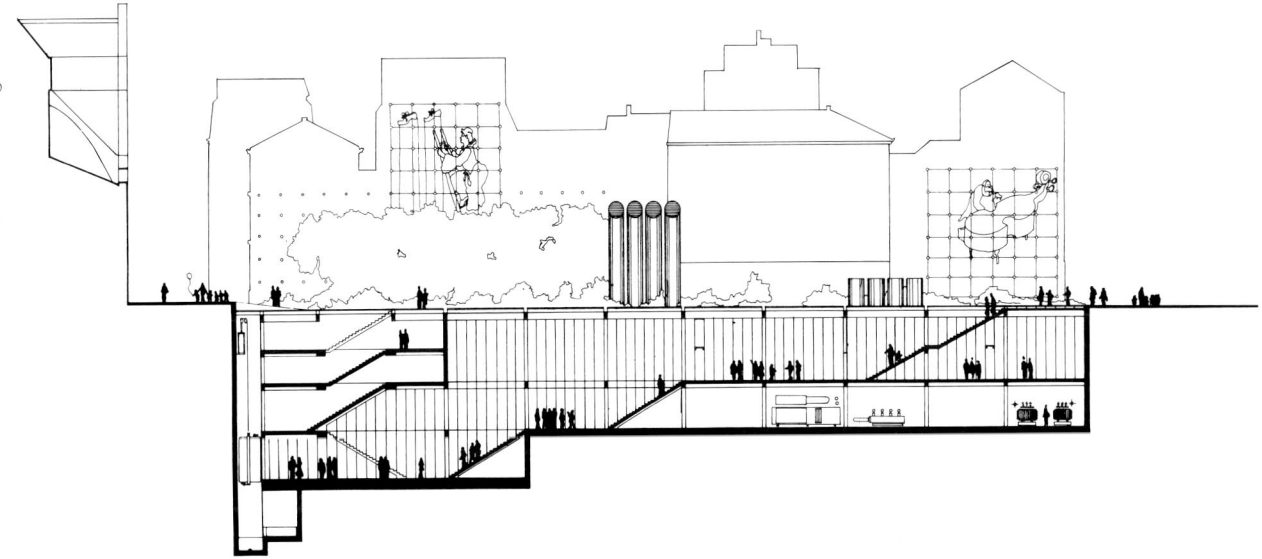

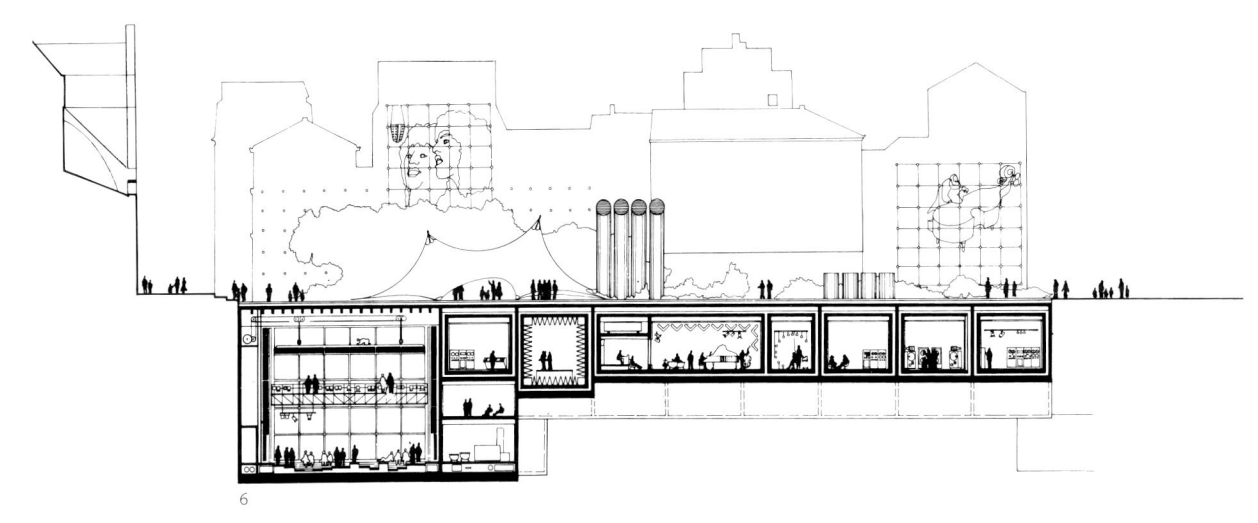

7

8

The interior of the building contains specialist research facilities including an anechoic chamber (7), recording studios (8) and the great hall (9) – an acoustically and volumetrically flexible performance space that can range in aural properties from cathedral to cupboard.

IRCAM

9

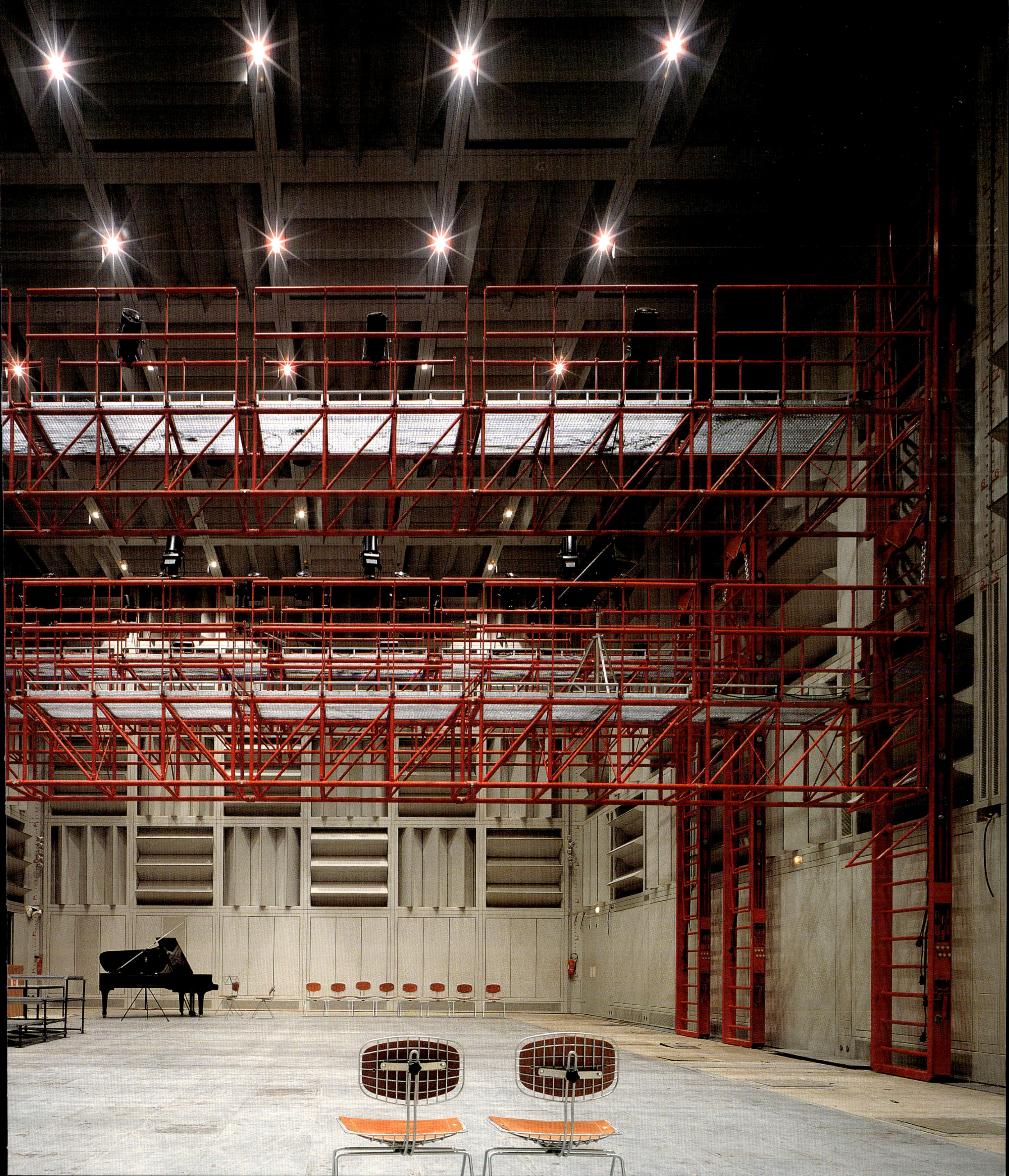

ARAM Module

Association for Rural Aid in Medicine, 1971

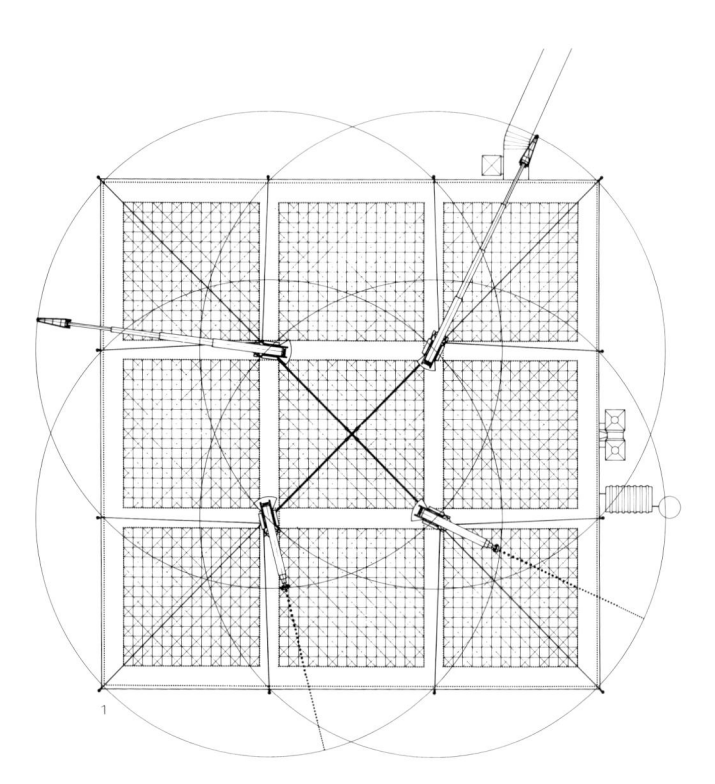

There has always been an idealistic, even utopian element in the work of Richard Rogers. When the campaigning American doctor, Lalla Iveson, came to Piano + Rogers asking for help with a hospital project for developing countries, she received an enthusiastic response. The intention was to produce a standardized hospital which could be airlifted to places where there was an urgent need for medical services – for example, areas affected by famine, war, epidemics or natural disasters. Dr Iveson believed that the hospital system had ceased to serve people's needs and that typical Western hospitals had developed into vastly expensive 'empires' which could never be afforded by developing countries. The aim was to give them not a second-best alternative, but a facility which could be adapted to their specific needs. If houses and factories could be made demountable and portable – and this was the idea behind the Zip-Up programme – why not hospitals? (This was an issue, coincidentally, to which Rogers' associates, Jan Kaplicky and Amanda Levete of Future Systems, were to return twenty years later.)

The imagery of the space race between the superpowers and of the UK's emerging North Sea oil industry underlie the ARAM designs, which are equally obviously related to those for the Pompidou Centre. The project, on which Rogers and Piano collaborated closely along with Tony Hunt as engineer, combines practicality with a degree of the fantastic. The ideas behind ARAM, including that of a free-standing structure on which services could be hung, were found not only in the Pompidou Centre but in Rogers' projects of a decade later, such as the Inmos factory and the Fleetguard Factory.

The project fitted in well with Piano + Rogers' concern with flexible space and adaptability. The hospital module consisted of a 'hard' core, the technical equipment and services needed to diagnose and treat patients, and a flexible space for beds – normally no more than 200, though this figure could be reduced to fifty for isolated locations. The entire structure, made of small-scale, standardized parts, could be transported, assembled by a non-specialist team directed by a few technicians, and quickly brought into operation. (A crane for assembly was built into the package.) Structurally, the module consisted of latticed steel columns, with lightweight trusses supporting space decks suspended from high-tensile steel cables. The floor space provided was interrupted only by the four main columns and amounted to around 2,500 sq.m. Services were to be mounted in voids above and below the 'activity' floor. Power and other services could be adapted to suit what was available locally. Standby generating equipment was provided within the module.

This project was another instance of architects and client in close empathy – using flexible but advanced technology to serve people was a central theme with Piano + Rogers. Photomontages showed the module erected in urban slums and African villages. The idea was, in fact, entirely practical and only a wider lack of will has prevented it being realized – no ARAM hospital was ever constructed.

The ARAM Module was a self-contained medical facility that could be built easily and deployed where needed (1). The concept was adaptable to many contexts, from deprived urban areas (2 & 3) to the rural heart of Africa (4). The servicing package could be adapted to suit local needs and resources.

B&B Italia Offices

Como, Italy, 1972–3

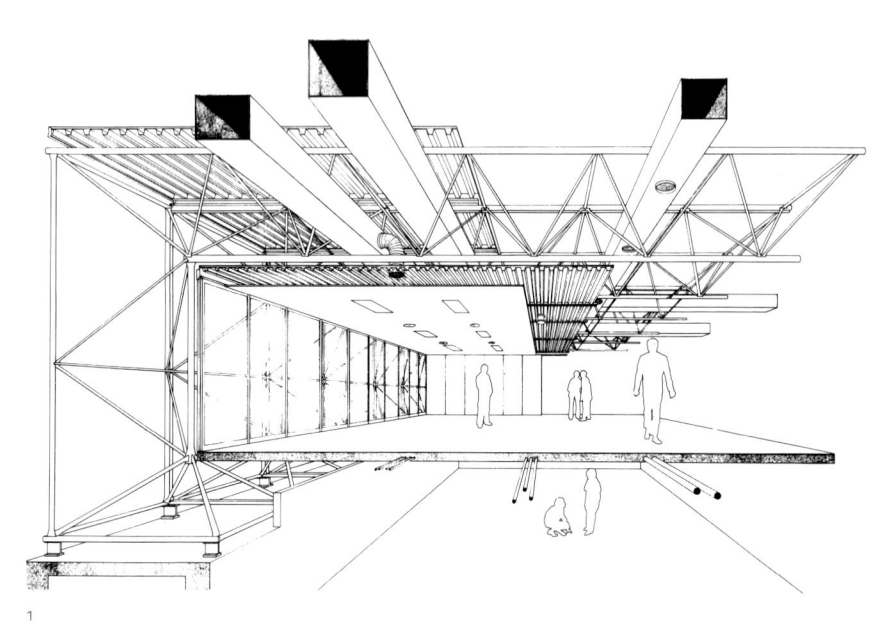

B&B, a large Italian furniture manufacturer, was run by Piero Busnelli, who much admired the designs for the Pompidou Centre and commissioned Piano + Rogers to design his company's new offices on a site adjacent to the existing B&B factory at Novedrate, Como. Busnelli wanted a prestige building that reflected the image of his company, with scope for expansion and internal changes.

Relatively modest in itself, the building is important as a 'small-scale dress rehearsal' for the Pompidou Centre, both structurally and aesthetically. The interior of the building is totally column-free, contained within a box suspended from a series of twenty tubular steel portal frames spanning 30 metres – just as the services at Beaubourg were to be fixed within the frame of the steel facade. Services are restricted to the perimeter, so that there are no fixed elements inside – walls and partitions can be freely moved around. The elevation of the building above the uneven ground leaves space for plantroom and storage underneath. A raised floor provides for extensive use of computers, while the double roof provides space for other services as well as encouraging the free flow of air to keep the building cool. The steel frame is painted blue, while service risers and vents are coloured red and yellow.

The sheer elegance of the B&B building is memorable. This was a conscious aim on the part of the architects, working both from Paris and from Piano's office in Genoa, with Cuno Brullmann as team leader before moving on to Paris to join the Beaubourg team. Lightness and transparency were the objectives: 'The idea was to reduce everything to a very slender structure, to a sort of filigree: at bottom, a formal and rather sophisticated exercise, an effort of stylistic and plastic research carried out with the components of metal supporting structures ... It was a work that required a great deal of patience, and some demanding acrobatics.' (Renzo Piano, *Renzo Piano Logbook*, 1997.)

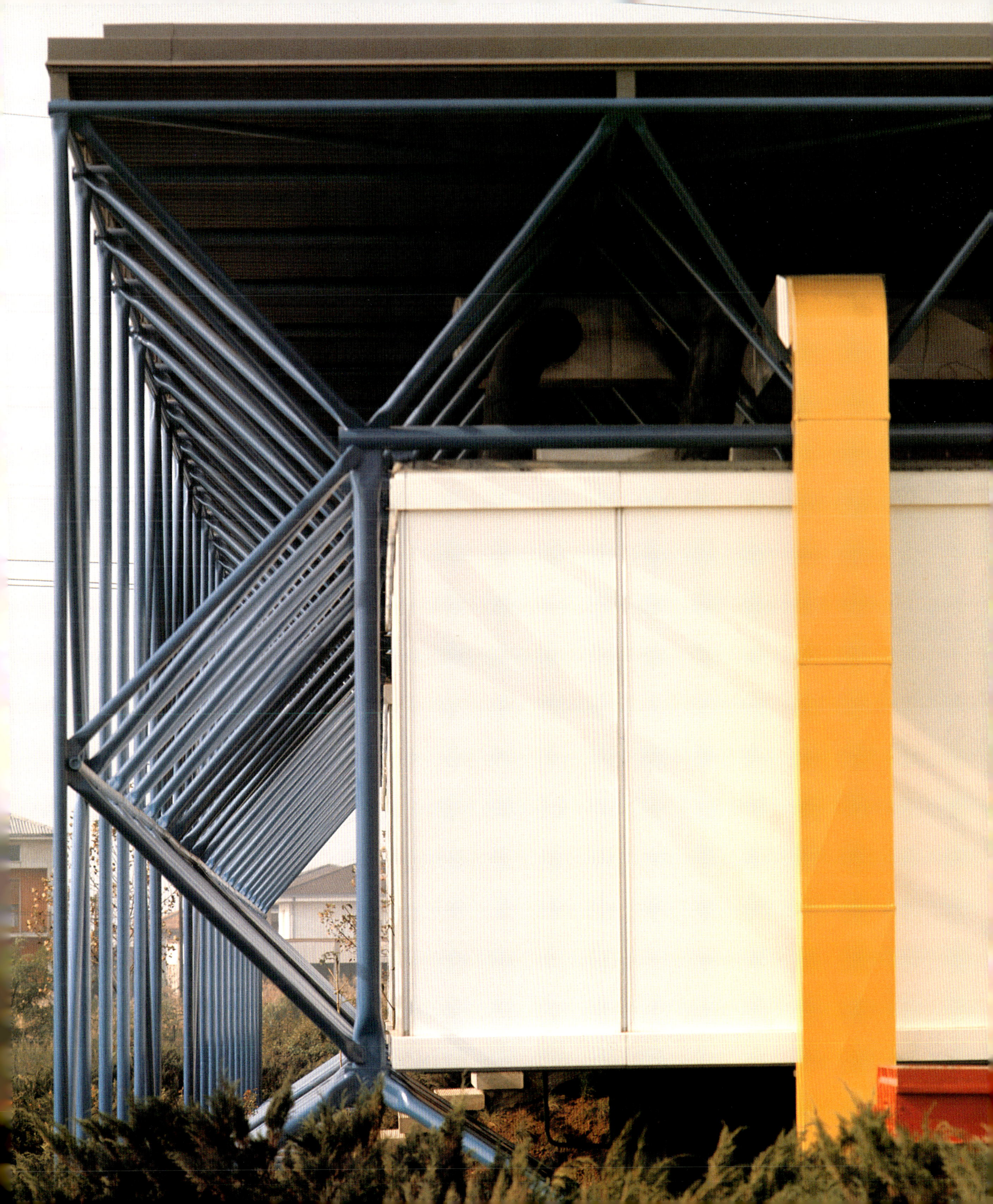

3

4

The structure of the B&B Italia offices consists of a series of latticed portal frames joined together (1, p142 & 7–9), within which the enclosure of office space is contained. The oversailing double roof provides effective and economical shade (2, previous page, 3).
The plan of the building (5) shows a great open space, completely column-free and almost infinitely flexible.
A glazed bridge links the office and the manufacturing facility (4 & 6).

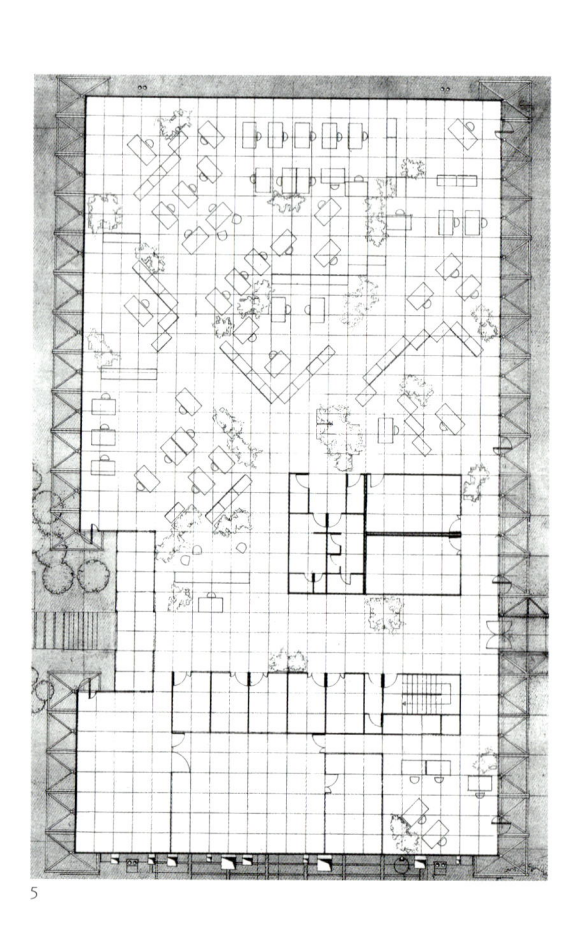

5

B&B Italia Offices

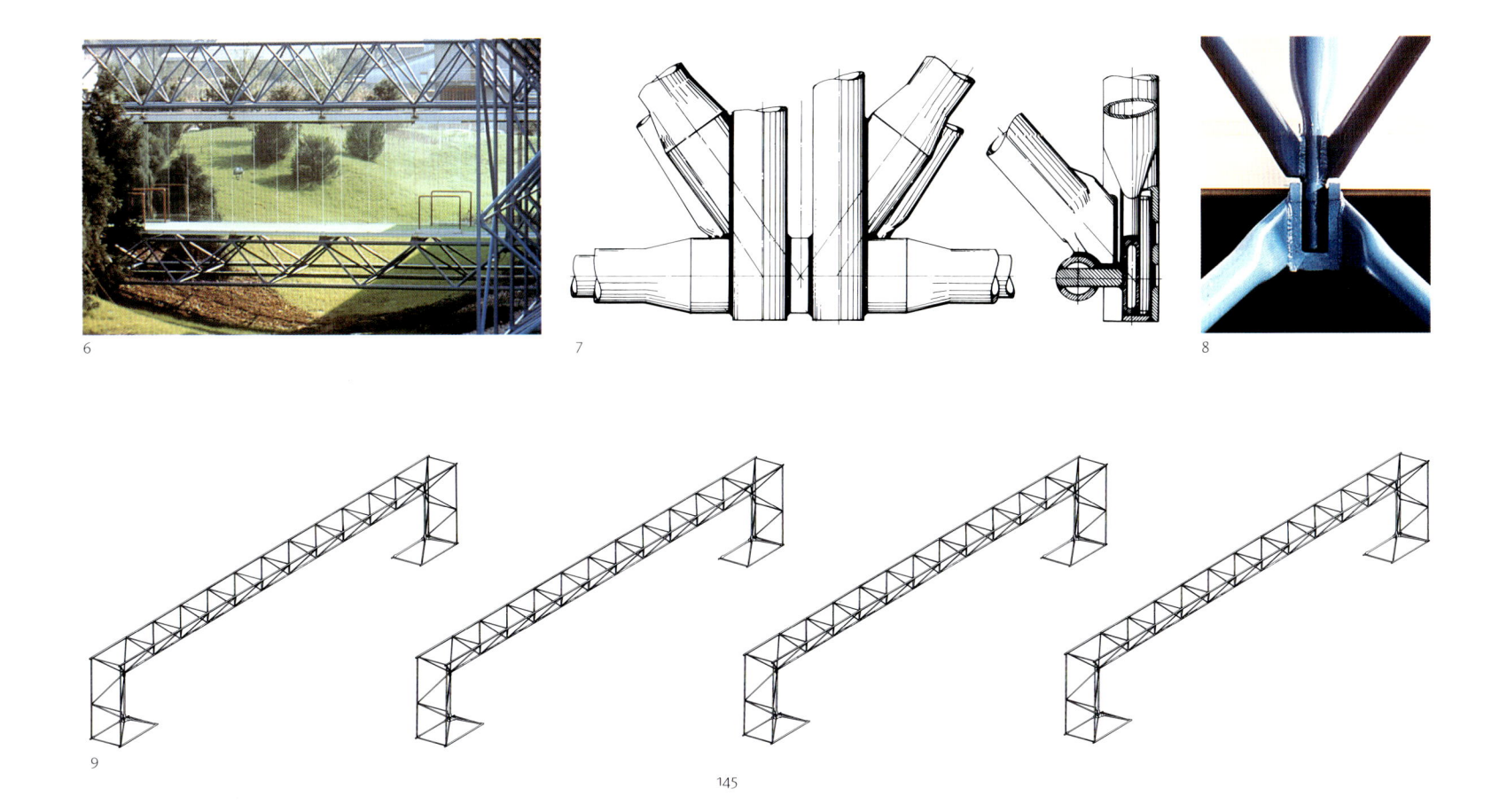

6

7

8

9

UOP Factory

Tadworth, Surrey, 1973–4

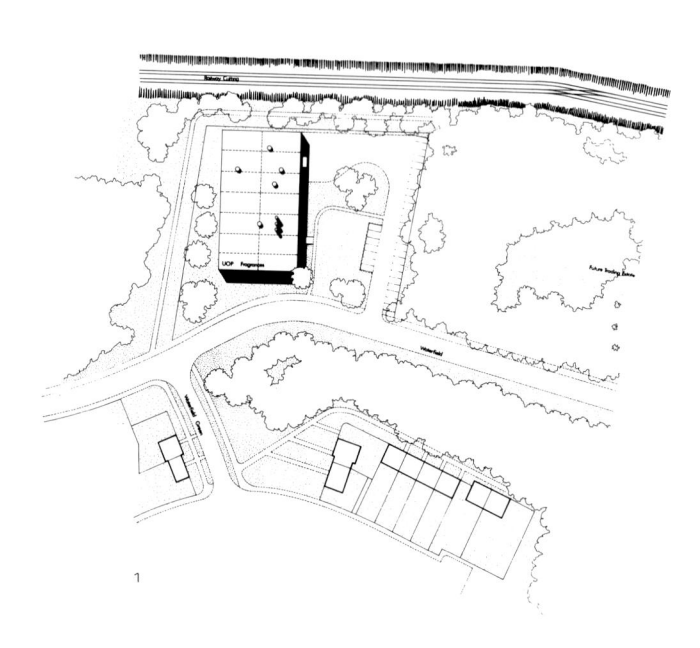

Richard + Su Rogers' highly innovative 1969 project for UOP, a development of Zip-Up principles applied to an industrial structure, had remained unbuilt, but the company later returned to Piano + Rogers with the commission for a factory on a new site at Tadworth. (The job was significant in providing work for the practice's 'London office' while the Pompidou Centre was being built and was run by John Young.) A pragmatic approach produced what the brief demanded: a flexible, high-performance building with scope for growth and change. Internal divisions between offices, laboratories and manufacturing were achieved with full height demountable glazed walls creating a feeling of spaciousness, affording long views throughout the facility and visual contact between employees working on different aspects of the company's business. Only the stores area, containing highly flammable compounds, was hidden from view behind a two-hour fire wall. The use of large sandwich wall panels (6" thick), sealed with neoprene, on a steel frame made for rapid assembly of the basic envelope.

The building stood apart from the general run of industrial structures being built in Britain at this period. Its economy, generosity of space and sheer verve – the use of colour was striking – impressed and seemed to point the way towards a new industrial vernacular. The building, widely published, helped to establish Rogers' reputation in the field of industrial building.

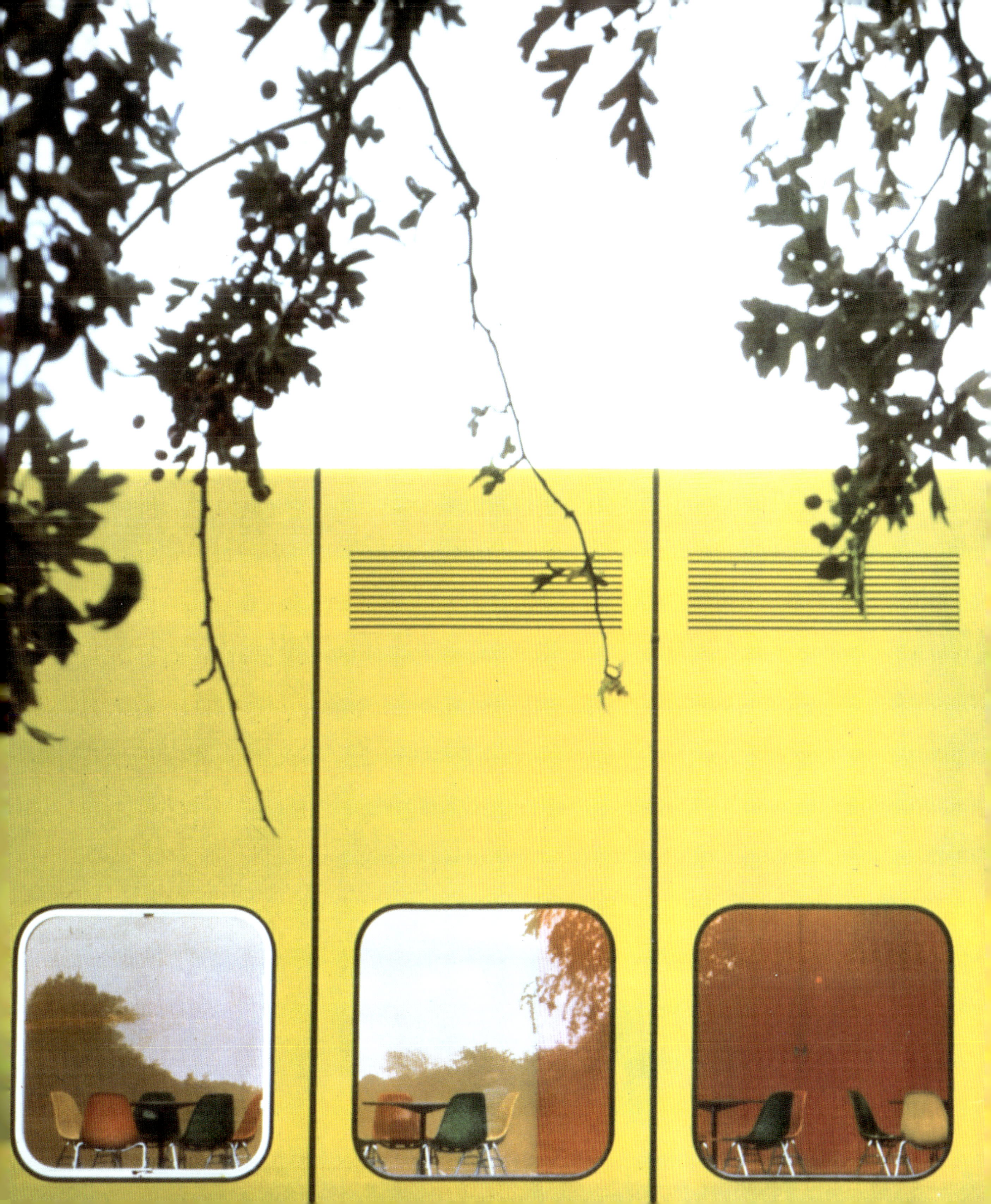

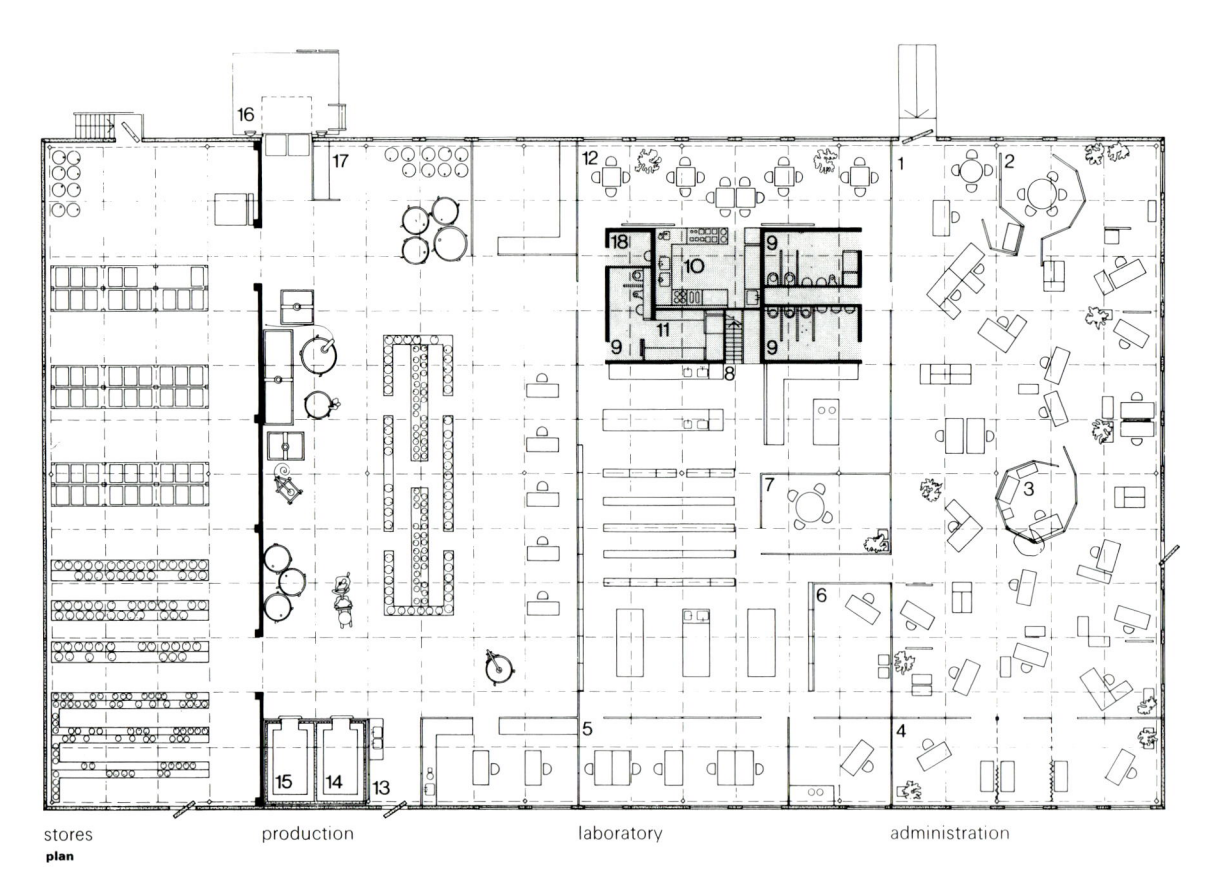

stores   production   laboratory   administration

plan

key
1. reception
2. meetings
3. business machines
4. executive/conference
5. perfumers
6. formula security
7. odour evaluation
8. up to plant
9. wcs
10. kitchen
11. lockers
12. canteen
13. wash
14. hot room
15. cold room
16. loading bay
17. despatch
18. first aid

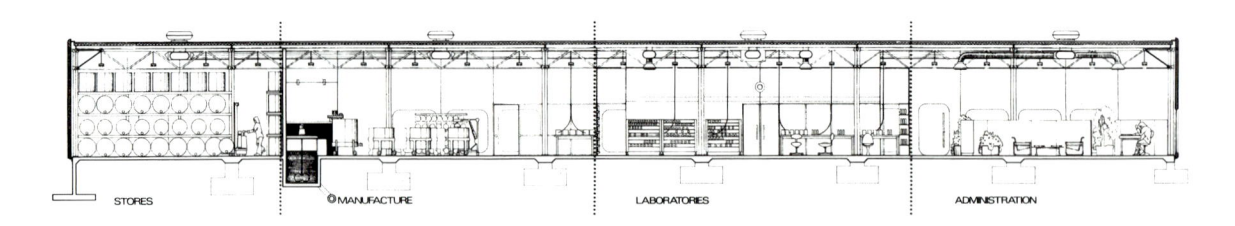

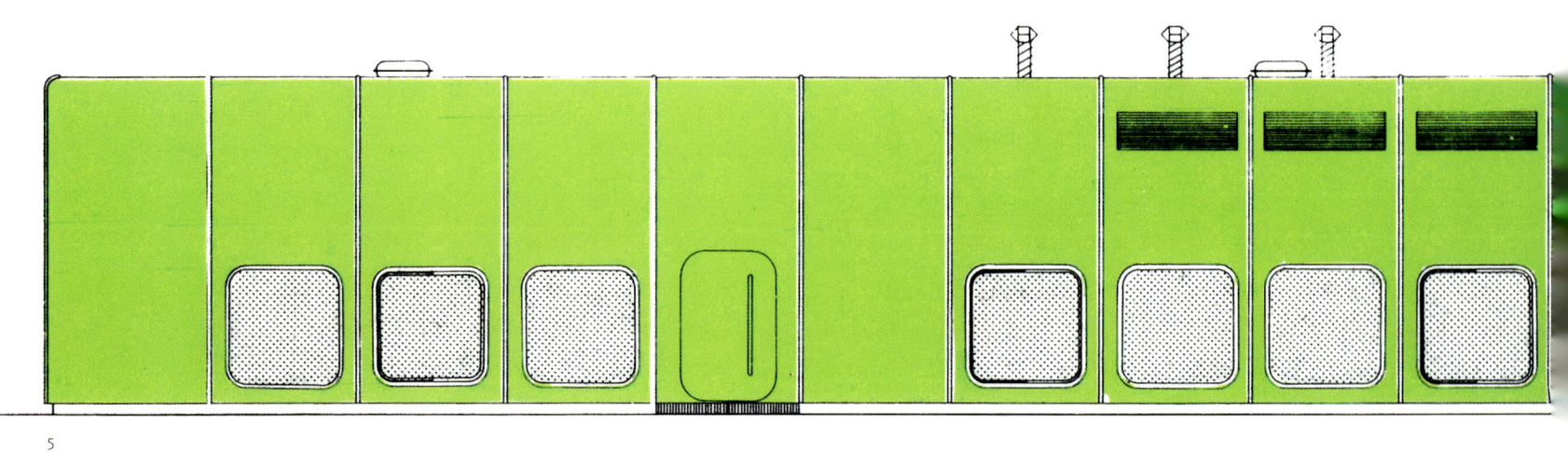

3

The UOP factory is an adaptable, industrial variant on the Zip-Up House, with an open flow space permitting wide variations in layout. The building, set in an open site (1, p146 & 6) was pioneering as a model for interchangeable office, research and manufacturing units (3 & 4). It was clad with prefabricated, full-height, glass-reinforced cement sandwich panels (2, previous page), interchangeable in response to the activities within (5).

STORES   MANUFACTURE   LABORATORIES   ADMINISTRATION

4

5

UOP Factory

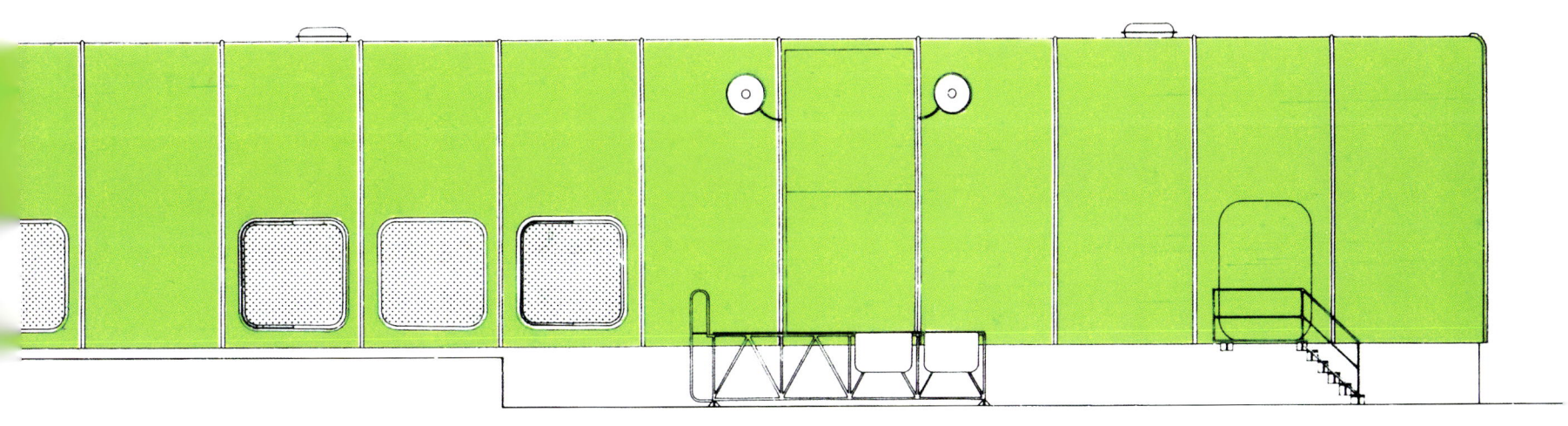

6

149

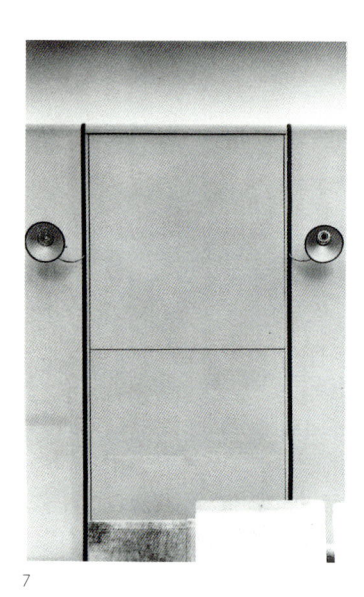

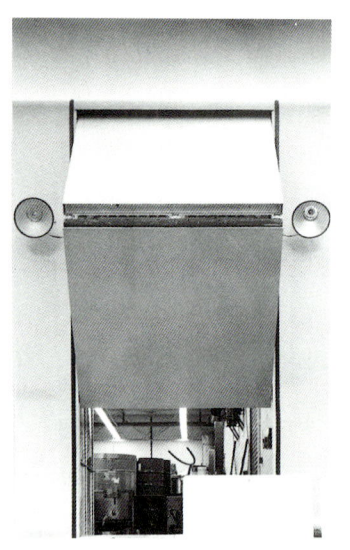

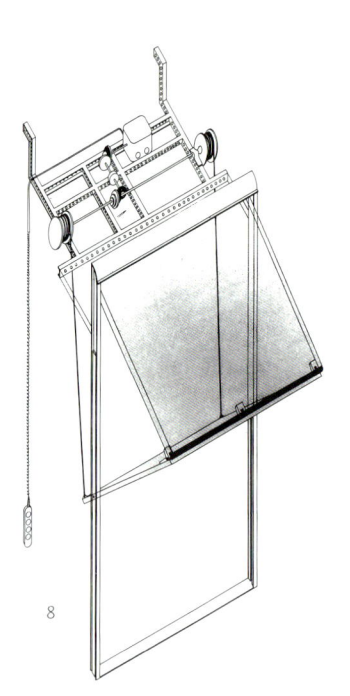

The storey-height panels with their innovative details (10) incorporated large windows for views out (9, 11 & 12) and a purpose-designed loading bay door (7 & 8).

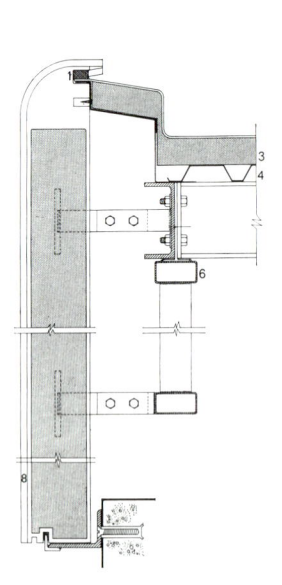

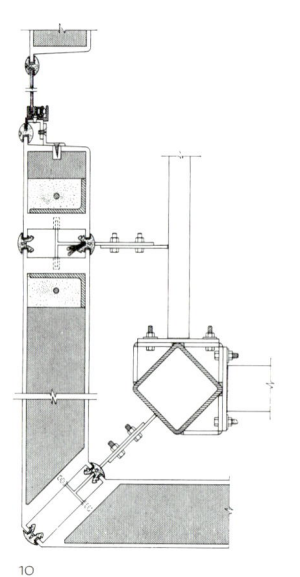

UOP Factory

11

12

151

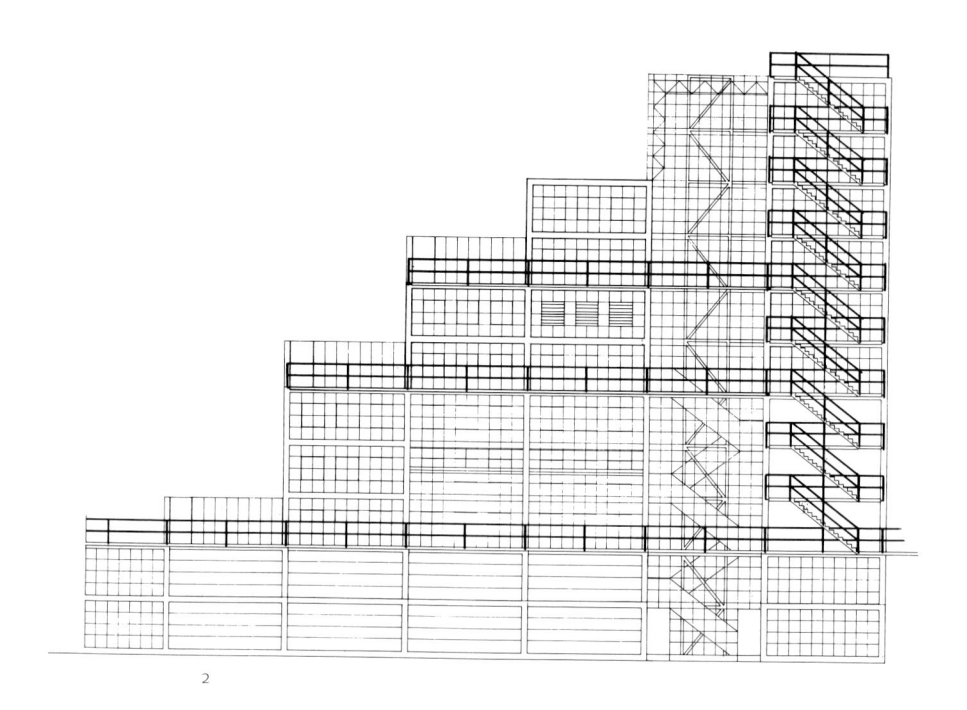

Park Road Development

London, 1973

Rogers' Park Road scheme was for a site to the north of an innovative apartment block by Farrell Grimshaw, squeezed in between the busy road and the railway tracks into Marylebone station, and was one of the most important projects in the London office concurrent with the Pompidou Centre. Unfortunately, it was not built.

The aesthetic of the mixed-use (sixty flats, 20,000 sq.ft. of offices, showroom, plus restaurant and parking) scheme was restrained and Miesian; intended to be relieved by the use of colour, it also reflected a concern for the sensitivity of the location. Its particular interest lay in an ingenious approach to plan and layout intended to insulate the residential element from the noise of traffic and trains, provide maximum privacy and capitalize on daylight. The residential space was split into two blocks, facing the road (with views beyond to Regent's Park) and rail tracks respectively. The latter block was stepped in section, with rooftop gardens to provide a noise baffle. The flats were served by an internal, planted atrium, crisscrossed with walkways – a radical alternative to the dark corridors found in old-style 'mansion' blocks. The atrium was to be of steel within the precast concrete structure of the building. Offices were also to benefit from day-lit internal courts. The scheme was a victim of the 1970s recession, but many of its ideas resurfaced in the Millbank Riverside Housing project a few years later.

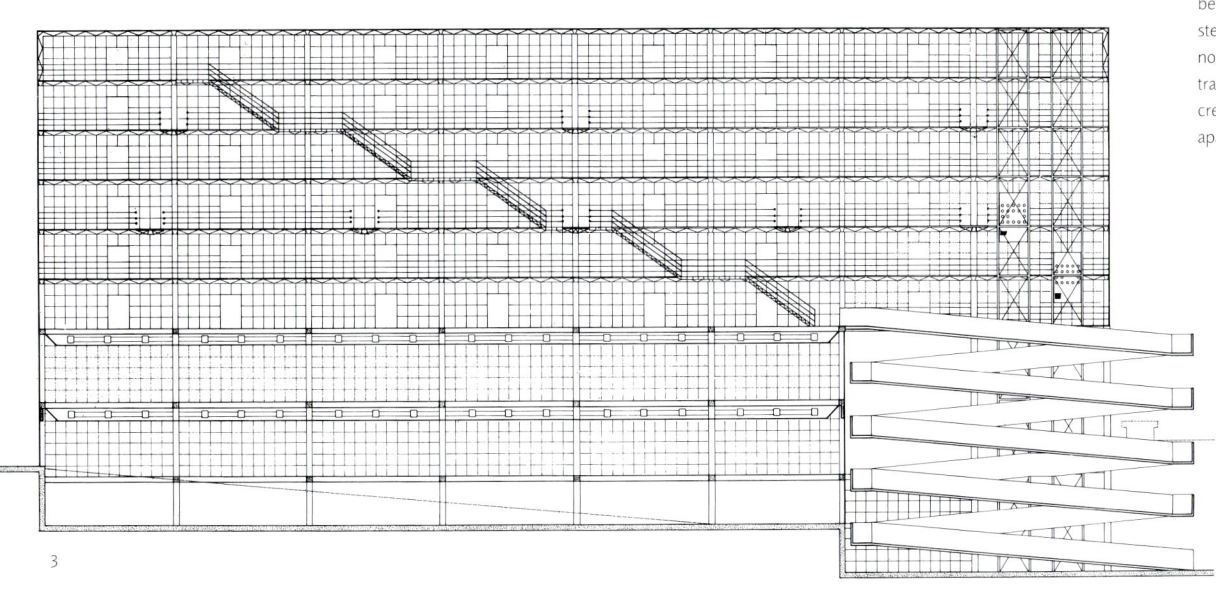

The Park Road project was designed for a site close to Regent's Park but sandwiched between a busy road and a railway line. The stepped section allows light in and provides noise protection from the adjacent train tracks. The landscaped internal courtyard created a communal focus with access to all apartments (1–7).

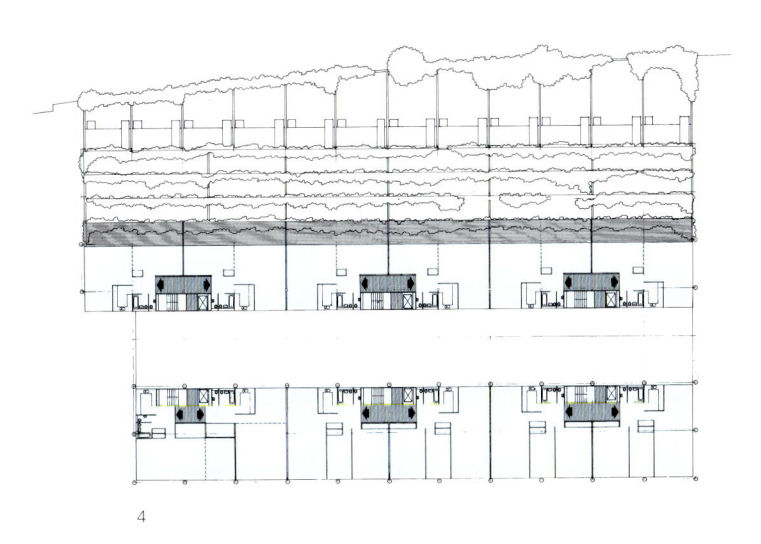

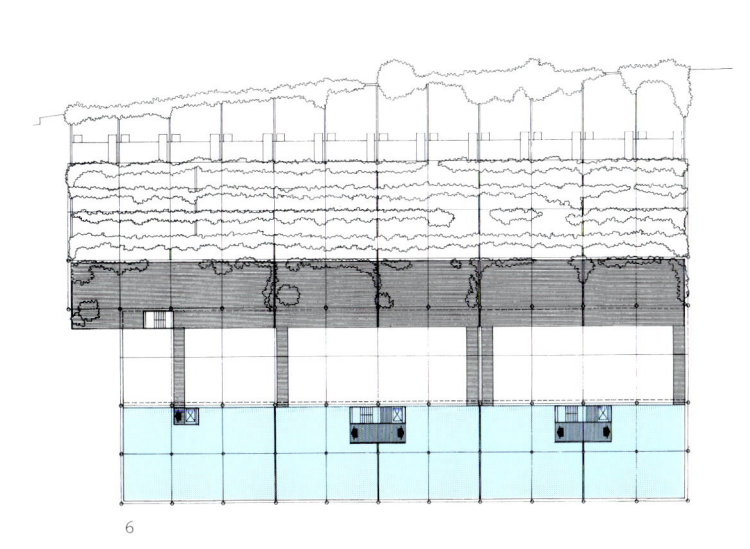

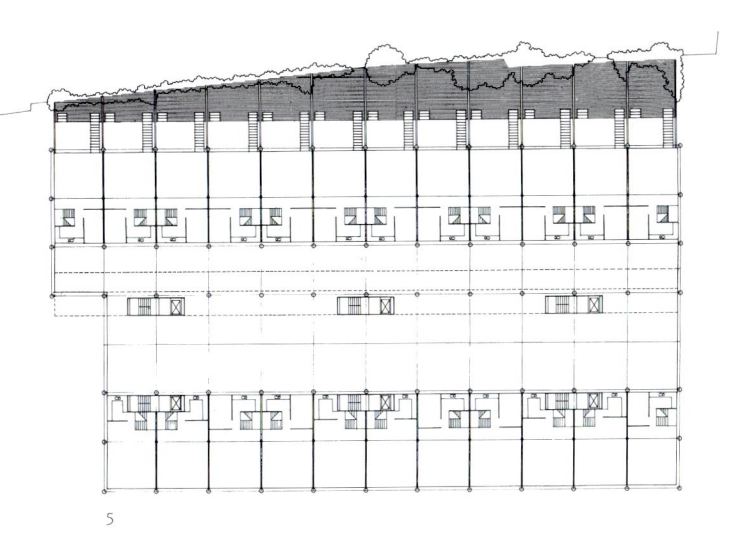

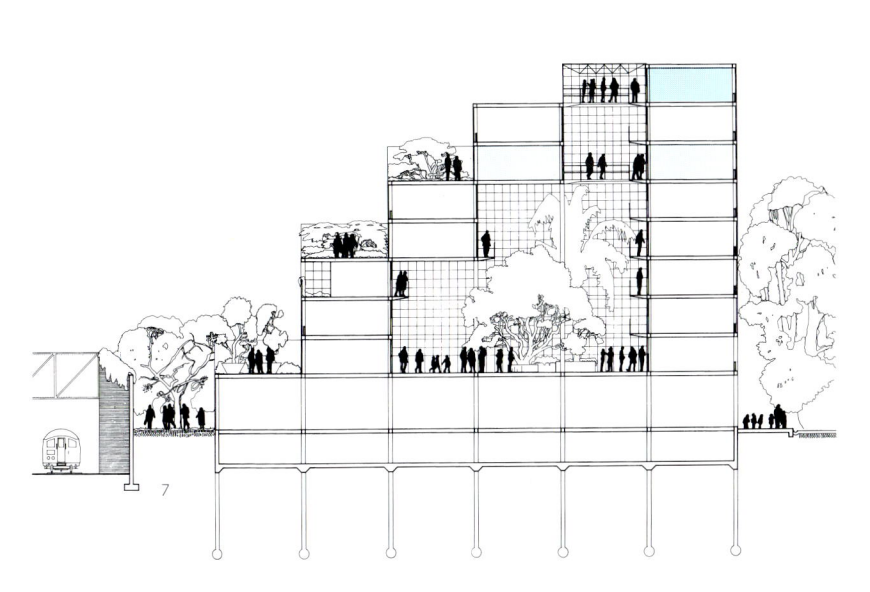

PA Technology Laboratory

Melbourn, Cambridgeshire, 1975

The PA organization, a major international research, management and development consultancy, commissioned Piano + Rogers to design a highly-serviced laboratories building with attached support areas and offices. The building was to be the British headquarters of PA Technology; a prestige building of around 2,500 sq.m. was envisaged for the first phase. The architectural style was open to discussion, but the client's initial preference was for a relatively conservative design. Rogers produced proposals for a great column-free, arched shed, covered in a single membrane and sunk into the landscape, with parking and service access in an open undercroft. Although this scheme was too radical for the client, the revised version as constructed incorporated a number of ideas from it, while containing others from earlier projects including the Rogers House at Wimbledon. The building is constructed on a solid, insulated concrete slab on which precast cruciform columns support a steel frame infilled with stressed skin plywood roof panels. The cladding system comprises an interchangeable mix of glass and insulated sandwich panels. Inside, partitions are entirely flexible, allowing spaces to be reconfigured at will. Laboratories are centrally located, with offices at the perimeter.

The servicing strategy allows easy maintenance, upgrading and rearrangement as functions within the building change. Services are suspended below the main slab at undercroft level, where parking is provided, as in the first proposal. The building carries a high degree of conviction – the reception area, for example, with its walls of glass bricks, exposed frame and use of bright primary colours, is defiantly un-corporate. The idea of submerging the building in the landscape remains in the form of the grass banks which mask the undercroft. The building was fully occupied as soon as it was completed and two additional phases of the scheme were completed in 1982 and 1984 respectively. PA Technology Laboratory is a worthy successor to Reliance Controls and led to further experiment, not least in another 'Patscentre', as they were known, designed by Rogers in the USA. It provided a model for the research and office buildings widely constructed on out-of-town sites during the 1980s, though few possessed its sleek and purposeful glamour. Most importantly for John Young, it was a Rogers building that really put its growth and flexibility credentials to the test, growing 300 per cent over seven years but looking calm and seamless straddling the crest of a hill.

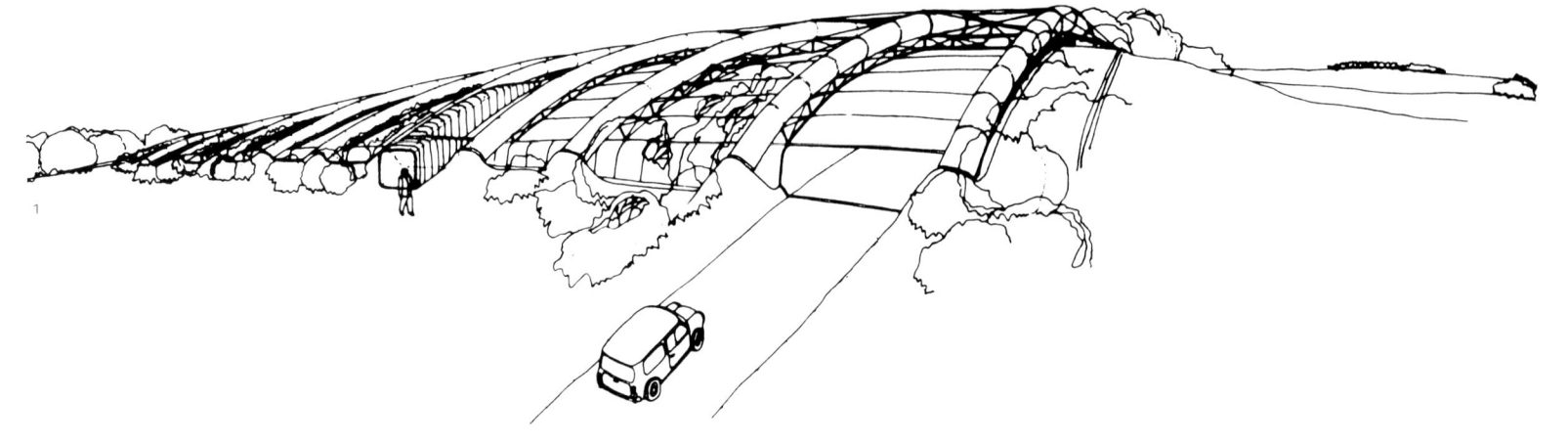

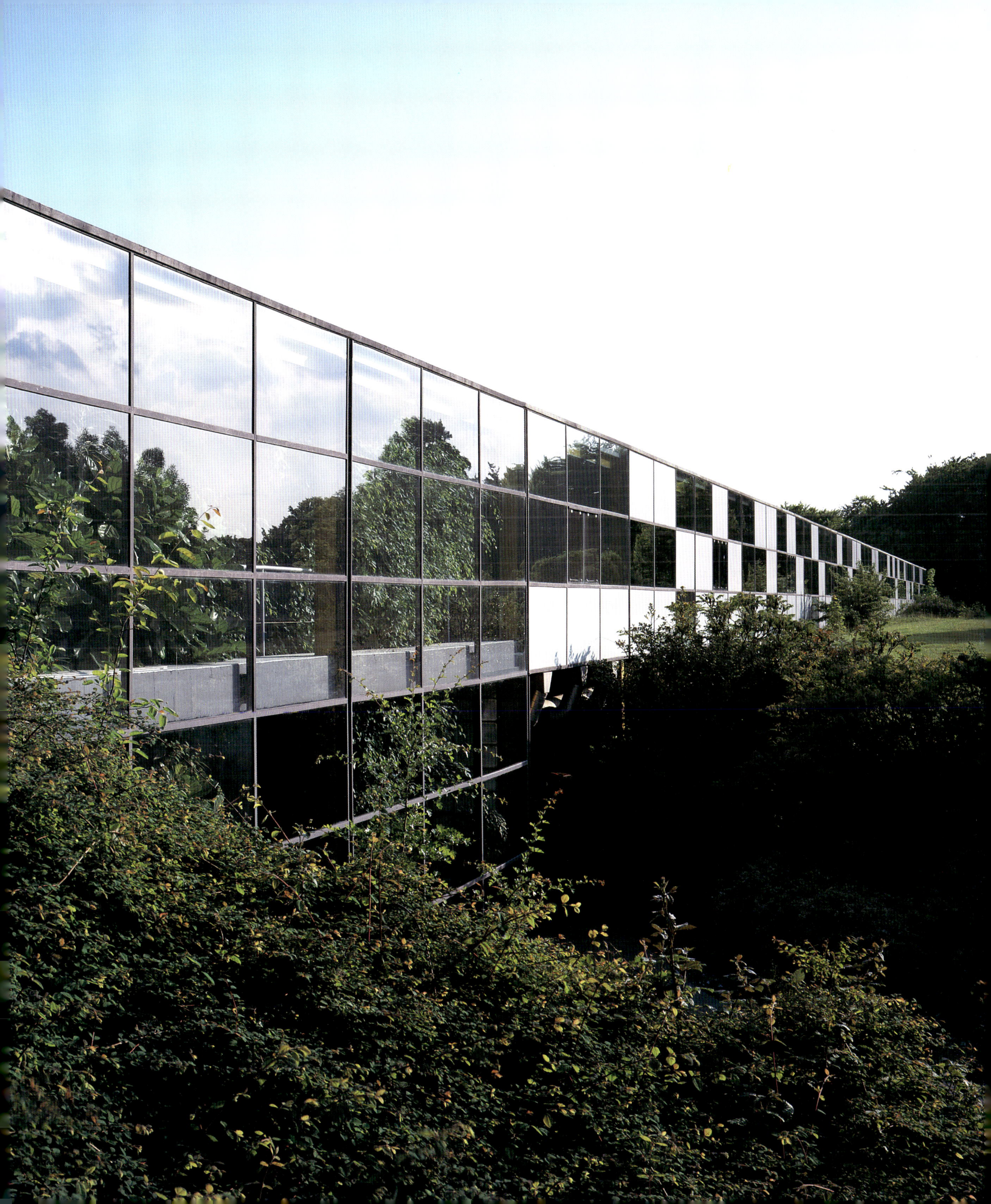

3

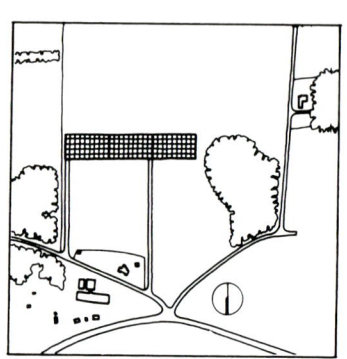

4

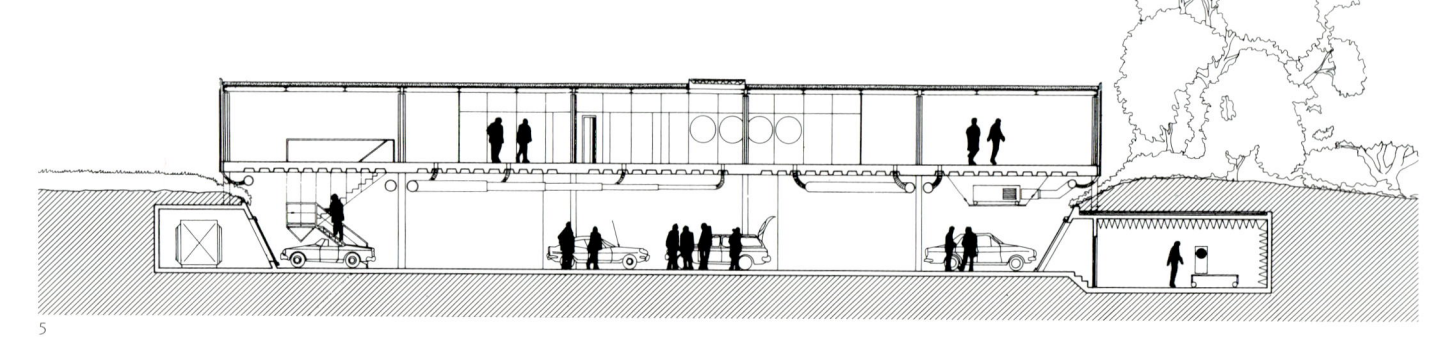

5

PA Technology Laboratory

The radical first scheme proposed an arched shed sunk in the landscape (1, p154). The building addresses the issues of integration and modern design within a green landscape (2, previous page & 3). It offers an adaptable interior configuration (6 & 7), opportunity for expansion (4) and concealment of parking (5).

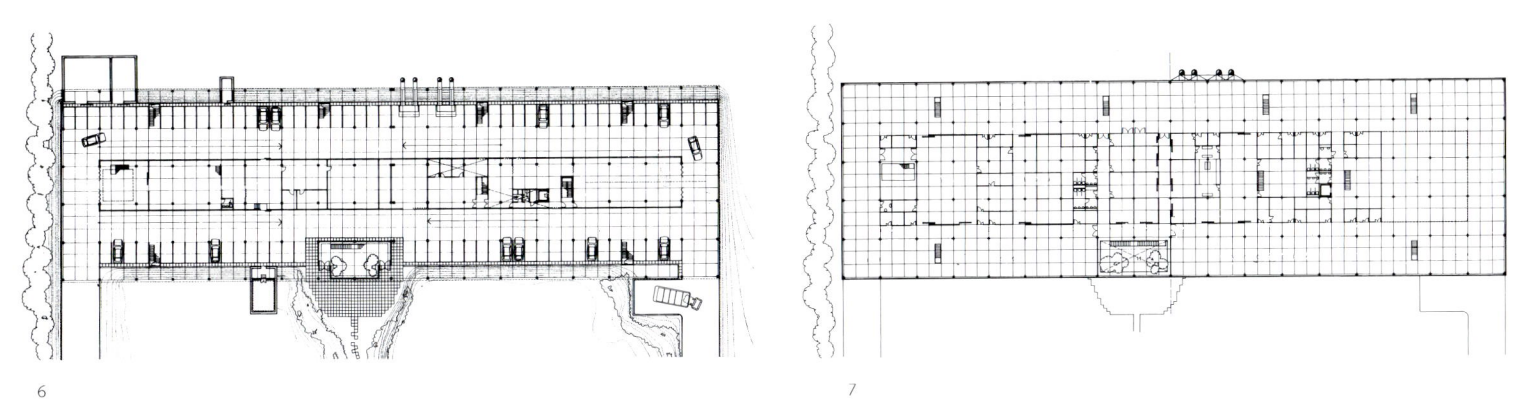

Services are suspended below the main slab of the building, on top of the parking and service zone (8). Solid and glazed panels are interchangeable.
The interior includes a double-height reception area at the centre of the building, planted and generously day-lit (10 & 12). Stairs lead directly from the building to the car park beneath (11).
An exploded axonometric (9) shows the main elements of the building system – a repetitive bay construction and sophisticated kit-of-parts.

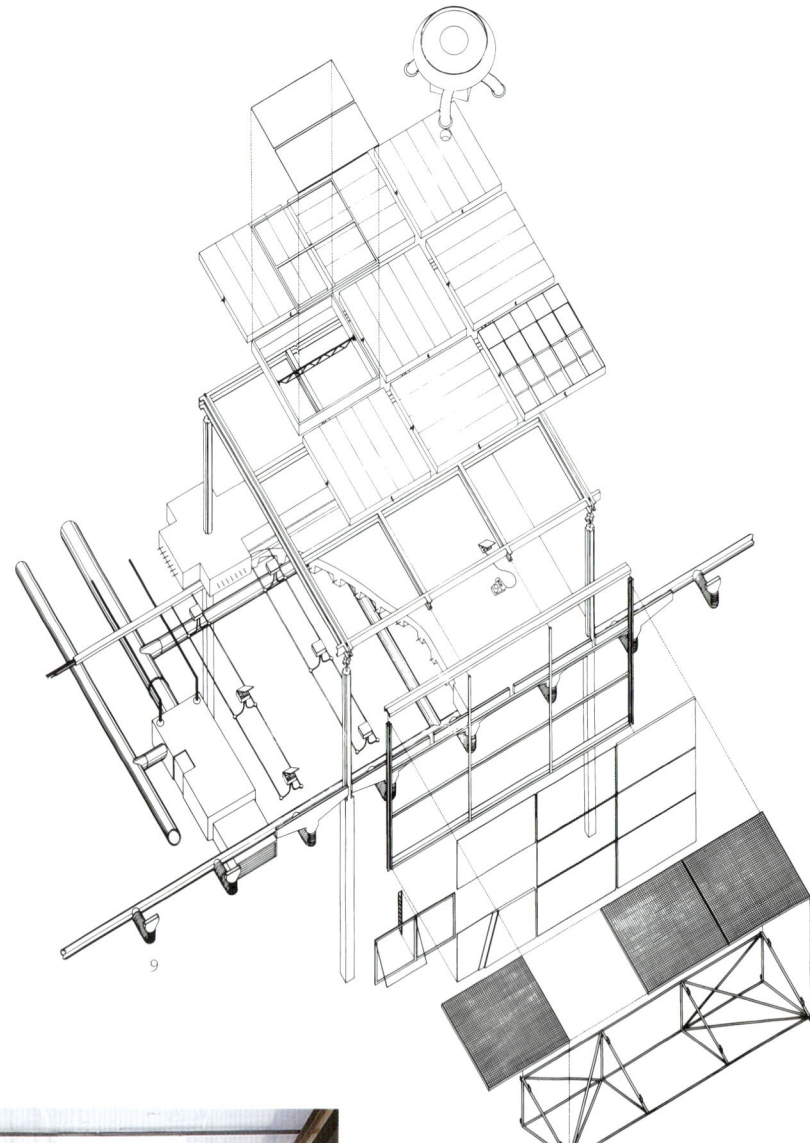

PA Technology Laboratory

12

Millbank Riverside Housing

London, 1977

The work carried out by the practice on the Park Road Development scheme in 1973 was not wasted. The stepped section and approach to natural lighting devised there were further developed at Millbank. The riverside site at Pimlico – adjacent to the northern end of Vauxhall Bridge – was, however, very different from that at Park Road. In the 1970s, the potential of the river had hardly struck most architects – many London developments simply turned their back on it. The Millbank scheme, however, capitalized on its setting, proposing apartments with very wide frontages to the river and generous terraced gardens. Flats were to be accessed through their own private gardens – like houses in the sky – and circulation was proposed along river walkways (the internal ramps connecting the floors were an echo of the Pompidou scheme, while lifts, which were to be accommodated in a detached service tower, provided a premonition of Lloyd's).

The underlying idea was of a riverside pier, the bones of which were to be composed of concrete while it was designed to support a framework of interchangeable steel components (a system which allowed a high degree of flexibility in the disposition of walls and windows). Here again, the affinity with Pompidou was clear. Unfortunately the scheme – along with other interesting projects for the area by a number of architects – came to nothing. In the end, Lacey, Jobst, Hyett built a monumental brick-clad development on the site.

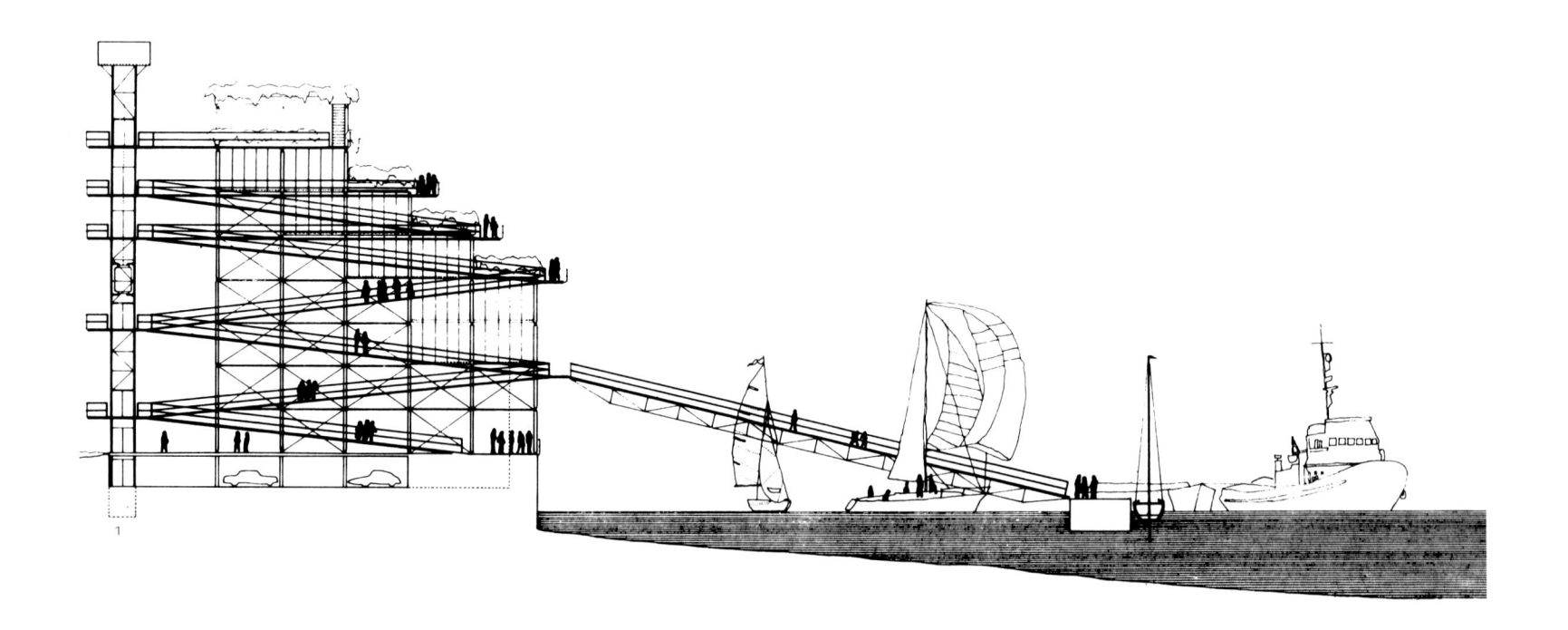

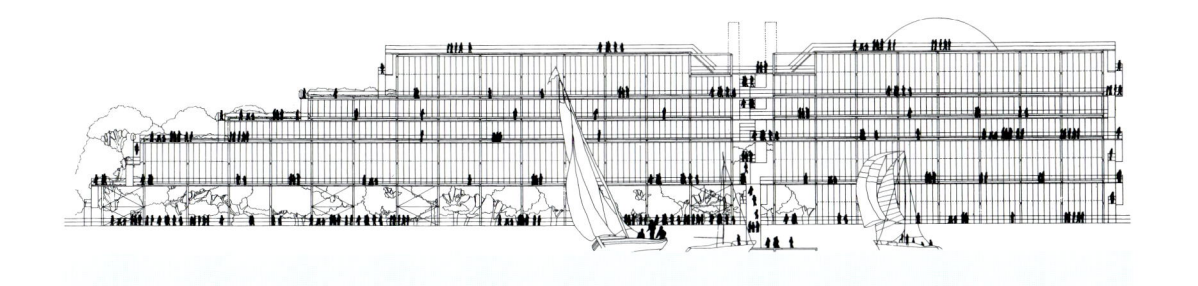

The Millbank housing project, never executed, applied the Kahnian language of 'served' and 'servant' spaces to a residential programme. Rigorous but romantic, the scheme was an early attempt by Rogers to address the particular issues of building on the banks of the River Thames (1–5).

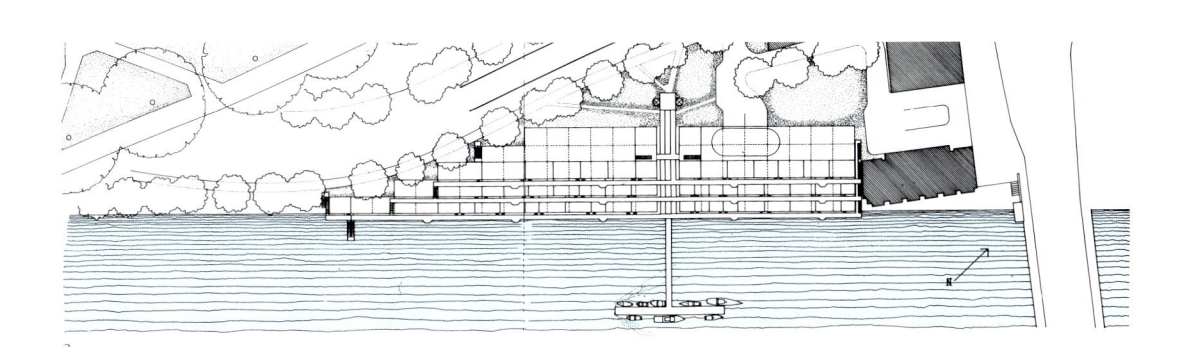

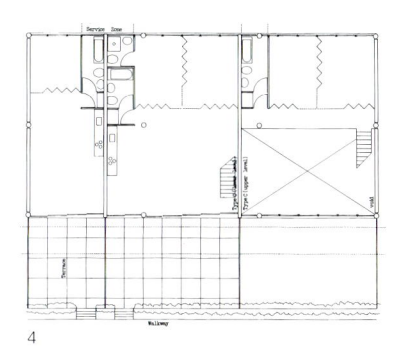

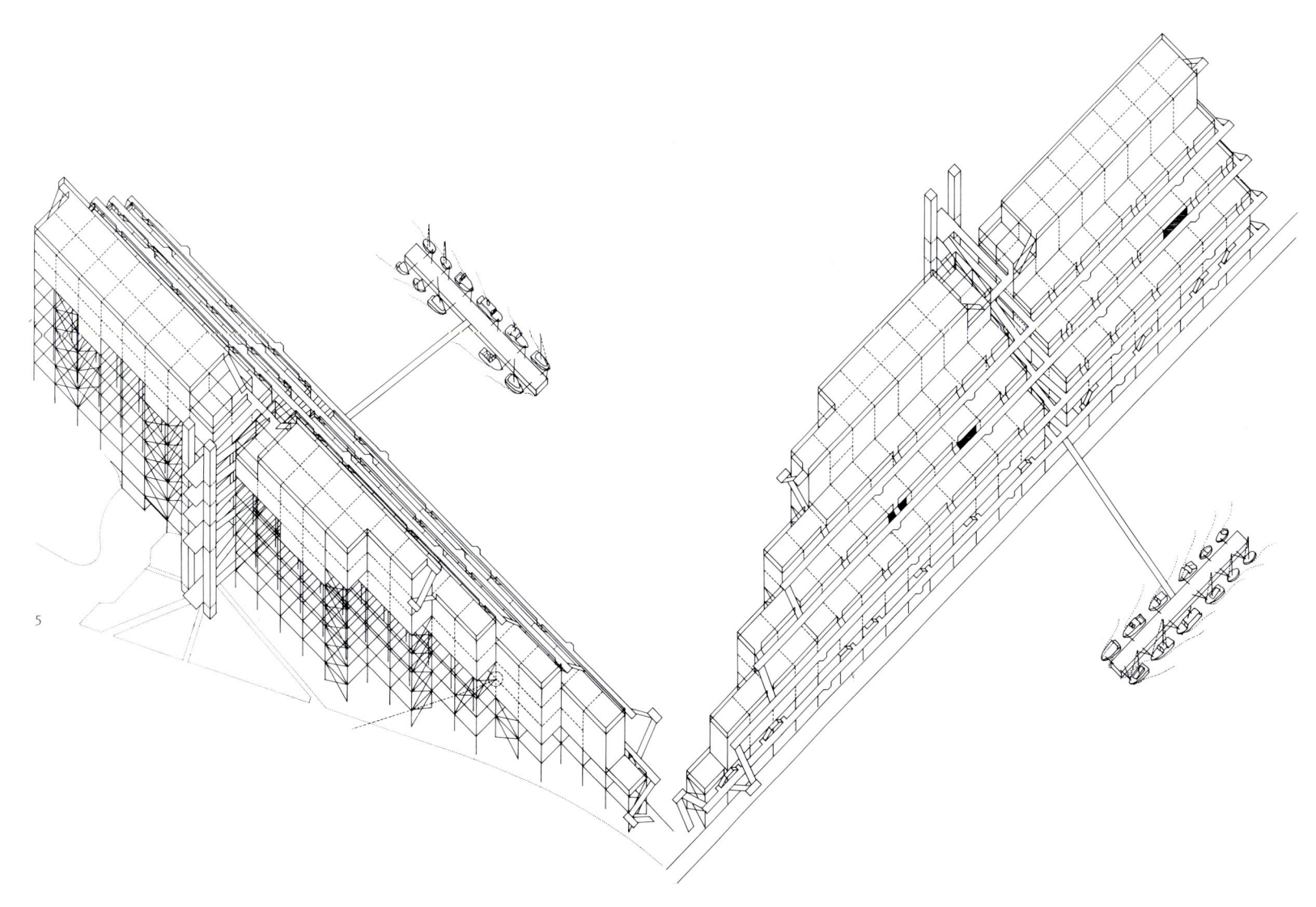

Richard Rogers Partnership

Origins, philosophy and ethos: a design community

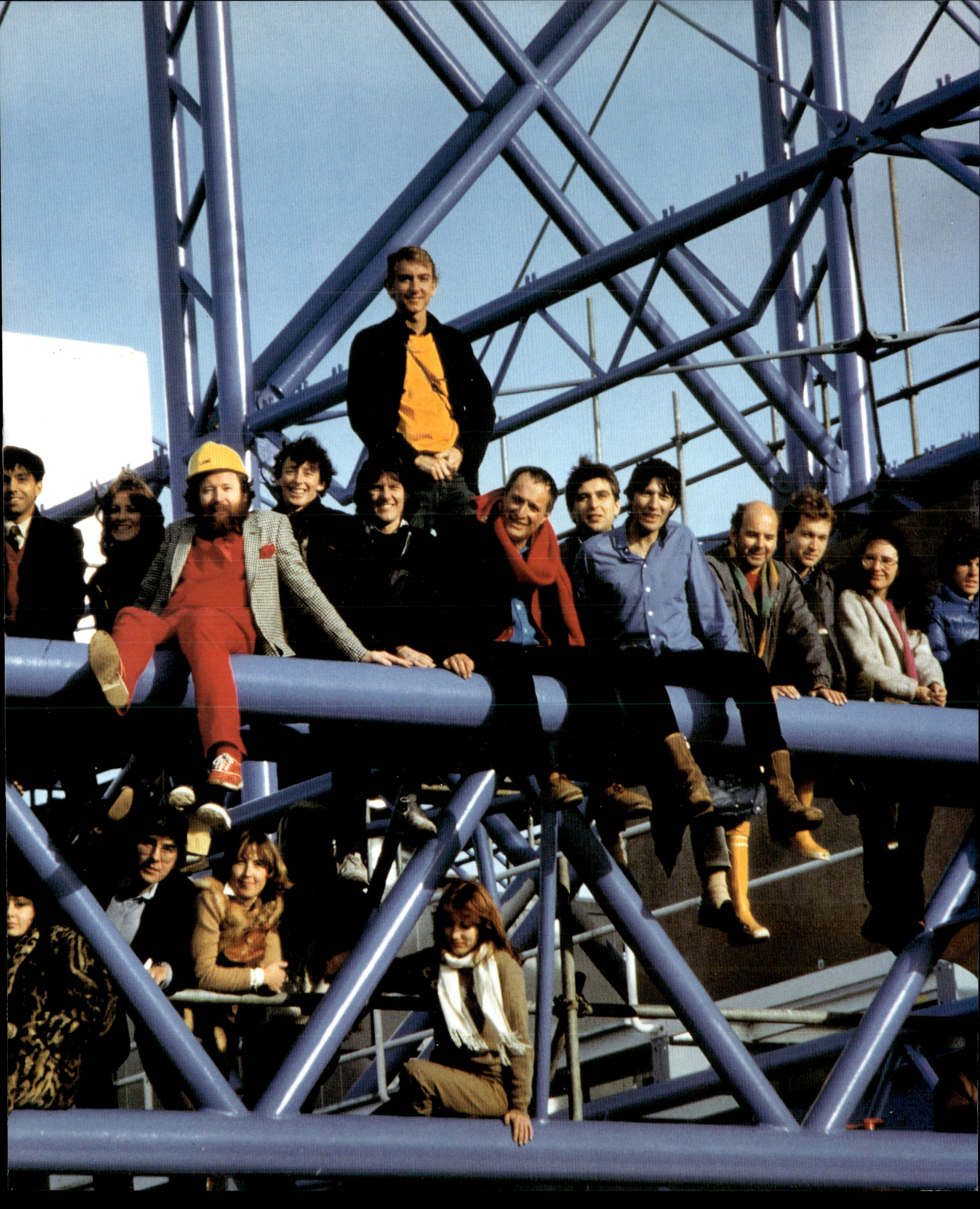

The Lloyd's Building confirmed Richard Rogers' pre-eminence on the British architectural scene: the award of the RIBA Royal Gold Medal for Architecture in 1985, as the structure was nearing completion, placed him among the hierarchy of the profession worldwide. His widening fame was the outcome not just of a growing body of commissions, but of his increasingly prominent role as the critic of conventional attitudes to architecture and urban design. Rogers' buildings did not simply *look* different – they posed cultural as much as architectural questions. What was a building for? What did it contribute to the public – as well as the private – good? How would it respond over the years to social and economic change? How was technological change to be reflected in the design of buildings? (Not, surely, by hiding new technology behind pseudo-historic facades.) Lloyd's summed up Rogers' perhaps unique ability, rooted in teamwork, to address these issues.

In retrospect, Lloyd's seems a near-miraculous achievement. Even before it was completed, the planning regime in the City of London had moved towards a conservative, conservation-led position, so that Rogers was not to complete another building in the City for over a decade. (His later involvement, in 1983, with a site at Whittington Avenue in the City ended in frustration: Rogers' concept of another radical building in the Lloyd's mould was arbitrarily dismissed. Indeed, City planners went so far as to suggest the models he might study – commercial buildings of the Victorian period replete with Gothic sculptures – in designing the exterior of the development. Rogers was prepared to compromise so far, but could not fall in line with the planners' prescriptions. The site was sold and a banal Post Modernist block was later built there, with the full support of the City.) Rogers is still vexed at the 'dogmatic' controls imposed 'by people who are first and foremost bureaucrats, lacking imagination, taste, creativity and theory'. He questions the need for aesthetic controls of this sort, pointing to the success of cities like Chicago where modern architects have been given a freer hand.

What was new at Lloyd's, at least in the British context, was the urban dimension – the building was arguably more significant for its contribution to the urban landscape than for its technical virtuosity. Lloyd's never made the generous concessions to the public domain that the architects had envisaged, with cafés, shops and the Nelson Collection as a public ground floor area. (After a few years, even the token public gallery was closed 'on security grounds'.) Yet the building's footprint is permeated by public space and it does not stand aloof and disconnected from its setting. Rogers related his building to the complex medieval fabric of the City. The proximity of Leadenhall Market was fortuitous and there were clear links between its iron and glass architecture and that of the new building. In its modest way, Leadenhall recalled the great galleries of nineteenth-century Italian cities. Lloyd's was not an isolated landmark, but part of an ever-changing urban organism. London, like Paris, seemed to offer enormous opportunities for architects who wanted to build in tune with, but not in obeisance to, history – all that was missing was the political will and the enlightened patronage. Lloyd's inaugurated an era in which Rogers addressed the needs and potential of London.

Lloyd's had further underlined the nature of Rogers' practice: its success was based on teamwork, which was developed as the very foundation of the office. John Young and Marco Goldschmied played key roles in the Lloyd's project and it also brought a younger generation into the office, some of them – like Graham Stirk, Amarjit Kalsi, Andrew Morris, Philip Gumuchdjian, Stig Larsen and Marcus Lee – to become mainstays of the firm in the 1990s. Others – like Richard Soundy, John Sorcinelli, Ian Davidson, Mark Guard, Malcolm Last, John McAslan, Jamie Troughton, Peter St John, Andrew Weston and Chris Wilkinson – went on to form their own practices and to become part of an acclaimed renaissance of British architecture. Lloyd's marked a watershed for the practice of Piano + Rogers. While Renzo Piano came to London as a gesture of support for the Lloyd's competition, in reality Piano + Rogers was two separate practices

The location for Antonioni's seminal film *Blow Up*, later to become the Richard Rogers Partnership's studio in Holland Park, London

John Young and Richard Rogers at the *Blow Up* studio, Holland Park, 1980

Interior view of the Holland Park studio

based in two different countries. Piano + Rogers was formally wound up and a new partnership – Richard Rogers + Partners (later Richard Rogers Partnership) – was formed. Lloyd's dominated the new Partnership for eight years and the fame and size of the practice grew apace in a period which became noted as a test-bed for research and innovation.

The founder directors with Rogers were John Young and Marco Goldschmied, with Mike Davies joining a couple of years later. Laurie Abbott – a veteran of Team 4 days – might well have been among them, but his inclinations were then, as ever, to maintain a degree of independence, with the freedom to pursue his own life, while maintaining a close association with the office. Davies had joined the Rogers' team at Pompidou, subsequently developing the office's fundamentally important research and development work and pushing it, in particular, towards energy-conscious, environmentally friendly design. Marco Goldschmied's talents as a strategist had been developed at Cambridge and confirmed at Lloyd's, and he rapidly came to occupy a dual role combining the planning and overseeing of projects with the financial management of the practice. Goldschmied acted very much as a foil to Rogers by not being afraid to 'tread on his toes'. John Young describes himself as 'first and foremost a constructor'. Making and detailing are his passions and they were fully exercised at Lloyd's. Young's fastidious concern for getting the details right underscored the work of the Rogers practice – to which he has been completely committed. Rogers, while also praising his significant understanding of spatial organization, calls Young 'a technical aesthete'.

Richard Rogers has always been the pivotal figure in the practice. It is Rogers, colleagues report, who drives the practice, the first to sense when a project is going off-course, with a clear view on what is needed to rescue it. Intuitive and romantic by instinct, a lover of grand gestures, of the accretive and the expressive, rather than the minimal or the refined, and a maker of architectural form in the tradition of his heroes Frank Lloyd Wright, Louis Kahn, Sant'Elia, Chareau and the Russian Constructivists, Rogers has been spokesman, critic, catalyst and, above all, inspirer. Yet Rogers is also a pragmatist, with an agenda for his work which extends beyond the purely architectural. It is Rogers, indeed, the dyslexic student whose attempts at drawing so depressed his AA tutors, who has given British architecture a new vision and underscored the vitality of the modern tradition internationally.

Visitors to the Rogers office – including the many members of the public interested in architecture but with no knowledge of its practice – are often excited to find that the staff are so enthusiastic, even fervent, about their work. There is a sense of the practice being a family without a rigid hierarchy; the founding, 'core' partners along with Laurie Abbott remain at the heart of the office, and there is a prevailing sense of continuity. Teamwork – whether within the organization or between it and key engineering (or other) consultants, such as Peter Rice, Tom Barker, Chris Wise or Klaus Bode – remains the guiding principle, as it was at Pompidou and Lloyd's, and the practice's written constitution brings a moral dimension into the business, enshrining ideas about community, teamwork, equity, collaboration and social responsibility. 'The practice of architecture is inseparable from the social and economic values of the individuals who practice it and the society which sustains it', the constitution states. 'We as individuals are responsible for contributing to the welfare of mankind ... ' The constitution defines a range of rules on ownership (the practice is entirely owned by charities, so no director has direct equity in the company or can pass control onto non-executive shareholders), pay (the highest paid director can only be paid six times the salary of the lowest paid architect of two years standing), profit (the company's profit is divided between employee profit sharing, contributions to charity and investment), charity (architects of two years standing are allocated a sum to be donated to a charity of his/her choice) and on eschewing work on military or

John Young and Richard Rogers with a detailed model of the entrance to the Lloyd's Building, 1983

The Lloyd's team (foreground, left to right): Sir Peter Green (Chairman of Lloyd's), Courtenay Blackmore (Lloyd's); (background, left to right): Geoffrey Ashworth (Monk Dunstone Associates), John Young (RRP), Marco Goldschmied (RRP), Peter Rice (Ove Arup), Richard Rogers (RRP), Mike Davies (RRP), Brian Pettifer (Bovis), Nick Ayres (Monk Dunstone Associates), John Smith (Bovis); Tom Barker from Ove Arup is missing from this photograph

The Richard Rogers Partnership office in Holland Park, London, c.1982

Richard Rogers and Marco Goldschmied at an Inmos site visit, 1982

environmentally damaging projects. The point of a constitution is to build a self-renewing dynamism into the practice/community and to head off the growth of a complacent hierarchy at the top.

Richard Rogers has never swerved far from the socialism which he espoused when still a schoolboy. His first job was in the Middlesex County Council, when public architecture was alive and well. The post-Pompidou Rogers practice was launched in a very different climate, as the Labour government in Britain steadily collapsed and was, in 1979, replaced by a Conservative one, led by Margaret Thatcher. As the UK economy recovered from the recession of the 1970s and the property market boomed, Britain – and especially London – was reshaped by market forces; Lloyd's – while a powerful statement about the public domain – was a commercial monument after all. After the debacle of the Cambridge shopping centre scheme in the 1970s, John Young had written: 'it is clear that the vastly different goals of a local community, a city council and a developer can never be one, and the professional team and the design become of secondary importance'. In the Britain (and increasingly, the world) of the 1980s, Rogers and colleagues, with Laurie Abbott as lead player, had to come to terms with the *realpolitik* of property development and a market-led economy. The saga of Coin Street was a 'baptism of fire' and a reflection of the radicalism and, to a degree, socialism which fired new recruits to the Rogers office. It epitomized what was to become, perhaps, Richard Rogers' most significant contribution to the British scene: his insistence that architecture must be conceived and practiced within an urban, political and economic context.

Coin Street is a minor thoroughfare on the South Bank of the River Thames, close to the South Bank arts centre and to Sir Denys Lasdun's National Theatre. Coin Street was surrounded by a sizeable area of vacant land and redundant industrial buildings, conveniently located close to the West End and City but ignored by developers

until the 1970s. The project which Rogers developed there for Greycoat Estates, which first approached the practice in 1979, was, however, to become a pointer to the future.

The first version of the Coin Street scheme was produced under pressure, since Greycoat (which owned only a third of the development site but had an option on the rest from the Greater London Council) faced an imminent planning inquiry – a number of possible development options were being examined with local community groups, backed by Lambeth Council, opposing the principle of office use on the site. The developers perhaps hoped that commissioning Rogers, whose Lloyd's building was much in the news, would help overcome objections – especially with a pro-market Tory government now in power. The image of the Pompidou Centre as a 'people's place' was also invoked.

The rejection of the Greycoat scheme in July 1980 was firm but not, it seemed, final. Rogers had been given little time to develop his ideas – 'Utopia takes a bit longer than two weeks', one critic commented. The government was concerned at the impact of commercial development on London's riverside. For Rogers, however, the river was not a problem but an enormous opportunity. Coin Street marked Richard Rogers' first engagement with the Thames, which was generally seen as an insuperable barrier between central London to the north and a cut-off hinterland to the south. Over the next twenty years, Rogers as architect, polemicist and urbanist, was to develop a contrary view: that the Thames represented an enormous opportunity as the lifeline and the true heart of London. The first version of the Coin Street scheme, described by Rogers as 'an open-ended infrastructure for local and city activities', contained all the elements of a new strategy. The offices were to be built around a great arcade, or galleria – a public space, with lots of shops, sweeping in a great curve from Waterloo Station to the river and culminating in a new footbridge to the north bank. At this period, the idea of a developer

John Nash's early nineteenth-century 'Golden Mile' plans for central London

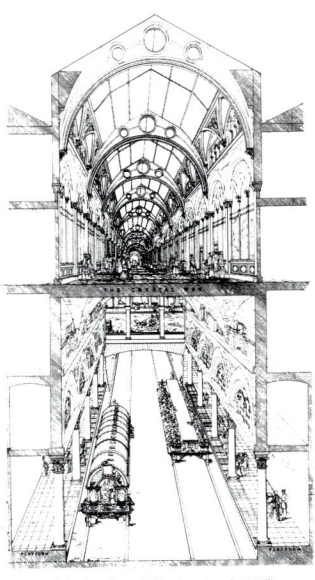

Proposal for the Crystal Way, London, by William Moseley, 1855

Galleria Vittoria Emanuele I, Milan, Italy – an inspiration for the Coin Street scheme

Coin Street scheme

providing a public amenity, such as a bridge, was novel. There would also be 20,000 sq.m. of housing alongside the 120,000 sq.m. of offices. This was to be a coherent, compact, mixed-use development with 98 per cent of the ground level being public/non-office space.

The decision letter issued by the Environment Secretary, Michael Heseltine – in a later incarnation, one of the promoters of the Greenwich Millennium Dome – ruled that the scheme constituted 'overdevelopment', but commented favourably on its mix of uses. Developer and architects were left to rethink their ideas. The scheme was modified and rethought even as the inquiry decision was awaited and critical opinion had swung firmly behind Rogers – 'the South Bank needs him – he should be given a chance', urged Colin Amery. 'Rogers has a chance of saving the South Bank', declared Peter Murray. 'It is surely obvious', commented *The Architects' Journal*, 'that if this imaginative scheme does not get planning permission, then the Coin Street area (and its vociferous residents) will be left to the mercy of a run-of-the-mill, straightforward commercial development'. The issue was not 'obvious' to Heseltine, but Greycoat and its architects were quick off the mark with revised proposals in the aftermath of his ruling. What adverse critics described as a 'Berlin Wall' of offices was broken down into a dramatic series of towers, structures with more than a hint of Lloyd's, linked by the great public galleria. There was more emphasis on linking the development to the existing street pattern via a series of 'gateways', as at Lloyd's, which seemed to grow out of the medieval street plan of the City of London. Indeed, the revised plans drew extensively on the thinking behind Lloyd's and as a result the megastructural elements were toned down. New planning applications were submitted to Lambeth and Southwark councils (the development crossed the borders of the two boroughs) at the end of 1980 and duly 'called in' by Heseltine in February 1981. A further public inquiry opened in April of that year.

In his evidence to the inquiry, Rogers explained that 'the aim is to create a linking and pulling riverside; a metropolitan, people magnet which will weave together the local environment, making the area a coherent whole, and give Londoners a meeting, working and living place on the South Bank'. The rhetoric was that of the Pompidou Centre – the development would create 'a dynamic place for those who live in the neighbourhood, those who work there, and for the tourists. It will be a centre where all can participate.' The solution to the problems of the area, Rogers argued, lay not in architecture alone but in a mix of activities and a radical dedication of the street level to public rather than private uses. The 480-metre long 'glazed street' at the centre of the Coin Street development would be 'full of light, sun and shade, with shops, restaurants and sports facilities mixing with the offices' (the latter confined to upper floors). It recalled the nineteenth-century 'Crystal Way' by William Moseley, a visionary – and unrealized – proposal for the West End of London. Conceding that much post-war development had produced hostile and anonymous environments, Rogers looked back to the achievements of the past, to Nash's replanning of central London, for example. Nash's work had stood the test of time. Rogers intended to ensure that his would do the same by designing for change. The servicing strategy would allow for long life and adaptability – 'the office or shop may become the workshop, the home or the university of tomorrow, or vice versa', he argued. The proposed mix of uses might change radically in the future. For the present, a substantial area of housing was proposed, most of it around Stamford Street with a smaller area on the riverfront, partly on the site of the Oxo Tower, a popular landmark but an obstacle to proper utilization of the site. The housing should be high density, Rogers argued, 'to generate a vigorous and interesting community'. (A mix of private and 'social' housing was envisaged.) Workshops, providing for light industrial and craft uses (including those servicing the South Bank arts centre and theatres), were provided. At the river end of the glazed street would be a large piazza, clearly modelled on the one at Beaubourg, suitable for open air markets, street theatre or concerts and balancing 'the more elitist activities of the rest of the South Bank', but with the particular attraction of a location directly on the riverside. Beyond would be the bridge, an elegant, almost ethereal structure linking the pedestrian route from Waterloo through to the north bank of the river, St Paul's and the City (this element was, however, dropped from the revised scheme at the developer's behest – it was seen as too controversial – to Rogers' chagrin). Rogers concluded his submission to the inquiry by stating: 'Today, probably for the last time, we stand on a knife edge as to whether this place will become the lively public activity area we have aimed at and dreamed about ... a place for all people. We have a unique opportunity. The choice is ours.'

The opportunity was lost. In the second, long-running, public inquiry the choice for London was stark: either Rogers' 'meeting, working and living place', which used the profits of commercial development to create public benefits, or the rented housing proposed by the Coin Street Action Group. Michael Heseltine ducked the issue by approving both. The Rogers scheme was described as 'an architectural solution commensurate with the metropolitan importance of the site ... a desirable form of development'. But the long delays had undermined the scheme and it was finally abandoned in 1984. The land reverted to the GLC and was passed on to the newly-formed Coin Street Community Group, which developed housing there, initially in an abject vernacular cottage manner out of keeping with a site so close to the heart of London. (Ironically, the later – far better – housing at Coin Street, together with the conversion of the Oxo Building, was entrusted to Lifschutz Davidson, a practice in which Ian Davidson, a sometime member of the Rogers office, was a partner.) 'Community architecture', a movement eagerly taken up in the mid-1980s by the Prince of Wales and promoted by his disciple, sometime RIBA President Rod Hackney, began to be associated, not unfairly, with sloppy and even reactionary design.

The protracted Coin Street story depressed and disappointed Rogers and his colleagues immensely; not least since they had been cast in the role of servants of the property industry and enemies of the community – there were even demonstrations outside the practice's offices in Holland Park. 'I felt we were fighting a totally unrealistic, essentially suburban view', says Rogers. 'But we suffered from an image problem. We were seen as Goliath to their [the community campaigners] David.' David won – 'and I suppose that the democratic system did triumph', says Rogers. The Coin Street project had, however, at least introduced Richard Rogers + Partners to the South Bank, where the practice was to return with a major scheme for the arts centre in the 1990s, and to the politics of development in London. At Coin Street, Rogers had worked with Stuart Lipton of Greycoat, an enlightened developer, subsequently the creator of Broadgate in the City and of Stockley Park (the model business park of the 1980s), who was later to become a fellow trustee of the Architecture Foundation, as well as Gary Hart in the legal team. (A further member of the team was Derry Irvine QC, later Lord Chancellor in Tony Blair's government.)

Richard Rogers took a pragmatic view of the property world, believing that private profit and public gain could be combined. The development project for London's National Gallery highlighted the potential of combining the two. The National Gallery needed an extension. The Thatcher government was not prepared to provide funding for it. So a bizarre – and ultimately fruitless – attempt was made to provide the requisite new galleries as a spin-off from an office scheme. The site, next to the National Gallery in Trafalgar Square, was that of Hampton's, a department store levelled by wartime bombs and subsequently left vacant, operating as a car park. Developers were invited to join up with architects and, in effect, make their bids for the site, which was government-owned. In return for a peppercorn lease on the land, the successful bidder would provide wall space on which would be hung the Gallery's collection of Renaissance paintings and, in return, would be allowed to build offices to fund the project. There were 79 submissions and seven were shortlisted by a jury chaired by Sir Hugh Casson, then President of the Royal Academy: Ahrends, Burton & Koralek with Trafalgar House; Spratley & Cullearn/Barratt Ltd; Skidmore, Owings & Merrill/London Land; Sheppard Robson/London & Metropolitan; Covell, Matthews, Wheatley/London & Edinburgh Trust; Arup Associates/Rosehaugh; and Rogers, working, on this occasion, with Trevor Osborne and Derek Park of the developers Speyhawk. All seven were put on display at the National Gallery in the summer 1982, and public comment then invited.

The Rogers scheme, in which Laurie Abbott and John Sorcinelli played key roles with Peter Rice as structural engineer, was a further development of the architectural language of Lloyd's, but far more important were the cultural and urbanistic influences flowing from Pompidou and Coin Street; this was another challenge to established ways of thinking about cities. The gallery space was contained within a rectangular structure, top-lit – services, including air conditioning, had to be concentrated at floor level – accompanied by a number of servant towers around its perimeter, providing access and escape routes, reminiscent of Lloyd's. The offices were to be provided in an irregularly-shaped structure, sitting below and clearly detached from the galleries – commerce subordinated to art in a brave attempt to defy the spirit of the Thatcher age. Keeping the offices quite separate left open the option of removing or converting them in the future.

A key consideration in the design was the skyline of the surrounding area. The main Regency facade of William Wilkins' National Gallery – a building which had never been much admired, even when new – focused on a weak and undersized dome. More emphatic were Nelson's Column, in the centre of the Square, and the elegant spire of James Gibbs' neo-classical church of St Martin-in-the-Fields to the east. To balance the spire of St Martin's, Rogers provided a new vertical element in his Gallery scheme: a tower with a restaurant and coffee shop on top, enjoying

Foster and Partners, Hongkong and Shanghai Bank, Hong Kong, 1979–86. Foster's entry to the 'Big Three' exhibition, 1986

James Stirling Michael Wilford & Associates, Neue Staatsgalerie, Stuttgart, 1977–84. Stirling's entry to the 'Big Three' exhibition, 1986

Richard Rogers at the Royal Academy with the model for 'London as it Could Be', his entry for the 'Big Three' exhibition

wonderful views of the heart of London.

The proposals were, indeed, radical, and came at a time when British architecture was about to face a powerful reaction from conservative, populist forces led by the Prince of Wales. The Rogers scheme made no attempt whatever to ape the architectural style of its neighbours by 'fitting in' – it stood apart from its Regency neighbour, to which it was barely attached, and superficially looked like a brazen attempt to build a mini-Pompidou Centre in London. Only when the visual relationship between the new building and the other elements in the square was considered did the radical contextualism of the project become clear. The galleries inside would have offered the same high degree of flexibility as those at Beaubourg – a move at odds with the conventional outlook of the National Gallery.

The real strengths of the scheme lay in its contribution to the 'public realm' (a notion which was itself regarded as radical in Thatcherite circles). Rogers conceived the National Gallery as part of the life of London, not an insulated temple of art. By elevating the galleries, Rogers was able to provide a clear and inviting pedestrian route through from Leicester Square behind the building to Trafalgar Square in front of it. A tunnel would then dip down beneath the road to emerge in the Square – 'closing the road was seen as simply too radical', says Rogers. 'It would have been dismissed out of hand – and had, in fact, been ruled out in the competition brief.' By providing shop units along the tunnel, the architects made the latter more inviting – and underpinned the financial viability of the scheme. It was an astute move and it was typical of Rogers that the urban diagram came first, considered in the light of the functional brief. The architectural form and details emerged later. The project was as much about the city as about housing paintings.

The National Gallery competition finalists were exhaustively analysed by press and critics and the exhibition of schemes attracted considerable public interest. Owen Luder, then President of the RIBA, weighed in on Rogers' side, declaring: 'This is the architecture of a man who says, "Sod you! This is the way it's going to be".' (Rogers believes that this forthright statement 'did more harm than good'. The scheme was designed, not as a defiant statement of principle but as a practical response to a client brief and to the wider needs of London.) Rogers' proposals won considerable public support, but polarized opinion – they were voted both the best and the worst entry. The winner of the competition was, in fact, the scheme produced by Ahrends, Burton & Koralek, who subsequently introduced a tower into their designs, conceding Rogers' point that the square needed a new vertical element.

ABK's triumph was, however, short-lived. After their scheme was lambasted in a speech at Hampton Court by the Prince of Wales in 1984, it was rejected by the government. The idea of combining galleries and offices was quietly dropped and, with the Sainsbury family providing financial backing (up to £30 million), a new competition was launched for galleries alone. The invited schemes were all in a broadly classical or post modernist mould – 'it was a club of

PoMos', says Rogers – and included designs by James Stirling, Jeremy Dixon + Edward Jones and Piers Gough. The eventual winners (in 1986) were Robert Venturi and Denise Scott-Brown, whose joky, sub-classical scheme was duly built and named the Sainsbury Wing. It provided adequate, if unmemorable (and totally inflexible), spaces for showing pictures, but failed utterly as public architecture. Where Rogers (and ABK) proposed a new landmark, Venturi Scott-Brown built a formless, recessive structure, meekly deferring to the platitudes of Wilkins and ducking the urban issues altogether.

Rogers' National Gallery scheme is one of the most remarkable of the office's unbuilt projects, not only for its striking form but equally for its assured approach to urban planning. It would have been a landmark in the advance of modern architecture in Britain. The victory of the traditionalists was extremely depressing for Rogers and his supporters. Trafalgar Square remained a battleground between opposing views of the city – at the end of the twentieth century his plans to reclaim the square for people were yet to be realized.

The early years of the Richard Rogers Partnership were rich in ideas but frustratingly thin in terms of executed schemes. The practice had to pay its way as a business, with no likelihood of the sort of public support given to architects in France. Yet its idealism remained undimmed. Philip Gumuchdjian, one of the younger generation recruited in 1980, recalls the office in those days as 'incredibly exciting. Britain seemed to be stuck in the mud and we were on a mission – the *enfants terribles* trying to pull it out, entering uncharted territory, baiting the establishment and sometimes annoying a lot of people.' Nevertheless there had to be fee-earning schemes. The projects for Napp Laboratories at Cambridge (1979), with a striking masted structure engineered by Tony Hunt (Rogers' long-standing engineering collaborator), and for Free Trade Wharf in London Docklands (1981), where renovation of historic warehouses was to be combined with a run of new flats along the Thames, remained unbuilt. The modest development of industrial units at Maidenhead, a project begun in 1982 under Pierre Botschi's supervision, was an elegant notch above the typical scheme of its sort, but hardly a major landmark. The Inmos Microprocessor Factory in South Wales *was* completed in 1982, producing a building which challenges the assumption that a concern for technology necessarily leads to 'functionalism'. The kit-of-parts building was developed by Mike Davies with Tony Hunt. Reyner Banham wrote of it: 'What Inmos emphatically offers is that Old Modern Movement dream of infinitely adaptable clear space between a floor plane below and a roof plane above, and thus belongs in a rich and authoritative tradition that runs back through the SCSD schools prototypes of Ezra Ehrenkrantz, Mies's Farnsworth House, Albert Kahn's wartime bomber plants, to the Barcelona Pavilion.' Yet the purism of Mies was, as always, absent. The look of the building reflected a pragmatic approach to the job it had to do: it appeared indeterminate and flexible, not a finite object.

While Coin Street and the National Gallery competition had ended in failure for the Rogers office, the public profile of the practice had been much raised and Richard Rogers had become a public personality in Britain. By the time that Lloyd's was opened in 1986, his architecture was sufficiently familiar to become a popular subject for newspaper cartoonists; Rogers was demonized by 'traditionalists', and lionized by those – including many young architects – who saw him as a source of renewal for modern architecture in Britain. He identified himself with the modernist cause, appearing as a witness at the public inquiry into Peter Palumbo's Mansion House Square scheme in 1984. (Rogers saw the attacks on the project as essentially reactionary and, alone of front-rank British practitioners, dared to have an intellectual debate and go into print in *The Times* against the Prince of Wales, who had openly objected to the scheme.)

It was Rogers' standing on the world scene that won him the Royal Gold Medal for Architecture in 1985. For all the vitality of the post-war architectural scene in Britain, few British architects had achieved international renown. Among those living, only Sir Hugh Casson came anywhere near the fame of a past master like Lutyens – and Casson was famous as an artist and wit rather than for his architecture. Casson's greatest achievement, perhaps, was to breathe new life into the hitherto stuffy Royal Academy of Arts, where high-profile exhibitions attracted the public in droves. In 1986 the Academy mounted a major exhibition of the acknowledged 'big three' of British architecture: Rogers, Norman Foster and James Stirling. Foster showed his monumental Hongkong & Shanghai Bank, and Stirling showed the Neue Staatsgalerie in Stuttgart, the masterpiece of the post modern classical manner he had adopted in the 1980s. The Rogers office exhibited not a completed building, but a vision of a revivified public realm – 'London as it could be'. This in the heyday of Thatcher's free-booting experiment in market economics – 'there is no such thing as society', the Prime Minister had declared.

Spectacularly shown in an installation, with a huge, water-filled model depicting the Thames, the exhibit developed the ideas of Coin Street and the National Gallery project. Integrating the South Bank into central London was a key concern. As in the Coin Street scheme, a new bridge, this time on the line of the existing Hungerford railway bridge into Charing Cross, itself a replacement of an elegant Regency footbridge, was proposed, with attached islands to animate the life of the river. The railway bridge, Rogers proposed, should become redundant, with the rail tracks terminating at Waterloo and a rapid transit system shuttling passengers across the river. The pedestrian route from Waterloo, across the South Bank, would continue up a pedestrianized Northumberland Avenue to Charing Cross and Trafalgar Square, itself to be largely closed to traffic and linked by a new route to Leicester Square. The Thames, Rogers believed, was the key to a more civilized London. The Victoria Embankment had thrown a busy road along the north bank of the river, so that Somerset House, for example, with its great arches which previously opened directly on to water, was isolated behind a wall of traffic. By digging a new road tunnel, partly below the river, the traffic could be removed and the riverside recreated as a public space. On the South Bank, the

Rogers proposals aimed to create new pedestrian routes between the arts centre and Waterloo Station, with the system of drab underpasses beneath the roads suppressed.

The chances of this vision coming to reality were, of course, nil and Rogers and his team, with Laurie Abbott and Philip Gumuchdjian to the fore, were well aware of that fact and quite unabashed. Their project, which attracted intense media interest, was a campaigning move, a statement of what *could* (and should) be rather than what was likely to happen in the short term. A more pragmatic approach prevailed, with Charing Cross station cemented permanently in place by Terry Farrell's air rights development on top of it. Waterloo Station became more significant after the opening of Nicholas Grimshaw's Waterloo International terminal there in 1990 – this focused attention on the future of the South Bank and brought Richard Rogers Partnership back as masterplanners for the reconfiguration of the arts centre and its surroundings. Richard Rogers' personal exasperation with the market-dominated thinking of the Tories drove him into an alliance with the Labour opposition, to active collaboration with Labour in the run up to the 1992 general election, and, in due course, to his becoming a Labour peer. In retrospect, 'London as it could be' was as important a project as any completed Rogers building. During the 1980s, the Rogers office was advancing technically, refining its approach to the hardware of buildings. Alongside, however, it was developing other themes which radically qualified the popular myth of 'High-Tech' as a determinist architectural language, spawned by an obsession with the machine. In the view of Graham Stirk (who joined the office in 1983 to work on Lloyd's) 'the hardware was incidental to the development of a social and intellectual philosophy of design. Being 'High-Tech' didn't rule out more traditional civic values, which technology could actually serve.'

Rogers' buildings have always been about movement and change – modern lifts and escalator banks enhanced mobility and animated the facades of buildings. Rogers used them as part of a vocabulary of design which scorned composition (in the way that term was used by the Post Modernists and neo-traditionalists) but placed a strong emphasis on the look of buildings and their relationship to streets and public places, the scale and grain of cities. Richard Rogers, like many other great architects, is no draughtsman, yet he always has a clear vision of the diagram of a building and a conception of the way in which it relates to its surroundings. Rogers' view of the city was, in this sense, more genuinely traditional than that of the various architects who backed the Prince of Wales' campaigns for pastiche cities. For Rogers, cities were places that posed questions – there were no certainties, no easy solutions. Both symbolic and functional, cities were meeting places. Public space was part of their very essence, yet it was being eroded by private needs and greed. The Modern Movement, with its stress on individual monuments, was partly to blame. A new, modern urban architecture had to be developed in tune with a renaissance of the public realm which meant 'giving the streets back to the people' – these concerns seemed

The Partners at the Lloyd's Building, 1986: John Young, Richard Rogers, Mike Davies and Marco Goldschmied

Celebrating the award of the RIBA Gold Medal to Renzo Piano at the Richard Rogers Partnership offices, 1989

Peter Rice

absent from the Prince's programme. Rogers' architecture was in harmony with his vision. It retained a fresh, even experimental quality which linked it to the work of a younger generation for whom the old Modern Movement dogmas were not just questionable (as they had been for Rogers in his youth) but were archaeological curiosities.

A short distance downriver from the South Bank, at Billingsgate, Rogers was able to realize a more specific element of regeneration. The former Billingsgate Market was earmarked for closure and redevelopment, its operations being transferred to the Docklands. With Horace Jones' handsome market building of 1874–7 – iron and glass inside and clad with classical details externally – demolished, the City Corporation would be able to sell the site for a large sum and was prepared to approve a large office development there. Fortunately, there were those who opposed this destructive approach – vigorously and with some imagination. SAVE Britain's Heritage, the conservation lobby group masterminded by Marcus Binney, was determined to save Billingsgate, while recognizing that the building could not be simply preserved as a monument. Binney admired the work of Rogers and had endorsed the Lloyd's project – though it involved demolishing a listed building. He asked Rogers for help with Billingsgate but the Rogers office was hard-pressed and initially suggested that Alan Stanton might be able to help. He produced a radical strategy for conservation, suggesting that the market could become specialized, Covent Garden-style shopping, with offices developed on an adjacent lorry park. Despite rearguard resistance from the City – and bogus claims that the building would collapse when the refrigeration was switched off – Billingsgate was listed by the government and demolition effectively ruled out.

The Rogers office subsequently took up the project of refurbishing Billingsgate into a dealing room. In the hands of Marco Goldschmied, Pierre Botschi and their team, the scheme became a benchmark for an approach which combined painstaking restoration of old work with radical new intervention. For Richard Rogers, there was nothing new in such thinking, which informed, for example, the brilliant restoration of the Castello Sforza in Milan done by Ernesto Rogers and his colleagues at BBPR; Rogers recalls seeing the project on site on one of his holiday visits to Italy. In Britain, the emphasis tended to be on 'keeping in keeping', though historically Ruskin and Morris – the founders of the conservation movement – had argued that any new addition to an old building should be in a contrasting style and should reflect the thinking of its own age.

The space available inside the building was increased by the addition of a new mezzanine floor at first floor level, suspended from steel hangers and supported by new steel columns at the perimeter. The top-floor 'haddock' gallery itself was retained intact, creating a strikingly simple and direct space. At basement level, accommodation was found for services and support amenities. The essence of the scheme was not structural change but a massive upgrading of services to support a thousand computers and many miles of cabling, a task which seemed daunting. So heavy were the servicing requirements – and so tight the constraints on adding to the existing building – that an additional plantroom had to be constructed, sunk into the mud 7 metres out into the river.

The Billingsgate scheme, completed in 1988, was a triumph in architectural and preservation terms. Even the Prince of Wales approved of it and wrote to Richard Rogers to praise the way in which it demonstrated the practicality of incorporating 'radically new uses in historic buildings without disturbing their integrity'. The Prince, who added 'I realize that this may not be the sort of accolade you want', enthused about the building's 'wonderful sense of space'. The City, which had tried hard to have the market demolished, now used it as a model example of creative re-use and restoration. The Billingsgate project had been, in fact, a trying experience, with the client's brief constantly changing and the introduction of a project manager complicating the task of the architects. Moreover, the rehabilitated building was never used by the client, whose operational requirements had changed, and remained empty for years before a new user eventually occupied it. Billingsgate remains, however, an exemplar of adaptive re-use and the restored riverside frontage of the market is a landmark on the Thames.

Some miles upstream of Billingsgate, the Richard Rogers Partnership was responsible for the renaissance of a less exalted group of old buildings. With Lloyd's underway and other work in hand, the practice needed a larger office and found one at Thames Wharf on Rainville Road in Hammersmith. The riverside site was occupied by a rundown oil depot, but included some solid and convertible brick warehouses among the tangle of sheds and tanks. Acquired in 1983, the buildings were partly converted to the company's offices, and partly refurbished as lettable workshop and office space for small, design-based firms. The remainder of the site was earmarked for housing, carried out to Rogers' design in 1984–7. The housing reflected a growing concern in the practice's work for contextual issues: extensive use of brick mirrored the neighbouring warehouses and was balanced by areas of glazing and projecting balconies in nautical-looking steelwork. Thames Wharf was to become a true home to the practice – John Young later carried out a dazzling design of one of the apartments there as his own London home. The opening of the River Café, run by Ruthie Rogers and her partner Rose Gray – both inspired cooks – reinforced its attractions.

The Richard Rogers Partnership

When Richard and Ruth Rogers returned to London after the completion of the Pompidou Centre, they lived in Richard's old flat in Hampstead. In 1984, they bought a pair of listed early nineteenth-century houses on the corner of Royal Avenue, facing Wren's Royal Hospital. Having abandoned long-cherished ideas of building a new house for lack of finding an available site, Richard Rogers accepted that the best alternative was a thoroughgoing refurbishment scheme. On a trip to Venice, Rogers drew up a sketch scheme in his hotel room. He admired the civility of the houses, but his instincts balked at the idea of living in a series of small rooms. By removing an entire floor, he would be able to create a lofty living space which focused, not surprisingly, on the kitchen. Ruthie Rogers, who initially had doubts about the sense of losing so much floorspace, recalls: 'I'd always wanted a room big enough to ride a bike around!' The entire internal structure of the houses was, in fact, stripped out and replaced with a new modern structural frame. Many of the detailed elements in the scheme were beyond the experience of the craftsmen. Only the involvement of Laurie Abbot and Nick McLean of Ove Arup & Partners, an engineer with a great deal of practical experience in rehabilitation, bridged the gap between the idea and its realization.

The new Rogers house was, Ruthie Rogers says, 'heaven – with all the family in layers'. The Rogers themselves slept in a gallery overlooking the main living space, accessed via a staircase designed by Laurie Abbott and Peter Rice. At ground and basement levels were flats for Ruth's mother and some of the Rogers children, others of whom were accommodated on the top floor of the house with its own staircase, acting as a refuge from the world of adults. Although Royal Avenue seemed to some a far remove from traditional notions of domestic comfort, it came into its own as a place for an extended family to gather and as a venue for some memorable parties. It reflected the same social and domestic ideals which had produced the Rogers House and Creek Vean. The house was launched with a bang. Richard Rogers' 50th birthday occurred around the time that work started on site and a dinner, with everyone in the office invited, was held in the shell of the building. Royal Avenue was a very personal project, yet it exemplified an inclusive vision of architecture and the city. Transparent, open and radical but within the framework of an historic square, it was a place of views, in and out.

The Rogers practice bears the strong stamp of Richard Rogers' own personality, but it has never been an autocracy. The diversity of the individuals who form the practice make it what it is. John Young, for example, with his passion for materials and components (reflected in his striking London apartment), Mike Davies, an enthusiast for 1930s architecture, restorer of a Berthold Lubetkin house and a passionate astronomer, and Marco Goldschmied, who retreats from London to a 1920s house close to the Solent. It is here that the Rogers office has its annual weekend away, with everyone in the office, plus partners and offspring, and a select group of associates and friends invited and accommodated in a string of local hotels. Few people, least of all the senior members of the firm, are missing. To the outside world, the weekend might seem rather frivolous; in the context of the practice, it is an essential occasion. The Rogers office is a very sociable place and it produces sociable architecture which uses a technological language, yet at its core embodies values which would have been familiar to the Renaissance architects whom Rogers has always so admired. Rogers has taken those values and rethought them for the present age: one of mass democracy, urban crisis and technological change. Rogers' achievement has been to ignore the sceptics who said that modern architecture was dead, and to prove that it still has the potential to make the world a better and happier place. Only by imagining the apparently impossible and striving to make it happen has he cracked the mould of caution and conservatism.

By the end of Lloyd's, the Partnership had assembled a team which would carry the practice through to the millennium and beyond – the partners in 1996 (left to right): Graham Stirk, Laurie Abbott, Andrew Morris, Amo Kalsi, Mike Davies, Marco Goldschmied, Richard Rogers, Lennart Grut, John Young and Ivan Harbour

Lloyd's of London

London, 1978–86

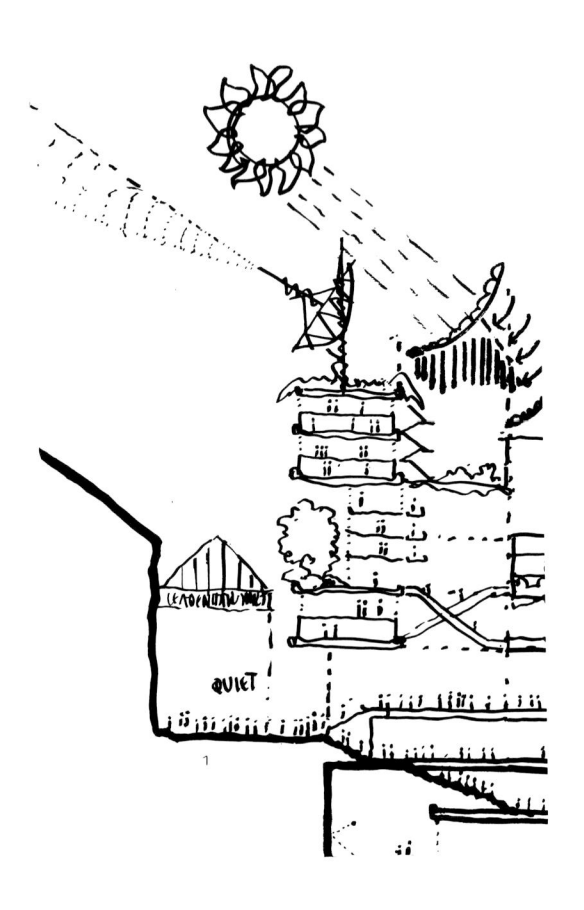

Completed in 1986, Lloyd's has become a symbol of London, and of the City of London in particular, as well as an emblem of the renaissance of British architecture in the 1980s. It is a radical and revolutionary structure; created for an historic and, in some respects, conservative corporation, it was designed to accommodate change. No new City building of the post-war era has so fearlessly rejected the compromise of historical pastiche – of 'keeping in keeping' – and yet none has made such a positive contribution to the historic locality in which it stands. At once forward-looking and, at the same time, evocative of some of the most captivating visions of the heroic age of modern architecture, Lloyd's is a building which is full of tensions and contradictions. A machine for making money? A place for people? An abstractly beautiful piece of sculpture? Lloyd's is all these and more. It appears, in retrospect, as the product of a heroic moment in British architecture. Yet Lloyd's was not the product of chance circumstances but of a unique process of partnership and collaboration; of inspired and intelligent patronage.

Lloyd's of London, the world's biggest insurance market, is a place which trades in, often huge, risks – it is a place that is neither static nor staid. Nor is it a monolithic corporate body, like the big banks and insurance companies which are its City neighbours. Lloyd's is a club, where the members elect the Committee and pay the administrative staff. It is a place for individualists, a fact which Richard Rogers and his team could never forget when they were designing its new headquarters.

When the Rogers practice first got to know Lloyd's in 1977, the famous City institution had moved the centre of its operations twice in half a century. Founded by Edward Lloyd in a coffee house in Tower Street, close to the Tower of London, in 1688, Lloyd's had left the coffee house era by the 1770s and found accommodation in the Royal Exchange – a token of its growing importance and respectability. It was to stay there until the 1920s when the sheer scale of its operations made a move inevitable. A site was acquired in Leadenhall Street and Sir Edwin Cooper, an architect who was a favourite with prestigious City institutions, was commissioned to design the new building. The site was, in fact, quite awkward, since most of the frontage on to the main thoroughfare of Leadenhall Street had been taken up by another Cooper-designed block, Royal Mail House. Completed in 1928, Cooper's building was soon inadequate in size. Luckily, Royal Mail House came on to the market and was acquired by Lloyd's in 1936. The two buildings were rather untidily joined together, producing a lot of circuitous corridors and inconvenient spaces.

In 1952 work started on a 'new' Lloyd's. The architect of the new building was Terence Heysham, who produced a suave but rather bland exercise in stripped classicism. It was linked to the 1928 building by a bridge above Lime Street.

It was the continued growth of Lloyd's during the 1960s and 1970s which made Heysham's building, designed to 'see Lloyd's into the twenty-first century', redundant. The Room, with a capacity of 1,500,

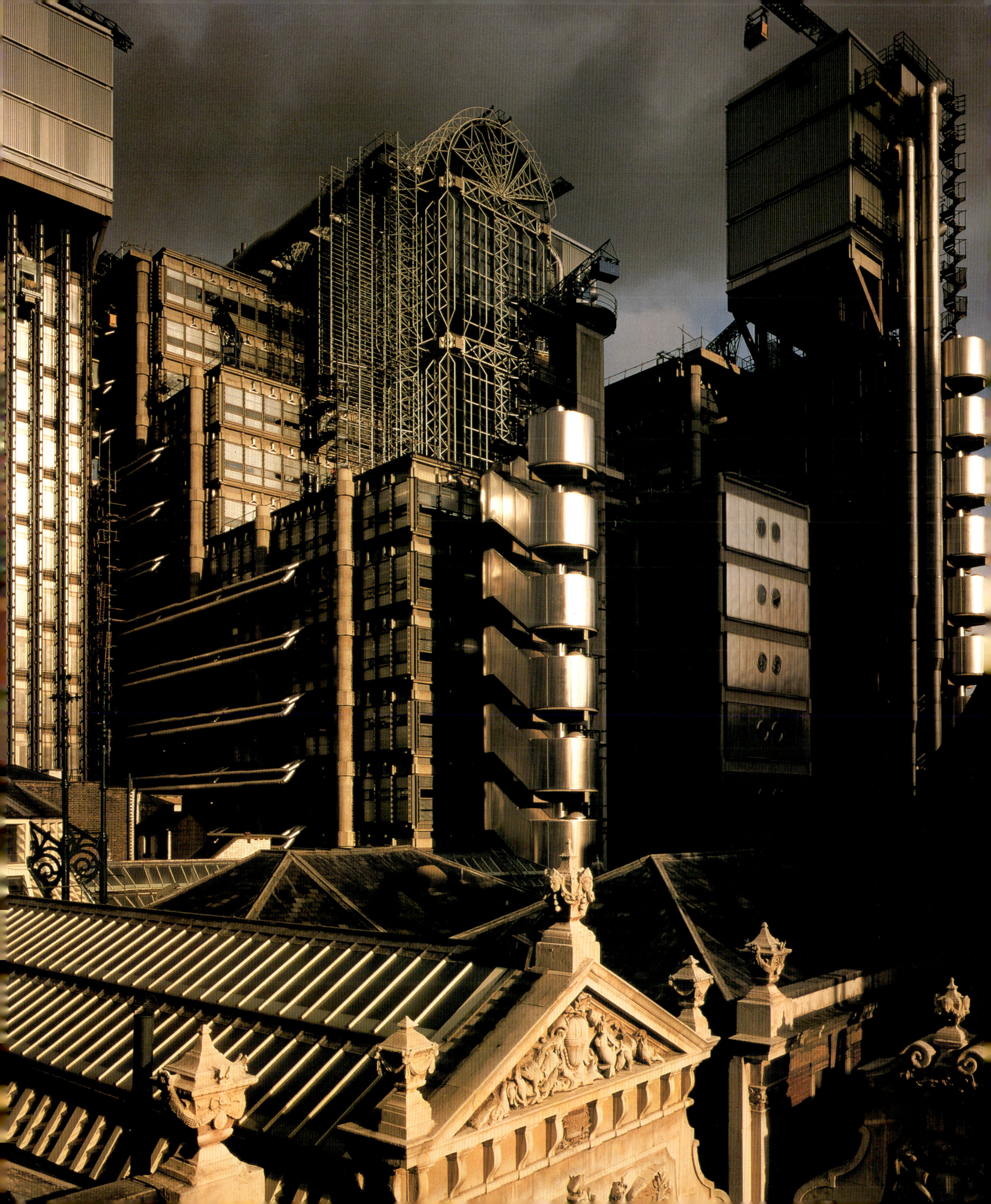

The Lloyd's building is set among a network of medieval streets at the heart of the City of London, south of Leadenhall Street (1 & 2, previous pages & 4).
The form of the building, with its working spaces ringed by a series of service towers (6), evokes the plan of a medieval castle (5). Rogers' competition proposal (3) did not suggest an architectural solution. Instead, a series of options for the future development of Lloyd's was explored before the architects concluded that redevelopment of the 1928 building was vital.
A new alleyway links Leadenhall Street to Leadenhall Market via a retained archway of the 1928 Lloyd's Building (7).

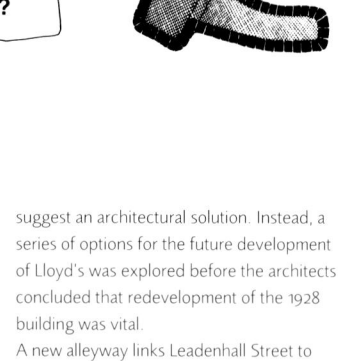

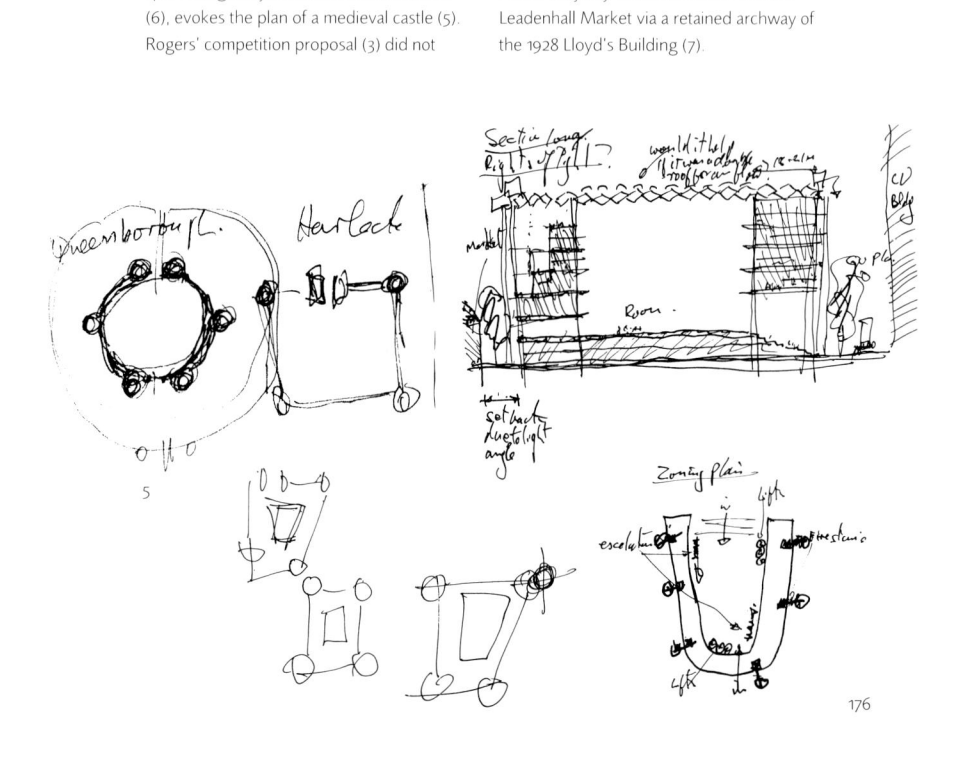

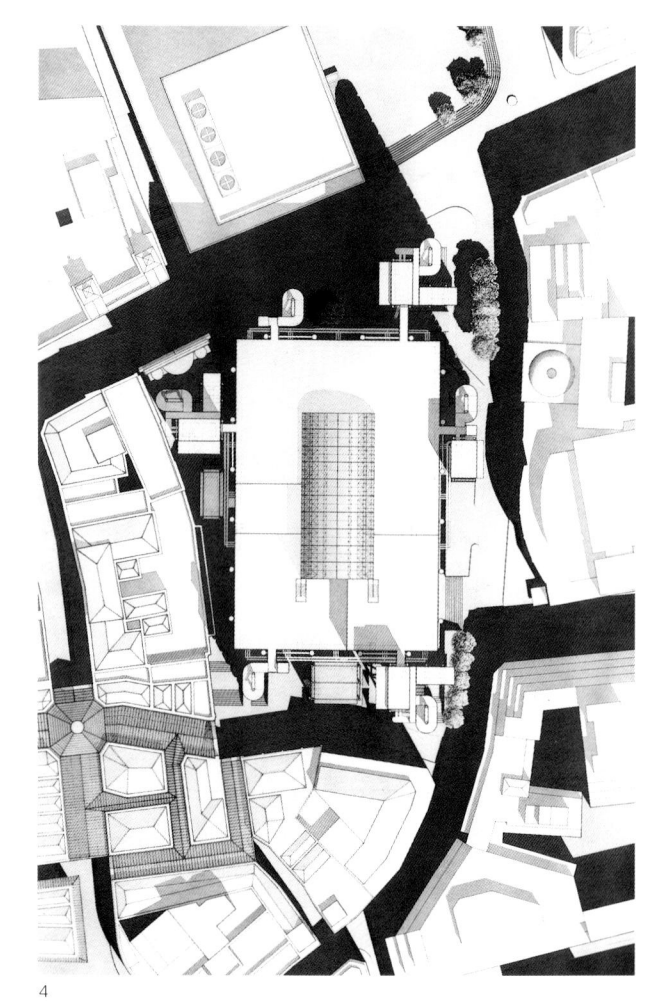

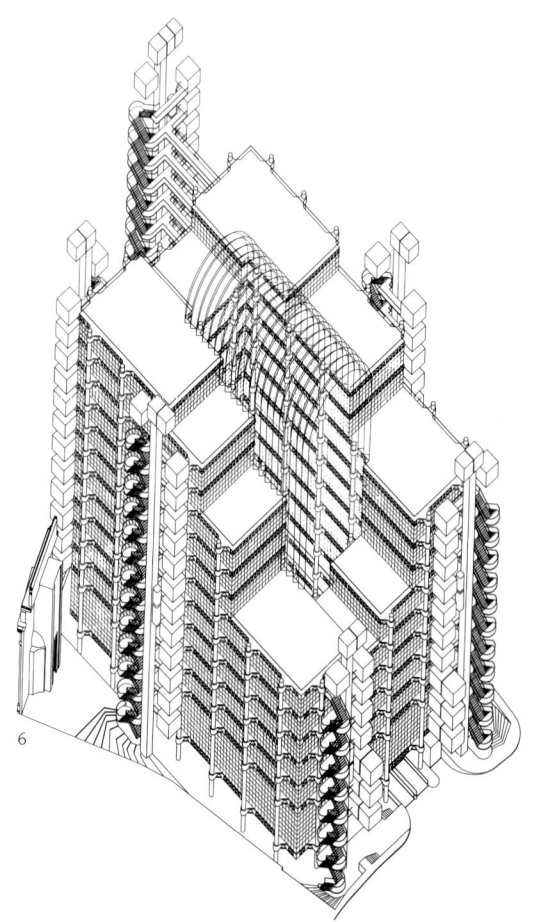

7

was simply too small. More underwriting space was needed – and quickly if Lloyd's was not to suffer. Lloyd's plans came to the notice of Gordon Graham, recently elected as President of the Royal Institute of British Architects, eager to see some of Britain's bright young practices get work and well aware that Lloyd's could be the British commission of the decade. Graham went to see Sir Ian Findlay, the Chairman, and advised him that Lloyd's should look not for a scheme but for a strategy – one priority was keeping Lloyd's in operation during the rebuilding process. 'I told Lloyd's to find an architect and work with him on a development strategy before even thinking about designs', Graham recalls.

Richard Rogers Partnership's victory in the Lloyd's competition was the outcome of the firm's response to Gordon Graham's formula – strategy first, scheme second. A flexible place of work, rather than a one-off monument, was required. It was not immediately obvious that the 1928 building had to go. The range of possibilities would be presented and the client invited to work through them with the architects, who offered twenty-six distinct options, including one providing for conversion of the Cooper building.

Lloyd's wanted continuity of trading, the potential for expansion and contraction, and the retention of the Room as a unified space, the historic heart of the institution. The architects looked at the two previous purpose-built buildings and concluded that, while built to last centuries, they suffered from an inability to accommodate change. It should be possible, they argued, to distinguish between those parts of a building which were permanent and unchanging and those areas which were subject to obsolescence and deterioration. Richard Rogers' interest in prefabrication, in the impermanent monumentality of the Constructivists and Archigram, and the dynamic visions of the Futurists (Antonio Sant'Elia especially) was reflected in Lloyd's, but the project was also strongly influenced by the work of Louis Kahn. It was Kahn's notion of 'served' and 'servant' spaces which impressed Rogers. At Pompidou, the perimeter walls had housed the services. In the case of Lloyd's, they were concentrated in towers in the manner of Kahn's Richards Medical Laboratories at the University of Pennsylvania.

A new building, Rogers believed, should take the form of a

The irregular and varied form of J.G. Street's Law Courts on the Strand (8), a response to the informal townscape of London, was one inspiration behind Rogers' approach at Lloyd's.
The building is primarily seen obliquely and in the context of narrow streets and alleyways (9), to which its 'Gothic' drama responds strongly. The only full view is from the Commercial Union Plaza (10).

'doughnut', with rings of underwriting space serviced from the perimeter encircling an atrium – in effect, the Larkin Building formula, though updated to take account of modern technical needs. Potential conservationist objections to demolition were assuaged by the proposal that the grand arched portal on Leadenhall Street be retained as a memory of the old Lloyd's.

Rogers' outline proposal report put to Lloyd's in June 1979 showed a building with all the essential elements of that eventually constructed. It was to total around 522,000 sq.ft. gross (375,000 sq.ft. net), a 66 per cent increase over the Cooper buildings and implying a plot ratio of around 7.9:1. The Redevelopment Committee of Lloyd's enthusiastically accepted Rogers' ideas, which centred on a central glazed atrium surrounded by galleries, some of which would be lettable offices. The concept offered Lloyd's a building with greatly enhanced value, and the element of flexibility (present from the beginning) produced a building which could respond to change. (Should the densely populated market expand upwards, it was possible to add on more service towers to provide for the greater numbers of people.)

There were key issues to be decided before a final design could be produced. First, would the new building contain just the Room and ancillary offices, or should it become the 'new' Lloyd's, with the Chairman's suite, committee room and Captains' Room transferred there? The Rogers team felt strongly that it should be exactly that and eventually managed to convince the client. The committee room took the form of a splendid Adam dining-room bodily transferred from the demolished Bowood House, Wiltshire, and relocated (in a badly cut-down form) in the Heysham building in 1957. It was now to move again. The Captains' Room, the architects proposed, should be sited on top of the new building, where members could enjoy fine views across the City. On this matter Lloyd's disagreed, and the restaurant went to the ground floor. The character of the ground level was a second subject for prolonged discussion. Rogers felt strongly that it should be a public space, encouraging City workers and tourists. A wine bar, coffee house and display area for Lloyd's treasured Nelson Collection would open off a central court, an irregular, amoeba-shaped space. The Lloyd's Committee did accept this idea, but intensified security concerns have effectively barred the public from Lloyd's, watering down the architect's vision of it as an extension of the City's streets, a retort to the hostile anonymity of most of its neighbours.

By early 1980 the detailed configuration of the new building had emerged, so that Rogers could present the scheme to the City in July of that year. The City finally approved the detailed plans in May of the following year, by which time demolition work (which had proved considerably more problematic than expected) was virtually complete. The basic 'doughnut' plan remained, but the building had emerged clearly as a forceful, dramatic new City monument. The most startling feature was clearly the external profile, punctuated by the servicing towers (modest, as it turned out, in comparison with

Lloyd's of London

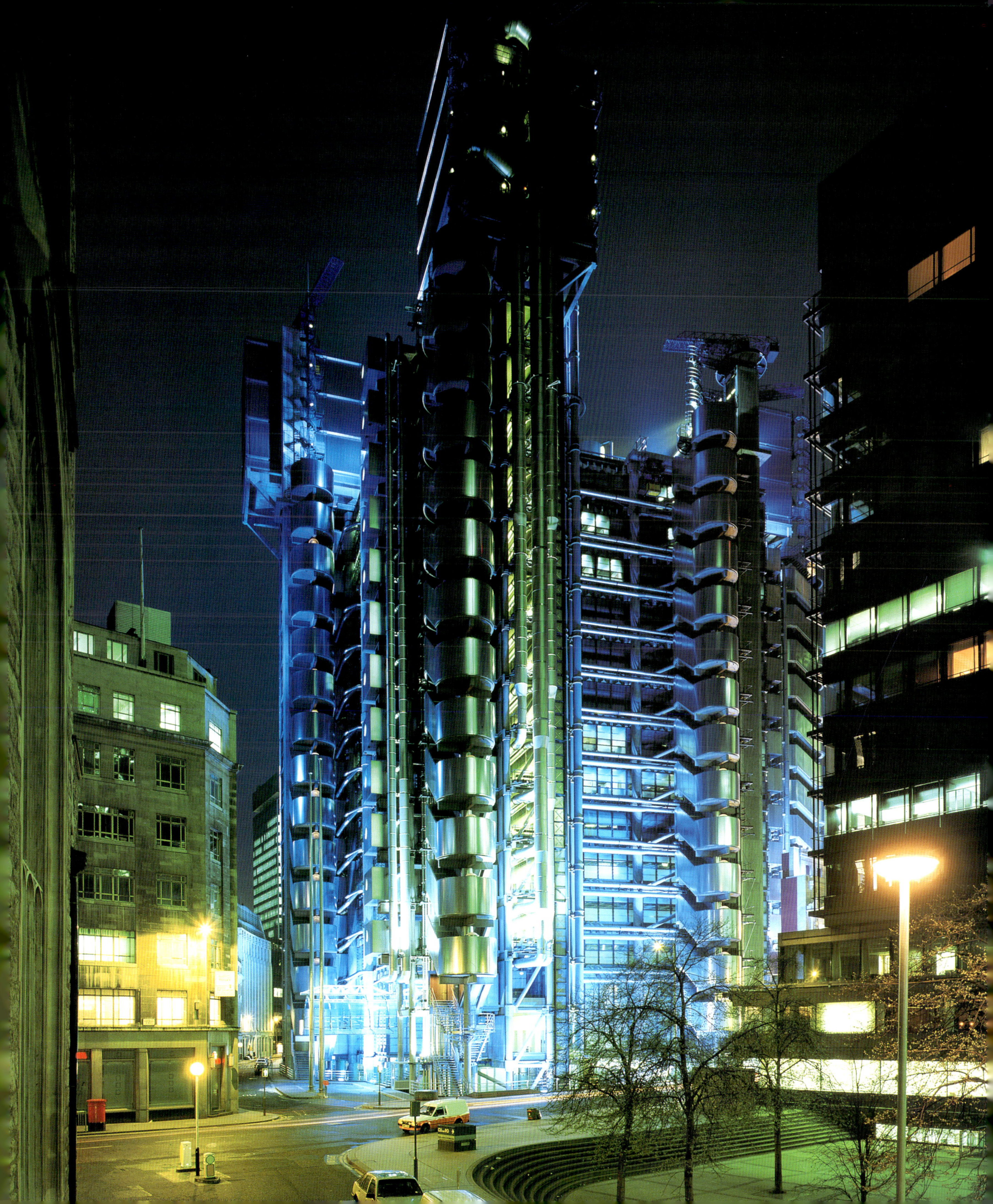

Dealing space for the Lloyd's insurance market is arranged around a full-height central atrium – escalators provide easy access to the first four levels (11). At lower ground level, general access, servicing and restaurant facilities are provided (12). Public space surrounding the exterior of the building gives partial public access. The service towers are ranged round the perimeter, a practical strategy but equally one which gives the building a dramatic skyline (13).

Lloyd's of London

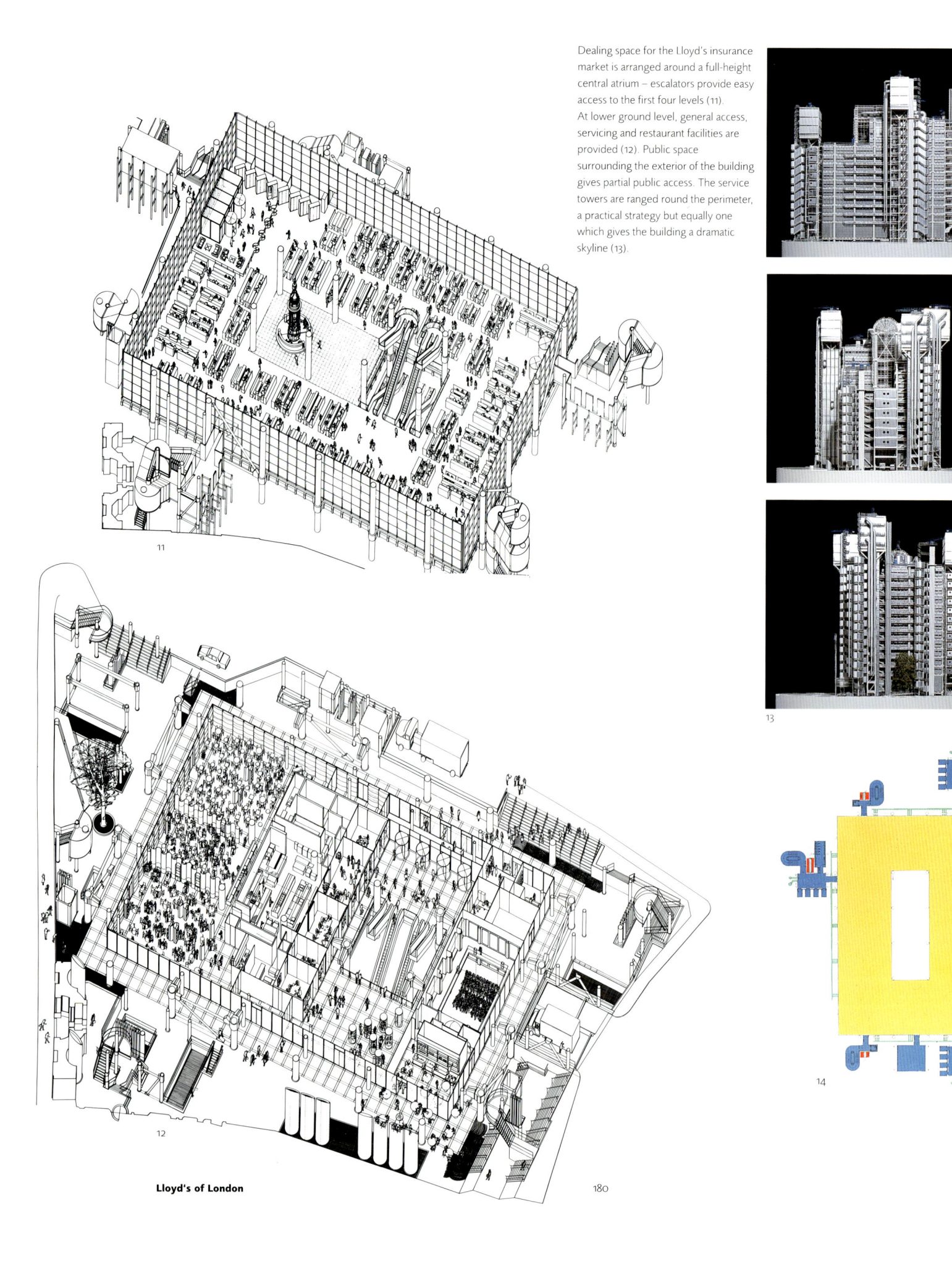

15   16   17

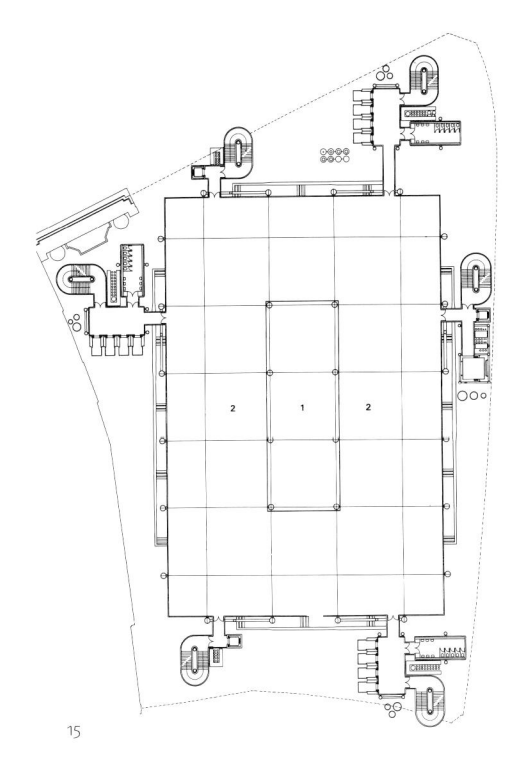

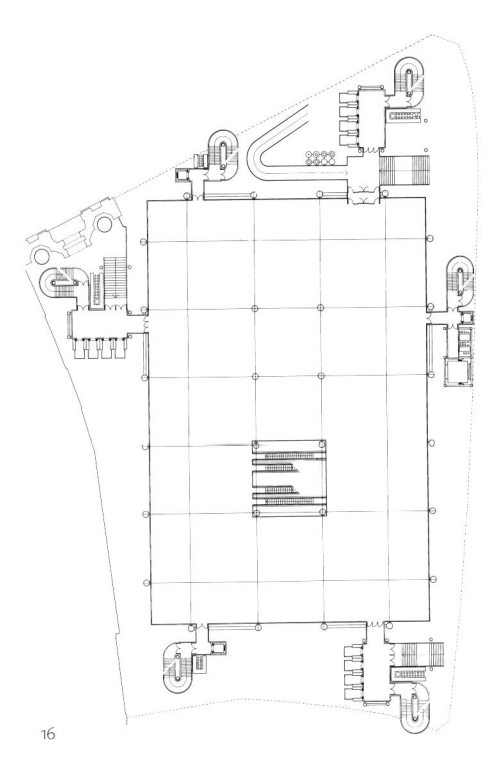

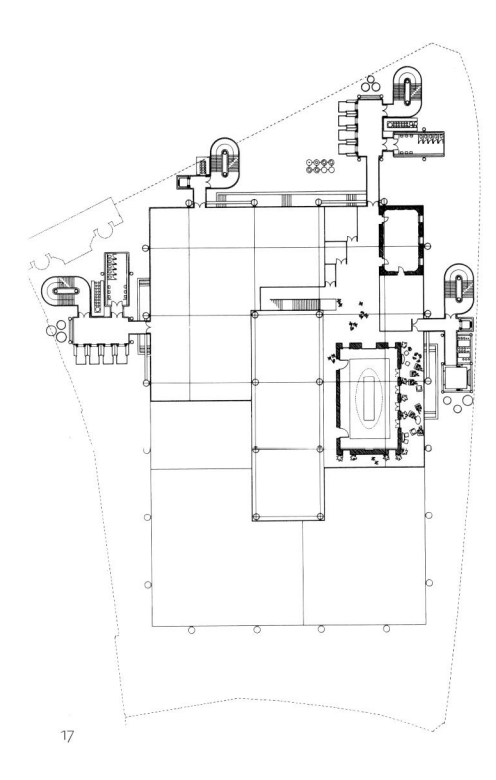

The location of the service towers allows totally uninterrupted usable floor space (14 & 16).
A central atrium (15) brings light down to the lowest levels of the building.
The upper levels (17) step down in a series of terraces towards Leadenhall Market.

those which were eventually built). Rogers initially envisaged Lloyd's as a steel structure, like the Pompidou Centre. The main columns were to be of stainless steel. Arup Associates had actually completed a City office block, Bush Lane House, on an exposed steel frame, water-filled as at Pompidou. But in the case of Lloyd's, the fire authorities were resolutely opposed to steel and not even Peter Rice was able to change their views. Rice advised against fighting for steel, since he felt the battle could be long and costly to the client. Rogers feared that a concrete building would be over-weighty and bulky, but in the event Lloyd's provided him with a chance to learn from the revered Kahn and, indeed, from American architects more generally. John Young and Courtenay Blackmore, Lloyd's head of administration, along with John Bathgate, Lloyd's project coordinator and Brian Pettifer of Bovis, recently appointed as management contractors for the scheme, went to the USA to study high-quality *in situ* concrete.

Although steel was rejected as a structural element, it was to be used for cladding the service towers – largely because of the fire officers' doubts about the safety of aluminium. The third element in the external look of Lloyd's was glass. Rogers' extensive use of translucent glazing on the building reflected his admiration for Pierre Chareau's Maison de Verre in Paris. Triple glazing, with rolled glass to achieve 'sparkle', was used. More than Pompidou, Lloyd's represented for Rogers the opportunity to bring together the themes which had preoccupied him since the days of his early partnership with Norman Foster. Given adequate funding, an enthusiastic and well-informed client and a distinct lack of obstacles ('there was a unique mood at the time: distinctly in favour of the new and radical', he says), Rogers was able to create a building which became (by the time of its completion) a defiant symbol of modern architecture under attack.

Test piling on the cleared site of the 1928 building had begun in March 1981, and work on the substructure began in June of that year. A sixty-six month-programme was adopted. Even with additions to the brief (extra servicing and more meeting rooms, in particular) the job was completed with a month to spare.

The commissioning and construction of the new Lloyd's, between 1977 and 1986, coincided with a period of rapid change in the way that financial dealings were conducted. Later in 1986, the so-called 'Big Bang', the electronic-based revolution in financial operations, was to inaugurate the greatest office building boom in London's history and to create the new 'office cities' of Broadgate and Canary Wharf. When Rogers won the commission, computers were scarce at Lloyd's (less than 4 per cent of underwriters used them) and many members, firmly attached to their traditional 'boxes' (a survival of coffee-house days) and to personal contact as the foundation of their business, expressed doubts that this situation would change. The Rogers team thought otherwise – and was of course proved right. By 1981, with the building on site, Lloyd's grasped the

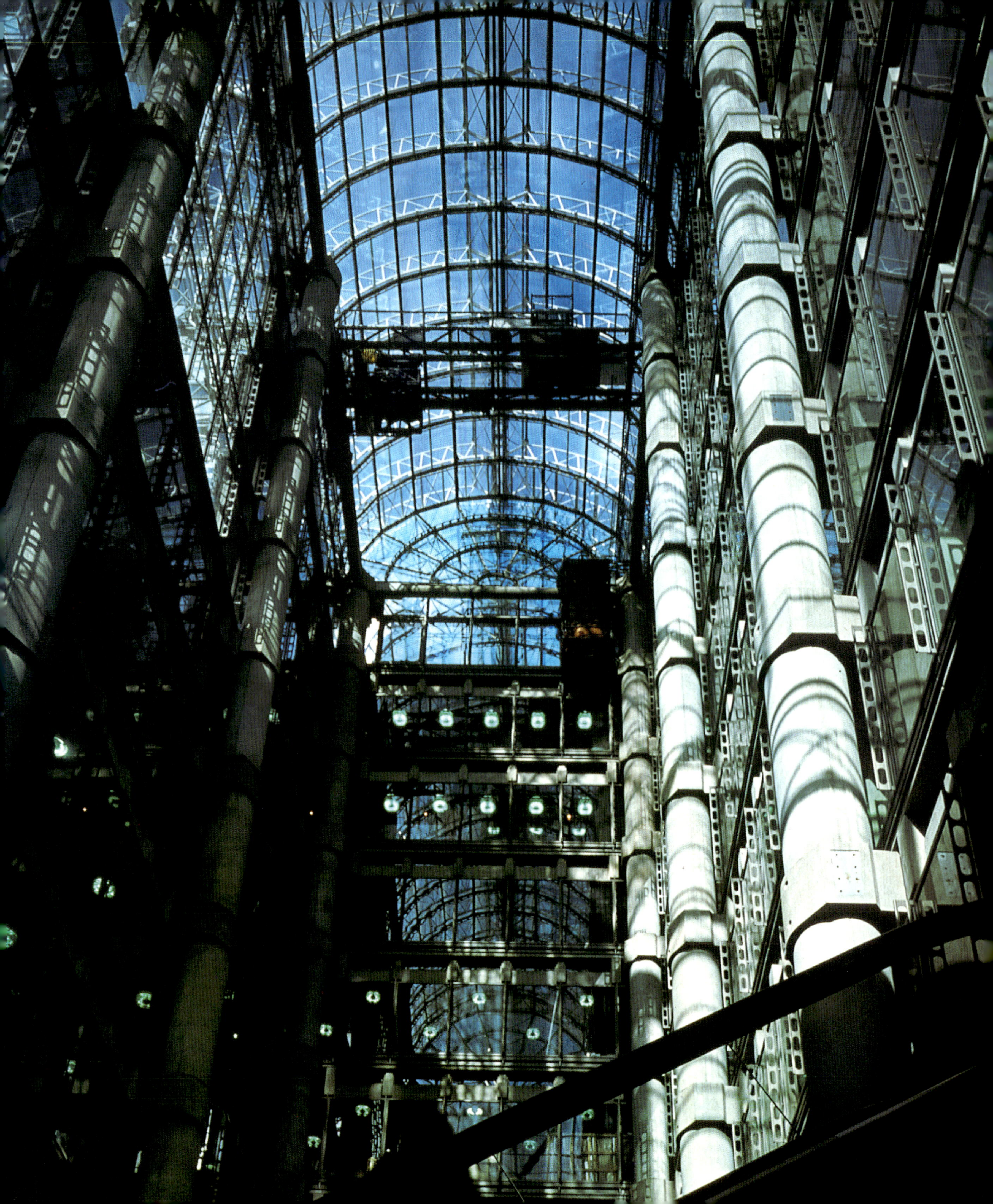

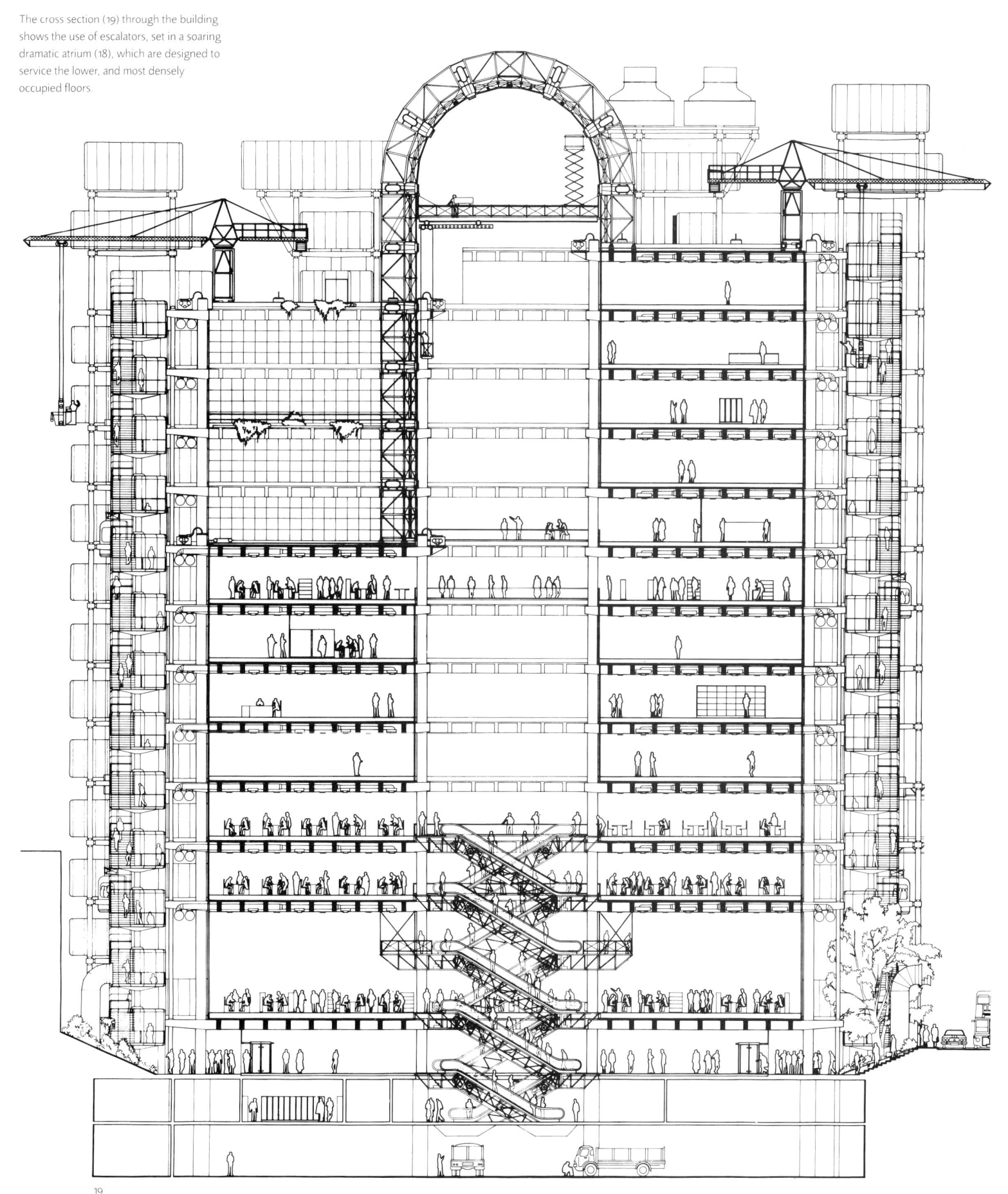

The cross section (19) through the building shows the use of escalators, set in a soaring dramatic atrium (18), which are designed to service the lower, and most densely occupied floors.

The 'Gothic' character of Lloyd's (20 & 21) is particularly appropriate to the tight streets of the City – nothing could be further removed from the bland and recessive classicism of Lloyd's 1958 building (22).
The towers form a powerful composition and bring together staircases, prefabricated toilet capsules, service risers and lifts (23–25).

Lloyd's of London

23

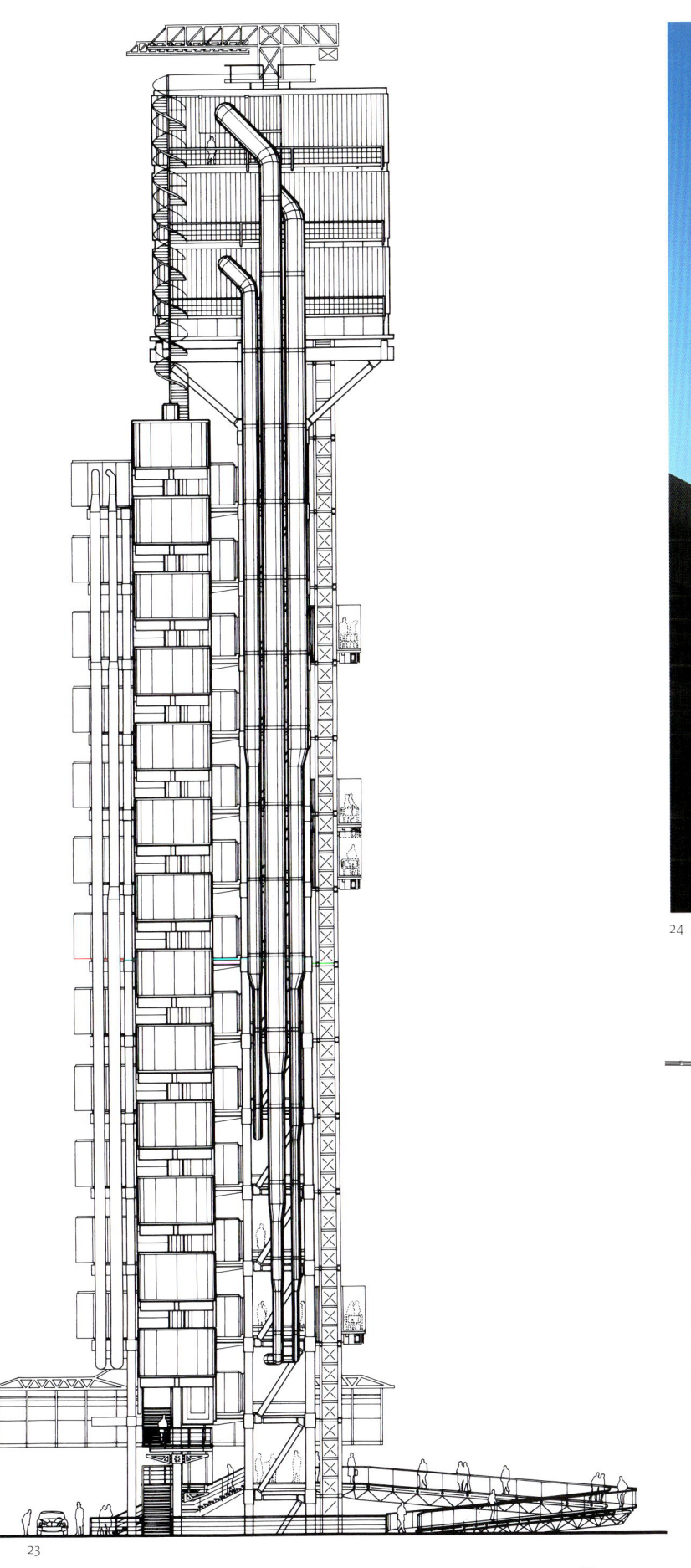

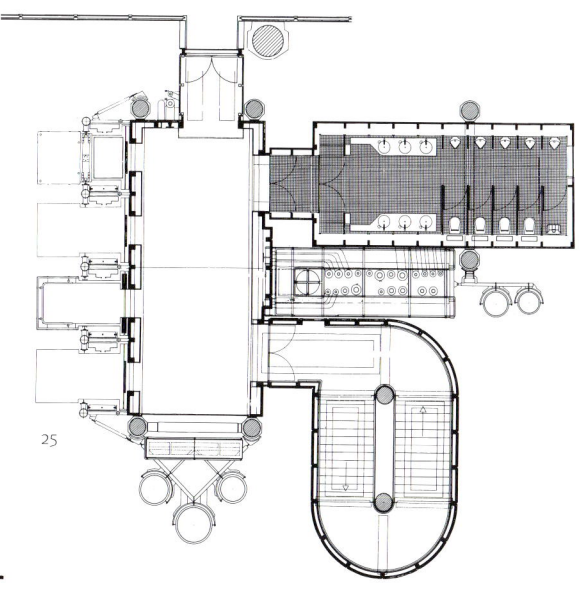

24

25

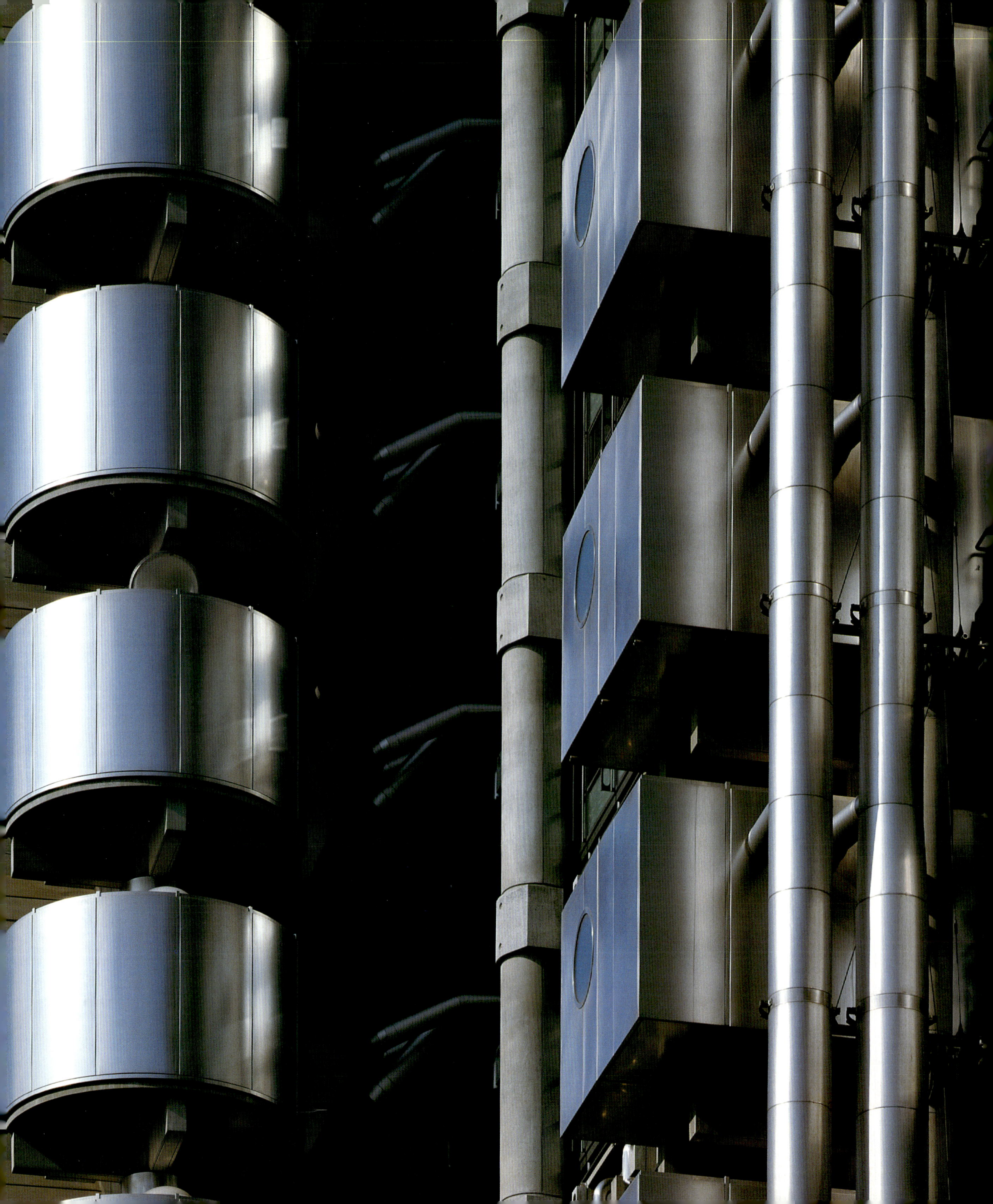

While the imagery of Lloyd's is that of the machine, the building makes use of fine materials like stainless steel, assembled with a craftsman's precision (26). In response to congested site conditions, widespread use was made of off-site prefabrication, such as the one-piece stair and riser extrusion (27–30).

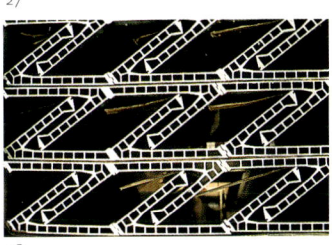

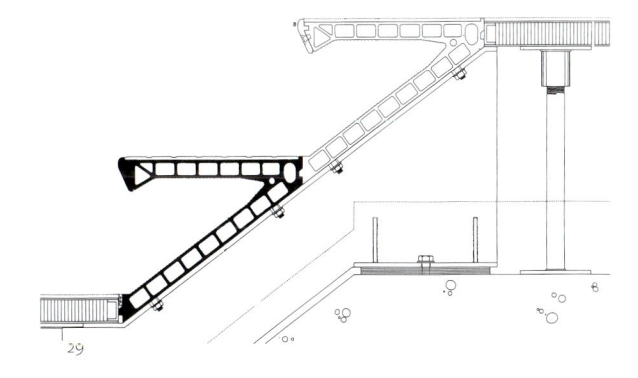

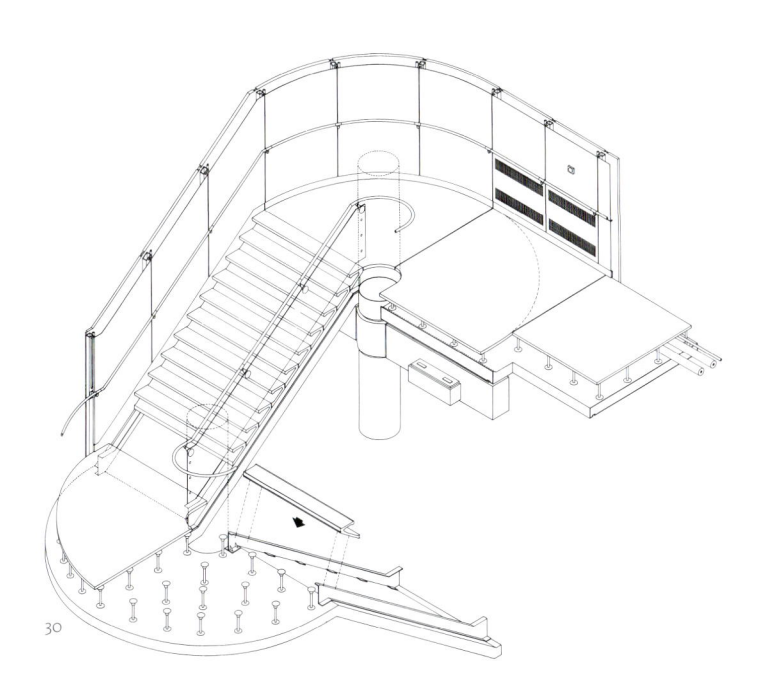

31

The American Airstream trailer was a point of departure for the fully-finished toilet capsule (31–34).
Accessed from the glazed lift lobbies, the all-glass lift capsules are celebrations of movement, riding up and down the outside of the building, thereby animating the exterior and providing delight for both the occupant and the passerby (35 & 36).

32

Lloyd's of London

33

34

35

36

188

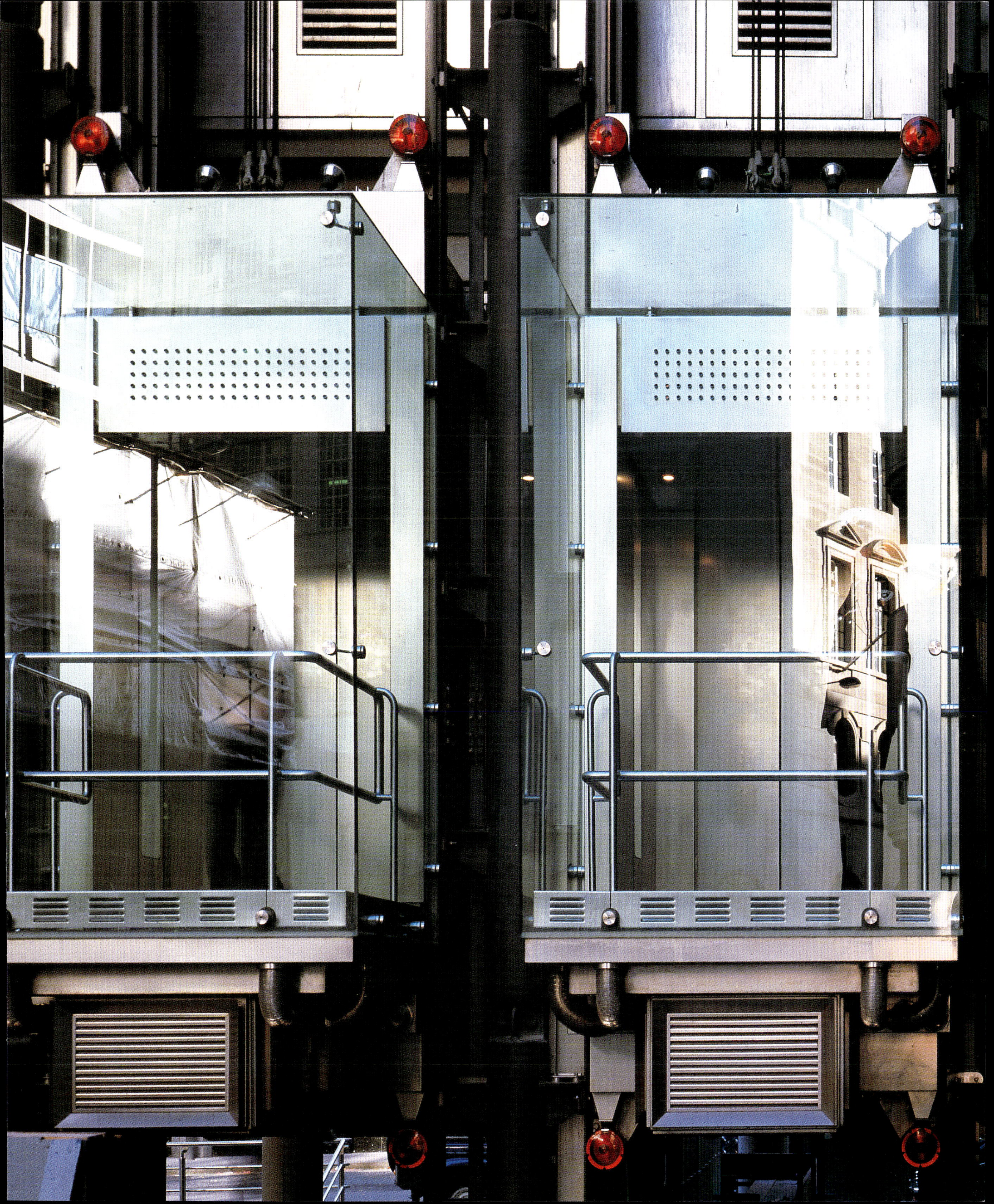

37

The clear separation of the main floor plate and the satellite towers (44) is reflected in the construction methodology, which uses predominantly *in situ* concrete for the main floor (40–42) and pre-cast elements for the towers (37 & 38).

Raised steel formwork for the floors creates a high level service zone above the grillage of beams (39).
Unlike the Pompidou Centre (which was built bay by bay) Lloyd's was built floor by floor (43).

38

39

40

41

42

Lloyd's of London

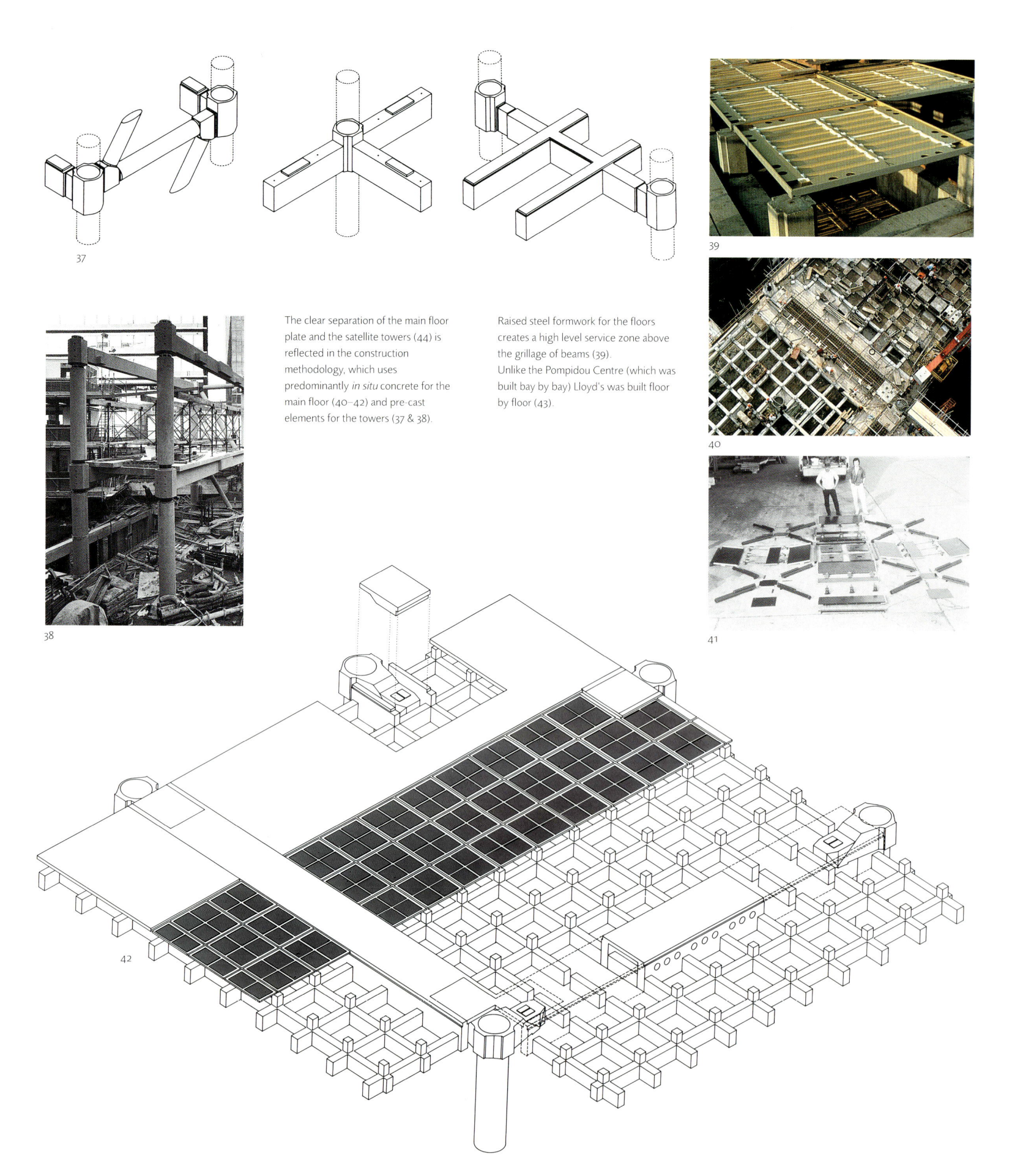

seriousness of the situation: the new building could (it was suggested) end up gravely under-equipped. A specialist firm, Point Consultants, had been brought in and their predictions of an almost universal use of information technology and computer terminals would require a doubling of the anticipated power provision with a consequent dramatic impact on cabling capacity and cooling. This had an inevitable impact on the look of the building, with the six service towers gradually losing the emphatically slim and expressive form which Rogers wanted and becoming bulkier and more dominant.

The essence of the Lloyd's servicing system is the use of the atrium form, concrete structure and triple-glazed cladding as active elements. Conditioned air is distributed through a sub-floor plenum into the offices, while stale air is extracted from above through the luminaires. The extracted air is passed to the perimeter of the building and forced through the triple-layered exterior glazing – ensuring an almost zero heat loss from the offices during the winter and reducing heat gain in summer. Heat from the return air is collected in the basement sprinkler tanks and re-used. The internal concrete soffits and slabs are 'heat sinks', absorbing heat during occupation and being cooled off overnight using naturally chilled night air. This allows cooling to follow a 24-hour cycle and reduces the peak cooling requirement. Air handling equipment is located at basement level and in four service tower plantrooms. Lloyd's illustrates Rogers' pronouncement that 'there is no such thing as high technology or low technology – simply appropriate

43

44

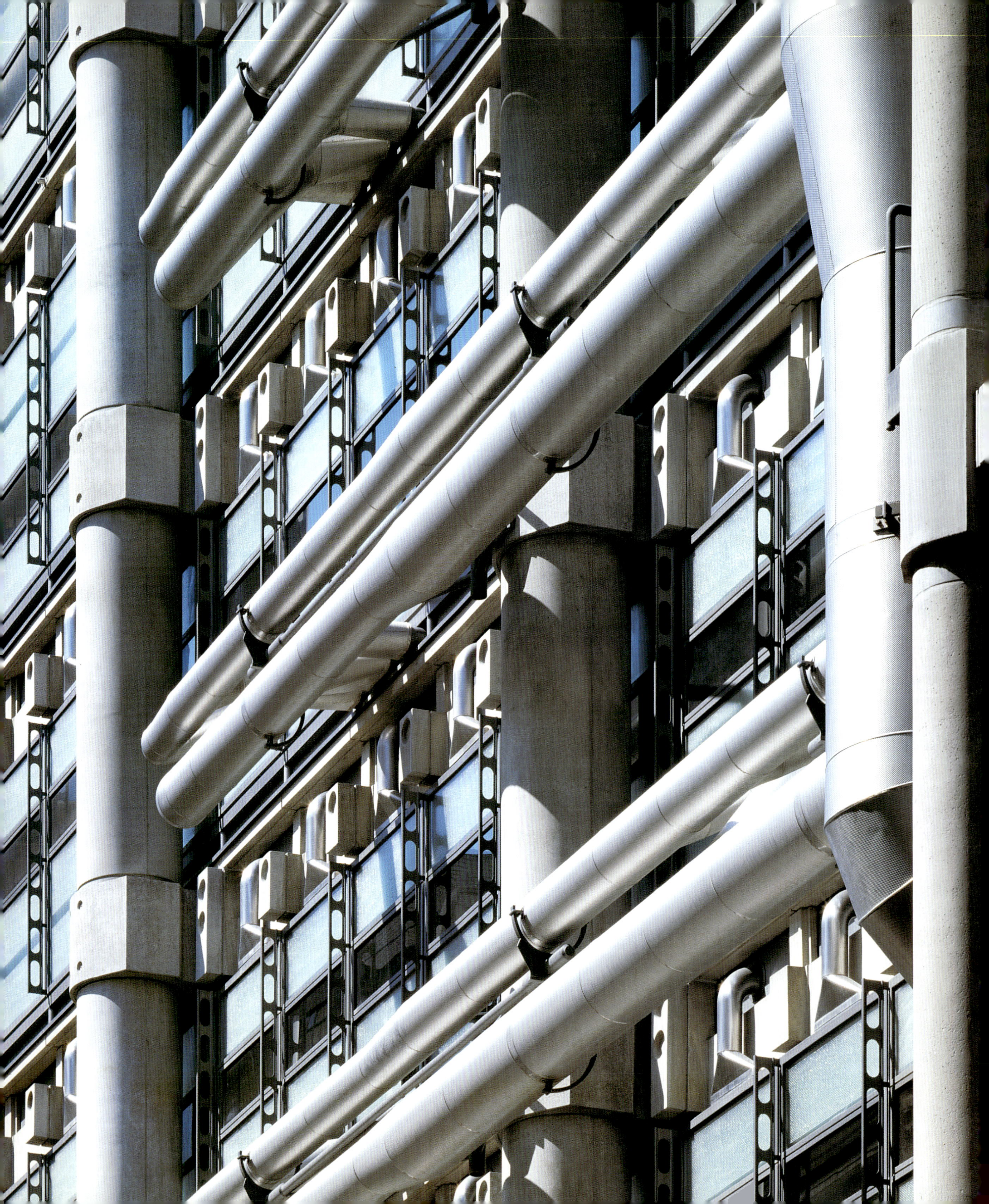

technology'. The basic form of the building is that of a large atrium, surmounted by a steel and glass arched roof, surrounded by galleries (twelve levels of them on the north side) which contain the bulk of the underwriting space and a variable amount of lettable space, depending on the changing accommodational needs of the Lloyd's market itself. The floors intended to be let are glazed to the atrium, while those which are part of the Room are left open. The floors were constructed on a grid by using beams with parallel sides and sharp arrises; Rogers emphasizes that the floor is a grid and not a solid, coffered slab – great care was taken to secure this effect. The floors are supported on reinforced concrete columns on a 10.8 x 18 metre grid. The load is transferred between the columns and the floor beams by means of a precast bracket – an arrangement which inevitably recalls the steel 'gerberettes' of the Pompidou Centre. Pre-cast 'yokes' cast into inverted U-beams transmit the loads of the floor grid to the perimeter columns via the brackets. The great columns, both on the exterior of the building and within the atrium, stand proud of the cladding, increasing the highly-articulated 'Gothic' effect of Lloyd's. External cross-braces are actually made of steel tube, concrete-cased for reasons of fire safety, which helped to maintain the spare slenderness of the exterior. It was proposed to leave the services within the concrete grid open to view, but the client demurred and the squares of the ceiling grid are filled with black metal panels which contain the light fittings.

The massiveness and weight of the interior of Lloyd's may come as a surprise after the predominantly metal and glass exterior, but the heaviness of the concrete superstructure is successfully balanced by the airy and elegant lightness of the atrium roof. This is a startling re-enactment of the Victorian drama of The Crystal Palace and the great nineteenth-century railway termini – though wrought iron is, of course, replaced by tubular steel. The roof sits, by means of steel brackets, on the main columns of the atrium. Its lattice steelwork is of painted rather than stainless steel – an economy measure.

The service towers, three of them principally for firefighting and escape and the other three for lifts, lavatories and risers, are the visual expression of the Kahnian doctrine of 'served and servant spaces'; the towers on the Gothic castle of Lloyd's. They provide access and escape routes by means of lifts and staircases – in an emergency the core building (which could have 6,000 people inside it) can be evacuated into the detached service towers within two and a half minutes. The precast concrete kit-of-parts of the service towers is not entirely independent of the main block of the building, as was proposed at one stage, but depends on a degree of restraint from the main building. The towers form a flexible framework for the ventilation plant, lifts, service risers and lavatories (the replaceable, potentially obsolescent parts of the building) attached to them. The cladding of the towers is entirely stainless steel (for reasons already outlined). Four towers carry major plantrooms, with mains services running vertically down the towers and connecting

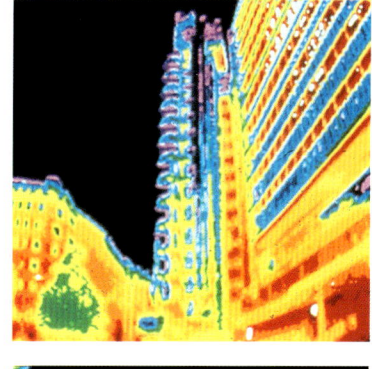

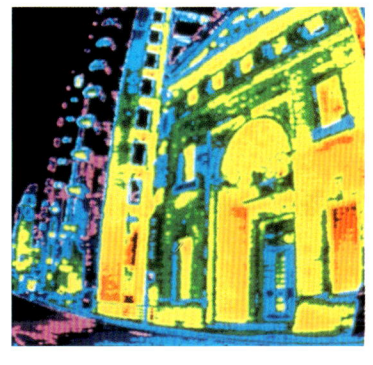

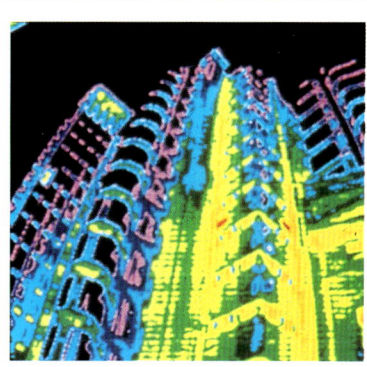

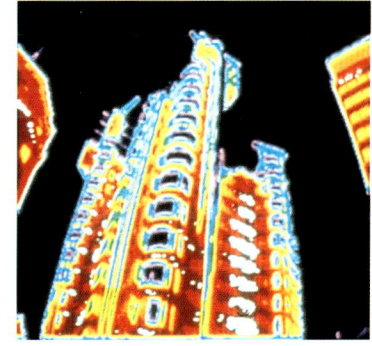

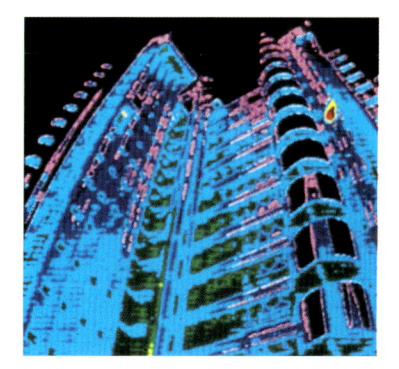

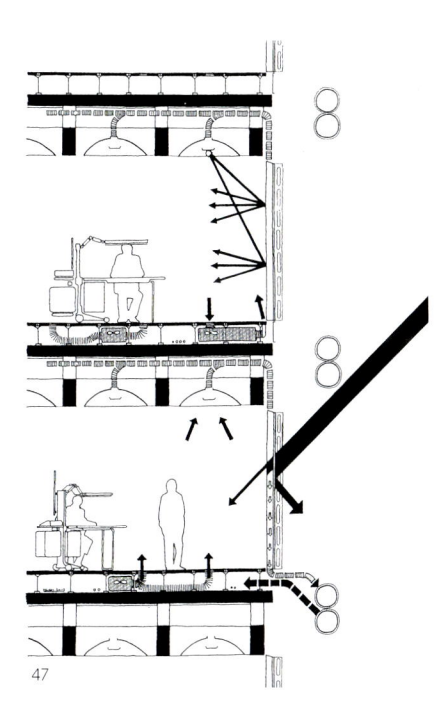

The all-glass facade contributes dynamically to the energy efficiency of the building by using the triple glazing as a return air plenum (47). An infra-red thermagraphic survey confirms the building's high thermal efficiency (46). The strong expression of services contributes to the aesthetic of Lloyd's (45).

into each level of the building. In contrast to the colour-coded service ducts of the Pompidou Centre, those at Lloyd's are cased in stainless steel, and are neutral in effect. The largest contain the air-conditioning, with lesser ducts for water, drains, power and electronics. On top of four of the six towers sit the plantrooms, grown from the slender turrets Rogers initially envisaged into massive steel-clad boxes. Sometimes criticized as clumsy and over-dominant, they nonetheless underline the subordination of traditional architectural concerns to the all-important functional needs of the users. All the towers are topped by service cranes, painted a jaunty blue and intended to allow both maintenance and the easy replacement of obsolete or worn-out equipment. Pre-assembling elements of the building made sense because of the very confined nature of the site.

A key part of the design strategy was that Lloyd's should be, like Pompidou, a place of movement. With the Room divided over a number of floors, it was vital that underwriters and brokers should be able to meet face to face without difficulty. Location had always been a contentious matter with Lloyd's members. A single-level room was impossible, but all parts of the Room had to be easily reached one from another. Rogers' strategy had always provided for the lifts to be located in the service towers, but the idea of external lifts ('wall-climbers') worried the client. Was this a practical idea, in view of the exposure of cars and mechanisms to the elements? Icing in winter might affect the operation of the lifts, while summer heat could make the glass-walled cars intolerable – especially if there were a power failure. A further fact-finding trip to the USA helped to assuage Lloyd's fears – here were external lifts which had worked well for years in a climate more extreme than that of Britain. The St Francis Hotel in San Francisco had depended on external lifts to

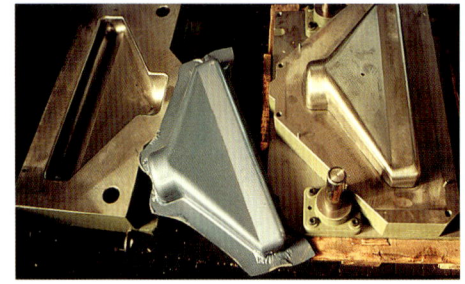

A stainless steel fishtail duct transfers air under pressure through the triple-glazed facade (48, 49 & 51).
At the base of the facade the air is extracted via horizontal ducts and returned to the plantrooms (50).

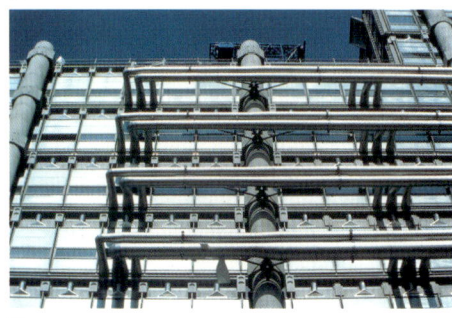

Lloyd's of London

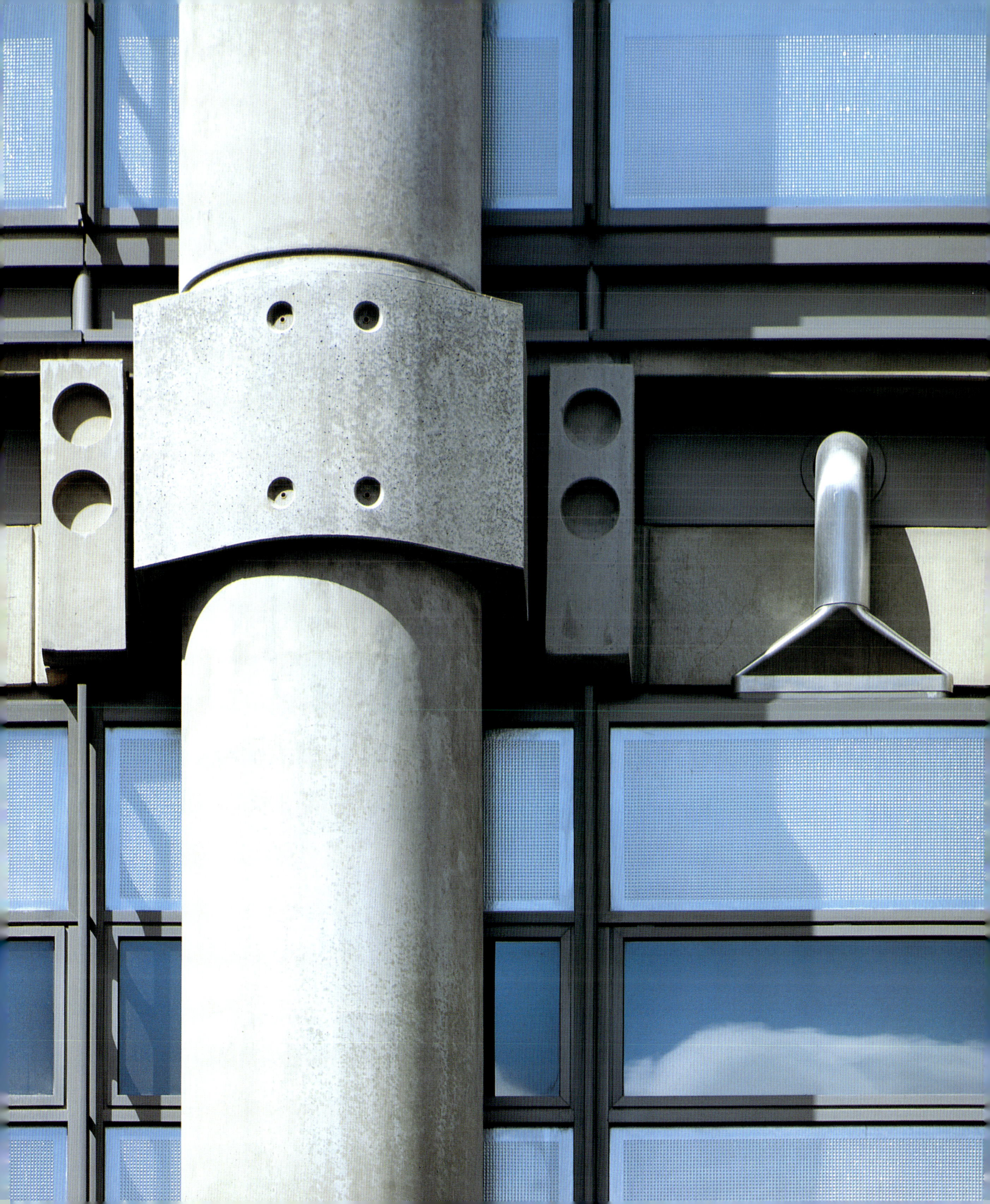

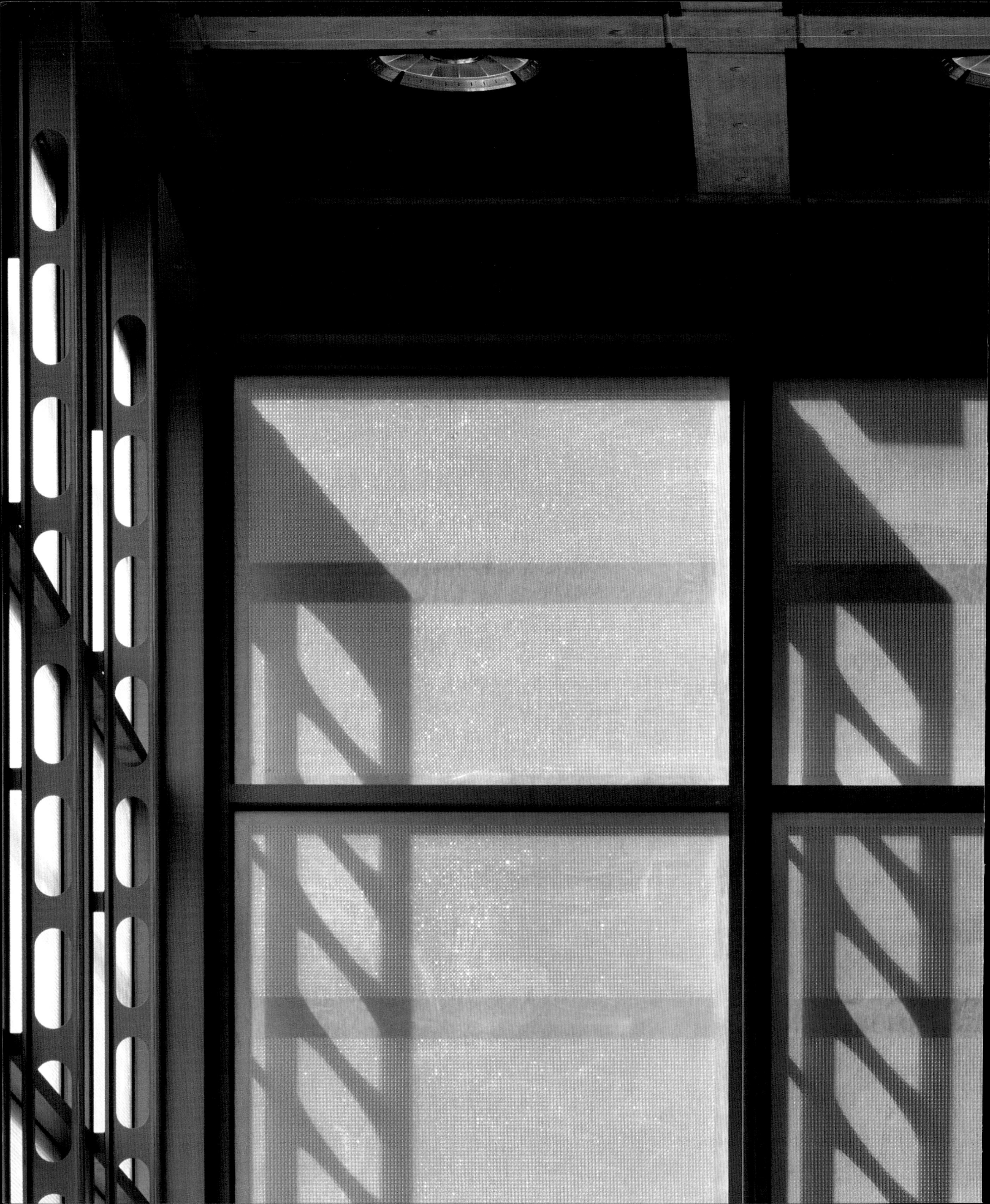

52 53

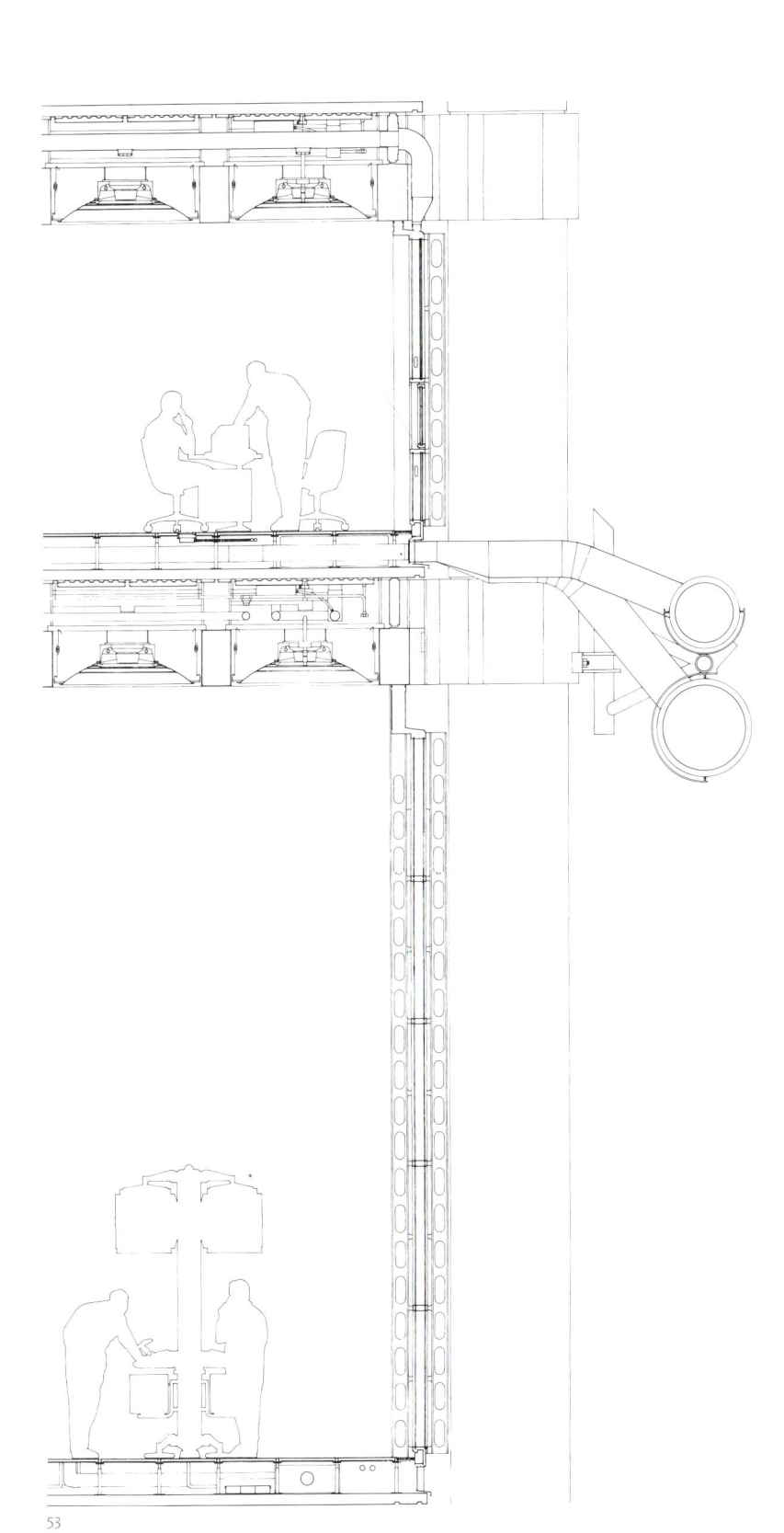

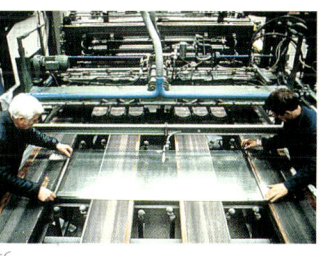

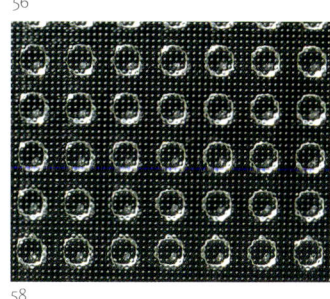

54

55 56

57 58

Inspired by the translucent glass blocks of the Maison de Verre (54), Rogers sought to create an animated play of light in both day and night conditions (52). This was achieved by passing molten glass through dimpled steel rollers to create a texture that both reflects and refracts light (55–58). The modular glass panels are framed in aluminium with perforated mullions (53).

The main entrance to Lloyd's is signalled by a great glazed canopy (61–64) which both echoes the atrium and evokes the character of the adjacent Leadenhall Market (59 & 60).

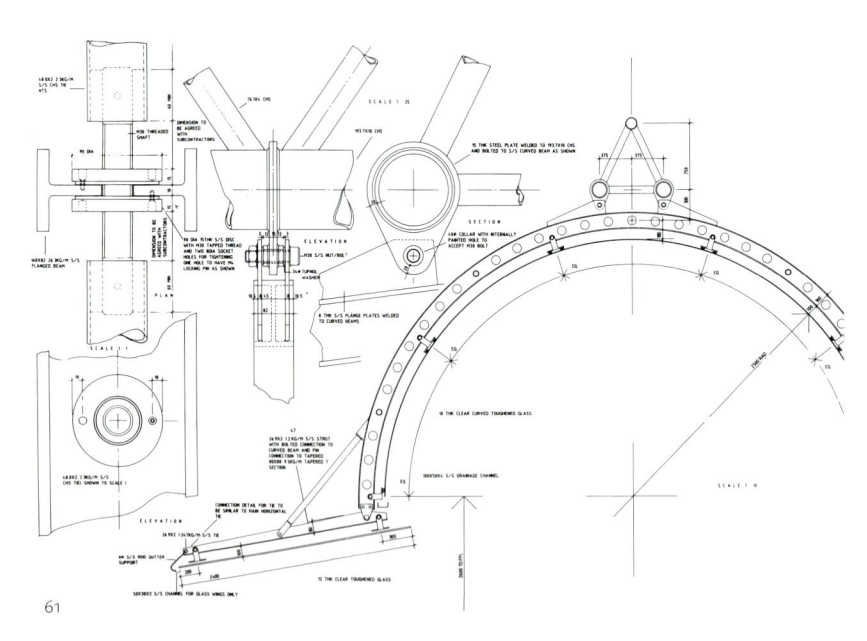

serve thirty-one storeys of rooms, without problems. In the event, the lifts at Lloyd's incorporated a wide range of fail-safe measures – de-icing equipment for cold winter days, for example, and air-conditioning units attached to the bottom of each car.

The escalators snaking up the face of the Pompidou Centre remain the single most popular feature of Piano + Rogers' early masterpiece. At Lloyd's, escalators were used to connect the floors used for underwriting – at first, only two gallery levels were earmarked for this purpose but a third was subsequently added and the escalators in fact end at the fourth level. Exposing the mechanism of the escalators behind clear glass panels was a way of 'celebrating' movement – like the glass lifts. The effect of the escalators when the Room is at work, with people hurrying from one floor to the next, is an essential ingredient of the character of Lloyd's, a striking embodiment of the fantasies of a Sant'Elia (or, for that matter, a Fritz Lang).

Richard Rogers defined his aim at Lloyd's as being 'to create poetry out of basic enclosure, by translating technology into form'. He has compared the building to Street's Law Courts on the Strand, London, a masterpiece of historicist street architecture in the hard Gothic style of the later nineteenth century. Lloyd's, says Rogers, 'is richly detailed and layered in section. It cascades down towards the existing lower buildings and upwards to the higher ones'. Rogers here makes analogies with very traditional architectural and urban values. Yet, he admits, the brief at Lloyd's implied 'a responsive, indeterminate architecture'. The building which resulted reflected Rogers' avowed search for 'a balance between permanence and transformation'.

It is this balance which is central to the character of the building, which is, in Rogers' view, 'history-conscious, energy-conscious, functional, of course, like all our buildings, and more dynamic than Pompidou'. It provided a working model for the buildings spawned by London's 'Big Bang' in being essentially inward-looking and user-

Lloyd's of London

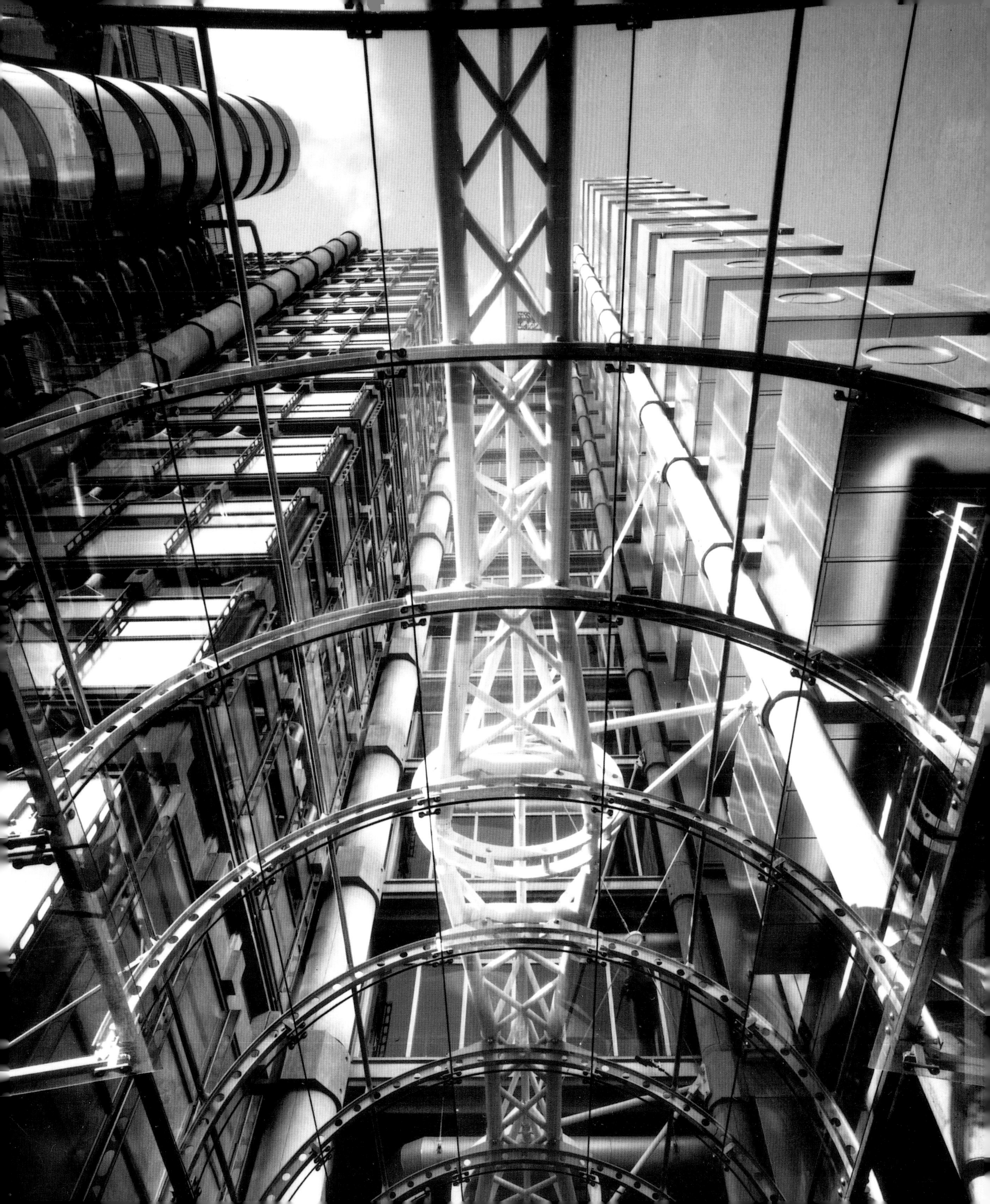

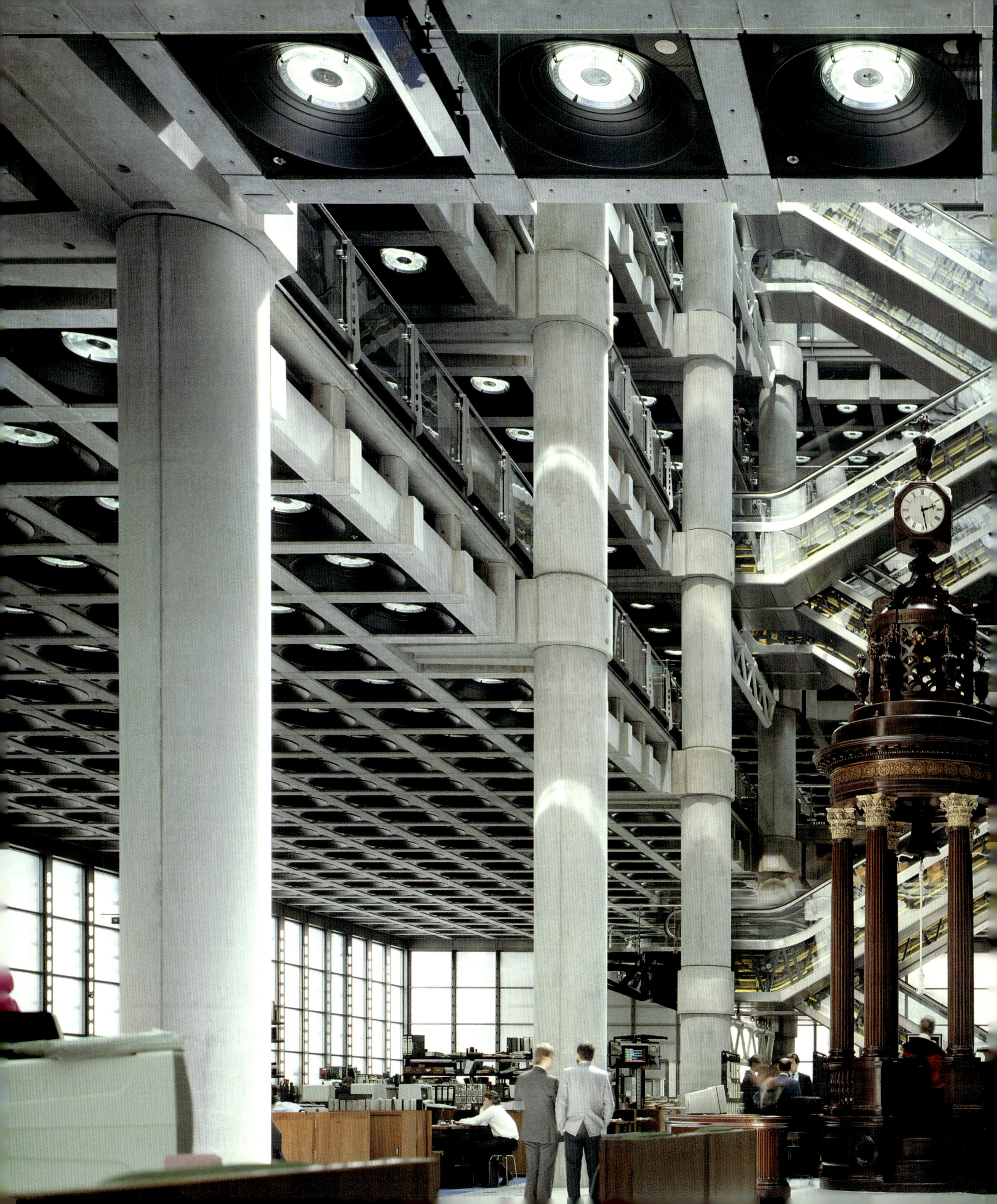

1418
BOURING/KENDRICK
PLEASE PHONE YOUR OFFICE EXT 5221
1420
SEASCOPE/BOTTING:
PLEASE PHONE YOUR OFFICE EXT 131
1421
N. HURST/OSULLIVAN
PLEASE PHONE YOUR OFFICE EXT 2142
1424
THO.HEATH/IND
PLEASE GO TO GALLERY 2
1424
J. PLUMER/BELL
PLEASE PHONE YOUR OFFICE EXT 238
SONY
TeleVideo

Lloyd's of London

67

68

'The Room' is one of the great interiors of London. The dynamism and drama inherent in the space are heightened by the bank of escalators linking all the working levels (65, previous pages, 66, 70, 71 & 72, overleaf). Public and private restaurant and bar facilities were located at the lower ground floor (67 & 68). Underwriters' boxes, the basic Lloyd's workstation, were designed as a pressed-steel structural chassis supporting a wide variety of finishes and technology options (69).

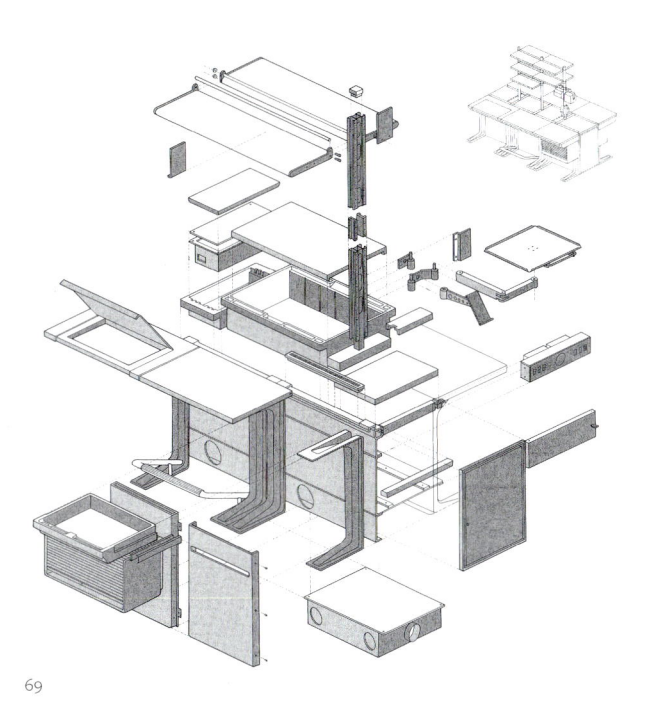

70

69

71

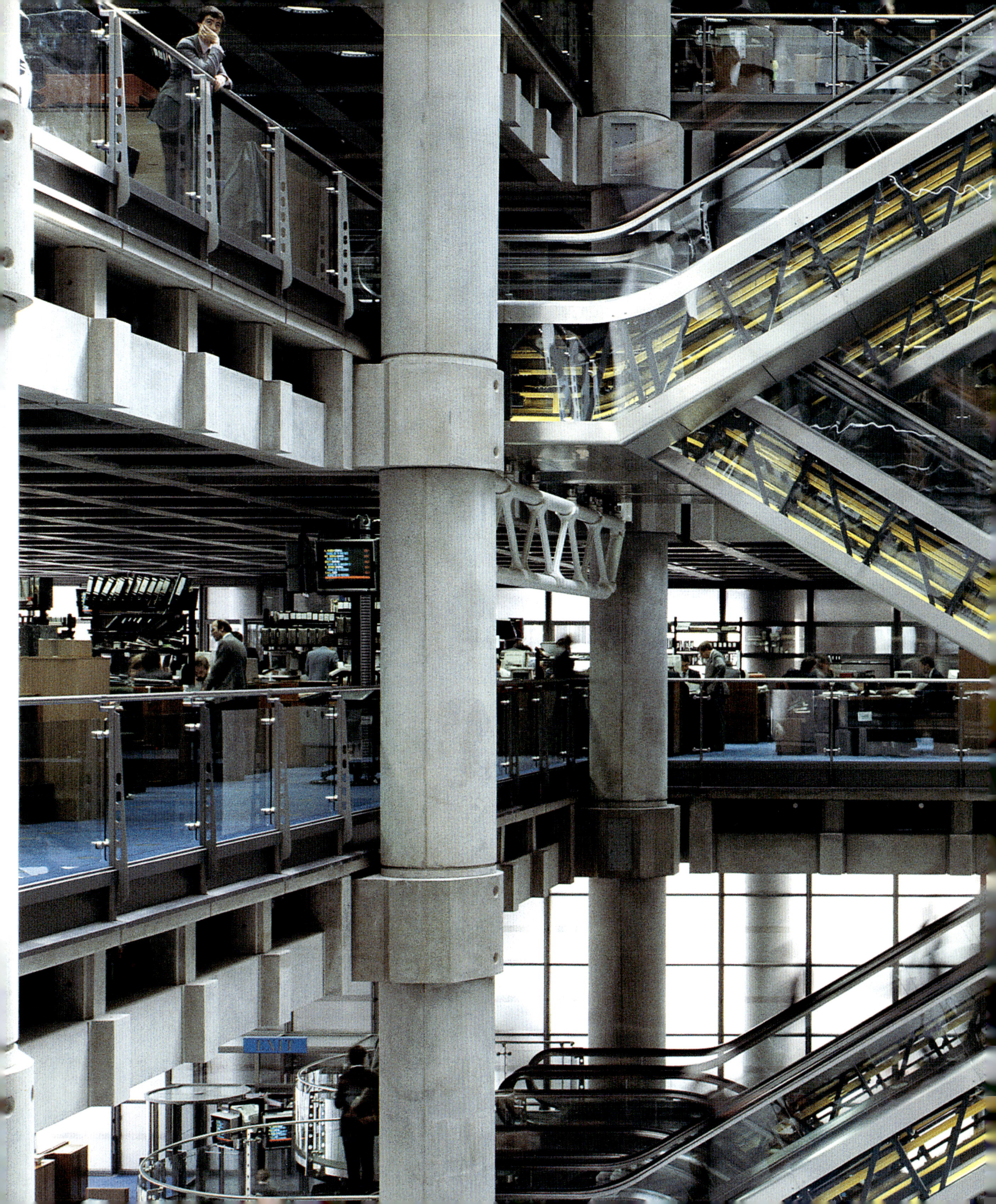

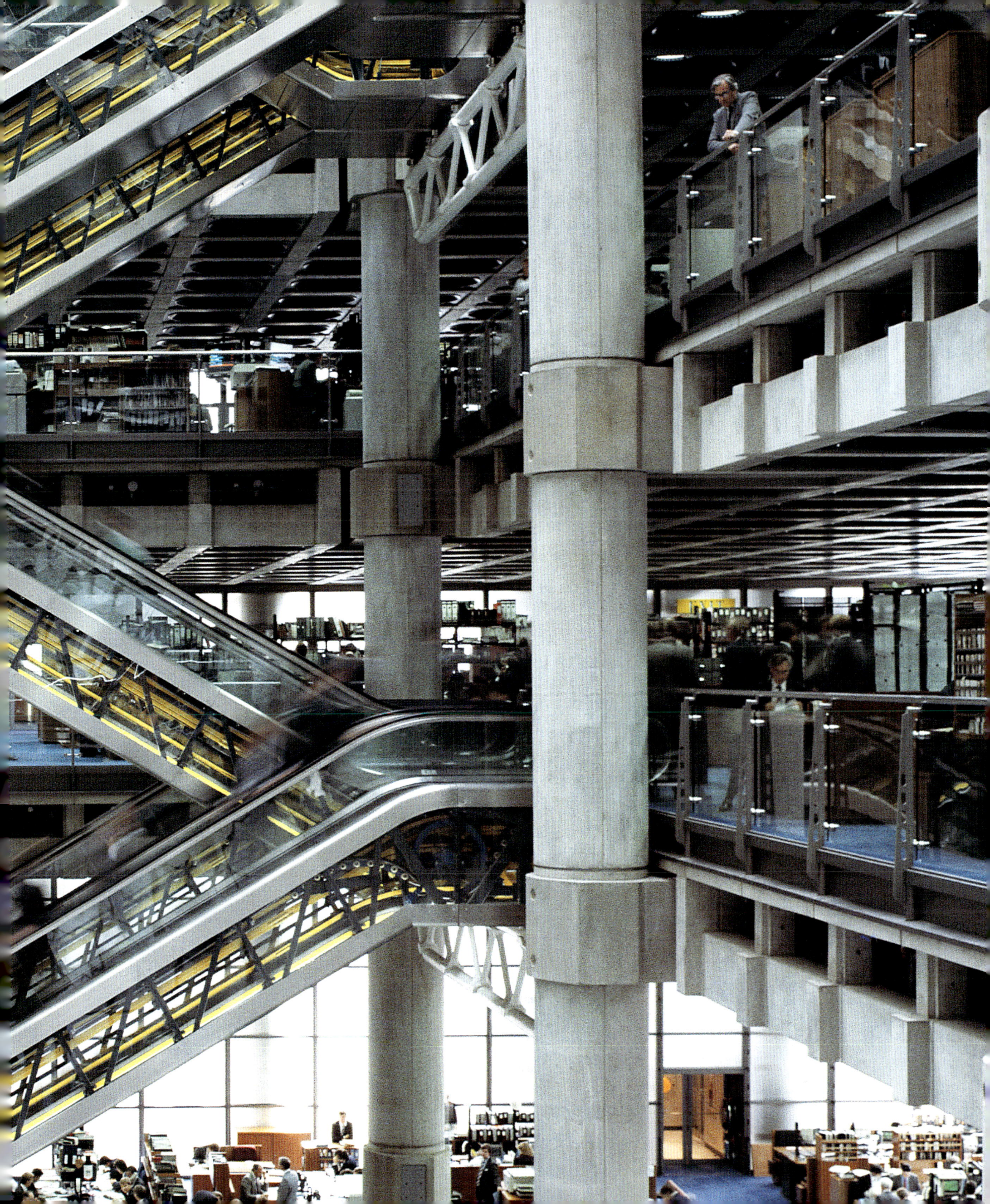

centred. In its flexibility, environmentalism and responsiveness to the changing shape of services, electronic and non-electronic, it is also a pioneer 'intelligent' building which Frank Duffy has described as 'one of the most advanced technological edifices in the world'. All of this depends on the basic strategy: core versus perimeter, 'served' and 'servant'.

If Lloyd's is a 'kit-of-parts', however, it is a kit of parts put together to impressive architectonic effect. Although Rogers has always looked longingly at the potential for an architecture of dematerialization, Lloyd's expresses the 'controlled randomness' which typifies his own finest work. Lloyd's is, far more than the classical building it replaced, a monument. The interior is, for all the activity going on, a place of overwhelming calm and order beneath the great columns and the soaring roof. The outside, for all the restless, mechanistic quality provided by the ducts, flues and lifts, has a grave permanence which is lacking in any of the post-war buildings in the vicinity.

Like a medieval cathedral, Lloyd's is detailed beautifully even in those places which the eye cannot see. Against all the odds, Rogers and his team gave conservative London a building which expresses the heroic age of modernism, a benchmark for everything built or proposed in the capital in the years that followed.

The lightweight atrium roof seems to float at the top of the robust concrete framework of the building bringing light to the heart of Lloyd's (74–76). There are views out of the atrium to the skyline of the City. Rogers' proposal for the Chairman's suite added a range of sumptuous materials to the basic palette; sadly it was not implemented (73).
The roofscape of Lloyd's has become a distinctive landmark in London's skyline (77, overleaf).

Lloyd's of London

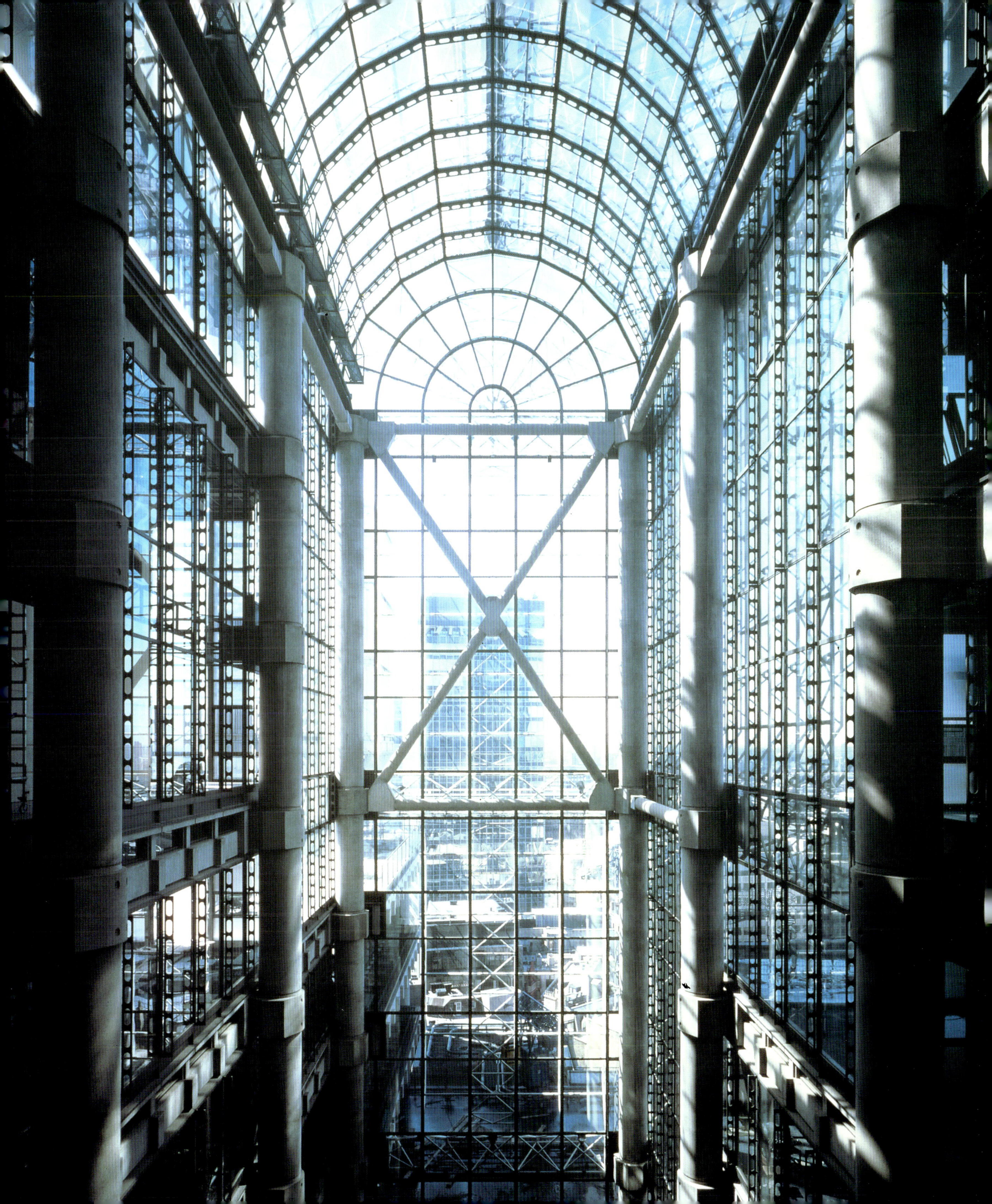

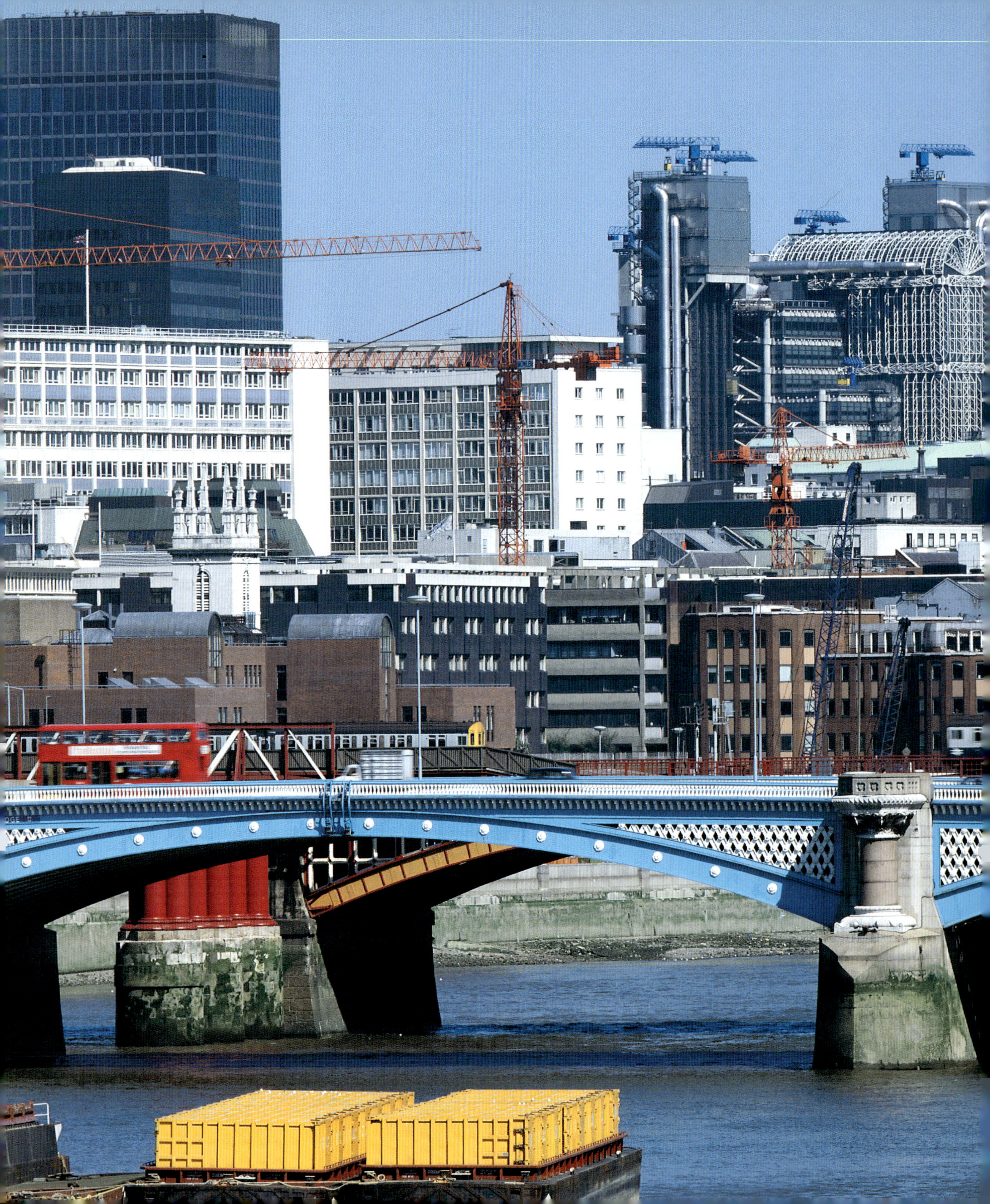

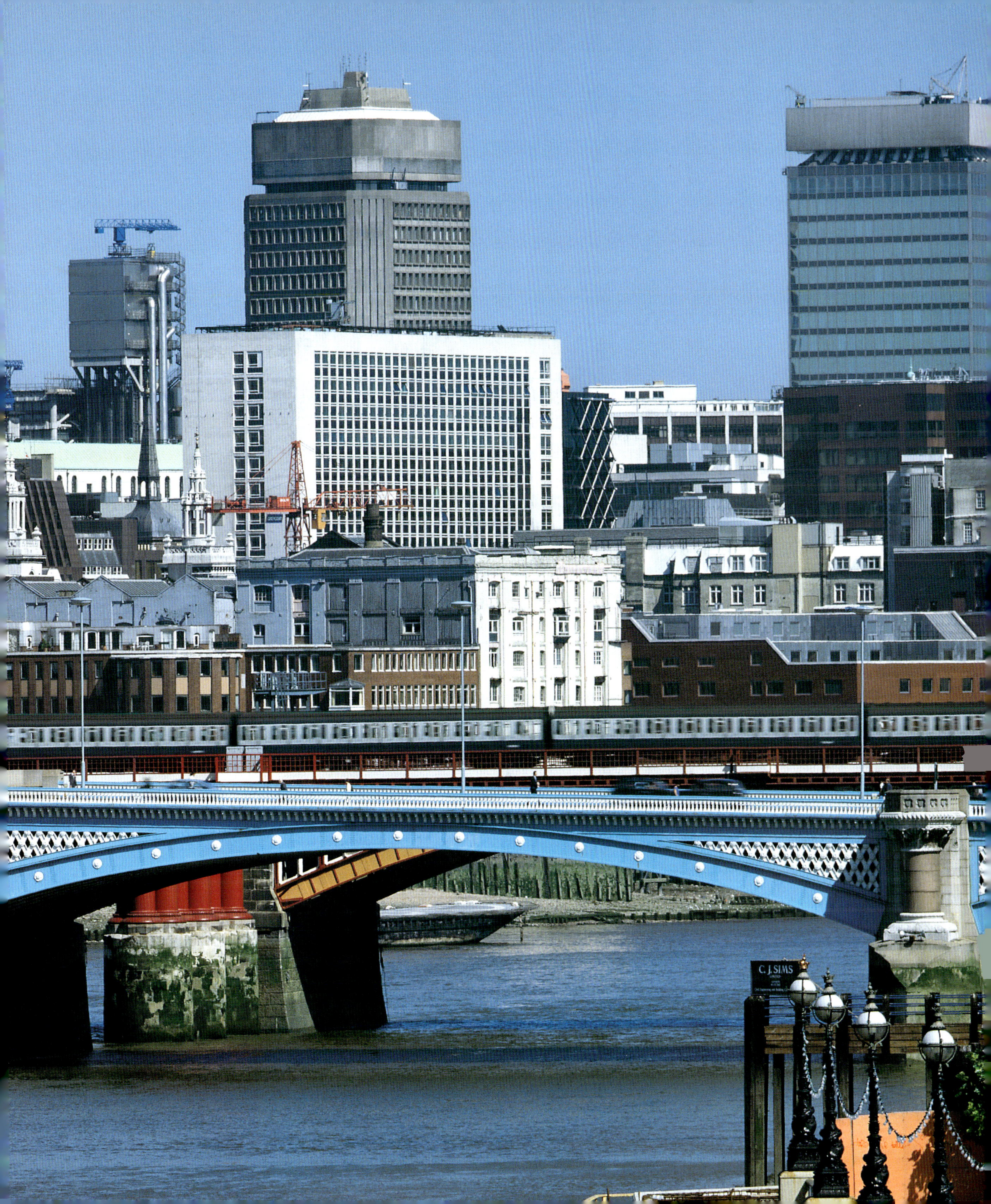
C.J. SIMS

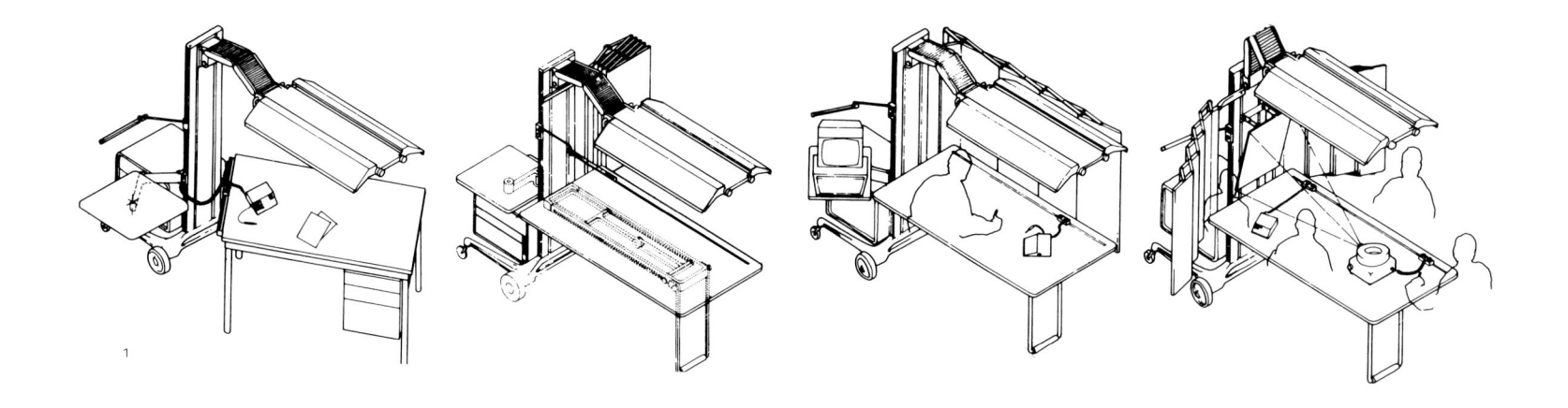

Third Generation Office
1978

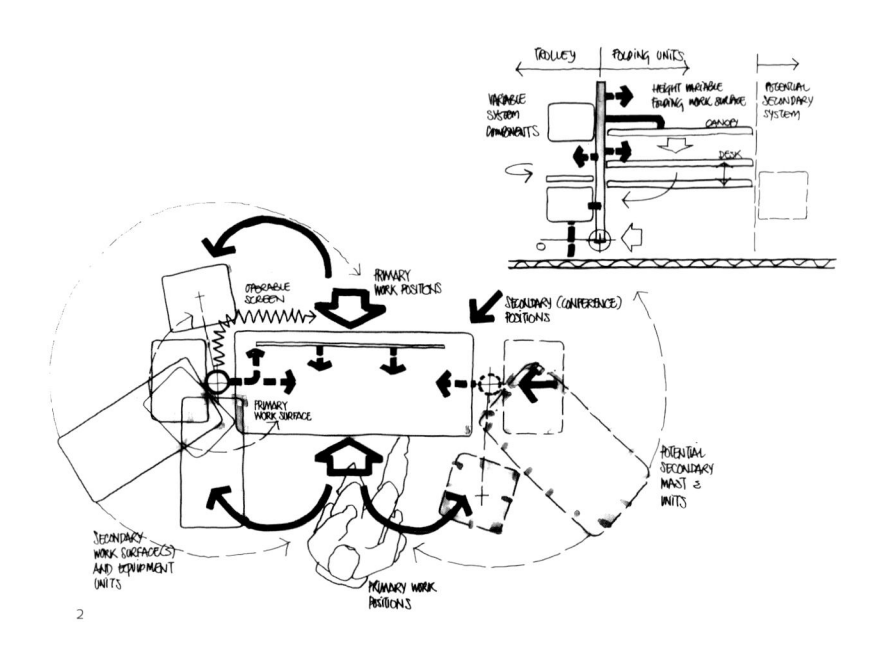

This project brings together perennial themes in Rogers' work – a vision of architecture as the means for creating a total working and living environment (reflected in his work for DRU and the interiors of the Pompidou Centre) and a concern for giving people control over their surroundings. Both are grounded on a commitment to the use of benign technology as a tool for human progress.

The office, Rogers felt, had gone through a major revolution when, after the Second World War, the concept of *burolandschaft* swept away all before it and a second generation of office fitouts was developed to meet the needs of a mobile, changing society. Working with manufacturers Knoll International, Rogers proposed new office systems which could respond to another office revolution – even in the 1970s, the impact of new information and communications technology was beginning to be anticipated. In the Third Generation (G3) Office fixed work stations would become as redundant as the rigid hierarchy which they reflected; the office was to be a place of interaction, not a clerical production line.

A third theme emerged in the Knoll project: the use of standardized components to provide an economical and flexible modern environment of portable work stations. The basic G3 units – linked to the central services of a building by means of a raised floor – incorporated storage, power, communications systems, air conditioning and even a compacting unit for waste paper disposal. Individual lighting units, moreover, would replace bland overall illumination. Though not put into production, the G3 concept underpinned Rogers' user-orientated fitout at Lloyd's.

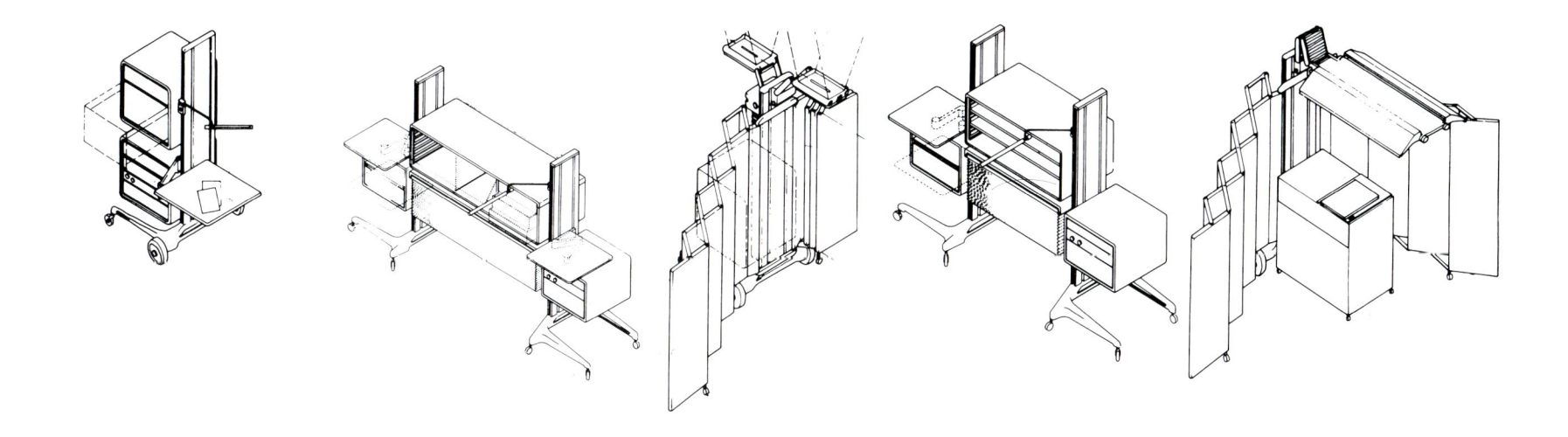

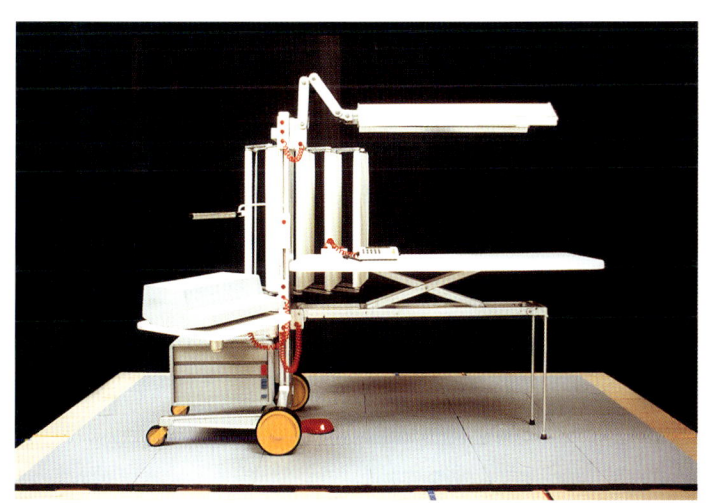

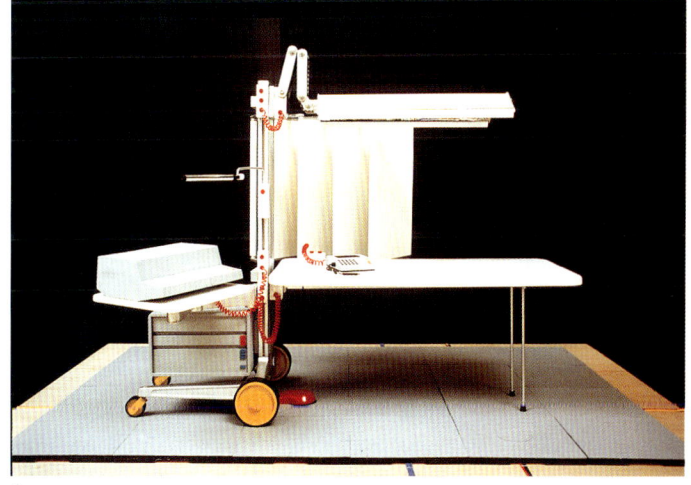

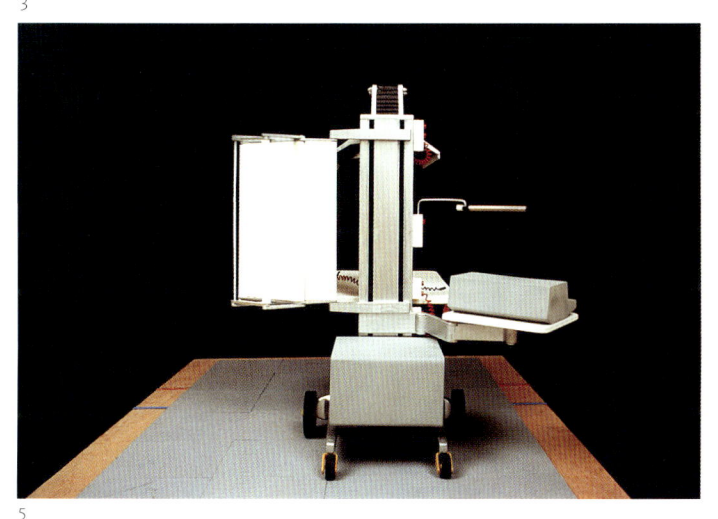

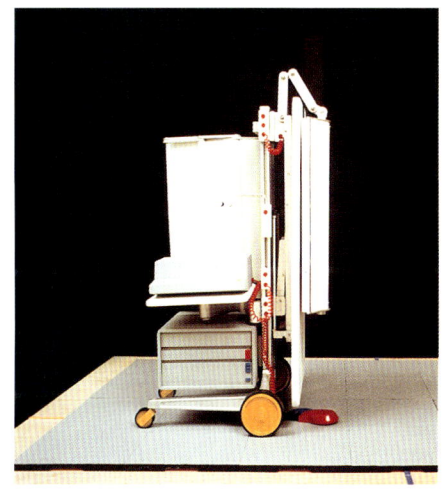

The basic G3 workstation could be adapted and augmented for the needs of users by deploying a set of standard components incorporating storage, lighting and other facilities.

A typical G3 desk configuration allowed users access to a number of different work positions. Desk height and other elements were adjustable.

The G3 unit was designed to fold up for storage and could be moved around the office, using services from a raised floor. it could even be taken home. The emphasis was on providing a strong element of user control over the working environment (1–6).

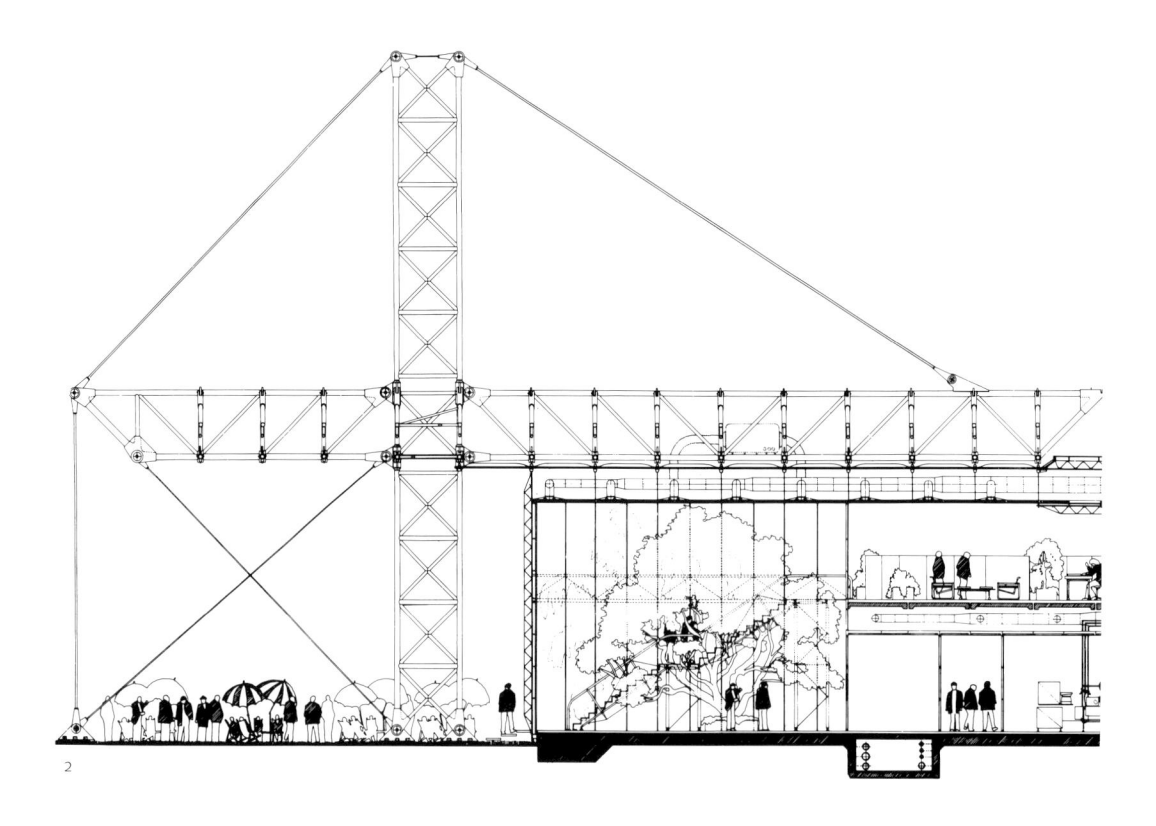

NAPP Laboratories

Cambridge, 1979

The proposed terrain for the NAPP Laboratories scheme was the Cambridge hinterland, an area which became a 'launch pad' for research and industry ensuring the university city's economic role in the UK economy. The client was a major pharmaceuticals company. The Rogers scheme, submitted for a competition, was not built but is of interest as one of several masted structures developed by the practice, and also as a way into understanding what was produced at Fleetguard, Inmos and the PA Technology Laboratories at Princeton.

NAPP demanded maximum flexibility with potential for change and expansion. The structural system, devised in association with Anthony Hunt, facilitated the provision of large spaces, but the masted form was equally valued for its 'landmark' potential – located at a main road junction, the building could be seen as a 'gateway' to Cambridge. Placing services in an intermediate zone, between the main structure and the internal envelope, avoided internal disruption and provided for easy updating and maintenance.

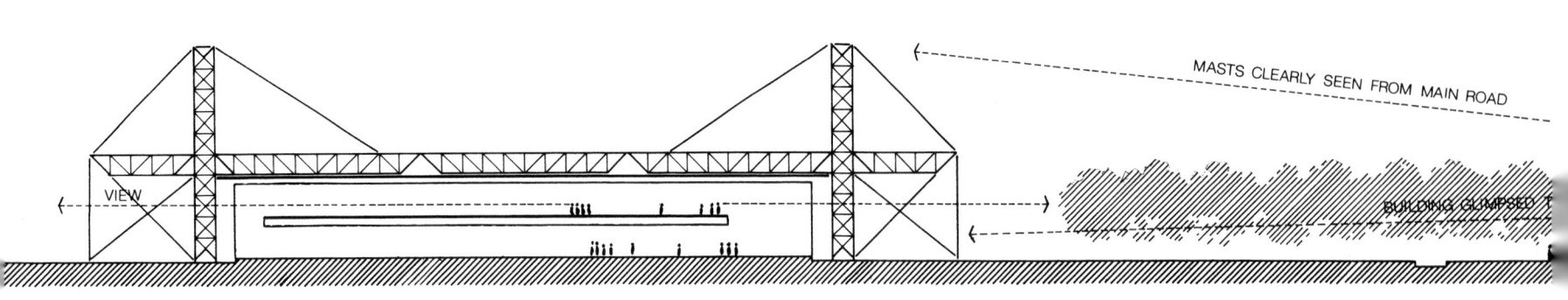

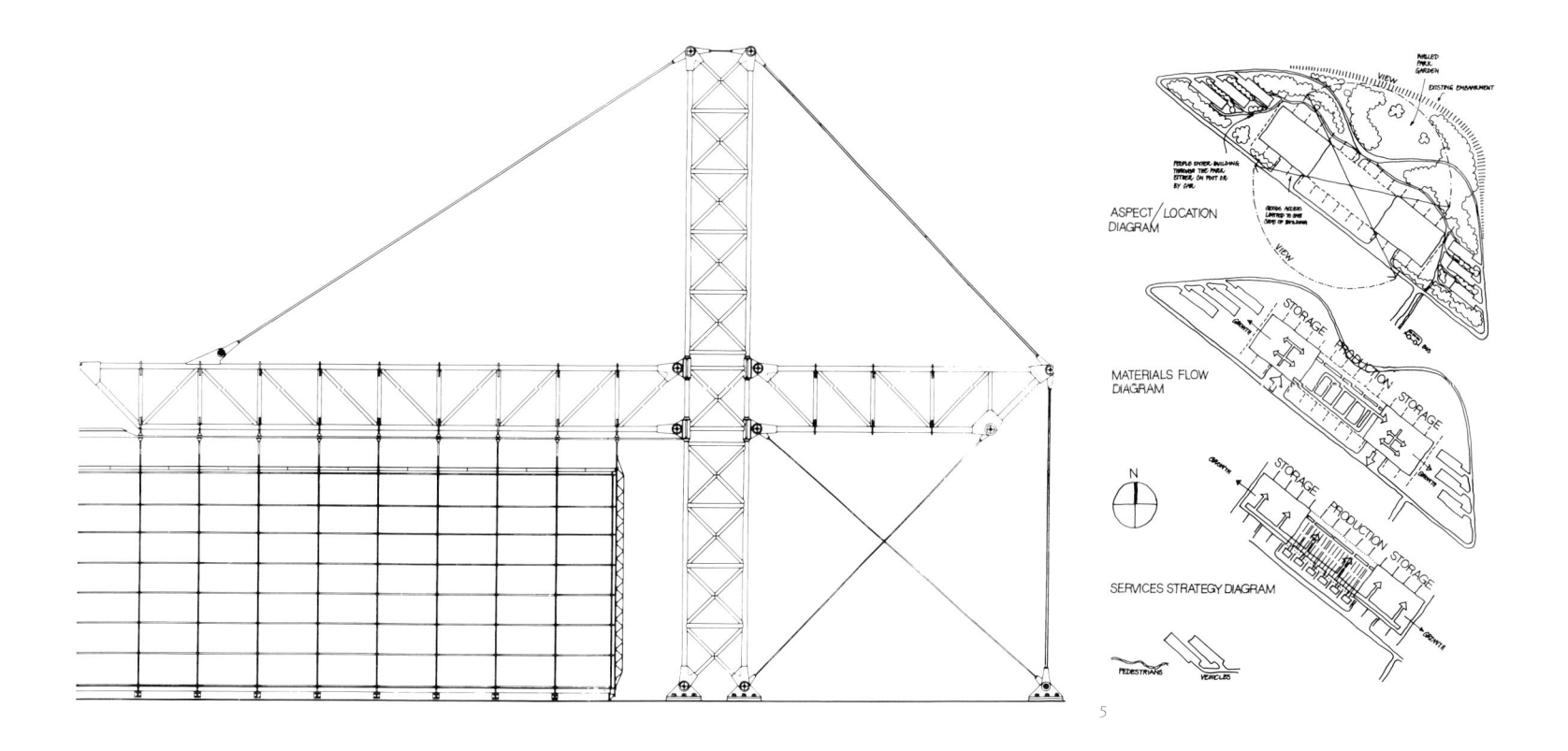

The unbuilt scheme for NAPP Laboratories outside Cambridge featured one of Rogers' masted structures – services were provided in an intermediate zone between the structure and the laboratory enclosure (1–5).

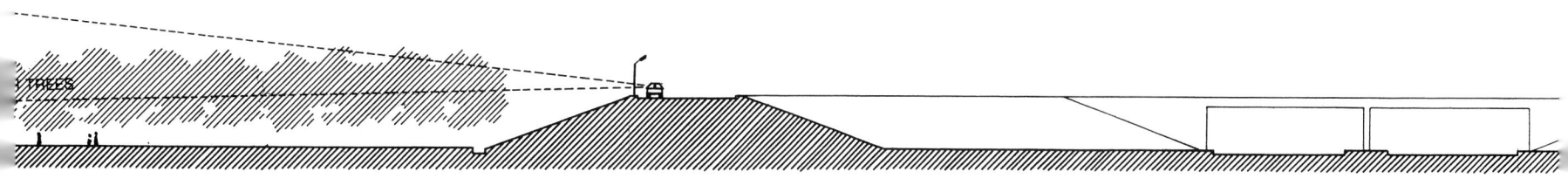

Fleetguard Factory

Quimper, Brittany, France 1979–81

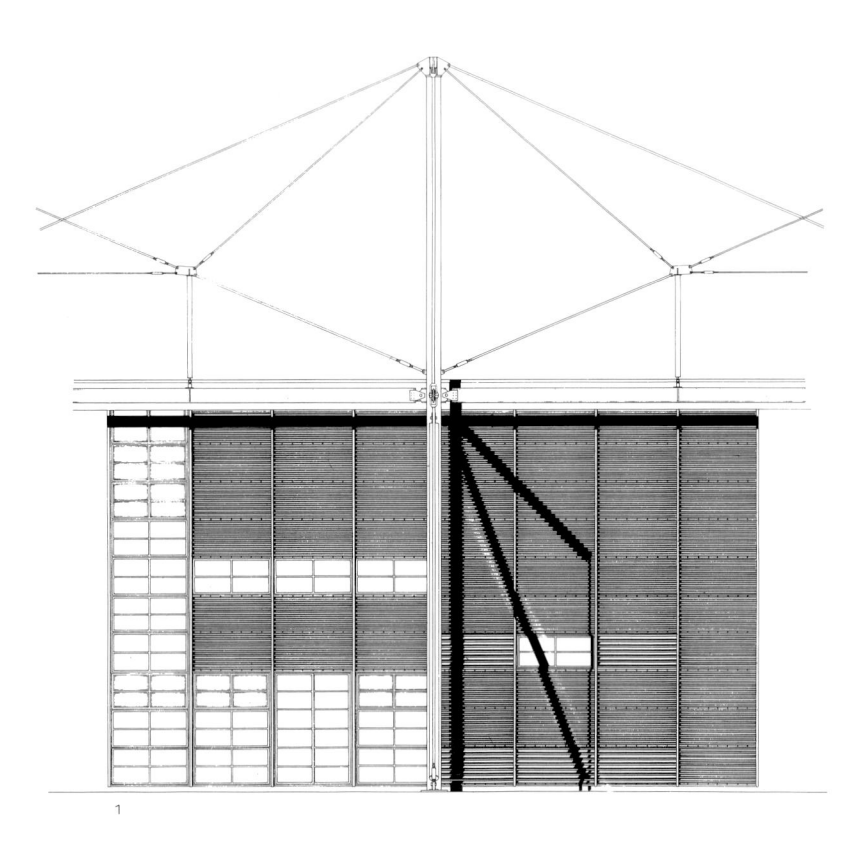

The Fleetguard Factory was the first project to be completed after the dissolution of Rogers' partnership with Renzo Piano. The client was the American Cummins company, which had a long and honourable record of architectural patronage in both the USA and Europe – Kevin Roche, who had worked extensively for Cummins in America, recommended Rogers to the company. Peter Rice headed the team from Ove Arup & Partners which advised on the structure of the building.

The brief was for the provision of a production facility for engine filters, along with warehousing and office space within the same volume – around 8,750 sq.m. in total, on a regular grid, with expansion potential for another 30,000 sq.m. on the site (close to Quimper, but on the edge of open country). The client wanted a high-value, flexible and expandable building which could equally be seen as a positive addition to – rather than a blot on – the green landscape, and an expression of the company's progressive image. Rogers addressed this brief with a scheme which remains a potent expression of his ability to combine modest cost and high style. The concept is simple, but it is realized with enormous flair; this is a large box in which the use of a suspended tension roof structure allows the largely open-plan interior to be kept free of obstructions and equally reduces the apparent height of the building in the landscape. Slender steel columns, stayed with cables, are the key to the structure – which has to cope with the heavy and uneven loadings resulting from the manufacturing processes. Services are inserted below the roof within the lofty interior, where they are accessible for maintenance and upgrading. The profiled steel cladding is merely suspended from the structure, so that an expansion of the building can be achieved from outside, with no disruption to operational functions. A band of high-level glazing introduces daylight into all parts of the interior.

By making use of the contours of the site and using excavated soil to further enhance the setting, Rogers achieved an element of drama within a basically practical agenda. The building is entered at the level of the mezzanine offices, via a lightweight bridge from the car park. There are views down into the huge production space accessed via a suspended staircase, its significance marked by the use of exposed service ducts, brightly coloured as at the Pompidou Centre. Externally, only one colour is used – a bright red for the masts and cables of the structure, a vivid expression of the basic rationale behind the building as well as a bold promotional device.

Sunk in provincial France and apparently matter-of-fact, Fleetguard is relatively little-known and far less celebrated than the much more rhetorical and expressive Inmos factory. Yet its elegant practicality shows the Rogers team working to a strict brief and transforming it to achieve something out of the ordinary.

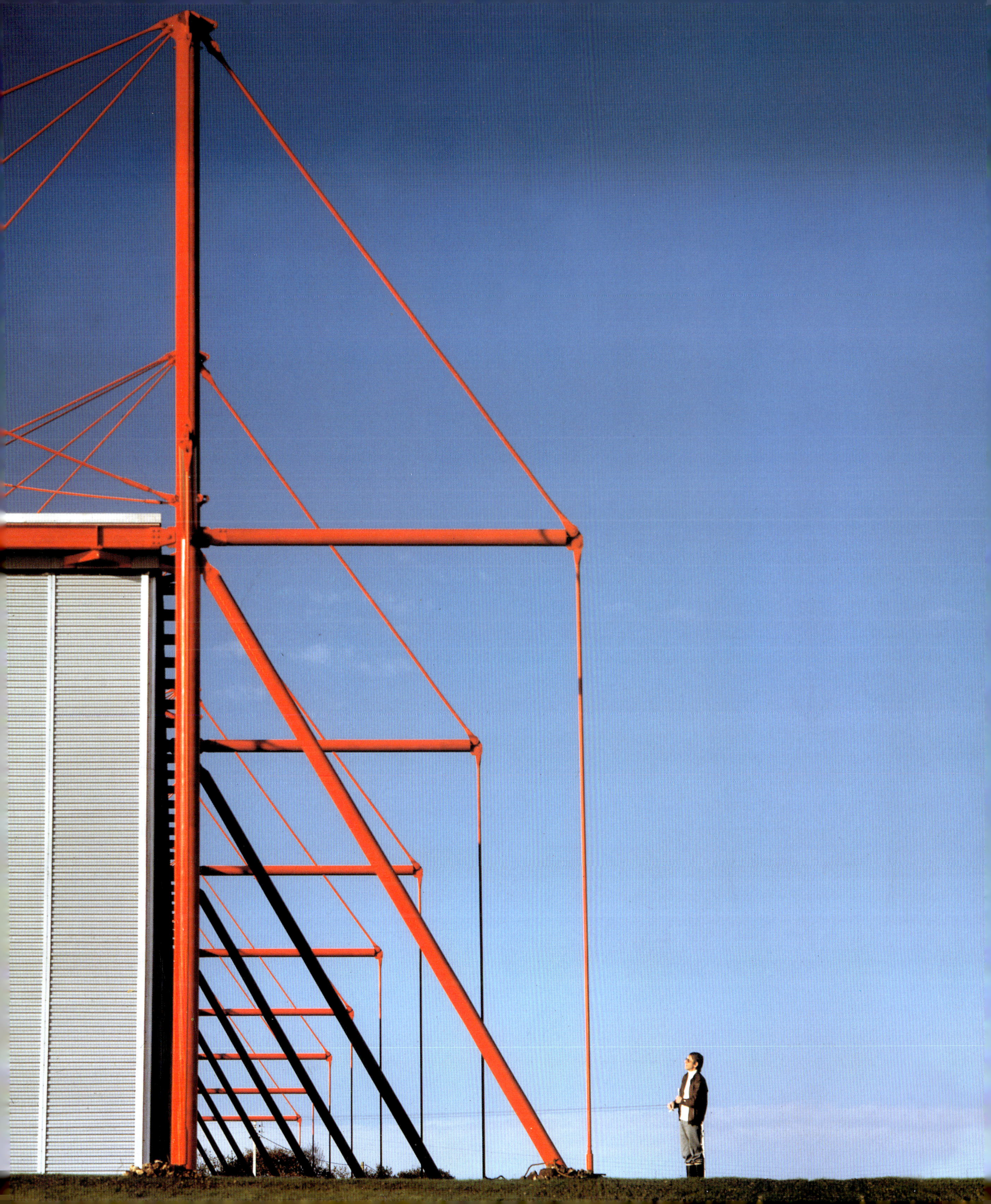

4

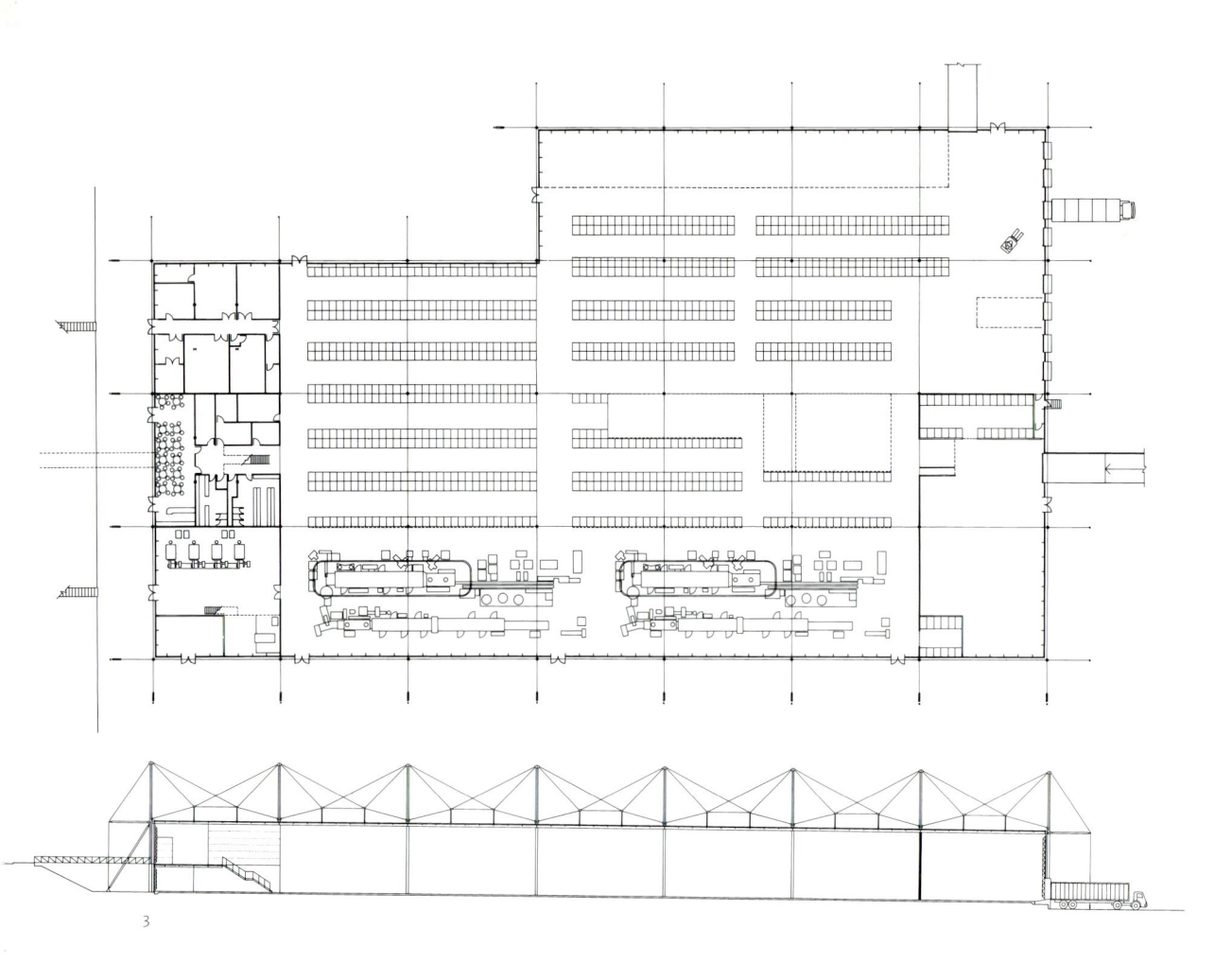

The Fleetguard plant (1 & 2, previous pages, 4 & 7), producing oil filters, was housed in a great masted shed. The masts, painted a brilliant red, acted as a powerful expression of the client's identity.

The masted structure was significant in producing, firstly, large areas of space unencumbered by internal supports and, secondly, a high degree of flexibility and potential for incremental growth (3, 5 & 6). The masts, with their suspension points, reduce the overall height, a desirable feature in its rural French setting.

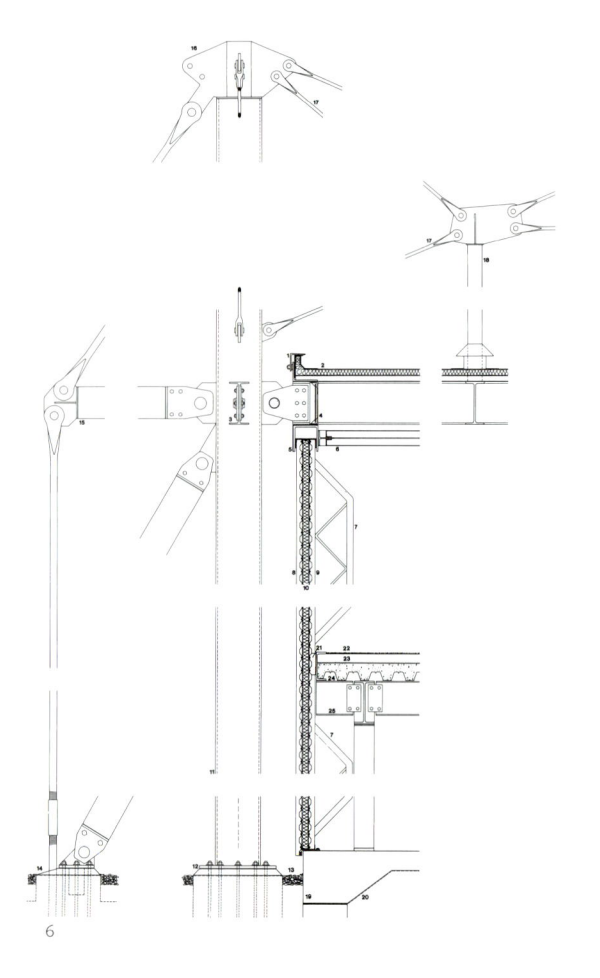

Fleetguard

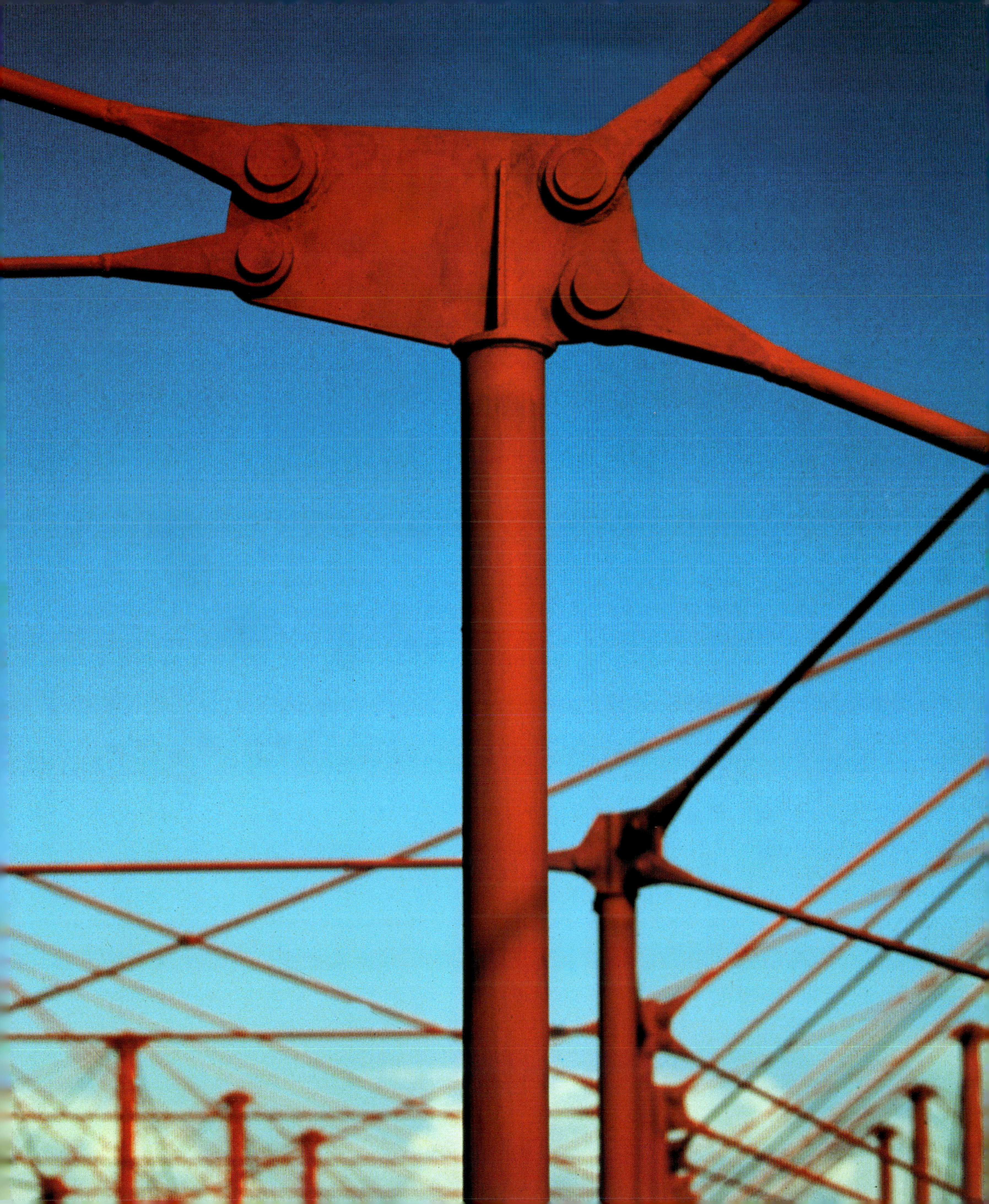

8

The building stands on a greenfield site, close to the town of Quimper. Care was taken to create a landscape setting which conceals parking and servicing, allowing the red masts to proclaim the plant's presence (8 & 9).
Internally, the production space is seen from a mezzanine office level, from which a lightweight staircase descends to the manufacturing and warehouse level (10–12).

9

Fleetguard

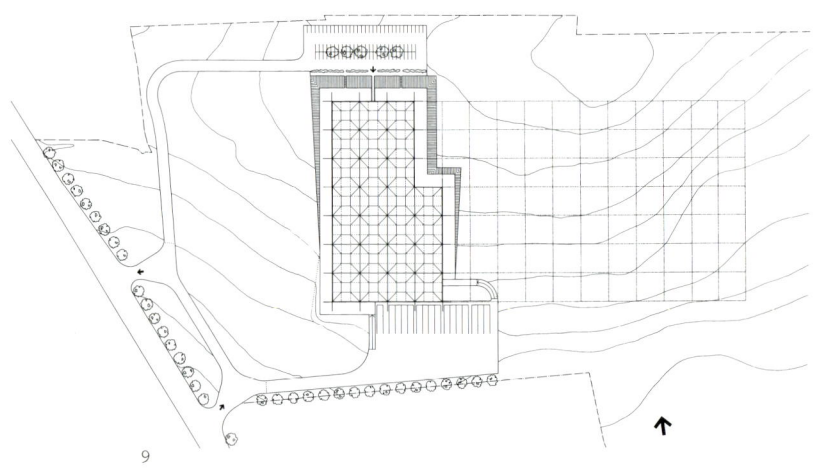

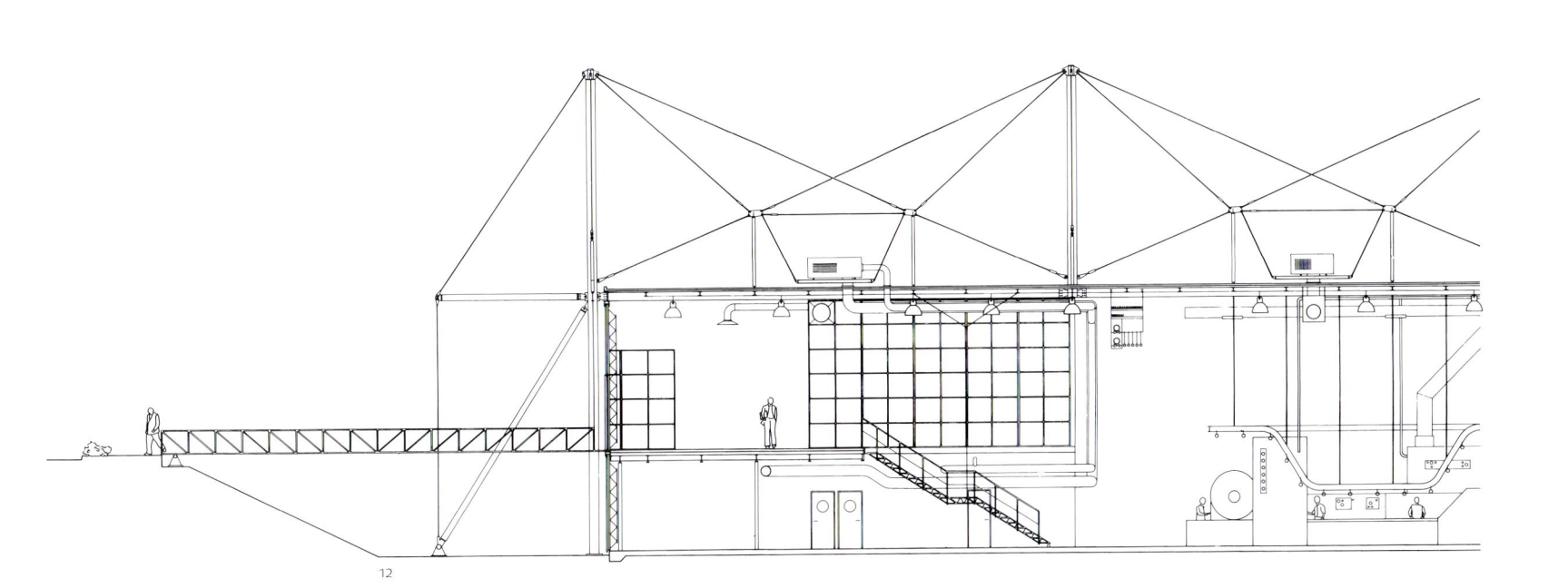

10

11

12

Coin Street Development

South Bank, London, 1979–83

The site for the Coin Street scheme was close to the South Bank arts centre, the National Theatre and Waterloo Station, in an area of London which, though close to the City and West End, retained expanses of vacant and undeveloped land as a result of wartime bombing and subsequent clearances. The intention was to create a major development of new offices, together with substantial amounts of housing, light industrial, retail and leisure space. The scheme was commercial in its rationale, but equally offered major public benefits – regenerating the area socially and economically, providing new employment and weaving it into the wider life of London. The Rogers practice became involved with the site in 1979 when the client, Greycoat Estates, faced a planning inquiry into its proposals for office development in the area.

The essence of the Rogers scheme remained constant throughout, though the scheme was much developed over the next four years. It provided for a great curve of buildings, focused on a glazed pedestrian arcade, extending from Waterloo Bridge to a point west of Blackfriars Bridge, from where a new footbridge would span the Thames thereby providing a pedestrian route from Waterloo Station to the City. The scheme was megastructural in its scope, which led to criticisms that it would dominate the locale; but it was developed to provide a civic, yet human-scaled framework for social and business life which offered an alternative to piecemeal commercial development. After the first version of the proposals was rejected in 1980, they were substantially redesigned, firstly, to reduce the element of offices and, secondly, to provide closer physical links with the existing street pattern. The architectural expression of the development became more emphatic, with the offices grouped in three distinct blocks, and with service towers – rising up to sixteen storeys in the manner of Lloyd's – punctuating the great sweep of the atrium to provide a dramatic skyline. A second public inquiry was held in 1981 and resulted in final approval, early in 1983, for the proposals – and *also* for rival proposals produced by local community activists. Partly as a result of opposition from the Labour-controlled Greater London Council (GLC), a major landowner in the Coin Street area, the Rogers scheme was abandoned in 1984.

Coin Street saw Rogers grappling with the problem of combining commercial profit with public benefits on a huge and controversial site and against a taut political background. (The launch of his scheme came soon after the election of Margaret Thatcher's Conservative government, which set out to abolish the GLC.) The aim was 'to create a public meeting place which optimizes the river and weaves together the isolated activities in the neighbourhood ... an open-ended flexible infrastructure capable of fostering a wide range of local and metropolitan activities...' In its final version, the scheme included 92,500 sq.m. of offices, 18,500 sq.m. of residential space – both speculative and 'social' – 10,500 sq.m. of shops and restaurants, 6,500 sq.m. of leisure use and a small area of light industrial space.

Rogers addressed the concerns of both the isolation of the South Bank arts centre, developed in the aftermath of the 1951 Festival of

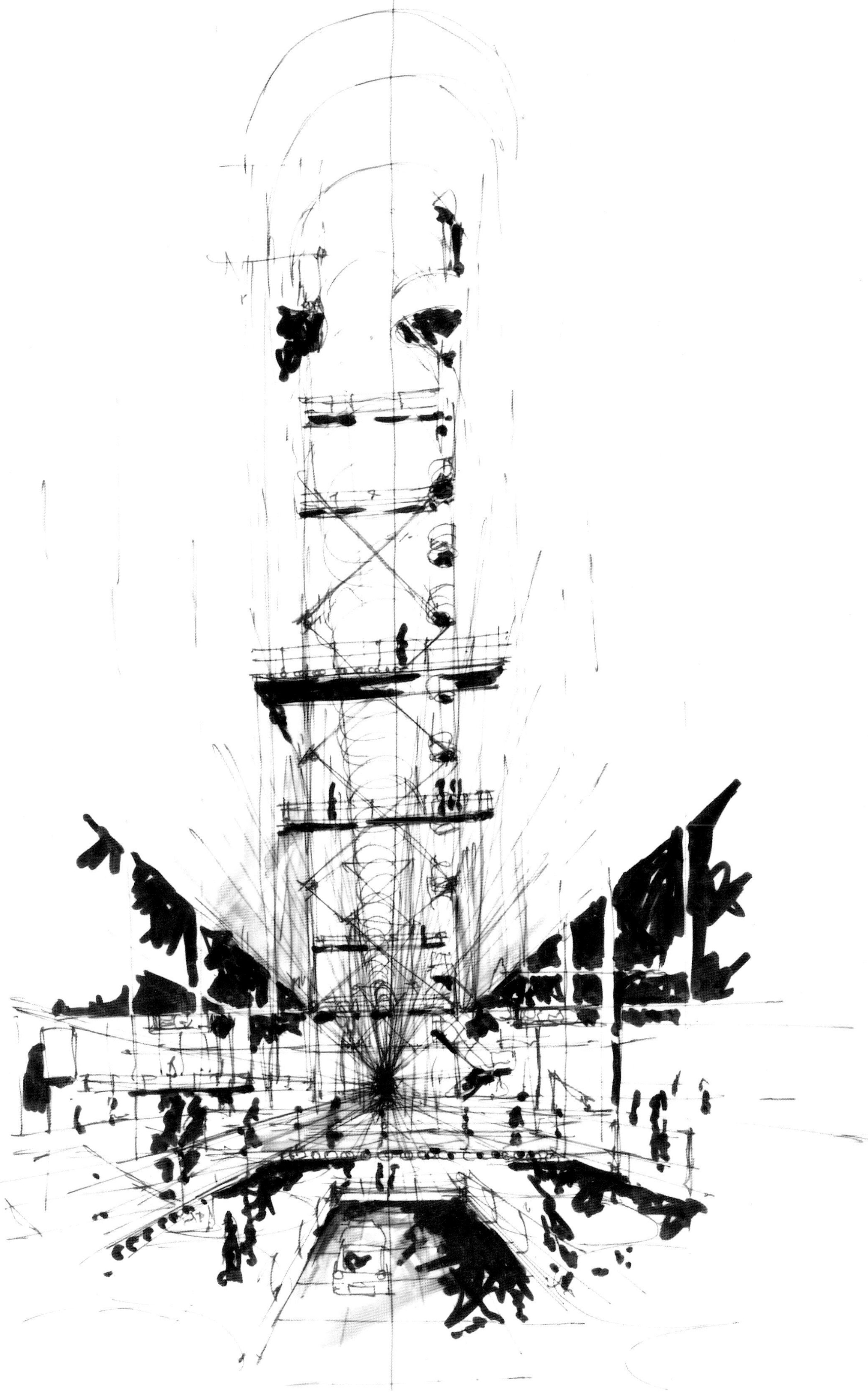

2

3

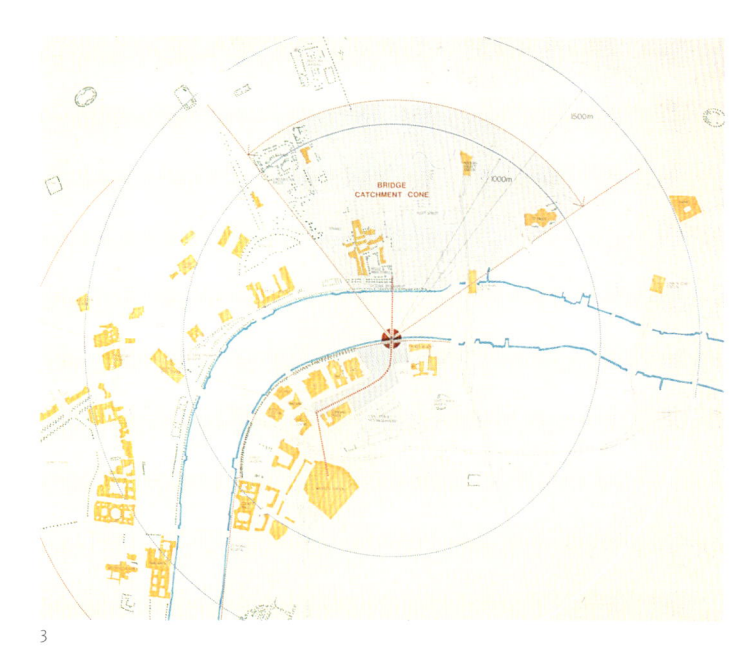

The Coin Street project was designed for a key site in London (3), a natural link between the cultural quarter of the South Bank and the City, to be connected by a great public galleria (1 & 2, previous pages). Superficially the scheme was a megastructure, yet the office space was broken down into a series of towers, producing a superb skyline, while the ground level space was almost entirely public. The scheme also included significant public space on the river (4 & 5).

Britain, and the neglect of the River Thames as a focus for London. The South Bank, it was argued, faced 'a crisis of place', being detached from the life of the capital. A flexible environment where all sorts of people could meet might produce a regenerating influence. The glazed arcade, a familiar feature of London and other British cities and seen to spectacular effect in the Galleria Vittorio Emmanuele in Milan, would be 'full of light, sun and shade', a meeting place for London – which had suffered from past failure to integrate buildings and public space – and particularly appropriate in the changeable British climate. The development would stitch together new and old, repairing a damaged urban fabric, and create new routes across the site while eroding the isolation of South London.

Coin Street is Rogers' great unbuilt scheme. It foundered for a variety of reasons, but they were largely political. Although the Thatcher government was anxious to give free rein to developers, there was strong pressure, which it heeded, to protect views along the river. The community campaigning group in the Coin Street area, bolstered by the election of a Labour GLC in 1981, opposed office development on principle and wanted only housing for rent built on the site. It dismissed as spurious Greycoat's claims to be benefiting the local community, ignoring the fact that virtually the entire ground level of the development would have been public space, not to mention the public piazza on the river. The polarized politics of 1980s Britain killed the scheme and left the South Bank in limbo, with only a banal, low-rise housing scheme on the Coin Street site. The architecture of the Rogers scheme was never fully developed and was given too little regard, yet the drawings, some of the best of them by Laurie Abbott, suggest a dynamic development of Lloyd's and look forward to the Rogers proposals for Paternoster Square, for Berlin's Potsdamerplatz and even for Shanghai. The controversy over Coin Street raised the temperature of the architectural and planning debate in Britain. The issues raised were to be further explored in the case of developments like Broadgate and Canary Wharf. With the abandonment of the Coin Street scheme, the South Bank lost a chance of benefiting hugely from the property boom of the 1980s, and the problems of the area remained only partially resolved in the late 1990s.

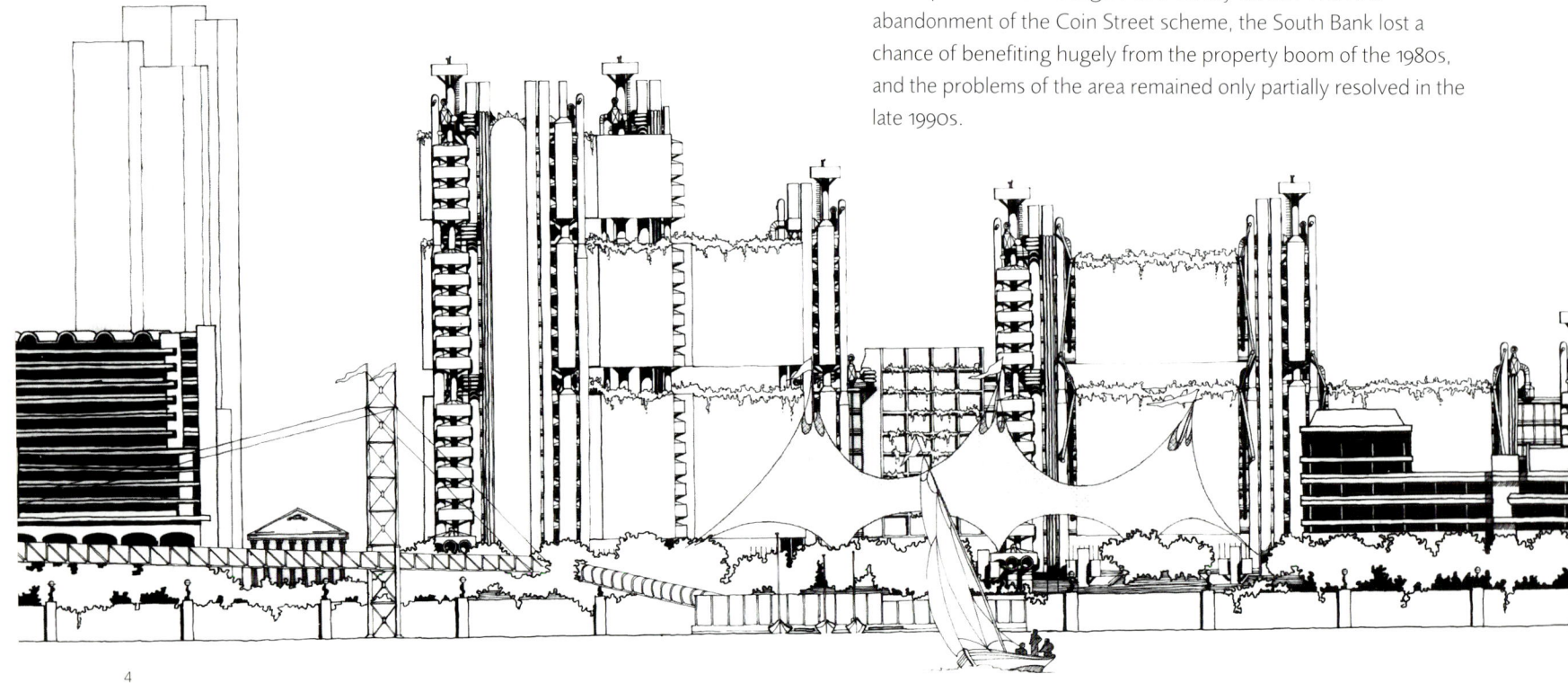

4

5

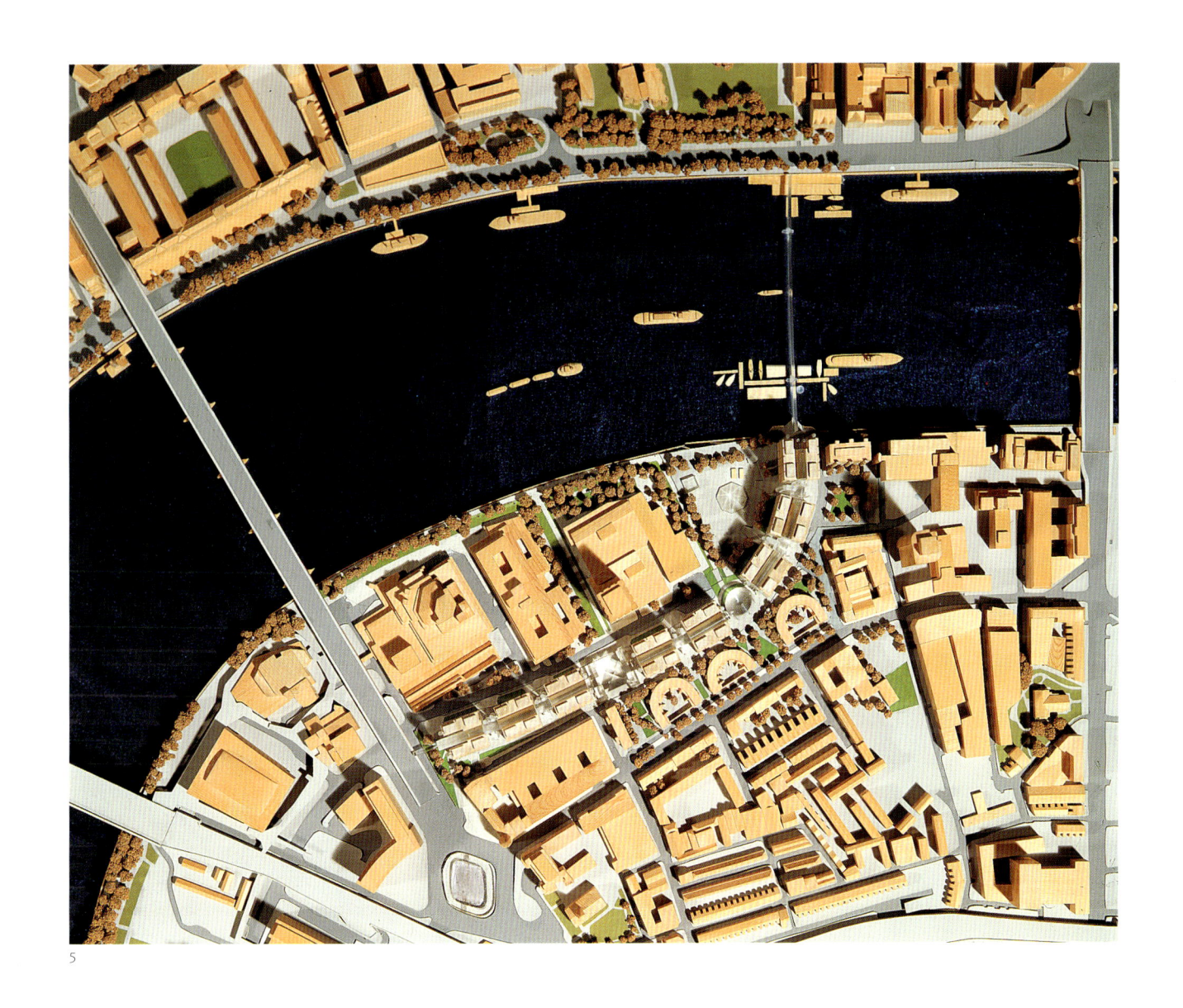

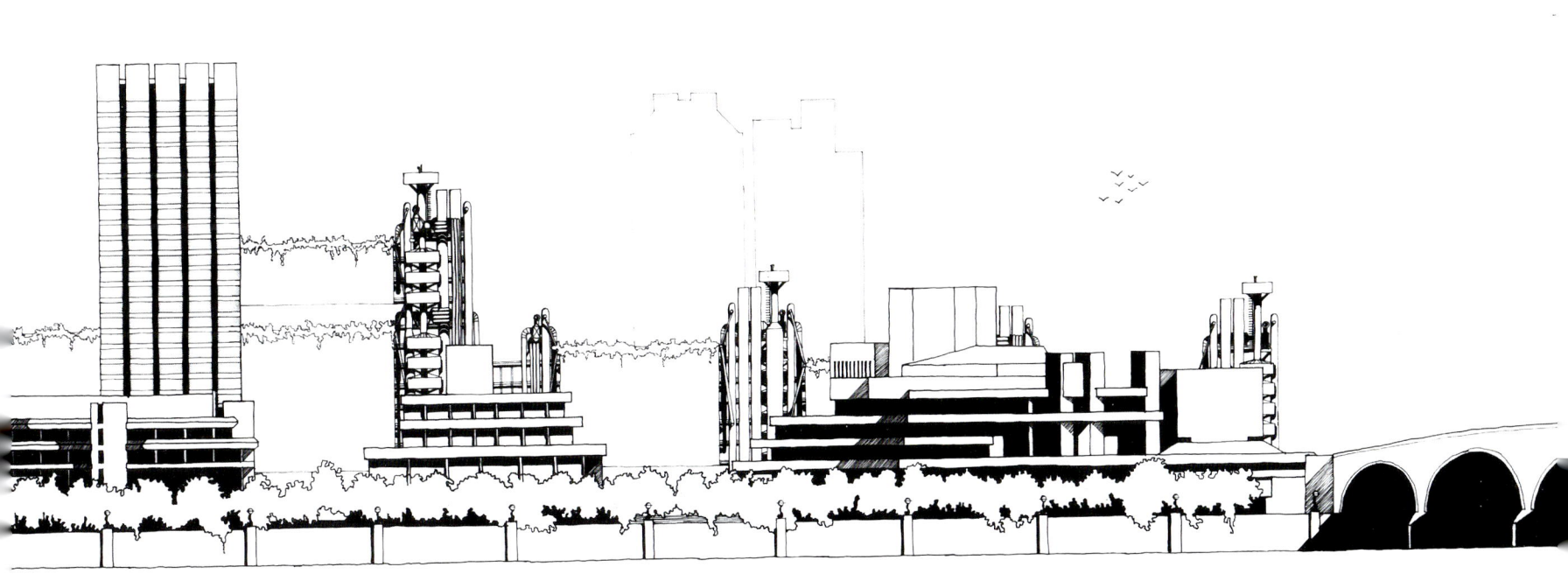

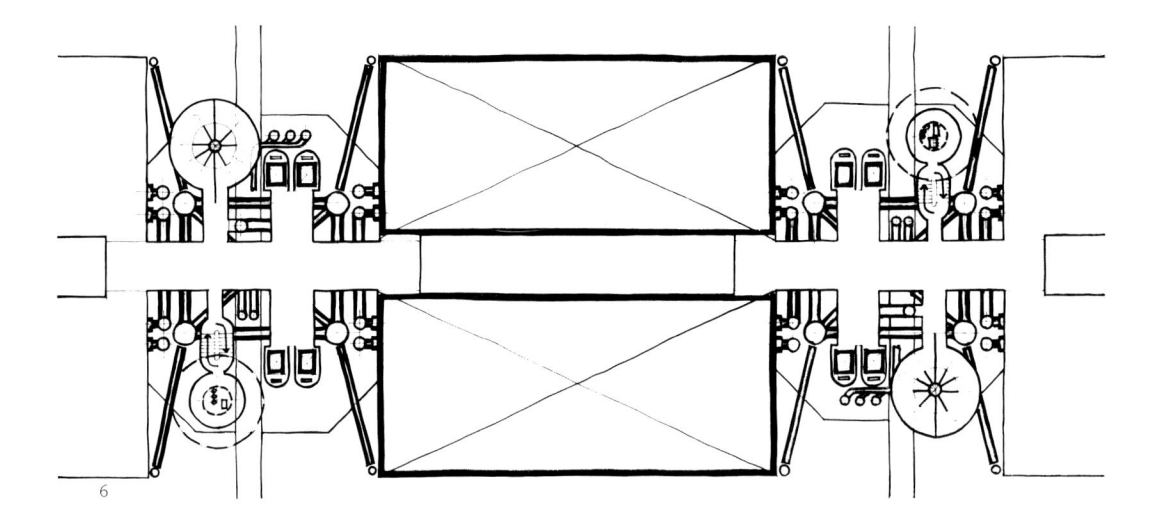

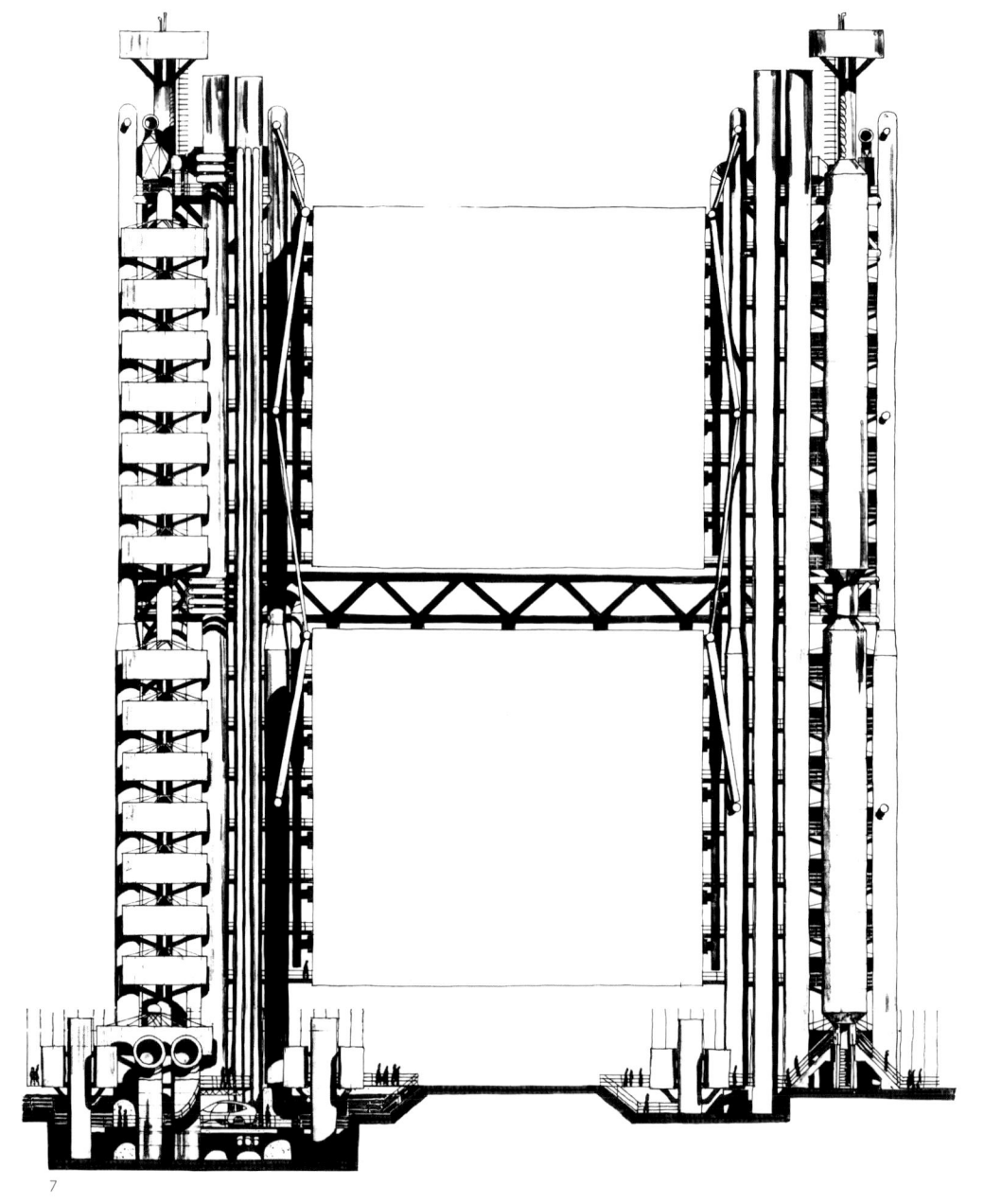

The architectural language of the scheme was clearly related to that of Lloyd's; service and structure towers punctuated the skyline, and offices were strung between them (6–8).

Coin Street Development

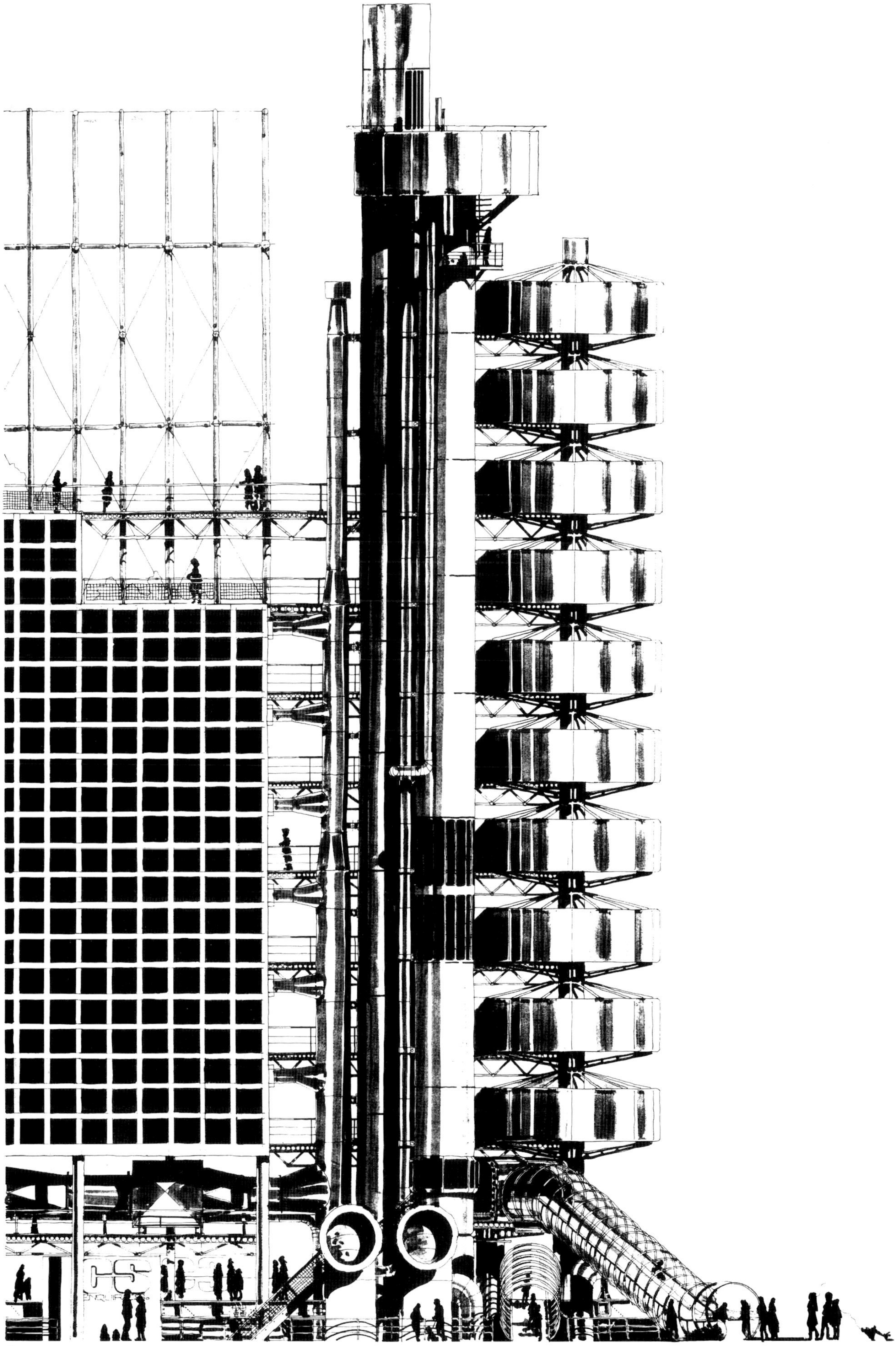

8

The development of London's long-neglected Docklands provided many opportunities for innovative architecture, though all too often exceptional sites were wasted on commonplace schemes. This eventually happened at Free Trade Wharf, situated off the Highway, the link road from the City of London to the Isle of Dogs. There were some existing warehouses of real quality, though utterly derelict, at the Wharf – a 6-acre site which offered ample space for new buildings. The assumption was that the development would be predominantly residential, though some shopping and other ancillary amenities could possibly be developed.

The obvious strategy was to restore the old warehouses, which stood well back from the river and close to the very busy road, as shops and restaurants along a new glazed galleria leading to the river. The new housing was to 'hug' the riverside, with every flat having a river view. The traditional corridor was eliminated in favour of access from lifts (one to every four flats) set in a dramatic run of service towers providing a strong, even emphatic, addition to the riverside. There were echoes here of the Coin Street development. The scheme was, however, not built. Some of the ideas behind it were incorporated into the Thameside housing schemes at Hammersmith and Battersea.

Free Trade Wharf

London, 1981

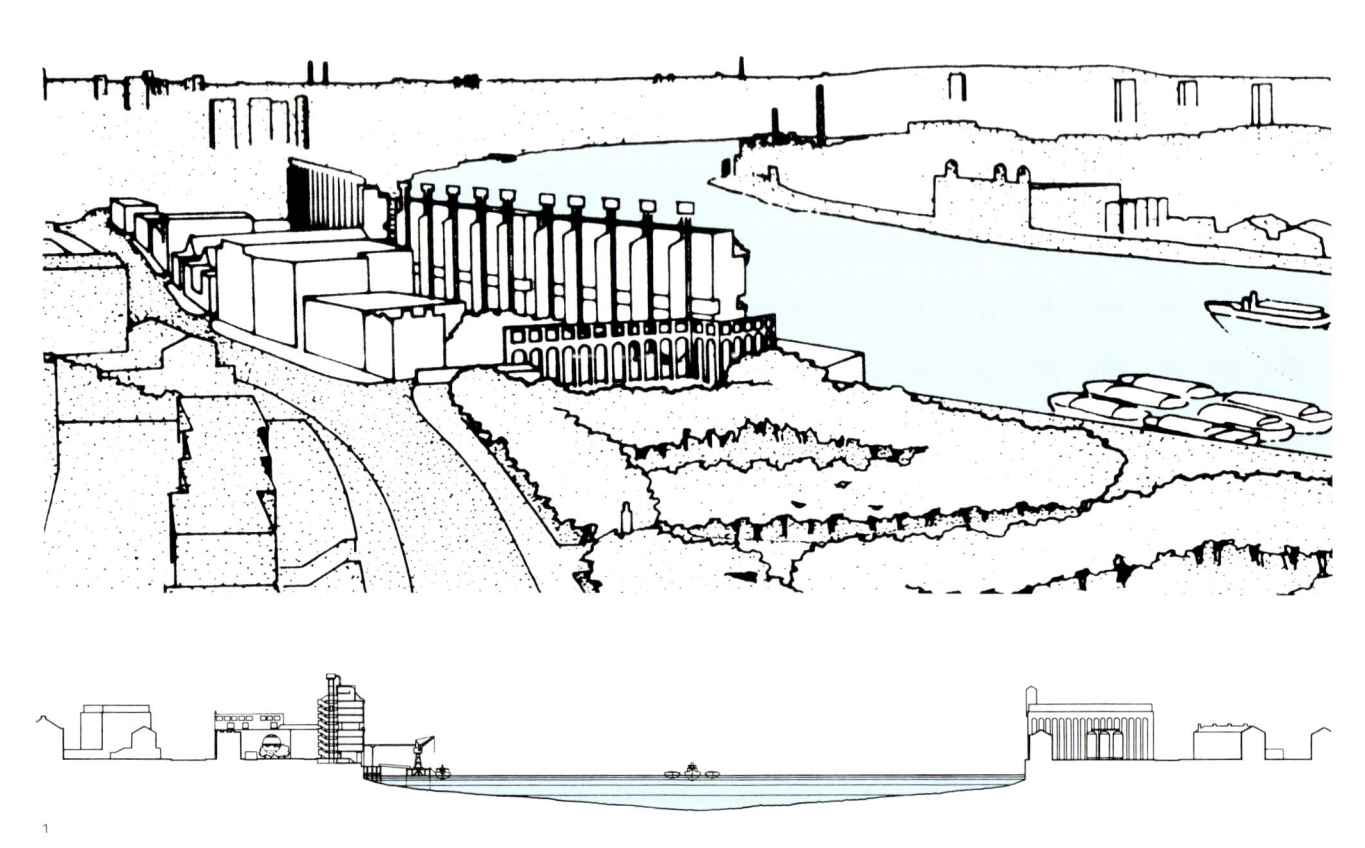

1

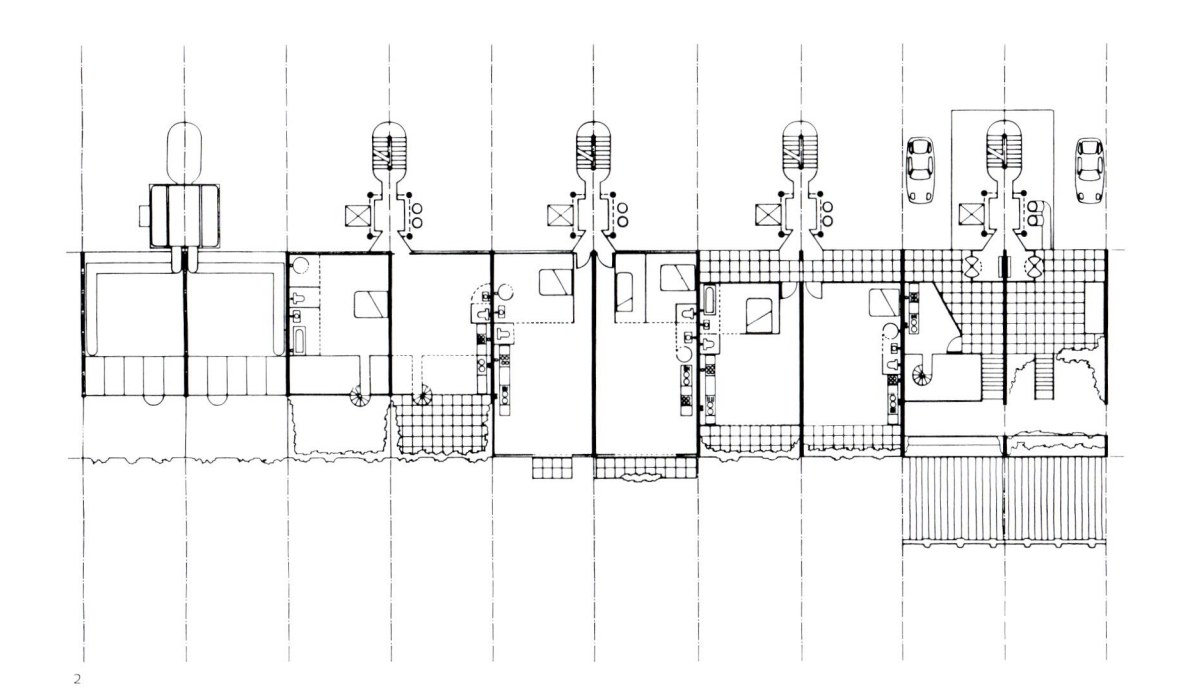

At Free Trade Wharf, as at Coin Street, Rogers addressed the issues of building on the Thames. The scale of the proposed apartment blocks recalled that of Docklands warehouses and silos. Staircase/service towers were again used to provide an element of drama in the skyline. Existing listed buildings on the site were to be retained (1–3).

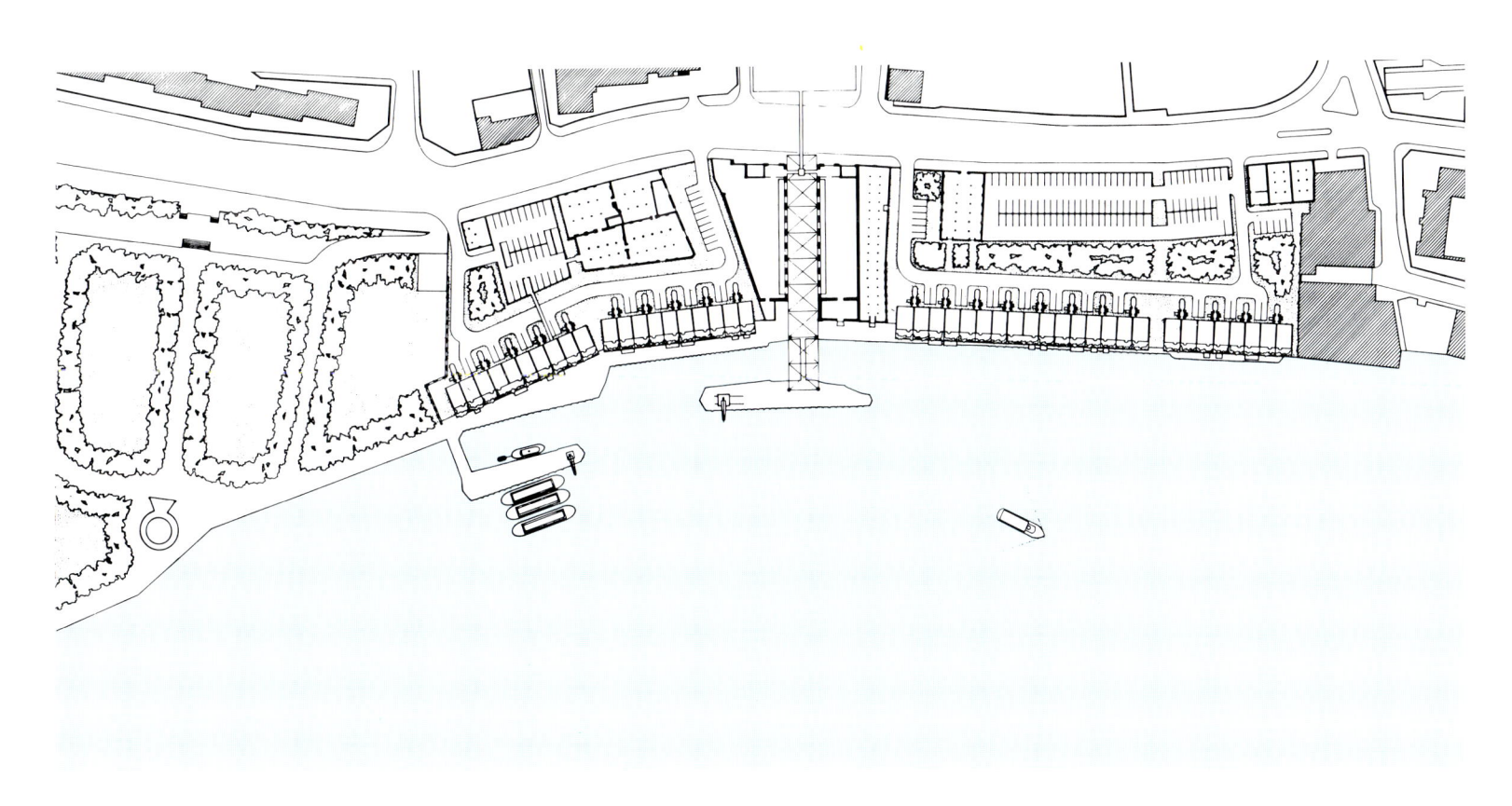

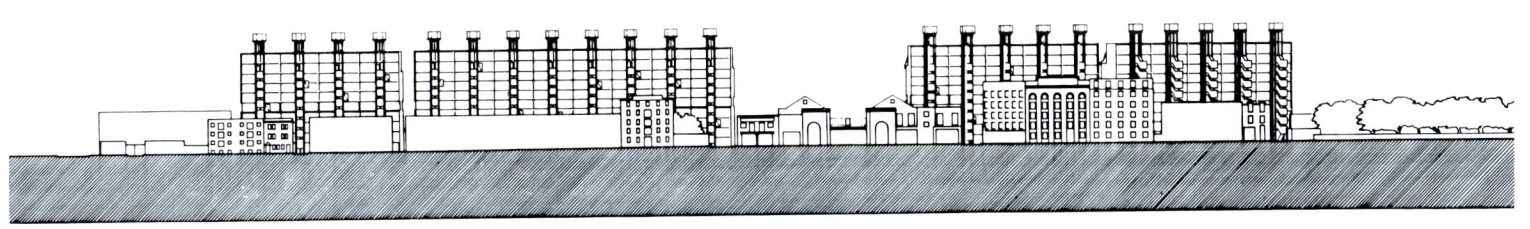

Inmos Microprocessor Factory

Newport, Wales, 1982

The Inmos Microprocessor Factory was the lateral descendant of the Reliance Controls Electronics Factory. Designed a decade and a half later, Inmos was built at a time when Britain's traditional industries were rapidly withering or being radically restructured, while new, electronics-based industries were seen as the key to the future. Despite its predilection for the dogmas of market economics, the Thatcher government of the 1980s accepted that the state should take a lead in promoting and even financing the growth of this new sector of the economy and continued the support given by its Labour predecessor for the Inmos project. Rogers' client was Ian Barron who was charged with developing a major British presence in the silicon chip industry (then largely the preserve of the American West Coast).

The initial work on the project had been directed towards developing a model factory, suitable for construction virtually anywhere – no specific site had been identified, rather like the earlier ARAM project in Piano + Rogers days. In the USA, where California's booming 'Silicon Valley' was the centre of the chip industry, factories were erected, expensively rebuilt and refitted and then torn down – all within a few years. This reflected the sheer dynamism of the new electronic age, but was wasteful, inconvenient and disruptive for management and research staff. (Since total cleanliness was vital, any building work generally meant that a factory had to shut down for its duration.) The brief to Rogers embodied the lessons of the American experience – adaptability and flexibility in use were now regarded as essential. An architectural framework was needed which could respond to ever-changing technical specifications – Inmos made it clear that these could be rewritten several times even while the building was being constructed. Added to the complete uncertainty on the siting of the factory (eventually located close to the M4 motorway in Gwent, South Wales) this posed major problems for the design team, which included Tony Hunt as structural engineer and quantity surveyors Hanscomb who had also been part of the Reliance Controls team.

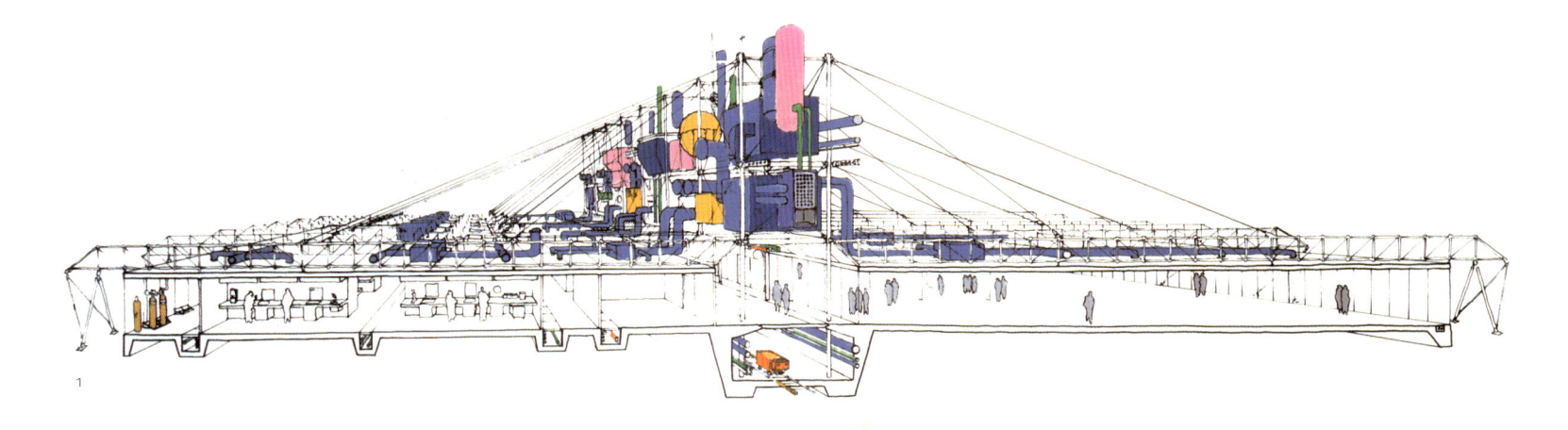

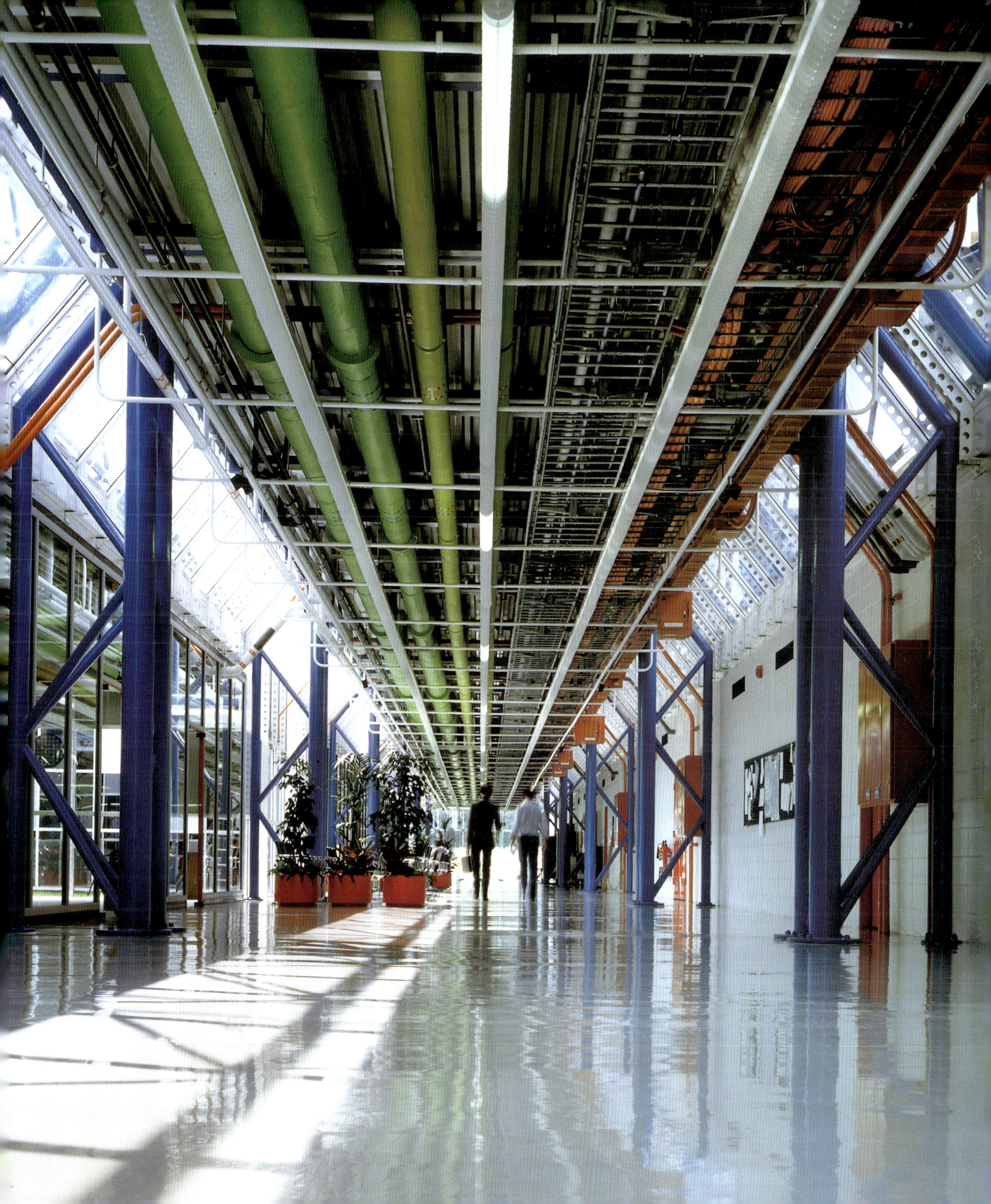

3

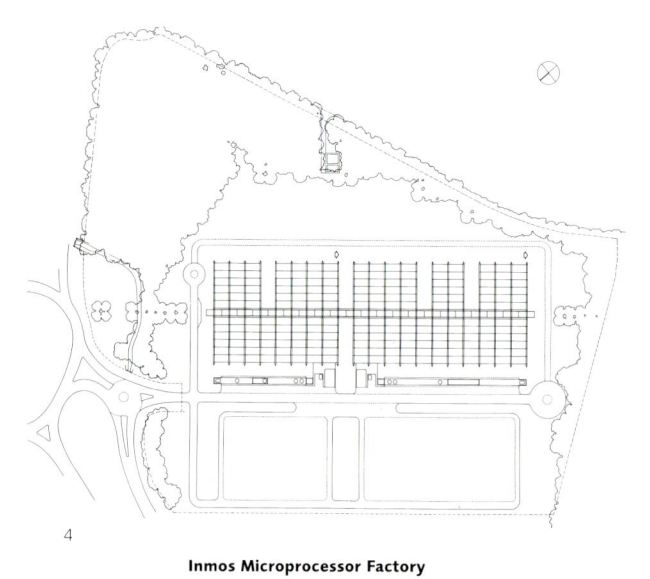

The heart of Inmos (1 & 2, previous pages & 5) is an internal 'street': a place for staff to meet as well as a circulation route and a reflection of Rogers' social approach to design. The Inmos Factory was designed without a definite site in mind. It was eventually located in Gwent (3 & 4) close to the M4 motorway, where it has become a startling local landmark.
The masted structure – related to, but far more radical than that of Fleetguard – allows column-free space to be provided in the wings, used respectively for actual microprocessor production and for office and social space. The internal 'street' joined the two halves (5).
The kit-of-parts of the services was disposed along the central spine (6 & 7).

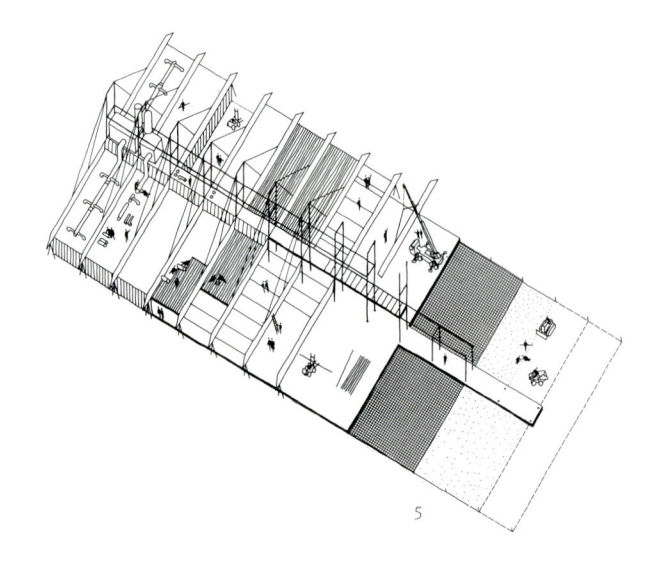

4

Inmos Microprocessor Factory

5

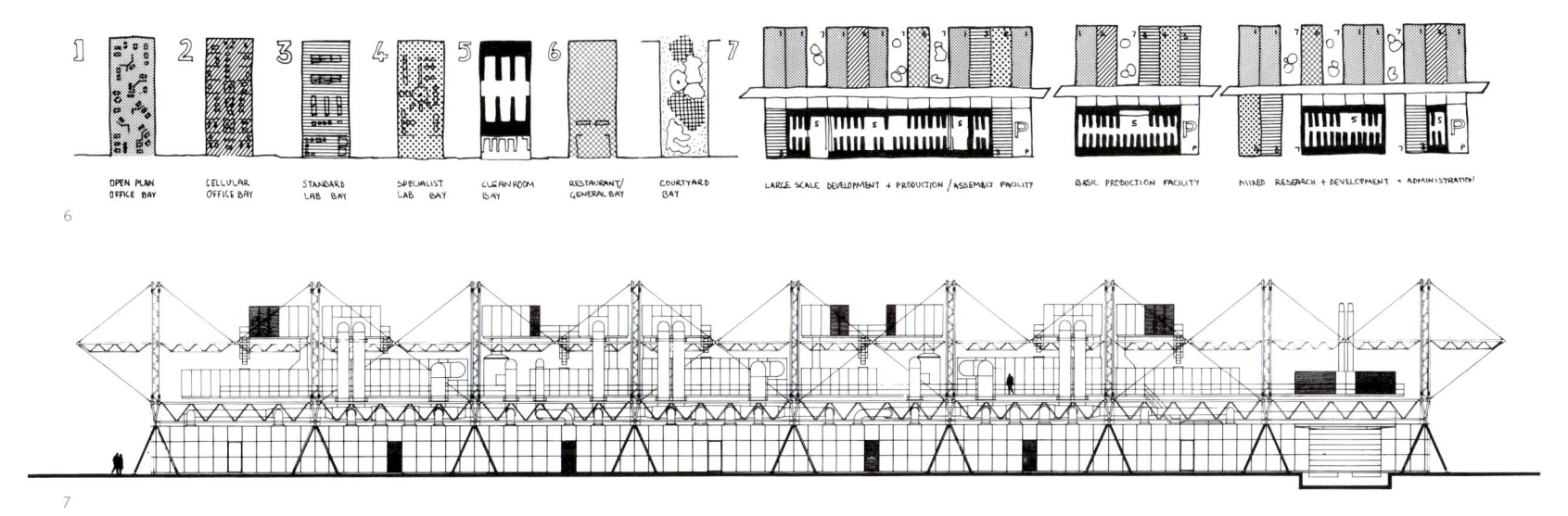

1	2	3	4	5	6	7
OPEN PLAN OFFICE BAY	CELLULAR OFFICE BAY	STANDARD LAB BAY	SPECIALIST LAB BAY	CLEANROOM BAY	RESTAURANT/ GENERAL BAY	COURTYARD BAY

LARGE SCALE DEVELOPMENT + PRODUCTION / ASSEMBLY FACILITY

BASIC PRODUCTION FACILITY

MIXED RESEARCH + DEVELOPMENT + ADMINISTRATION

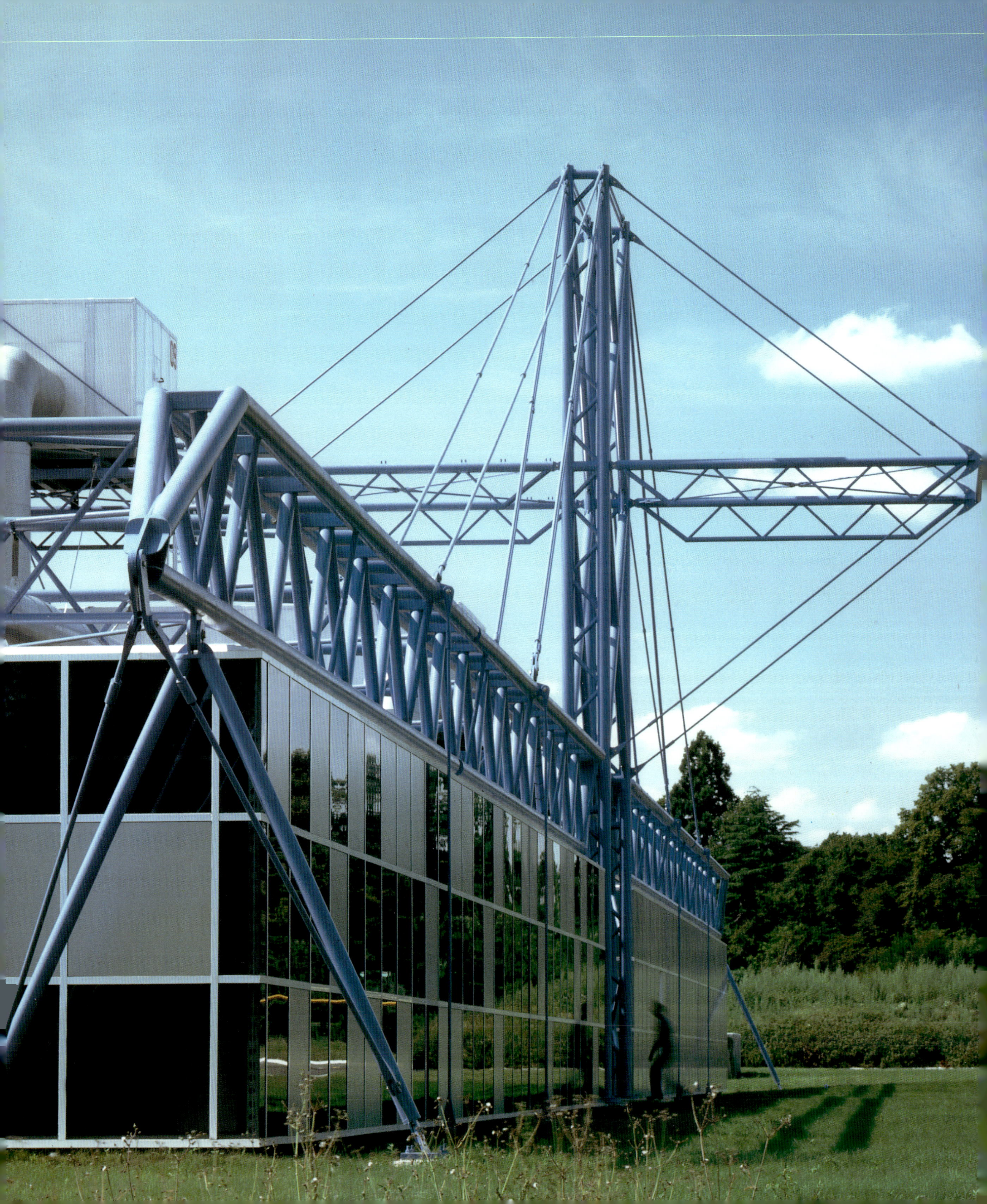

A number of design parameters were, however, established early on in the project. These focused on flexibility of layout and services, with 'clean' rooms entirely free of columns and totally protected not only from dust particles but from potentially destructive vibration. The building had to be fast-track – ready for operation within one year of starting on site – and capable of being expanded while operations continued. (The life of the building was envisaged as no more than seven years, but it was still in operation in the late 1990s.) Finally, the client wanted a high-profile, flagship building, a visible symbol of the technological leap forward which it represented, not a dumb shed in the American tradition.

The Rogers team, which was led by Mike Davies with Pierre Botschi overseeing construction, adopted a kit-of-parts approach allowing for a high degree of off-site prefabrication. The central element in the scheme is an extendable spine, containing a 106-m. long internal 'street' for circulation, flanked by very wide, column-free wings. One of the wings, built to a 36 x 13 m. module, houses the production area – the 'clean room' – while the other contains offices and support space, including a cafeteria. The 'street' is the meeting place, with seating areas and reception for visitors (who are under constant supervision). The production area is protected by a zone of locker rooms where employees change into the 'space suits' which are a further precaution against contamination. Structural support for the wings is provided by a system of tension rods from the top of the central spine – no internal support is needed. The connection to the roof trusses is by means of a pin-joint – only the 'H' frame of the

Services are concentrated in a series of containers on top of the central spine allowing easy maintenance for rapid upgrading in line with the changing needs of the users (9–11).
The masted structure (12) has a practical logic. Equally it was no accident that it gives the building a strong symbolic presence (8).

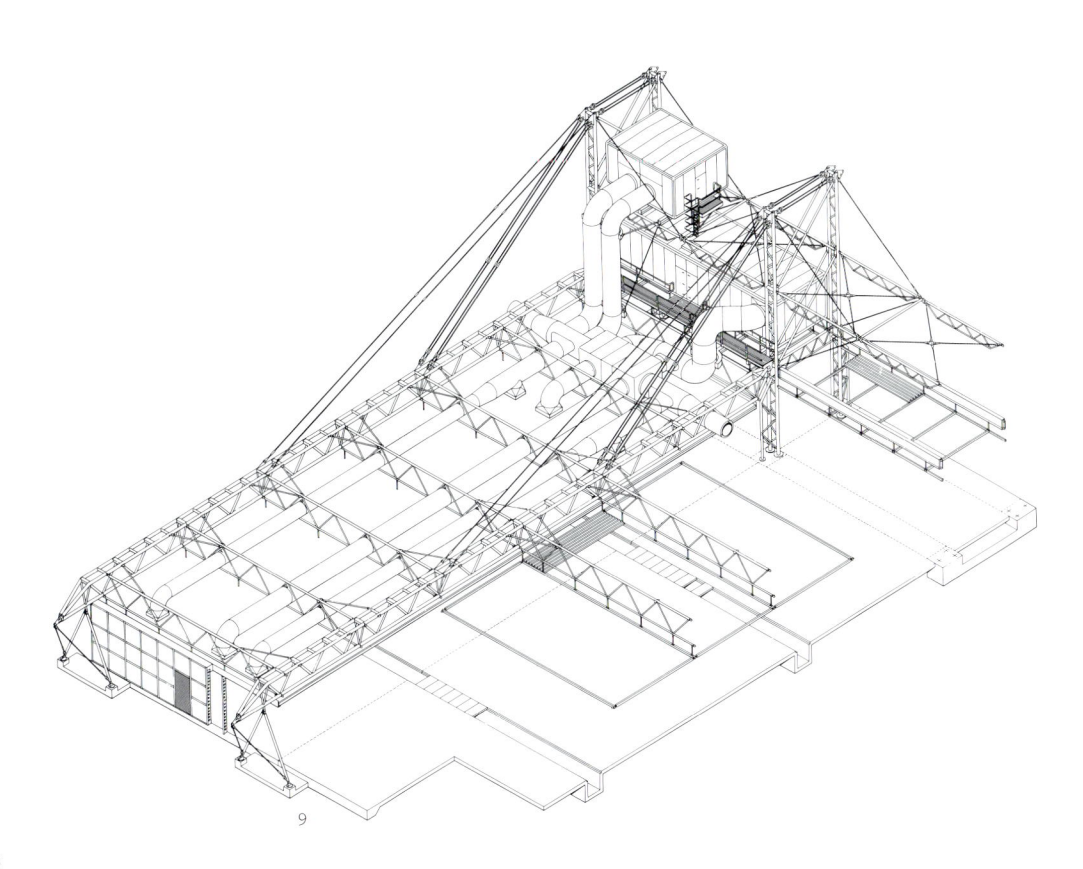

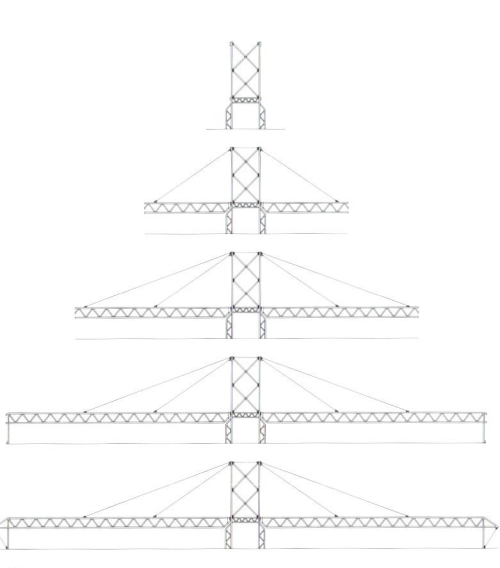

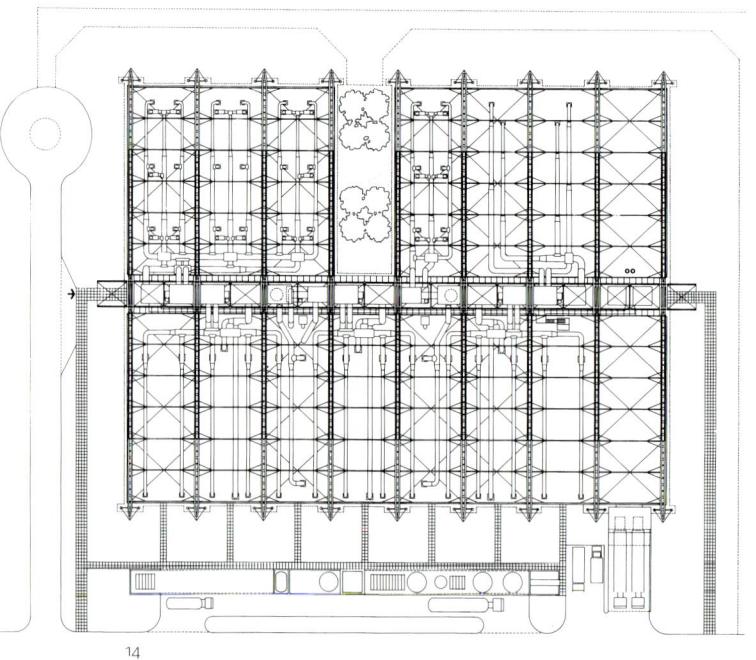

Inmos Microprocessor Factory

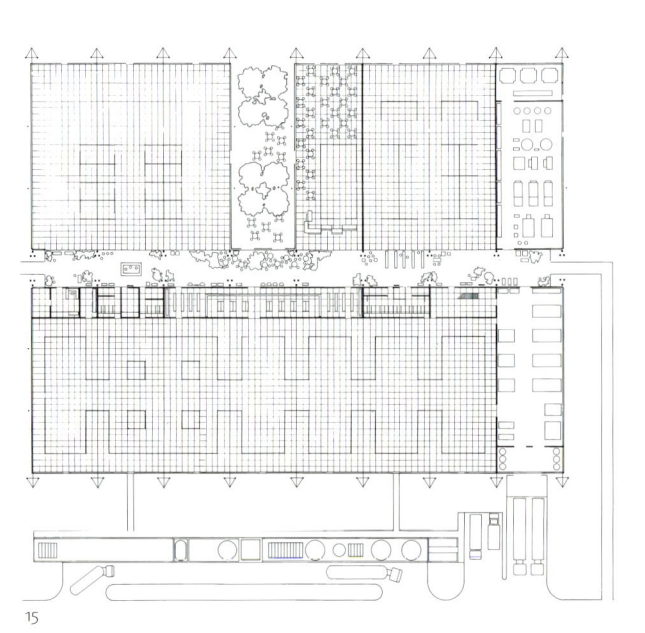

The central 'street' is a dynamic space using the services to startling aesthetic effect (13). The plan (14 & 15) is vigorously practical and reflects the exigencies of the production process in its location of clean production on one side of the spine and support and recreation facilities on the other (16). The interior of the production area is highly secure and highly serviced – in the 'clean' zone staff wear protective clothing to avoid contamination (17–19).

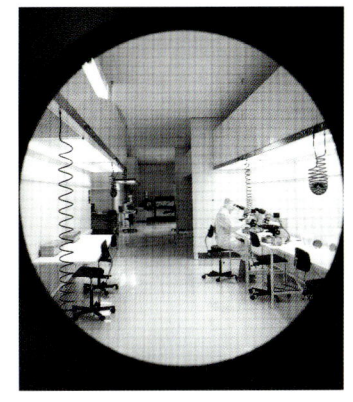

central spine is rigid. Services are mounted on top of the spine and piped to the wings – a random display of services, as depicted in early versions of the scheme, was ruled out in favour of containment within a uniform series of boxes, from which ducts snake across the flat roofs to serve the spaces below. These boxes can be removed or augmented as the need arises. The cladding is a flexible system, allowing the users to freely alter the walls by selecting from a range of solid, opaque or transparent panels. Not surprisingly, the production wing is clad in solid sandwich panels, while the appearance of the office/support wing is a random-looking mix. The latter irritated Reyner Banham (who wrote an incisive – and generally positive – critique of Inmos). Banham criticised 'the lack of conviction that makes this side of the building the weakest part of a very strong design'. For Mike Davies, however, the 'speckled' wall makes sense in the context of a flexible building which adapts to users' needs – it is almost a symbol of flexibility. (In his 1981 article on 'A wall for all seasons', Davies had declared that 'a polyvalent wall as the envelope of a building will remove the distinction between solid and transparent ... The polyvalent wall is ... a chameleon skin adapting itself to provide best possible interior conditions.')

Banham's piece addressed the 'functionalism' of Inmos. 'The air of conviction that pervades almost every part of the design', he wrote, 'seems to derive, as in naval architecture, from a sense of necessity, a feeling that nothing could be other than the way it is. As in the best nautical design, much of that necessity is rhetorical (the way things ought to be) or superstitious (the way things feel right) as often as it is rational or pragmatic, but the main thing is that it should be understood to be there.' Banham contrasted Rogers' approach with that of the International Style, 'when unquestioned custom or rigid rules could guide the designer through the blank passages where necessity could not come to the aid of art'.

The suspended structure of Inmos had been previewed in the Fleetguard manufacturing and distribution centre, but Fleetguard, despite its verve, was matter-of-fact alongside Inmos. In many respects – colour, expressiveness, the use of services as sculpture – Inmos echoed some of the key themes of the Pompidou Centre. Pompidou was a public building, visited by millions annually. Inmos was a highly secure, rarified environment. Yet the central 'street' of Inmos provided one of the most potent images seen of Rogers' ability to create social space for people. Like Pompidou, Inmos was compared to a great ship, moored, on this occasion, on a flat industrial site close to the Bristol Channel. Banham, typically, got to the root of the nautical analogy. Inmos was designed to function with the smooth efficiency of an ocean liner, but it was also designed to look good. The emphatic form of the building – actually not unlike a vast aircraft, with fuselage and wings – was echoed in the designs for PA Technology Laboratories, Princeton. There the imagery of the structure was pushed to extremes. Inmos, in comparison, for all its hyperbole and demonstrative display of virtuosity, has a straightforward modesty which suggests that the architecture really is an inevitable consequence of structural and functional necessity. In this sense, Inmos comes close to being a perfect expression of the intentions behind Rogers' architecture.

National Gallery Extension

London, 1982

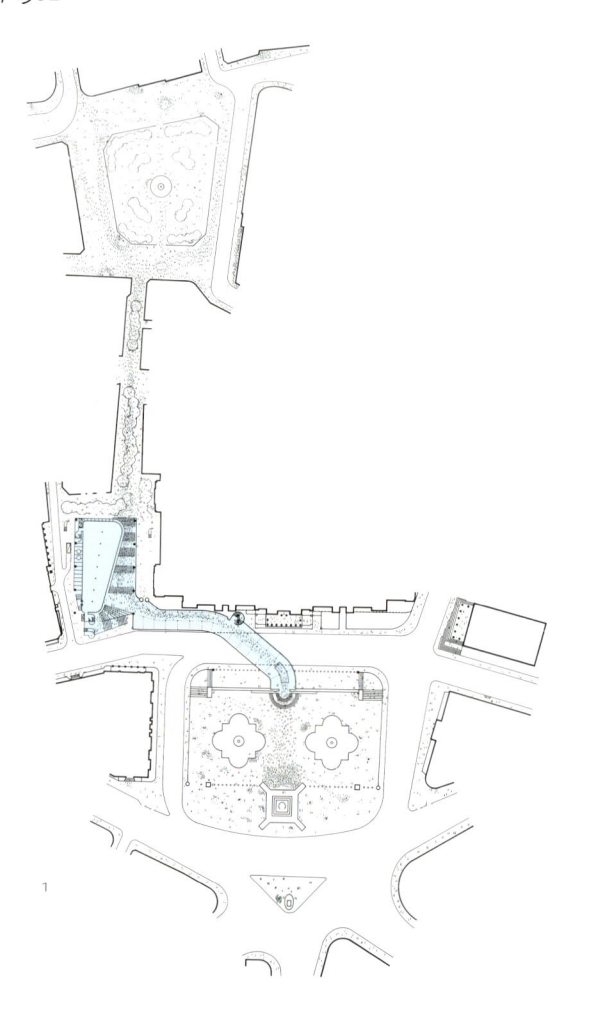

The competition for an extension to the National Gallery in Trafalgar Square was launched at the end of 1981. Architects, linked to developers, were invited to produce a scheme which combined offices and gallery space; the former to fund the latter – intended to house the collection's Renaissance pictures and extending to at least 500 ft. in length – on the 'Hampton's' site (the name of a former department store situated there), just east of the Gallery. The winning developer was to be given the site, valued at over £6 million. Of seventy-nine entries, seven were shortlisted in May 1982, and invited to develop their proposals. Among the seven was the Richard Rogers Partnership.

The Rogers scheme was a daring development of the ideas behind the Pompidou Centre, but cast in the architectural language of Lloyd's. The brief for the project was extremely unsatisfactory – and eventually proved unworkable – but Rogers addressed it with bravado, placing the offices in a separate structure subordinate to the galleries which were to be, as a provision of the brief, naturally lit from above. The provision of services had to be carefully considered to leave the roof space clear, so all environmental services were located at floor level. At roof level, daylight was to be filtered through sunscreening rooflights fitted with control louvres. A lighting grid was integrated to supplement the natural lighting when the latter fell short of normal requirements. The servicing grid allowed for a high degree of flexibility within the building, so that galleries could be reconfigured as required – a provision which did not necessarily appeal to conservative curatorial opinion. The principal access to the galleries took the form of a ramp from street level, with secondary access and escape facilities located in 'servant' towers around the perimeter. A tall tower, intended to balance the vertical element of the spire of St Martin-in-the-Fields church at the west end of the National Gallery, was to be topped with a restaurant and viewing gallery. Although this feature could have been seen as rather gratuitous, it attracted public support for the scheme and a tower was later incorporated into the winning scheme by Ahrends, Burton & Koralek.

More significant, perhaps, than the architecture of the Rogers scheme was its strategy for public space. The National Gallery, one of the most popular tourist attractions in Britain, was cut off from Trafalgar Square by a busy road. Rogers proposed a subterranean galleria, diving beneath the road to take pedestrians directly into the Square. A clear route below the new building would lead directly to Leicester Square, the acknowledged heart of the West End, behind the building.

Rogers proposed a new landmark for London, a cultural building which made a clear statement about change and was linked to a radical view of the city. In the end, a conservative solution, which simply deferred to the weak Regency frontage of the National Gallery, was adopted, but Rogers' proposals informed the 'London as it could be' project of 1986 and fed into the practice's searching analysis of London. Although the Rogers scheme came nowhere near being built, it was significant in establishing Rogers as a major force in the replanning of late twentieth-century London.

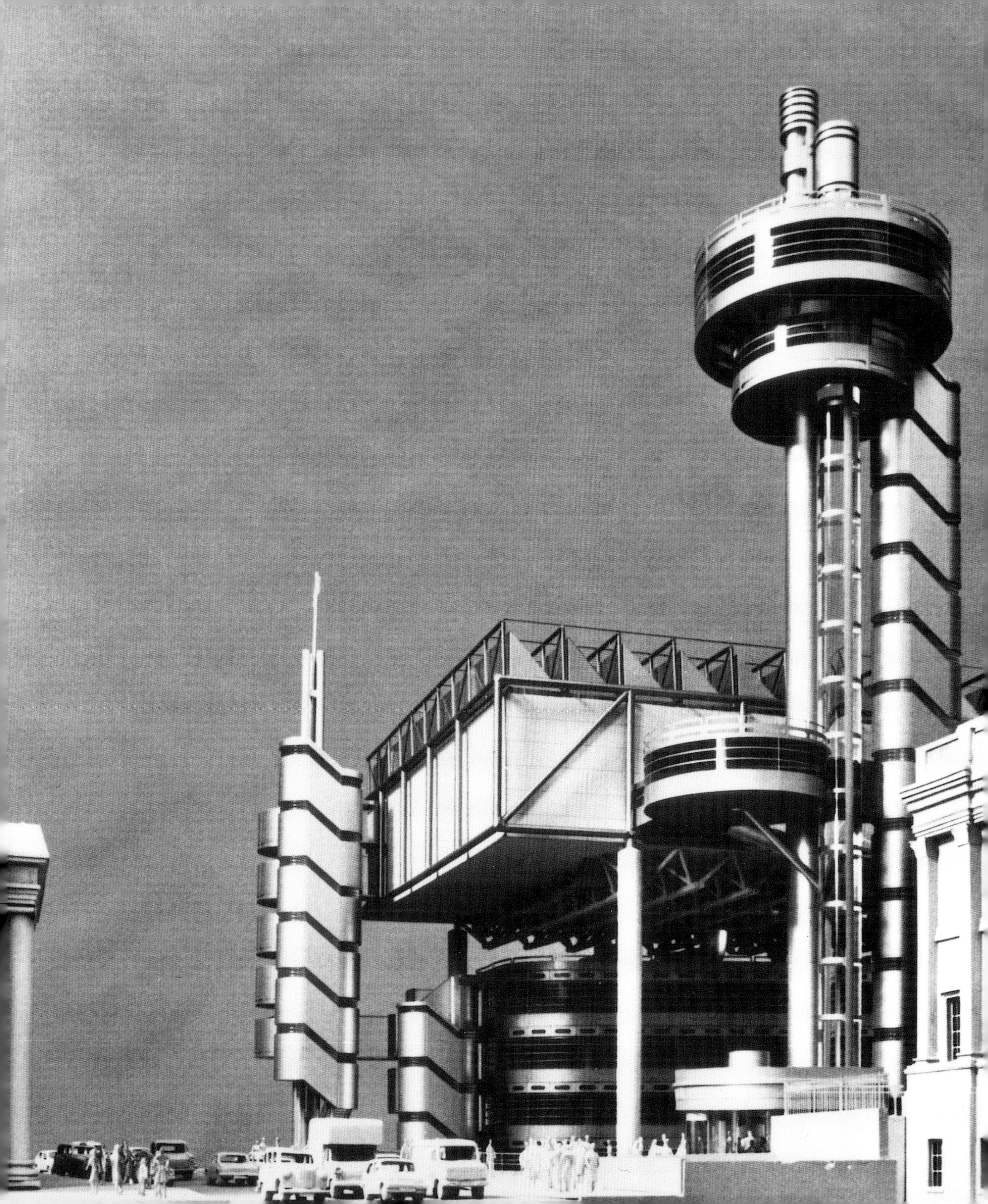

Rogers' scheme (1 & 2, previous pages, 3 & 6) was visually striking – the inclusion of a tower with the public gallery (5) was a popular move. The tower was conceived as a counterpoint to that of Gibbs' St Martin-in-the-Fields church across Trafalgar Square (4).

More important than the architectural language (8) was the strategy for creating public space, by which a clear route was provided from Leicester Square into Trafalgar Square, accessed by an underpass from the National Gallery (7).

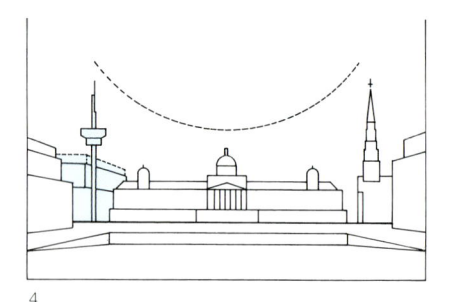

3

4

5

National Gallery Extension

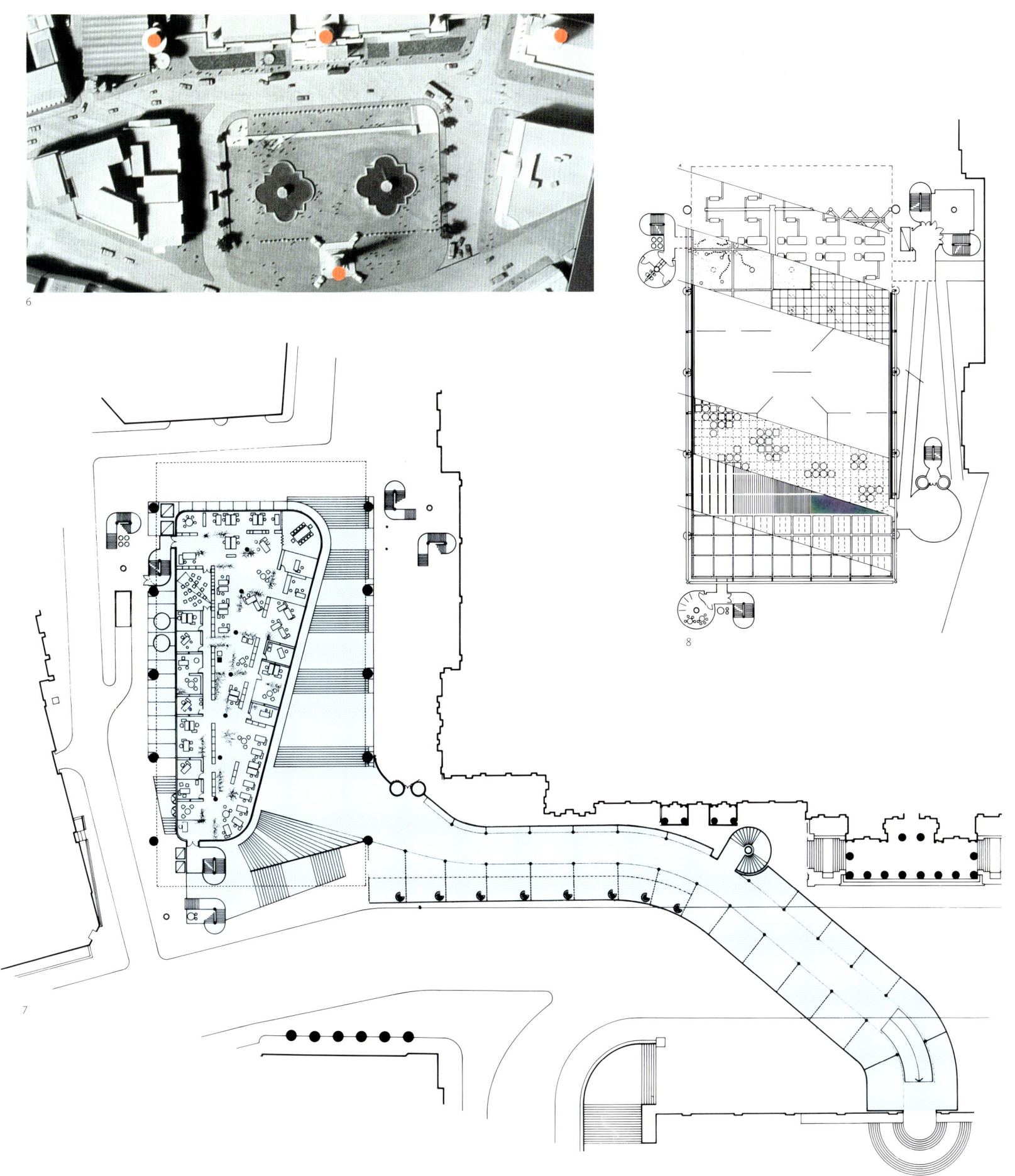

6

7

8

9

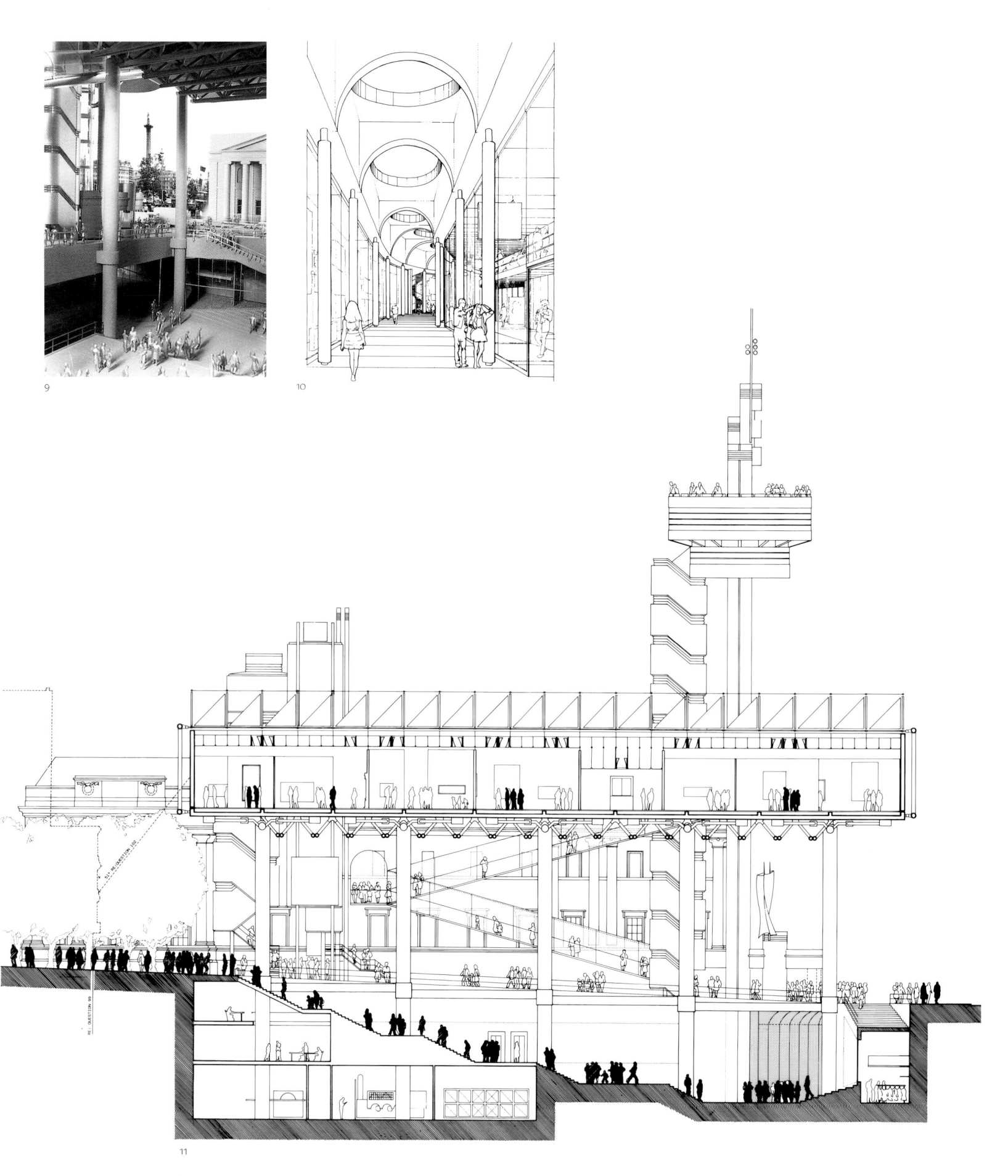

10

11

National Gallery Extension

240

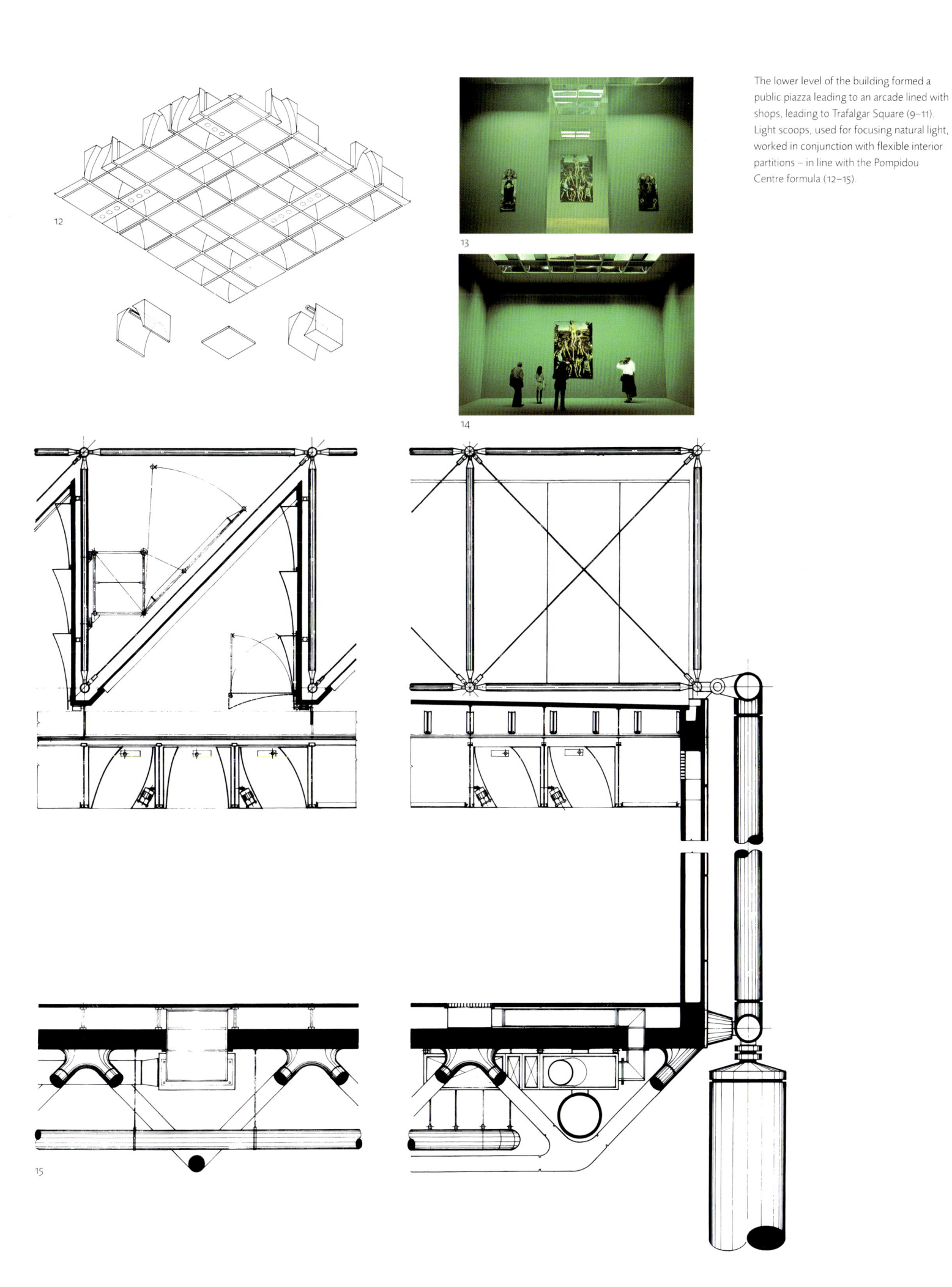

The lower level of the building formed a public piazza leading to an arcade lined with shops, leading to Trafalgar Square (9–11). Light scoops, used for focusing natural light, worked in conjunction with flexible interior partitions – in line with the Pompidou Centre formula (12–15).

PA Technology Laboratories

Princeton, New Jersey, 1982–5

The PA Laboratories ('Patscentre') project at Princeton followed on naturally from the building which Rogers completed for PA's operation in Britain in the mid 1970s and from the active collaboration which followed between the two companies. The plan took its cue from Inmos (perhaps the key Rogers project of the period): a central circulation/interaction spine, 8 m. wide, flanked by single-storey wings (containing, in this instance, offices and laboratories) spanning 22.8 m. The structure too was based on similar principles – the use of a prefabricated kit of parts which could be rapidly assembled, and of a cable structure emanating from the central spine to give support to the roofs of the wings. At Princeton, however, where the wings were of a much smaller span than those of Inmos, a fully-fledged cantilever structure was not used. Instead, the roof beams are supported both from above, using the system of tie rod cables, and by means of columns at the beam ends. Although the central A frame, coloured a bright red, does not perform the same critical role as its equivalent at Inmos, it is more clearly celebrated (or 'heroicized' as Michael Sorkin commented) and made into a frankly sculptural object. (The masts of the A frame are, in fact, supported on the portal frame which is the basic structure of the whole building.) The platform containing the services – here frankly exposed, rather than boxed-up as at Inmos – is neatly slotted into the A frame, again with the aim of making a point about the nature of the work going on in the building.

The engineering of the PA Technology Laboratories was both more pragmatic and more demonstrative than that of Inmos, yet the desired effect was achieved – internal spaces free of columns with scope for rearrangement and extension. The use of translucent cladding provides a remarkable quality of daylighting for the interiors. At night, the building glows gently. The structure was a rare American excursion for the fully formed Rogers manner – colourful, extrovert and rich in symbolism.

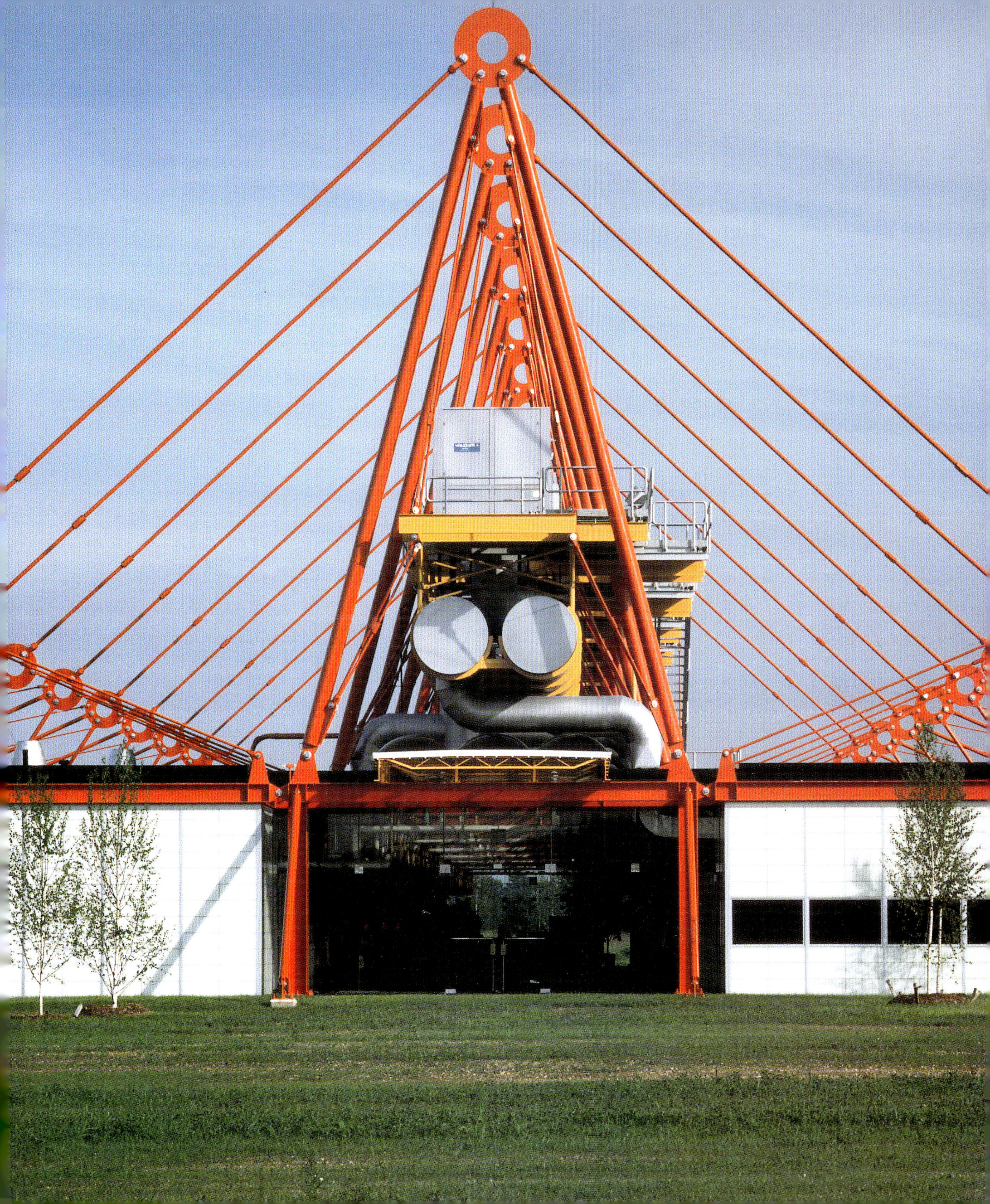

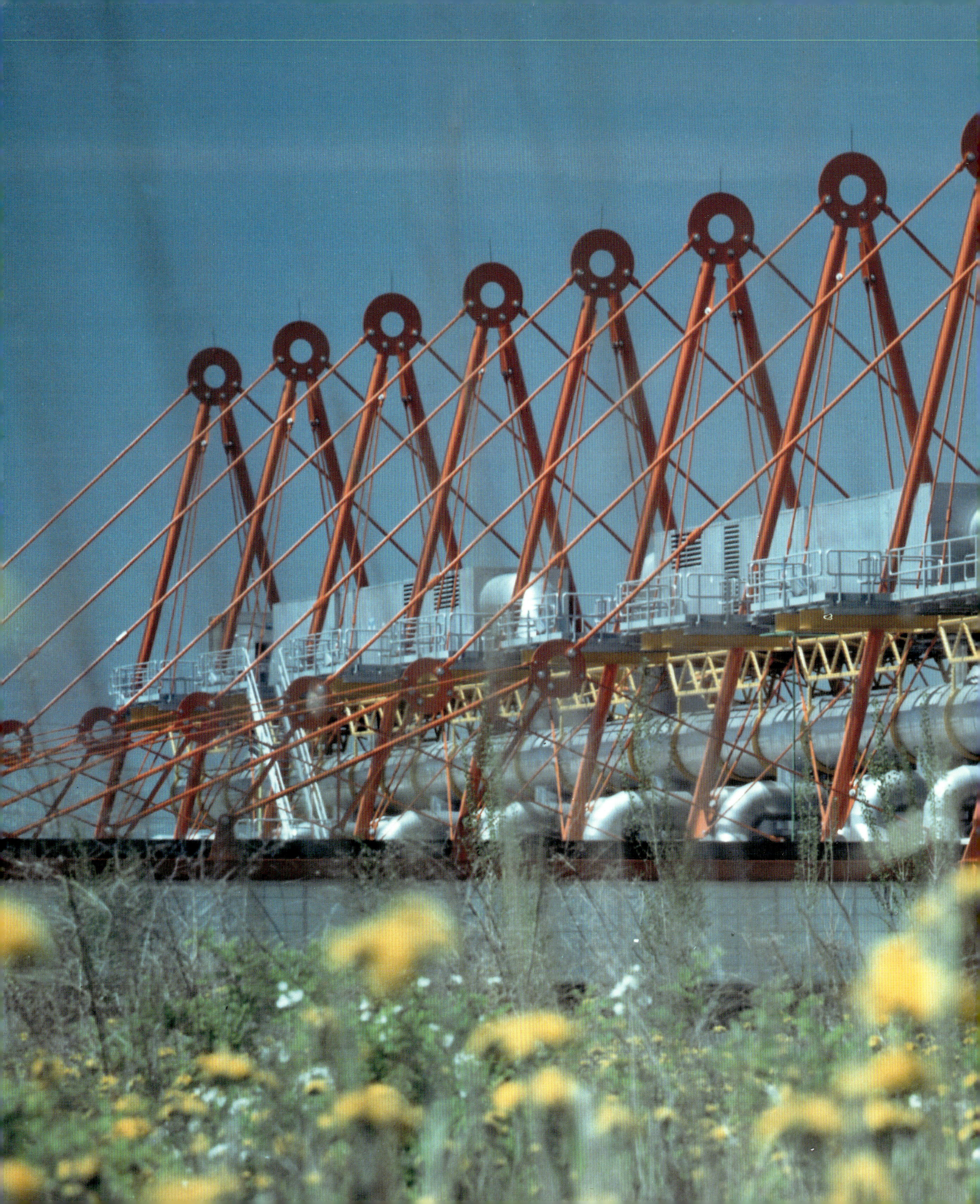

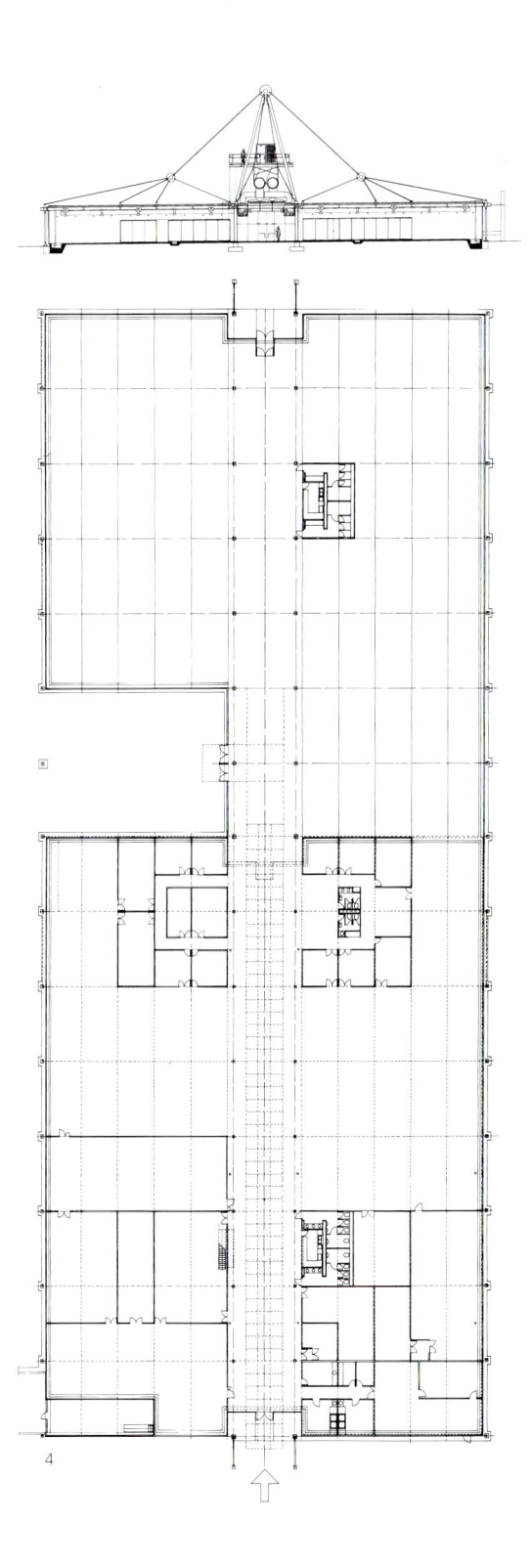

Patscentre, Princeton, designed to be a landmark object (1 & 2, previous pages), bears a marked resemblance to Inmos (3). A central spine of circulation and services (4) divides the working spaces, less highly serviced and more flexible in use than those at Inmos.

5

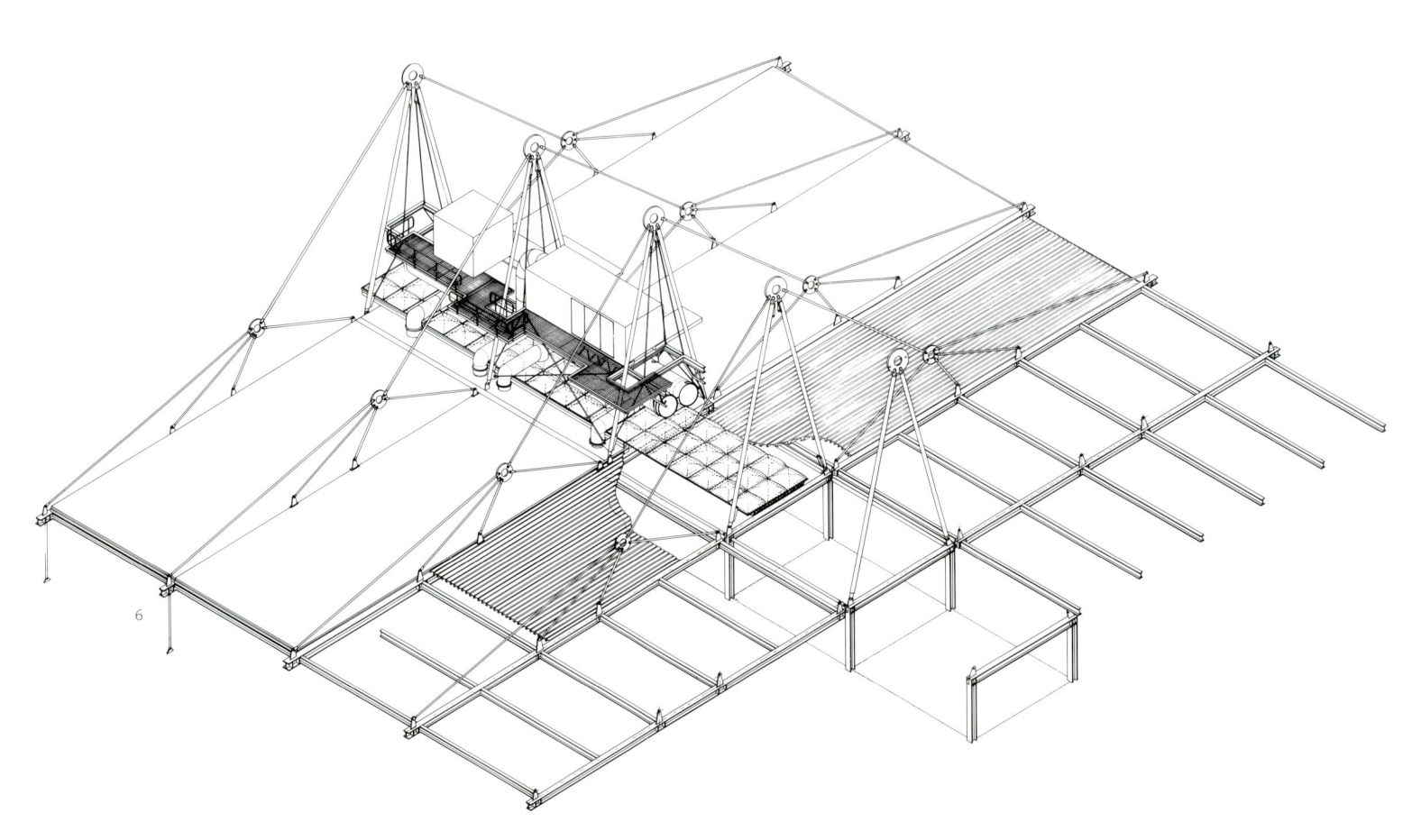

6

PA Technology Laboratories

246

7

The building is a colourful, sculptural form in the landscape (5).
The structural form applies the lessons of Inmos to create open-plan working space off a central thoroughfare (6).
Interiors are made luminous (9 & 10) both by the use of a translucent cladding system (7) with a band of clear glazing to give views out and by top lighting through the open-masted structure (8).

8   9   10

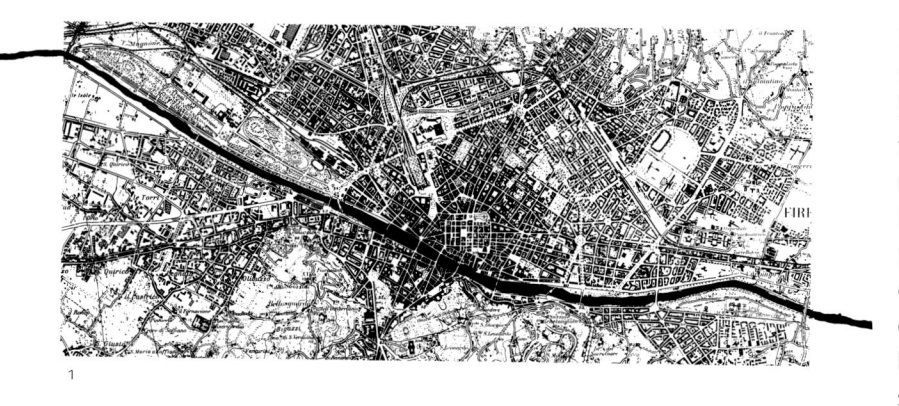

Florence was Richard Rogers' native city, yet the strategic study for reviving life along the banks of the Arno had equal significance for his adopted home, London. The Arno masterplan certainly helped to inspire the proposals for the banks of the River Thames contained in the 'London as it could be' proposals in 1986. In Florence, as in London, nineteenth-century civic improvement had produced roads along the riverside and, by the late twentieth century, heavy motor traffic cutting off the river from the city. The city of Florence sought ways to restore life to the riverside and break down this division. Rogers proposed to create a linear park stretching five miles along the Arno, extending from the city centre to the suburbs. This was to be achieved by reclaiming the banks of the river and, where necessary, extending them out with piers and pontoons designed by Laurie Abbott and engineered by Peter Rice. For the greater part of the year, except when the river is in flood, the banks would be populated by stalls, cafés, tents and performers. The new walkway was to be paved in the local *pietra serena* with planted green areas.

The project was never realized, yet it was an important one for Rogers, who was commissioned to work in a city which was not only his own birthplace, but one of the key 'heritage' sites of the world. In Britain, reactionary attitudes prevailed but in Italy there was a willingness to see contemporary design at work in an historic context.

Arno Masterplan

Florence, Italy, 1983–4

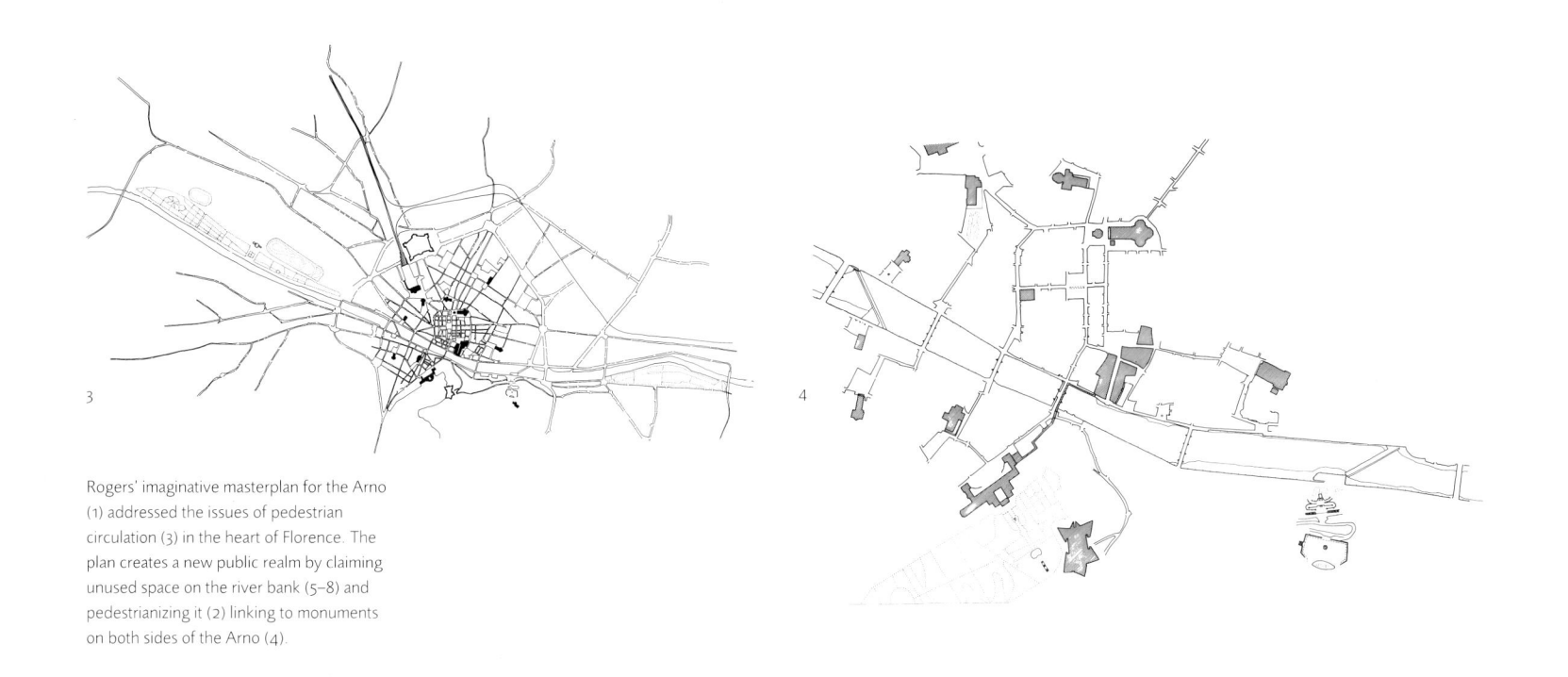

Rogers' imaginative masterplan for the Arno (1) addressed the issues of pedestrian circulation (3) in the heart of Florence. The plan creates a new public realm by claiming unused space on the river bank (5–8) and pedestrianizing it (2) linking to monuments on both sides of the Arno (4).

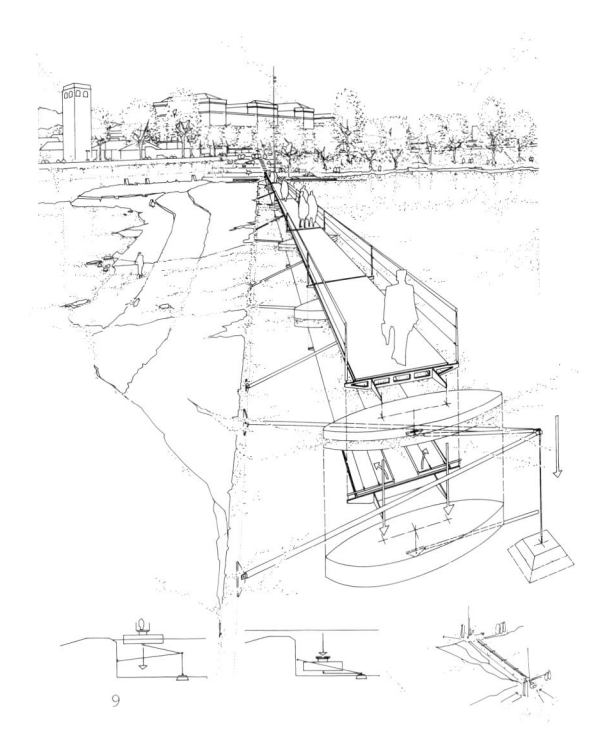

The banks of the Arno were transformed by means of both fixed and demountable interventions. Cafés, shops and kiosks – which could be brought into use in summer, combine with more permanent elements of paving and landscape to create a linear park (9–21).

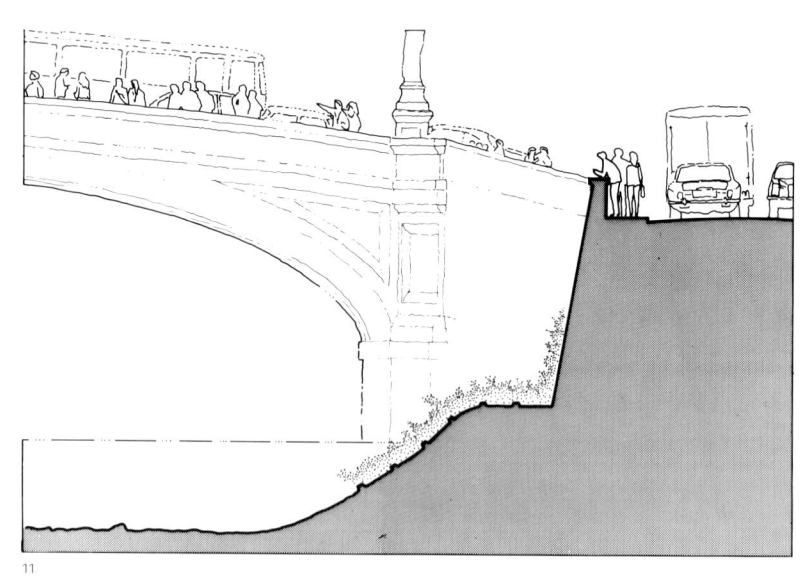

Arno Masterplan

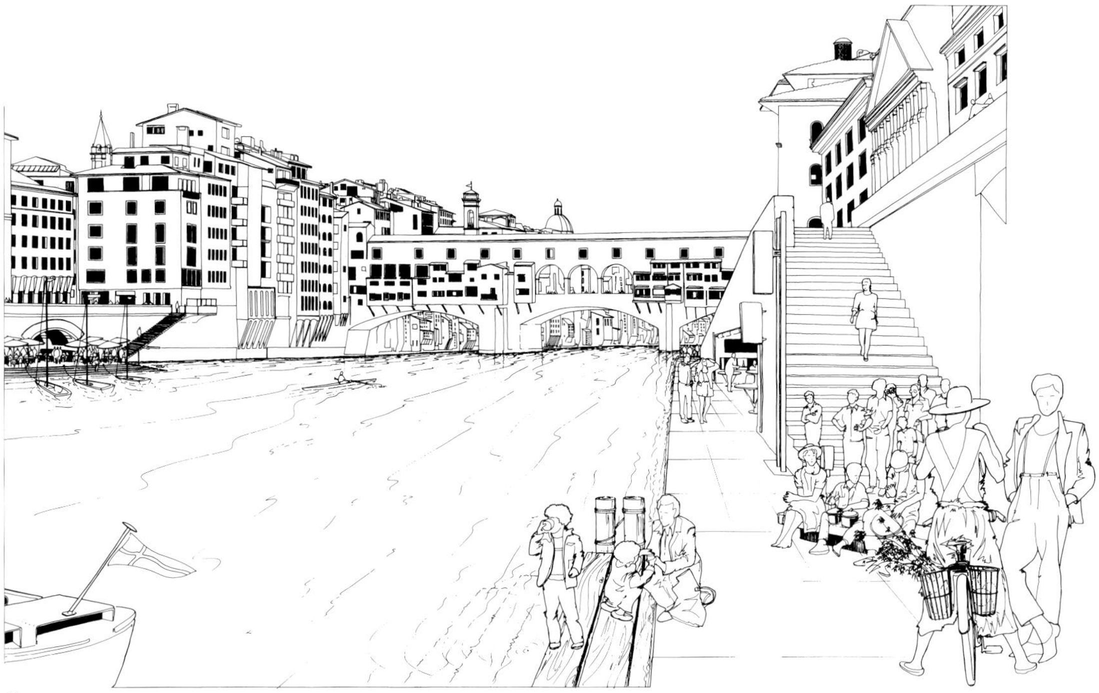

15

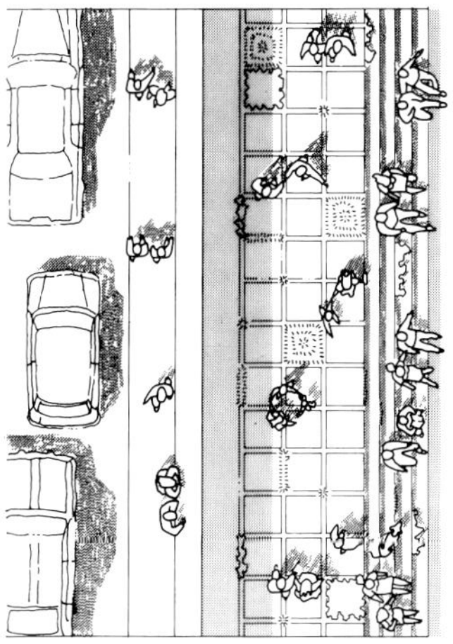

16

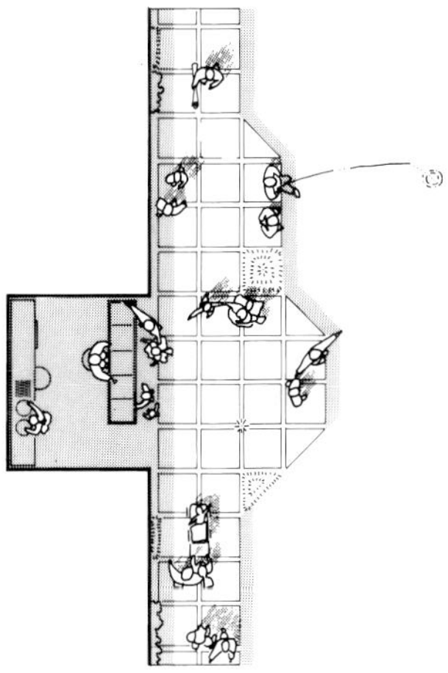

17

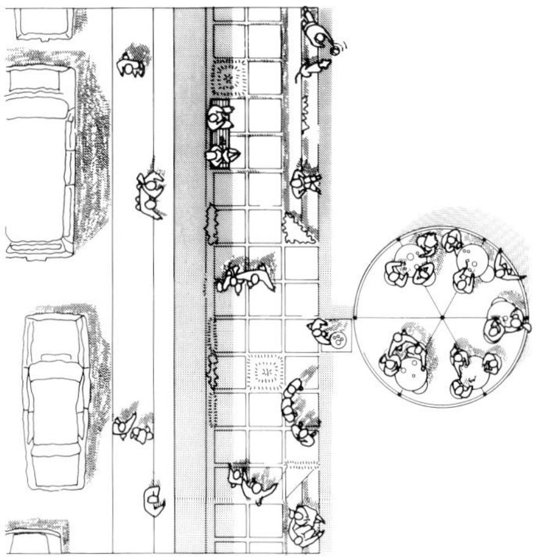

18

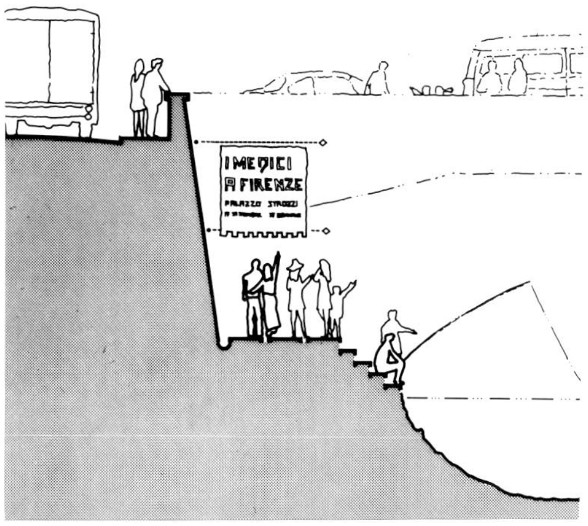

19

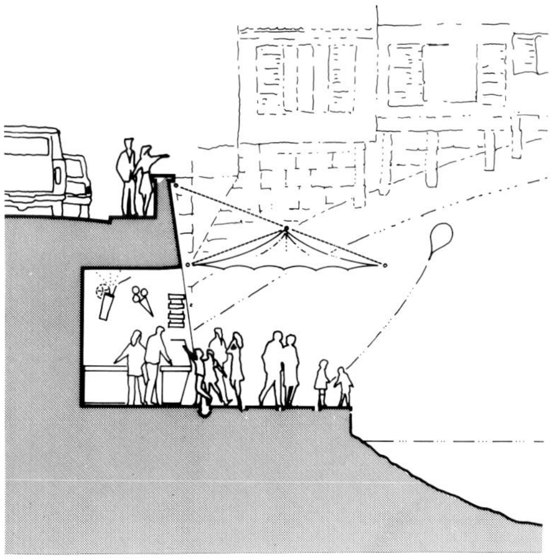

20

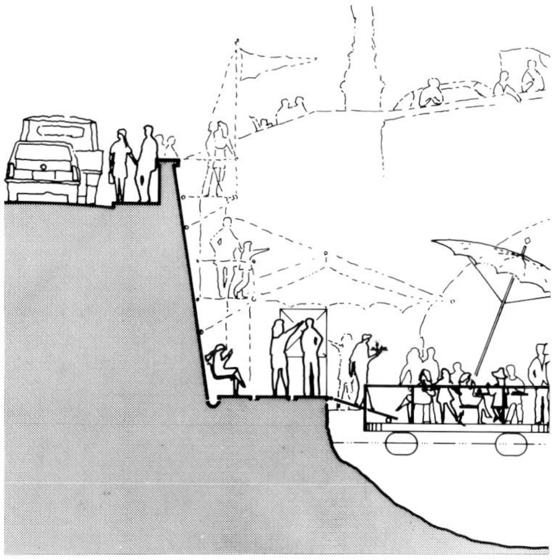

21

Industrial Units

Maidenhead, Berkshire, 1984–5

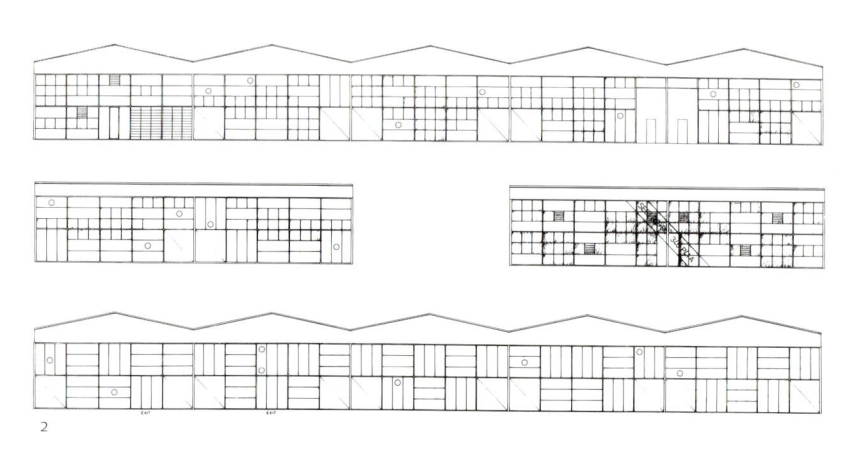

Alongside the innovative and exploratory projects of the 1970s and early 1980s, all too often unbuilt, Rogers continued to evolve a new industrial vernacular – low cost and undemonstrative, but significant in building on the lessons of the Reliance Controls Electronics Factory and other completed schemes.

Economy was a high priority in the Maidenhead project – two units of 2,500 sq.m. each, built speculatively and intended for use by a range of potential tenants. The scheme was essentially simple and not revolutionary in structure: 14.5 m. primary trusses supporting pitched secondary trusses. The cladding system was fixed directly to the steel frame in 3 m. modules.

The units possessed a basic elegance and quality of detailing which set them apart from much industrial building of the period. The 'informal randomness' of the cladding, mixing solid and transparent elements and using bright colours, was typically Rogers reflecting a determination to fit form to function and to facilitate great flexibility in internal layout rather than to prescribe the activities of users.

3

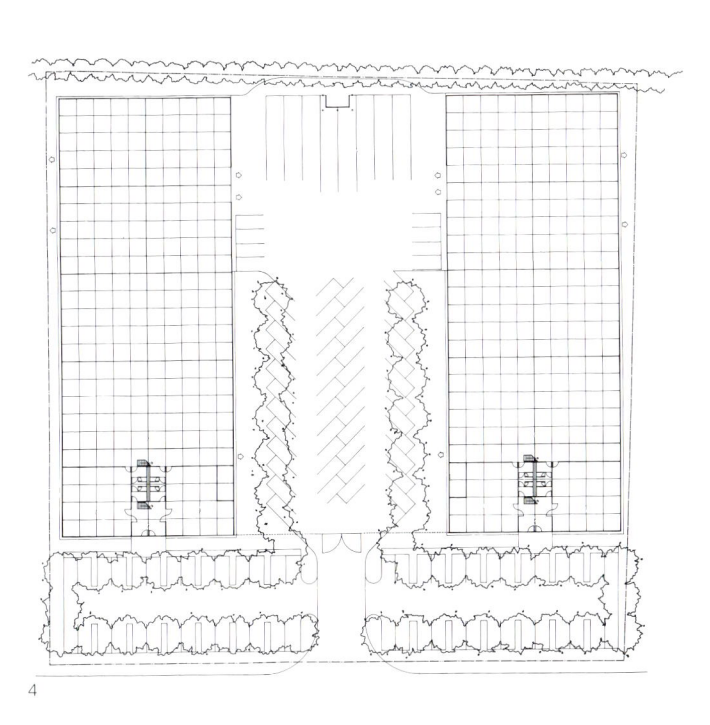

5
The industrial units in Maidenhead applied the lessons of previous projects to the design of spec-built warehousing. The use of colour, the mixture of solid and transparent panels and the glazed clerestory produced a representative Rogers elevation (1–5).

Thames Wharf

London, 1984–9

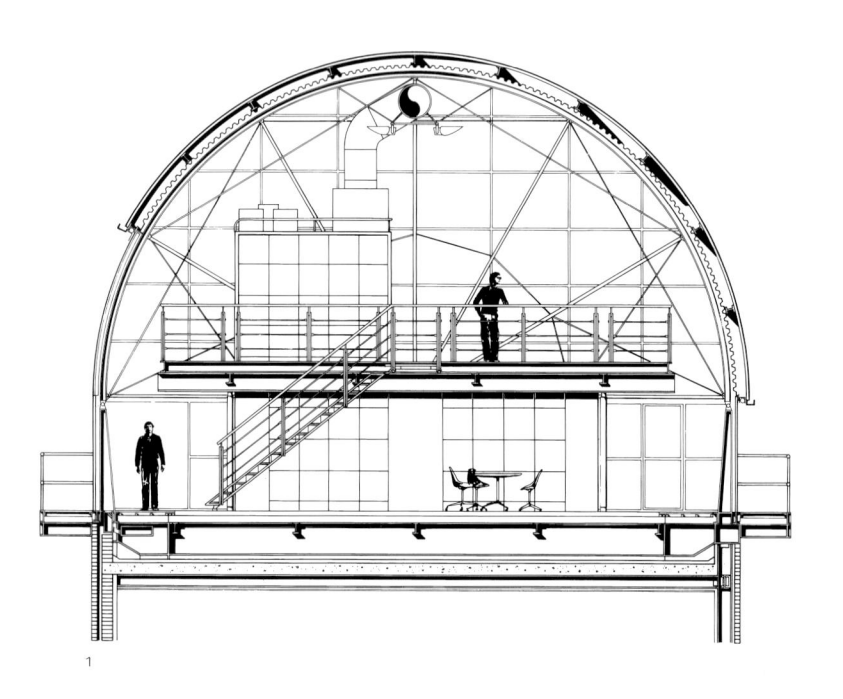

The site at Thames Wharf, Hammersmith, was acquired by Richard Rogers and his partners in 1983 as the location for the practice's new offices. It was then a redundant industrial complex, containing a group of substantially built early twentieth-century warehouses – sunk in a later accretion of sheds and oil tanks. The hinterland of the site is a mesh of prim Edwardian terraced streets behind the Fulham Palace Road, where the 1960s Charing Cross Hospital provides a dominating landmark. The development of industry along the riverside in the nineteenth century had cut off the river from the surrounding area.

The site was developed in 1984–7 as practice offices, lettable workshop and office units – both these elements in refurbished former warehouse blocks – and new housing. The conversion of the existing blocks was relatively straightforward. Unlike Billingsgate Securities Market, they were not listed and could be altered at will, although in practice structural alterations were kept to a minimum. A double height entrance lobby is the principal intervention in the Rogers offices. Over the years, it has developed as an informal gallery where models of projects are shown on steel racks. Throughout the building, new elements are of a frankly industrial character and are brightly painted. Furnishings are equally colourful. The approach in the other converted buildings is equally straightforward. A key element in the regeneration of the site was the development of the River Café (opened in 1987) on the ground floor of the block extending along Rainville Road. The café, which evolved into an internationally-rated restaurant, faces on to a landscaped area extending to the newly created river walkway. (The landscaping was designed by Rogers' old Team 4 colleague, Georgie Wolton.) A sizeable area of public space was laid out where there had been no previous public access.

Thames Wharf was a commercially shrewd undertaking, but the idea behind the development was equally that of making a community. The lettable offices are largely occupied by architects and design-related professionals, for whom the River Café is a useful amenity. One of the architectural practices based there is Lifschutz Davidson, responsible for the spectacular, two storey rooftop extension to the Rogers office completed in 1991 and designed in association with Rogers. With its great semi-circular roof, the extension provides a lightweight expression of the activities carried on below. Commissioning Lifschutz Davidson was a deliberate move of patronage, an encouragement to a young firm which has since enjoyed considerable success – even succeeding, where Rogers failed, in building on the Coin Street site.

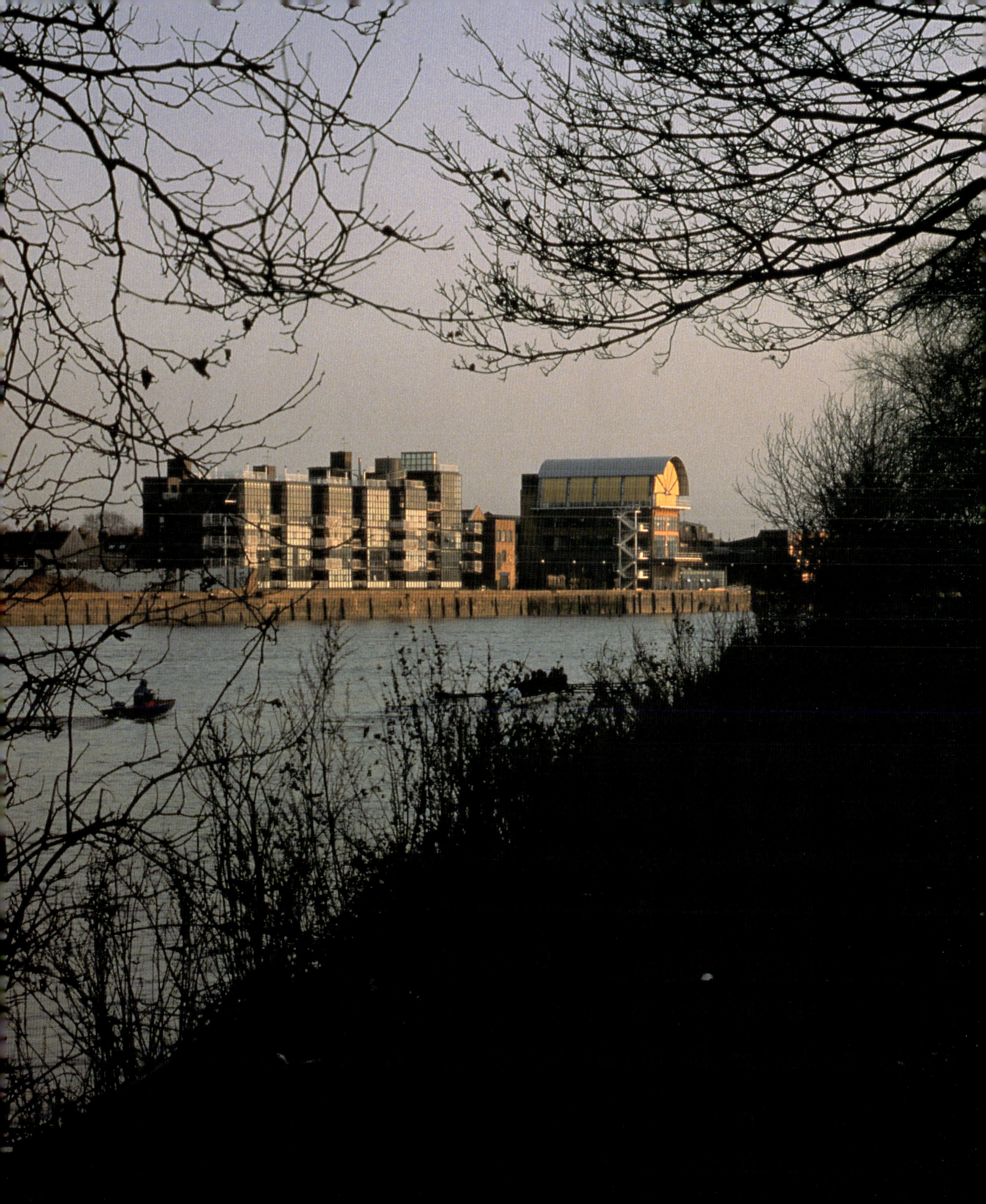

3

4

5

6

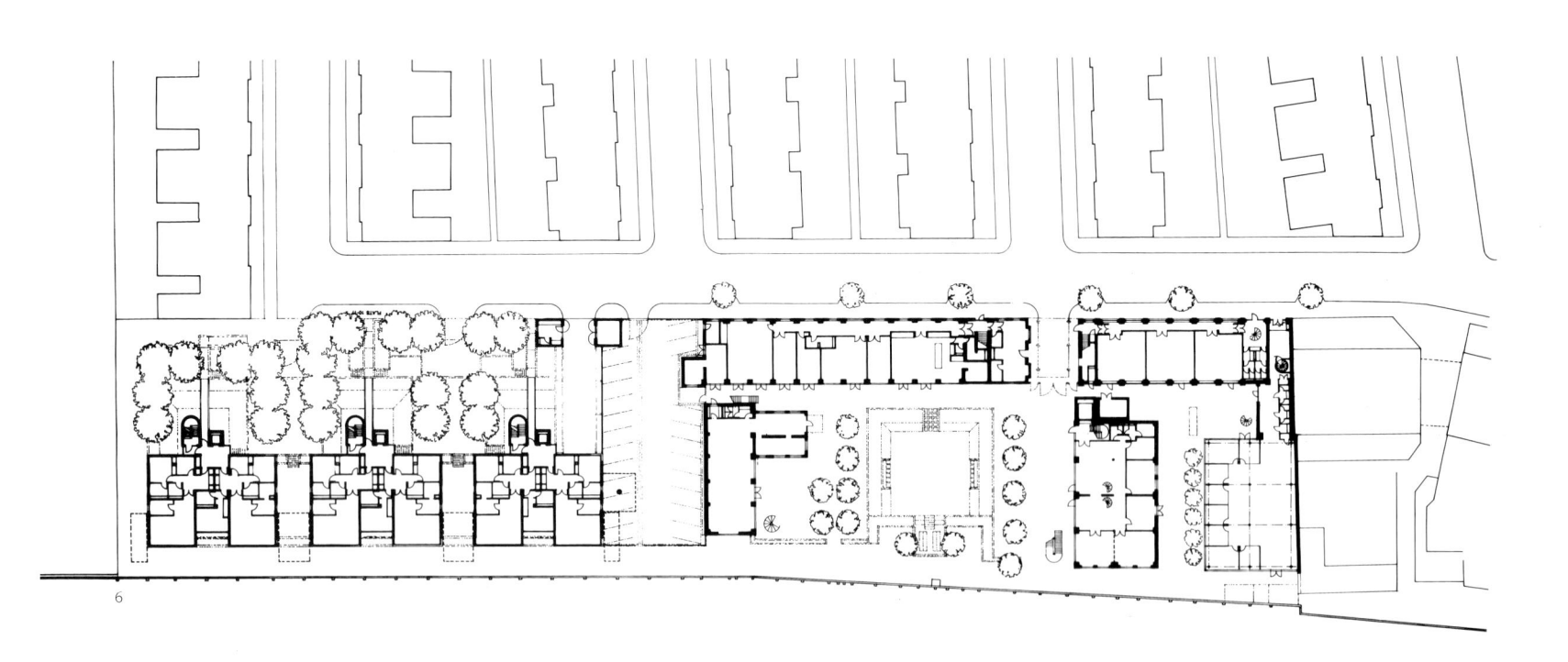

7

Thames Wharf

8

9

10

The site at Thames Wharf was occupied by good quality nineteenth-century industrial buildings – sunk in a sea of sheds and tanks (3–5 & 7). The redevelopment (2, previous page) of the site (6) has retained everything of value, while generous public open space, including a riverside walk, has been provided (8). The River Café occupies the ground floor of one of the blocks (9 & 10). Others contain small office and workshop units as well as offices of the Richard Rogers Partnership (1, p254 & 11, overleaf).

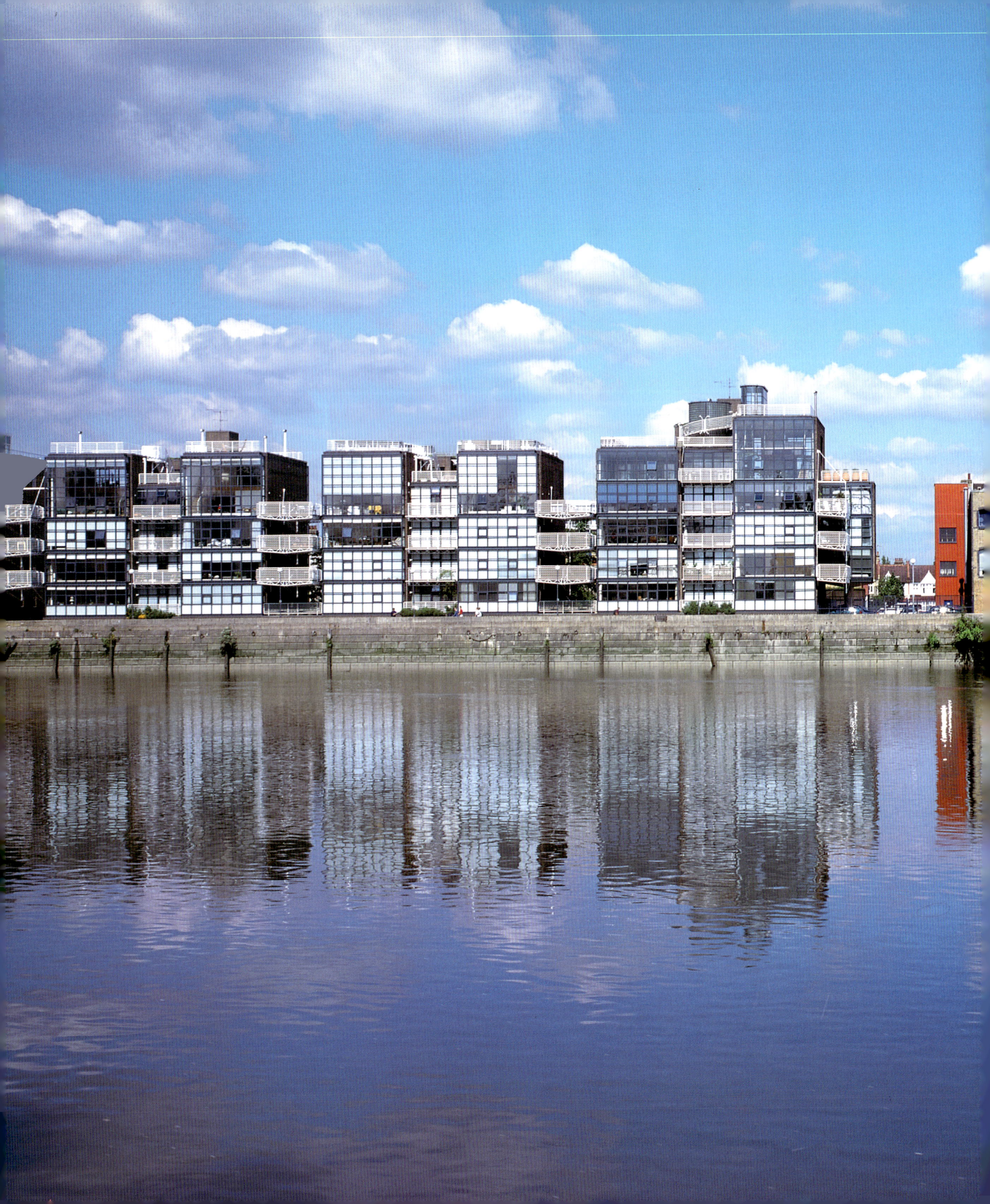

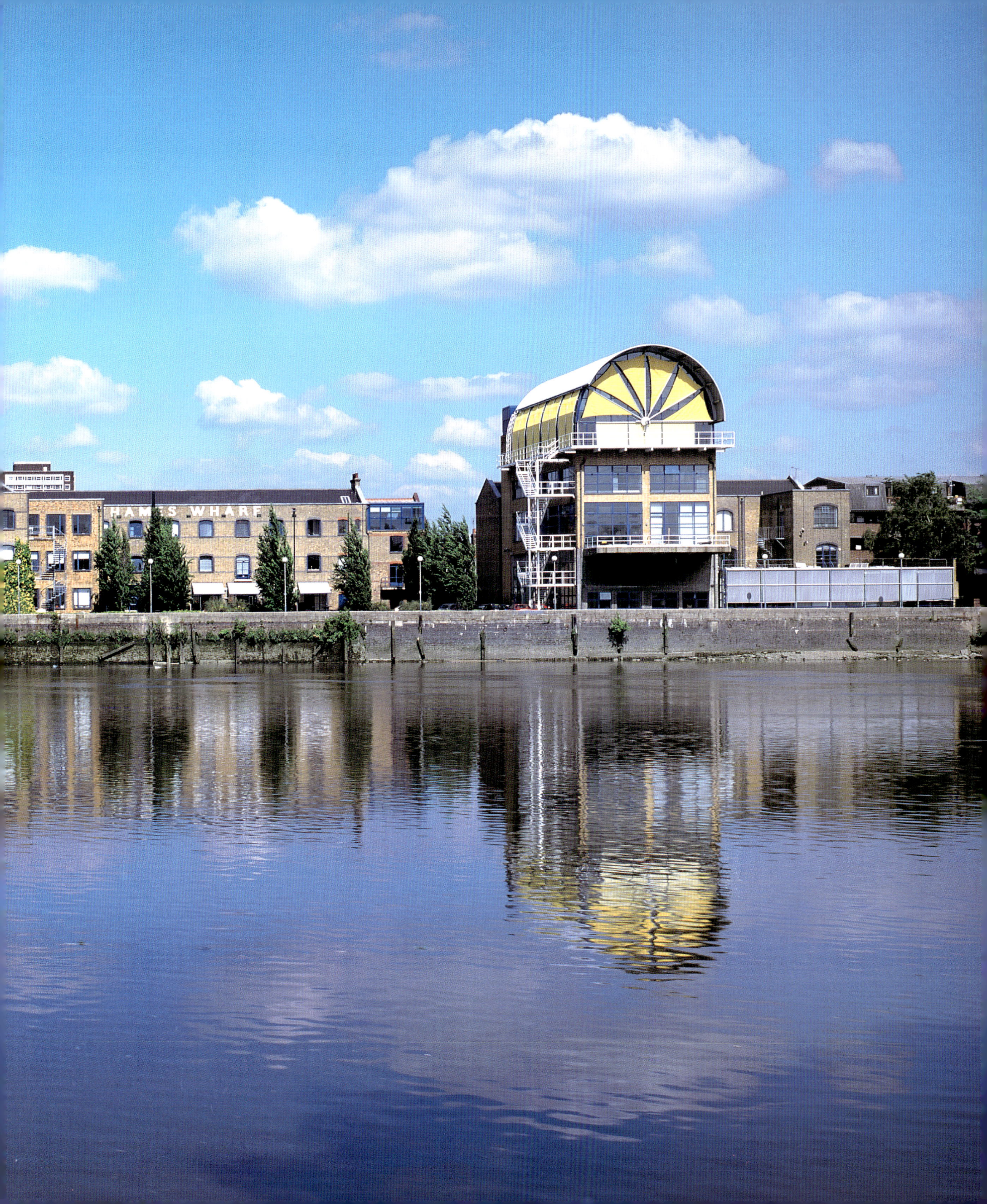

The Rogers office occupies an entire block of Thames Wharf. It was extended upwards in 1987. The new top floor is capped by a great arched roof (15).
The Rogers office provides a visible local landmark (16). Nearby streets now have free access to the riverside, previously sealed off and inaccessible.

The interiors of the Rogers offices include a double height entrance (14) – a showcase for models of Rogers' schemes. The glazed roof extension (13) uses retractable blinds to reduce solar gain (12).

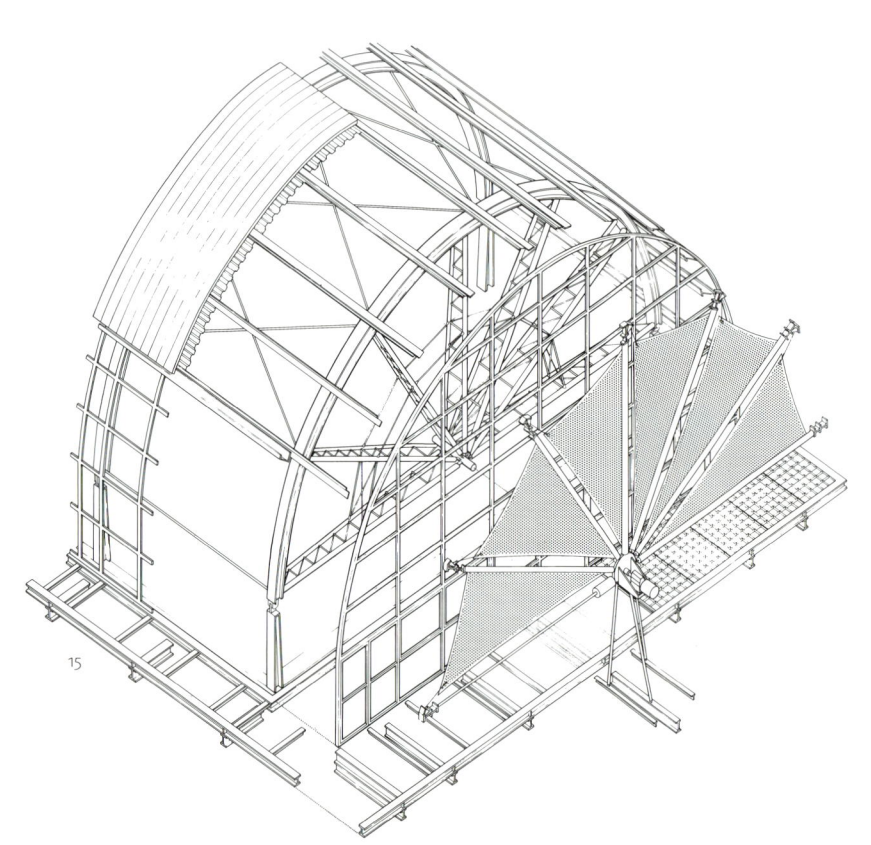

Thames Wharf

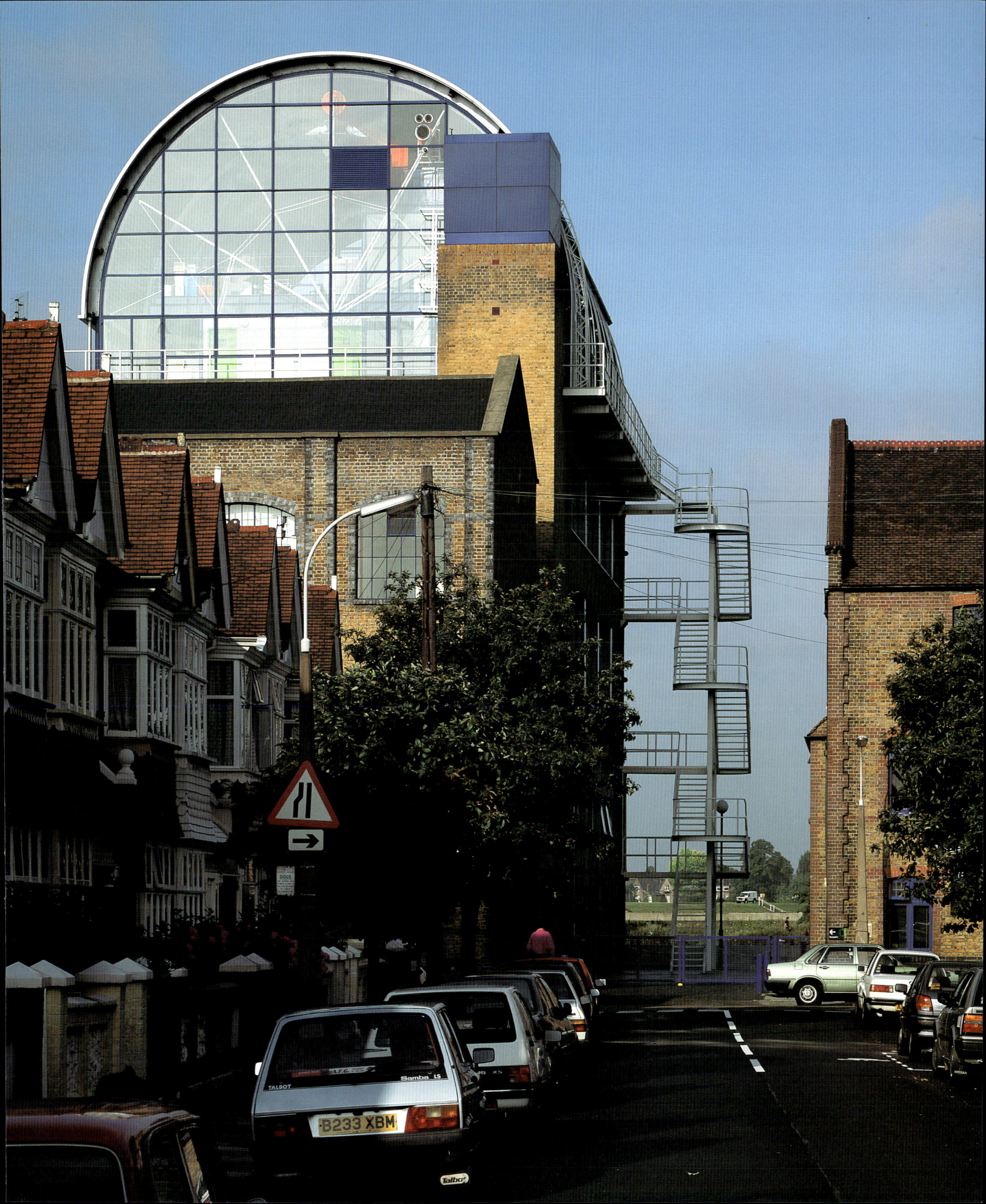
TALBOT
Samba LS
B233 XBM
Talbot

Thames Reach Housing 1984–7

Rogers had been persistently thwarted in his early attempts to build housing – as opposed to houses. Housing was a key part of the development plan for the Thames Wharf site, though it was – inevitably for the 1980s – built by a private developer rather than a public agency. The development incorporated the new public walkway along the river, extended as a result of the Thames Wharf project, and was arranged in three blocks, their height carefully related to that of the adjacent converted warehouses and of the nearby terraced houses.

From the river, in fact, the blocks read as a single unit, clad in glass and steel and linked by steel bridges which provide glimpses through to the river from neighbouring streets. The riverside frontage is strongly modelled, with boldly projecting balconies. To the rear, on the street frontage, extensive use is made of brick to reinforce the contextuality of the buildings. The brick is of a dark hue, contrasting with the golden stock brick of the cleaned and refurbished warehouses and the windows are informally arranged.

The stepped windows light the ancillary bedrooms of the apartments. Living rooms and master bedrooms are placed on the river front. Kitchens and bathrooms are accommodated in central cores. Lifts and stairs are detached from the blocks into servant towers in the manner of Louis Kahn. From the street, the rhythm of semi-circular and rectangular projections, contrasted with lightweight, white-painted steelwork, is a powerful and austere presence.

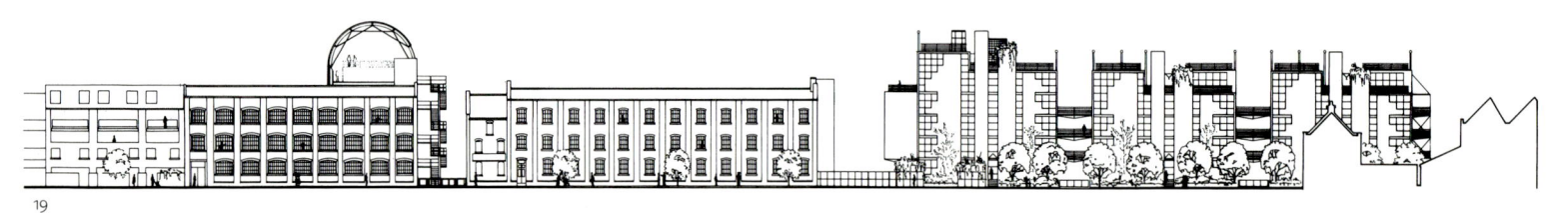

On the river elevation the housing is fully glazed (18). To the street, it has a more discreet and solid look, with brick to echo the character of the immediate area (19 & 20). The new flats have nautical balconies overlooking the Thames (17).

THAMES REACH
1-9

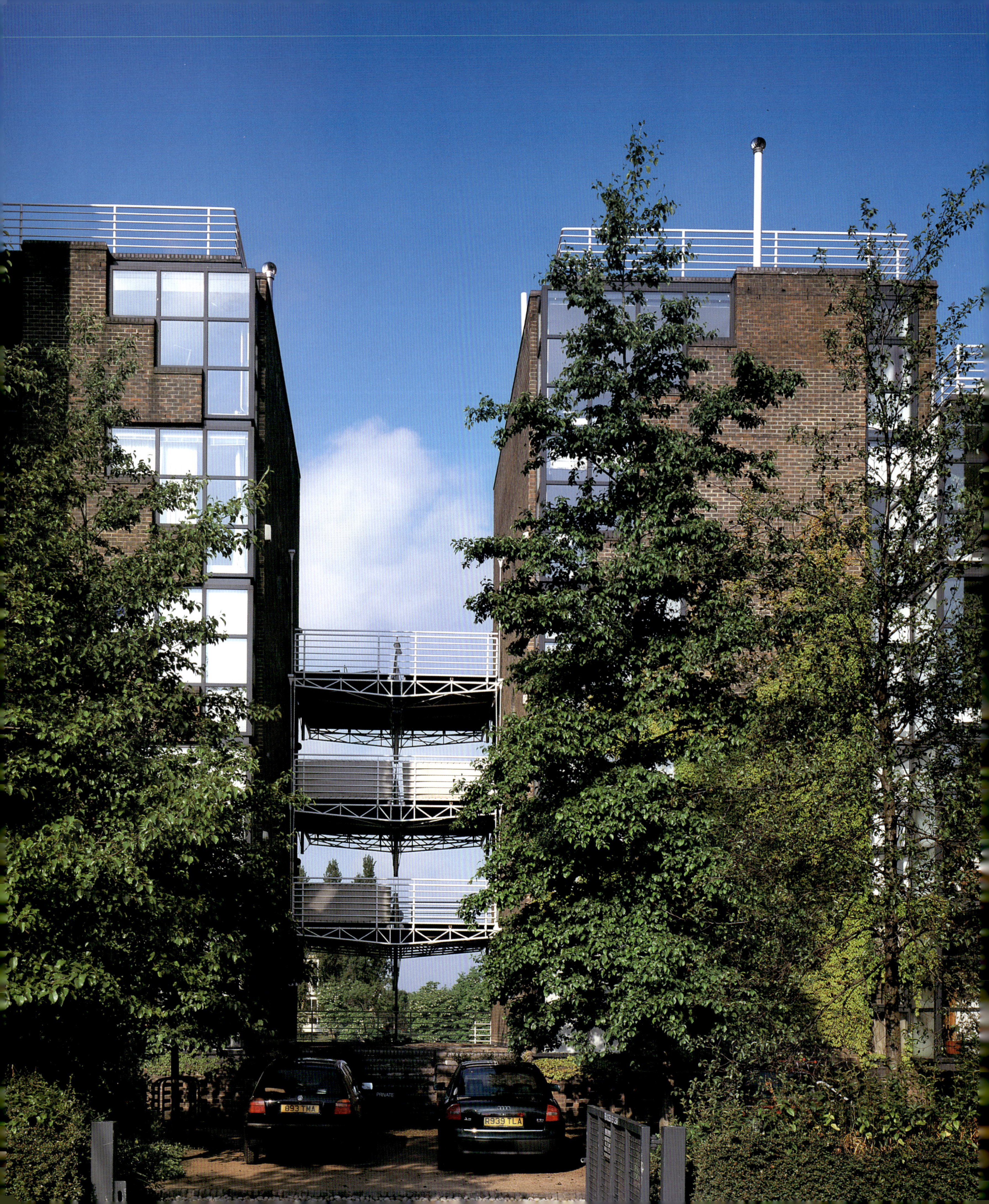
B93 TMA
R939 TLA

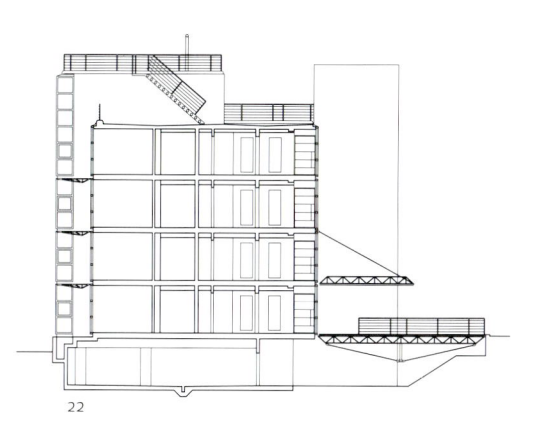

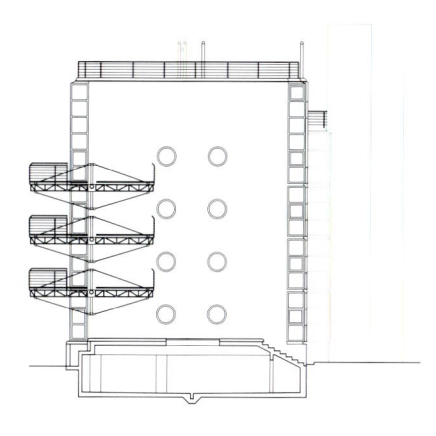

The plan and section of the apartment blocks is designed to provide residents with optimum views from living and bedrooms (22 & 25).
Generous balconies cantilever over the River Walk (23). The spaces between the blocks, bridged by slender suspended balconies, provide views through to the river beyond (21 & 24).

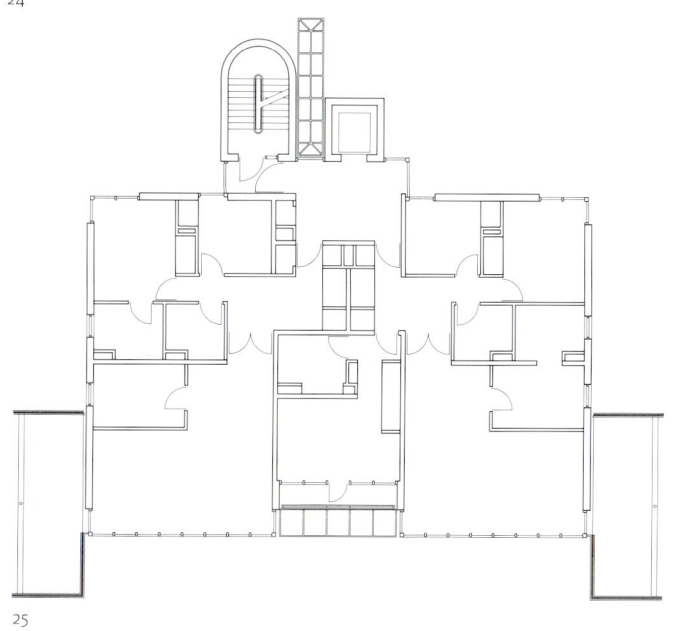

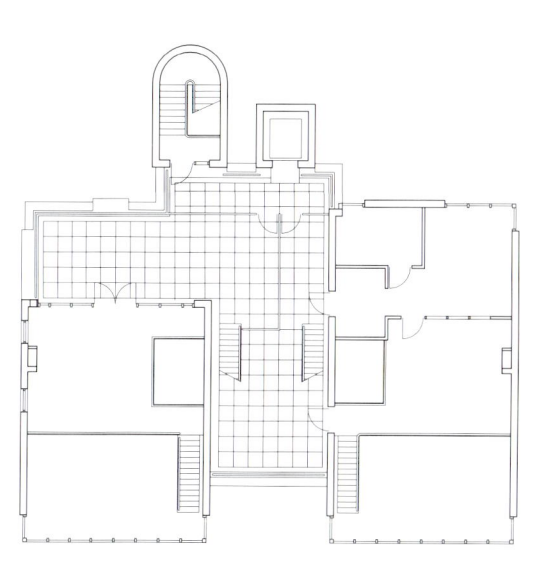

26

The Deck House 1986–7

The apartment which Rogers' partner John Young created on the top floor of the housing development at Thames Reach forms part of the living and working community on that site. The apartment was constructed, in tandem with the completion of the housing, in the shells of two conventional flat units in the easternmost block of the development. Only the rooftop bathroom tower and observatory indicate that something out of the ordinary lies below.

Young is proud to be called, as was Jean Prouvé, a 'constucteur'. He takes delight in fine building and in the components which make up a building or interior and wanted to make a home which celebrates craftsmanship and the appropriate use of good – though not necessarily rare or precious – materials. Young's concern is to use ordinary materials to best effect even if they are not ones normally associated with domestic interiors. Nor is Young's vision of domestic bliss one of conventional comfort or convenience – to choose to live so close to one's office is a brave move. It is no accident that the apartment was begun in the year that the Lloyd's Building (in which Young was heavily involved for eight years) was finally completed.

Flexibility and adaptability – a refusal to allow fixed structures and spaces to determine or prescribe a certain way of working or living – have been features of Rogers' architecture from the early years and Young's apartment is radical and made for change and mobility. Within the double height of the living space, with spectacular river views, hangs (literally) the open sleeping platform. From here a staircase ascends to the bathroom and look-out. Young is a sailor and it shows – both the idea of this ensemble and the way it is realized, along with the use of teak, tubular metal and cables, evoke the world of boats. The bathroom tower is a free-standing structure, a steel frame infilled with translucent glass blocks, with a roof of clear glass.

The other half of the apartment, entered through the kitchen area, is used as a workroom, with a small apartment, for the use of guests, behind. Young's fervent dislike of normal domestic clutter is evident here – books, for example, are not displayed but stored away, with other possessions kept in huge mobile storage units of burnished stainless steel, like the coffers of a great archive. There is no more furniture than necessary – just a selection of classic Modern items and one piece of art. Models of classic cars, boats and trains are shown in cases. Young takes delight in unlikely, slightly incongruous elements, such as the circular industrial heating elements, manufactured in Texas, mounted on the living room wall.

According to Young, 'the apartment celebrates process and materials, collisions, connections, the way things work and the skill of the craftsman. It is essentially about detail, density of detail and the role that an accumulation of appropriate details plays in shaping the whole. A container to show off a collection of jewel-like artefacts, a celebration of the intricacy of construction.' But the apartment is also an inspirational space which renews the dialogue between architecture and lifestyle, which is so strongly expressed in that favourite of Rogers and Young, the Maison de Verre.

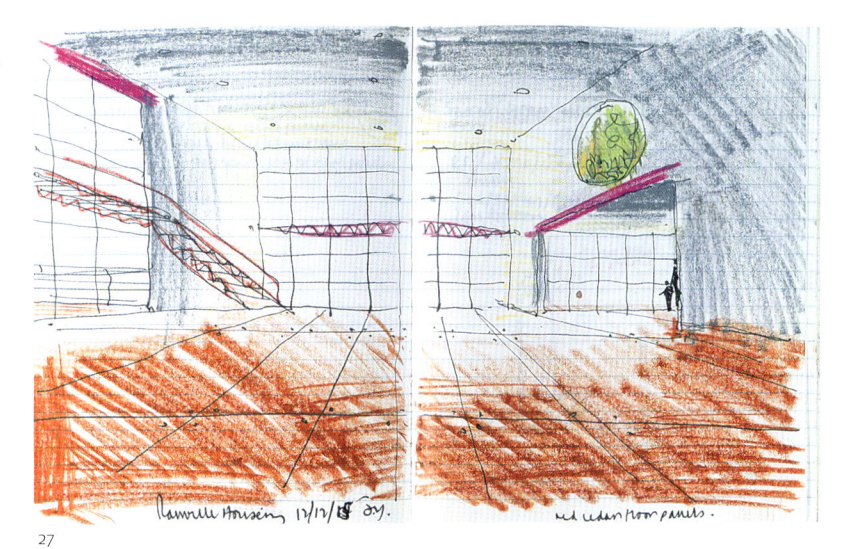

John Young's private apartment at Thames Reach – the Deck House – occupies the entire top floor of one block. The apartment celebrates the intricacies of construction and craftsmanship. The design for the apartment reflects a radical approach to living. A suspended sleeping platform accessed by stairway (28) replaces a conventional bedroom. The double height living room is a spectacular space (26 & 27).

29

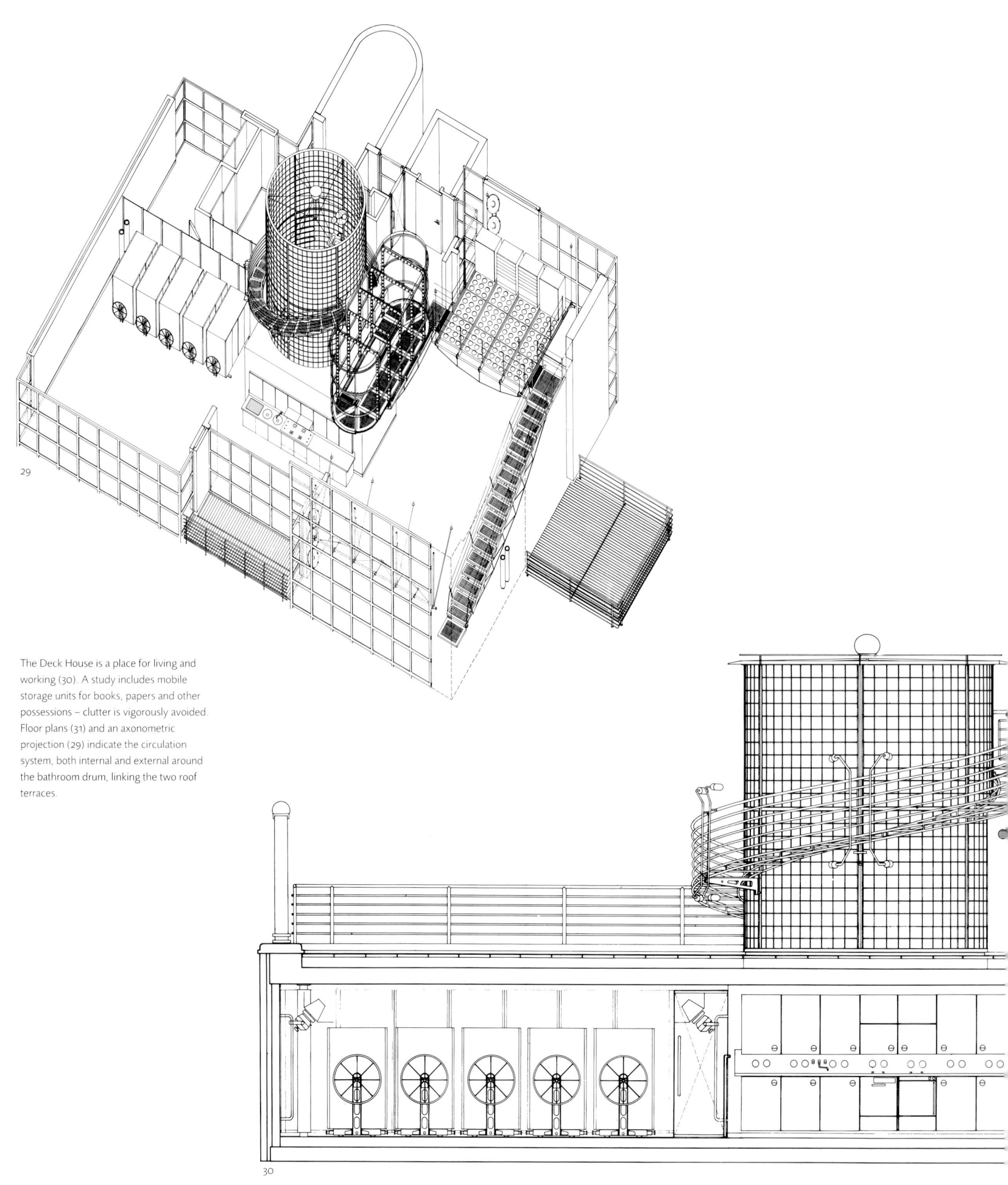

The Deck House is a place for living and working (30). A study includes mobile storage units for books, papers and other possessions – clutter is vigorously avoided. Floor plans (31) and an axonometric projection (29) indicate the circulation system, both internal and external around the bathroom drum, linking the two roof terraces.

30

Thames Wharf

31

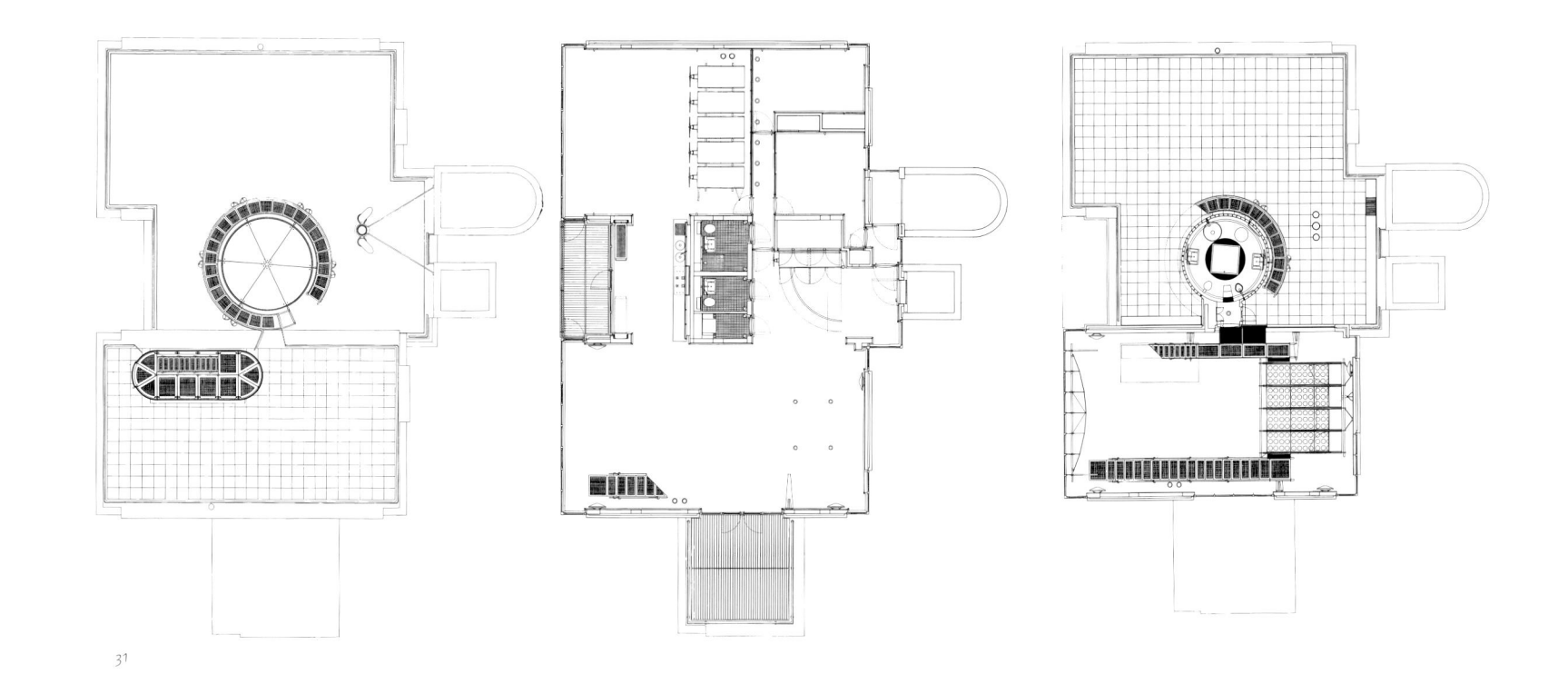

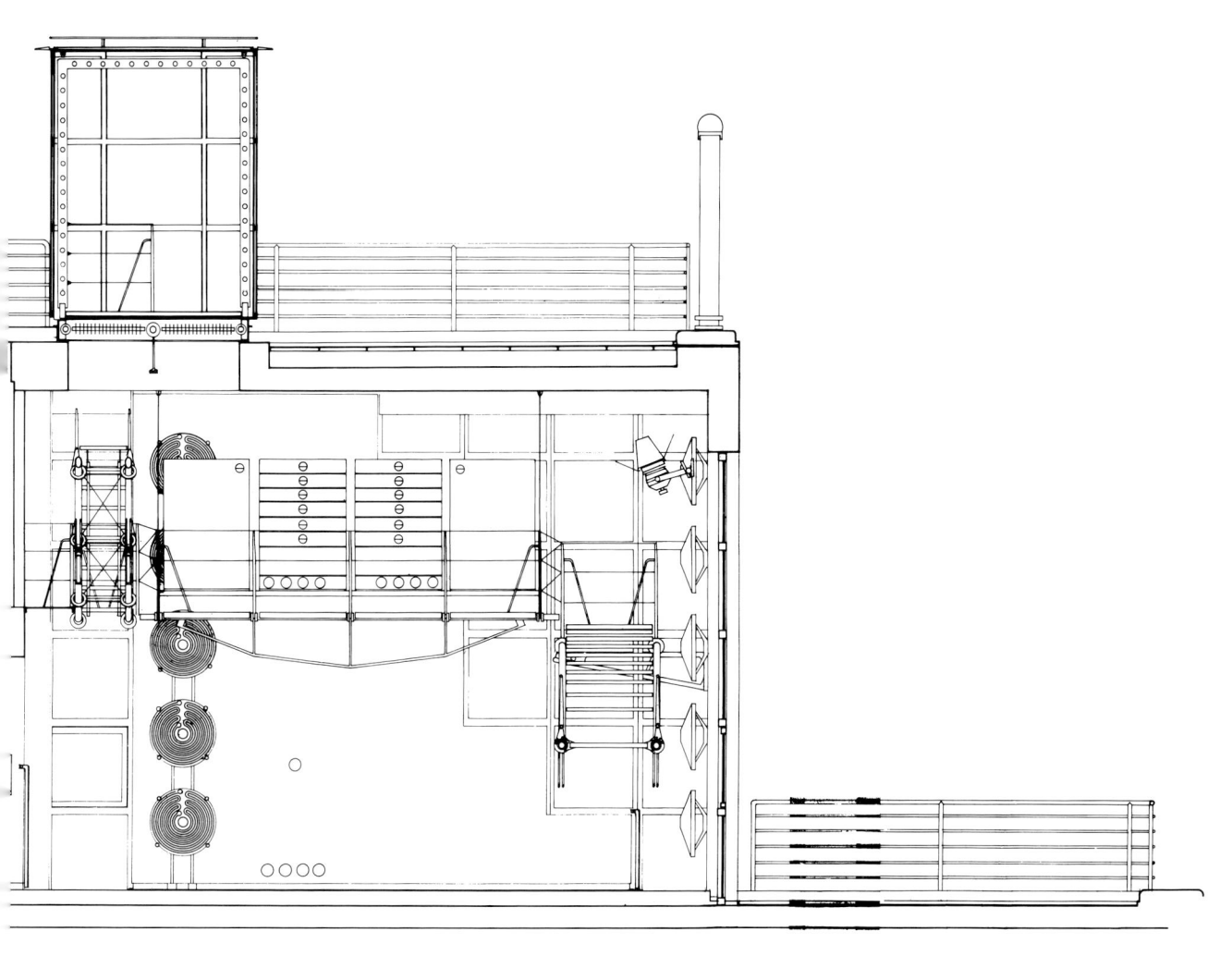

32

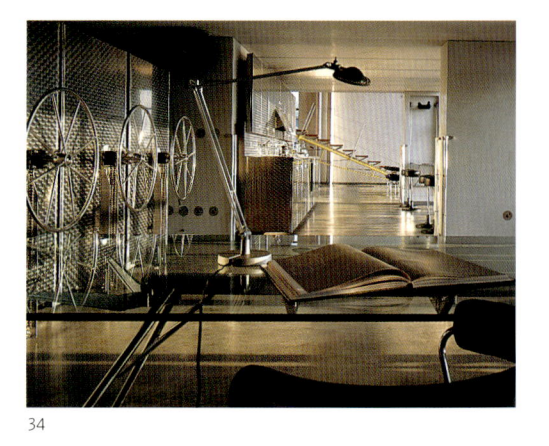

33

34

35

36

The apartment reflects Young's interests in craftsmanship and in components. A progression through the apartments leads from the lift into the living area (32) with views of the river beyond, through the kitchen (33) to the study (34). From the living area the shallow stair (35) leads up to the sleeping platform of concrete panels studded with glass lenses (36).
The use of clear and opaque glass, as in the rooftop bathroom, is a striking feature of the apartment (37–39).

37

38 39

The plan (5 & 7) is at the core of the Linn Products scheme: a production and research building (2 & 3) is connected to an automated warehouse block. The natural contours of the rural site are put to good use and the context respected (6) to create a third level (4) below the main production space with a triple-height reception area (1).

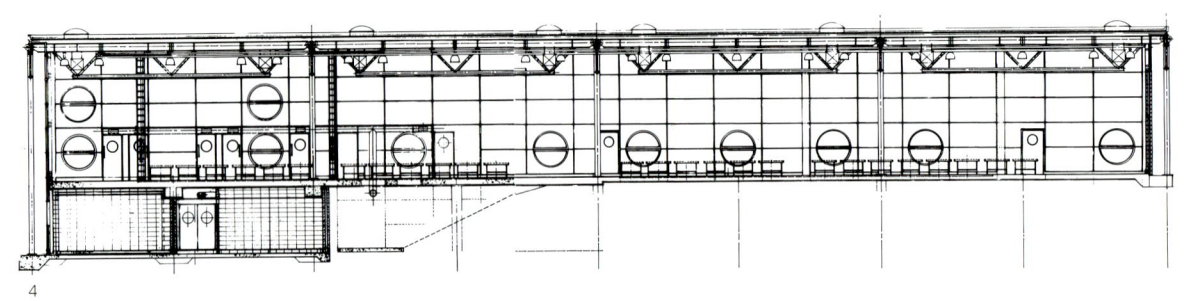

Linn Products

Glasgow, 1985–7

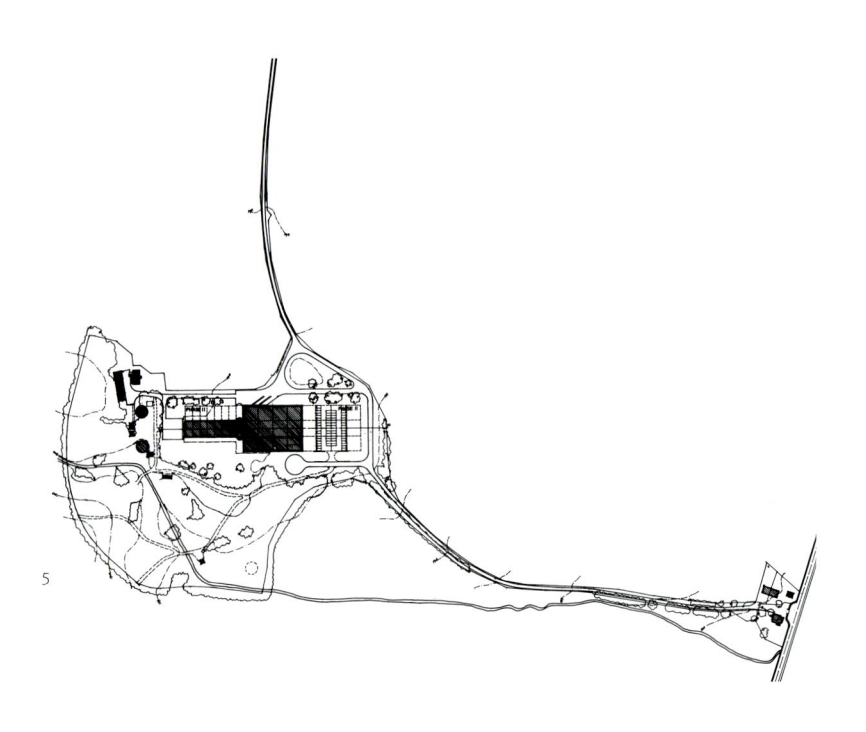

The essence of the Linn Products scheme is its ingenious plan, devised to suit the needs of a highly-automated audio equipment manufacturer. All the business activities were to be under one roof. Two rectangular blocks are linked: one houses administration, production, assembly and research, partly in an undercroft contrived within the slope of the site; the second building is a highly-automated warehouse supplying components via robotic carts to the production lines. Repetitive structural and cladding systems allow for easy expansion if required.

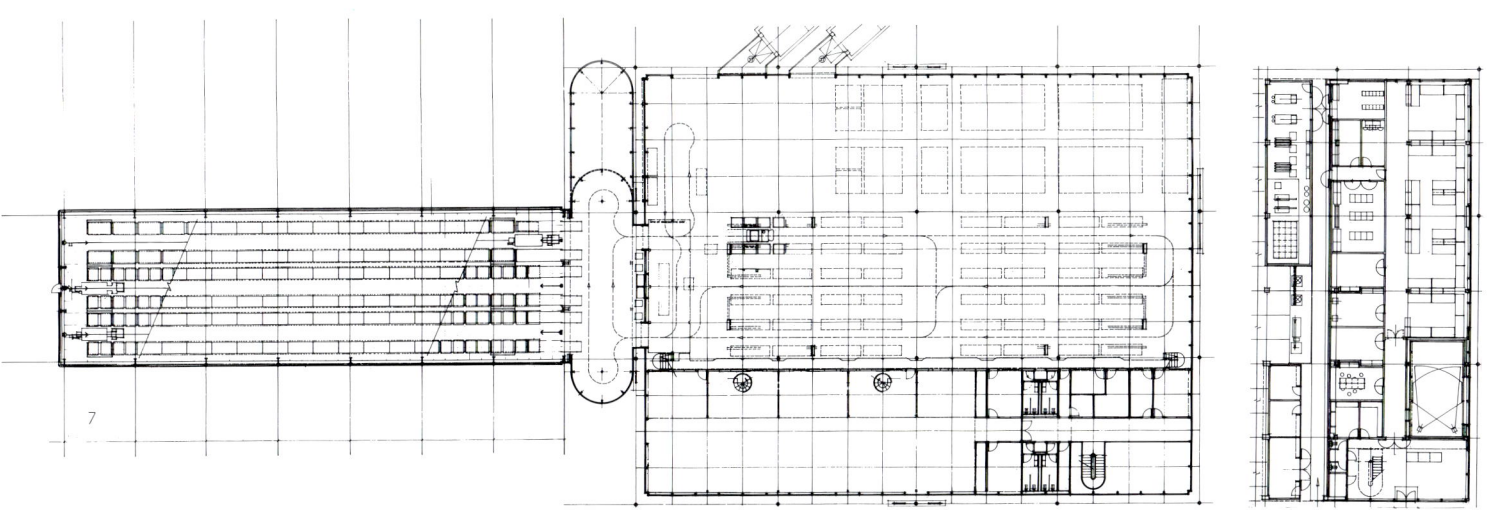

6

7

273

Billingsgate Securities Market

London, 1985–8

The restoration and conversion of Billingsgate, from redundant fish market into state-of-the-art dealing floor, was a highly significant project for the Rogers office. Conversion and rehabilitation had become an increasingly significant aspect of architectural practice in Britain during the 1970s, a reflection, in part, of public disquiet over the neglect of 'heritage'. The arguments for saving old buildings were partly sentimental but were also practical: reuse made financial sense. Other European countries, notably Italy, had stricter provisions than Britain for the protection of historic buildings. The City of London, which had suffered badly from wartime bombing, had destroyed many more buildings in the decades after the war, generally to make way for mediocre new developments.

Billingsgate became a test case for the new conservationist ethos. The City, which had built a new market in the Docklands, wanted to sell the old building (by Horace Jones, 1874–7) for redevelopment. Conservationists, led by Marcus Binney of SAVE, demanded that it be retained and asked the government to list it. An outline scheme by Chrysalis Architects (in which Mike Davies was a partner) helped to demonstrate that the market could be profitably retained and reused and it was – to the dismay of the City – listed. With demolition made extremely difficult, if not impossible, the City looked for a buyer. One eventually emerged, in the form of Citibank - a major American bank seeking electronic dealing floor space in London. The market's large main floor was judged to be ideal for this new use.

As found, the building, measuring 64m x 59m, consisted of a ground floor trading area - surrounded by cellular offices on three sides and open to an impressive timber, iron and glass roof – a gallery (the 'Haddock Gallery') extending across this principal space at second floor level, in a north/south direction, and a brick-vaulted basement supporting the superstructure and itself resting on a 3m thick concrete floor slab. No subdivision of the principal market space was likely to gain approval, though there was scope for changes in the ancillary parts of the building. The retention of the market space was entirely compatible with the needs of the new users, but it was clear that a massive upgrading of services would be required, to support both a permanent workforce of over 500 and a massive amount of electronic equipment.

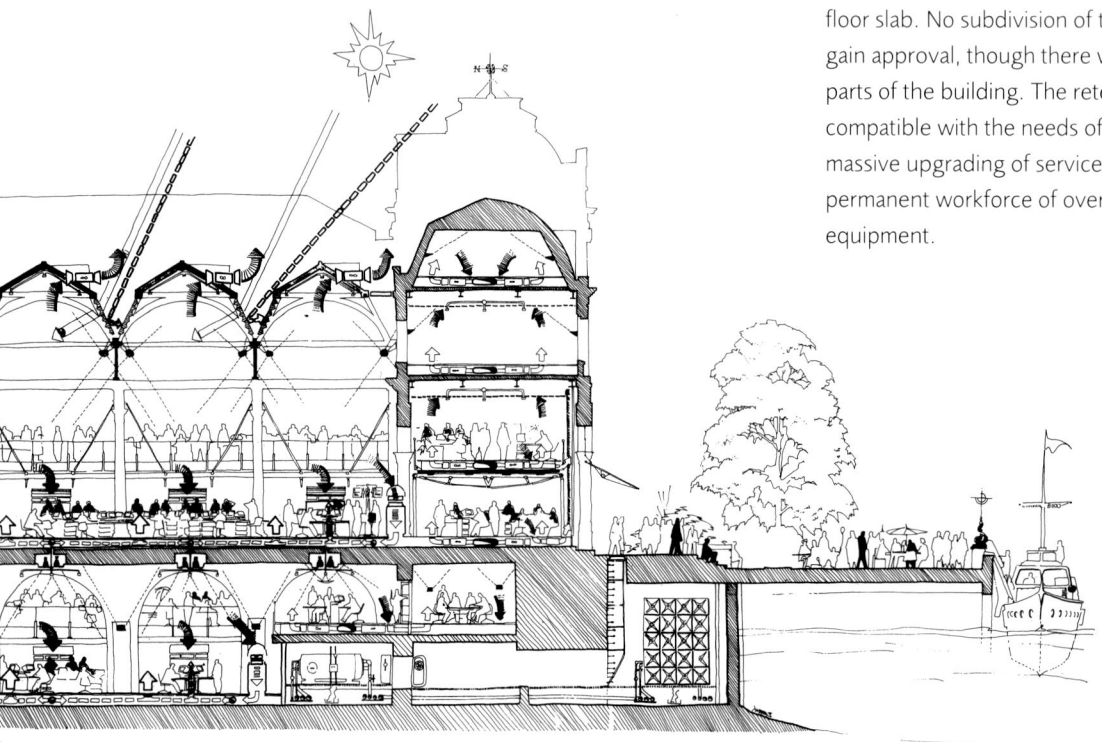

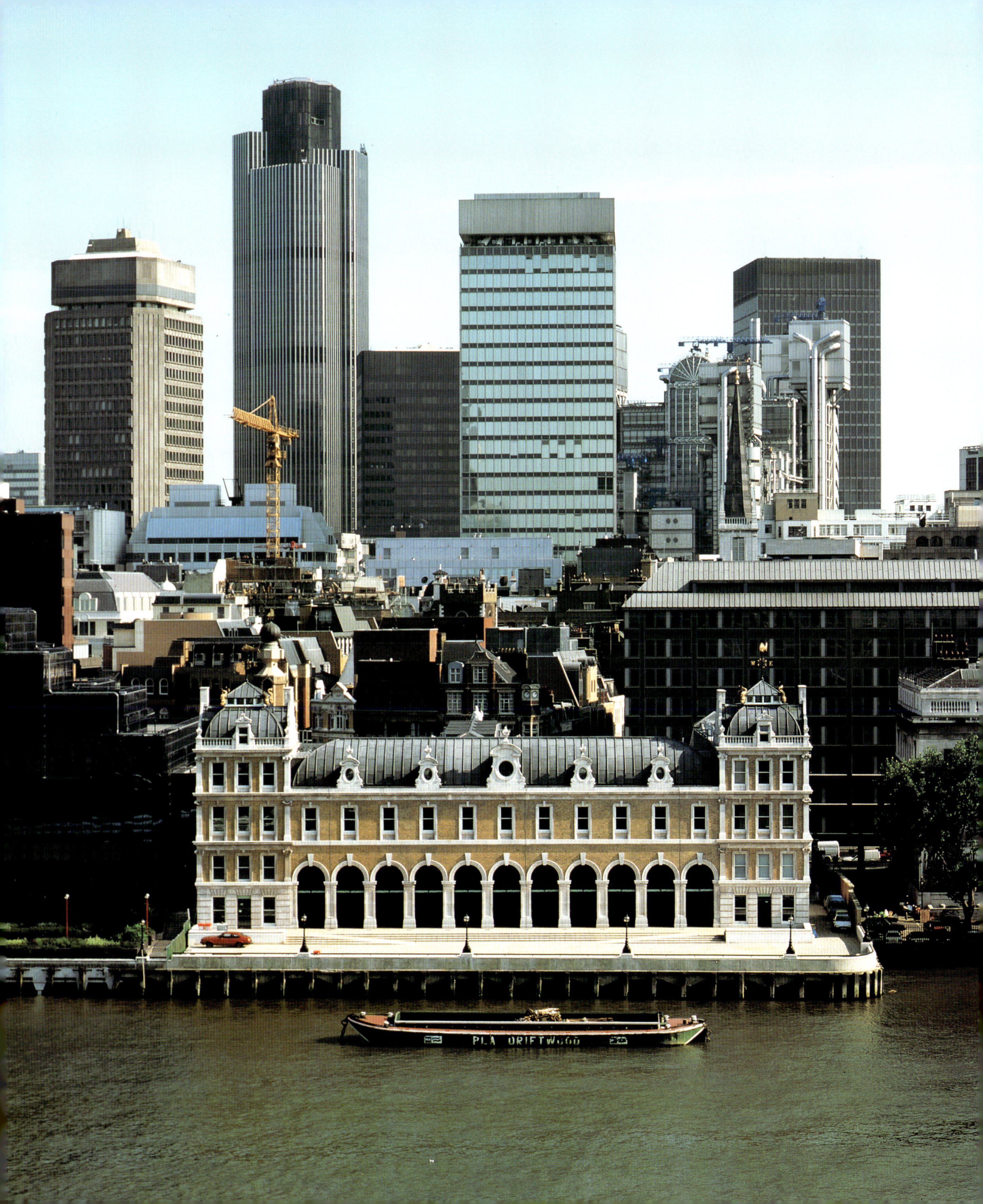
PLA DRIFTWOOD

Billingsgate Market was a fine example of Victorian architecture and had long been the centre of the wholesale fish trade (3 & 4). After the market moved out, however, the building faced demolition.
Rogers' transformation of Billingsgate included a painstaking restoration of the Victorian exterior (1 & 2, previous pages & 5) where missing details were carefully reinstated.

Faithful repair and the restoration of missing features was an important element in the Billingsgate project. The timber roof structure, for example, needed major overhaul, with the replacement of rotten members. Lead coverings were replaced in the traditional manner. Externally, the market regained its lost splendour. Inside, its inherent qualities were enhanced by the refurbishment. Lighting was a key consideration, both aesthetically and functionally. Conventional glass in the main roof and that of the Haddock Gallery was replaced by prismatic glazing units, which excluded direct sunlight and glare and filtered in a steady north light. A frameless glazed screen wall – using glass 2.5 cm thick to ensure soundproofing – set back beyond the street elevation provided further natural light and a sense of transparency and contact with the outside world. Artificial lighting for the new dealing floor was provided using fluorescent linear fittings to give both up and down-light, supplying ideal conditions for screenwork and highlighting the historic structure.

The major intervention into the old building was the construction of a new mezzanine floor of lightweight reinforced concrete supported by hangers from the Haddock Gallery. The floor of the Haddock Gallery was structurally reinforced to permit heavier loadings. New floors were introduced into the perimeter office wings. A new reinforced concrete floor slab was laid over the brick vaults to transfer loads from the new superstructure to the existing substructure.

At basement level, extensive alterations, including the insertion of intermediate floors across part of the space, were made to provide for the insertion of services. Full air conditioning was installed, with air handling on the main floor level conducted through a raised floor into specially designed perimeter units, striking objects in their own right. Chilling units were located in the basement. The high servicing requirements of the refurbished building necessitated the construction of an additional plant room under the river bank for water storage tanks.

Billingsgate was a very challenging project and gave the lie to the idea that conversion is a less demanding exercise than building new. It set a new standard for historic refurbishment in Britain and demonstrated that the insertion of uncompromisingly new work into old buildings could be a positive addition. Unfortunately, that lesson has not always been heeded and local planning authorities and statutory bodies continue to demand copies of past styles. The approach at Billingsgate was, in fact, more American than British, reflecting the application of a close analysis of the historic fabric and its potential for change and embracing the latter, rather than regarding it as a necessary evil.

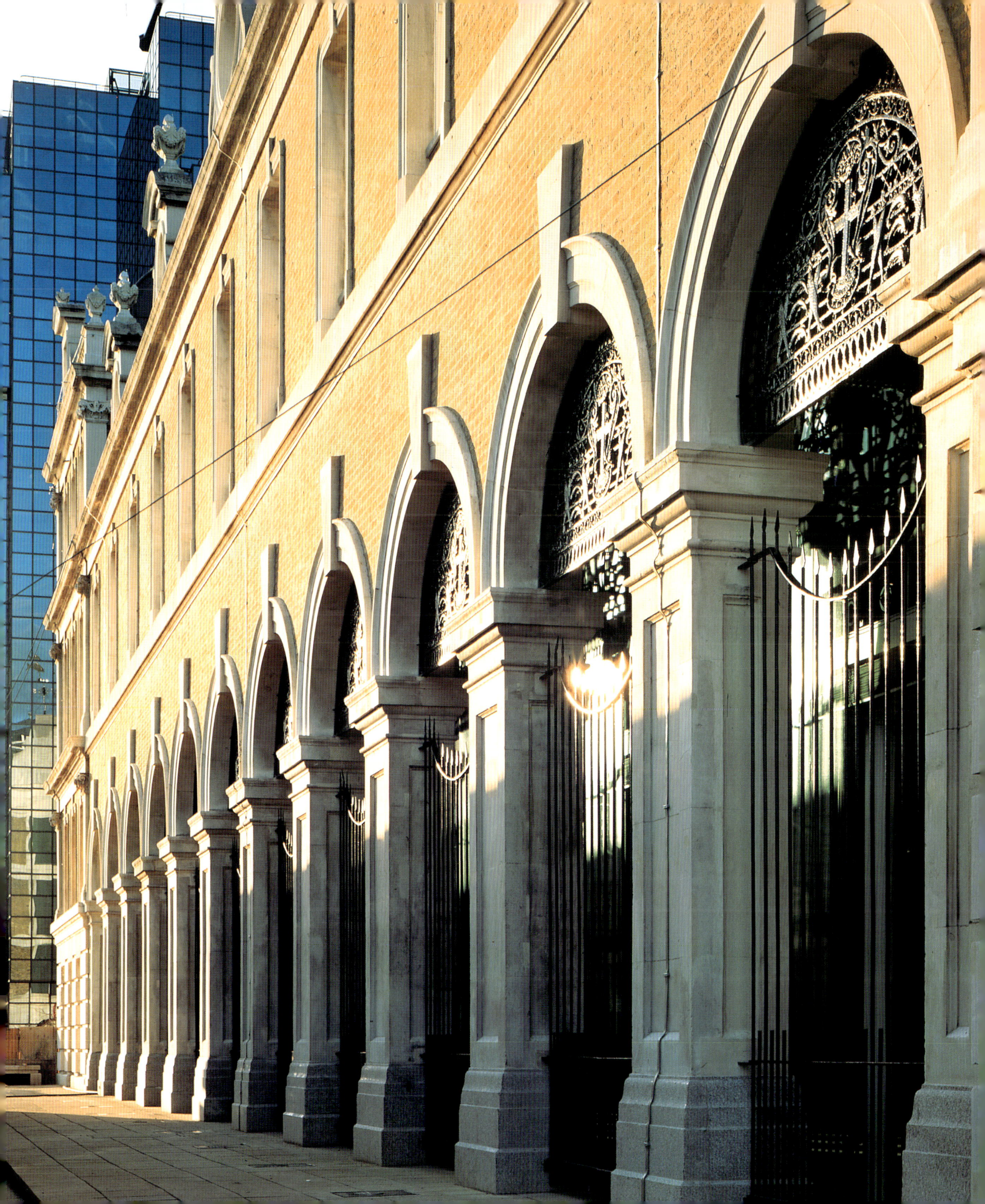

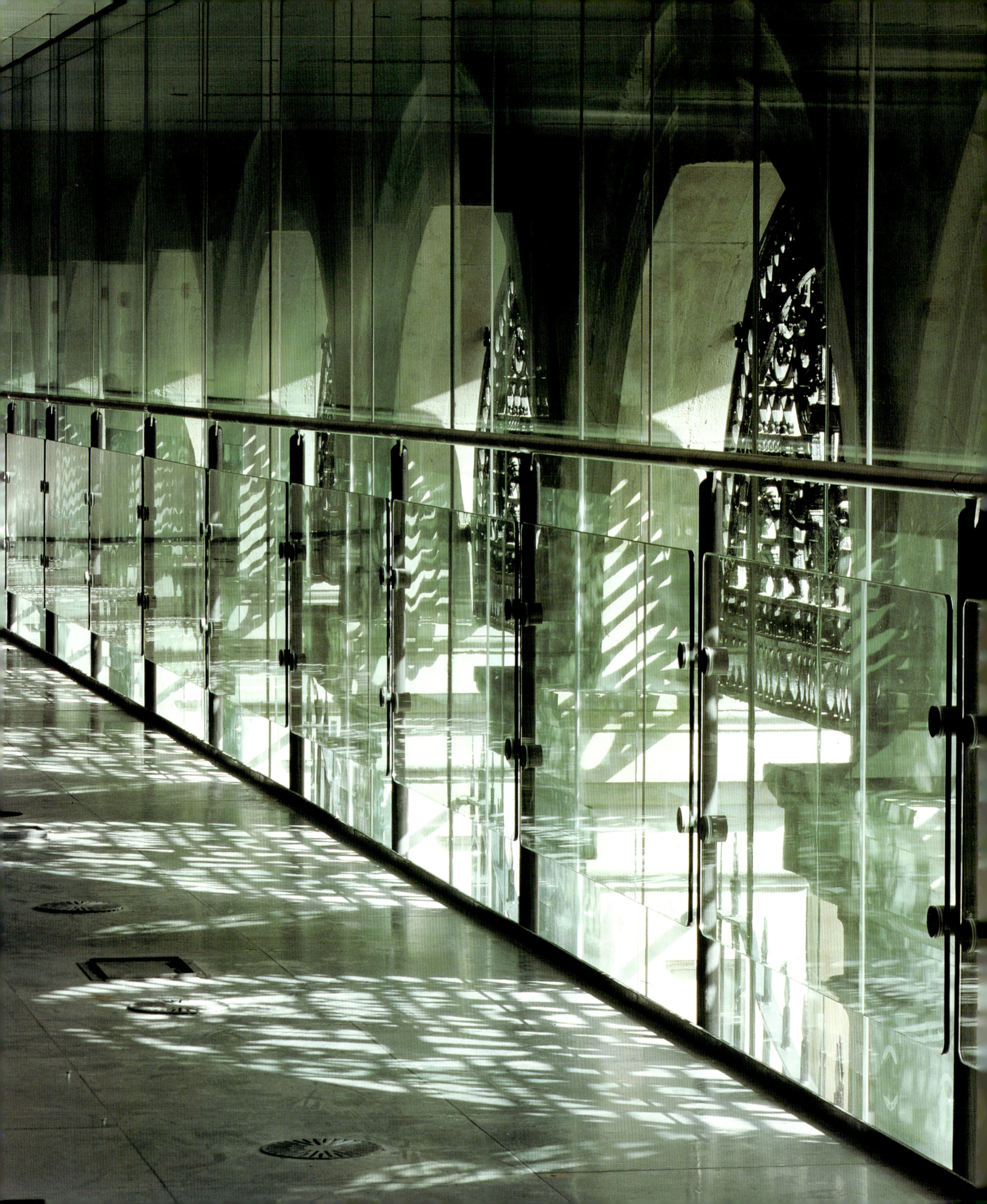

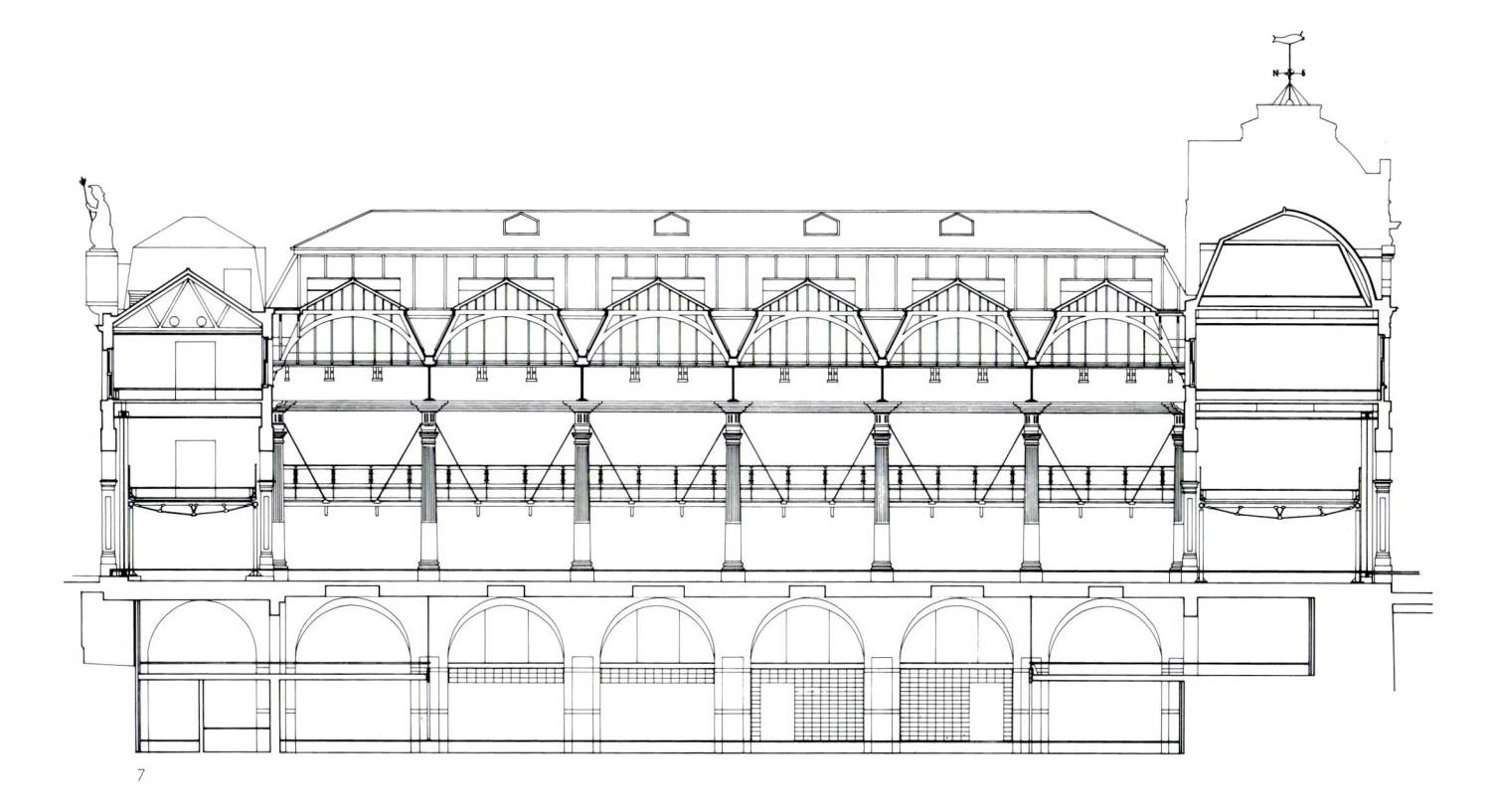

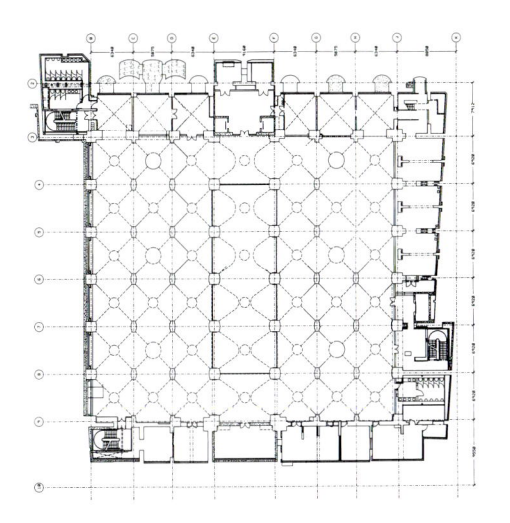

The old market was ideally suited for the intended new use of a trading floor, while the basement was used for servicing and restaurant space (8). Heavy plate glass panels were sensitively fitted behind Victorian iron gates to eliminate street noise and pollution (6).

The section of the building (7) shows how a new mezzanine suspended from the old structure was inserted to increase the amount of useable space. These insertions by Rogers were unmistakably contemporary (9) and typical of Rogers' interest in lightweight steel structure.

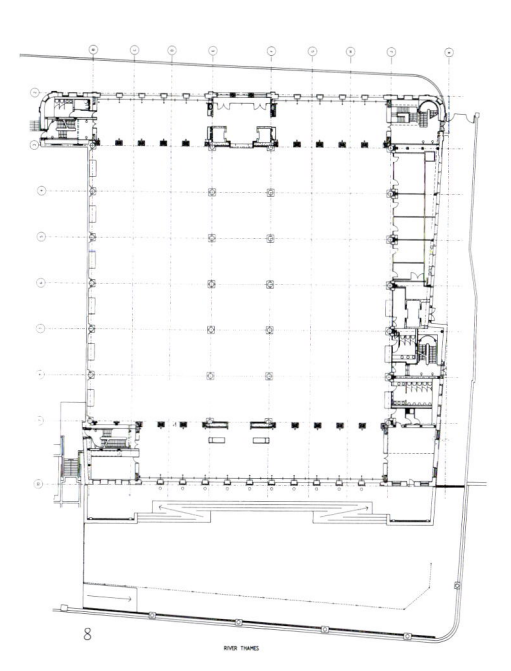

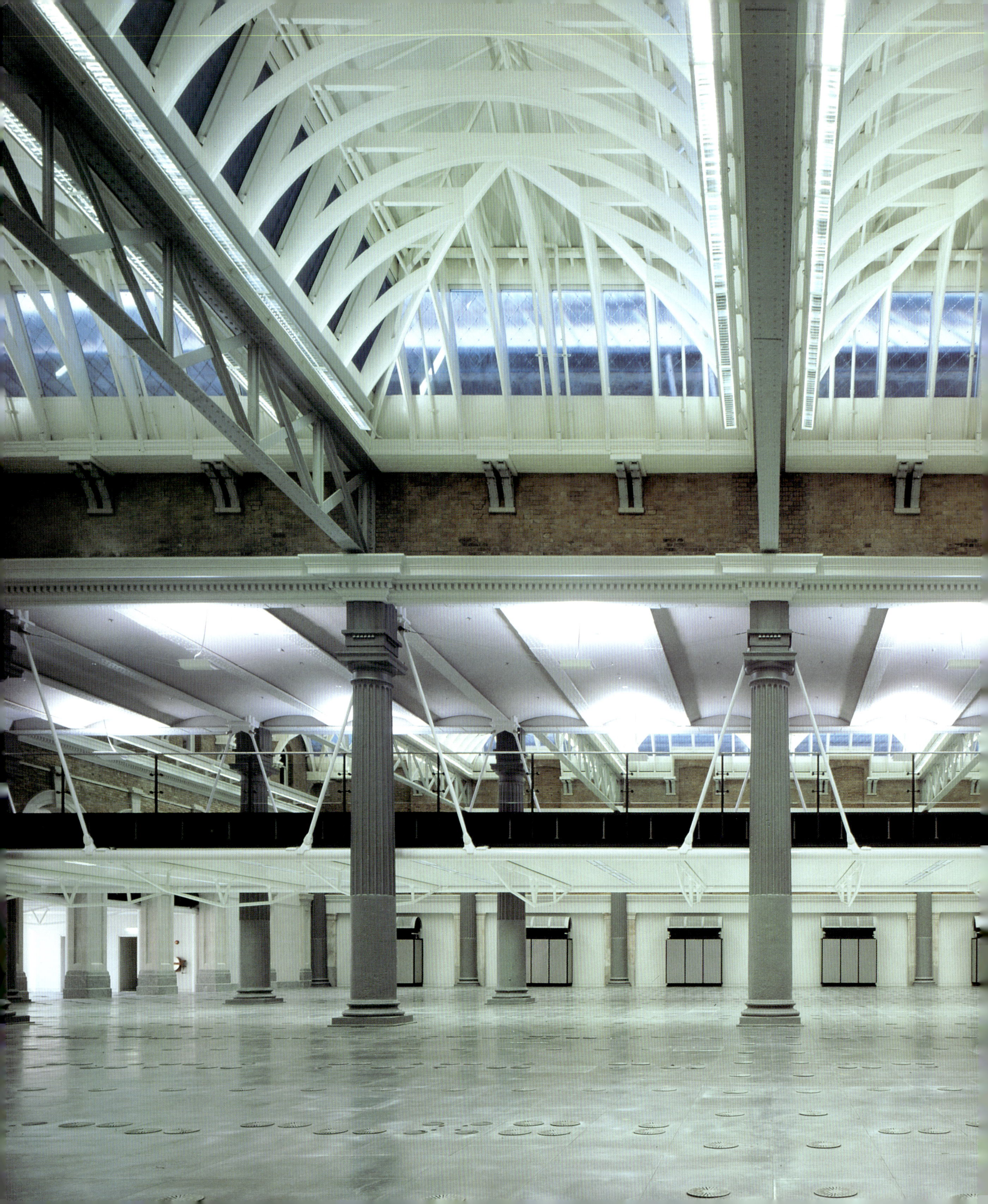

The reconstructed interior balances careful restoration with striking new interventions (10–12).
Historic spaces including the undercroft, used for services, and the Haddock Gallery were restored for new uses (13 & 14).

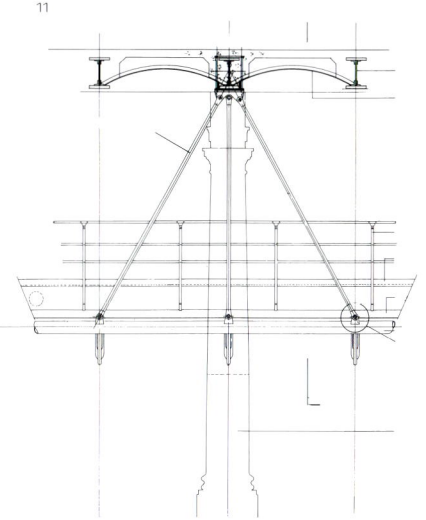

Centre Commercial St Herblain

Nantes, France 1986–7

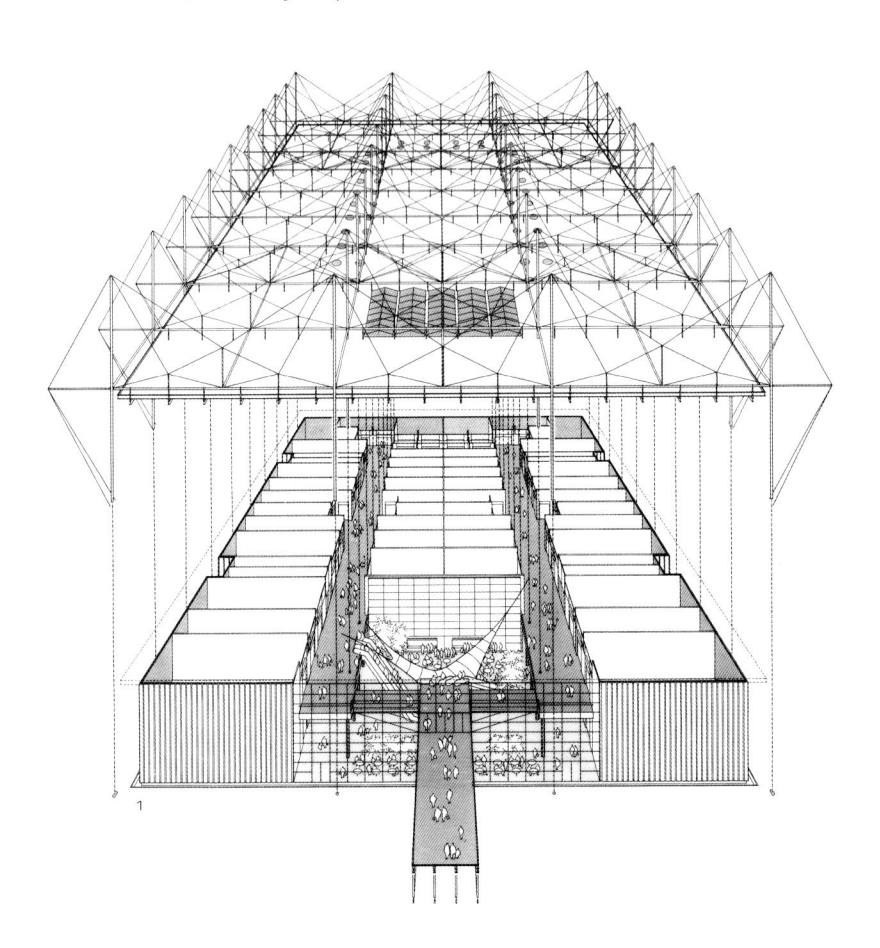

The Centre Commercial at St Herblain is modest by the standards of many of its contemporary (and later) out-of-town retail developments – just 21,000 square metres (gross). It firmly eschews the trashy Post Modernist rhetoric of so many such schemes in favour of a superficially straightforward shed which takes its cue from the earlier Fleetguard Factory not so very far away from it.

Low cost and quick construction were prime requirements of the client, who wanted a scheme which could be adapted to other sites. The Centre is entered, like Fleetguard, by way of a steel bridge, leading into a double height reception area. Use of a masted roof structure keeps internal supports to the minimum. Shops are arranged on two levels, with services clearly exposed and brightly coloured. This project applied the imagery of the Pompidou Centre, not inappropriately, to the world of retailing – the shopping centre is a public (or semi-public) place.

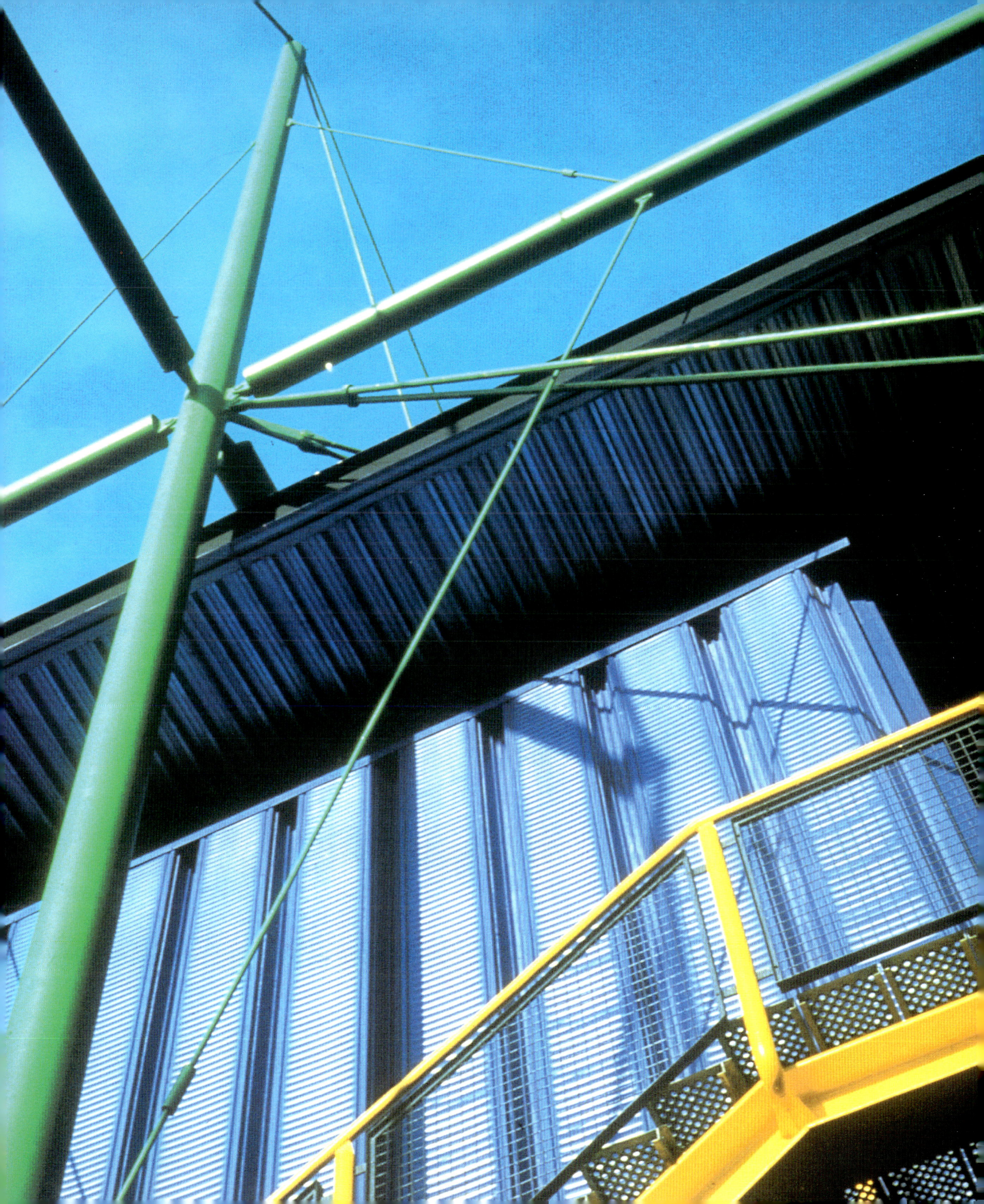

3

The Centre Commercial adapted the masted structure of Fleetguard for the purposes of retailing (2, previous page & 3). The combination of suspended steel structure and use of colour raise the tenor of the nondescript retail campus (1, p282 & 4).

A very careful attention to detail and the use of vivid colours to code principal elements set the building apart from the usual run of retail sheds (5–7).

4

Centre Commercial St Herblain

5

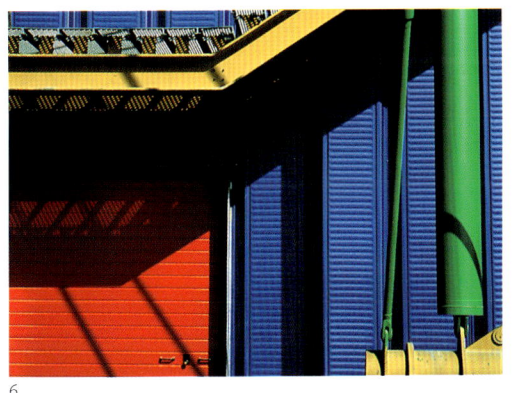

6

7

285

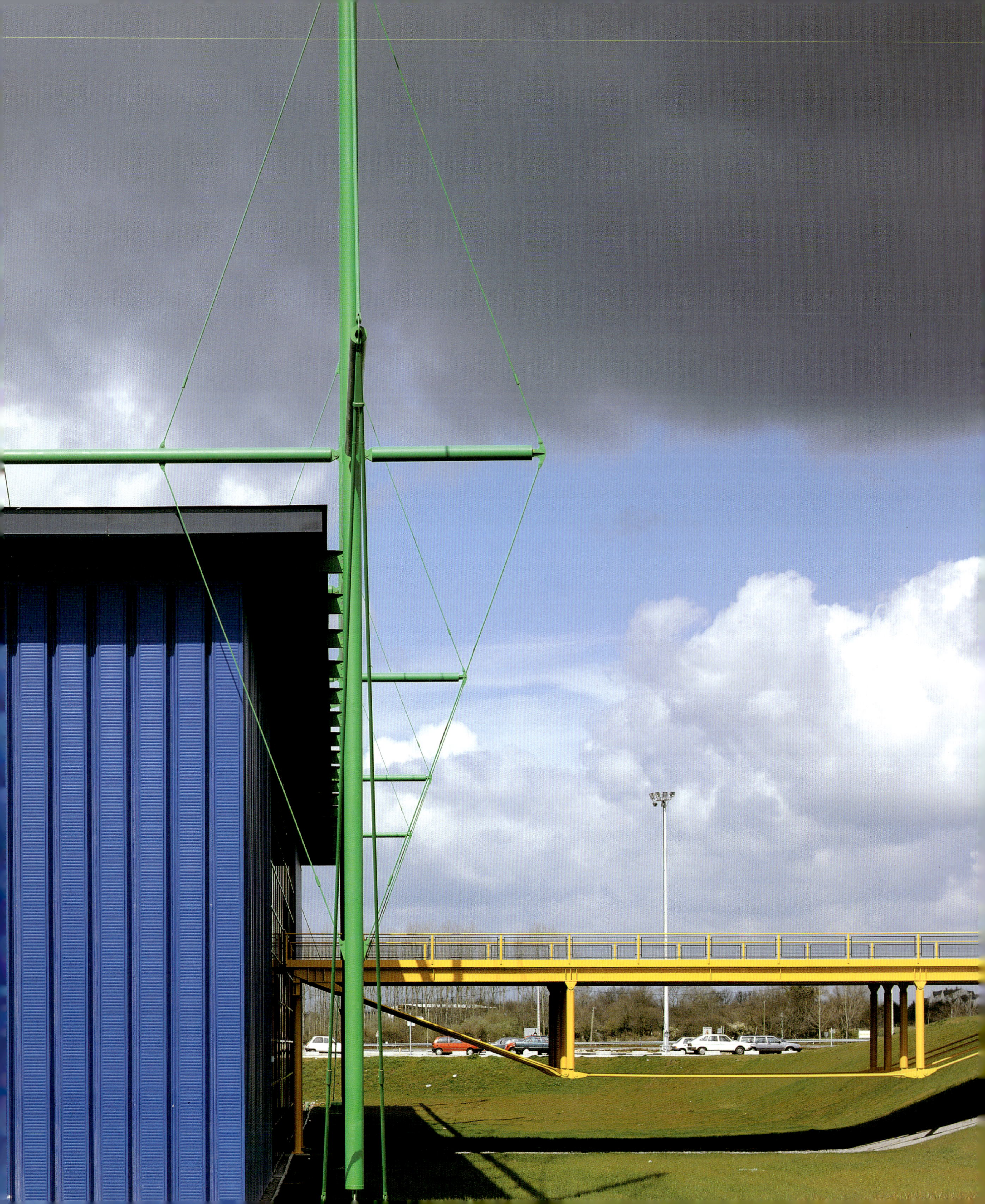

A steel causeway leads from the car park into a large entry foyer (8 & 9).

Escalators link the retail levels (10) which are characterized by brightly coloured exposed services (11). Tension and compression elements are clearly expressed in the mast-base detail (12).

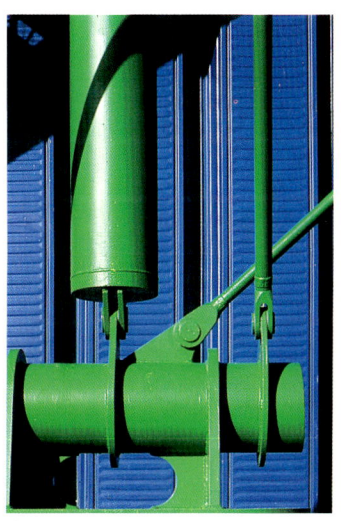

London as it could be

London, 1986

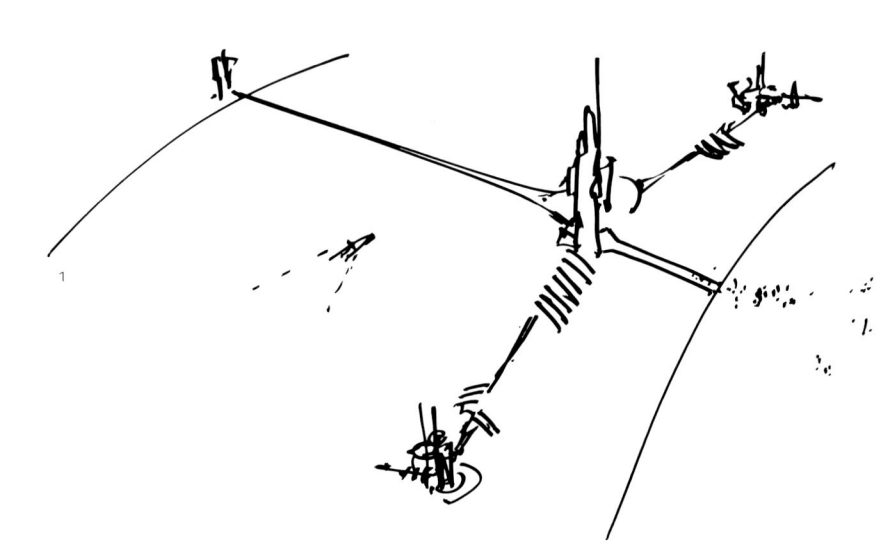

The experience of Coin Street and the National Gallery competition fed into the Rogers segment of the major exhibition at the Royal Academy in 1986, devoted to the work of Rogers, Norman Foster and James Stirling – the 'big three' of British architecture.

Both Foster and Stirling showed major new buildings – the Hongkong and Shanghai Bank and Stuttgart Neue Staatsgalerie respectively. But Rogers chose instead to explore ideas about London's public realm, breaking the mould imposed by geography (notably the presence of the River Thames) and history (which had trapped the life of the capital in a net of established and seemingly immutable transport links). Rogers refused to accept the established order. The river became, in the Royal Academy project, not a barrier but a link between north and south. A bridge, based on that proposed for Coin Street, leapt across the Thames, bearing a rapid transit system and a pedestrian way from the South Bank (and Waterloo Station) to a pedestrianized Northumberland Avenue (a broad an dignified street which has always seemed to lead nowhere) and so to Trafalgar Square. The existing railway bridge, always excoriated as a blot on river views, was to be removed and the railway terminated at Waterloo, leaving the undistinguished Charing Cross station as a potential development site. Trafalgar Square itself was to be largely pedestrianized and the road barrier between its central area and the National Gallery removed. Although the project could be described as visionary – and therefore dismissed as impractical – it provided for the real needs of London. Traffic, it was accepted, could not simply be

2

'London as it could be', exhibited at the Royal Academy in London, presented Rogers' vision of the metropolis in which the River Thames became a focus of activity rather than a gulf between the northern and southern banks (1 & 2).

3

4

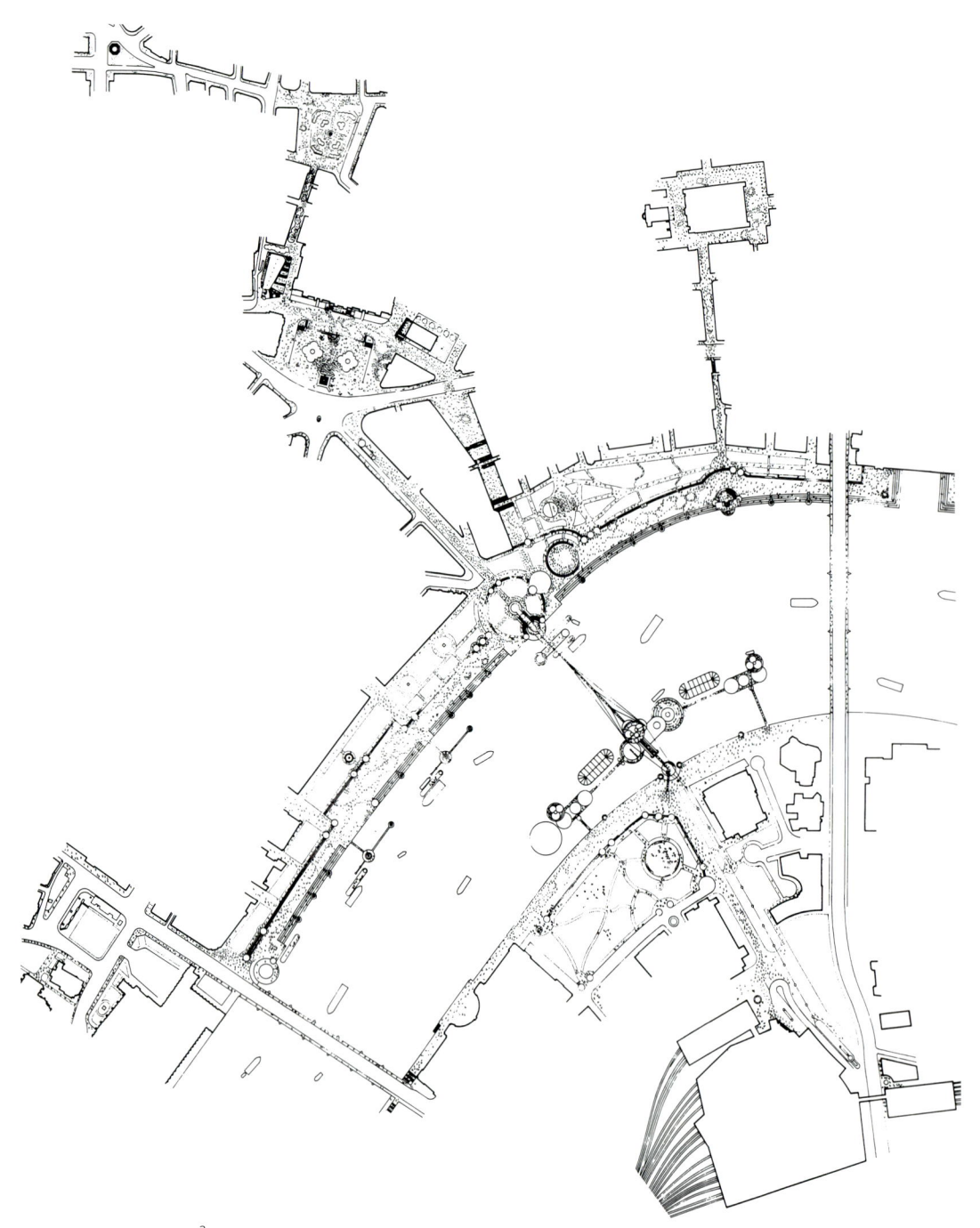

A study on two axes (3): north–south from Piccadilly Circus to Waterloo Station and east–west from Parliament to Blackfriars Bridge.
A radical approach was taken to traffic – no longer allowed to dominate the riverside but relocated to a new submerged highway. This created a pedestrianized linear park, open to the river and weaving together existing public gardens (4).
An eighteenth-century watercolour of Somerset House as it was (5).

5

London as it could be

6

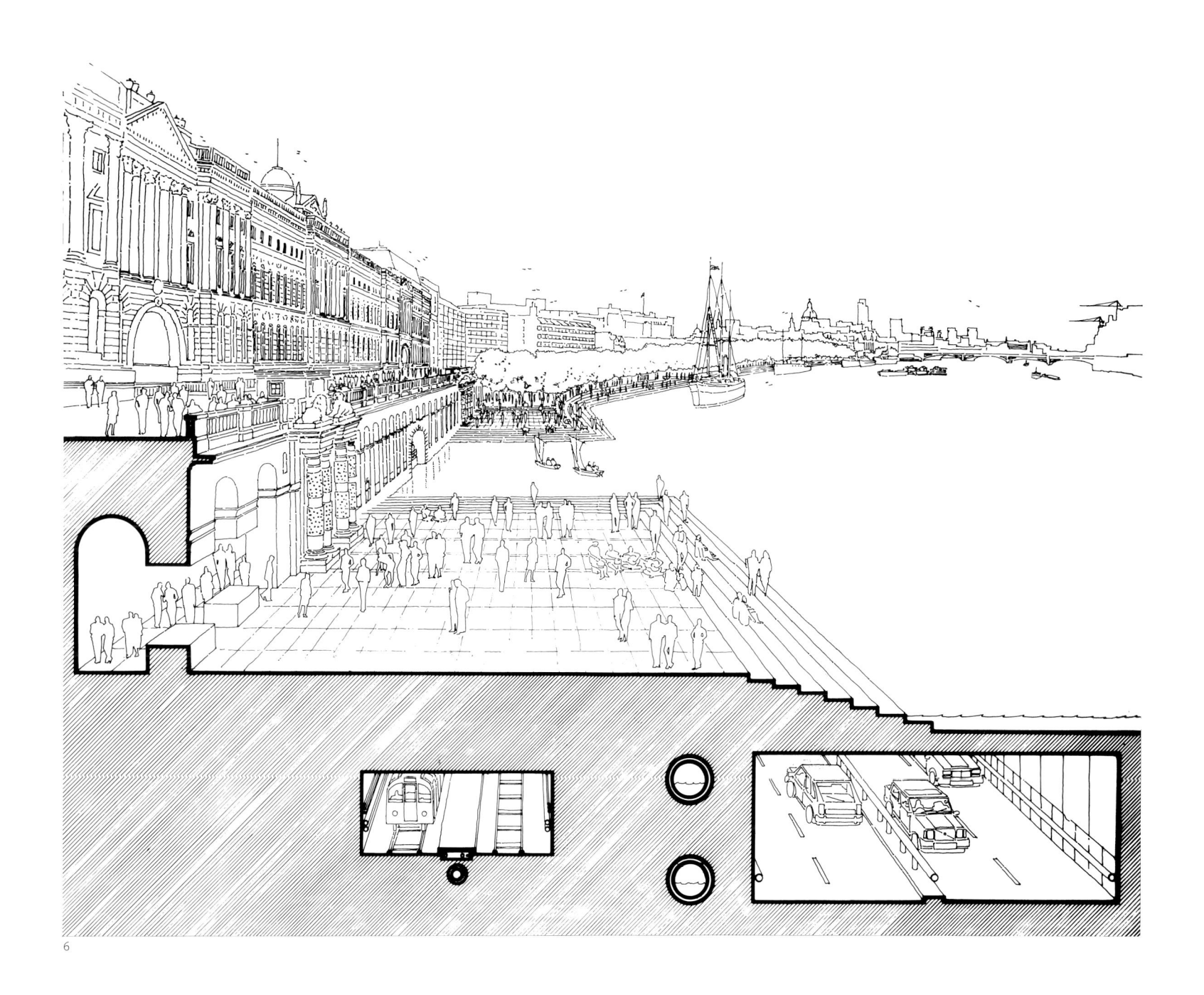

The restoration of Somerset House's relationship to the river was made possible by the relocation of the road (6–8) and the provision of a water garden in its original position.

7 8

9

10

A network of pedestrianized places and routes reclaimed Trafalgar Square as a public meeting place (9, 11 & 14).
Rogers created a strong, new direct connection between the South Bank and Trafalgar Square by means of a pedestrianized route along Northumberland Avenue (10 & 12).

11

12

London as it could be

13

14

15

16

Opening the terrace in front of the National Gallery allowed free pedestrian movement and the possibility of a sculpture garden (13 & 15).
The removal of Charing Cross Station opened-up a dramatic pedestrian route to the river and clear visual links from north to south banks (16).

17

The aim was to reclaim London's riverside, which had been turned into a highway and transform it into a place for the people (17–19).
On the South Bank the closure of roads and the removal of the obtrusive rail viaduct opened up a gateway to the Thames and a visual link to Trafalgar Square; also providing a better entry to the Royal Festival Hall (20, 21).

18

London as it could be

19

20

21

295

22

23

The Hungerford railway bridge (22 & 27) which replaced an elegant early nineteenth-century suspension bridge by Brunel (25), had long been regarded as an ugly intrusion into the river's views. Earlier projects to provide a dignified link to the South Bank had failed (23 & 26).
Rogers proposed a new pedestrian bridge, with an underslung shuttle ferrying people from Waterloo Station to Trafalgar Square (24 & 28).

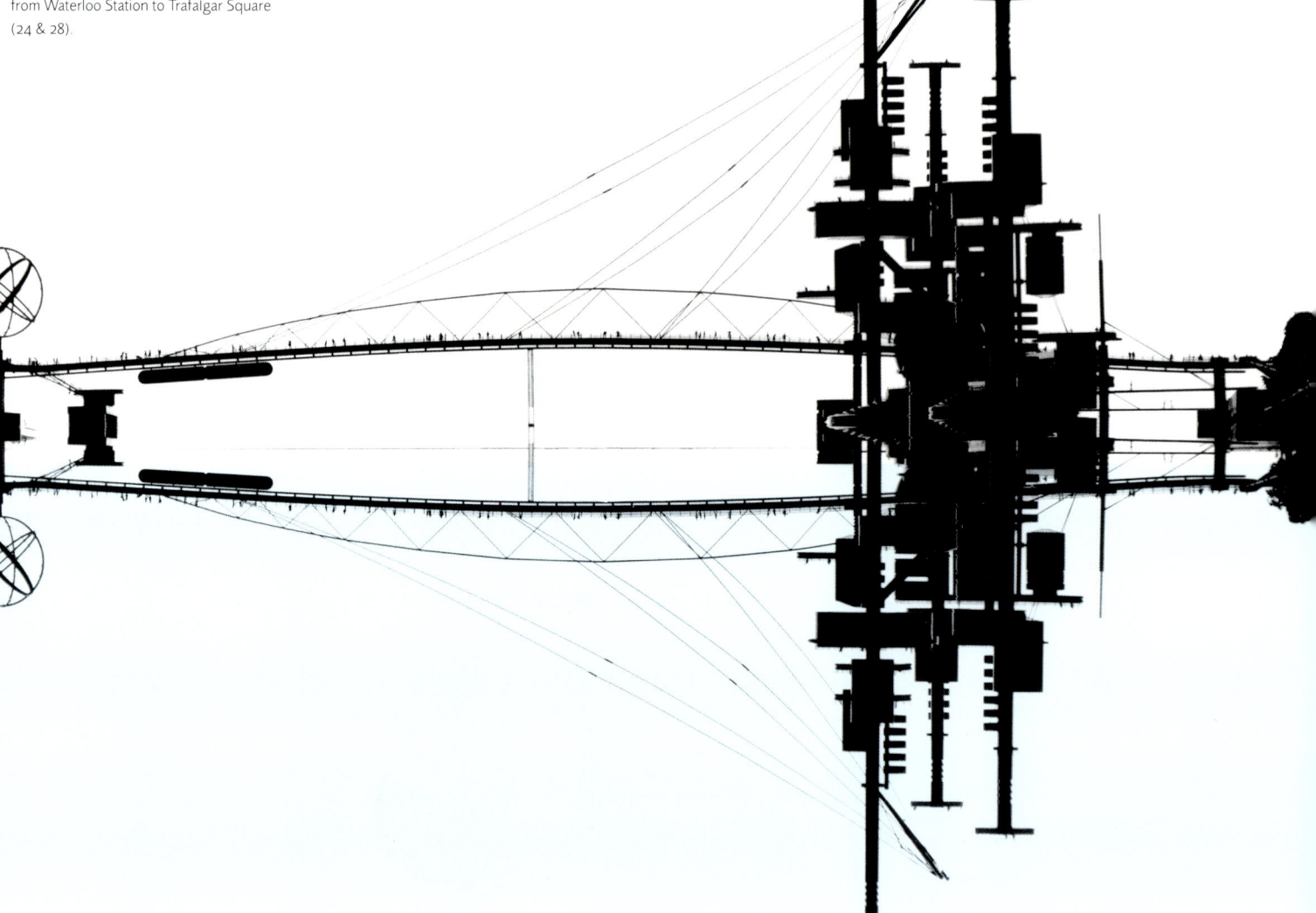

24

London as it could be

25

26

27

28

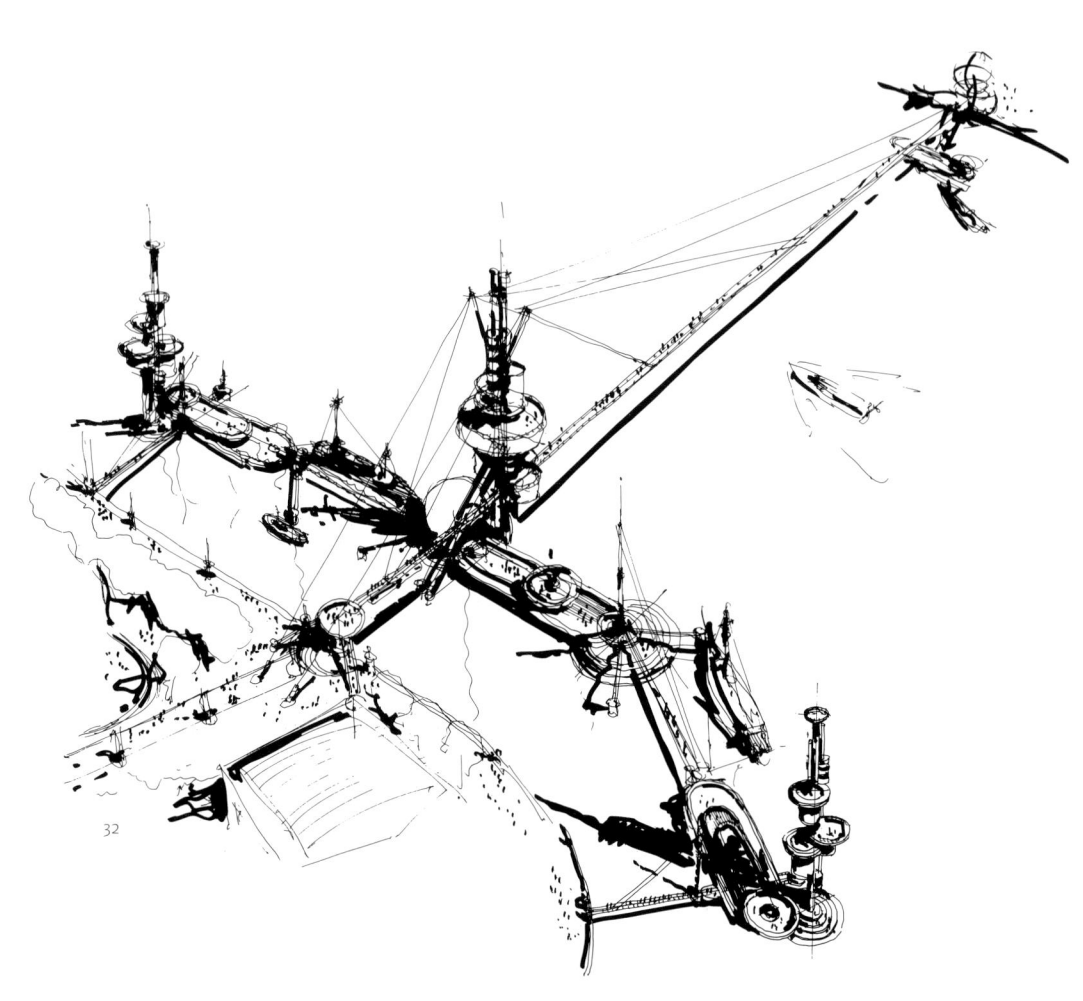

The new bridge and floating islands contained shops, galleries and restaurants on the water, populating the river and breaking the scale of it as a barrier (29–33).

London as it could be

banished in one remove. A new high speed road would extend along the Embankment, but below ground level, leaving the riverside itself as a vibrant new public realm for pedestrians.

The imagery of 'London as it could be' was undeniably futuristic but the project was urban rather than architectural in intent. The new islands proposed in the Thames derived their form from North Sea oil platforms as much as from buildings, though their shapes echoed those of Coin Street and Lloyd's. They were seen not only as a means of funding change but as an approach to populating the river, where new boat services would provide a high-speed link between South Bank, City and West End.

The project was a reaction to the 1980s development boom. It focused on space rather than buildings. More than any other project, it placed Richard Rogers at the head of a movement for reform in London, a capital deprived of leadership and vision. Its ideas remained alive into the 1990s, though some of them – like the removal of the Hungerford bridge – were rendered impossible by later developments. The Architecture Foundation, which Rogers was to chair, and the thinking of the Labour Party, which launched a campaign to restore a central authority to London, were both beneficiaries of the proposals.

'London as it could be' exemplifies the spirit of the Rogers office in the 1980s. Having finally completed a major London building, Lloyd's, the practice could have turned away from the radicalism of its earlier work. Instead, it built on the lessons of the Coin Street and National Gallery schemes and committed itself to a campaign for better cities.

Royal Avenue

London, 1987

The success of the Billingsgate refurbishment lay in the counterpoint of old and new, of restoration and innovation. Converting historic buildings involves constraints but, Richard Rogers argues, 'architecture is made out of constraints. The success of a building can be measured by how well one has resolved these constraints. Problems often have to be turned upside down in order to be understood.' At Royal Avenue, Rogers achieved transformation, a complete fusion of an old building and radical new design.

Richard and Ruth Rogers (who had been living in a modest flat in Hampstead) bought two early Victorian listed houses in 1983, on the corner of Royal Avenue, Chelsea, which were to form their London home. Their natural instinct had always been to build a new home, but finding a suitable site in central London on which an innovative new house could be built proved impossible. A radical conversion was a viable alternative, given the attractions of the Chelsea site, though the public exterior at Royal Avenue had to remain more or less completely unchanged. (The existing wooden sash windows, for example, largely rotten, had to be remade in exact replica.) The interior was undistinguished, and had been poorly reinstated after war-time bomb damage. Two houses became one – transforming the narrow verticality of the typical London house, with its many small rooms. Rogers says of Royal Avenue: 'it is common for barns to be converted into houses, with their big spaces split up into small rooms. We converted a house into a barn!'

The two houses were of five storeys. There was no garden, but there was a flat roof with wonderful views across to Wren's Royal Hospital, a building which Rogers had always admired. Richard and Ruth were attracted by the views, but above all they wanted space and light, of the order they had enjoyed in their flat in Paris' Place des Vosges, during the construction of the Pompidou Centre. A corner site, with green space on one side and the urban rigour of the nearby King's Road, on the other, had clear appeal. Le Corbusier's Domino House project had been critical in freeing houses from the tyranny of fixed walls and partitions and provided an agenda for the modern house. Even more relevant was the exemplar of Rogers' beloved Maison de Verre, where Chareau and Bijvoet had created a series of flowing modern spaces within the container of an old structure.

The transformation project, which involved totally gutting the houses, was based on a strategy for extended family living. Space had to be found for children and for Ruth's parents, who had moved to Britain. The children's flats were provided at basement and top floor levels and accessed by a new spiral staircase, which is contained within a central core and connects all five floors of the building. Dr and Mrs Elias' apartment was formed on the ground floor. The Rogers' own domain was on the first and second floors, which were turned into a single, huge, 7 m. high space, lit by two rows of windows. (Initial ideas to open up the whole interior to roof level quickly proved too costly.) A mezzanine gallery was formed within the space as a sleeping area, accessed via an extremely lightweight staircase. A prominent steel I-beam supporting the mezzanine could be read as a reference to the Maison de Verre. The principal living area is approached from the street

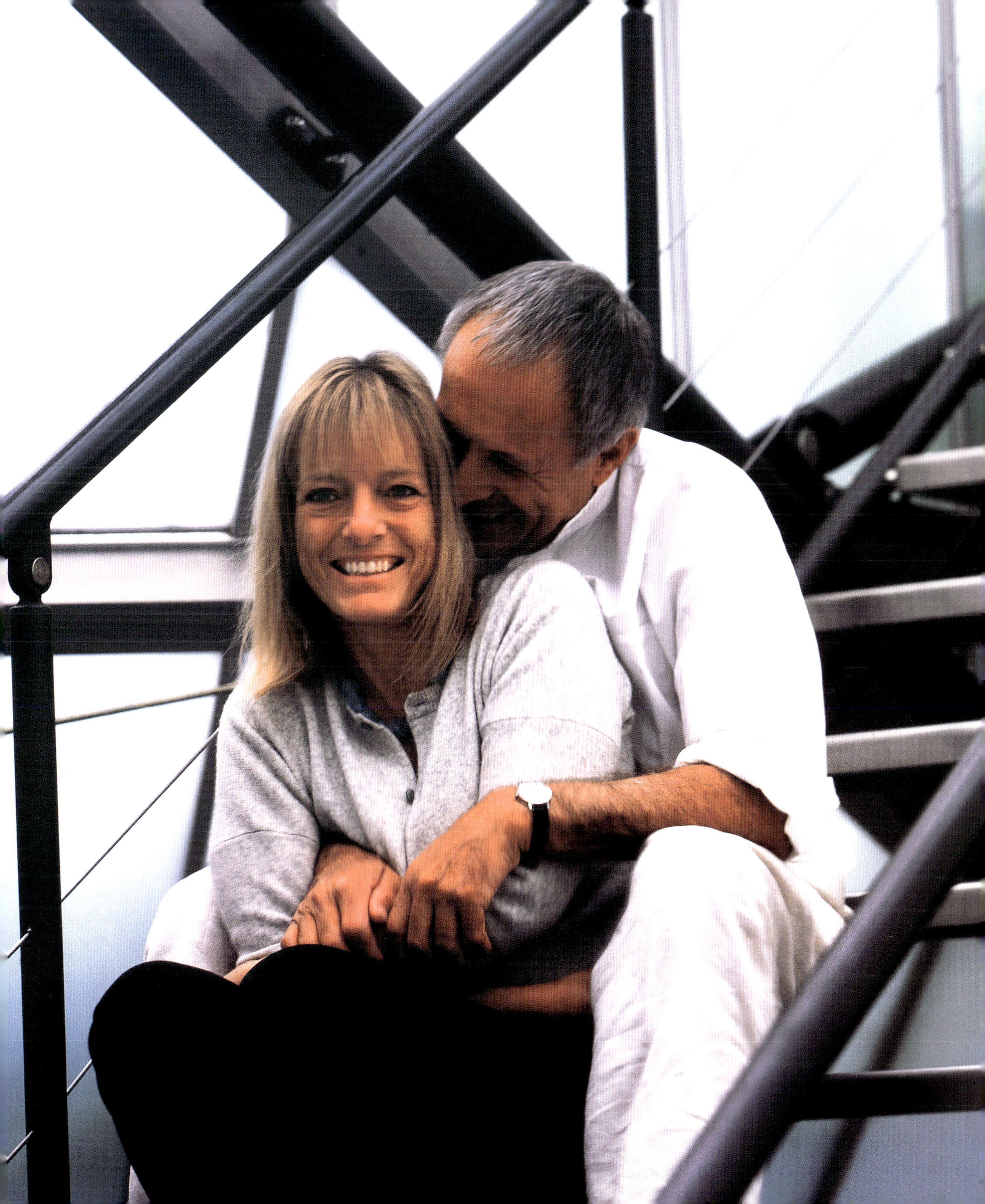

by way of a new, bridge-like staircase, located within a glazed extension which stands in what was a dank back yard. This is a serene space of diffused light. From here, one passes into the brilliantly lit living area. Rogers' friends often call this the 'piazza' and it is a marvellous place for entertaining. When empty, Rogers relishes the lack of enclosure and the qualities of the space for the display of large works of art.

Since the house was completed, the former top floor flat has been converted into a bedroom and is approached from a new staircase, taking off from mezzanine level. The former sleeping gallery is now used as a study. This is not a house for privacy or seclusion. Richard Rogers, influenced by the lifestyle he had seen on America's West Coast, wanted a house 'where you can hear, see, smell everything'.

In this spirit, the kitchen is not a separate room (though a clearance and storage area is set in an alcove, part of a central service core which includes a small cloakroom a level below). Instead, cooking is integrated into the main living space, as a public activity and something to be celebrated and enjoyed. The fittings are of an industrial toughness and rigour and include an island unit descended from that installed at Creek Vean. The Rogers house is made for extended family use and for entertaining. The lofty interior comes into its own when a party is held there. It carries forward the tradition of sociable space established during the 1960s at Creek Vean and the Rogers House in Wimbledon.

The home of Richard and Ruth Rogers at Royal Avenue, Chelsea, is housed behind early nineteenth-century facades (3); but it is a radically modern environment. Rogers made a virtue of working within an historic structure, creating uncompromisingly modern interiors behind period frontages, removing walls and floors to create a great flowing volume (1 & 2, previous pages, & 5). Entry from the street level is via a translucent glazed conservatory (4 & 6).

Royal Avenue

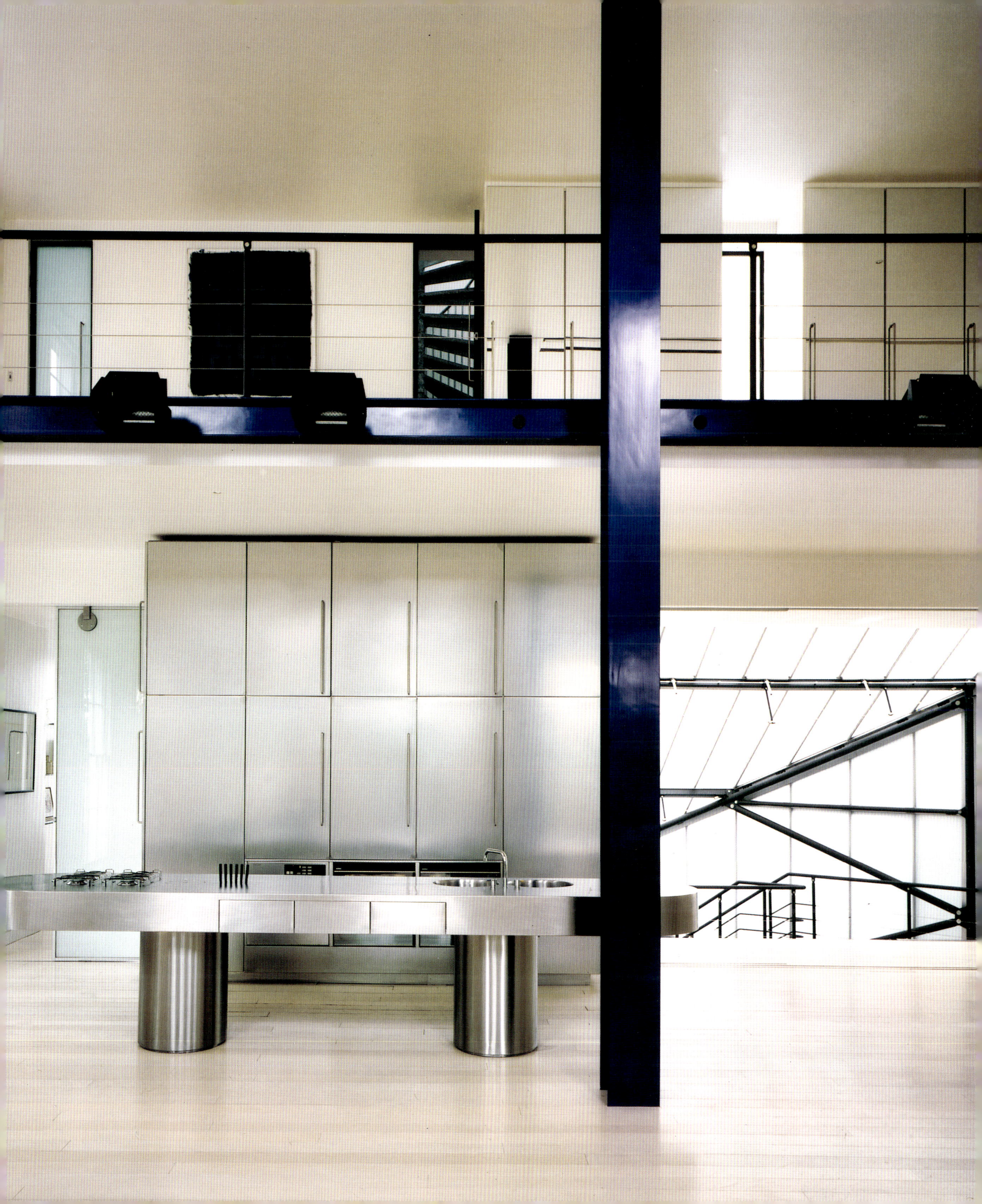

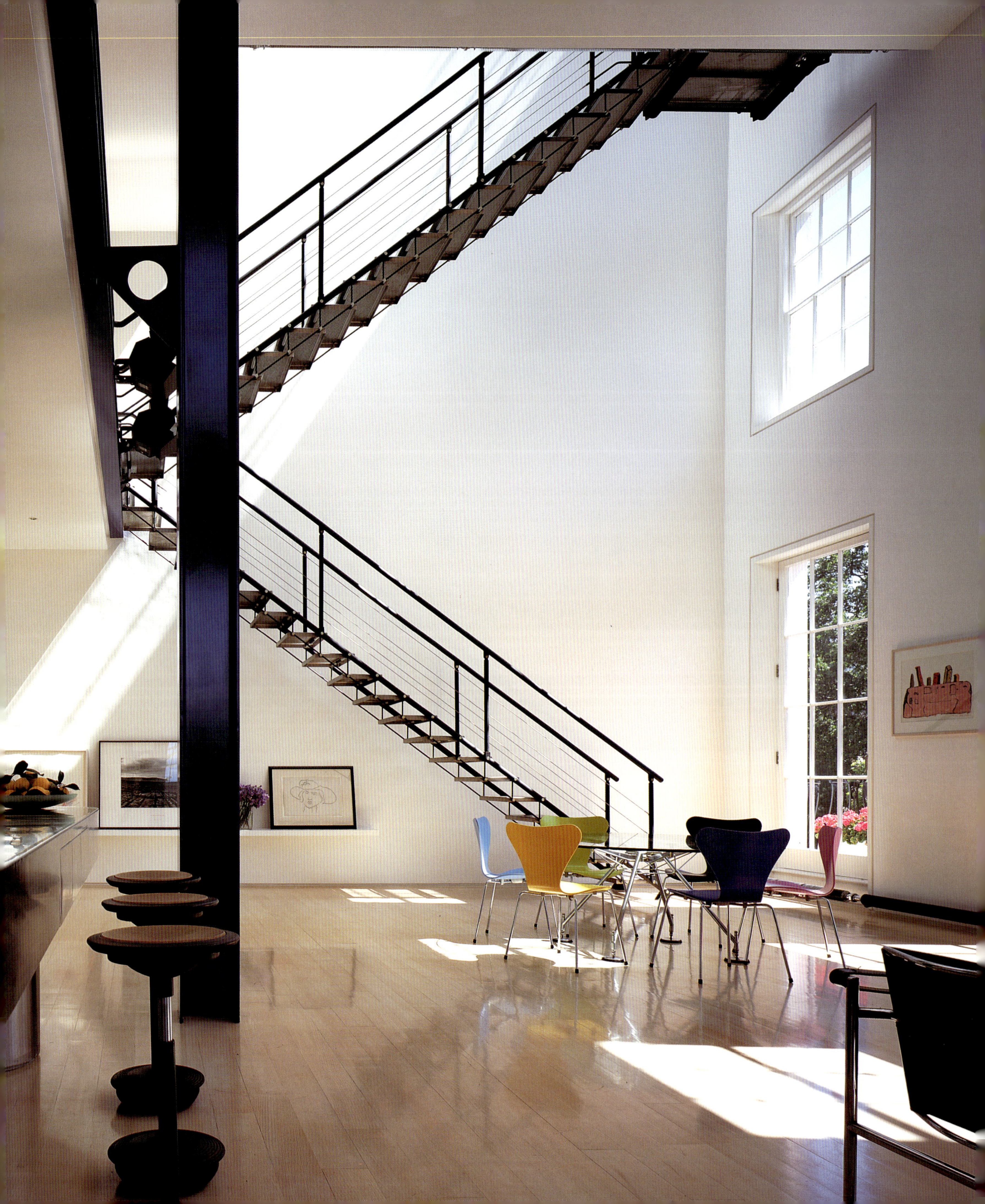

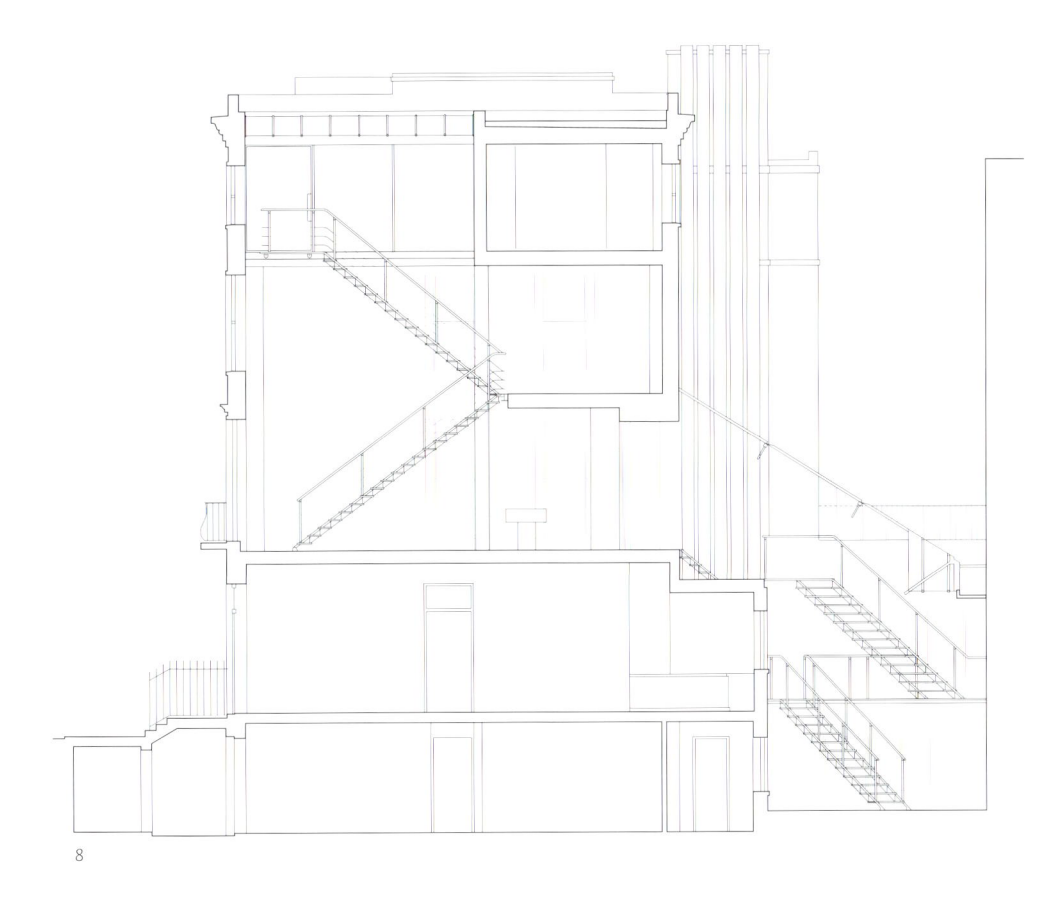

Internal floors were removed to create a vast double-height space (8). From the living room (11), a roof-lit staircase leads to the top floor bedroom (10 & 13) via a study mezzanine (12). At the highest level, a roof terrace commands impressive views of Wren's Royal Hospital and the River Thames beyond (9). Flats for members of Rogers' extended family are provided at top-floor level.
The main living space, with the kitchen area integrated, is sparsely furnished and forms a fine setting for works of art (7).

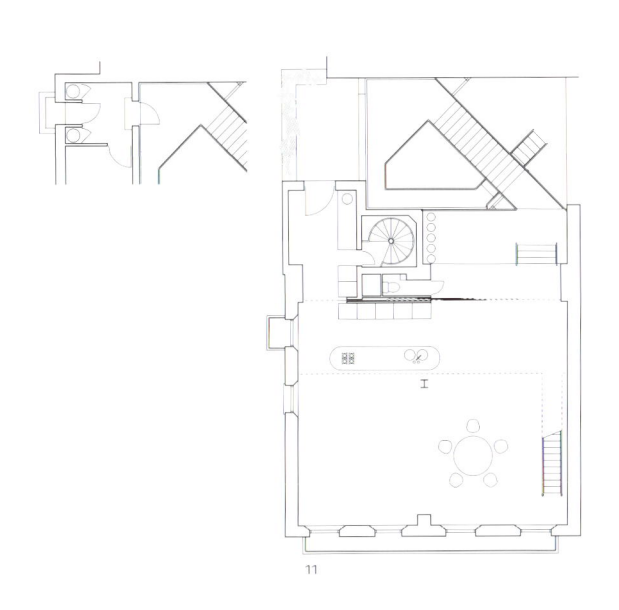

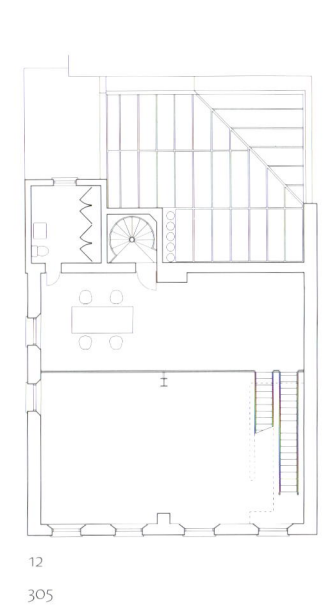

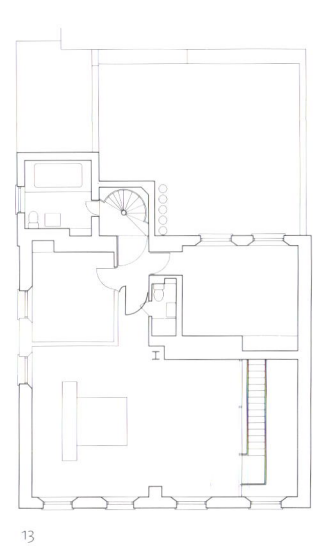

Complete List of Works 1961–87
Index

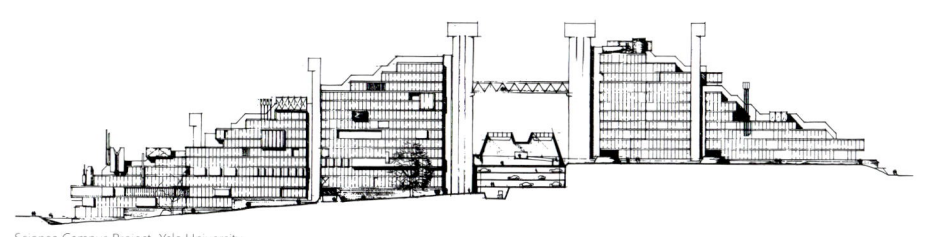

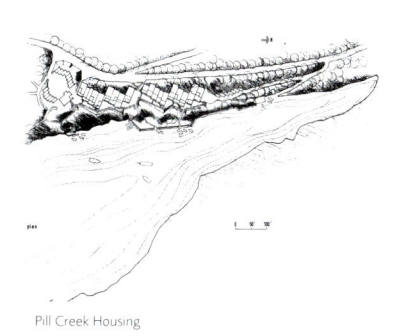

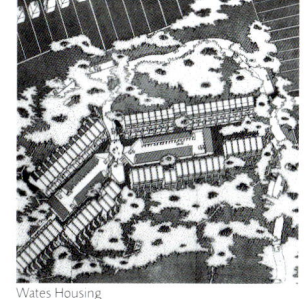

Science Campus Project, Yale University

Homefield School

Creek Vean

Pill Creek Retreat

Pill Creek Housing

Wates Housing

Jaffe House

1961	1963	1964	1965	1966
Team 4				

Science Campus Project Yale University
New Haven, Connecticut
1961
Team
Norman Foster, Richard Rogers

Pill Creek Retreat*
Feock, Cornwall
1963
Client
Marcus and Rene Brumwell
Team
Norman Foster, Wendy Foster, Frank Peacock, Richard Rogers, Su Rogers
Structural Engineer
Anthony Hunt Associates
Landscape Architect
Michael Branch

Pill Creek Housing
Feock, Cornwall
1964
Client
Marcus Brumwell/ Groveminster Investments
Team
Laurie Abbott, Norman Foster, Wendy Foster, Richard Rogers, Su Rogers
Structural Engineer
Anthony Hunt Associates
Quantity Surveyor
GA Hanscomb Partnership
Landscape Architect
Michael Branch
Awards
Architectural Design Project Award 1964

Homefield School
Sutton, Surrey
1965
Client
Homefield School
Team
Norman Foster, Wendy Foster, Richard Rogers, Su Rogers

Wates Housing
Coulsdon, Surrey
1965-67
Client
Wates Built Homes Ltd
Team
Sally Appleby, Norman Foster, Wendy Foster, Frank Peacock, Richard Rogers, Su Rogers, John Young
Structural Engineer
Anthony Hunt Associates
Quantity Surveyor
Wates Ltd/GA Hanscomb Partnership
Awards
Architectural Design Project Award 1965

Creek Vean*
Feock, Cornwall
1966
Client
Marcus and Rene Brumwell
Team
Laurie Abbott, Norman Foster, Wendy Foster, Richard Rogers, Su Rogers
Structural Engineer
Anthony Hunt Associates
Quantity Surveyor
GA Hanscomb Partnership
Landscape Architect
Landscape Design Partnership
Main Contractor
Leonard Williams Ltd
Awards
RIBA Award for Work of Outstanding Quality 1969

Jaffe House*
Radlett, Hertfordshire
1966
Client
Mr and Mrs Anthony Jaffe
Team
Norman Foster, Wendy Foster, Frank Peacock, Maurice Philips, Richard Rogers, Su Rogers
Structural Engineer
Anthony Hunt Associates
Quantity Surveyor
GA Hanscomb Partnership

* indicates built project

Reliance Controls Electronics Factory

Rogers House

Yorke Mason House

Sports Centre

Murray Mews Housing

Spender House

Witham Workshops

Zip Up Enclosures

Seaside Housing

Universal Oil Products (UOP) Factory

Housing, Healy Homes

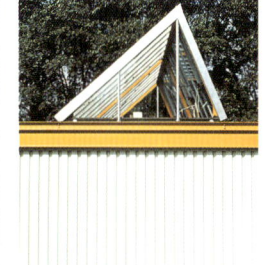

1967

1967
Richard + Su Rogers

1968

1969

Reliance Controls Electronics Factory*
Swindon, Wiltshire
1967
Client
Reliance Controls Limited
Team
Norman Foster, Wendy Foster, Frank Peacock, Richard Rogers, Su Rogers, Mark Sutcliffe
Structural Engineer
Anthony Hunt Associates
Services Engineer
G. N. Haden and Sons Ltd
Quantity Surveyor
GA Hanscomb Partnership
Main Contractor
Pope Brothers
Awards
Architectural Design Project Award 1966
Financial Times Industrial Architecture Award 1967

Murray Mews Housing*
London
1967
Client
Mr and Mrs Franklin, Mr and Mrs Williams, Mr de Marco
Team
Laurie Abbott, Sally Appleby, Norman Foster, Wendy Foster, Frank Peacock, Maurice Philips, Richard Rogers, Su Rogers, John Young
Structural Engineer
Anthony Hunt Associates
Quantity Surveyor
GA Hanscomb Partnership

Spender House*
Ulting, Essex
1967–8
Client
Humphrey and Pauline Spender
Team
Richard Rogers, Su Rogers, Richard Russell, John Young
Structural Engineer
Anthony Hunt Associates
Quantity Surveyor
GA Hanscomb Partnership
Main Contractor
Tanner and Wicks
Represented British Architecture at Paris Biennale 1967

Rogers House*
London
1968–9
Client
Dr and Mrs Rogers
Team
Pierre Botschi, John Doggart, Ingrid Morris, Richard Rogers, Su Rogers, Richard Russell, John Young
Structural Engineer
Anthony Hunt Associates
Services Engineer
H Bressloff Associates
Quantity Surveyor
GA Hanscomb Partnership
Landscape Architect
Landscape Design Partnership
Represented British Architecture at Paris Biennale 1967

Witham Workshops
Witham, Essex
1968
Client
Tanner and Wicks
Team
Richard Rogers, Su Rogers, John Young
Structural Engineer
Anthony Hunt Associates

Zip-Up Enclosures
1968–71
Team
Sally Appleby, John Doggart, Marco Goldschmied, Richard Rogers, Su Rogers, John Young
Structural Engineer
Anthony Hunt Associates
Services Engineer
Max Fordham
Quantity Surveyor
GA Hanscomb Partnership
Awards
Prize winner 'House for Today' competition 1968
RIBA Research Award 1970

Yorke Mason House
London
1968
Client
Mr and Mrs Aubrey Yorke Mason
Team
Sally Appleby, Richard Rogers, Su Rogers, Peter Southgate, John Young
Structural Engineer
Anthony Hunt Associates
Quantity Surveyor
GS Hanscomb Partnership

Seaside Housing Project
1968
Team
Sally Appleby, Richard Rogers, Su Rogers, Peter Southgate, John Young
Structural Engineer
Anthony Hunt Associates

Sports Centre
New Ash Green, Kent
1969
Client
Span Ltd
Team
John Doggart, Richard Rogers, Su Rogers, John Young
Structural Engineer
Anthony Hunt Associates

Universal Oil Products (UOP) Factory
Ashford, Kent
1969–70
Client
Universal Oil Products (UOP)
Team
Richard Rogers, Su Rogers, John Young
Structural Engineer
Anthony Hunt Associates
Services Engineer
H. Bresloff Associates
Quantity Surveyor
GA Hanscomb Partnership

Housing, Healy Homes
Dublin and Cork
1969
Client
Healy Homes
Team
Richard Rogers, Su Rogers, John Young

Complete List of Works 1961–87

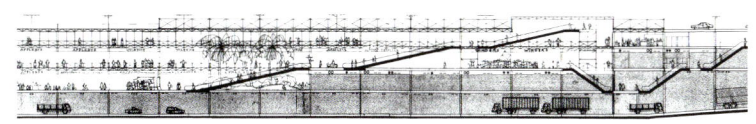

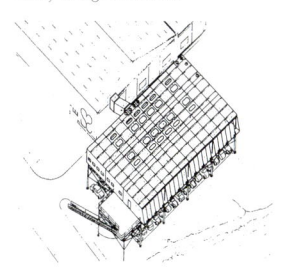

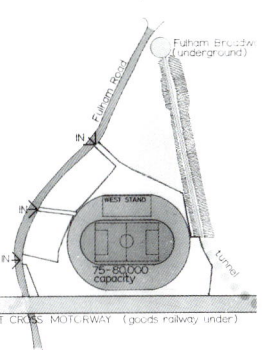

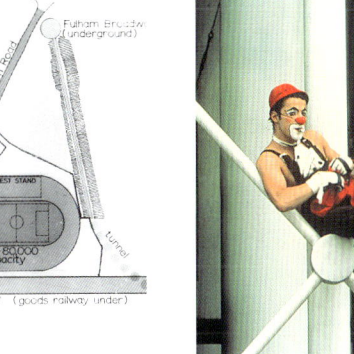

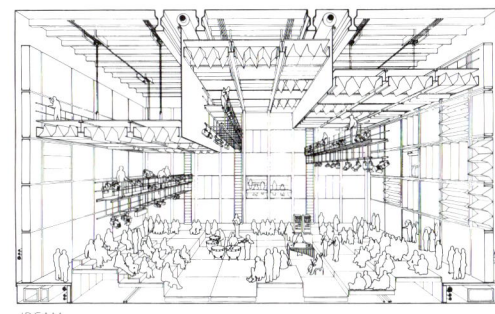

Fitzroy Burleigh Central Area

Burrell Collection Competition

Pompidou Centre

Sweetheart Plastics

Design Research Unit Roof Extension

Chelsea Football Club

Pompidou Centre

IRCAM

1970

1971
Piano + Rogers

Design Research Unit Roof Extension*
London
1969–71
Client
Design Research Unit
Team
Sally Appleby, Pierre Botschi, John Doggart, Marco Goldschmied, Andrew Holmes, Jan Kaplicky, Renzo Piano, Richard Rogers, Su Rogers, John Young
Structural Engineer
Anthony Hunt Associates
Services Engineer
Max Fordham
Quantity Surveyor
GA Hanscomb Partnership
Main Contractor
F. G. Minter

Fitzroy Burleigh Central Area
Cambridge
1970
Client
Jesus College and Samuel Properties
Team
Marco Goldschmied, John Lyall, Ingrid Morris, Alphons Oberhofer, Richard Rogers, Su Rogers, John Young
Structural Engineer
Kenchington Little and Partners
Services Engineer
John Bradley Associates
Quantity Surveyor
GA Hanscomb Partnership

Sweetheart Plastics
Gosport, Hampshire
1970
Client
Sweetheart Plastics
Team
Hugh Chapman, Richard Rogers, Su Rogers, John Young
Structural Engineer
Anthony Hunt Associates
Quantity Surveyor
GA Hanscomb Partnership

Chelsea Football Club
London
1970
Team
Marco Goldschmied, Richard Rogers, Su Rogers, John Young
Structural Engineer
Ove Arup and Partners
Graphics/
Corporate Identity
Wolff Olins

Burrell Collection Competition
Glasgow
1971
Team
Marco Goldschmied, Renzo Piano, Richard Rogers, Su Rogers, John Young
Structural Engineer
Anthony Hunt Associates
Services Engineer
Max Fordham

Pompidou Centre*
Paris
1971–7
Client
Ministère des Affaires Culturelles/ Ministère de l'Education Nationale
Team
Partners in Charge
Renzo Piano, Richard Rogers
Competition
Sally Appleby, Peter Flack, Gianfranco Franchini, Marco Goldschmied, Jan Kaplicky, Su Rogers, John Young
Sub Structure and Mechanical Services
Walter Zbinden with Hans-Peter Bysaeth, Johanna Lohse, Peter Merz, Philippe Dupont
Superstructure and Mechanical Services
Laurie Abbott with Shunji Ishida, Hiroshi Naruse, Hiroyuki Takahashi
Facades and Galleries
Eric Holt with Michael Davies, Jan Sircus
Programme/Interiors
Gianfranco Franchini
Internal/External Systems
Audio-Visual
Alan Stanton with Michael Dowd, William Logan, Noriaki Okabe, Rainer Verbizh
Environment and Piazza, Scenographic Spaces
Cuno Brullmann
Co-ordination and Site Supervision
Bernard Plattner
Furniture Systems
John Young with Francois Barat, Helene Diebold, Jacques Fendard, Jean Huc, Helga Schlegel
Administration
Francoise Gouinguenet, Claudette Spielmann, Colette Valensi
Other Contributors
Ken Allinson, William Carmen, Chris Dawson, Tony Dugdale, Alphons Oberhofer, Judith Raymond, Martin Richardson, Philippe Robert
Structural Engineer
Ove Arup and Partners
Services Engineer
Ove Arup and Partners
Quantity Surveyor
Ove Arup and Partners
Graphics
VDA Group
Main Contractor
Grands Travaux de Marseilles
Awards
International Union of Architects August Perret Prize for most outstanding international work 1975–8

IRCAM*
Paris
1971–7
Client
Ministère des Affaires Culturelles/Ministère de l'Education Nationale
Team
Mike Davies, Alphons Oberhofer, Noriaki Okabe, Renzo Piano, Bernard Plattner, Richard Rogers, Ken Rupard, Jan Sircus, Walter Zbinden
Structural Engineer
Ove Arup and Partners
Services Engineer
Ove Arup and Partners
Quantity Surveyor
Ove Arup and Partners
Acoustics
Peutz and Associates
Scenographer
G. L. Francois
Main Contractor
Grands Travaux de Marseilles

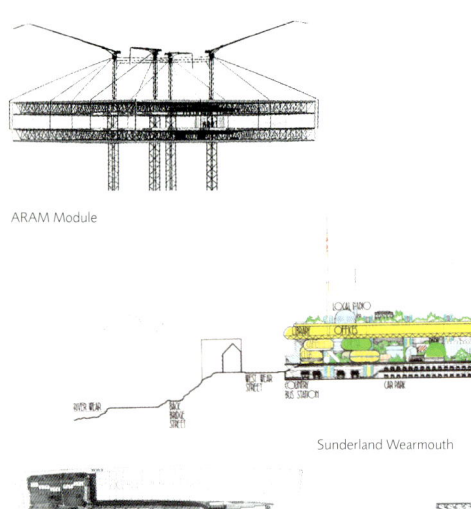

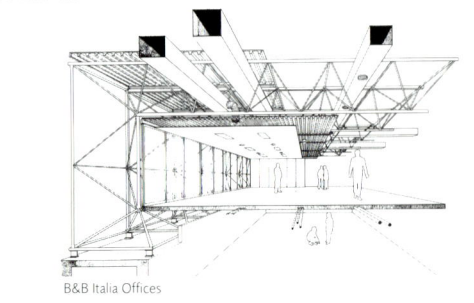

ARAM Module

Sunderland Wearmouth

UOP Factory

PA Technology Laboratory

Housing, Globe Construction

B&B Italia Offices

Park Road Development

1971

1972

1974

1975

ARAM Module
1971
Client
Association for Rural Aid in Medicine Inc, USA
Team
Marco Goldschmied, Renzo Piano, Richard Rogers, Su Rogers, Peter Ullathorne, John Young
Structural Engineer
Anthony Hunt Associates
Services Engineer
Max Fordham

Housing, Globe Construction
Basildon, Essex
1971
Client
Globe Construction
Team
Marco Goldschmied, Eric Holt, Renzo Piano, Richard Rogers, Su Rogers, John Young

Sunderland Wearmouth
Sunderland, Tyne and Wear
1972
Client
Sunderland Borough Council and Laurence Vanger
Team
Marco Goldschmied, Richard Rogers, Peter Ullathorne, John Young

B&B Italia Offices*
Como, Italy
1972-73
Client
B&B Italia
Team
Cuno Brullmann, Flavio Marano, Renzo Piano, Richard Rogers
Structural Engineer
Flavio Marano

UOP Factory*
Tadworth, Surrey
1973–4
Client
Universal Oil Products (UOP), Fragrances Division
Team
Sally Appleby, Rita Bormioli, Peter Flack, Marco Goldschmied, Eric Holt, Renzo Piano, Richard Rogers, Peter Ullathorne, Niki van Oosten, Neil Winder, John Young
Structural Engineer
Anthony Hunt Associates
Services Engineers
Max Fordham, Cressey Wilder Associates
Quantity Surveyor
Monk Dunstone Associates
Landscape Architect
Landscape Design Partnership
Main Contractor
James Longley & Co Ltd
Awards
British Steel Corporation Structural Steel Design Award 1975
RIBA Regional Award Commendation 1975

Park Road Development
London
1973–5
Client
Company Developments Limited/Aston Martin Lagonda
Team
Sally Appleby, Marco Goldschmied, Nigel Greenhill, Andrew Holmes, Angela Jackson, Irini Kiladiti, Renzo Piano, Luis Renau, Richard Rogers, Richard Soundy, Peter Ullathorne, Niki van Oosten, George Xydis, John Young
Structural Engineer
Felix J. Samuely and Partners
Quantity Surveyor
Monk Dunstone Associates

PA Technology Laboratory*
Melbourn, Cambridgeshire
1975–85
Client
PA Management Consultants Ltd
Team
Phase 1
Sally Appleby, Michael Burckhardt, Peter Flack, Marco Goldschmied, Don Gray, Alphons Oberhofer, Renzo Piano, Richard Rogers, Richard Soundy, David Thom, Peter Ullathorne, Neil Winder, John Young
Phase 2
Pierre Botschi, Mike Davies, Sally Eaton, Marco Goldschmied, John McAslan, Richard Rogers, John Young
Phase 3
Pierre Botschi, Mike Davies, Marco Goldschmied, Nathalie Moore, Brendan O'Neill, Mark Roche, Richard Rogers, John Young
Structural Engineer
Felix J. Samuely and Partners
Services Engineer
Hancock Design Co-ordinates, David W.G. Bedwell and Partners, YRM Engineers, Cressey Wilder Associates
Quantity Surveyor
Gleeds
Landscape Architect
Landscape Design Partnership
Main Contractor
Phase 1: R. G. Carter (Kings Lynn) Ltd
Phases 2 and 3: Rattee and Kett Ltd
Awards
Financial Times Industrial Architecture Award 1976
RIBA Regional Award 1977

Simmons Electrical

Place des Vosges Apartment

Elias House

Fleet Air Arm Museum

English Industrial Estates

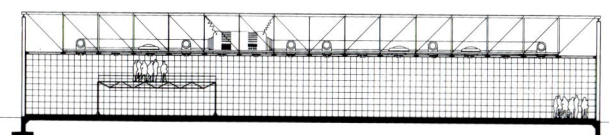

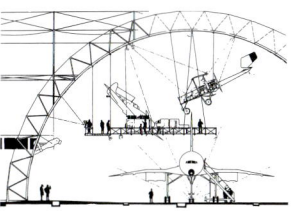

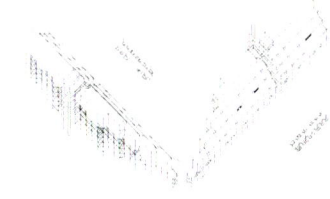

Millbank Housing

Lloyd's of London

1976

1977

1978
Richard Rogers Partnership

Simmons Electrical
Tadworth, Surrey
1975
Client
Simmons Electrical Ltd
Team
Marco Goldschmied, Renzo Piano, Richard Rogers, Richard Soundy, John Young

Place des Vosges Apartment*
Paris
1975
Client
Richard & Ruth Rogers
Team
Judy Bing, Richard Rogers, Ruth Rogers, Ken Rupard, John Young

Elias House
Northpoint, Long Island, USA
1976
Client
Fred & Sylvia Elias
Team
Marco Goldschmied, Richard Rogers, Richard Soundy, John Young

English Industrial Estates
Gateshead, Tyne and Wear
1976
Client
English Industrial Estates Competition
Team
Jill Anderson, Judy Bing, Marco Goldschmied, Jamie Mill, Richard Rogers, Graham Simpson, Richard Soundy, John Young
Structural Engineer
Ove Arup and Partners
Quantity Surveyor
GA Hanscomb Partnership

Millbank Riverside Housing
London
1977
Client
Crown Estates Competition
Team
Judy Bing, Marco Goldschmied, Richard Rogers, Richard Soundy, John Young
Structural Engineer
Peter Rice
Quantity Surveyor
Hanscomb Partnership

Fleet Air Arm Museum
Yeovilton, Somerset
1977
Client
Fleet Air Museum and Taylor Woodrow
Team
Laurie Abbott, Marco Goldschmied, Richard Rogers, Richard Soundy, John Young
Structural Engineer
Ove Arup and Partners

Lloyd's of London*
London
1978–86
Client
Corporation of Lloyd's of London
Team
Directors
Mike Davies, Marco Goldschmied, Richard Rogers, John Young
Project Administrator
Richard Marzec
Analysis
Laurie Abbott, Julia Barfield, Simon Colebrook, Ian Davidson, Malcolm Last, John McAslan, Michael McGarry, Tim Oakshott, Henrietta Salvesen, Kiyo Sawaoka, Richard Soundy
Substructure
Chris Wilkinson with Marcus Lee, David Mark, Peter McMunn, Jamie Troughton
Superstructure
Richard Soundy with Colin MacKenzie, Maureen Diffley
Main Cladding and External Works
Stephen Le Roith with Graham Fairley, Ivan Harbour, Elizabeth Post, Niki van Oosten
Service Tower Cladding
Frank Peacock with Amarjit Kalsi, Peter St John, Clare Strasser
Services
Graham Anthony with Robert Barnes, Kieran Breen, Graham Stirk, Peter Thomas, Andrew Weston
Plantrooms
Michael Elkan with Joseph Wilson
Mechanical Systems
Stig Larsen

Interiors
Eva Jiricna with Mark Guard, Philip Gumuchdjian, Roger Huntley, Andrew Jones, Kathy Kerr, Andrew Morris, Robert Peebles, Stephen Tsang, Yasu Yada
Administration
Susan Blyth, Julianne Coleman, Janet Dunsford, Wendy Judd, Sue McMillan, Caryn Roger, Georgina Savva, Judy Taylor
Structural and Services Engineers
Ove Arup and Partners
Quantity Surveyor
Monk Dunstone Associates
Rights of Light
Anstey Horne and Co
Planning Consultant
Montagu Evans
Acoustics
Sandy Brown Associates
Catering
GWP Associates
Audio Visual
Theatre Developments Ltd
Lighting
Friedrich Wagner of Lichttechnische Planung
Signs/Graphics
Pentagram Design Ltd
Modelmakers
Tetra Design Services Ltd
Management Contractor
Bovis Construction Ltd
Awards
Civic Trust Award 1987
Financial Times Architecture at Work Award 1987
Eternit 8th International Prize for Architecture Special Mention 1988
RIBA National Award 1988

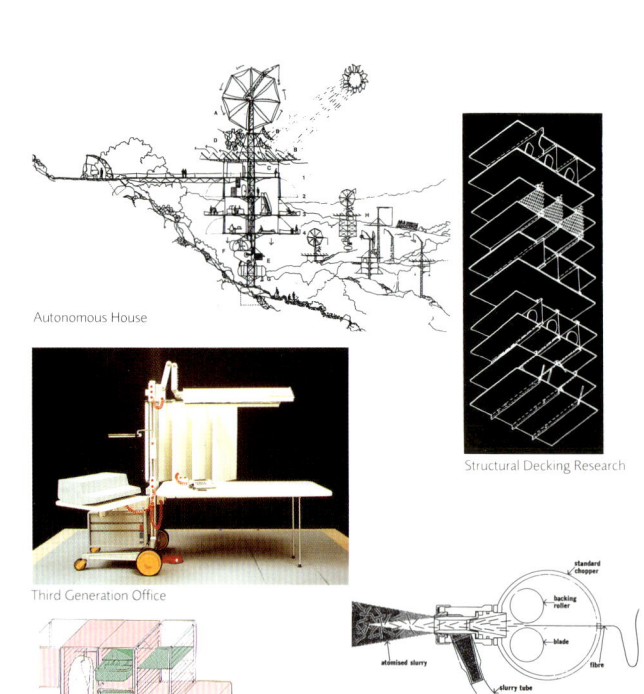

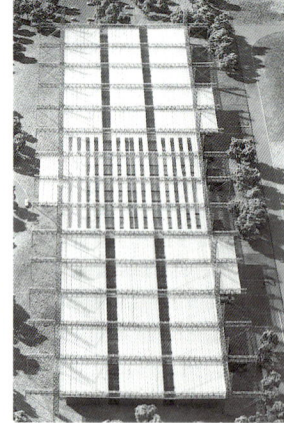

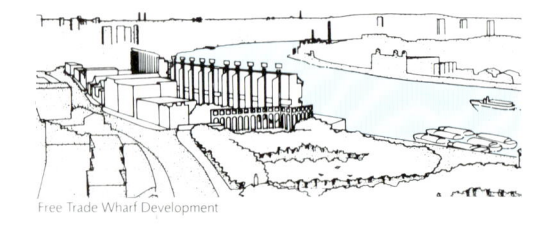

Autonomous House

Third Generation Office

Flat Pack Storage Systems

Structural Decking Research

Glass Reinforced Cement Research

NAPP Laboratories

Fleetguard Factory

Coin Street Development

Free Trade Wharf Development

1978

1979

1981

Autonomous House
Aspen, Colorado
1978
Client
Steve Martin
Team
Mike Davies, Marco Goldschmied, Richard Rogers, John Young, with PA Technology (Rogers Patscentre)

Third Generation Office
1978
Client
Knoll International
Team
Simon Connolly, Mike Davies, Marco Goldschmied, Amarjit Kalsi, Roger Huntley, Richard Rogers, Alan Stanton, John Young, with PA Technology (Rogers Patscentre)
Services Engineer
Ove Arup and Partners

Flat Pack Storage Systems
1978
Client
Knoll International
Team
Mike Davies, Marco Goldschmied, Roger Huntley, Richard Rogers, John Young

Glass Reinforced Cement Research
1978–9
Client
Pilkington Brothers
Team
Mike Davies, Marco Goldschmied, Richard Rogers, Richard Soundy, John Young with PA Technology (Rogers Patscentre)

Structural Decking Research
1979
Client
Ayrshire Metals Company
Team
Simon Connolly, Mike Davies, Marco Goldschmied, Richard Rogers, John Young with PA Technology (Rogers Patscentre)

NAPP Laboratories
Cambridge
1979
Client
Napp Laboratories
Team
Mike Davies, Marco Goldschmied, Michael McGarry, Sue McMillan, Richard Rogers, Richard Soundy, John Young
Structural Engineer
Anthony Hunt Associates
Services Engineer
Derek Clapton and Partners
Quantity Surveyor
GA Hanscomb Partnership

Fleetguard Factory*
Quimper, France
1979
Client
Fleetguard International Division of Cummins Engine Co/Ville de Quimper
Team
Ram Ahronov, Sally Eaton, Ian Davidson, Marco Goldschmied, Kunimi Hayashi, Amarjit Kalsi, Sue McMillan, Richard Rogers, Richard Soundy, John Young
Structural and Services Engineer
Ove Arup and Partners
Quantity Surveyor
Northcroft Neighbour and Nicholson
Project Manager
Fleetguard International Corporation
Awards
Concours de Plus Beaux Ouvrages de Construction Metallique 1982
Constructa-Preis 1986

Coin Street Development
London
1979–83
Client
Greycoat Commercial Estates Ltd
Team
Laurie Abbott, Mike Davies, Jan Dunsford, Marco Goldschmied, Philip Gumuchdjian, Amarjit Kalsi, Sue McMillan, Andrew Morris, Tim Oakshott, Richard Rogers, John Sorcinelli, Peter Thomas, Chris Wilkinson, John Young
Structural and Services Engineer
Ove Arup and Partners
Traffic Engineer
W. R. Davidge and Partners
Quantity Surveyor
Gardiner and Theobald

Free Trade Wharf Development
London
1981
Client
Spoolbest Ltd/LDDC
Team
Simon Colebrook, Marco Goldschmied, Philip Gumuchdjian, Gennaro Picardi, Richard Rogers, John Sorcinelli, Alan Stanton, Niki van Oosten, John Young
Structural Engineer
Ove Arup and Partners
Quantity Surveyor
GA Hanscomb Partnership

National Gallery Extension

PA Technology Laboratories

Inmos Microprocessor Factory

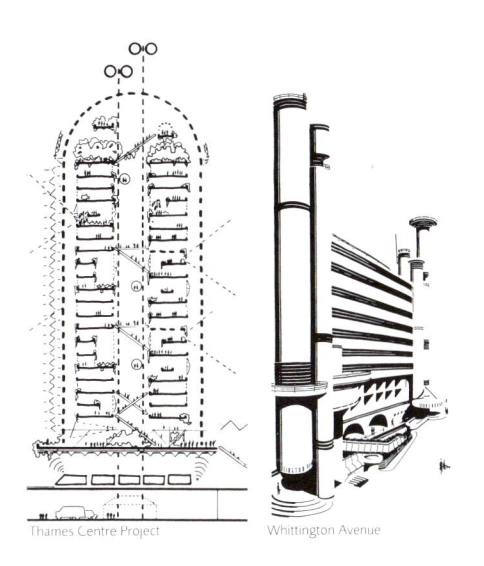

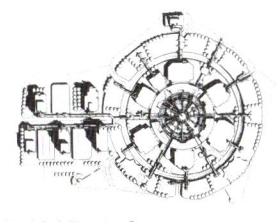

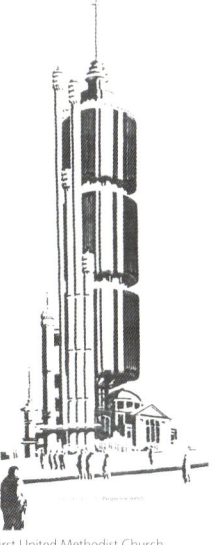

1982

Thames Centre Project

Whittington Avenue

Arno Masterplan

North Park Shopping Centre

First United Methodist Church

Industrial Units

1983

Immos Microprocessor Factory*
Newport, Wales
1982
Client
Immos Ltd
Team
Julia Barfield, David Bartlett, Pierre Botschi, Mike Davies, Sally Eaton, Michael Elkan, Marco Goldschmied, Kunimi Hayashi, Tim Inskip, Peter McMunn, Richard Rogers, John Young
Structural Engineer
Anthony Hunt Associates
Services Engineer
YRM Engineers
Quantity Surveyor
GA Hanscomb Partnership
Contractor
Laing Management Contracting Ltd
Awards
Eurostructpress Award 1983
Financial Times Architecture at Work Award Commendation 1983
The Structural Steel Design Award 1982
Constructa-Preis 1986

National Gallery Extension
London
1982
Client
Speyhawk plc/Secretary of State for the Environment
Team
Laurie Abbott, Julia Barfield, Mike Davies, Marco Goldschmied, Philip Gumuchdjian, Di Hope, Sue McMillan, Andrew Morris, Gennaro Picardi, Richard Rogers, John Sorcinelli, Richard Soundy, Peter St John, Peter Thomas, John Young
Structural Engineer
Ove Arup and Partners
Services Engineer
YRM Engineers
Quantity Surveyor
Axtell Yates Hallett

PA Technology Laboratories*
Princeton, New Jersey, USA
1982–5
Client
PA Consulting Services Inc
Team
Ram Ahronov, Pierre Botschi, Mike Davies, Marco Goldschmied, John McAslan, Gennaro Picardi, Richard Rogers, John Young, in association with Kelbaugh and Lee Architects (USA)
Structural Engineer
Ove Arup and Partners/
Robert Silman (USA)
Services Engineer
Ove Arup and Partners/
Syska and Hennessy, Inc (USA)
Quantity Surveyor
GA Hanscomb Partnership/
GA Hanscomb Associates Inc (USA)

Thames Centre Project
London
1983
Client
British Rail
Team
Richard Rogers Partnership, Ahrends Burton and Koralek, John Hawkes, Ove Arup and Partners, Monk Dunstone Associates

Whittington Avenue
London
1983
Client
Speyhawk Limited
Team
Laurie Abbott, Mike Davies, Marco Goldschmied, John McAslan, Richard Rogers, John Sorcinelli, Graham Stirk, John Young
Structural Engineer
Ove Arup & Partners
Services Engineer
YRM Engineers

Arno Masterplan
Florence, Italy
1983–4
Client
Council of the City of Florence
Team
Mike Davies, Marco Goldschmied, Philip Gumuchdjian, Andrew Morris, Gennaro Picardi, Richard Rogers, Alan Stanton, John Young, with Claudio Cantella
Hydraulic Engineer
Enrico Bougleux

North Park Shopping Centre
Houston, Texas, USA
1984
Client
Nasher Paragon
Team
Laurie Abbott, Mike Davies, Marco Goldschmied, Richard Rogers, John Young, in association with Omniplan Architects

First United Methodist Church
Seattle, Washington, USA
1984
Client
First United Methodist Church
Team
Laurie Abbott, Mike Davies, Richard Rogers, in association with Broome, Oringdulph, O'Toole, Rudolf and Associates

Industrial Units*
Maidenhead, Berkshire
1984–5
Client
Speyhawk Land and Estates Limited
Team
Pierre Botschi, Mike Davies, Marco Goldschmied, Tim Inskip, Richard Rogers, Karenna Wilford, John Young
Structural Engineer
Anthony Hunt Associates
Services Engineer
YRM Engineers
Quantity Surveyor
GA Hanscomb Partnership
Awards
Civic Trust Award Commendation 1986
BSC Colorcoat Building Award 1985

Thames Wharf – River Café

Royal Opera House

Linn Products

Thames Wharf – Richard Rogers Partnership Offices

Thames Wharf – Thames Reach Housing

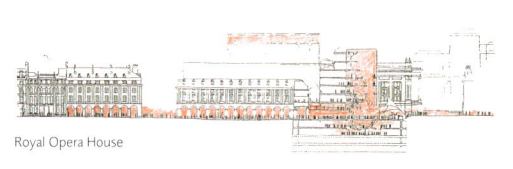

Thames Wharf – The Deck House

375 Hudson Street

1984

1985

Thames Wharf – Richard Rogers Partnership Offices*
London
1984–9
Client
Marco Goldschmied, Richard Rogers, John Young
Team
Pierre Botschi, Mike Davies, Patrick Davies, Marco Goldschmied, Tim Inskip, Peter Jennett, James McGrath, Nathalie Moore, Gennaro Picardi, Mark Roche, Richard Rogers, Neville Smith, Graham Stirk, Karenna Wilford, John Young
Roof Extension
with Lifschutz Davidson Ltd
Structural Engineers
Anthony Hunt Associates
Ove Arup and Partners
Services Engineers
Rosser and Russell
Ove Arup and Partners
Quantity Surveyor
GA Hanscomb Partnership
Landscape Architect
Georgie Wolton
Planning Consultant
Montagu Evans
Main Contractor
Woolf Construction Ltd, Tarmac Cubitts, Woolf Construction Ltd (roof extension)
Awards
Structural Steel Design Award Certificate of Merit 1992

Thames Wharf – River Café*
London
1984–9
Client
Rose Gray, Richard Rogers, Ruth Rogers
Team
Pierre Botschi, Rose Gray, Shehab Kasmai-Tehran, Stig Larsen, Richard Rogers, Ruth Rogers, John Young
Main Contractor
Tarmac Cubitts

Thames Wharf – Thames Reach Housing*
London
1984–7
Client
Croudace Construction Ltd
Team
Peter Angrave, Paul Cook, Ian Gibson, Marco Goldschmied, Sarah Granville, Ian Hopton, Tim Inskip, Janette Mackie, Mark Roche, Richard Rogers, John Young
Structural Engineer
Hay Barry and Partners
Services Engineer
The Sinnett Partnership
Quantity Surveyor
Melvyn Newell
Landscape Architect
Rendel + Branch
Main Contractor
Croudace Construction Ltd
Awards
RIBA Housing Design Awards 1989

Royal Opera House Competition
London
1984
Client
Royal Opera House
Team
Mike Davies, Marco Goldschmied, Philip Gumuchdjian, Gennaro Piccardi, Richard Rogers, Graham Stirk, John Young

Thames Wharf – The Deck House*
London
1986–9
Client
John Young
Design Team
John Young with Peter Angrave and Amarjit Kalsi
Structural Engineer
Ove Arup and Partners
Hay Barry and Partners
Services Engineer
The Sinnett Partnership
Quantity Surveyor
Melvyn Newell
Lighting Consultant
Lighting Design Partnership
Audio Visual Consultant
Michael Holden
Main Contractor
Croudace Construction Ltd.
Awards
RIBA National Award 1991

Linn Products*
Glasgow
1985–7
Client
Linn Products Ltd
Team
Kieran Breen, Tim Colquhoun, Mike Davies, William Firebrace, Marco Goldschmied, Colin MacKenzie, John McFarland, Richard Rogers, John Sorcinelli, John Young
Structural Engineer
Ove Arup and Partners
Services Engineer
YRM Engineers
Quantity Surveyor
GA Hanscomb Partnership
Main Contractor
Balfour Beatty

375 Hudson Street
New York, USA
1985
Client
Tishman Speyer Properties
Team
Laurie Abbott, Mike Davies, Marco Goldschmied, Philip Gumuchdjian, Richard Rogers, John Young, in association with Richard Roth Architects

Complete List of Works 1961–87

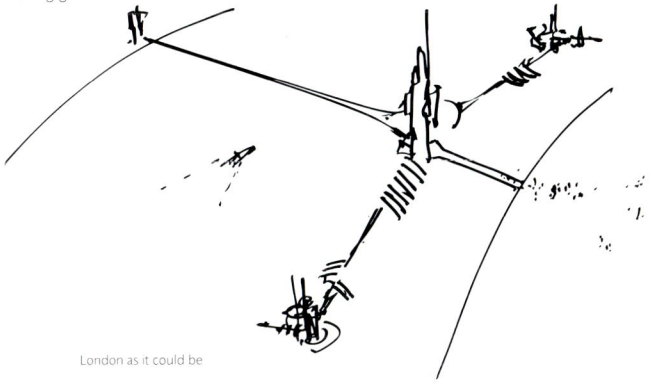

Billingsgate Securities Market

Centre Commercial St Herblain

London as it could be

Centre Commercial Forum d'Epone

Royal Avenue

1986

1987

Billingsgate Securities Market*
London
1985–8
Client
Citibank/Citicorp
Team
Tom Alexander, Peter Angrave, David Bartlett, Pierre Botschi, John Cannon, Philip Chalmers, Tim Colquhoun, Mike Davies, Patrick Davies, Sally Draper, Marco Goldschmied, Ian Hopton, Shahab Kasmai-Tehran, Lester Korzilius, Clodagh Latimer, Mary Le Jeune, Amanda Levete, Kevin Lewenden, Avtar Lotay, John Lowe, Ernest Lowinger, Luke Lowings, Janette Mackie, Richard Marzec, Arif Mehmood, Malcolm McGowan, Natalie Moore, Frank Peacock, Mark Roche, Richard Rogers, Seth Stein, Peter Thomas, John Young
Structural and Services Engineer
Ove Arup and Partners
Quantity Surveyor
GA Hanscomb Partnership
Lighting Consultant
Lighting Design Partnership
Main Contractor
Taylor Woodrow Management Contracting Ltd
Awards
RIBA Regional Award 1988
RIBA Award 1989
Civic Trust Award 1989
BBC Design Awards finalist 1990

Centre Commercial St Herblain*
Nantes, France
1986–7
Client
Groupement Rhodanien de Construction
Team
Kieran Breen, Philippa Browning, Mike Davies, Pierre Ebbo, Florian Fischotter, Marco Goldschmied, Lennart Grut, Werner Lang, Stig Larsen, Richard Rogers, Stephen Spence, John Young
Structural Engineer
Ove Arup and Partners/RFR
OtH Rhone-Alpes
Interior Design
B & FL
Quantity Surveyor
Thorne Wheatley Associates
Awards
Concours des Plus Beaux Ouvrages de Construction Metallique 1988

London as it could be
London
1986
Client
Royal Academy
Team
Laurie Abbott, Philip Gumuchdjian, Stephen Pimbley, Richard Rogers
Structural Engineer
Ove Arup and Partners
Exhibition Design
John Andrews, Philip Gumuchdjian

Centre Commercial Forum d'Epone
Epone, France
1986
Client
Groupement Rhodanien de Construction
Team
Kieran Breen, Philippa Browning, Philip Chalmers, Paul Cook, Mike Davies, Pierre Ebbo, Florian Fischotter, Marco Goldschmied, Lennart Grut, Werner Lang, Stig Larsen, Ernest Lowinger, Andrew Morris, Richard Rogers, Stephen Spence, Benjamin Warner, John Young
Structural Engineer
Ove Arup and Partners/RFR
OtH, Rhone-Alpes
Quantity Surveyor
GA Hanscomb Partnership
Interior Design
B & FL

Royal Avenue*
London
1987
Client
Richard and Ruth Rogers
Team
Laurie Abbott, Tim Boyd, Marco Goldschmied, Eva Jiricna, Andrew Morris, Richard Rogers, Ruth Rogers, John Young
Structural and Services Engineer
Ove Arup and Partners
Quantity Surveyor
Hanscomb Partnership
Main Contractor
J and J. J. Stanford

Page numbers in *italic* refer to illustrations. Headings and page numbers in **bold** indicate main entries.

A

Aalto, Alvar 33
Abbott, Carl *10*, 12
Abbott, Carol *11*
Abbott, Laurie *11*, 97, *97*, 166, 171
  joins Team 4 13
  on Creek Vean 15
  the Pompidou Centre 95, 98, 99, 118
  in RRP 165, *173*
  National Gallery extension 168
  and the Royal Avenue house 173
  and the Arno Masterplan 248
Adam, Robert 178
Ahrends, Burton & Koralek 169, 170, 236
Albini, Franco 8
Alexander, Christopher 16
American Airstream trailer *63*, *188*
Amery, Colin 167
Antonioni, Michelangelo 164
Appleby, Sally *94*
Appleyard, Bryan 16
ARAM (Association for Rural Aid in Medicine) Module (1971) **140-41**, 228, 310, *310*
Archigram group 60-61, 93, 94, 106, 177
The Architects' Co-Partnership 60
Architectural Association (AA) 9, 11, 12, 14, 20, 61, 65, 67, 94, 96, 165
Architectural Heritage Year (1975) 101
Architecture Foundation 168, 299
Arno Masterplan, Florence, Italy (1983-4) **248-51**, 313, *313*
Arno River 248, *249*, *250*
Ashworth, Geoffrey 165
Atelier 5 15, 24, 28
Autonomous House, Aspen, Colorado (1978) 64, 82, 100, 312, *312*
Avon Trading Estate, West London 67
Ayres, Nick 165

B

B&B Italia Offices, Como, Italy (1972-73) **142-5**, 310, *310*
Banham, Reyner 17, 61, 66, 94, 170, 235
  Megastructure: Urban Futures of the Recent Past 94
Barker, Tom 96, 98, 99, 109, 165, *165*
Barron, Ian 228
Bathgate, John 181
BBPR 8, *8*, *9*, 172
Beaudouin & Lods 94
Behrens, Peter 56
Bennett, TP 60
'Big Bang' (1986) 181, 198
'Big Three' exhibition (1986) *169*, 170, 288
Bijvoet, Bernard *13*, 300
Billingsgate Securities Market, London (1985-8) 172, 254, **274-81**, 300, 315, *315*
Bilsby, Leslie 24
Binney, Marcus 172, 274
Black, Misha 11, 65
Blackmore, Courtenay *165*, 181
Blair, Tony 168
Blow Up (film) 164
Bode, Klaus 165
Booker empire 18
Boots 60
Boots factory block, Nottingham 17
Bordaz, Robert 92, 96, 97, *97*, 99, 102
Bormioli, Rita *96*
Botschi, Pierre 65, 67, 170, 172, 233

Boulez, Pierre 97, 99, 102, 134, *137*
Bovis 165, 181
Bowood House, Wiltshire 178
Branch, Michael 14-15, 33
Britain
  electronics industry 16
  the 'new' British architecture 18
  post-war school building programme 13
  renaissance of British architecture 164
Broadgate, City of London 168, 181, 222
Brullman, Cuno 96, 99, 118, 142
Brumwell, Joe *11*
Brumwell, Marcus 9, 11, 14, *14*, 15, 22, 28, 30, *30*, 33, 38, 60, 88
Brumwell, Rene 9, 11, 14, *14*, 15, 22, 28, 30, 33, 35, 38, 60
Brunel, Isambard Kingdom 296
Brunelleschi, Filippo 8
Brynmawr rubber factory 86
Buchanan, Peter 92
building industry 15, 16, 26, 62
Burolandschaft 67, 210
Burrell Collection Competition, Glasgow (1971) 67, *94*, 309, *309*
Bush Lane House, London 181
business parks 50, 168
Busnelli, Piero 142

C

California 12, 13, 101
Cambridge 66, 212
Cambridge University 60, 67, 165
Camden Mews, Camden Town 44, 64
Campaign for Nuclear Disarmament (CND) 60
Canary Wharf, London 181, 222
Case Study houses, California 12-13, *13*, 50, 63, 68, 72, 94
Casson, Sir Hugh 60, 168, 170
Castello Sforza, Milan 172
Centre Commercial Forum d'Epone, Epone, France (1986) 315, *315*
Centre Commercial St Herblain, Nantes, France (1986-7) **282-7**, 315, *315*
Centrepoint tower, London 60
Chamberlin, Powell & Bon 94
Chareau, Pierre *13*, 165, 181, 300
Charing Cross Station, London 171, 288, *293*
Charles, HRH the Prince of Wales 168, 169, 170, 171, 172
Cheeseman, Georgie (later Wolton) 9, 13, 19, 254
Chelsea Football Club, Stamford Bridge (1970) 67, 93, 309, *309*
Chermayeff, Serge
  at Yale *10*, 11, 20, *25*, 38
  balance of 'community' and 'privacy' 11-12, 15, 24, 25
  influences Team 4 11-12, 16, 28, 38
Chrysalis Architects 95, 96, 274
Chrysalis II 101
CIAM 9, 18
Citibank 274
City of London 164, 167, 168, 172, 174, *176*, 178, 274
A Clockwork Orange (film) 40
Coin Street Development, London (1979-83) 16, 66, 166-7, *167*, 168, 170, **220-25**, 226, 254, 288, 299, 312, *312*
Colquhoun, Alan 9, 14
Commercial Union Plaza, London *178*
'community architecture' 168
Constructivism 11, 94, 106, *126*, 165, 177
Cooper, Sir Edwin 174, *177*, 178

Cornell University 67
Cornwall 33, 35, 63, 82
Cot House, Pill Creek, Cornwall 14, 15
Covell, Matthews, Wheatley/London & Edinburgh Trust 168
Creek Vean, Feock, Cornwall (1964-7) *11*, 14, 15, 16, 22, *23*, 24, **28-37**, 38, 40, 50, 53, 62, 64, 72, 173, 302, 307, *307*
Crittall family 61
Crompton, Dennis 95
Crown Hall, Illinois Institute of Technology, Chicago 17
Crystal Palace, London 193
Crystal Way, London proposal 167, *167*
Cullinan, Edward 18
Cummins company 214
Cummins Engines building, Darlington 17, 86

D

Darbourne & Darke 44
Dartington 30
Davidson, Ian 164, 168
Davies, Mike *171*
  the Chrysalis practice 95, 274
  the Pompidou Centre 95-6, *96*, 99
  and IRCAM 99, 118, 134
  in the 'R&D end of Piano + Rogers' 100, 165
  launches 'Chrysalis II' 101
  the Lloyd's Building 165
  in RRP 165, *173*
  the Inmos building 170, 233, 235
  restores a Berthold Lubetkin house 173
Dawson, Chris 96
Design Research Unit 9, 11, 60, 64, 65, 65, 67, 88, 210
Design Research Unit Roof Extension, Aybrook Street, London (1969-71) 65, 66-7, **88-9**, 309, *309*
Diamond, Ralph 66
Dixon, Jeremy 44
Docklands, London 172, 226, *227*, 274
Doggart, John *61*, 64
Dome of Discovery, Festival of Britain 9
Domino House project 300
Donat, John 16
Dowd, Mike *96*
DRU *see* Design Research Unit
Duffy, Frank 206
Dugdale, Tony 95
Dupont company 63, 80

E

Eames, Charles & Ray 12, *15*, 16, 18, 56, 62, 72
Eames House, Pacific Palisades, California *15*, 61
Ede, Jim 33
Ehrenkrantz, Ezra *13*, 64, 170
Elias, Dr & Mrs 300
Elias House, Northpoint, Long Island, USA (1976) 311, *311*
Ellwood, Craig 12, 16, 18, 68, 72
'energy crisis' (1970s) 65, 101
English Industrial Estates, Gateshead, Tyne and Wear 311, *311*
Entertainments Centre for Leicester Square, London 92, 93
Evans, Eldred 11, 14, 35

F

fabric structures 67
Fal estuary 22, *23*, 28
Fallingwater, Bear Run, Pennsylvania 28
Farnsworth House, Illinois 22, 170

Farrell, Terry 171
Farrell Grimshaw 152
Feock, Cornwall 14, 15, 22, 35, 38
Festival of Britain (1951) 9, 60, 220, 222
Financial Times Award for Industrial Architecture 18, 100
Findlay, Sir Ian 177
First United Methodist Church, Seattle, Washington, USA (1984) 313, *313*
Fitzroy Burleigh Central Area, Cambridge (1970) 66, *66*, 100, 166, 309, *309*
Flack, Peter *94*, 96
Fleet Air Arm Museum, Yeovilton, Somerset (1977) 311, *311*
Fleetguard Factory, Quimper, France 140, 212, **214-19**, 230, 235, 282, *284*, 312, *312*
Fletcher & Stewart offices, Derby 18
flexibility 15, 40, *56*, 95, 106, *131*, 144, 160, 169, *245*, 267
Florence 8, 248, *249*
  Cathedral 8, *9*
Fordham, Max 82
Foster & Partners 169
Foster Associates
  early industrial schemes 18
  formed 18, 50, 60
  Goldschmied and 65
Foster, Norman *10*, 11, 18, *19*, 26, 56, 63-4, 95, 96, 100, 170
  entry to the 'Big Three' exhibition 169, 170, 288
Foster, Wendy (née Cheeseman) *10*, 13, 18, *19*
Franchini, Gianni *94*, 95, 99, 102, 118
Franklin, Dr Owen 16, 44, 65
Free Trade Wharf Development, London (1981) 170, **226-7**, 312, *312*
Freud, Ernst 14, 28
Fuller, Buckminster 63, 94
Fun Palace scheme 93-4, 96
Future Systems 65, 140
Futurism *126*, 177

G

G3 concept 210, *211*
Gabo, Miriam *19*
Gabo, Naum 11, 15, 16, *19*
Gailey, Dennis 14
Gairinger, Ricardo (RR's maternal grandfather) 8
Galleria Vittoria Emanuele I, Milan 167, *222*
Gardella, Ignazio 8
Gaulle, Charles De 92, 102
Genoa 92, 101, 142
Gerber, Heinrich 98
gerberettes 98, *99*, 112, *113*, *114*, 118, *193*
Gibb, James 168, *238*
Gibberd, Frederick 11
Giscard d'Estaing, Valéry 99, 134
Glass Reinforced Cement Research (1978-9) 312, *312*
glass reinforced plastic (GRP) 67, 88
glazing 15
  raked 38
  triple 181, *193*, *194*
Goldfinger, Erno 18
Goldschmied, Marco 18, 65, *65*, 66, 67, *94*, 95, 96, *96*, 100, 101, 102, 165, *165*, *166*, *171*, 172, 173, *173*
Gough, Piers 170
Gowan, James 14, 16, *17*
Graham, Gordon 177
Grande Arche, La Defense 129
Gray, Milner 11
Gray, Rose 172

Greater London Council (GLC) 13, 166, 220, 222
Green, Sir Peter *165*
Greenhill, Nigel *96*
Greenwich Millennium Dome *19*, 167
Greycoat Estates 166, 167, 168, 220, 222
Grimshaw, Nicholas 171
Grut, Lennart 95
  the Pompidou Centre *96*, 98, 118
  a director of Richard Rogers Partnership 98
  in RRP *173*
Guard, Mark 164
Gumuchdjian, Philip 164, 170, 171

H

Hackney, Rod 168
Les Halles, Paris 92, 102
Hampton Court Palace, Middlesex 169
Hanscomb 228
Happold, Sir Edmund (Ted) 67, *67*
  and the Pompidou Centre 92-3, 95, 95, 102
Harbour, Ivan *173*
Hart, Gary 168
Healy House, Sarasota, Florida 11
Heinz 60
Hepworth, Barbara 14, *14*, 33, 35
Heron, Patrick 33
Herron, Ron: Cities Moving Project *93*
Heseltine, Michael 167, 168
Heysham, Terence 174, 178
Hill, Jim 98
Holmes, Andrew 100
Holt, Eric 99, 118
Homefield School, Sutton, Surrey (1965) 307, *307*
Hongkong and Shanghai Bank, Hong Kong 18, *169*, 170, 288
'The House for Today' competition (1969) 63, 80
Housing, Globe Construction, Basildon, Essex (1971) 310, *310*
Housing, Healy Homes 308, *308*
Hulten, Pontus 118
Hungerford railway bridge, London 170, *296*
Hunstanton School, Norfolk 9, *17*
Hunt, Anthony 14, 15, 17, *19*, 53, 62, 80, 140, 170, 212, 228
'The Hut', Dorking, Surrey 22

I

IBM Cosham 56
Ideal Home Exhibition (1969) 80
Industrial Units, Maidenhead, Berkshire (1984-5) 170, **252-3**, 313, *313*
inflatables 94, 96
Inmos Microprocessor Factory, Newport, Wales (1982) 100, 140, 166, 170, **228-35**, 242, *245*, 313, *313*
Institute of Contemporary Arts exhibition 'This is Tomorrow' (1956) 61
IRCAM (Institut de Recherche & Coordination Acoustique Musique), Paris (1971-7) 97, 99, 109, 118, *133*, **134-9**, 309, *309*
Irvine, Derry, QC 168
Ishida, Shunji 99
Italian Industry Pavilion, Osaka World Fair (1970) *66*, 92

J

Jaffe House, Radlett, Hertfordshire (1966) 15-16, **40-43**, 307, *307*

James Stirling Michael Wilford &
    Associates 169
Jeremy Dixon + Edward Jones 170
Jesus College, Cambridge 66
Johnson, Philip 12, 20, 95, 106
Jones, Horace 172, 274
Jordan, Robert Furneaux 9

K
Kahn, Albert 170
Kahn, Louis I. 12, 18, 20, 21, 161, 165,
    177, 181, 262
Kalsi, Amarjit 164, 173
Kaplicky, Jan 65, 66, 67, 89, 94, 101,
    140
Kettle's Yard, Cambridge 33
Killick, John 9
Knoll International 210
Koenig, Pierre 12, 13
Kubrick, Stanley 40
Kurokawa, Kisho 95

L
Lacey, Jobst, Hyett 160
Lambeth Council 166, 167
Lang, Fritz 198
Lapidus, Morris 60
Larsen, Stig 164
Lasdun, Sir Denys 18, 60, 166
Last, Malcolm 164
Law Courts, Strand, London 178, 198
Le Corbusier 9, 10, 18, 94, 300
Leadenhall Market, London 164, 176,
    198
Lee, Marcus 164
Leeds University scheme 94
Legnano, Italy: Sanatorium 9
Leicester Square, London 169, 170,
    236, 238
Leicester University Engineering
    Building 16, 17, 18
Lescaze 30
Levete, Amanda 140
Lifschutz Davidson 168, 254
lightweight construction 40, 50, 92,
    96, 279
Linn Products, Glasgow (1985-7)
    272-3, 314, 314
Lipton, Stuart 168
Littlewood, Joan 93
Lloyd, Edward 174
Lloyd's Building (1928) 174, 176
Lloyd's Building (1958) 174, 177, 178,
    184
Lloyd's of London, London (1978-
    86) 18, 160, 165, 167, 168, 170, 171,
    172, **174-209**, 210, 267, 299, 311, 311
    and Richards Medical Research
        Laboratories 12
    clear delineation of the structure
        and the services 18, 20, 56
    use of full-scale mock ups 62
    the Room 174, 177, 178, 194, 203
    escalators 183, 198, 203
    lifts 184, 188, 194, 198
    'Gothic' character 184, 193
    thermal efficiency 193
Lock, Max 15
Lombard, François 92
London 16, 164
    Georgian 12
London County Council Architects 61
London County Council (LCC) 60
'London as it could be', London
    (1986) 169, 170-71, 248, **288-99**, 315,
    315
Lubetkin, Berthold 173
Luder, Owen 13, 169
Lutyens, Sir Edwin 170
Lyons, Eric 16, 24, 38

M
McAslan, John 164
MacCormac, Richard 18
McLean, Nick 173
Maison de la Publicité, Paris 94, 102
Maison de Verre, Paris 9, 13, 94, 129,
    181, 197, 267, 300
Maison du Peuple, Clichy 93, 94
Maison Tropicale, Maxeville 64
Manchester University 11
Mansion House Square scheme 170
Marais district, Paris 102, 104
MARS Group 60
Martin, Sir Leslie 9, 10, 11, 14, 18, 60
Masaccio 8
mass-production 13, 16, 63
Merello, Benedetto ('Benny') 95, 99
Middlesex County Council 166
Mies van der Rohe, Ludwig 12, 13, 16,
    17, 17, 18, 22, 23, 56, 60, 61, 152, 170
Milan, Torre Velasca 8, 9
**Millbank Riverside Housing,
    London** (1977) 100, 152, **160-61**, 311,
    311
Miller, John 35
Mitterand, François 99
Modern Movement 9, 94, 129, 171
Monk Dunstone Associates 165
monocoque construction 82
Moore, Henry 14
Morandi, Giorgio 63
Morris, Andrew 164, 173
Morris, William 172
Moseley, William 167, 167
**Murray Mews Housing, Camden
    Town, London** (1967) 16, 38, **44-9**,
    50, 62, 65, 72, 308, 308
Murray, Peter 167

N
Nairn, Ian 17-18
NAPP Laboratories, Cambridge
    (1979) 170, **212-13**, 312, 312
Nash, John 167, 167
**National Gallery Extension,
    London** (1982) 168-70, **236-41**, 288,
    299, 313, 313
National Gallery, London 293
National Theatre, London 166, 220
Nelson Collection, Lloyd's of London
    178
Nelson's Column, Trafalgar Square,
    London 168
neoprene 15, 62, 63, 72
New Ash Green 16
New York 10, 12
Newby, Frank 93
Newport school project (unbuilt) 18
Nicholson, Ben 14, 14, 33, 35
Niemeyer, Oscar 95
Nitschke, Oscar 94, 102
No 1 Poultry scheme, City of London
    18
North Park Shopping Centre, Houston,
    Texas, USA (1984) 313, 313
North Sea oil industry 140, 299
Northern Polytechnic 96
Northey Avenue, Cheam 62, 72

O
Oberhofer, Alphons 96
Okabe, Noriaki 99
Oosten, Niki van 96
Osaka Expo 70 66, 92, 96
Osborne, Trevor 168
Otto, Frei 67
Ove Arup & Partners 173
    and Team 4 13
    RR's first contacts 67
    Structures Group 3 67, 95
    and the Pompidou Centre 92-3, 99,
        102, 109, 118
    the furniture system 131
    the Lloyd's Building 165
    the Fleetguard Factory 214
Oxo Tower, London 167, 168

P
**PA Technology Laboratories,
    Princeton, New Jersey, USA**
    (1982-5) 212, 235, **242-7**, 313, 313
**PA Technology Laboratory,
    Melbourn, Cambridgeshire**
    (1975-85) 100, **154-9**, 310, 310
Palumbo, Peter 60, 170
Paolozzi, Eduardo 61
Paris 99, 142, 164
    office in an inflatable 94
Paris riots (1968) 92, 93, 102
Park, Derek 168
Park Road Development, London
    (1973-5) 100, **152-3**, 160, 310, 310
Parker, Sir Peter 16, 50
Paternoster Square, London 222
Peacock, Frank 19
    joins Team 4 13, 14
    on the Rogers-Foster partnership 18
Peressuti, Enrico 9
Pettifer, Brian 165, 181
Philips, Maurice 19
Piano, Renzo 65, 66, 67, 94, 96, 97
    joins Richard + Su Rogers 65
    Genoa team 67
    innovative use of materials 92
    the Pompidou Centre 94-5, 97, 99,
        99, 102, 109
    extends IRCAM 134
    and the Lloyd's competition 164
    RIBA Gold Medal 171
Piano + Rogers 64, **90-161**, 94, 96,
    97, 98
    formed 65, 92, 95
    end of tie-up with DRU 67
    the design process for the
        Pompidou Centre competition
        94-5
    wins the Pompidou competition
        95, 102
    the London office 100, 146
    wound up 164-5, 214
**Pill Creek Housing, Feock,
    Cornwall** (1964; unbuilt) **38-9**, 40,
    307, 307 variant (1968) 38
**Pill Creek Retreat, Feock,
    Cornwall** (1963) **22-3**, 24, 28, 307,
    307
Place des Vosges Apartment, Paris
    (1975) 99, 300, 311, 311
Place St Merri, Paris 133, 134
Plattner, Bernard 99, 118
Pompidou, Georges 92, 93, 97, 99,
    102, 109, 134
Pompidou Centre, Paris (1971-7)
    56, 67, **90-133**, 134, 140, 142, 160,
    165, 166, 167, 168, 177, 181, 193, 194,
    210, 214, 236, 241, 282, 300, 309,
    309
    RR's ideology 9
    Archigram's influence 61
    and the Fitzroy Burleigh Central
        Area project 66
Piano + Rogers' scheme 95, 96-9, 102
    other competitors 95
    the team 95-6, 96, 97, 99, 101,
        102, 118
    excavation work 97, 99, 109
    giant walls of information 98, 98, 99,
        102, 104, 106
    'jelly mould' scheme 97, 98, 106
    refurbishment 109
    the piazza in use 123
    the escalators 126
    the furniture system 131
pop culture 60, 61, 94
Post Modernism 101, 164, 171
Potsdamerplatz, Berlin 222
Powell & Moya 60
Prairie houses 12
prefabrication 12, 15, 64, 92, 113, 117,
    148, 177, 184, 187
Price, Cedric 93, 94, 96, 106
Prouvé, Jean 62, 63, 64, 93, 94, 95,
    106, 129, 267

Q
Quimper, France 214, 218

R
Read, Herbert 11
Read, Sophie 19
**Reliance Controls Electronics
    Factory, Swindon, Wiltshire**
    (1967) 13, 15, 16-18, **50–57**, 61, 62,
    64, 67, 68, 71, 72, 86, 100, 154, 228,
    308, 308
Renzo Piano Building Workshop,
    key members 99
Renzo Piano's office-workshop, Genoa
    66
Rice, Peter 165, 172
    friendship with RR 67
    and the Pompidou Centre 93, 95, 96,
        98, 99, 99, 118, 129
    and Sydney Opera House 95, 96
    RR on 96, 129
    Bordaz on 96
    the Lloyd's Building 165
    National gallery extension 168
    the Fleetguard Factory 214
    and the Arno Masterplan 248
Richard + Sue Rogers 58-89, 61
    formed 60
    and DRU 60, 64, 88
    Piano joins 65
    mass production 82
Richard Rogers + Partners 165, 168
Richard Rogers Partnership
    162-305
    origins 18, 61
    offices in Holland Park 164, 166, 168,
        171, 173
    formed 165
    teamwork 165
    the RRP team 173
Richards Medical Research
    Laboratories, University of
    Pennsylvania, Philadelphia 12, 13, 177
Ritchie, Ian 101
RMIM 60
Roche & Dinkeloo 17
Rogers, Ermengarde Gairinger
    ('Dada'; RR's mother) 8
    influence on RR 8
    and the Rogers House 62, 62, 63,
        76, 76
    accomplished potter 63, 76, 80
Rogers, Ernesto 8, 8, 9, 9, 72, 80, 172
Rogers, Richard
    background 8, 9
    education 8, 9, 10, 11, 12, 14
    influences 8-9, 11, 12, 18, 20, 60,
        63, 302
    first American visit (1961) 12
    partnership with Foster 12, 13, 15,
        18, 20, 21
    urban masterplans 21
    socialism 60, 63, 166
    sense of continuity of use 63
    teaching 67, 101
    RIBA Gold Medal 164, 170
    entry for the 'Big Three' exhibition
        169, 170, 315, 315
    on 'appropriate technology' 191, 193
    continuity 9, 76
    expressive drama 15, 20, 235
    landscape 35, 76
    space and light 35
    colour 56, 67, 72, 121, 194, 214, 216,
        235, 242, 247, 252, 253, 284, 287
    family 76, 82
    identity 76
    'hierarchy' idea 112
Rogers, Ruth (née Elias; RR's second
    wife) 96, 98, 99, 100, 101
    the River Café 172
    and the Royal Avenue house 173,
        300
Rogers, Su (née Brumwell; RR's first
    wife) 9, 19, 35, 61
    education 11, 60
    first American visit (1961) 11
    and Team 4 13, 18
    divorce 67
    resignation 95
    and the Pompidou Centre 94, 102
Rogers, Dr William Nino (RR's father)
    8, 8, 62, 63, 72
Rogers House, Wimbledon
    (1968-9) 18, 62-3, 62, 63, 63, 68,
    72-81, 154, 173, 302, 308, 308
Rome, Nolli plan 8-9
Rosenauer, Michael 60
Royal Academy of Arts 170, 288, 289
Royal Avenue, Chelsea, London
    (1987) 35, 173, **300-305**, 315, 315
Royal College of Art, London 61
Royal Exchange, London 174
Royal Festival Hall, South Bank,
    London 9, 60, 294
Royal Hospital, Chelsea 173, 300, 305
Royal Institute of British Architects
    (RIBA) 168, 169, 177
    Creek Vean wins an award 35
    RR lecture (1976) 100-101
Royal Mail House, London 174
Royal Opera House Competition,
    London (1984) 314, 314
Rudolph, Paul 11, 20, 30
Ruskin, John 172
Russell, Richard 61

S
Saarinen, Eero 18
Safdie, Moshie 95
Sainsbury Centre, University of
    East Anglia 64
Sainsbury family 169
Sainsbury Wing, National Gallery,
    London 170
St Francis Hotel, San Francisco 194, 198
St John, Peter 164
St Martin's-in-the-Fields church,
    London 168, 236, 238
St Merri's church, Paris 133
St Paul's Cathedral, London 168
Saint Phalle, Niki De 133
Samuel properties 66
Samuely, and Team 4 14
Samuely, Felix 11
San Francisco 12
Sandberg, Willem 97
Sant'Elia, Antonio 94, 165, 177, 198
SAVE Britain's Heritage 101, 172, 274
Saynatsalo Town Hall 33
Schindler, Rudolf 12, 18
Schinkel, Karl Friedrich 56
**Science Campus Project, Yale
    University, New Haven,
    Connecticut**
    (1961) **20-21**, 307, 307
Science Museum, La Villette 129

Scott-Brown, Denise 170
SCSD (School Construction Systems Development) programme, California 13, *13*, 50, 170
Scully, Vincent *11*, 12
Seaside Housing Project 308, *308*
Second World War 60, 63, 129
Seifert, Richard 60
Shalev, David 35
Shanghai 222
Shepheard, Peter 60
Sheppard Robson/
London & Metropolitan 168
Siedlung Halen housing scheme, Berne 15, 24, 28
Siegrist House, Venice, Florida 11
'Silicon Valley' (UK) 50
'Silicon Valley' (US) 228
Simmone Electrical, Tadworth, Surrey (1975) 311, *311*
Sircus, Jari 96
Skidmore, Owings & Merrill (SOM) 12, 18, 60
Skidmore, Owings & Merrill/London Land 168
Skylon, Festival of Britain 60
Smith, John *165*
Smithson, Alison 9, 17, *17*, 18, 20
Smithson, Peter 9, 17, *17*, 18, 20, 61
Snowman, Nicholas 99, 134
Solomon R. Guggenheim Museum, New York *12*, 12
Somerset House, London 170, *290*, *291*
Sorcinelli, John 164, 168
Soriano, Raphael 12, 13, 16, 68, 72
Sorkin, Michael 242
Soundy, Richard 164
South Bank Centre, London 60, 99, 134, 167, 220, 222
Southgate, Peter 64
Southwark Council 167
Span Homes 16, 24, 38
Speight, Sadie (later Martin) 11
Spence, Sir Basil 18, 60
Spender, Humphrey 61-2, *71*
Spender, Stanley 61
Spender House, Ulting, Essex (1967-8) 18, 61-3, **68-71**, 72, 308, *308*
Speyhawk 168
Sports Centre, New Ash Green, Kent 308, *308*
Spratley & Cullearn/Barratt Ltd 168
Stahl House, Hollywood *13*
Stansted Airport 56
Stanton, Alan 96, *96*, 99, 100, 101, 118, 172
Stedelijk Museum, Amsterdam 97
Stirk, Graham 164, 171, *173*
Stirling, James 14, *17*, 61
as RR's tutor 11, *11*, 18
and Reliance Controls 16-17, 50
one of the 'big three' of British architecture 18, 170
entry to the 'Big Three' exhibition *169*, 170, 288
Stockley Park 17, 50, 168
Street, J G *178*, 198
Structural Decking Research (1979) 312, *312*
Studio, Oak Park, Illinois *12*
Stuttgart Neue Staatsgalerie *169*, 170, 288
Stuttgart Staatsgalerie 18
Summerson, John 12
Sunderland Wearmouth, Sunderland, Tyne and Wear (1972) 310, *310*
Sutcliffe, Mark 13-14
Sweetheart Plastics (1970) 64, 309, *309*
Sydney Opera House 95, 96

T
Taliesin, Wisconsin 12
Tate Gallery trustees 8
'Tate of the West', St Ives 35
Tatlin, Vladimir: drawing of the *Monument to the Third International* 93
Team 4 1-57, *10*, *19*, 63, 101
influences 11-12, 15, 16, 18, 38
founded (1963) 13
staff recruited 13
Su Rogers' role 13
Branch house project 14-15
the abandoned Coulsdon scheme 16
the Reliance Controls project 16-18, 50, 56
dissolution of (1967) 18, 60, 67, 88
'technology transfer' 12
Tensile Steel and Reinforced Polyester Structure, Genoa (1966) 66
Thames Centre Project, London (1983) 313, *313*
Thames Reach Housing, London (1984-7) 262-5, 267
Thames River 160, *161*, 166, 170, 172, 222, *227*, 248, 262, 288, *289*, *290*, *291*, *293*, *294*, *296*, *299*, 305
Thames Wharf, London (1984-9) **254-71**
Thames Wharf-Richard Rogers Partnership Offices, London (1984-9) 172, 254, *257*, *260*, 314, *314*
Thames Wharf-Riverside Café, London (1984-9) 172, 254, *257*, 314, *314*
Thames Wharf-The Deck House, London (1986-9) 267-71, 314, *314*
Thatcher, Margaret (later Baroness) 166, 168, 170, 220, 228
Third Generation Office (1978) **210-11**, 312, *312*, 375
Hudson Street, New York, USA 314, *314*
Tingueley, Jean 133
Trafalgar House 168
Trafalgar Square, London 168, 169, 170, 236, *238*, *241*, 288, *292*, *294*, *296*
Trieste, Italy 9
Troughton, Jamie 164
Tubbs, Ralph 9
Twitchell, Ralph S 11

U
UCLA (University of California at Los Angeles) 96
Ullathorne, Peter 96
United States
RR's first visit (1961) 11, 12
West Coast 12, 16, 18, 50, 56, 60, *76*, 228, 302
Unity Temple, Oak Park, Illinois 12
Universal Oil Products (UOP) Factory, Ashford, Kent (1969-70) 64, **86-7**, 100, 146, 308, *308*
Universal Oil Products (UOP) Factory, Tadworth, Surrey (1973-4) 64, 100, **146-51**, 310, *310*
Utzon, Jørn 95

V
Venice 173
Venturi, Robert 170
Verbitz, Reiner *96*
Viollet-le-Duc, Eugène 129

W
Waterloo Station, London 166, 171, 220, 288, *290*, *296*
Wates, Neil 16, 24

Wates Housing Project, Coulsdon, Surrey (1965; unexecuted) 16, **24-7**, 307, *307*
Watney's brewery 65
Watts urban workshop, Los Angeles 96
Webb, Michael *92*, 93
Westminster City Council 65
Weston, Andrew 164
Whittington Avenue, London (1983) 164, 313, *313*
Wilkins, William 168, 170
Wilkinson, Chris 164
Wilson, Harold (later Baron Wilson) 60
Wimbledon Common 72, 76
Wise, Chris 165
Witham Workshops, Witham, Essex (1968) 66, 308, *308*
Wood, Christopher 33
Wolton, Georgie *see* Cheeseman, Georgie
Wren, Sir Christopher 173, 300, *305*
Wright, Frank Lloyd *11*, *12*, 18, 61, 72, 165
Scully and 11, 12
influences Team 4 15, 16, 28, 30, 33

X
Xydis, George 96

Y
Yale University *10*, 11-14, 16, 38, 60
Yorke Mason House, London (1968) 308, *308*
Young, John 18, 61, *61*, 65, 67, *94*, 96, 101–101, 146, 154, *164*, 165, 171, *173*
joins Team 4 13
and the Zip-Up House 63-4
and the Cambridge development 66, 166
and the Spender House 68
and the Pompidou Centre 95, 99, 102
and the Lloyd's Building *165*, 181, 267
Thames Wharf Deck House 172, 267-71
YRM 18, 60

Z
Zbinden, Walter 99, 118
Zip-Up Enclosures (1968-71) 18, 63-4, *63*, **82-5**, 86, 88, *89*, 100, 140, 146, *148*, 308, *308*

Photographic Acknowledgments

All drawings courtesy of Richard Rogers Partnership, unless otherwise specified. Image sources are listed where possible, but the publisher will endeavour to rectify any inadvertent omissions.

ADMM: p64TR; Alinari: p9BL; Arcaid/Richard Bryant: Back cover; p74/5; p80T; p95BL; p122; p169T,C; p179; p184L,BR; p185TR; p186; pp192; p195; p196; p198CB; p200/1; p203TL,CL,TR; p204/5; p207; p208/9; p252T; p253T; p257T; p260T,CR,BR; p261; p262TL; p265TR; p266; p270TL,TC,TR,B; p271CL,BL,BC; p277; p278; p280; 281TR,CR,BR; p283; p284B; p287BR; p294/5T; p301; p302TL,TC,B; p304; p305TR,CR; Arcaid/Richard Bryant & ERCO Lighting: p289; Arcaid/Brecht-Einzig: 36L; p37BC; Arcaid/Richard Einzig: p4; p10BL; p17CR; p30TL,TC; p31; p32; p34; p36BR; p37BL; p41; p42; p43T; p76CR; p77BR; p78/9; p80BC,BR; p87TC; p89T,BR; p118TL,TC; p127; p126TL; p130T; p135; p136T,B; p138BL; p139; p147; p150BL; p151L,R; Architectural Association: p61BL; Architectural Association/©Bill Chaitkin: p9BR; Architectural Association / E. McCoy & Foster Associates: p7; Ove Arup & Partners: p67BR; p95BL; p190BR; p194BL; Otto Baitz: p243; p246T; p247T,BL,BR; Berengo Gardin: p18T; British Film Institute: p164BL; Cuno Brullmann: p145CL; Brumwell Family: p59; Camera Craft: p23T; Martin Charles: front cover; p117CR; p118TR; p119; p123T; p124/5; p126TC,TR; p128; p129BR; p130BL; p186TR; p198BL; p203BR; p188BL,BCL,BCR,BR; Peter Cook: p175; p182; p189; p194TL; p272TL,TC,TR; p273T; p283; p284/5T; p285BL,BR; p286; p287TC,TR,BC; The Daily Telegraph: p61BR; Richard Davies: p180TR,UCR,CR; p290TR; p298TL,CL,TC; p299; ©Michel Denance: p172TL; Domus/Casali: p143; p144CL; p144/5T; p145CR; John Donat: p45; p46; p47T,C; p48, p49BL,BR; p104B; p130BR; p131BC,TR,BR; p176TR; p184CR; p188TL; p197BC,BR; p206TL; p237; p238TL; p239TL; p240TL; p253BR; p256BL; Barry Dunnage: p247BC; Eames Office © 1989, 1999 www.eamesoffice.com: p15; ESTO/© Ezra Stoller: p22TR; p23BR; Florian Fischotter: p77T,BL; Norman Foster/Foster & Partners: p20/1B; p21CR; p26B; p49TR,CL; p51; p52T,C; p53T; p54/55T; p56CR,BL,BR; p57; Y. Futagawa & Associates: p13CL; p129TR; Janet Gill: p202; The Guardian/Martin Argles: p165BL; Ron Herron: p93BC; Andrew Holmes: p62TR; p63TC; p69; p70TC,TR,B; p94TR; p149T; p158TL,BL; p159; © Hulton Getty/Haywood Magee: p14TC; Pat Hunt: p69; Timothy Hursley: p303; Shunji Ishida: p96C; Katsuhisa Kida: p155; p156/7T; p257BL; p258/9; p263; p264; p265C; Ken Kirkwood: p73; p81; p215; pp216TR; p217; p218; p219TL,TR; p229; p230/1; p232; p233TR,CR; p234T; p235TL,TR,C,CR; p244/5; ©Balthazar Korab Ltd: p13T; p17CR; Stephen Le Roith: p197CL,CR,BL; Network/Mike Abrahams: p165BR; The Observer: p169B; Eamonn O'Mahony: p80BL; p83; p84T,B; p108T,B; p255; p275; p279BR; p294/5T; Rondal Partridge: p13BC; Renzo Piano Building Workshop: p66BL,CL,CR,BR; p67BL; p103; Matteo Piazza: p166TL; Archives du Centre Georges Pompidou: p105BL, p106T; © Ken Powell: p19BR; Justin Pumfrey: p2; Marc Riboud: pp123BL,BR; Richard Rogers Partnership Archive: p7; p8T,CL,CR; p10TL,TR,UC,BR; p11TL; p19TL,CR; p54/5B; p59; p61BR; p65TR; p94CR,LC,BR; p96TL,TC,TR; p97TL,TR,BR; p98TL,TR,CL,BL; p99TR; p101; p163; p164BC,BR; p166TR; p167TL,TR; p171BR; p178TL; p197TR; RIBA Library Photographs Collection: p10LR; Philippe Ruault: p285CL; Alain Salaun: p93TR; Yuri Semenov/©Graham & Nina Williams: p19TR; Patrick Shanahan: p191TR; Julius Shulman: p13BL; Grant Smith: p173BR; Alison & Peter Smithson Architects: p17TR; ©SPADEM: p 64TL; Harry Sowden: p190CL,TR,CR; p194BL; Courtesy Mary Stirling: p11TR; SYGMA/Henri Bureau: p92BL; ©Telegraph Weekend Magazine/Patrick Shanahan: p171TR; Jocelyn Van Den Bossche: p211,CL,CR,BL,BR; Bernard Vincent: p96; p107B; p112T,CL,BL; p113TL,BL,R; p114TL,TC,TR,C; p115TL,CL,BL,TC,C,BC; p116T,BL,BCL,BCR,BR;

p117TL,TC,TR,BL,BR; VIVA / ©Jacques Minassian: p91; Felicitas Vogler: p14TL; Friedrich Wagner: p241TR,CR; Paul Wakefield: p120/1T; p126B; p129TL,TC; p132/3; p199; Michael Webb: p92BR; Matthew Weinreb: p206BL; Frank Lloyd Wright drawings are Copyright © 1999 The Frank Lloyd Wright Foundation, Scottsdale, AZ: p12TL,TR; Office of Public Affairs Yale University: p11TC; John Young: p62TL; p158BC; p187CR; p194CL; p266; p267TR,BR;

Author's Acknowledgments

This book is the outcome of more than a decade of collaboration and, indeed, friendship with the members of Richard Rogers Partnership, which began when Richard Rogers asked me to Thames Wharf to talk about the future of London. Among the many members of the practice who helped me to write the book, John Young was a constant and untiring source of information, advice and positive criticism. Two former members of the office, Philip Gumuchdjian and Fiona Charlesworth, were also instrumental in the project. I am also grateful to Richard Rogers' partners Mike Davies and Marco Goldschmied and to Laurie Abbott for their thoughts and reminiscences, to the staff of the press office and to Susan Smallcomb, Rebecca Ivatts and Annette Main.

Of the many owners of Rogers buildings who helped, the late Dada Rogers and Rene Brumwell stand apart – it was a privilege to see the Rogers House in Wimbledon and Creek Vean through their eyes.

Thanks are also due to Jimmy Brumwell, Norman Foster, Tony Hunt, Jan Kaplicky, John McAslan, Martin Pawley, Frank Peacock, Renzo Piano, the late Peter Rice, Ruthie Rogers, Su Rogers, Alan Stanton and Jack Zunz for help freely given.

I am grateful to David Jenkins, formerly of Phaidon Press, who invited me to write this book, and to Anita Moryadas, Paul Harron, Sophia Gibb, Paul Hammond and Karl Shanahan who patiently and expertly saw it through to completion.

Phaidon Press Limited
Regent's Wharf
All Saints Street
London N1 9PA

First published 1999
© 1999 Phaidon Press Limited

ISBN 0 7148 3746 6

A CIP catalogue record of this book is available from the British Library.

All rights reserved. No part of this publication may be reproduced, stored in a retrieval system or transmitted in any form or by any means, electronic, mechanical, photocopying, recording or otherwise, without the prior permission of Phaidon Press.

Printed in Hong Kong